The 115th New York
in the Civil War

The 115th New York in the Civil War

A Regimental History

MARK SILO

Foreword by John J. Hennessy

McFarland & Company, Inc., Publishers
Jefferson, North Carolina, and London

The present work is a reprint of the illustrated case bound edition of The 115th New York in the Civil War: A Regimental History, *first published in 2007 by McFarland.*

LIBRARY OF CONGRESS CATALOGUING-IN-PUBLICATION DATA

Silo, Mark, 1951–
The 115th New York in the Civil War :
a regimental history / Mark Silo ;
foreword by John J. Hennessy.
p. cm.
Includes bibliographical references and index.

ISBN 978-0-7864-7720-3
softcover : acid free paper ∞

1. United States. Army. New York Infantry Regiment, 115th (1862–1865) 2. New York (State)—History—Civil War, 1861–1865—Regimental histories. 3. United States—History—Civil War, 1861–1865—Regimental histories. 4. Soldiers—New York (State)—Registers. 5. New York (State)—History—Civil War, 1861–1865—Registers. 6. United States—History—Civil War, 1861–1865—Registers. I. Title. II. Title: One Hundred and Fifteenth New York in the Civil War.
E523.5115th .S55   2013   973.7'447—dc22   2007007214

BRITISH LIBRARY CATALOGUING DATA ARE AVAILABLE

© 2007 Mark Silo. All rights reserved

No part of this book may be reproduced or transmitted in any form or by any means, electronic or mechanical, including photocopying or recording, or by any information storage and retrieval system, without permission in writing from the publisher.

Cover photograph: Lieutenant Nicholas DeGraff and Sergeant Elbert Slingerland (courtesy researcher and collector Lance Ingmire of Saratoga, New York)

Manufactured in the United States of America

*McFarland & Company, Inc., Publishers
Box 611, Jefferson, North Carolina 28640
www.mcfarlandpub.com*

Contents

Foreword		1
Preface		3
1	Camp Mohawk to Charles Town • "I fear they will have bad luck"	5
2	Chased from Maryland Heights • "We could easily have held"	15
3	White Flags at Harpers Ferry • "It was like a dagger to every heart"	26
4	Penned in Chicago • "Our boys are very unruly"	34
5	Fire and Consequences • "Thunder clap from a clear sky"	43
6	Idle Year in the South • "Even in paradise itself"	52
7	Olustee • "Like a mountain of adamant"	68
8	Bottled on Bermuda Hundred • "Nothing has been accomplished"	89
9	Brief Triumph at Cold Harbor • "The boys felt ugly"	108
10	War in Trench and Crater • "What a fearful thunder"	120
11	Decoying at Deep Bottom • "We were mowed down like grass"	138
12	Fort Gilmer and Darbytown Road • "It looked like suicide"	149
13	Two Calls on Fort Fisher • "Win or die"	161
14	Peace and Home Again • "Great rejoicing! Our fighting is ended"	181
15	Epilogue • "Your colors have been foremost in the fight"	192
Afterword • "Riding a white horse and carrying the U.S. flag"		199
Appendix A: Chronology of the 115th New York		201
Appendix B: Regimental Roster		205
Notes		279
Bibliography		297
Index		303

Foreword
by John J. Hennessy

The shades that distinguish one regimental history from another are often subtle indeed. The vast majority of modern regimental histories tell largely the same story—usually of a regiment fighting in one of the major armies (most commonly in the Eastern Theater) involved in the major battles (Gettysburg usually is the focal point), with similar tales of woe and triumph. This is not to diminish these studies; some of them are excellent and important. But we have to acknowledge the familiar rhythm of their pages and, most often, their relentless pursuit of new detail on Gettysburg, Antietam, Chickamauga, or (more recently) Joshua Chamberlain.

This book by Mark Silo is different. No, it doesn't depart from the methods used by historians like Pullen (20th Maine), Wilkinson (57th Massachusetts—maybe the best regimental history ever done), and Moe (the 1st Minnesota). But it deals with a unit, the 115th New York, that trod ground and suffered adventures virtually unknown to those authors and their more famous subjects.

It might not have been so, save for one untoward incident in late 1862. After being captured by Stonewall Jackson's Confederates at Harpers Ferry in September 1862, the 115th New York was sent (with other regiments) to Camp Douglas in Chicago to sit out their parole. While the unit was there, barracks at the camp caught fire, and the accusatory glare of the government settled on the men of the 115th. The other regiments with which the 115th had surrendered at Harpers Ferry eventually joined the Army of the Potomac and fought at Gettysburg. The 115th, marked as recalcitrant by the government, instead received assignments out of the mainstream.

The result is a journey (and a book) that will carry readers to places most have never been, through experiences unknown to the war's famous regiments. Most of the Civil War was in fact waged away from the glare of the east-coast press; indeed, most historians agree that militarily the war was won and lost *outside* of Virginia. To reaches beyond Virginia the 115th went, joining campaigns on the Carolina Coast (visiting Hilton Head long before it was fashionable to do so); in Florida, where the regiment fought prominently at Olustee; and finally concluding the war as part of Benjamin Butler's Army of the James, engaging in months of tedium and battle at Petersburg.

Their story is not the exception. Tens of thousands of Union soldiers fought for and at important places beyond the span of the Army of the Potomac (bear in mind, only about 10 percent of all Union soldiers served in that army; the rest were cast about the South, waging war in the same way the 115th did). It is for this reason that the story of the 115th is important: Their service reflects the many forms and the many paths taken by the Union in the quest for victory.

Mark Silo, who lives in upstate New York, has crafted the story of his historical neighbors in the 115th by spending years poring through newspapers, manuscripts, books, archives, memoirs, official records, and virtually anything else that sheds light on the service of this group of men from the mostly rural counties west and north of Albany. This is the story of more than a regiment—it is the story of a community going to war. Community leaders become officers; everyday men become soldiers. In unison they departed domesticity for a wartime experience that would transform their lives. They would play a part in a drama that would transform a nation.

I have read hundreds of published regimental histories dealing with the Civil War; I've read many dozens more that never found their way into print (sometimes with good reason). Most, even if well done, are forgettable simply because they tell a story so familiar. Few have I enjoyed more than this one—the story of these men from New York who, by a quirk of governmental injustice, found themselves cast to the Civil War's literal edge. Out there on the edge they saw and experienced things that stood at the heart of the national experience of civil war: emancipation of families who had been in bondage for generations; combat on a large scale; the emergence of black troops; widespread destruction that helped bring the Confederacy to its knees.

Mark Silo has mined huge amounts of source material that reflects vividly on these and other topics. His use of that source material is truly exceptional. The result: a woven story that is both excellent history and engaging narrative—an important chronicle of common men on an uncommon quest for survival and triumph.

John J. Hennessy is the author of several books, most notably *Return to Bull Run: The Campaign and Battle of Second Manassas*. Formerly a historian at Manassas Battlefield, he is now the Chief Historian/Chief of Interpretation at Fredericksburg and Spotsylvania National Military Park.

Preface

Sometime during the night of August 31–September 1, 1862, the path of the 115th New York Volunteer Infantry veered away from that being followed by most new Union regiments from the northeastern states. At the railroad junction at Relay House south of Baltimore, the train carrying the regiment's thousand recruits to war turned westward toward Virginia's Shenandoah Valley rather than continuing on to Washington, D.C. From this moment onward the 115th was diverted from the mainstream of events. The railroad switch that moved them away from the mainline track during the middle of the night started the 115th on an odyssey that encompassed 34 months, 6,000 miles, 800 casualties, and a story that is unique among the fighting Union units of the Civil War.

Sixty-seven veterans of the 115th have told this story through their diaries, letters, memoirs, and recorded testimony. The wealth of material that these men left enables this history of their regiment to be more than a simple chronicle of events. The words, emotions, and sentiments of the volunteer soldiers who lived the events are the core of this work; without them it would be dry and unfinished.

These sixty-seven veterans can best be thanked by telling their story well. If I have accomplished this, it is only because of help provided by many people who I can thank more directly, including Kelly Farquhar and Violet Dake Fallone of the Montgomery County Department of History and Archives; Michael Pilgrim and Michael Musick of the National Archives and Records Administration; Richard Sommers of the U.S. Army Military History Institute; Barbara Gail Bulfin of the Fort Lauderdale *Sun-Sentinel*; Tom DuClos, Jim Gandy, and Michael Aikey of the New York State Military Museum; Michael Andrus and Robert K. Krick of the National Park Service; A. Wilson Greene of the Pamplin Historical Park; Hector Allen, Historian, Town of Oppenheim, New York; Richard Bellinger of St. Johnsville, New York; Roger D. Hunt of Gettysburg, Pennsylvania; Charles Mood of Pembroke Pines, Florida; Donald Oakley of Amsterdam, New York; Paul Quinn of Troy, New York, who kindly assisted with digital formatting; and many friends from the Capital District Civil War Round Table, including Bob Keating, Bruce Venter, Sue Knost, Bob Johnson, and Margaret and Richard Becker. Blake Magner of Collingswood, New Jersey, turned the author's rough sketches into maps.

Local historian Jim Morrison of Gloversville, New York, has spent years accumulating information about the roles of his town and county in America's colonial wars and in the Civil War. When Jim learned of my project with the 115th, he sent me all the source material he had on the regiment and shared all of his new discoveries as my work continued, all without being asked. Material he gathered from local newspapers was of particular value. Jim's generosity is enormously appreciated.

Dan Lorello of the New York State Archives dealt patiently with my many inquiries and always passed along any 115th New York material he came across in his work at the Archives. He closely read the draft manuscript and provided many valuable insights. Most importantly, Dan was this amateur's sounding board on many issues relating to research, writing, and publication.

John Hennessy is the Chief Historian at Fredericksburg and Spotsylvania National Military Park in Virginia, but became a friend and associate during his service with the New York State Office of Parks, Recreation, and Historic Preservation and the Capital District Civil War Round Table in Albany. John read many early chapter drafts and provided numerous invaluable suggestions; his long term loan of several volumes of the *Official Records* was a blessing; and I am very grateful for his excellent Foreword. But his most critical contribution was the whirlwind weekend he spent with me finding and tramping the 115th's obscure battle sites in the Richmond area—a weekend mission that jump-started the writing phase of this book.

This work owes much to the contributions of indefatigable researcher and collector Lance Ingmire of Saratoga, New York. While Lance's main interest is the 95th New York, he also had forebears in the 115th. Unfortunately for him but very luckily for this author, his uncounted hours on line and in moldy archives have invariably turned up ten 115th items for every one on the 95th, and Lance has generously shared his 115th finds while only occasionally venting over his frustration with the 95th.

My gratitude to my family—Kap, Dan, and Caitie—is boundless. Dan and Caitie changed from fun little kids into fine young adults as I worked my way through the story of the 115th New York, while somehow their mother remained ageless. They all supported the many winter evenings when I disappeared to my basement office to retreat into the 1860s, and they all enjoyed (or obligingly tolerated) several jaunts across campsites and battlefields in Maryland, Virginia, North Carolina, and Florida. There are no words sufficient to express my love and appreciation for them.

Mark Silo
Loudonville, New York

1

Camp Mohawk to Charles Town

"I fear they will have bad luck"

On the sunny late summer's morning of August 29, 1862, a large crowd packed the center of the village of Fonda, New York, a Mohawk Valley railroad town where the tracks ran parallel to Main Street and the train station stood opposite the county courthouse. In neat rows in the center of the raucous assembly stood one thousand young men in crisp blue uniforms. Speeches by prominent citizens inspired the newly minted soldiers; the cheers of the crowd excited them; and with tearful goodbyes they embarked to whip the Confederacy. Amidst the tumult, however, there stood at least one young woman who had her doubts. "It is Friday, and I am sorry to see this regiment start today," one of the recruits heard her say. "I fear they will have bad luck." Two and a half weeks later when the entire regiment had become prisoners of war, the young private who overheard her remark wondered if she was telling her friends, "I told you so." As things turned out, her ominous words would spring to his mind many times over the next three years.

That very morning, at Bull Run in northern Virginia, southern rebels were dealing federal forces yet another crushing blow. It would prove the low point of a long spring and summer of false hope and defeat for the Union cause. But no one in the cheering Upstate New York crowd yet knew about that. The folks in the noisy gathering believed they were doing something that would make a difference in the great conflict that gripped their nation: they were sending the boys of the sparkling new 115th New York Volunteer Infantry off to war.[1]

A few short weeks earlier on July 1, as General George B. McClellan's ponderous advance on Richmond stumbled and stalled on the Virginia Peninsula, President Lincoln issued a call for 300,000 new volunteers to suppress the rebellion. The following day New York Governor Edwin Morgan declared the state "ready and more than willing" to respond to the President's summons. He divided New York into recruiting areas, most of which corresponded to state senatorial districts, and charged each with raising a new regiment of one thousand men. The citizens responded briskly, and with astounding speed New York State became a vast military recruiting area.[2]

Patriotic fervor ran high. The July 4, 1862, edition of *The Daily Saratogian* ran the text of the Governor's speech calling for volunteers. The paper followed with a series of frequent, impassioned pleas for recruits "to rally once more into the ranks of the army, to punish Treason, and save the Government from final disgrace and overthrow."[3]

The governor appointed regimental commanders, usually men recommended by organizing committees within the districts. These men would be commissioned as colonels and begin to assemble their regiments. Other aspiring officers soon besieged the fledgling colonels with offers to raise one of the ten companies that formed an infantry regiment. Once they won the recommendation of the colonel and the required approval of the governor, these men would be rewarded with commissions: second lieutenant when they mustered thirty recruits, first lieutenant when the figure reached forty, and captain when they enrolled the company minimum of eighty-three men. One hundred men composed a standard company. "Authorizations to raise companies were issued daily by the hundred and every nerve and muscle were strained to keep pace with the popular ardor and to provide for the swarms of recruits.... Enlistments day after day exceeded by far any period of the war," recalled one beleaguered state official.[4]

The 115th New York was one of the numerous volunteer infantry units formed during this period. Its creation came in response to the call for a regiment to be recruited from New York's Fifteenth Senatorial District, a large, rural upstate region. On July 5 the governor appointed a local organizing committee, and by the end of July regimental officers had been named and recruiting was well under way. By the end of August the 115th New York was raised and mustered, and the excited crowd at Fonda had sent it off to war.[5]

The Fifteenth Senatorial District encompassed the contiguous but disparate counties of Saratoga, Montgomery, Fulton, and Hamilton. The towns and cities in these counties were assigned recruiting quotas in proportion to their populations. Saratoga County, with thriving villages along the Hudson and Mohawk Rivers and growing communities around the famous spas at Ballston and Saratoga Springs, would provide half of the thousand recruits. Montgomery County, astride the ancient transportation corridor of the Mohawk River and the parallel Erie Canal and railroad, sent most of the balance of the regiment. Fulton County, to the north of Montgomery County, where the industrial and agrarian river valley gives way to the Adirondack foothills, provided one full hundred-man company and part of a second. Sprawling Hamilton County, in the heart of the sparsely populated Adirondack wilderness, filled its quota with part of one company.[6]

Lincoln's July 1862 call for 300,000 troops was his second request for volunteer soldiers. James E. Reid, who responded by enlisting in Company C of the 115th at Ballston Spa, felt a need to explain why the men of the regiment had waited until this latter summons:

> We find the youth of 18 who had been counting the months for a year past, could now join his brothers at the front, nothing daunted by the reports of dangers, privations, etc., that came from every source. The young man of more mature years, who had not previously enlisted because of the sacrifices he would be forced to make, could no longer quench the fires of patriotism that filled his whole soul. The man of a family, who now had the promise from those upon whom he could depend, that his loved ones should not suffer for the necessaries of life, could no longer be restrained at home, and such an element responded to the call for 300,000 more.[7]

Government enlistment bounties, which Reid failed to mention, provided additional incentive. The U.S. Congress enacted a bounty of $25 upon muster to any volunteer enlisting for three years. In addition, on July 19 Governor Morgan enacted a $50 state bounty for new recruits. It also became a matter of community pride to meet the local quotas speed-

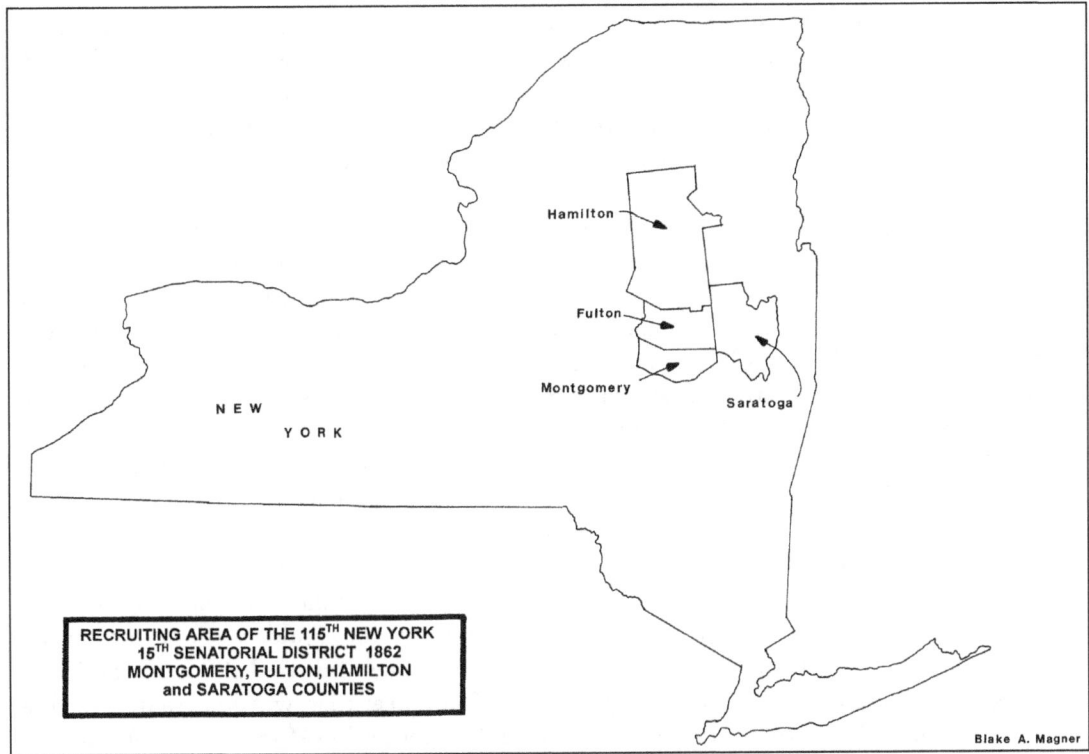

ily and special town meetings and rallies aided recruiting. Prominent citizens, businesses, and local governments provided further inducements. The Reverend Dr. John Wayland offered $20 to each of the first five men enlisted in the village of Saratoga. A paper manufacturing company in Rock City Falls offered to continue paying half wages to any of its employees who volunteered. The Fulton County Board of Supervisors called a special session to authorize a monthly stipend of $4.00 to be paid to the family of each volunteer for twelve months. In Moreau the town board borrowed money in order to offer $50 to each volunteer who stepped forward, and succeeded in enrolling its quota of twenty-two men within four hours.[8]

How strong a role these cash bonuses played in bringing out recruits is speculative, but as hundreds of men stepped forward in the wake of ghastly casualty lists reported from Virginia and in a time of unbridled patriotic ardor, one suspects that the money was only a sweetener. As the chaplain of the 115th later said, "The regiment was enlisted at a time when large bounties did not tempt the cupidity of men, and most of our men enlisted out of pure patriotism." Whatever their individual motivation they responded swiftly. For example, in just fifteen days Reid's company not only enrolled its full complement of one hundred men, but sent a surplus of fourteen recruits to another company. Most were young, averaging twenty-three years of age, and they came from every profession and trade common in Upstate New York, though mechanics and farm laborers predominated. As one of the new soldiers recalled, it was hard to leave "pleasant homes, fond parents, loving wives, idolized children and other loved ones," but leave they did.[9]

The man commissioned to lead the regiment, forty-one-year-old Simeon Sammons, farmed the same land north of Fonda from which his forebears had marched to serve in the American Revolution and the War of 1812. Sammons joined the local militia regiment at age seventeen and within a few years rose to become its commander. He served in a number of prominent local positions including town supervisor, president of the county agricultural society, chairman of the county Democratic committee, and member of the state legislature. Sammons offered his services and became the district committee's immediate choice as colonel of the new regiment. He would prove worthy though not without controversy.

The newly commissioned colonel threw himself into the task of preparing a camp to receive his regiment. By noon on the day after his appointment Sammons had contracted for material, and "before the sun went down thirty men were engaged in the construction of barracks." The new regimental headquarters, alternately known as Camp Fonda or Camp Mohawk, rose quickly on a level plain near the Sammons family farm. The colonel issued orders to the recruiting officers that all the men should report there by August 19 and hundreds of men soon converged on the camp.[10]

Once his recruits arrived Sammons's task became that of transforming them, as Captain William Shaw later phrased it, "from the status of free American citizens to that of so many mere automatic machines." Shaw called the initial attempts at drill a mockery, but the men willingly devoted themselves to learning the arts of military discipline. While they worked at drill, the camp stood open to all visitors. As Shaw recalled, the men enjoyed "the most magnificent picnic of their whole lives. Our stay at Camp Fonda was but one continuous gala day." The major complaint—not for the last time—involved the food. The men griped about butter "strong enough to walk alone," and beef that, when chewed, formed a "sort of India rubber ball." They would soon find butter and beef in any form to be rare commodities.[11]

Colonel Simeon Sammons, of a prominent local family in Fonda, New York, raised the 115th and became its commander. He earned the respect of his soldiers but several of his officers plotted to remove him. He entered two battles with the regiment and was shot in both (Lance Ingmire Collection).

The stay at Camp Mohawk lasted ten days—ample time for a magnificent picnic, but too brief for any meaningful military training. Urgent calls from the warfront for more troops abbreviated the preparations of the 115th and dozens of other raw regiments like it. Time did not permit them the luxury of proper training, so on the morning of August 29 the regiment formed up and marched the two miles into Fonda where that cheering crowd awaited them. Bands played and speeches were made, but the focus of the event was the presentation of two flags, national and state colors, from the ladies of the district. Hearts swelled and each man, according to Captain Shaw, "made a solemn but silent vow to protect those ensigns of liberty and freedom, even with their own heart's blood."[12]

With emotional farewells the men boarded first-class passenger cars and steamed down the Mohawk Valley en route to save the Union. More cheering crowds attended their passing at Amsterdam and Schenectady and, just forty miles from Fonda, they disembarked at Albany where Governor Morgan reviewed the regiment. Adjutant Thomas Horton wrote that the governor greeted the

Camp Mohawk, where the recruits of the 115th New York assembled in August 1862, is located near Colonel Sammons's home and farm north of Fonda, along today's Route 30A (collection of the Montgomery County Department of History and Archives, Fonda, New York).

115th with lavish compliments. At a hotel near the State Capitol the men were "bountifully refreshed with all the good things that the old Dutch city could ... afford." They then ferried across the Hudson River, boarded second-class cars, and headed for New York City.[13]

For some the refreshment enjoyed at Albany included hard liquor, which made for a lively train trip through the Hudson Valley. "While some were stupefied, others were jolly and happy, then again some would be delirious," recorded Captain Shaw. Private James Montaney's consumption in the capital city distorted his reason. He determined to leave the thirty mile per hour train "for more Albany water" and slipped out a window. His comrades spent that night at the Park Barracks in New York City, giving Montaney up for lost, but he suddenly reappeared the next morning just in time for roll call. His desperate leap from the train had landed him on a grassy railroad embankment down which he rolled into the Hudson. He then managed to walk to the nearest station and board another train.[14]

That evening the regiment made a slow sail across New York Harbor on a transport ship. Waterborne passages would become routine for the 115th, but this was their first and almost all of the men stayed on deck to enjoy the cool sea air. At Amboy, New Jersey they boarded a train for Philadelphia, this time in "rickety emigrant cars," remembered James H. Clark who mustered in as a private from Clifton Park in Saratoga County and later wrote a regimental history.[15]

On their journey the regiment had been accompanied by the Cayadutta Cornet Band of Fonda, as an "ornamental appendage" according to Captain Shaw, who quipped that the band could play anything but poker. As the soldiers marched from the train station to an abundant breakfast at the Philadelphia Soldier's Retreat, the group played the *Star Spangled Banner*. The men found it a hilarious critique of the musicians' ability when a Quaker gentleman in a broadbrim hat approached and asked, "Will thou instruct thy men to play something besides *God Save the Queen*, as that tune is distasteful to the descendants of the founder of our city?" Shaw conceded that it may have been possible that some band members were playing the offensive *God Save the Queen* while others "were no doubt blowing away" at several other tunes.[16]

From Philadelphia the regiment made the rest of its journey in freight cars. The men noted the downgrading of the travel accommodations on each leg of their journey and soon realized it was but a mild portent of things to come.[17]

Sergeant Nicholas DeGraff of Company D went to sleep as the train left Baltimore expecting to wake up in Washington. The soldiers assumed the national capital to be their destination, as it was for most new Union regiments. But the 115th New York was not destined to do things as most regiments did. At Baltimore Colonel Sammons received instructions ordering the 115th to proceed to Harpers Ferry, Virginia. As a result, at a railroad junction just below Baltimore, the regiment made its first turn away from the mainstream, turning westward on the Baltimore and Ohio Railroad. They made their next stop at 5:00 a.m. on September 1 at Sandy Hook, Maryland, where they spent a few leisurely hours.[18]

The village of Sandy Hook nestled along the base of towering Maryland Heights, wedged between the mountainside and the Potomac River. Between the historic river and the row of shops and homes that formed the village ran both the Baltimore & Ohio tracks and the old Chesapeake & Ohio Canal. Here the men received their first issue of weapons. Some companies got the favored British Enfield rifled muskets, while others got Belgian rifles, which the caustic Captain Shaw described as, "worth just the price of so much old iron in an ordinary junk shop."[19]

While the new soldiers excitedly grasped their weapons of war, they wondered at getting only three to five rounds of ammunition apiece. "What are we to do when we have fired these? Run?" asked one man.

"Yes," responded another with rookie bravado, "you are to fix bayonets and run at them with cold steel."[20]

As they clutched their new muskets and peered across the Potomac at secessionist Virginia, their chagrin over the limited supply of ammunition was natural. But by the strange fate of this regiment they would soon be stripped of all ammunition by the Confederate army, and later denied the right to bear arms by their own Union army.

While his men lounged at Sandy Hook, Colonel Sammons continued on to Harpers Ferry for orders. He returned with word that the companies of the regiment were to be separated and stationed along the railroad to guard the tracks. This came as bad news to this group of young men just forming a regimental identity. Lieutenant Colonel George Batcheller called it unpleasant information. Fortunately, the separation did not last long.[21]

At two that afternoon the New Yorkers boarded another westward train. A mile from Sandy Hook, as they crossed the bridge over the Potomac into Harpers Ferry, Virginia, Nicholas DeGraff recalled that, "silence reigned supreme, except the noise made by the slowly moving train." Directly on the bridge itself lay the railroad turnout that represented the junction of the Baltimore & Ohio Railroad with the Winchester Railroad. At this point the 115th made another turn away from the mainstream, bypassing the federal garrison and stronghold at Harpers Ferry, and took the Winchester Railroad into the Shenandoah Valley. "All idea of Harpers Ferry being our destination was dispelled," remembered James Reid. As the train rolled past Harpers Ferry, Reid continued, "candles were then lighted and rations hunted out for the evening meal. These consisted of crackers and cheese, the latter being the first and last we had issued to us by the government during our term of service."[22]

Just beyond the Ferry the breakup of the regiment commenced. One company stayed near Harpers Ferry at Halltown and five more at Charles Town,[23] eight miles west of Harpers Ferry, where Colonel Sammons set up his headquarters. Two companies continued several miles farther along the railroad to Summit Point, arriving there at midnight. The final two, Companies A and C, traveled two more hours to Opequon Bridge, eight miles short of Winchester, which at that time was the most advanced Union position in inland Virginia.[24]

Little over forty-eight hours after leaving their home state and not two weeks after their initial assembly, the 115th arrived at the front. "Of course we were surprised at finding ourselves in the face of the enemy so soon. We had no opportunity to drill or learn anything of the art of war," recalled Sergeant DeGraff. The commander of the companies at Opequon Bridge, Lieutenant Colonel Batcheller, complained that "we had only five rounds of ammunition, and one half of my men did not know even how to load or fire a gun." Wild rumors of lurking rebel guerrillas soon engulfed the regiment. Despite these frightening tales, and the 115th's location being "pretty far advanced for greenhorns," DeGraff considered it an honor to be placed in a forward position. "We felt proud in being considered worthy of such a trust, and determined to do our duty."[25]

At Opequon Bridge Batcheller was warned that the area was infested with rebel cavalry. He and the other officers advised the men to keep their guns at the ready and to remain dressed overnight. James Reid found all of this "not very reassuring for an all night's sleep," but the night passed quietly. At Summit Point where two companies of the 115th had been placed in support of the 8th New York Cavalry, the men heard warnings that they might be attacked at any moment. And back at Charles Town, Lieutenant Henry X. Devendorf noted the unsettling effect of "signal lights of the rebels dancing on the different mountain tops." Nerves ran raw for these green recruits, weary from four days of travel and far from home, most for the first time.[26]

On September 2, after their restless night at Opequon Bridge, Companies A and C

Lieutenant Colonel George Sherman Batcheller was a Harvard-trained lawyer and a state legislator before joining the 115th at age 26. He left the regiment within a year after disagreements with Colonel Sammons (Lance Ingmire Collection).

formed into line and twenty-five-year-old Lieutenant Colonel Batcheller led them on a reconnaissance of the countryside. James Reid remembered a long afternoon "marching thru fields, climbing fences, crossing ditches, etc." The soldiers remained wary of local folks observing their movements, concerned that by night "these innocent looking farmers could be miles away as informers," or might, as Reid feared, "join bands of skulking guerillas."[27]

Most of the tales of guerrilla depredations and rebel advances that passed among the regiment were pure rumor, but they were firmly rooted in the fact that Robert E. Lee and his Confederate army, emboldened by recent successes and anxious to move the war out of Virginia, had turned northward. In three days of battle from August 28–30—while the 115th New York enjoyed its festive sendoff at Fonda—Lee engineered a decisive victory over Union General John Pope at the Second Battle of Bull Run. The rebel commander then aimed the 55,000 men of his Army of Northern Virginia toward the Potomac.

As a result there was frantic activity at Winchester. Since General Thomas J. (Stonewall) Jackson had humiliated three separate northern armies in the Shenandoah Valley that spring, Winchester represented the most forward point of Union occupation in the historic valley. It also represented the Union's most advanced non-coastal position in all of Virginia. With Lee's army operating northeast of Winchester the Yankee hold on the town had become tenuous, and on the afternoon of September 2 federal troops prepared to evacuate. Soon after dark shouts of "Fire!" awoke the townspeople. The departing troops had torched the railroad depot and a row of warehouses full of material they could not carry away with them. A frightening explosion punctuated the inferno when they blew up the powder magazine at Fort Garibaldi, the Union works northwest of town. The blast could be heard twenty-five miles away at Charles Town. The arrival of a small band of Confederate cavalry in Win-

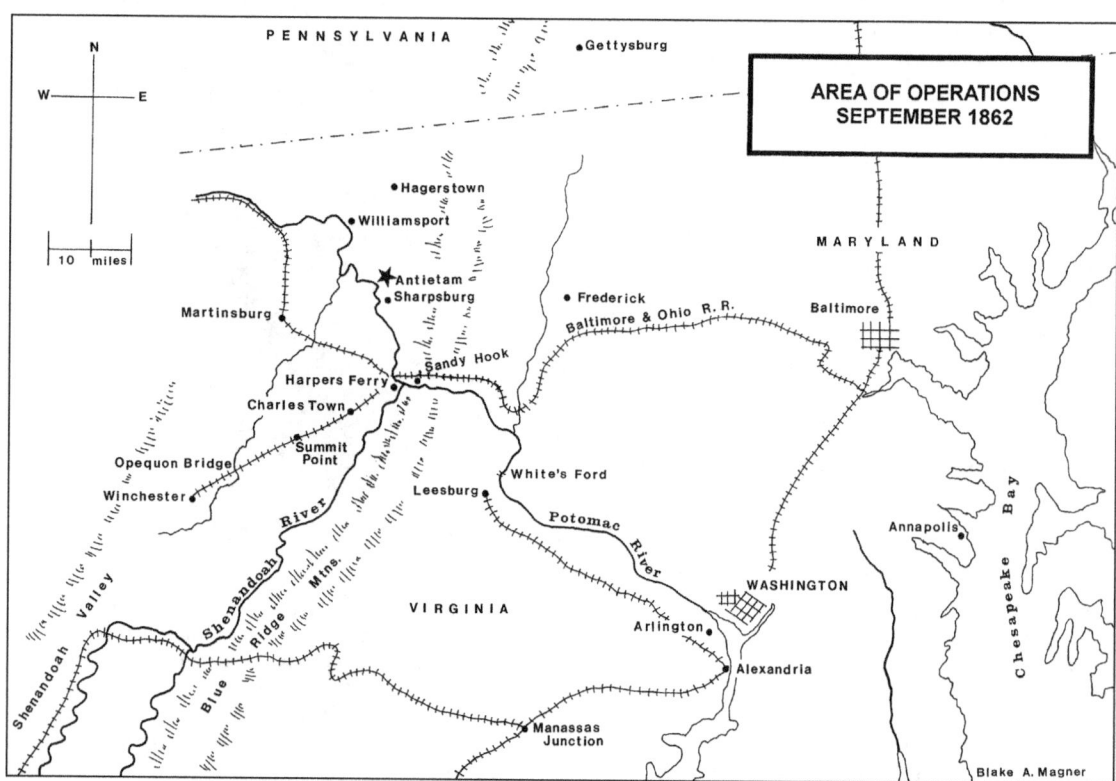

chester the next morning marked just one of the ninety-six times the town changed hands during the Civil War.[28]

At midnight the two companies of the 115th at Opequon Bridge were suddenly roused into heavy marching order, which meant to gather up all their equipment and get ready to move. "There was considerable confusion and excitement, intensified by hearing heavy explosions from direction of Winchester," wrote Reid. Two trains loaded with material not destroyed by the departing federals arrived from Winchester bringing news of the evacuation. Over noisy protests from the alarmed railroad crews, Batcheller detained the trains until the 115th loaded its baggage and horses aboard.[29]

Shortly afterwards Companies A and C followed the trains, marching along the track towards Charles Town. Within a mile Union cavalry pickets halted the column, demanding the countersign. Batcheller had to be summoned from the rear, a circumstance that created a stir among some of the men. They felt that their commander should be in front of the troops. Batcheller explained that he marched at the rear of the column "to look out for pursuers or surprises." At Summit Point Companies G and H of the 115th were roused from sleep at midnight when the 8th New York Cavalry "dashed down the road with a clatter that made the hair on our heads stand," as Sergeant Clark recalled. The companies rushed into line then merely waited there until 9:00 a.m. when they fell in with their comrades from Opequon Bridge and hastened to Charles Town.[30]

Back at Charles Town the rest of the regiment awaited them and treated the tired and hungry arrivals to a meal of pork, hardtack, and coffee. Charles Town had been an exciting stop for the regiment. The place had achieved considerable renown just a couple of years earlier as the site of the judgment and execution of "that poor old fanatic" John Brown. Two hundred men of the 115th quartered inside the local courthouse where the highly publicized trial and sentencing had taken place, some of whom claimed to feel Brown's ghost stalking about. In addition to its John Brown related notoriety, Charles Town represented the men's initial firsthand view of "Secessia," and they sent home many letters describing the place and its people. DeGraff gave this description:

> Charleston seemed a nice village. Had before the war about 3000 inhabitants but now all that are left are women, children, and Negroes. All the men are in the Rebel army. The ladies, so-called, do not deign to notice us and show their contempt for the Yankees in every way they can.[31]

The reunited regiment set out for Harpers Ferry, a march DeGraff described as very somber and sad. The regiment's first strategic movement was a retreat, and the men knew nothing of the circumstances provoking the retrograde move. The march grew sadder still when Private James English became the 115th's first casualty, accidentally shot during a scuffle with a fellow Company D private, Winslow Burton. Burton had been drinking and English tried to disarm him. As he did so "the scoundrel Burton" fired, the ball passing through English's wrist and forcing amputation of his right arm. Burton himself later suffered an even crueler fate, dying of chronic diarrhea in an army hospital in New York City.[32]

As evening approached on September 3 the regiment halted near Bolivar Heights, a prominent ridge just west of Harpers Ferry. The men felt exhausted, particularly those who had set out from Opequon Bridge the previous midnight. "We quickly divested ourselves of equipments and dropped to the ground for a rest," noted Corporal Reid. Men from the 111th New York, a western New York unit that had left home just a week earlier than the 115th, greeted their newly arrived comrades with kettles of much appreciated coffee that

they distributed by corresponding companies, i.e., Company A of the 111th serving Company A of the 115th, etc. The soldiers downed a supper of hardtack and bivouacked on the cold ground with "nothing but mother earth for a bed, and the blue arched, starry, decked heavens for a covering."[33]

Left: James English enlisted at Florida in Montgomery County. He lost his right hand to an accidental shot by a drunken comrade soon after the 115th entered service (New York State Military Museum).

2

Chased from Maryland Heights
"We could easily have held"

Lieutenant Colonel Batcheller called Harpers Ferry, Virginia, "that celebrated point."[1] The historic town is situated on the triangle of land formed by the junction of the Shenandoah and Potomac Rivers. This location put it at the mouth of the Shenandoah Valley, astride both the Baltimore & Ohio Railroad and the Chesapeake & Ohio Canal, and on the border between Confederate Virginia and Union Maryland. It housed a massive federal rifle works and arsenal, the targets of John Brown's ill-fated raid in 1859. Added to these circumstances—any one of which would have given the town vital strategic importance—was Harpers Ferry's location northwest of Washington, D.C., within a natural transportation corridor extending from the Shenandoah Valley into Pennsylvania. An enemy in possession of Harpers Ferry would pose an alarming threat to Washington, Baltimore, Harrisburg, or Philadelphia. That control of the Ferry would be hotly contested throughout the Civil War was foreordained.

The natural setting of Harpers Ferry is one that no visitor is likely to forget. Overlooking the town from the Maryland side of the Potomac stands Maryland Heights, whose steep rocky face rises abruptly a thousand feet above the river. Its counterpart on the Virginia side is Loudoun Heights, not quite as steep or high as Maryland Heights but imposing nonetheless. These heights, towering above the rivers that merge at their base, dominate the village of Harpers Ferry. A mile and a half west of the village is the long ridge of Bolivar Heights, which stretches from the Potomac on the north to the Shenandoah on the south. Bolivar rises only a relatively modest 300 feet above the river, but it sits astride the only land approach to the town. This spectacular geography makes a beautiful setting for sightseers but a troubling one for soldiers. Harpers Ferry stands at the bottom of a natural basin: its strategic importance and natural beauty are rivaled only by its tactical vulnerability.

On their first morning at Bolivar, September 4, 1862, the 115th received orders to pitch tents and set up camp. But their tents had not yet caught up with the regiment and did not arrive until just before dark. The tired soldiers set them up and gratefully bedded down but only moments later, "the long roll beat... and 'fall in' rang out upon the night air," recorded Sergeant DeGraff. "We all turned out on the double quick to find that one of our pickets, John A. Hubbard of Company A had been fired on and severely wounded." Shot in the foot

Harpers Ferry, 1865. This view looks down the Potomac River with the nose of Maryland Heights on the left and Loudoun Heights in the distance. The Shenandoah River flows in from the right, or west, in front of Loudoun Heights. The railroad bridge had been destroyed when the 115th New York was here in 1862. They crossed the Potomac to fight on Maryland Heights on a pontoon bridge (National Archives and Records Administration).

by a supposed guerrilla, Hubbard suffered the misfortune of being the first combat casualty of his regiment. Afterwards Colonel Sammons called for volunteers to strengthen the picket line and several men stepped forward while the rest returned to the tents.[2]

Right after roll call the next morning orders came to take down the tents the men had erected in hurried disarray the previous night and reassemble them into a more orderly camp. It took several hours and, as one soldier recalled, "a good deal of measuring and blowing," to establish a regimental campground with neat rows of tents. The tired men then repaired to the conical Sibley tents to catch up on lost sleep, but no rest was to be had. Within an hour orders came again to strike tents and prepare to move on. The regiment marched just a half-mile, formed in line of battle, and spent the night in the open. The following morning, September 6, the weary 115th marched to the crest of Bolivar Heights and pitched tents for the third time in forty-eight hours, this time in a camp they would call home for the next eleven days. Had the New Yorkers not been fatigued by interrupted sleep and sobered by Hubbard's wounding, these apparently pointless gyrations might have seemed comical. Their first week in service had brought a clear taste of the frustrating and always inexplicable cycle of marching, waiting, marching some more, and waiting some more that is a staple of military life.[3]

From their perch on Bolivar Heights the men of the 115th enjoyed a marvelous vista looking out over the village of Harpers Ferry toward the river confluence and down the eastward flowing Potomac beyond—a view dramatically framed by the Heights of Maryland and Loudoun. "A splendid location," wrote DeGraff, "Can see the country for miles around." But even these new soldiers, not two weeks removed from civilian life, perceived the threat imposed by the higher ground on either side. "How insignificant Bolivar did appear in comparison with its pretentious rivals," noted Reid, an observation to which he affixed an ominous postscript: "Coming events cast their shadow before."[4]

Soldiers from the nearby 9th Vermont drifted over to visit with the newcomers from New York. Besides offering helpful hints on how to pitch tents, one Vermonter regaled a captivated group from Company B with tales of his war experiences. As one of his listeners recorded:

> He told of charges and counter-charges, of victories and defeats, and of terrible carnage on both sides; whole companies seeming to be swept away in their endeavor to gain and hold this or that position. We looked at him in amazement, wondering how it was possible for even one to have escaped. Our mouths were open, our hair on end, and cold chills were creeping up our backs.

As the men of the 115th grilled the Vermonter with anxious questions, he related that all this action had taken place in Virginia, adding that the 9th's toughest fight came at the Battle of Shiloh. Most of the New Yorkers knew that Shiloh was in Tennessee, and they abruptly realized that their visitor's war stories were just so many fish stories. They quickly sent the bogus hero packing. Indeed, the 9th Vermont was nearly as new to the army as the 115th.[5]

At Bolivar Heights the 115th joined a newly formed brigade with the 39th and 111th New York Infantry regiments and two batteries of artillery. The brigade was placed under the command of Colonel Frederick D'Utassy of the 39th New York. A colorful, polyglot New York City regiment, the 39th was composed of companies of Germans, Hungarians, Swiss, Italians, French, Spanish, and Portuguese, and called the Garibaldi Guards after the renowned Italian revolutionary. D'Utassy, himself a Hungarian revolutionary, was described by Captain Shaw as "a blustering foreign gentleman, who was possessed of more gab than brains." Shaw's was a pinpoint description of D'Utassy, whose exaggerated claims about his military experience in Europe were later revealed as pure bluster.[6]

D'Utassy's Brigade was one of four brigades into which Colonel Dixon S. Miles, the Union commander at Harpers Ferry, organized his ten infantry regiments. Only three of the ten possessed any combat experience—the 32nd Ohio, 60th Ohio, and the 39th New York—and Miles spread these outfits out among the green regiments. The Garibaldi's of the 39th had seen some minor

Captain William Shaw was wounded in action twice while leading Company E of the 115th (Lance Ingmire Collection).

battle action at First Bull Run in July of 1861 and in the Shenandoah Valley Campaign against Stonewall Jackson in the spring of 1862.[7]

On Sunday September 7th the 115th formed in line for inspection by their new brigade commander. Colonel D'Utassy seemed pleased with the regiment's appearance and delivered a short address. Expressing his belief that some drilling and discipline would bring the new units to combat readiness, D'Utassy told the men he would be "proud of the privilege to lead you on to victory." Afterwards the 115th gathered for a religious service where they first met their chaplain, Reverend Sylvester W. Clemens. A Vermonter who had spent twenty-two years as a traveling preacher, Clemens was affiliated with the Methodist Episcopal Church of Troy, New York. He was the only chaplain the regiment would have and, by James Clark's estimation, "probably worked harder than any chaplain in the army.... He did not hesitate to go where the bullets flew if his work took him there."[8]

Most of the 115th's first week at Bolivar consisted of camp duty and drill, but many found time to visit Harpers Ferry. Lieutenant Colonel Batcheller recalled finding "little else here besides the troops and Ruins Ruins Ruins!" In a letter published in the *Cohoes Cataract*, Private Almon Stone of Company H provided this description for the folks back home:

Almon Stone enlisted at age 18 at Halfmoon in Saratoga County. He served as a private with the 115th throughout the war.

> The village is a hard looking place, being about half destroyed, having changed hands several times during the war.... The scenery here is beautiful, but the villages are the meanest looking places I ever saw. Half of the buildings are log shanties whitewashed ... and look as though they were built before the Revolution. The people are as old fashioned as their houses, without any enterprise.... If they are the F.F.V.s [First Families of Virginia] I don't know what the S.F.V.s, or Second Families must be.[9]

On September 5, twenty-five men of Private Stone's Company H went out to investigate a hilltop house near Bolivar Heights that supposedly exhibited signal lights visible to the enemy. Several unidentified men who had been seen skulking around quickly vanished as the blue-clad detail approached. The northerners demanded entry from the lady of the house, and their search produced a cache of material stamped *U.S.* In the barn the soldiers poked their bayonets into piles of hay to rout out any hiding rebels, but none were found. They did discover several barrels of cider but they dared not drink any for fear it might be poisoned. Instead they offered a cup to a young black man who happened by. "The colored individual soon drained it to the dregs and handed the empty cup back with a 'Thank you, sah,'" recorded Sergeant Clark. "Being satisfied with the experiment, the whole party drank heartily." By this time a number of local ladies had gathered and begun to hurl insults at the Union soldiers. "Some of them turned up their noses and threw back their heads to show their disgust." The New Yorkers did not respond and returned to camp.[10]

Twice the troops at Harpers Ferry received false news of the defeat of Stonewall Jackson. Nonetheless the men expected battle at any time. Still harboring illusions as to what a battle would be like, Nicholas DeGraff bought a large Colt's Navy revolver. He secured seventy-five cartridges the next day and declared himself "prepared to slaughter the gray backs at close quarters and on short notice." The gray backs would soon be at close quarters, but neither DeGraff nor any of the other 11,000 Union troops at the Ferry got the opportunity to offer much resistance.[11]

While the men of the 115th New York adapted to soldier life in western Virginia, Robert E. Lee and his Confederate Army of Northern Virginia moved into Maryland. On September 4 the rebels began crossing the Potomac at White's Ford, twenty miles east of Harpers Ferry, and sprawled into western Maryland over the next week. Much of their energy would soon turn toward the 115th and their Union comrades: Harpers Ferry was about to become the focal point of the Civil War.

Nicholas DeGraff left the family farm at Tribes Hill at age 20 to join the 115th. The observant and sensitive DeGraff saved his wartime letters and diaries and wrote a post-war memoir, providing rich and colorful detail to the story of his regiment (New York State Military Museum).

Lee had not been in command of his army very long, having assumed its leadership just three months earlier. At the time, the federal army of General George B. McClellan was literally within sight of Richmond after a two month advance up the Virginia Peninsula between the York and James Rivers. The audacious Lee assumed command on June 1 after the wounding of General Joseph E. Johnston at the Battle of Seven Pines. Lee swiftly turned back McClellan's threatening hordes then, with McClellan safely sealed up against the James River below Richmond, Lee turned his attention to a newly formed Union army under John Pope. The Confederates crushed Pope's Yankees at the Second Battle of Bull Run in late August, the fight raging while the 115th New York received its festive sendoff at Fonda on August 29. With both federal armies in flight, Lee wrote to Jefferson Davis on September 3 that he found "the present to be the most propitious time" to push into Union territory. In less than one hundred days Lee had moved the war away from the very gates of Richmond and into the North.[12]

As the rebels entered Maryland the two

defeated Union armies regrouped around Washington. Lincoln placed McClellan in command of the merged forces and a chastened Pope was exiled to battle the Sioux in Minnesota. McClellan quickly readied his federals to counter Lee's invasion. Meanwhile, the rebels stood squarely between the main Union army around Washington and the Union outposts at Harpers Ferry and in the Shenandoah Valley.

Lee assumed that the federals would evacuate Harpers Ferry as soon as he moved his force between there and Washington. Indeed General McClellan argued vehemently that Harpers Ferry should be abandoned—not only did he fear for the safety of the garrison, McClellan also wanted its 11,000 men added to his own force. But Henry Halleck, Lincoln's general-in-chief in Washington, remained determined to hold on to the Ferry. He overruled McClellan and on September 7 ordered Colonel Miles to stand fast. As a result Lee was forced to contend with an enemy force that threatened his rear, compelling him to halt his northward advance and strike at Harpers Ferry.[13]

Lee's plan called for the division of his army into four parts. Jackson's Corps would move out first by making a sweeping march via Williamsport, Maryland, and re-crossing the Potomac back into Virginia. Then Jackson was to chase the small Union garrison out of Martinsburg and seal off Harpers Ferry from the west. Lee ordered a second contingent, consisting of two divisions under Major General Lafayette McLaws to seize Maryland Heights and capture the enemy forces at Harpers Ferry. Lee's third prong, the division of Major General John G. Walker, was to cross the Potomac east of Harpers Ferry, move up the Virginia side of the river, and take possession of Loudoun Heights. Lee and the rest of the army would move west and cross the South Mountain range, which would shield them from McClellan's pursuit and where they could re-unite all their forces following the capture of Harpers Ferry.[14]

The Confederates moved out of Frederick, Maryland on September 10. The three forces moving against Harpers Ferry were expected to complete their assignments by September 12. Dividing an army into four parts in enemy territory was a bold action, especially so when the divided forces would be separated by major rivers and mountain ranges. Moreover, to expect the separate elements to cooperate in a major operation over many miles and complete it in two days was extraordinary. But such was Lee's confidence in his men and his disdain for McClellan and the other federal commanders. His audacious plan would succeed but not within his overly ambitious timetable.

Although they encountered no resistance in taking Martinsburg, Jackson and his 11,500 men did not reach Harpers Ferry until September 13. The 2,500-man Union garrison at Martinsburg evacuated as Jackson's Corps approached, hastily retreating to Harpers Ferry. Walker's 3,400 rebels, unopposed like Jackson's, also took until September 13 to carry out their assignment—that of occupying Loudoun Heights. The 8,000 Confederates under McLaws reached Maryland Heights on the 12th but did not take control until the 13th. McLaws's was the only rebel contingent to meet Union resistance as Lee's pincers encircled Harpers Ferry. As McLaws fought his way up Maryland Heights, the 115th New York would get its first taste of battle, playing a small role in a feeble federal attempt to repel the southerners.[15]

With the garrison from Martinsburg falling back on Harpers Ferry together with a few other contingents of federal troops that had been guarding railroad lines, Colonel Miles's total force at the Ferry grew to nearly 14,000 men, most of them as raw as the 115th New York. These inexperienced Unionists sat in the vulnerable natural basin of Harpers Ferry with 23,000 seasoned rebel fighters closing in on them. It would have been a daunting prospect for any commander, but Dixon Miles was particularly unsuited for the task. Accused of being drunk at the First Battle of Bull Run in July 1861, he was removed from field duty and relegated to the supposedly safe garrison command at Harpers Ferry. Now, as hindsight would soon reveal, the crisis facing the garrison would be amplified by Miles's own ill-conceived preparations for its defense.[16]

As he established his defensive strategy at Harpers Ferry, Miles erroneously perceived his chief threat to be an enemy approach from the west. Accordingly he placed 7,000 of his 14,000 troops along the crest of the natural defense line of Bolivar Heights. D'Utassy's Brigade held the right end of this line, nearest the Potomac River. Miles posted another 2,000 men on Maryland Heights as well as a formidable "Naval Battery" of big guns on a small plateau between the Potomac and the crest of the Heights. He remained unconcerned with Loudoun Heights, feeling that its terrain would be inaccessible to Confederate artillery and that, in any case, it would be dominated by the Naval Battery on Maryland Heights. As a result neither a man nor a gun was stationed on Loudoun Heights.[17]

Miles's deployments were misdirected: he needed to do everything possible to hold the dominating high ground of Loudoun and Maryland Heights. Events would soon prove this, and it was certainly clear in retrospect to the 115th and the others who shared their fate. "General Stonewall Jackson himself could not have arranged matters more favorably for the rebels than our own generals did," wrote James Clark. "The men were willing and eager to fight, but were powerless to do good."[18]

During the morning of September 12 Confederate General McLaws, a robust and profusely bearded Georgian, sent his lead elements up an abandoned forest road into Solomon's

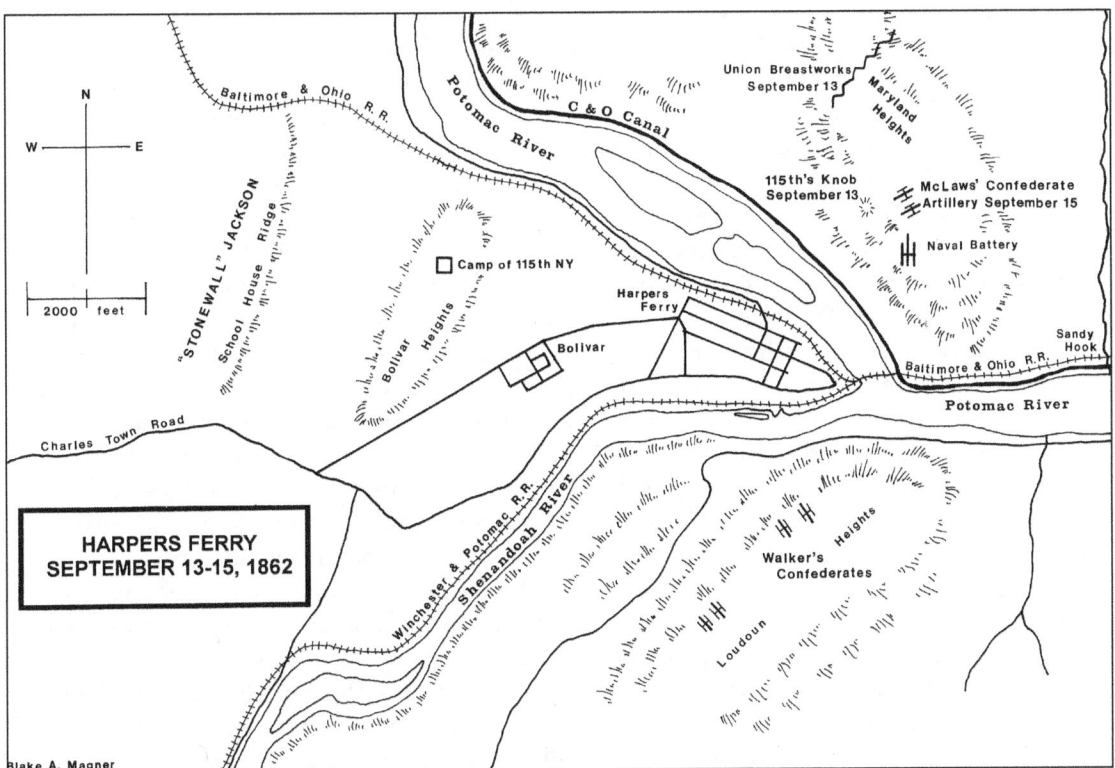

Gap. This gap, four and a half miles above the southern nose of Maryland Heights, is a shallow pass in the high elongated ridge that extends north from the Heights. The rebel force consisted of veterans of Joseph Kershaw's South Carolina brigade and William Barksdale's Mississippi brigade. A few Rhode Island cavalrymen met the Mississippians as they approached Solomon's Gap, but the overmatched New Englanders quickly gave way. From the Gap the rebels turned southward and began a slow, wary march along the rugged and narrow crest of the ridge. Before long they encountered a Union picket line consisting of two companies of the First Maryland Infantry and one from the 32nd Ohio. After a brief exchange of fire the outgunned federals withdrew and the southerners continued their advance.[19]

As this skirmishing took place, Colonel Miles sent reinforcements across the Potomac from Bolivar Heights—the 39th and 126th New York, and two companies of the 115th. Once on the Maryland side, the 39th and 126th ascended Maryland Heights toward the sound of the firing. The detached 115th Companies A and E were sent to Sandy Hook at the southern base of the Heights.[20]

Stretching across the Heights at its highest elevation the federals had constructed a line of log and stone breastworks with an abatis of tangled branches placed four hundred yards in its front. The Yankee skirmishers contesting the Confederate approach eventually fell back behind these defenses, where additional federal troops were stationed. Meanwhile the reinforcements from Bolivar headed toward this same point. As evening darkened, the rebels neared the abatis. The waiting northerners greeted them with a flame of musketry, and after a brief exchange the Confederates halted for the night. The decisive fight for Maryland Heights would come with the dawn.[21]

"This morning opened with the boom of cannon and the crash of musketry, and we were soon convinced that it was not a Fourth of July celebration as had been our previous experience. The firing was over on Maryland Heights," recalled Sergeant DeGraff. As September 13 dawned with the 115th's introduction to the din of war, DeGraff and the other eight companies of the regiment remained at Bolivar Heights. But while his men got breakfast Colonel Sammons received orders to move his command across the Potomac toward the sounds of battle. "In a few minutes we were on our way," wrote eighteen-year old John Dye of Company K who complained that he never got his meal. Leaving Company B behind to picket their camp, seven companies of the 115th hustled through Harpers Ferry, crossed the pontoon bridge that spanned the Potomac, and started up the steep west face of Maryland Heights. Companies A and E, detached to Sandy Hook the previous day, had also moved toward the sound of the guns that morning and were already on the mountain.[22]

Kershaw's South Carolinians led the morning assault against the Union positions atop Maryland Heights. Pushing aside a few skirmishers, the southerners encountered the abatis, manned mainly by the 126th New York, a western New York regiment that had left home just three days before the 115th. These rookies withstood the determined rebel veterans only briefly before falling back to the stronger line of prepared breastworks. Constructed two days earlier, these works spanned the crest of the Heights, anchoring on a steep rock outcrop on the Union right and fading into the forest on the left, where the western flank of the Heights sloped sharply away toward the Potomac.

The 126th joined a very fragmented Union force behind this line. Full and partial regiments from three different brigades were represented, many as green as the New Yorkers, and no single leader held command over all the federal units. Disciplined, experienced

Confederate troops with veteran leaders bore down on this amalgam of untested Union troops. Although poorly prepared and overmatched, these northerners offered a determined resistance for a time, but after heavy fighting in which Colonel Eliakim Sherrill of the 126th was seriously wounded, some of the defenders panicked and the rest melted away in a confused retreat.[23]

Back on Bolivar Heights Colonel Miles learned of the accelerating disaster on Maryland Heights and sent a message over to Colonel Thomas Ford of the 32nd Ohio, the ranking Union officer there. "You will hold on, you can hold on," Miles demanded, "until the cows' tails drop off." Ford commanded only a portion of the troops on the Heights and, even had Miles's strange exhortation been more timely, the Ohioan would have been unable to stem the rebel advance. Miles's cheerleading came too late. While standing on Bolivar within the camp of the 115th, Miles watched in horror as his troops began their hasty retreat from the crest of Maryland Heights. The 115th's Chaplain Clemens, who had remained at camp while most of the regiment rushed to Maryland Heights, heard Miles vent his rage. "God Almighty! What does that mean?" he roared. "They are coming down! Hell and damnation!" Sergeant Clark, who had stayed in camp due to illness, recorded that Miles wheeled his horse and "dashed down the hill like a madman to learn the cause."[24]

Most of the routed federals fled down the west slope of Maryland Heights toward the Potomac. Others fell back to a secondary line of works near an observation tower. It was at this point, as the disaster unfolded, that Companies A and E of the 115th completed the climb from Sandy Hook and emerged onto the crest of Maryland Heights. They joined the small force near the tower still trying to hold back the oncoming Confederates. "When we arrived at the lookout we received the first fire from the Johnnies," remembered William Scorsby of Company E. "We then took a position in low log breastworks." Here they engaged in a lengthy duel with rebel skirmishers.[25]

Lieutenant Willett Ferguson of Company A stood exposed on top of the breastworks and blazed away at the rebels. He fought like a tiger according to Clark. Luck was with the courageous thirty-year-old Ferguson, who until joining the army had been a merchant in Fort Plain in Montgomery County. He escaped injury though a sharpshooter took deliberate aim at him several times. Sergeant Stephen Morris of Ferguson's company was not as lucky. A ball passed through his cap inflicting a bloody scalp wound. As he fell blinded by his own blood, Morris exhorted his mates, "Give it to them!" Fortunately for the few federals remaining on Maryland Heights, the Confederates did not energetically press their advance. The exchange of skirmish fire went on for a couple of hours; then at about three o'clock, the northerners received orders to fall back and they headed down a narrow woods trail toward safety.[26]

As Companies A and E faced enemy fire for the first time on the crest of Maryland Heights, seven more companies of the 115th underwent their own baptism of fire on the west side of the mountain. These men had rushed from Bolivar, through Harpers Ferry, across the Potomac and up the slope to the Naval Battery. As they ascended they passed some of the wounded being carried down the mountain, including their own Sergeant Morris. Colonel Miles, who had relocated to Maryland Heights, ordered Colonel Sammons to take his regiment to a knob that jutted out of the mountainside about a quarter-mile in front of the Naval Battery. Miles feared this knob could be used by the Confederates as a position from which to threaten the big Union guns and sent the 115th New York forward to occupy and protect the knob from any rebel encroachment. Sammons led his men through the dense woods to their assigned position.[27]

"We saw a few of the enemy and several shots were exchanged," recalled John Dye. The Confederates they encountered were seasoned Mississippians of Barksdale's brigade, acting as flankers for the rebel advance along the crest of the Heights. One of the southerner's shots pierced the thigh of Captain William Smith, leader of Dye's Company K, gracing Smith with the dubious distinction of being the first officer of the 115th wounded in battle. Smith, a carriage maker from Amsterdam, recovered from his wound and commanded his company throughout the remainder of the war.[28]

Aside from seeing a few of the enemy—"very few indeed," according to Colonel Sammons—the regiment was totally isolated on their little knob. Not another federal soldier could be seen and the men had no way of knowing what other forces from which army might be nearby. The cannons of the Naval Battery continually fired over their heads into the woods beyond, but that provided little comfort to the New Yorkers. Asked later what he thought the big guns were shooting at, Sammons could only reply, "I presume at the enemy, somewhere."[29]

The 115th held this position for about three hours. Above the noise of the artillery they could hear the sound of the skirmishing at the crest where Companies A and E were among the federal troops still sparring with Kershaw's South Carolinians. Finally, wrote Reid, "discouraging reports came that our forces were driven from their works on the mountaintop and the enemy in full possession." A messenger soon arrived and handed Sammons orders to fall back to Harpers Ferry and the 115th pulled out. Moving back toward the Naval Battery, the seven companies from the knob met Companies A and E, down from their fight at the crest.[30]

At the battery the reunited regiment beheld a dismaying sight. "To my utter astonishment," wrote an irate Lieutenant Colonel Batcheller, "I saw the large siege guns, which had been our boast and pride, indeed our main strength and defense, dismounted and spiked and the whole works abandoned by our forces." The other New Yorkers shared Batcheller's shock and disappointment with the day's events, including James Reid. "The evacuation of the Heights was ordered," he recalled. "The doom of Harpers Ferry was sealed. We quietly but sullenly marched down, crossed the river, and returned to our former position on Bolivar Heights." The regiment had played a minor roll on a cheerless day for Union forces, but would claim one small honor—the 115th New York was the last federal unit to leave Maryland Heights.[31]

The soldiers found little comfort back at their camp on the crest of Bolivar Heights as the situation there was little more secure than on Maryland Heights. Clouds of dust to the west revealed that thousands of Confederates (Stonewall Jackson's main force) now threatened the Union line on Bolivar from that direction. Danger loomed to the south also, where the men saw signal flags flashing from Loudoun Heights, disclosing that General Walker and his detachment of rebels had seized that high point and opened communication with Jackson. With McLaws now in possession of Maryland Heights, General Lee's pincers had closed upon Harpers Ferry according to plan. As Corporal Reid wrote, "We were now completely surrounded."[32]

The night of September 13, remembered Sergeant DeGraff, "closed in around us and found a sad company." His regiment had lost five men wounded during the day and the situation spread before them at Bolivar portended graver business ahead. Even these inexperienced soldiers could quickly grasp the danger of their position. Along the Union lines the frustrated troops began to cast blame for their predicament, particularly the army's lamentable performance on Maryland Heights. Thousands echoed Batcheller's bafflement at the loss of that critical position: "The cause of the evacuation of Maryland Heights is indeed a mystery to me—we could easily have held." Many fingers would be pointed in the days and decades ahead.[33]

That evening wrote Reid, "Long lines of campfires in the direction of Jackson's army were constant reminders of the presence of our would-be captors." A dispatch from Colonel D'Utassy confirmed what the men already surmised—the garrison at Harpers Ferry was completely surrounded and the Confederates would likely attack at daybreak. "Let our watchword and rallying cry then be 'Victory or Death!'" D'Utassy exhorted. Each man in the 115th received eighty rounds of ammunition and the regiment was ordered to fall in for action promptly at four the next morning.[34]

The long day had ended. In two separate contingents the 115th had tasted enemy fire for the first time—a fairly warm skirmish for two companies at the crest of Maryland Heights, and a few shots for seven others at the knob. Lieutenant Henry Devendorf wrote his wife, "You can never conceive of the excitement that there is manifested in a battle. I tell you there is great music in the roar and thunder of the cannons and continuous fire of musketry." Reid recorded that as darkness brought the day to a close, "all firing ceased, and the stillness of death reigned along the lines until morning."[35]

3

White Flags at Harpers Ferry

"It was like a dagger to every heart"

As the Union soldiers at Harpers Ferry awakened on September 14 they expected the swarms of rebels that encircled them to attack at any moment, but the southern lines remained quiet. The only visible activity by the enemy was the purposeful waving of the signal flags by which the Confederate forces communicated. Federal artillerists lobbed a few shells in each direction to challenge the rebels, but even this hostile gesture brought no response. The morning passed while Jackson's men completed their final preparations.[1]

In the early afternoon Jackson began to tighten the noose. "About 1:00 p.m. watchful eyes saw a puff of smoke on Loudoun Heights," wrote Corporal Reid. "There she goes," cried soldiers as they heard the roar of the enemy's guns and watched the shells arc toward them. "As they, the cursed rebels, discharged a piece the smoke would puff forth and rise gracefully in the air. The shell and the report would reach us at the same time," wrote Sergeant DeGraff. The Confederates launched these initial shots at Union artillery positions on Bolivar Heights and within the village of Harpers Ferry. An hour later McLaws's rebel guns on Maryland Heights joined the cannonade, aiming their shells at the north end of Bolivar Heights, the position held by D'Utassy's Brigade including the 115th. Finally enemy batteries to the west of Bolivar Heights joined the bombardment and the rebel barrage "came screaming and groaning from nearly every direction."[2]

William Jennings of Company C was playing tourist in Harpers Ferry when the shells began to fall. Determined to be with his regiment should it go into battle, Jennings made a mad dash for Bolivar Heights "through shot and shell ... right through the hottest of the fire." The thirty-nine-year old sergeant wrote that he wanted to be sure that, should he be hit, "someone would be able to say they saw me fall in Liberty's Cause."[3]

Cannon thundered through an afternoon that one of the 115th remembered being as beautiful "as ever adorned the month of September." Blue and gray artillery units fired at one another and the infantrymen on Bolivar Heights felt like mere spectators. "To us the whole business, so to speak, was new and novel," wrote Reid. "There was danger enough to keep us on the alert, but not enough to in any way terrify us." Remarked Batcheller, "We had the opportunity of witnessing an artillery battle ... without partaking of its dangers." The foot soldiers looked on in fascination although they found it frustrating to have no chance to return the fire. As Jennings recorded, "Those were trying hours, for we were commanded to stand still until further orders. The most momentous time in the life of a soldier is to stand firm under fire without being allowed to return the compliment."[4]

The men of the 2nd Illinois Light Artillery dueled with their rebel counterparts from a position adjacent to the camp of the 115th. The midwesterners became a focus of both the enemy's fire and the New Yorkers' admiration. "We took real pleasure in watching the gunners stand up to their work. They seemed unmindful of danger although they were the real targets of the enemy's aim." Curiosity impelled some of the spectators to drift toward the Illinoisans' position for a better view of the action. As Reid described, "In defiance of the danger, the inclination of our boys to see all that was to be seen took many of them in close proximity to our batteries." Some of the incoming shells failed to explode, and a number of the excited young men of the 115th put themselves farther into harm's way in order to dig up these undetonated rounds for a closer look. Not completely reckless, they at least waited long enough to assure that the fuses had burned out before approaching them.

The regiment remained in camp for the first several hours of the rebel bombardment. Luckily not a man was injured during this time, "although hair-breadth escapes were numerous." Eventually orders came to move a short way down the east slope of Bolivar Heights to a position that provided greater protection from the shellfire. The men kept a hopeful eye out for the friendly forces they believed must soon be coming to their rescue and false reports circulated of approaching federal forces. During the afternoon great clouds of dust rose up from the roads west of Bolivar, indicating significant troop movements and bringing renewed hope to the trapped soldiers. "But, alas," as a rueful William Scorsby of Company E recalled, "it was Jackson's troops moving into position, as we soon learned." Indeed, Stonewall Jackson was readying his infantry to strike.[5]

The sound of distant cannon fire also heartened the federals. It came from the northeast, the direction in which they knew McClellan's army to be operating. McClellan had moved his troops out of Frederick, Maryland that morning and they spent the day fighting their way over South Mountain and toward Lee. McClellan dispatched three couriers to Colonel Miles at Harpers Ferry via three different routes but none made it through the ring of Confederates surrounding the Ferry. Just as well perhaps, for the couriers carried a promise that would never be fulfilled. "You may count on our making every effort to relieve you," assured McClellan's message. "Hold out to the last extremity. You may rely on my speedily accomplishing that object."[6]

Miles also sent a team of couriers to find McClellan. He instructed them to "try to reach somebody that had ever heard of the United States Army, or any general of the United States Army, or anybody that knew anything about the United States Army, and report the condition of Harpers Ferry." These riders galloped up the Potomac, crossed the river near Antietam Creek, and headed east over South Mountain, dashing around three sets of enemy pickets along the way. They managed to complete their mission where McClellan's triad of messengers had failed, reaching McClellan at Frederick on the morning of September 14— at the same time the Confederates began shelling Harpers Ferry.[7]

McClellan sent Miles's couriers on to General William Franklin, who commanded the Army of the Potomac's left wing. At that time Franklin was attempting to seize Crampton's Gap in South Mountain, just ten miles from Harpers Ferry. McClellan ordered Franklin to drive Confederate General McLaws from Maryland Heights and then to relieve Miles and his garrison. Miles's couriers reached Franklin at 3:00 p.m. just as Franklin's corps succeeded in forcing its passage through Crampton's Gap. But instead of pressing on toward the Ferry, Franklin rested his troops for the night. There would be no relief for the troops penned in at Harpers Ferry.[8]

Near 6:00 p.m. in the evening of September 14, as General Franklin's troops settled down to supper, the 115th and the rest of D'Utassy's Brigade were ordered into marching formation on Bolivar Heights. This move brought them under enemy fire, as described by James Reid:

> This line was on the crest of the Heights, and when we formed we became a conspicuous target for many of the batteries of the enemy. They seemed to open on us with every available gun. The shells literally rained among us from front, flank and rear, tearing up the ground at our feet, or screeching through the air over our heads in solid or fragmentary form. It was a severe trial for new troops, but excepting a few cases of dodging—an act performed invariably after the particular danger had passed—not a man of our regiment left the ranks, but preserving a stoic-like indifference, we awaited orders.[9]

Casualties remained light. "It was marvelous—indeed Providential—how our men escaped," wrote Batcheller. "Few had been wounded and none killed by these terrible engines of death." John Dye recalled that Colonel D'Utassy rode among the 115th at this point. Noticing some of the men futilely dodging the shellfire, the Hungarian born D'Utassy shouted, "Ton't pe afrait, poys; de shells vat vistles vill neffer do you haarm." D'Utassy had just finished his heavily accented exhortation when a shell flew past him. "It was seen that he could dodge as quick as the most expert and artful dodger we had," noted Dye.[10]

The blustering Frederick George D'Utassy shared his men's frustration with their lot at Harpers Ferry. As soon as Maryland Heights was evacuated, he began pleading with Colonel Miles for authorization to lead a force back into Maryland to retake that critical point. Miles considered such a move fruitless, saying "Damn it! It is too late." Despite the commander's resistance, D'Utassy sent a detachment from the 65th Illinois and 39th New York back across the Potomac. They climbed to the Naval Battery, found it unoccupied by the enemy, retrieved four spiked field pieces, and brought them back to Harpers Ferry. D'Utassy later spoke grandly of his bold return to Maryland Heights although he had not personally accompanied the troops.[11]

These moments at the siege of Harpers Ferry represented the zenith of D'Utassy's checkered military career. He had secured his officer's commission with claims of long experience in the Austrian army and service in the Crimean War. He led the 39th New York for an undistinguished year before being elevated to brigade command just before the Confederate arrival at Harpers Ferry. Afterwards D'Utassy's career careened downhill. Several months later he was arrested for failing to post a proper guard at his camp, and soon thereafter was exposed as a charlatan and an embezzler. His European military experience was discovered to have been nothing more than a clerkship in a quartermaster's department. The Hungarian was drummed out of the army and sentenced to a year at Sing Sing for submission of fraudulent vouchers and other charges. He ended up as an insurance salesman in Cincinnati.[12]

Still in his full glory on Bolivar Heights on September 14, 1862, D'Utassy ordered the regiments of his brigade off the crest of the Heights in an attempt to distance them from the pesky Confederate shells. The troops filed to the northern end of Bolivar Heights, turned left, and descended a path down the western slope. As the 115th's Company C turned off the hill a shell whistled past the men's heads and landed several feet behind the last man in line, satisfying William Jennings that "a kind providence had spread his shield" over the regiment. Another shot passed directly over Colonel Sammons and lodged unexploded in the ground under Batcheller's horse as he rode behind Sammons.[13]

At the western base of Bolivar Heights the brigade again turned left and marched into a line parallel to their former position on the crest. This maneuvering placed the 115th on the right of the brigade line and thus on the extreme right of the entire Union line on Bolivar Heights. In this position the rise of the Heights protected their backs and Confederate artillery on Maryland and Loudoun Heights ceased to be a problem. But the brigade line now stood closer to Confederate batteries on Schoolhouse Ridge, a parallel elevation west of Bolivar Heights where Jackson had aligned his corps. The southern gunners quickly spotted the brigade and made it a focus of their fire. The 115th and D'Utassy's other units hugged the low ground along the foot of Bolivar Heights until darkness finally halted the day long cannonading.

Throughout the afternoon the men had watched as waves of rebels moved into position along Schoolhouse Ridge, and now nothing but a few farm fields separated the regiment from the fearsome soldiers of Stonewall Jackson. James Reid wondered about the wisdom of their position. No earthworks or pickets protected their front and in their rear Bolivar Heights rose sharply. On its slope lay a tangled jumble of downed trees, effectively cutting them off from any retreat back up to the crest. Ironically, during the previous week the 115th had served on a detail assigned to clear-cut the crest—felling the very trees that now seemed to entrap them. Batcheller wrote that he and his men "counted upon an assault at night or at daybreak the next morning." Said Reid, "It was do or die, and every soldier nerved himself for the expected contest."[14]

The slumber of the nervous soldiers was soon interrupted but not by the all-out enemy assault they feared. Union musketry awoke them. The firing started on the far left of the federal position and spread toward the 115th. The men of the regiment jumped to their feet and, as DeGraff recorded, "along the whole line our boys blazed away finely." But no Confederates were to be seen. The men could never quite establish what had ignited the shooting spree, but offered several theories. Far off to the left near the Shenandoah River, some of Jackson's men were moving into position on some high ground that the northerners had left unoccupied. This triggered some shots by Union pickets that perhaps carried along the line, or the outbreak may have been directed against enemy cavalry, which Sammons later told D'Utassy he distinctly heard approaching. Batcheller afterward claimed to have learned from the rebels themselves that the regiment's fire resulted in some casualties among southern cavalry scouts and their mounts. Sammons even reported one man wounded by the elusive enemy's return fire. Some of the men, however, simply concluded that they had been firing at cornstalks, not Confederates. John Dye admitted he could not actually see any targets, but he fired five shots during the phantom skirmish. Within minutes orders came to cease fire, quiet was restored, and the weary soldiers returned to bed.[15]

This eventful day had been the 115th's second Sunday in the field, leading the devout Sergeant DeGraff to conclude that "there was no Sabbath laid down in army regulations." William Jennings went out on guard duty, stationed in the no-man's-land between Bolivar Heights and Schoolhouse Ridge, protecting his slumbering comrades and "wishing that morning or the brave McClellan would come." Of morning at least he could be certain.[16]

On September 15, 1862, the Confederate gunners resumed their bombardment just as soon as they had sufficient daylight to see well enough to cut fuses for their shells. The 115th

New York had already been up and in line for an hour expecting the rebel onslaught, but no southern infantry appeared. One man later wondered, "Why did not the infantry attack us? We were becoming impatient to return some of this fearful fire." Instead, as DeGraff recalled, "Battery after battery opened on us again."[17]

"The rebels had not been idle during the night," wrote eighteen-year old Private Almon Stone. He noticed that the shellfire came from several points where no rebel gun batteries had been located the previous evening. Most disconcerting was the appearance of enemy artillery overnight on the unprotected high ground southwest of Bolivar, near the Shenandoah. This position allowed Jackson's gunners to pour flank fire along the federal Bolivar Heights lines. Rebel infantry was also there readying an assault. In yet another failure of Union command this ground had been left undefended. The southerners took the hill against minimal resistance and, crowed Confederate General A.P. Hill, "the fate of Harpers Ferry was sealed." The wooded hillside at their backs offered the 115th some shelter from this enfilading fire, and the regiment fell back among the trees. Directed to lie down and await further orders, the men passed the time "listening to the wiz and bang of bursting shells and laughing at the ridiculous evolutions of some of the more timid ones as the shriek of a shell would sound uncomfortably near."[18]

The men cheered D'Utassy as he again rode among them. "Keep up coot courage," he implored, "and keep your powder dry, mine fine fellows." D'Utassy halted when he discovered a woman talking with one of the 115th. "Vat you do here, Vomans? You vill take de courage from mine men!" The lady was Mrs. Lucy Bertrand, wife of Private Lewis Bertrand of Company C who had accompanied the regiment to war as a laundress. In a firm voice she replied, "Colonel, if your men will stand as long as I will you need have no fears of them." Reassured, D'Utassy disappeared from view. James Reid remembered that the brief incident provided a timely lift to drooping spirits.[19]

The 115th had crouched in the woods for an hour when the regiment's drum major, Joshua Ripley, arrived from camp shouting news. He claimed he had heard that the whole Union garrison was about to surrender. His comrades ridiculed the idea but it quickly proved true when D'Utassy returned to the regiment. "His countenance betrays his errand before his lips utter the words," wrote Reid. The brigade commander sought out Colonel Sammons and announced, "General Miles has surrendered de place, and you will blease march your regiment on de color line, and stack arms."[20]

D'Utassy had just attended a council of war which Colonel Miles held on Bolivar Heights. Miles appeared there early that morning, reviewed the situation, and summoned his brigade commanders. He feared the impending rebel attack, deemed the Union position hopeless, and thought it advisable to surrender without further bloodshed. Some of his subalterns sternly resisted the idea, notably D'Utassy who argued that they should attempt a fighting escape. But the council ultimately supported Miles with a unanimous decision to surrender. At 8:30 a.m. the white flags went up.[21]

The action stunned the troops in the federal ranks; they had been surrendered without a fight. "Our men were frantic with rage," wrote Lieutenant Thomas Horton, adjutant of the 115th. "The cruel news spread with lightning speed throughout the whole army, and immediately one universal cry of indignation went up to heaven," anguished Sergeant Clark. "It was like a dagger to every heart. Strong men wept like children, and thousands were in tears." Certainly the young soldiers realized their predicament, but actual damage suffered during two days of rebel shelling remained fairly light. The

115th was typical in that it had sustained just ten casualties, none killed. The men also believed that time was on their side—they were sure that McClellan was marching to their rescue and that the garrison ought to hold out as long as possible. They felt they had not yet been tested and were not nearly ready to quit. "At that moment I would not have turned aside for the most deadly missile," George Batcheller declared in a letter home to his sister. "For the first time our men were weak. We all wept, for we felt that this great national disgrace was unnecessary."[22]

"To the men of the 115th the treason of Miles is too apparent," concluded Horton, echoing the majority sentiment. "Colonel Miles has played into the enemy's hands from the first," reasoned another man, no doubt calling to mind the events on Maryland Heights two days earlier. Whether or not Miles betrayed his country would be argued among the veterans for the rest of their lives and is still debated by historians. But he was no traitor, simply the wrong man in the wrong place. Miles's poor leadership and the impossible situation he faced combined to doom Harpers Ferry.[23]

Several rebel batteries kept firing after the Yankees hoisted their white flags. One Confederate artillery officer, whose guns stood opposite the 115th, recorded that when he thought he saw a white flag he immediately went to report it to his superior. The commander "could not or would not see it" and ordered that the shelling go on. "Damn their eyes, give it to them," he demanded. The gunner returned to his battery and resumed firing, but at a slowed pace. The rebel shelling continued as the 115th ascended Bolivar Heights pursuant to D'Utassy's order to return to the crest and stack arms. Sergeant DeGraff judged that the shelling continued for twenty minutes after the white flags went up. Officers from both sides scrambled to put a stop to it and the firing ceased, but too late: it had already inflicted a couple of significant casualties.[24]

A fragment from one of the last of these shots pierced the side of Private John Vanbrocklin of Company A producing a mortal wound. The unfortunate eighteen-year old died on October 6, becoming the 115th's first fatality. At the time of his death Vanbrocklin shared a hospital tent with Captain William Smith, who had been shot at the knob on Maryland Heights. Smith advised Vanbrocklin's family in Johnstown that the private "was doing well untill inflimation [sic] set in and struck to the vital parts and carried him off.... He had all the care and medical skill that could be bestowed upon him." Smith put the boy's mother in touch with the hospital chaplain. She asked the chaplain to forward her son's effects and to have his body sent home for burial. The chaplain wrote back to offer sympathy and prayers and further bad news. He had been transferred and could not arrange to ship her son's remains, but advised that he had carved John's name on both a wooden headstone and his coffin to help her find him. And, as if all this were not enough, he had to advise the grieving mother that the hospital had been beset by thieves and someone had stolen all of her son's things. "Oh dear how hard this is," she wrote.[25]

Colonel Miles was also a casualty of the late rebel fire. As he proceeded down the east slope of Bolivar Heights with an aide a shell struck just behind him and shrapnel tore through both of his legs. He died the next day. Given the recriminations the old soldier would surely have faced, it was a merciful shot. DeGraff called it good news when he learned of Miles's death saying, "he richly deserved his fate." Private John Dye was assisting the 115th's regimental surgeon Richard Sutton when reports of Miles's demise first reached the soldiers, and he listened as the doctor asked a passing officer if the reports were indeed true. Dye claimed he would remember the reply for as long as he lived. "Yes," answered the officer, "he's dead and damned by this time, the old traitor."[26]

Things moved rapidly after the surrender as General Lee urgently needed his detached contingents to return to him. General McClellan and his Army of the Potomac, having forced their way across South Mountain the previous day, were closing on Lee's position along Antietam Creek near Sharpsburg, Maryland. The Confederates at Harpers Ferry, anxious to rejoin Lee, acted quickly to complete their work among the captured garrison. "We soon had plenty of visitors. The jubilant southerners came in squads and acted on the principle that 'to the victor belong the spoils,'" recalled Corporal Reid. "In the mean time—and it was mean enough," complained DeGraff, "a guard of the detested rebels were placed around us and we were prisoners indeed."[27]

Captives and captors "mingled freely and held conversations about the war," recorded Lieutenant Devendorf. Close inspection of the victorious rebels startled the Union men. In a letter to his wife Devendorf did his best to describe the southerners:

> They had nothing to eat but green corn and apples for over a month and the men looked as though they were walking skeletons with clothing on.... Why, Sarah, one half of the rebels had no shoes or boots. They were dirty and filthy. One rebel told me he had not washed or combed his hair for over three months. In fact they glory in their shame—the worse they look, the better they feel. It was impossible to tell the officers from the men. They were all alike the sufferers of poverty and hunger.[28]

James Reid enjoyed exchanging pleasantries with his captors, but was also taken aback by their condition:

> Their clothes and general appearance contrasted strangely with our well-dressed, cleanly appearance. Every conceivable article of head-gear and the poorest of its kind seemed in vogue with them. Sleeveless coats and legless pants partially covered these war-begrimed veterans; whereas it would have been difficult to have found a whole pair of shoes in all the number we saw.

George Batcheller deduced the ragged Confederates to be "surely earnest men or they would not—they could not—like to fight as they do."[29]

The victorious rebels "despoiled the camps of anything that was loose," wrote Reid. He added the grateful note that the southerners did not pilfer any personal belongings from Union soldiers and he wondered if the Yankees would have been as lenient under reversed circumstances. But the Confederates were in great need of horses and grabbed all they could find, including the mounts of Colonel Sammons and Lieutenant Colonel Batcheller. They seized these horses not knowing that they were Sammons's and Batcheller's personal property, violating the terms of the surrender which stated that all officers would be allowed to keep their horses. Batcheller complained to rebel General A.P. Hill, who Jackson had placed in charge of the surrender proceedings. Hill placated Batcheller by issuing the meaningless order that the horses should be returned if found.[30]

The Confederates were quick to collect that most treasured prize of the Civil War, the flags of vanquished units. The loss of these unit emblems to the enemy was the greatest disgrace a soldier could suffer, but thanks to some fast action the 115th New York managed to avoid this ignominy at Harpers Ferry. Determined to save their banners some quick-thinking men removed the regiment's flags from their staffs and hid them under their clothes. The resourceful soldiers wrapped pieces of tent cloth around the stripped flagstaffs and covered them with the oilcloth coverings used for flag storage. Before long some Confederate officers, loaded down with numerous colors wrested from other northern units, came to the 115th and demanded their flags. They were handed the bogus banners. "The rebs took them without noticing the exchange," wrote a relieved DeGraff. "The colors were restored to the regiment a few days later ... to the joy and surprise of all."[31]

Some men defied their captors by wrecking equipment before it fell into rebel hands. Batcheller broke his sword by ramming it into the ground and bending it until it snapped. Lieutenant Ferguson "dashed his sword to atoms against a stone." DeGraff buried his Navy revolver. Many others smashed their muskets.[32]

The troops spent a few hours fraternizing with the enemy and pondering their fate before learning that they would be paroled, an arrangement by which captured men swore an oath that they would not serve against the Confederacy until officially exchanged for enemy prisoners. After taking the oath the captives remained in the custody of their own army but could not fight until exchanged. News of the parole arrangement failed to soothe a concerned Robert Fox, a corporal in Company C. Fox told his mates that he feared the parole would apply only to privates and that he and the other officers would be imprisoned in Richmond. This brought a good laugh from his comrades who were quicker than Fox to discern that "a corporal's chevrons were not a very distinguishing insignia."[33]

The parole indeed applied to all men and officers and parole procedures occupied the entire afternoon and evening of September 15. The Union regiments formed up, the parole statement was read to them, and the men raised their right hands and pledged to abide by it. Officers signed parole papers on behalf of their commands, and the men returned to their camps. "Night came on and we lay ourselves down on the ground to sleep (those who could)," wrote Nicholas DeGraff, "a forlorn set of fellows—soldiers armless, defenseless, and prisoners."[34]

4

Penned in Chicago

"Our boys are very unruly"

Eleven thousand paroled prisoners filed out of Harpers Ferry on the morning of September 16, 1862, starting an eighty mile, five day trek to Annapolis, Maryland. "Our march was a rapid pace," remembered James Reid, "probably accelerated as much by the desire of the enemy to get rid of us as by our desire to get beyond their immediate control." The Confederates at the Ferry were in a desperate hurry to rejoin General Lee and the balance of his army along the banks of Antietam Creek, where they awaited battle with George McClellan and the Army of the Potomac.

Heat, fatigue, and blisters marked the journey across Maryland, and many soldiers lagged behind their units. Despite halting several times to give the stragglers a chance to catch up the 115th covered twenty-two miles on the first day, marching from Harpers Ferry to Frederick, Maryland. A horrible stench pervaded the field near Frederick where the regiment bivouacked. The next morning the men discovered that they had camped in an area used several days earlier to butcher cattle to feed the troops of the Army of the Potomac as they passed through in pursuit of Lee. "Mutterings of discontent were heard on every side, while not a few cursed the officer who selected such a place for our bivouac," complained Corporal Reid.[1]

The mood brightened abruptly as the 115th assembled to resume the march, a joyous buzz spreading among the men as they saw their regimental flags unfurled and waved before them. Most of the soldiers had not been privy to the ruse that saved the banners from Confederate hands, and they greeted the unexpected sight of the "glorious emblems" with delight. "Loud huzzas" erupted from the ranks, wrote Corporal Reid. "Great was the joy manifested by the boys when the colors were brought out," recalled William Scorsby.[2]

During that day, September 17, the men could hear sounds of heavy firing off toward the west: McClellan and Lee had finally clashed along the Antietam. The parolees trudged eastward as the bloodiest day in American history played out within earshot.[3]

When the parolees departed Harpers Ferry the rebels allowed them to pack only two days' rations of pork and hardtack. This meager fare could hardly satisfy thousands of young men, so the pursuit of edibles became a constant theme of the march across Maryland, and it dominated later recollections. The soldiers remembered orchards of ripe peaches that they bought from local farms at six for a penny, fields of corn which they quickly stripped bare, generous citizens who shared whatever they had with the passing soldiers, and foraging to supplement their diet in any way possible.[4]

No one had a sharper instinct for a meal than Sergeant DeGraff. As the regiment turned off the road into its chosen campsite for September 18, DeGraff spotted a hog in a nearby field. He handed his recovered Navy revolver to Private Bill Nutt and told him to go shoot the hog. "We soon heard him banging away and the hog squealing." DeGraff sent some other men to help Nutt fetch the hog back to camp while he went to a nearby farmhouse to beg some salt for the anticipated feast. At the house DeGraff saw the farmer talking to Lieutenant Colonel Batcheller and heard Batcheller saying, "We do not allow such things, and if you can find out what soldiers killed your hog we will make them pay you its full value." The bold twenty-year old stayed and got his salt before double-quicking back to camp to tell his friends what he had heard. "Of course there was no hog meat in sight after that," he noted.

Later on the march DeGraff's stomach and his revolver got him into more trouble when he discovered a flock of turkeys in a farmyard. DeGraff left the marching column with his lieutenant's permission, went into the farmyard and dropped one of the turkeys with his pistol. As he turned proudly back to the road he was "confronted by a dashing colonel of one of the regiments accompanied by his glittering staff." They forced him at sword point to drop the turkey and placed him under arrest. The farmer came to the scene and good-naturedly told "the superb colonel" that the young soldier could keep the turkey. But the colonel escorted DeGraff back to the 115th and "with a great flourish" turned him over to Colonel Sammons with a request that he be properly punished. Sammons promised to attend to it, and the natty colonel went on his way. DeGraff feared for his sergeant's stripes but never heard any more of the incident except in jokes.

At the end of that day's fourteen hour march the regiment bivouacked in a woodlot. Two thousand hungry parolees had preceded the 115th to the spot and had picked the area clean of any available victuals, leaving the regiment stuck with only their sparse army rations. "Oh, how I wished for that turkey," pined DeGraff.[5]

The main body of the 115th arrived at Annapolis on the evening of September 21. James Reid who had reached Annapolis about two hours earlier wrote, "I shall never forget the way the regiment looked on its arrival, after a tramp of about 125 miles [Reid overestimated] through Maryland dust and heat. Foot-sore, tired, and above all hungry, and yet, after a sumptuous repast, the boys began to sing, and in fact were ready for anything that might come up for amusement."[6]

"Annapolis City is not a pretty town," declared James Clark. He found most buildings "fast going to decay," and "the marts of trade" mostly closed—casualties of the war. Continued Clark:

> The military have full possession of the city, and armed bands of soldiers meet you at every corner; while one person here, and another there, with an arm or a leg cut off, are seen in every street. The Naval Academy, and almost all of the fine public buildings serve as hospitals for sick and wounded soldiers, who arrive from the cruelty of rebel dungeons.

A huge encampment near Annapolis served as a collecting place for paroled federal prisoners of war and was accordingly dubbed Camp Parole. The Harpers Ferry troops joined many thousands of other parolees who had preceded them into the camp and the city.[7]

Annapolis was crowded but offered plenty to eat. On the evening of their arrival the boys enjoyed "a hearty meal for the first time in many days," according to Clark. The next morning Nicholas DeGraff and some others went swimming in Chesapeake Bay and found its waters rich with fish, crabs, and other bounty. On each day of their stay at Camp Parole the men returned to the bay. James Reid and friends hunted oysters by walking barefoot in the shallows where they harvested the bivalves with their feet. They found the oysters so abundant that it became difficult to transport their haul back to camp. Reid solved that problem by turning his longjohns into a sack. He said that when he filled the drawers with oysters and slung them across his shoulders he looked like a farmer "with a pumpkin in each end of a bag."[8]

Lieutenant Colonel Batcheller judged the men of the 115th "very much demoralized" when they arrived at Annapolis. "To restore their soldierly bearing and dignity" he held a dress parade each afternoon. One soldier thought the dress parades seemed odd as the men had no rifles to carry. Nonetheless, after the second of these assemblies Batcheller declared success. In a letter to his sister he reported that his men's spirits and health had returned. The rank and file of the regiment would more likely have attributed any uplift in morale to their romps in Chesapeake Bay and their full stomachs. Batcheller's letter also recounted the miserable story of the loss of Harpers Ferry, but concluded on a hopeful note:

> We have in this little time experienced more of war and its perils and hardships than many regiments who have served from the beginning of the war. It has been a valuable experience to both officers and men, and should we be so fortunate as to be soon exchanged and go into another action we will prove that the surrender at Harpers Ferry was not caused by any weakness of the 115th Regiment.[9]

Camp Parole buzzed with speculation about the ultimate fate of the parolees. "There are a thousand rumors afloat about what disposition the Government will make of us, but nothing official is known," wrote one soldier. The men hoped to be furloughed home to await their official exchange as had been a common practice earlier in the war, but they were quickly disabused of this notion when all of the Harpers Ferry prisoners were ordered to Camp Douglas in Chicago to await their exchange.[10]

The rumor mill held that the Harpers Ferry men would be sent west from Chicago to fight Indians, a story rooted in an order issued by U.S. Secretary of War Edwin Stanton on September 24 directing the parolees to Minnesota to join General Pope. As the troops left Camp Parole and marched to the Annapolis waterfront on September 25 they believed that they were en route to the American frontier and a bout with the Sioux. But sometime during the next few days as the Harpers Ferry thousands rolled westward, the army changed its plans and this order was never carried out. The parolees' destination, as it turned out, would be less adventurous but equally dangerous—internment in a crowded Chicago prison camp.[11]

The soldiers of the 115th were among 2,500 men crowded "like herring in a box" aboard the former Hudson River transport *City of Norwich* for the slow sail up the Chesapeake to Baltimore. In spite of the crowding they enjoyed the cruise. Less enjoyable was the two-mile march from the dock to the railroad station through the streets of Baltimore, a city infamous for its southern sympathies. Residents along the route mocked the disarmed prisoners. "We were treated with great contempt," remembered Lieutenant Devendorf. Some of the hostile locals went so far as to remove the handles from their pumps in order to deny drinking water to the soldiers. The sneers and meanness of the citizens were "enough to make a saint swear," according to Chaplain Sylvester Clemens who "felt like threshing every one who looked pleased, and kicking every wench who showed the white of her eye."[12]

The dejected parolees boarded trains and began a slow and uncomfortable ride westward with forty soldiers stuffed in each box car. The crowded cars wound along the Susquehanna River, passing through tunnels over one thousand feet long, past coal mines, and over terrain of "the wildest kind of place for a railroad," recalled Sergeant DeGraff. At 4:00 a.m. on Saturday, September 27, after thirty-three hours on the rails, the troops disembarked at Pittsburgh where the men enjoyed their first inkling that the folks at home did not view them as shamed and defeated. "It put new heart into the boys. They began to feel like men again," rejoiced Chaplain Clemens. They enjoyed a sumptuous breakfast in a grand hall bedecked with a banner reading *Pittsburgh Welcomes Her Country's Defenders*. Henry Devendorf wrote his wife, "I tell you, we did have a tiptop meal, and the best of it was, we were waited upon by very handsome ladies (Don't get jealous)." The splendid breakfast moved Corporal Michael Rice of Company C to exclaim, "If this be war, I hope we may never have peace."[13]

Indeed, from western Pennsylvania to Chicago the journey became "one continued, grand ovation," a memory the men cherished the rest of their lives. Crowds formed all along the route to greet and cheer the Harpers Ferry prisoners. At every stop they were hailed and feasted with everything "the thoughtfulness of a generous and patriotic people could devise," recalled a thankful James Reid. "Ohio and Indiana were not to be outdone, and our welcome within their borders was no less generous. If we had captured Jackson's army instead of being captured by it we could hardly have commanded greater attention."

At Lima, Ohio, "the people brought out bread, pie, apples, etc., urging them on us," wrote DeGraff. And at Delphos "the people could not do enough for us." Colonel Sammons and Chaplain Clemens made speeches to the crowd gathered at Fort Wayne, Indiana, where, noted St. Johnsville native Corporal John Reardon of Company E, "seemingly the whole population turned caterers.... Every conceivable article of food and fruit tempted our appetites." Sergeant Clark particularly remembered the stop at Fort Wayne where the town's young ladies ran the welcoming committee and lavished feminine attention on the regiment. Similar scenes occurred elsewhere in the Hoosier State.[14]

Reid called the trip "the grandest ovation of modern times." DeGraff gratefully proclaimed: "What a glorious people! Who would not suffer privations for a nation such as ours?" Some men vowed to return to the midwest after the war to find wives and settle down. Decades later a terminally ill John Reardon, thinking back on his regiment's benefactors, ascribed a motive to their kindness: "No doubt that nearly all of them had more or less near kin in the army of whom they were seriously thinking while making life pleasant for us."[15]

The triumphant tour ended anticlimactically when the train carrying the rank and file of the 115th arrived in Chicago on the dark and rainy night of September 28. The railroad crew rudely ordered the soldiers off the cars, and the men found themselves on their own to find rest and shelter. The fact that the regiment's officers rode on a separate train no doubt abetted the trainmen's surly attitude. The troops sought refuge from the stormy night as best they could. Remembered James Reid, "Many chose the prairie, others searched the R.R. tracks for empty cars, while several of us wandered to the lakeside some distance away and spread our blankets under the trees." Clark and six friends spent the night in a kind Irishwoman's barn, despite her husband's drunken threat to "kill every mother's son of yee's. ... ye murderin' spalpeens." The downpour escalated and little sleep was had. In the morning the soggy travelers made their various ways to nearby Camp Douglas where they were met by their officers, whose train had arrived several hours after the enlisted men's.[16]

The *Ballston Journal* of October 7, 1862 reported the 115th's arrival in Chicago and presented a brief summary of its first month in service:

The 115th has been in two battles, in several skirmishes, has marched 175 miles, slept on the ground without covering 15 nights, and traveled in all about 1500 miles, passing thru 9 states, in the short space of thirty days!.... This is an astonishing record. We doubt whether history can furnish a parallel.

The *Journal* was a bit liberal in what it termed battles and skirmishes, but it had the mileage right. The Civil War odyssey of the 115th New York Volunteer Infantry had gotten under way in earnest.[17]

Camp Douglas was constructed soon after the outbreak of the war to serve as an organizing area for the many new army units being raised in northern Illinois. Just south of Chicago and close to the shore of Lake Michigan, the camp was named for the recently deceased Senator Stephen A. Douglas, whose home stood within sight. The camp sprawled across 160 acres, within which elongated frame buildings enclosed a number of open squares. Earlier in 1862, following the Union victories at Fort Donelson, Shiloh, and Island Number Ten, it had been pressed into use as a prisoner of war camp. Nearly 9,000 captured Confederates had vacated Camp Douglas just before the Harpers Ferry parolees began rolling in.[18]

The Harpers Ferry contingent overwhelmed Camp Douglas, and three regiments—the 9th Vermont, 39th New York, and the 115th—were sent on to the adjacent Illinois State Fairground. After seeing the condition in which its former residents had left Camp Douglas, these men cheerfully moved to the fairground where they quartered in horse stables. They found the stables in good condition and made themselves at home with six to nine men occupying each stall. "Each stall is 10 by 15 ft. square & never been used by the looks," Nicholas DeGraff wrote home to his father. "We put 8 boys in each & with boards & nails they soon began to look more like living than anything of the kind we had seen before."[19]

Getting enough to eat—that all-important concern of the common soldier—proved no problem during the regiment's seven weeks in Illinois. "If they will only let us alone a little while we will get fat," wrote DeGraff. "We have fresh beef nearly every day, all the coffee we want, and excellent bread and butter." The troops showed their usual initiative in supplementing government rations. "We could get any extra provisions we wished to buy at reasonable prices, vegetables being sold in camp daily," recorded John Reardon.[20]

A number of men from James Reid's Company C did some creative rule breaking to get a regular supply of fresh milk. They noticed that a small herd of dairy cows passed behind their quarters each evening. By scattering cabbage leaves and other bovine delicacies at their back door, they put the cows into the habit of stopping by to graze and be milked by some of the former farm boys of the 115th. They avoided detection by the herd's owner by partially milking several of the cows instead of fully milking any of them. Despite the good supply of foodstuffs some found grounds for complaint. Clark griped about a shipment of tainted rations with "bacon alive with maggots, the bread hard, sour, and black, and the sugar the color of sand." However, on November 3 Regimental Surgeon Richard E. Sutton reported to Colonel Sammons that the regiment enjoyed an abundant supply of good quality food.[21]

Officers assembled the regiment daily for drills and roll calls, but the men still had plenty of time on their hands and sought to fill it. "Of course where there are so many gathered together there will be something going on to pass the time," explained Lieutenant Devendorf. Lake Michigan drew men for bathing in the fair early autumn weather. Many went sightseeing, readily obtaining the required passes or simply not bothering with them.

The nearby home and grave of Stephen A. Douglas drew numbers of curious onlookers, and everyone found their way into Chicago. DeGraff rode all around the young city on trolleys and enjoyed the view from a high platform on a city courthouse:

> On one side Lake Michigan. On the other the rolling prairie. The ship canal dividing the city through its principal part. Masts of vessels could be seen moving among the buildings. The street cars and steam cars, sails dotting the lake with the din and noise of the business world below us, gave us a very good idea of the push and enterprise of Chicago.[22]

Camp activities included impromptu athletics. Lieutenant Colonel Batcheller gave the regiment a "fine foot ball with which the boys had immense sport." Later, as the weather turned wintry, the men naturally turned to the sport of "snow balling." Alcohol also provided diversion for those so inclined. "The supply of liquor to be had near the camp was plenty and easily gotten," noted a disapproving Reardon. Drinking contributed to a decline of discipline and had at least one fatal consequence. Thirty-four-year old Sylvanus Dodds, returning to camp from a foray into Chicago, "was run over by a train and horribly cut up. Canteens of whiskey were found on his body which told their own story."[23]

Letters to and from home provided a vital lifeline for the soldiers throughout the war, but the 115th's internment following the surrender at Harpers Ferry magnified homesickness and the desire to communicate with loved ones. DeGraff implored his brother to "write all you can think of. It is very interesting to me to hear of every little incident." Devendorf wrote often to his wife and baby, weaving emotional messages with descriptive accounts of his military experiences. "I confess I wish I could step in and give you and our dear baby a sweet kiss," he wrote in one letter. "Oh, how often I look at the miniatures and what pleasant thoughts arise while looking at those I so fondly love. Absent but ever near and dear in imagination."[24]

The men did what they could to enhance the comfort of living in cramped quarters designed for horses. DeGraff and his stall-mates constructed a desk and seat, shelves, tables, benches, and bunks for their room in the stables. And after a chilly autumn night on October 21 they each chipped in 71 cents to buy a secondhand stove. "Now we are all O.K. for a long stay," concluded DeGraff.[25]

In another company Orderly Sergeant George Curreen, a religious man who led groups of his mates into Chicago to attend church, worked at constructing a stool. The less pious Private George Millham watched him for a time, then asked, "Orderly, do you suppose God sees everything?"

"Yes," replied Curreen.

"Well," said Millham, "He will laugh like hell when he sees that stool."[26]

Officers attempted to keep order by establishing a routine of meals, roll call and drill but despite such efforts lack of discipline became a constant problem. "Our boys are very unruly," wrote DeGraff. Many men (classified by Corporal Reardon as "chronic kickers who were not fit to be in the army nor out of it") protested that prisoners of war were not obliged to drill and routinely avoided the regimental assemblies. Writing to his sister on the evening of October 31, DeGraff joked that he had been surprised that day to see the large size of his company as it mustered for pay. "When we go out for drill we cannot get half of them out. But coming out for pay is a horse of another color."[27]

It did not aid matters when several of the 115th's officers, including the colonel, the chaplain, and the surgeon, were called to Washington to testify before the War Department commission investigating the surrender of Harpers Ferry. The absence of key leaders from all the Harpers Ferry units contributed to troubles of varying magnitude throughout Camp

Douglas, as did the inexperience of the remaining officers, the idleness and lack of purpose in the camp, the uncertain future, and strong drink.[28]

The records of the 115th describe dozens of courts martial involving charges of drunkenness, profanity, disobedience of orders, theft, and absence without leave. Sentences for those found guilty could be extra drill, confinement, or forfeit of pay. Typical was the November 3 case heard against Private John McKnight. The forty-two-year old Saratoga County man of Company I faced charges of drunkenness, disobeying orders, and disrespectful language. McKnight got loudly drunk on three straight nights, ruining the sleep of many other soldiers. When Corporal Daniel Sherman ordered McKnight to quiet down and go to bed, McKnight told Sherman to "stop his noise and go to hell." When Sergeant Jeremiah Bovee intervened, McKnight raged that he "would not be driven to bed by a son of a bitch." The accused pleaded guilty to all charges and was sentenced to carry a knapsack filled with thirty pounds of rocks for one hour per day for two days.[29]

A significant number—over a hundred men from the 115th—simply went home, taking *French leave* as the soldiers called it. The army had another term for it—*desertion*. While some "deserted from sheer depravity," as suggested in a story in the *Ballston Journal* of October 21, others as the *Journal* explained,

George Curreen of Ballston in Saratoga County mustered in as a sergeant and received promotion to lieutenant on the day after the Battle of Olustee. He was wounded in action twice and left the regiment because of illness in December 1864 (New York State Military Museum).

"innocently believed that after they were paroled the government had no further control over them, and that they were at liberty to go where they pleased." Most eventually returned to the regiment and suffered minimal consequences such as demotion in rank.

Deserters also faced peer pressure as their actions dishonored their comrades and communities. The *Ballston Journal* article listed the names of all absent soldiers from Saratoga County and called for them to be punished. In a letter to his family in Amsterdam, DeGraff made it a point to list the names of men deserted from his company. Captain John Kneeskern, leader of the 115th's Company B, did the same in his October 12 note to a friend back in St. Johnsville. While most generally disapproved, the men shared a common view that such French leave did not compare to desertion in the face of the enemy.[30]

While the 115th New York had its share of problems, they were mild in comparison to other units. As early as October 3 the commandant at Camp Douglas became alarmed about the conduct of the Harpers Ferry troops. When he received a dispatch ordering their regimental officers to return east for the War Department hearings, he responded, "If I order the officers to Washington I am sure to have a mutiny tomorrow." He called the Harpers Ferry men "perfectly disorganized," and singled out the 39th and 125th New York for being especially insubordinate. Fires, generally ascribed to arson, broke out regularly at Camp Douglas, and the barracks of several regiments were destroyed. Captain Kneeskern called Camp Douglas "a Dirty filthy place." On October 12 he reported, "The Soldiers had it on fire last [night] and Sware they will burn it to ashes. They are raising hell all over Camp."[31]

The men of the 115th claimed innocence of the worst of the mischief. Colonel Sammons later asserted that his regiment, "performed every duty required of it cheerfully and without murmuring," and that they "destroyed no property, public or private." Upon his return from Washington he complimented the men on their good conduct. On one occasion the 115th was detailed to rebuild a stockade fence at Camp Douglas that other troops had destroyed, and on another the regiment served on guard duty. The men of the 115th later pointed to these assignments as proof that they had not been as bad as the other fellows. Eventually troops from the regular army arrived to watch over troubled Camp Douglas.[32]

October gave way to early winter. Frost appeared on October 14 and snow squalls marked October 25. The turn in the weather intensified the growing discontent. Idleness and boredom displaced the initial excitement of young men in new territory. "We have had nothing much to do," lamented DeGraff on October 31. Adding to the volatile mix, diseases associated with crowded, unsanitary conditions struck a growing number of soldiers. "Almost all of the regiment were more or less sick by the first of November, and large numbers soon died." The first to die in Company D was eighteen-year old Chauncy Snyder, Jr. "Poor Chauncy. A young life so full of promise ended," wrote DeGraff. Snyder and his father had enlisted together in July in Amsterdam, New York. Chauncy, Sr. served in the 115th throughout the war, but would lose another son in service with the 115th before the fighting concluded.[33]

The disintegrating situation alarmed Colonel Sammons and he attempted to relocate his command. He wrote directly to Governor Morgan and to New York State's Adjutant General Thomas Hillhouse, asking their intercession in having the 115th moved to its home state. To both Morgan and Hillhouse he sent copies of a November 3 report from the regimental surgeon, Dr. Sutton, who had treated 757 soldiers in the previous three weeks, including as many as 252 in a single day. He attributed the declining health to "the poisonous miasma generated in this climate," and recommended that "unless these troops can be speedily removed to some more elevated country, in my opinion, you have only to wait the tedious wearing away of winter to find your regiment decimated by disease and disorganized by sickness." The 115th would soon leave Chicago but not before forty men perished.[34]

By November hopeful rumors of the eagerly-awaited prisoner exchange pervaded camp, but as each report proved false, the misery only deepened. Frustration mounted day-by-day along with the sick list, and spirits sank with the temperature. Wrote a downcast DeGraff, "Our camp is a lake of mud, the air is heavy and damp, and it is all one can do to keep his spirits up. And some of the boys, I am sorry to say, keep them up by pouring them down."[35]

On November 19 DeGraff sat down to write to his brother. He mentioned a story in the morning paper that the Harpers Ferry parolees had been exchanged and ordered to Washington. For weeks DeGraff, who kept a diary and penned frequent letters home, eagerly recorded the many rumors and reports of exchange that circulated through camp. None of the stories proved true, and by this date DeGraff was cynical of the constant camp gossip. "It is not believed," he wrote. "The camp is full of rumors all the time and if I was to believe half of them it would make me dizzy headed." DeGraff's missive went on to describe the gloomy weather and the rapidly lengthening sick list. He assured his brother that he was healthy and had even put on some weight since leaving home, and enclosed some photos of himself. Sergeant DeGraff was still composing his letter when his friend Lieutenant Thomas Wayne came by with momentous news. This time the reports were true! Colonel Sammons had just received a dispatch confirming that the 115th was to depart Chicago the next day and would soon receive their exchange.[36]

"We bade goodbye to Chicago with few regrets," wrote James Clark. "Farewell, paradise of mud, city of stairs, rats, and beer saloons. Goodbye shivering fevers, wretched horse stalls, and rotten bacon. Farewell!" With such sentiment an eager 115th rose at 4:00 a.m. on November 20 to flee their Illinois confinement. They impatiently waited through the day until finally at 3:00 p.m. the order came to form into line and prepare to march.[37]

As the regiment, now about eight hundred men strong, stood in line outside their stables-turned-barracks, an event occurred that brought little notice at the time, but would prove pivotal in the career of the 115th New York Infantry. The quarters they had called home for the last seven weeks caught fire, the blaze quickly engulfing the flimsy structures. "The flames fanned by the stormy wind soon laid the detested horse stables in ashes with very few regrets on our part at the time," recorded Corporal Reid. Some 115th men rejoiced at the destruction, waving hats and cheering. Soldiers of the 9th Vermont and 39th New York attempted to subdue the flames, but no one in the 115th broke ranks to assist them. "We were not detained, but marched directly to the cars," wrote Reardon.[38]

As the fire raged, the 115th boarded a waiting train. "As we looked back towards our late camp we saw through the smoke the long lines of smouldering ruins of the horse stables and indulged, perhaps, in too many exclamations of joy at the devastation," Reid later recorded, thinking back on the fire and its ultimate impact on the 115th. But on November 20, 1862 these men were more concerned with what lay ahead than behind. They took just as much notice of boarding first-class passenger cars for their return to the east as they did of the burning barracks. The Chicago fire proved "a sad conflagration" for the 115th, as one of the regiment's later chroniclers put it. "Little did the brave men then imagine what trials, suffering, and insults awaited them."[39]

5

Fire and Consequences
"Thunder clap from a clear sky"

The 115th sped out of Chicago and retraced its journey across the country without all the fanfare and feasting that marked their westward trip. They had only two meals during a two-day ride that brought them to Baltimore at sunrise on November 23, 1862, but the men did appreciate traveling in first class passenger cars. In Baltimore they enjoyed a good breakfast before boarding livestock cars for a forty mile trip to Washington, D.C. that took several hours. Reaching the capital city on the evening of November 23, the men ate supper at the Soldier's Relief facility near the U.S. Capitol, and bivouacked on the floor of an adjacent building.[1]

The next morning many of the soldiers took advantage of some idle time to visit the Capitol. Private Joshua Ripley of Company A wrote of "the lofty and spacious rotunda, the splendid statuary, and unequaled paintings with which the immense building is decorated." After visiting the seat of his nation's government James Clark became "deeply impressed with the necessity of defending Washington against every foe."[2]

Later that morning the 115th reassembled and marched across the city. "Every soldier was on his good behavior and our quite full ranks made a very creditable display in our march through the streets," recalled James Reid. People stopped to watch the regiment pass by and judged the New Yorkers approvingly with remarks such as "fine lot of men," and "good stuff there." Crossing the Long Bridge over the Potomac, the 115th "trod the sacred and bloody soil of Virginia once again." There the men found they had outdistanced their tents and spent a frigid, sleepless night on bare ground.[3]

On the morning of November 25 the regiment formed camp on Arlington Heights within view of the buildings of Washington, in an area known as Camp Chase. Since the war's start in 1861 multitudes of Union soldiers had occupied Camp Chase, and thousands were encamped there when the 115th arrived. Private Ripley counted fifteen other camps within sight. He roamed several miles through the surrounding country and reported "not a square rod but a tent has been erected at some time during the war." Trees and fences had long since gone to firewood, and even green grass was a rarity. Ripley wrote:

> You should see the ruinous and devastating effects of the war in this rich and beautiful region.... Houses are deserted and pillaged and used for stables and barracks.... I passed by a once splendid mansion and out the parlor window a cavalry horse had his head, taking a very

cool survey of the destroying influence of war on the beautiful lawn and grounds surrounding the house. No doubt some very sagacious reflections were passing through his head on the foolish and wicked passions of his masters.[4]

Shortly after arriving at Camp Chase, the 115th received orders to prepare to spend the winter there and went to work constructing winter quarters. Log huts began to spring up, equipped with straw bedding and other necessaries secured by these veteran scroungers from Camp Douglas. With the finishing touch of wood stoves, within a couple of days the men had themselves fixed up "snug as a bug in a rug," according to John Reardon.[5]

On the first of December the 115th formed in dress parade and gratefully heard the order announcing their official exchange. The next day the men received Enfield rifled muskets and the regiment began sharing in guard duty around Camp Chase. Paroled prisoners no longer, the proud New Yorkers could once again consider themselves active soldiers for the Union.[6]

Other than outfitting their own quarters, the 115th performed little duty at Camp Chase. The regiment's officers remained lackadaisical about drill. James Reid recalled that "time passed slowly with us.... The days passed off pleasantly and with comfort, but the long cold nights were dreaded." Some diversion came from visiting with friends at the camp of the 153rd New York, six miles distant. The 153rd hailed from the same area of New York State as the 115th and had mustered into service at Camp Mohawk soon after the 115th departed.[7]

Just seventeen days into the anticipated winter's stay at Camp Chase the men of the regiment were surprised by orders to pack up and leave. On December 12, grumbling about

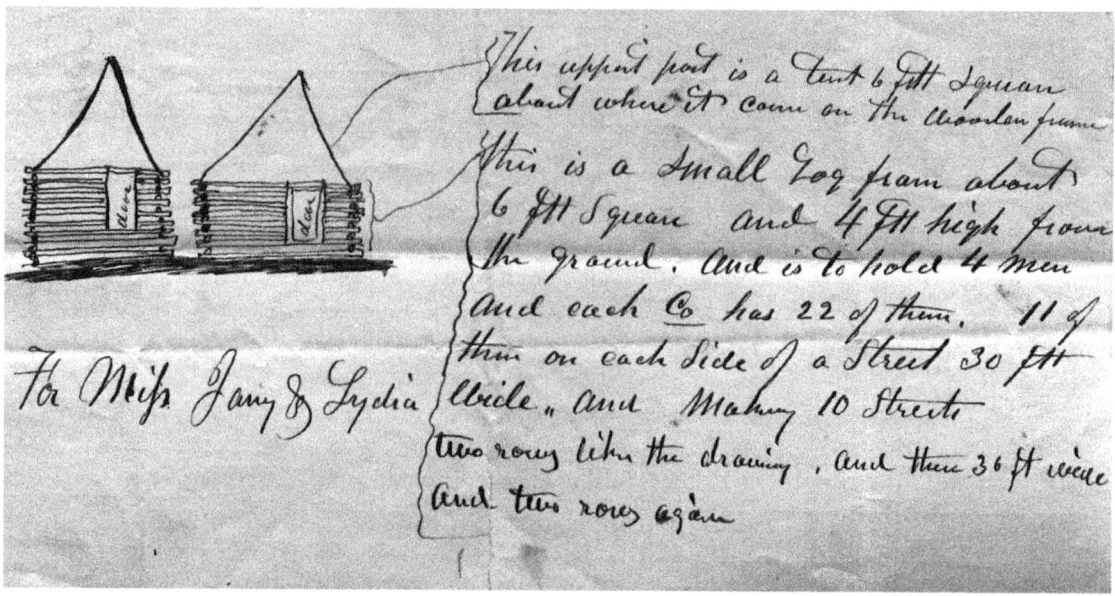

Colonel Sammons sent this drawing home to his daughters with a letter in late 1864. It reads: "For Miss Fanny & Lydia. This upper part is a tent 6 ft square about where it come on the wooden frame. This is a small log frame about 6 ft square and 4 ft high from the ground. And is to hold 4 men and each Co has 22 of them. 11 of them on each side of a street 30 ft wide. and making 10 streets two rows like this drawing. And 30 ft wide and two rows again" (Collection of the Montgomery County Department of History and Archives, Fonda, New York).

the wasted efforts sunk into their winter quarters, the 115th marched several miles to Hunter's Creek, a mile outside Alexandria, Virginia. The site had been vacated recently by Vermont troops so the men dubbed it Camp Vermont. Advised once again to settle in for a long stay, the regiment built winter huts for the second time. Cold, snow, and mud plagued northern Virginia in mid-December as the men devoted themselves to constructing their new homes. Soon more than two hundred log houses stood in neat rows. Wrote Colonel Sammons, "I am feeling very proud of my camp.... I hope they will let us remain in winter quarters here."[8]

But it was not to be. On Christmas Eve, a mere fourteen days into his unit's second winter encampment, Sammons received orders to move on and the grumbling redoubled. "We have apparently been driven about by adverse winds and waves," griped Lieutenant Martin McMartin, the 115th's quartermaster. "Here we are again, our dreams of a long rest in winter quarters rudely dispelled," groused DeGraff. "Just as we are putting on the finishing touches we are ordered to vacate and leave them for some other regiment to enjoy.... The boys are terribly out of humor."[9]

On the day after Christmas the regiment of disgruntled New Yorkers marched to the wharf at Alexandria, boarded transports, and set sail down the Potomac and into Chesapeake Bay. "We are designated now by common consent Flying Infantry, and no doubt have honorably won the distinction," wrote the colonel. Sergeant DeGraff's next letter advised his family that "the Flying Regiment has made another move." And Dr. Richard Sutton, the regimental surgeon, sported a new dateline on his correspondence:

"Gov. Morgan's Flying Infantry
Head Qtrs. 115th Reg't N.Y. Vols."[10]

The orders given to Colonel Sammons on Christmas Eve directed the 115th to Fortress Monroe, a key federal stronghold at the mouth of Chesapeake Bay. Then, just fifteen minutes before his unit broke camp on December 26, new orders came sending them instead to Yorktown. The frustrated colonel told his wife that his mind was "completely exercised," but he would carry on. "It is a soldier's duty to cheerfully submit to all orders and try our best to accomplish whatever may be required of us.... We must all, however, earnestly and faithfully do our duty to ourselves our God and our Country." Sergeant DeGraff echoed this theme and declared his wish for action: "If we can do more for our beloved country ... I say go. I hope if we get in a battle we may give a good account of ourselves. We enlisted to help put down this cursed rebellion, and hope we may have a hand in the ending of this dreadful war and at no distant day."[11]

The sail toward Yorktown took the 115th past Mount Vernon, affording them a good view of George Washington's estate. The soldiers passed time practicing their marksmanship on the plentiful waterfowl of Chesapeake Bay. Arriving at Yorktown on December 28, the 115th found a fine new ready-made home, soothing some of the frustration of abandoning the two sets of huts constructed during the previous month. A neat field of Sibley tents stood waiting for them, each of the conical shelters equipped with a stove, cooking supplies, and prepared bunks recently abandoned by the 29th Maine. "A quick survey of the camp convinced us that this was the Eldorado of all camps," recalled Corporal Reid. "Our boys were soon housekeeping in most improved style, with no regrets wasted on leaving our Hunter's Creek camp."[12]

Warm, clear weather greeted the arriving 115th, as did local citizens peddling cheap seafood. "We expect high living for a while," crowed one of the delighted soldiers.

Sightseeing again provided diversion for the young men, who enjoyed visits to the site of the 1781 British surrender to George Washington, and to the siege works used by McClellan's army in its ill-fated advance on Richmond the previous spring. But the most often recalled feature of the 115th's stay at Yorktown was the abundance of oysters that the boys could get effortlessly and cheaply. "Everybody dined on oysters three times during the day. They sold at forty cents per gallon, and the soldiers ate them fried, stewed and raw."[13]

As the year 1862 concluded, the 115th's spirits ran high. "The weather is mild and genial," Dr. Sutton wrote a friend back home. "Our dwellings are warm and comfortable, and upon the whole we are more pleasantly situated and have less sickness than at any time since we took the field." A soldier who wrote to the *Fulton County Republican* under the pen name Septimus reported, "Our camp is pleasantly situated on the southern bank of York river, about 1½ miles distant from Yorktown, and is one of the pleasantest locations to be found in this section of the country."[14]

The men received long awaited pay on New Year's Eve, and on New Year's Day a shipment of packages arrived full of good things from home. Even a shipment of turkeys, chickens, and ducks that had rotted en route failed to dampen the mood; on the contrary, it inspired an impromptu parade. Recorded James Clark: "The poultry was covered with ugly blue mould, and spoiled, and extensive preparations were made to bury them with military honors." A funeral procession formed and wound through the camp, complete with a coffin, a drummer boy slowly beating the dead march, an honor guard with ceremonially reversed weapons, a sexton with shovel, and a following of "mourners and sufferers, who were sadly weeping, with onions in their eyes." Spectators laughed heartily except for a couple of officers who voiced their disapproval. "Pity such narrow minds," concluded Clark.[15]

Four months into their term of service, with memorable travels and travails already behind them, the 115th finally got some serious military training at Yorktown where they began a daily regimen of company and regimental drill. In his entry for January 10, 1863, one diarist reported, "Had the same battalion, company, and squad drills; went through the manual of arms, the wheels, the facings, the loadings and firings, until our bones ached again." But the men recognized the benefits of the hard work. Reid was glad to replace useless duties with those that would make him an effective soldier. He believed each man "should be moulded into a machine that would kill." The 115th's progress also pleased DeGraff. "As we become more proficient," he noted, "the work becomes more interesting. Officers and men vie with each other for perfection."[16]

An early test of the regiment's readiness came on January 3, 1863. After nightfall Colonel Sammons suddenly galloped into camp from Division headquarters, a mile and a half away in Yorktown. Soon the long roll sounded, summoning the regiment to fall in ready for action. The excited men jumped from their bunks, grabbed their weapons, lined up and quick-marched the distance to headquarters, where they again formed in line awaiting orders. The alarm proved false—just a drill—but the regiment's efficient response pleased the men and their officers. Only twenty-two minutes passed from the long roll to the regiment being ready for action, including the 1½ mile march. From this time on the promptness of its formations became a matter of consistent pride with the 115th.

On this occasion the story circulated that the whole affair resulted from a wager between Colonel Sammons and the Division commander, General Erasmus Keyes. Sammons's boasting on his regiment provoked Keyes to bet Sammons that the 115th could not complete the maneuver in less than thirty minutes. The colonel's boys won the bet for him, and he and his regiment became favorites of General Keyes. Afterwards according to Corporal Reid, the 115th "owned the place during the remainder of our stay, having won the esteem of the commanding general."[17]

On January 7 General Keyes approached Sammons and asked how many men the 115th could send on a raid against the enemy. The colonel answered, "All you want," and Keyes asked for seventy-five. He wanted to mount a raid against a rebel supply depot at West Point, Virginia, where a railroad line from Richmond crossed the Pamunkey River, a major tributary of the York. The expedition consisted of naval gunboats, two hundred cavalrymen, and the infantrymen of the 115th led by Captain William McKittrick of Company C. They encountered no resistance and, without loss of a man or horse, captured or destroyed tons of supplies and torched a number of railcars and buildings.[18]

The winter at Yorktown proved as brief as the winters at Camp Chase and Camp Vermont. A pattern quickly growing all-too-familiar repeated itself when, on January 21, 1863, orders came to break camp and prepare to move. "We are earning the name of the Flying Regiment, but we do not seem to be doing much service in the way of causing the rebels to lay down their arms," lamented DeGraff. Back home, the *Fulton County Republican* gave its readers a report on "the migratory history of the 115th Regiment."[19]

General Keyes addressed the New Yorkers as they assembled to board the large ocean steamship *Matanzas* for an unrevealed destination. "I must say that I sincerely regret to part with so fine a body of men, but you are ordered elsewhere," said Keyes. He wished the regiment well and expressed his confidence that the 115th would always do its "full duty faithfully and patriotically." Corporal Reid remembered the general's voice being "tremulous at times." The emotional level of the general's speech suggests that perhaps Keyes was one of the few officials privy to the strange fate that awaited the 115th New York.

The *Matanzas* departed on January 22. During a stop at Fortress Monroe, Colonel Sammons learned that his regiment was bound for Hilton Head Island off the coast of South Carolina and he received sealed orders to be given to the commanding officer at Hilton Head upon arrival. "Little did we dream that those sealed orders contained a sentence of cruel banishment for a crime of which we were innocent," recalled DeGraff.[20]

Early on the three day voyage to Hilton Head, smooth sailing and frolicking schools of dolphin gave a holiday air to the new experience of ocean travel. But roughening seas brought the inevitable seasickness. According to Corporal Reid:

> With the first appearance of this troublesome and unwelcome malady there was a good deal of hilarity exhibited and jokes cracked on this and that afflicted one as they rushed to the rail to pay tribute to old Neptune. But the punster of one moment was quite liable to be engaged in a retching process the next.... The expression of one comrade quite fully stated the condition of all. He declared he had thrown up everything but his shoes and had started the soles on them.

Another soldier left a brief but very clear description of his bout with seasickness: "Oh what a feeling of goneness and misery."[21]

Arriving at Hilton Head, the Flying Regiment established another new camp, adjacent to the beach and overlooked by the heavy guns of the island's defensive works. The soldiers spent a couple of days settling in, then on the evening of January 30, 1863 the regiment assembled for dress parade and heard the contents of those fateful sealed orders. The men of the 115th New York knew what it felt like to be the defenseless targets of day long cannonading, but no experience could prepare them for the bombshell that now landed among them. Colonel Sammons, "with tears streaming down his face and voice tremulous with emotion, told us the story of our debasement." He read his men this official pronouncement:

> The 115th Regiment New York Volunteers has been reported by a Court of Inquiry as guilty of setting fire to the barracks at Camp Douglas, Chicago, about the 20th November last by which act the buildings were destroyed. The Secretary of War directs that the regiment be immediately sent to the Department of the South, and that after it is disembarked an order be issued stopping its pay.[22]

Shock pervaded the ranks of the 115th, as described by Corporal Reid:

> This order, bringing as it did the first intimation of the charges and verdict against us, came, so to speak, as a thunder clap from a clear sky.... Charges, trial and judgment had been made upon us without according to us our just right of defense.... We were banished to this island and our camp located where it was overlooked by many heavy guns.[23]

The men of the 115th found themselves disgraced, under arrest, and without pay due to accusations which they believed false. In DeGraff's words:

> The 115th Reg't New York Vols. have met with a great misfortune. The noble 1,100 who marched so gallantly from point to point willingly bearing fatigue and exposure if in so doing they might aid in putting down this accursed rebellion, are in banishment.[24]

Though stunned, they maintained composure. "Notwithstanding the false charges and harsh, cruel sentence, the regiment preserved its dignity and discipline, and with the exception of a murmur of surprise, completed the parade in fine, soldierly bearing." Once back in camp, as all the implications of the situation began dawning on the men, they grew agitated. The greatest indignation concerned the secrecy of the proceedings against them. As Reid put it, "hundreds of thousands of dollars are annually spent in the defense of the most hardened criminals, who are given the benefit of every doubt in the long chain of evidence, while in our case every man had been judged guilty without a hearing."[25]

The irate soldiers, looking back on their sojourn since leaving Chicago, attributed their numerous camp shifts to a conspiracy to prevent them from learning about the proceedings against them, thus denying them an opportunity to defend themselves. They also resented the intimidating location of their campsite, where the guns of the fort looked down upon them. And of course they recognized that they had been assigned to an island "away down here in this God-forsaken country, where the men could not escape if they tried." Some advocated mutiny but others argued that such action would "invite utter annihilation."[26]

During its stay at Hilton Head the 115th was often divided and assigned to do menial manual labor. The men saw such treatment as a means to weaken and disgrace them. The reactions of their Union comrades-in-arms also cut deeply. "Officers and privates were daily insulted." Colonel Sammons claimed "the officers of my command generally were averse to mixing up in social intercourse with the officers of other regiments under the impression that they were looked upon as unworthy." Some of the ills that the men of the 115th saw as consequences of the Camp Douglas fire may have been more imagined than genuine, but to these proud men they were real enough. "A more disheartened body of men probably did not belong to the service."[27]

In Chicago ten weeks earlier, on the day following the portentous barracks fire, Camp Douglas commander Daniel Tyler named a Board of Inquiry to investigate. The officers comprising the Board convened the next morning, November 22, 1862, and met over a five day period. The testimony of Colonel George Stannard of the 9th Vermont and four of his men made up most of the hearing. Two brief written statements comprised the remainder of the proceeding, the first submitted by two members of the 39th New York and the second by General Tyler himself.[28]

The joint written statement of Sergeant A. Louis Bona and Corporal Henry Palmer of the 39th was the only testimony that directly implicated the 115th. Their statement, dated November 21, 1862, was composed of a single sentence:

> We personally saw on the day of the departure of the 115th Reg. N.Y.V. some members of this Regiment taking fire brands in their Barracks located near to ours, and after our thinking the fire was made purposely.

Testimony from members of the 9th Vermont established the events surrounding the blaze but did not directly connect the 115th with its origin. The Vermonters agreed that flames erupted nearly simultaneously in three different locations within the quarters of the 115th. The doors to the rooms where the fires started were found fastened, while all the other doors in the quarters remained unlocked. These recollections clearly indicated arson.

Just before the blaze broke out, Colonel Stannard had seen some soldiers around the barracks, whom he identified as men of several regiments including the 115th, as well as some local citizens. Stannard testified that the first fire started while he was attempting to prevent civilians from looting the building. One of the other 9th Vermont witnesses said he saw some soldiers heading around the burning barracks and into the street, but he did not identify them as men of the 115th. None of the 9th Vermonters actually saw anyone set the fires or exit the rooms where the flames broke out. All the witnesses agreed that the 115th stood outside the barracks, "drawn up in line preparatory to leaving," at the time the conflagration started. They also agreed that, while many others rushed to fight the fire, no one from the 115th did so. Indeed, Vermonter J. H. Bisbee testified that "some of them seemed to be rejoicing. They were looking on and I heard some loud conversation. Once or twice I saw some hats waved."

While others struggled against the raging fire, the 115th marched out of camp without offering help. Were they good soldiers who would not break ranks without orders or a group of men unanimously pleased at the destruction of their loathed quarters? Were the cheers those of vandals or more like those of excited youths taking boyish pleasure at the burning of the schoolhouse? Some of the 115th still cheered as they looked back from their railroad cars at the smouldering ruins of their barracks.

General Tyler wrote his statement on November 24 and introduced it to the Board of Inquiry the next day. In it he related a conversation between himself and Colonel Sammons that took place on November 20, three hours before the 115th left camp. He said that Colonel Sammons "observed in a jocular manner, 'The boys are very merry at the idea of going away and have already begun to burn their bunkboards,' or words to that effect." Tyler took the jocular Sammons's words seriously: "Seeing the probable end of such disorder I exclaimed 'What, sir, burn the bunkboards? You call this being merry? It is the beginning of insubordination and will end in burning up the barracks,' or words to that effect." Tyler went on to say that he commanded Sammons to preserve order, and had him carry a written directive to Colonel Stannard indicating that Tyler would hold Stannard personally responsible for safeguarding the 115th's barracks.

Tyler's account of his exchange with Sammons has a ring of hindsight to it, though it does offer clues into his reasons for blaming the 115th for the fire. But his testimony does not establish any facts relating to the fire nor substantiate any direct involvement by anyone from the 115th. The men of the regiment saw other motives for Tyler's enmity, believing that Tyler held a grudge toward the 115th stemming from their attempts to be removed from his command at Camp Douglas. This notion was fueled by Colonel Sammons when he addressed the regiment on February 8, 1863, as he prepared to embark for Washington to initiate a belated defense against the arson charges. He attributed the accusations against the 115th to the influence of a "powerful enemy" presumed by the troops to be Tyler. After all, Sammons had gone over Tyler's head when he wrote directly to the Governor Morgan and the state's adjutant general informing them of the woeful conditions prevailing within Tyler's command and seeking the regiment's transfer from Chicago. Sammons had also managed to have an order of Tyler's countermanded when Tyler attempted to move the 115th from the Illinois State Fairgrounds into Camp Douglas, an action that could not have set well with Tyler.[29]

Along with Tyler, Colonel Stannard and his men presented testimony implicating the 115th although none indicated eye-witnessing any act of arson. They too could have had extra motivation for scapegoating the 115th since the 9th Vermont failed in its assignment to protect the barracks from destruction.

The Board of Inquiry submitted the record of its proceeding to General Tyler on November 27, 1862. In a cover letter transmitting the transcripts they made no judgment of guilt or innocence but did make one significant statement: "The Board regrets the absence of the 115th." The affair belonged to Tyler, and remained concealed from the accused until they unsuspectingly lined up on Hilton Head Island on January 30, 1863.[30]

By the time Colonel Sammons revealed the news of the repercussions of the Chicago blaze to his men, he had already applied for a leave of absence to go to Washington. He wanted the War Department to reopen the hearing so he could defend his regiment, prove its innocence, and ask that it "be reinstated to [its] former position in the Army and ... cleared from the stain that now rests upon it." Sammons and the 115th's other officers prepared for the colonel's mission to Washington by quickly putting together statements offering their versions of the facts surrounding the fire. On February 8 these affidavits were read to the men, after which the colonel stepped forward and addressed them, appearing "very much affected as he spoke." He vowed to do all in his power to clear their names and told them he had obtained his leave and would depart for Washington the next day, armed with the statements and prepared to enlist aid from influential allies back home in New York.[31]

Sammons's own statement—written before he had seen the earlier statement of General Tyler—presented his account of his interview with Tyler just prior to the fire. Sammons said he had gone to see Tyler at his own initiative to suggest that Tyler dispatch a guard to protect the 115th's quarters. Tyler immediately issued such an order and his adjutant put it in writing. This was the order making Stannard responsible for the protection of the barracks that Sammons then hand-carried to Stannard. Sammons's statement recalled that as soon as his command formed in line outside the barracks and before any fire erupted, "their vacant quarters were filled with straggling citizens and soldiers belonging to the 9th Vermont and 39th New York."[32]

Captain David Kittle of Company I, acting adjutant of the 115th on November 20, 1862, certified that after the regiment had lined up outside Colonel Sammons ordered him to return to the 115th's barracks to look for any stragglers. He found none. When he again left the barracks the fire had not yet started but there were already civilians and soldiers of the 9th and 39th milling in and around the 115th's quarters.[33]

Lieutenant Frank Barnum of Company I stated that Colonel Sammons detailed him to remain in Chicago to apprehend and collect all stragglers, deserters, and the sick. Forty-five minutes after the 115th's train embarked, Barnum visited the scene of the fire. There he found officers and soldiers clustered around the charred barracks. "On my inquiry how the fire originated the invariable answer was the coal stoves in the quarters had been stolen both by citizens and soldiers after my regiment had left their barracks, and in the haste to get them away the fire had been thrown into the straw and on the floor thus causing the conflagration." This version of the cause of the fire echoes through all of the reminiscences of the veterans of the 115th.[34]

Armed with these and other statements, Colonel Sammons got his hearing at the War Department and successfully obtained the desired result. The 115th received emphatic absolution from the charges of setting the fire. The report of the second hearing fully exonerated the regiment and restored its honor and military status. The Secretary of War even ordered a paymaster to proceed immediately to Hilton Head with the men's back pay. "The charge is shown to be a wicked calumny," the *Daily Saratogian* informed the concerned folks back home. The men at Hilton Head learned of their redemption on March 17, and both Colonel Sammons and the paymaster arrived on the same steamer on March 25. "Contentment and happiness resumed their sway," recalled Reid. DeGraff wrote that Sammons "is loved by all his men now more than ever before."[35]

In spite of the testimony of the 115th that every man was in line and accounted for when the fire broke out—a statement very difficult to make with complete assurance when dealing with over eight hundred individuals—and in spite of the subsequent acquittal of the regiment, it is impossible to conclude with certainty that one man or several did not in fact sneak off and commit the arson. But even if this did occur, the other men of the regiment could be justifiably indignant that they had been collectively judged guilty and disgraced before the army without any opportunity to defend themselves. The case against them had been inconclusive at best, the closed-door proceeding outrageous, the mass judgment unfair, and the punishment demeaning and unmerited.

Beyond the immediate results and "debasement" following the fateful blaze, the incident had a broad impact on the subsequent career of the regiment. "It is fair to presume," as James Reid wrote in his reminiscences, that if not for the fire the 115th New York would have taken a place in the Second Corps of the Union Army of the Potomac as did the other regiments brigaded with it at Harpers Ferry, "sharing the glory now so fully accorded those gallant veterans." The Second Corps went on to fight through the titanic battles of the eastern theater whose very names still evoke awe and emotion. But the 115th, as Reid continued:

> While its banners are not inscribed with the names Gettysburg, Wilderness, Spotsylvania, Appomattox, and several other of the great contests, there are inscribed on their scarred folds the names of numerous engagements, small in comparison to those mentioned, but of such severity as to carry a casualty list exceedingly high.[36]

The Flying Regiment was destined, as the result of its Chicago Fire, to fight and bleed at the fringes of the Civil War, moving from theater to theater to toil in battles essentially lost to history and of marginal consequence to the war's outcome. Even so, these fringes witnessed no shortage of bloodletting. In its odyssey through the Great Rebellion the 115th New York would suffer more battle casualties than most of the regiments with which it had been aligned prior to its "cruel banishment," and would become recognized among the Union's Fighting 300. But, as the regiment settled in on Hilton Head Island, these bloody fields still lay well ahead of them.[37]

6

Idle Year in the South
"Even in paradise itself"

At the outbreak of the Civil War, federal leadership adopted a strategy imposing a naval blockade on the Confederacy. But when the hostilities began, the United States military maintained control of only two seacoast installations within the seceded states—Hampton Roads, Virginia, at the mouth of the James River, and Key West, Florida. With 3,500 miles of southern coastline to cover, an early priority of the Union war effort was to secure additional bases to support the blockade. A prime objective was Port Royal Sound in South Carolina, which has been termed the finest natural harbor on the southeast coast. Port Royal lies far enough south to be an all-weather port and is situated about halfway between the important Confederate port cities of Charleston and Savannah, less than 50 miles from either. These qualities made Union strategists choose Port Royal as the desired base for the Atlantic blockading squadron.

St. Philips Island and Hilton Head Island flank the two and a half mile wide entrance to Port Royal Harbor on the north and the south. On each island Confederates built well-armed artillery fortifications to defend the harbor, but they quickly proved inadequate. On November 7, 1861, a federal fleet approached and opened fire, chasing the rebel defenders from the forts after a bombardment of several hours. Northern troops occupied the area, and Hilton Head became the headquarters of the Union Army's Department of the South and an important base of support for blockade operations and for staging land and sea offensives against other targets on the Confederate seacoast.[1]

By the time the 115th New York arrived in January 1863, the village of Hilton Head, at the northeast point of its namesake island, had blossomed into a military and commercial boomtown. The post served every need of an occupying army of more than 20,000 soldiers, from bakeries to sawmills. Government buildings dominated the town, including a huge arsenal that housed enormous reserves of munitions. James Clark of Company H, who had just been promoted from sergeant to lieutenant, boasted of the "Yankee enterprise" conspicuous at Hilton Head. Calling to mind the Carolinians who fled the Union takeover, he speculated that "when the runaway planters come home again they will, no doubt, be a little astonished at the vast improvements."[2]

Several days prior to the arrival of the 115th, a local Union newspaper reported Hilton Head "beginning to command an importance not only as a military and naval post, but as

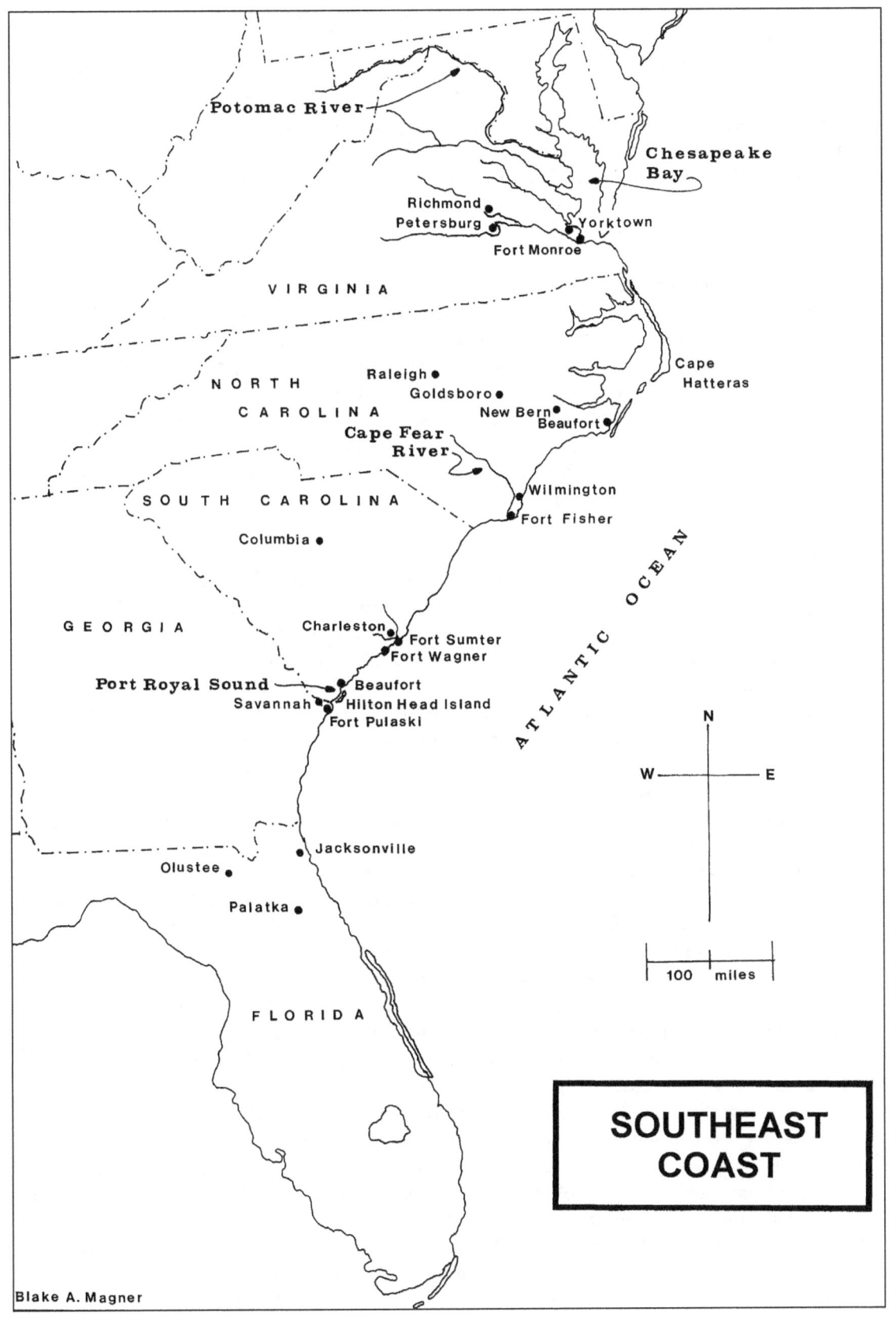

a place offering many business advantages to the enterprising classes who are now daily arriving from the North in pursuit of employ and business." Many sutler's stores, saloons, photographic studios and other establishments sprang up as businessmen from the North arrived in the wake of the occupation. Three different entrepreneurs published local newspapers for the consumption of Union troops: *The Free South*, *The New South*, and *The Palmetto Herald*. Clark recorded, "The sandy streets are generally crowded with people. Some of the merchants sell an incredible amount of goods, and, I need not say, realize large profits."[3]

Not all of Hilton Head bustled. After the jolting news about the Chicago fire followed by their banishment to the island, the 115th quickly settled into a humdrum camp life. The routine was monotonous, with company and battalion drills and dress parade occupying just two or three hours per day, and camp fatigue duties requiring only a brief morning cleanup. "We have plenty to eat and nothing to do," lamented Nicholas DeGraff.[4]

In a February 9 letter to his parents DeGraff reported that "the energy has all gone out of the officers." Colonel Sammons echoed DeGraff's observation: upon his return from Washington, he "found that the order disgracing the regiment had been a severe blow to their ambition, and there was not wanting some evidence of despondency." The 115th's mood could not have been helped by the scattering of the regiment across the island in various manual labor details soon after its arrival. Companies D and E went to work constructing a new fort on the north shore of the island about seven miles from the regiment's main camp. Company B labored at coaling vessels at Seabrook, six miles distant on the west side of the island. Other 115th men served on smaller work details around Hilton Head. Garret Van Derveer, Captain of Company A, complained that the regiment's exoneration seemed to mean only that they were "to stay and do just as we have been doing since we landed: dig ditches, build forts, shovel coal, unload and load vessels at the dock, &c., &c."[5]

Sickness also served to scatter the regiment. As in Chicago and Virginia, disease struck when troops settled into stationary camps and increased dramatically the longer they stayed in one place. "As the scourge of disease spread tentmate lines and even company lines disappeared, and the whole regiment became a brotherhood in care and sympathy," recalled James Reid. "Many hours of many days did members of the regiment spend at regimental and general hospitals, at the bedsides of fever-stricken soldiers."[6]

The healthy men found plenty of time on their hands. While some decried the monotony, others took an interest in the unfamiliar environs. DeGraff's lively interest in the natural world brought him endless diversion. "This country is so different from our own climate. Vegetation, birds, animals are all strange, that I find great enjoyment in running about hunting, gathering shells on the seashore, &c." DeGraff continued exploring throughout the 115th's year in South Carolina and remained an avid naturalist for the rest of his life.[7]

Colonel Sammons became fascinated with mockingbirds, which he recalled singing from midnight until daylight. "It has the power of mimicking all kinds of birds and, what is most wonderful, it will mew like a cat and then like a kitten," Sammons told his daughter. "When it first came for a time it kept the greater part of all in camp awake and many denounced it. Now, however, all are pleased with it and it is a great pet with all." The colonel even arranged to have an old former slave raise some mockingbirds for him as she had previously done for her master.[8]

Other men found fascination with snakes, alligators, and sharks, which they discovered in plentiful supply. Many species of snakes inhabited the island which required the soldiers' constant vigilance as they moved about. An eight foot adder attacked a Company H man as he walked in the forest. His call brought forth a comrade who slew the adder with an axe he had been using to make tent poles. Another soldier suffered a rude shock when he chopped into a hollow log he was splitting for firewood and out came a black snake six feet long. James Clark saw a cavalryman halve a very resilient snake with his saber, then watched in awe as the severed head slithered off into the brush.[9]

The men also needed to be wary of the alligators that inhabited the island's numerous wetlands. Jacob Brown of Company B reported that the regiment's drinking water came from a "marsh ware is inhabited by them Butiful reptiles the Aligater." When a party of wood-cutters from Companies H and K spotted an alligator, one man grabbed his rifle and put a bullet in its head. The soldiers dragged the wounded beast onto dry land with ropes. "The alligator showed fight and swept his ugly tail around in all directions, with a force that would have cut a man in two, had he been within reach," recalled James Clark. John Reardon related how he and a group from Company B discovered another alligator and promptly opened fire. "He was a tough customer requiring three or four shots to end him," Reardon noted. The cooks grabbed the six foot reptile's tail and concocted a stew that fed the entire company. Corporal Reardon pronounced it "very palatable."[10]

The need for vigilance did not end at the seashore. One day a shark passed between the beach and some swimming soldiers. Shouts from men on land warned the swimmers who then looped toward shore in the direction opposite the shark's. Their comrades watched anxiously until their circuitous swim brought them safely back to the beach. Another eight foot shark got caught in a fishing seine. Soldiers pulled him onto the beach, drawing a crowd of onlookers eager for a close-up view. Among them was Private Philip Christie, a cook in Company C. Deciding that boiled shark might make a good change of diet, Christie procured a chunk of shark meat and served it to his mates who declared it "as tough and stringy as palmetto wood" and even worse than military rations.[11]

Easily the most vividly remembered of all the denizens of Hilton Head were also the smallest—the tiny sand fleas that terrorized the soldiers. Corporal Seely Conover of Company B placed the fleas "above all things to torment us here ... You can't sleep more than an hour or so on account of their tormentings." Others described them as "the greatest plague we have here" that could "murder by inches." DeGraff complained of being covered with blotches where he had been bitten. The pesky intruders "appeared to have been created hungry and never tired in attempts to appease that hunger, especially delighting in human gore," wrote Reid. "He was never early nor never late, but always at his post of duty.... Your turnings, twistings, scratchings, diggings, striking, etc., are of no avail. His fleaship is master of the situation."[12]

The black people who inhabited Hilton Head were just as foreign to these Upstate New Yorkers in Dixie as the sharks and alligators. Around a thousand slaves had worked on the twenty-four plantations covering the fifty square miles of Hilton Head Island. Their former owners and overseers fled rather than face Yankee domination, leaving the slaves to fend for themselves. As the northerners spread their control over adjacent territory, more and more blacks came seeking the protection of the federal army. DeGraff described a group of several hundred brought in with a Union regiment returning from a raid on the mainland: "They were a forlorn looking lot, poorly clad, half starved, etc."[13]

These contrabands, as they came to be called, fell under the jurisdiction of the northern soldiers. While they received generally good treatment, they were almost universally regarded as objects of curiosity rather than fellow human beings. Colonel Sammons, for example, wrote a letter to his young daughter in which he described "little pickaninnies blacker than black." He joked that he might bring home a dozen or two who "would be quite handy about the house." He even suggested that she poll family members as to what size and color blacks they would like. His letter ended with a postscript reading, "P.S. Listen closely and hear if Mother don't say I have got Sambo on the brain."[14]

Corporal Conover, who enlisted at Canajoharie at age twenty-one, told a friend at home how the soldiers used black children for entertainment. Violin, fife, or banjo music "would set them all a-dancing and their little wooly heads would be bobbing up and down. ... a comical looking set." At other times the New Yorkers would gather some black children together then let loose a "dog that would chase a negro as quick as a fowl ... There would be a great scattering. You would see heels flying in every direction."[15]

The soldiers quickly became engaged in commerce with the Hilton Head blacks. True to his customary form, DeGraff scoped out the island's culinary potential, and within a couple days of landing reported, "oysters are very plenty. Negroes bring them to us for 5¢ per pint. Sweet potatoes are plenty and cheap. I saw some fine brook trout brought in camp by Negroes. They say they are plenty on the island." Corporal Alonzo Van Evera of Company B engaged in a different sort of commerce. He took up preaching among the deeply religious blacks of the neighborhood, his Sunday collections netting him about $2.00 a week.[16]

In addition to the contrabands, the northerners came in contact with black men who wore the same blue Union army uniforms they did. "Negroes in Uncle Sam's clothes was an interesting, though a common sight," wrote Sergeant DeGraff. These Colored Troops, as the army officially labeled them, were among the earliest participants in the controversial federal policy of recruiting blacks to serve in the army. The Port Royal area became the focus of this effort when General Rufus Saxton, a division commander in the Department of the South, received authority from the War Department to raise 5,000 troops from among the contrabands. "The government has concluded to organize colored troops and we have the first of them here, organized into regiments with white officers," noted DeGraff. "This looks odd but will, I think, do good service."[17]

Private Reuben Wells of Company E exaggerated in a June 4 letter to his wife in Mayfield Corners, Fulton County, when he reported "som six thousand niggars soljers" at Hilton Head. This was wishful thinking, prompted by rumors claiming that the white troops could go home as soon as, in Wells's phrase, "anuff nergroes gits heare two guard the island." James Clark, like many of his fellows, was amused by local dialects. He asked one of the slaves-turned-soldier how he enjoyed being in the army and recorded the man's response as, "Oh yes Massa, we all berry willin' to be a soger, we all Yankee now.... We all j'ined de Lincoln army, massa."[18]

The black soldiers, as DeGraff predicted, went on to do excellent service in the Union cause. The 115th New York would remain associated with black troops throughout its fighting career.

Much of the work undertaken by the 115th and the other units around Port Royal Sound came in preparation for military operations against Charleston. Charleston was known to northerners as the radical hotbed of secession in the years before the war and the site of the conflict's birth at Fort Sumter. Its capture was a coveted objective of the Union war effort and the long-awaited expedition got under way on Good Friday, April 3, 1863, after a full year of preparation. The plan called for a naval squadron of nine ironclad ships to bombard Fort Sumter and Charleston Harbor's other fortifications into submission. Troop transports would follow the warships, carrying 10,000 infantrymen assigned to seize the despised rebel city.[19]

The 115th did not go with them. The New Yorkers and two other regiments remained behind in support. They did not miss much. The navy returned unsuccessful, outgunned and unable to surmount the obstructions placed by the Confederates to impede entry into Charleston Harbor. Army units established some outposts on sea islands which would serve as staging areas for later assaults, but most of the troops returned to Port Royal without seeing any action. The 115th's Captain Van Derveer quizzed some of the returning men about the abbreviated campaign. All they could tell him was that they had done nothing. Van Derveer then dejectedly warned his brother, a surgeon in the 66th New York, that "to judge what will happen by what has happened, it will be many years before this rebellion is put down by our armies and fleets."[20]

While most troops of the federal Department of the South futilely probed Charleston, the 115th had labored at the wharves, loading and unloading the ships shuttling supplies to the troops on the Charleston expedition. After several days at this duty, DeGraff began to grumble, "We are growing tired of work at the docks. Seems too much like work that the Negroes ought to be doing instead of us. Besides we enlisted to shoot rebels and save the Union."

Nicholas DeGraff's letters home detailed every aspect of his experiences, the dull and the exciting. Nick, as his family referred to him, stayed in frequent touch with the folks back on the farm at Tribes Hill outside of Amsterdam, New York. He left there at the age of twenty to enlist in the 115th, mustered in as a sergeant in Company D, and thrived in the army. He commented repeatedly on his good health, and in one letter noted that he had gained fourteen pounds since joining up.

DeGraff's missives describe all he had seen and done, disclosing an observant young man with an upbeat outlook. He reported on his many explorations around Hilton Head Island, the gaudy seashells, and the strange flora and fauna. Each evening he attended prayer services and enthusiastically noted the numbers of men who turned out to declare their faith. His gripe about the dock work being more fit for blacks is one of his few complaints and reveals that even dutiful Christians of the time viewed blacks as an inferior caste of humans.

On one of his island forays DeGraff and tentmate William McKay wandered two miles up the shore collecting shells. Their stroll was cut short by a natural cul-de-sac formed by a wide stream crossing the beach in their front, a large swamp at their left, and the ocean on their right. As they about-faced to return to camp, a practicing artillery battery began firing toward the beach in front of them. DeGraff and McKay were trapped with water on three sides and bombs falling on the fourth. When a shell burst in the sand a short distance ahead, they made a dash for safety. "Into the swamp we went, and after a hard struggle succeeded in reaching the timber and security. We sat down to recover from our fright and laugh at the plight which we were in."

On another occasion DeGraff strolled along a creek accompanied by Lieutenant Thomas Wayne. They visited three plantations whose owners DeGraff reported as being "over in rebeldom." He found the elegant plantation buildings occupied by contrabands and falling into decay, though still commanding scenic settings and surrounded by groves of live oaks, magnolia, and orange trees. Nick returned to camp with a bouquet of flowers plucked from plantation gardens.

At dress parade on June 4 Colonel Sammons announced DeGraff's promotion to second lieutenant and directed him to don the shoulder straps symbolizing his new position as a commissioned officer. The proud but modest DeGraff found having to return the salutes of other soldiers "rather bewildering," but he managed to adapt to his lofty new status, soon ordering new uniforms and moving into officer's quarters.[21]

In early June Union leadership at Hilton Head initiated a series of raids into the interior intended to capture supplies, to find black men to fill more regiments of Colored Troops, and to injure the enemy in any way possible. These incursions generated controversy: some federal officers zealously torched anything southern whether of military value or not, while others objected to such wanton destruction. A raid which burned Darien, Georgia, for

Newly-promoted Lieutenant Nicholas DeGraff and his friend Sergeant Elbert Slingerland in a tintype they had taken at Hilton Head (Lance Ingmire Collection).

example, touched off a bitter dispute in which Colonel Robert Gould Shaw, the Boston Brahmin leader of the 54th Massachusetts, appealed to the governor of his home state for relief from such duty.[22]

On June 2 Companies B and E of the 115th were detailed to take part in another such raid. These two companies, with small detachments from other regiments, boarded transports and sailed to Fort Pulaski, Georgia, where six companies of the 48th New York joined them. Colonel William Barton of the 48th, who would later lead the 115th into some of its severest combat, commanded the expedition. After picking up the 48th, the boats doubled back northward and landed the force on the mainland opposite Hilton Head Island, near the town of Bluffton, South Carolina.

William Flint, a cook from Company B who remained behind at Hilton Head, heard "heavy cannonading all the forenoon" on June 4 as, just ten miles away, the gunboats accompanying the small expedition shelled the woods around Bluffton in order to scatter any rebels that might be in the area. Later that day Flint wrote dramatically that the cannonading had ceased and "what the result will be remains to be told."[23]

The result of the raid was anything but dramatic. The federals entered Bluffton unopposed and burned it to the ground with just one building, a church, left standing. As the northerners set sail for the return trip, some Confederates arrived and opened fire. Recalled Company B's John Reardon, "A few well directed volleys sent them back. The boats then moved out. We had no casualties."[24]

The raid on Bluffton did not test the soldiers, nor did it accomplish much. But the action-starved men of the 115th found it something to crow about. Unfortunately, the reports of the raid carried in *The New South* and *The Free South*, while listing the other units involved, failed to mention the 115th. One of the regiment, who signed himself as "True Soldier of the 115th," sent the clippings back to his hometown paper, *The Daily Saratogian*, along with a letter setting the record straight—he wanted everyone at home to know that his unit had seen some action. The result of the raid, as summed up by "True Soldier" and printed in *The Daily Saratogian*: "Bluffton that was, is no more."[25]

As the South Carolina weather turned sultry in the spring of 1863, sickness in the 115th reached alarming levels. In the first week of June the roll listed 130 men confined to quarters by illness or being treated in hospitals. Several had already died. At this time the regiment showed a total of just under 800 men on its rolls. In his letter to the Saratoga paper "True Soldier" blamed fatigue duty for the regiment's failing health. He listed such duty as "loading and unloading vessels, with goods from coal to broadcloth, commissary's articles, and ordnance; digging out old ditches filled with all kinds of refuse; taking up the dead and reburying them on other grounds, besides any amount of policing," and declared that "northern men cannot endure it." He felt that the 115th bore an unfair share of such duty and concluded, "If we could have less fatigue, I think we could have less sickness." Colonel Sammons agreed and took action. "Believing that much of this sickness was caused by excessive fatigue duty I obtained permission to have the regiment removed to Beaufort," he wrote a few weeks later. At last the regiment would be reunited, and it moved on with hopes that its duties would be more military in nature and that its health would improve.[26]

Beaufort, South Carolina, is on Port Royal Island, twelve miles from Hilton Head. Port Royal Island is not on the seacoast but is situated at the western end of Port Royal Sound. As the 115th marched through town after landing on June 28, the men made note of the town's fashionable homes and exquisite yards. James Clark called Beaufort "the Saratoga of South Carolina." Within a few days the regiment, by now accustomed to setting up long-term camps, had comfortably settled in at Beaufort and John Reardon found it "more pleasant here than at Hilton Head. Water is better and we have more grass, less sand and flies." Nonetheless, grim reality quickly dashed the hope that relocation would bring improved health. "For a long time after our arrival in Beaufort death continued to visit our ranks nearly every day, and a long row of graves soon helped to fill up the graveyard. Typhoid fever and chronic diarrhea made our camp a great hospital, and everything wore a sad and gloomy look," recalled Lieutenant Clark. While Clark exaggerated when he reported that death visited daily, the 115th New York was well represented in the weekly reports of soldier deaths carried in *The Free South*.[27]

Disease plagued the entire Department of the South. During the summer of 1863, 20% of all soldiers reported ill on an average day. Health problems in the 115th greatly exceeded this norm. In early August the regiment's sick list numbered 230 men, over 30% of the total roster, by then down to 736. Perhaps the lengthy fatigue duty did contribute to the problem as the men theorized. Certainly the time the 115th remained in stationary camps with poor sanitary conditions—while most of the Department went off campaigning—aided the spread of disease.[28]

Private Kelley Tulloch of Company D caught one of the camp fevers but recovered. He had been hospitalized for a month when he wrote his Cousin Ellen in Schenectady about his illness. "I ame in the hosptal yet but I ame on the gaine a littel now." He complained more about the cure than the illness: "It went purtty tuff for a wile at first for I thought that they was trying to starve me.... All that I got was one cup of tea and a half a slice of toste at a meal." His recovery brought culinary rewards. "I thought I would starve shure nouf but I made out to stand it and now I git all that I can eat ... We have roste beef and salt beef, pork, mouton, beens, rice, harring, pickels, cabbage, rice poodens, bread poodens, and appels saus ... they don't get all of this things in the Company." Private Tulloch went on to mention other foods he wished Cousin Ellen to send him—clearly his health was, as he said, "on the gaine." Tulloch, aware of his deficient English, closed his letter with a plea that Ellen "loork over all blunders and excuse all mistakes."[29]

While the move to Beaufort brought no immediate improvement in health, it did bring a welcome reduction in manual labor duties. They did little stevedoring and no construction work; in fact, through July and August the regiment had little to do. Meanwhile most of the soldiers around them once more left the 115th behind and went off to fight Confederates. As the regiment settled into its new camp the rest of the Department of the South made another stab at Charleston. After the futile expedition in April, General Quincy Gillmore took over command of the Department. A West Pointer from Ohio, Gillmore arrived

Commissary Sergeant Harvey C. Christie was one of at least 14 men from the 115th who died of disease at Hilton Head (New York State Military Museum).

in early June 1863 intent on taking Charleston, and doing it soon. By the middle of June Union artillery and supplies began quietly moving out of Port Royal Sound. The offensive started with a successful landing and assault on Morris Island on July 10. The Union forces occupied three-quarters of the length of the island, halting their advance within a few hundred yards of an earthen Confederate bulwark called Fort Wagner.[30]

Morris Island, four miles long and nowhere more than a half-mile wide, lay between the Atlantic and a quilt of impassable salt marshes. At its northern tip Confederate Fort Gregg guarded the entrance to Charleston Harbor. Fort Wagner stood less than a mile south of Gregg, straddling the entire width of the island at a point where it narrowed to just one thousand feet. In front of Wagner an inlet cut the width of the island to a mere seventy-five feet. Fort Wagner and its rebel garrison lay squarely between the Union army and its objective.[31]

On the morning of July 11 federal infantry made a gallant assault on Fort Wagner and received a bloody repulse. A week later on July 18, they tried again with the same result. On this occasion the battle was closely witnessed by Fred Goodrich of Company H of the 115th. Goodrich, a twenty-six-year old private from Halfmoon, was at the front serving as a courier hauling dispatches between General Gillmore and his field commanders. He had to interrupt one of his rides in order to let the assaulting lines of infantry pass by, then watched their charge. He later described the scene:

> The word was given and away they went. But oh how they fell. Great gaps a rod wide was made in their ranks at each discharge of the Rebel guns. But on they went through the moat, over the parapet into the fort. And such yelling from both sides. The blows fell thick and fast. I could hear them as the men clubbed their muskets and fought hand to hand. I could hear them crash as they struck deep into the brain and through the flashes could see them sink down to the earth. I stood and watched and listened and I saw our men falling back slowly.

Of the 5,000 northerners who made the vain assault 1,515 became casualties, including 242 men of the 48th New York, a regiment that would soon be closely aligned with the 115th.

Concluding that the fort could not be taken by storm, the troops lay siege, slowly digging their way closer and closer while both army and navy relentlessly shelled Fort Wagner and the many other Confederate installations around Charleston. Back at Beaufort, the rest of the 115th "could plainly hear the thunder of the great guns," but could only wonder and wait to learn the outcome. The campaign ended anticlimactically: the rebels abandoned Fort Wagner and Morris Island on September 6, but the federal navy still could not master Charleston Harbor and the campaign fizzled. Charleston remained in rebel hands through nearly the end of the war.[32]

The July 18, 1863 assault on Fort Wagner not only added hundreds of names to the casualty lists, it also created an enduring American military legacy. The 54th Massachusetts, a regiment composed of free blacks recruited in the north, spearheaded the infantry attack. The 54th fought with spirit, ability and courage, and absorbed egregious losses. This did not represent the first time African-Americans had gone into combat, nor the first time a black unit fought well, but this event got a great deal of publicity and served to prove the worthiness of black troops to remaining skeptics in the military, the federal government, and the northern public.[33]

Many of the 54th's wounded were transported to Beaufort where a fatigue detail from the 115th assisted them in landing. "The colored heroes," as DeGraff referred to them, received encouragement from the 115th and invited the New Yorkers to visit them in the hospital. In reporting the scene, *The Free South* declared that none who witnessed it would ever voice any "word of scorn or contempt for Negro soldiers.... At that moment our volunteers saw suffering comrades in the black men, and the tender hand and strong shoulder was extended as readily to them as to their fairer compatriots."[34]

Hearing the guns, loading the supplies, and helping the wounded were as close as the 115th came to the Charleston expedition. Newspaper reports of the July Union victories at Gettysburg and Vicksburg were as close as the regiment got to those momentous actions. Meanwhile, the men of the regiment passed their time on Port Royal Island working various duties around camp, visiting their sick and dying comrades, trying to escape the heat, and finding amusement where they could. For the 115th New York idleness, not action, remained the primary staple of military life.

Many soldiers enjoyed playing cards, but their officers frowned on Sunday card games. On Sunday, August 2, a private in the 115th was caught playing euchre and ordered "on the barrel," a punishment designed to disgrace a soldier before his peers, as well as to inflict physical discomfort. It involved standing on a barrel on public display for a length of time, with a sign or some other emblem advising passersby of the offender's violation. In this case the ace of hearts was pinned to the private's back. After a while a captain strode up and asked the man how he liked *that* game. The soldier replied that "it was all very nice, but he wished someone would come along with the 'right bower' and take him off." The officer got a laugh out of his response and ordered the man released.[35]

Winslow Burton of Company B, out on guard duty on a dark night, heard something approaching and three times called out challenges. Reports of rebel spies had recently circulated, so when no one replied to his calls the nervous sentry fired into the brush. He heard something drop. Several men went out to investigate and found a dying ox. Burton's shot had ripped through the animal's ribs. A comrade reported great happiness in camp as a detail of men butchered Burton's ox.[36]

When James Reid left camp one morning for sentry duty he found John Hutchinson of Company C, the man he went to relieve, sound asleep. He awakened Hutchinson and advised him to get out of the oppressively hot sun, but the indignant Hutchinson retorted that he just wanted to be left alone. This exchange might have remained a trivial memory of a bad sunburn, but two days later Hutchinson, until then quite healthy, came down with typhoid fever and was dead within two weeks.[37]

While at Beaufort the regiment received a detachment of 164 new recruits who the surgeon called "a strange medley of men." They differed from the earlier volunteers of 1861 and 1862 who enlisted mainly out of patriotism. By 1863 more men were attracted to the army by greatly enlarged enlistment bounties, while others were drafted involuntarily under a national conscription act enacted in March 1863. Some were substitutes, who received $300 from drafted men who paid them to serve in their place under a provision of the conscription law. While a number of the new troops proved good soldiers, several deserted at the first opportunity. Such "bounty-jumping sharpers," as one officer called them, might reappear elsewhere and enlist again in a different unit to collect another bounty or substitute's fee. DeGraff recalled running into trouble with some of the new men while acting as officer of the guard. "There are many bad men among them, New York City toughs, gamblers, pickpockets. Some were active in the late draft riots. They smuggle whiskey into camp, get drunk, gamble in their tents, quarrel and fight among themselves."[38]

Large numbers of men from the regiment served in Beaufort as members of the provost guard, or military police. Newly promoted Major Ezra L. Walrath of the 115th became Provost

A group of 115th men relaxing in camp and hamming it up for the camera. This photograph includes Peter Keck, Job Harlow, Seely Conover, and William Miller, but it is not known who is who (Lance Ingmire Collection).

Marshal and recruited the familiar men of his regiment—as many as 200 at a time—to form his post guards. James Reid recalled this assignment as a lot of echoing "all's well" and summed it up as "more or less red tape nonsense."[39]

During the summer of 1863 as his regiment languished in Beaufort, Colonel Sammons's attention turned to defending himself against a group of his own officers attempting to oust him from command. He had earned the respect of most of his men and provided them with able leadership. But while he worked tirelessly attending to the needs of his unit, he did not instill strong discipline. The regiment's attention to drill remained sporadic, perhaps reflecting that Sammons's only prior military experience had been with local militia—more a social than a martial organization.

Colonel Sammons's letters home reflect a simple family man. He wrote his young daughters frequently, often sending samples of South Carolina trees and flowers and other memorabilia. His letters to his wife reveal a man more concerned with his own family affairs and personal creature comforts than with military affairs and personal ambition. During the entire stay in Carolina he attempted continuously, but unsuccessfully, to gain a furlough to visit home.

A number of the 115th's subordinate officers became dissatisfied with Sammons. No doubt the regiment's scattered affairs, its tedious duties, and its non-inclusion in the military missions of the Department of the South served to amplify objections to the colonel's style of leadership. A small cabal arose among these officers and they succeeded in having Sammons court-martialed. Lieutenant DeGraff remained loyal to Sammons and recorded, "A conspiracy has been hatched by some of our shyster officers against our noble and beloved Colonel Sammons."[40]

The cabal did a poor job. They compiled nine trifling and stale charges against Sammons, small transgressions the colonel allegedly committed against various soldiers of the 115th going back to the beginning of its service a year earlier. For example, Sammons's accusers alleged that he had employed three privates as personal servants. All three testified that

Headquarters of the 115th at Hilton Head. Colonel Sammons sent this drawing home in one of his letters (Collection of the Montgomery County Department of History and Archives, Fonda, New York).

they worked for the colonel as orderlies, clerks, couriers, or horse hostlers, not servants. Sammons was also accused of berating, threatening, or striking several men during the march across Maryland in September 1862. Testimony, including that of Sammons's alleged victims, revealed that these soldiers were straggling and insubordinate and that the colonel was doing his job by trying to move them along.

An altercation that Colonel Sammons had with Lieutenant Colonel George Batcheller in December 1862 led to a charge that Sammons, "without cause or provocation whatsoever" called Batcheller a "God damned son of a bitch" and threatened him with raised fist. The testimony of several witnesses established that an argument began when the two men disagreed over the placement of some baggage. As tempers rose, Batcheller accused Sammons of "improper intimacy" with another man's wife and Sammons yelled, "You damned scoundrel, if you repeat that I will knock your head off."

"I repeat it then," Batcheller replied.

Sammons shook his fists and Batcheller called for pistols, but cooler heads intervened and the argument ended. The colonel's conduct may well have been unbecoming, but he argued that he was provoked and that his "honor and manhood required that the foul and slanderous imputation be silenced."

The court-martial, composed of officers from other regiments, not only acquitted Sammons on every particular of the allegations but it also called the charges "frivolous and vexatious accusations growing out of personal ill will and animosity." As Sammons wrote his wife, "The plot, however well laid, failed most signally."[41]

During the court proceeding Sammons made several references to his main accuser. Although he did not name any one individual, he probably meant Captain Walton W. French of Company F. Immediately after the verdict clearing Sammons, French was admonished by Brigadier General Rufus Saxton, division commander on Port Royal Island:

> The Brigadier General commanding desires to be informed if you consider a General Court Martial is the proper instrument through which you can vent your spleen, your ill will, your personal animosity and bitter feelings against your commanding officer. It would certainly seem so in the present instance as the officer whom you so pointedly maligned has been acquitted of every charge and the specifications thereof which you, in the exercise of your malicious spirit, have seen fit to cause him to be arraigned and tried upon.[42]

Sammons later wrote that he had "no difficulty with Capt. French having never exchanged an unpleasantry with him nor about him." He therefore concluded that French was acting on behalf of others, but he did not mention who those others might be. It is not clear which officers wanted Sammons removed, but there are a number of candidates. DeGraff named his own Company D's Captain Sidney Lingenfelter as a principal conspirator, adding that "a smaller pattern of a man, nor a greater coward cannot be found in the regiment." Also, the failed cabal had identified Lingenfelter as one of Sammons's victims, accusing Sammons of calling Lingenfelter a "damned son of a bitch," when he discovered him riding in a coach that Sammons and three other officers had hired during the 115th's trip across Maryland in September 1862.

It is hard to imagine that the action against Sammons could have taken place without the involvement of Lieutenant Colonel Batcheller. An ambitious and influential young man, Batcheller had argued to the point of violence with Sammons, left the 115th to serve on Department headquarters staff soon after arriving at Hilton Head, and resigned from the army shortly after Sammons was acquitted. Batcheller was a lawyer, perhaps one of the targets of DeGraff's reference to the "shyster officers" who provoked the Sammons court-martial.[43]

There is no doubt where lay the sympathies of most of the regiment. Just before the court-martial proceeding, nine officers of the regiment signed a petition praising their colonel and pleading that nothing be done "that may have a tendency to embarrass him in the discharge of his duties." The enlisted men presented Colonel Sammons with a black horse and riding tack at a ceremony highlighted by a speech delivered by Private George Millham. The speech paid extensive tribute to Sammons and recounted his constant efforts on behalf of his men and his determination and success in clearing the 115th of blame for the Camp Douglas fire. "It is you who has done all this, notwithstanding your immediate assistants, from whom you was justified in expecting more aid than you received, [who] have one by one left us. They are remembered by us, and their course is known to all."

Sammons replied with a speech of his own, expressing his gratitude and praising the men, but not responding to Millham's remark about the other officers. *The Free South* reported on the ceremony and concluded that "this exhibition of the feeling of his men is very creditable to Colonel Sammons." The sordid affair ended well.[44]

In early October 1863, right after the Sammons court-martial, the 115th was sent to the west end of Port Royal Island, where the Coosaw and Broad Rivers separated the island from the mainland. At that time these rivers defined the frontier between Union and Confederate territory, and the regiment's responsibilities included guarding a front of several miles of shoreline. They remained on advance picket duty for twelve days, returned to Beaufort for November, and then returned to the front for the first nineteen days of December.

During the periods at the front the 115th encountered no hostile rebels, but they did get to know some friendly ones. During the night and despite orders against it, the northern and southern soldiers conversed across the wide rivers, and even boated back and forth to meet and barter. Coffee, salt, newspapers, and calico were popular trade items. One Sunday night a man of the 115th and a rebel on the opposite shore told each other what they had for dinner that day. On learning that the Yankees received a ration of whiskey, the rebel replied, "All very fine, sir. Would like to get a little whiskey from you, sir. Would pay a tall price just now, sir.... Reckon you would shoot if we slid over, sir, and have a little bit of trade, sir?" But the presence of officers forced the thirsty Confederate to be rebuffed.[45]

In spite of the byplay with the enemy, the men found the outpost routine monotonous. "During days we have literally nothing to do," wrote DeGraff. Colonel Sammons complained about having the same duties each day. Indicative of the dull routine were the horses used to patrol back and forth along the riverbanks. So inculcated had these four-legged veterans become in their daily rituals, that they needed no guid-

DURING THE WAR

Dr. Carrington Macfarlane became the regimental surgeon for the 115th at Hilton Head in July 1863, and served with it through the rest of the war. He published this wartime photograph of himself in his memoir *Reminiscences of an Army Surgeon* in 1912.

ance in carrying the mounted guards between posts. They stopped instantly when a sentinel shouted a challenge, and moved on when their rider gave the countersign, all without prompting.[46]

These horses may have been content, but the men were ready to move on, as attested to by Dr. Carrington Macfarlane, who had replaced Richard Sutton as regimental surgeon in July. A native of Oswego, New York, Macfarlane served in the 24th New York and the 81st New York before being promoted to surgeon of the 115th. When he first joined the 115th in Beaufort, Macfarlane found the regiment "as near being in paradise as it was possible for live men to be." But writing of late 1863 he recorded, "Weeks and months passed here ... in an idyllic manner, and yet for all that we were not entirely happy. Even in paradise itself one would become discontented with nothing to do."[47]

Speculation over impending action flared in late December when the 115th joined a newly formed all–Empire State brigade with the 47th and 48th New York under the command of Colonel William Barton of the 48th. "To be brigaded with such troops was by us interpreted as an early advance on the enemy," explained James Reid, well aware that the 48th had lost heavily on the walls of Fort Wagner. The 115th would spend several notable months as part of Barton's Brigade. No action followed immediately, but the soldiers underwent a stern training regimen. Captain John Kneeskern of Company B called Colonel Barton "a damn fool to drill." Despite inevitable grumbling the routine of drill helped rid the regiment of its Hilton Head malaise. The five hour per day grind resulted in an efficiency which Lieutenant DeGraff found "filling the boys with pride as they catch the rhythm of the swinging step of the veterans, among whom the 115th is now classed." He also recorded that "the strictest discipline now exists in our large camp; a place and time for everything and woe to the laggard and the careless and indifferent."[48]

The drilling and discipline under Colonel Barton would pay dividends for the 115th. The upgrading of the regiment's readiness came with splendid timing, for it proved a prelude to active campaigning. The New Yorkers soon sailed away from the tedium of South Carolina and into all the action they could imagine.

Its idle year in the south at an end, the 115th resumed its ill-starred odyssey through the Civil War. The events of their first 18 months in service had amply fulfilled the early portent of bad luck. Surrender, captivity, mass arrest, disease, inaction, and squabbling among the officers thus far branded the regiment's career. They now entered the shooting war, and misfortune followed along.

Colonel William Barton of the 48th New York commanded the brigade with which the 115th served through several months of battle (Roger D. Hunt Collection).

7

Olustee

"Like a mountain of adamant"

A bored Simeon Sammons may never have been more mistaken than when he told his wife, in a letter dated January 24, 1864, that "at present there is no prospect of a move here." The 115th's commander clearly did not belong to the Department of the South's strategic inner circle, then busily preparing an invasion of Confederate Florida. Sammons and his regiment would be among the southbound expeditionary force that sailed less than two weeks after his faulty prediction.[1]

Since becoming the third southern state to secede from the Union in January 1861, Florida had remained largely ignored by both sides. Federal forces maintained a number of coastal installations in Florida, valuable in supporting the blockade, and the Confederacy drew Florida men and material to battle fronts elsewhere. But by the beginning of 1864 political, commercial, and military interests combined to focus renewed attention on the state. A businessman named Lyman D. Stickney, called "the most notorious of the early Florida carpetbaggers," maneuvered within all of these interests to generate the impetus for a federal occupation. Modern scholars have credited Stickney with playing an influential role in instigating the Florida campaign of 1864.[2]

Stickney, of Union-occupied St. Augustine, held the office of Federal Tax Commissioner in Florida, a position that gave him a role in the confiscation of property from absent (and non-tax-paying) southern owners, as well as the opportunity to profit from it. He also represented northern shareholders in the Florida Railroad Company who looked to Stickney to protect their investment. Nothing would profit Stickney and his employers more than a federal occupation of Florida, or better still, the state's return to the Union.

Stickney angled in every way possible to bring about these events. He traveled to Washington in September 1863 to visit his boss, Secretary of the Treasury Salmon P. Chase. At the time Chase was a serious contender to unseat Abraham Lincoln as Republican party candidate for President in the 1864 election. Stickney tried to convince Chase that military occupation could lead to Florida's seeking readmission under a pro–Chase government. The opportunistic Stickney found another chance to wield influence when in December 1863 Lincoln issued a proclamation creating a procedure for loyal interests in the South to return their states to the Union. Stickney did not hesitate to play both sides—he wrote to the President's personal secretary John Hay to describe the pro–Union efforts he was making in

Florida, and to invite Hay to Florida to become the repatriated state's representative in Congress.

Stickney also visited General Quincy Gillmore, the commanding officer of the Union's Department of the South, to convince him of the benefits that would follow occupation of Florida, including potential promotions for Gillmore's army friends. He found a sympathetic listener in Gillmore, who was anxious to achieve military distinction but still stymied in his long effort to take Charleston.[3]

On December 15, 1863, Gillmore applied to the War Department for approval of a Florida expedition. In response he was advised that "the matter had been left entirely to [his] judgment and discretion." He then received an unusual letter directly from the President dated January 13, 1864, which began, "I understand an effort is being made by some worthy gentlemen to reconstruct a loyal State government in Florida." Lincoln advised Gillmore that he was sending John Hay south to work with Gillmore on Florida's repatriation and made clear that he wanted "the thing done in the most speedy way possible."[4]

More than political maneuvering and military ambition lay behind the Florida mission. Gillmore recorded four objectives for the campaign: (a) to secure Florida products such as cotton, lumber and turpentine; (b) to stop the flow of beef to Confederate armies (estimates ranged as high as two thousand head of cattle shipped weekly from Florida to rebel forces, principally in Georgia); (c) to recruit troops for black Union regiments from the large slave population; and, (d) to "inaugurate measures for the speedy restoration of Florida to her allegiance," as directed by the President.[5]

Having determined his course of action and duly explained it to his superiors in the War Department, Gillmore set the initiative in motion. He chose Brigadier General Truman Seymour to lead the mission and on February 4 directed Seymour to embark without delay. From that point things moved rapidly. The 115th's Surgeon Macfarlane later called his memory of this period "dreamlike and hazy ... one exciting event followed so quickly by another, all mixed and beaten by the hand of time, memory becomes a delightful salad, sweet and bitter, mustard and oil, all deliciously blended."[6]

On February 5 orders reached the 115th New York to pack six day's rations and sixty rounds of ammunition and board the steamer *Delaware*. The ship put to sea at first light the next morning, part of a Union flotilla of thirty-five vessels. Midmorning February 7, just over twenty-four hours after sailing, the expedition arrived at the mouth of the St. John's River in northern Florida. They waited for the incoming tide to aid them across the bar, then steamed upstream reaching Jacksonville "just as the sun was sinking in the west, and the sky was a blaze of glory."[7]

Gillmore took precautions to keep word of his intentions from leaking. He gave the federal naval force blockading northern Florida only one day's notice of the friendly fleet's approach and the soldiers were not informed of their destination until well after they boarded the *Delaware* and took their southerly course in the Atlantic. Gillmore's stealth paid quick dividends, the element of surprise securing a virtually unopposed landing for his force. Not two dozen men represented the Confederate army in Jacksonville when the Union troops arrived. These few rebels quickly took flight though one managed to shoot the second mate of the Union flagship as he secured his ship to the dock. The first northerners to land, black infantrymen of the 54th Massachusetts and some horsemen of the 1st Massachusetts Independent Cavalry, struck off in pursuit of the sniper but as Lieutenant DeGraff recorded, the rascal escaped.[8]

Jacksonville taken with no further resistance, Barton's Brigade advanced a mile beyond the town and camped for the night. Noted John Reardon, "Jacksonville has the appearance of having been a nice little town [but] the gas works, R.R., hotel and other public buildings have been destroyed, injuring the appearance very much. Before the war the place may have contained two thousand souls." DeGraff wrote his father that "Jacksonville is about half as large as Amsterdam [New York] and was once a nice place."[9]

Barton's Brigade awoke February 8 to a heavy frost and orders to prepare to march at a moment's notice. That moment did not arrive until five in the afternoon when Barton's men moved out behind the cavalry brigade of Colonel Guy Henry. Their objective was Camp Finegan, eight miles distant, the largest Confederate base in the area. The rapid approach of the Union cavalry took the 350 rebels at Camp Finegan by surprise. Unprepared, the startled southerners made a hasty exodus, chased for several miles by Henry's horsemen who seized five cannon as a reward for their hard ride.[10]

The 115th and other northern infantry arrived at Camp Finegan in the wake of the fleeing rebels and their mounted pursuers. Surgeon Macfarlane recorded that the southerners fled in precipitate confusion, leaving behind a merry feast for the invaders, who quickly discovered that Camp Finegan was home to an abundance of turkeys, chickens, ducks, and geese. "The order to charge hen-coops was given," related Clark, "and the soldiers soon swept away all poultry from before them until the feathers flew in all directions. Such a cackling and gobbling was never before heard in eastern Florida." Captured pork and beef rounded out the menu. "The carnage was terrific and the memory of that massacre has always been a sweet morsel to roll under the tongue," concluded Dr. Macfarlane. A sated John Reardon quipped sarcastically that he regretted the rebels' rapid departure as the boys of the regiment wanted to thank them for the unexpected largesse.[11]

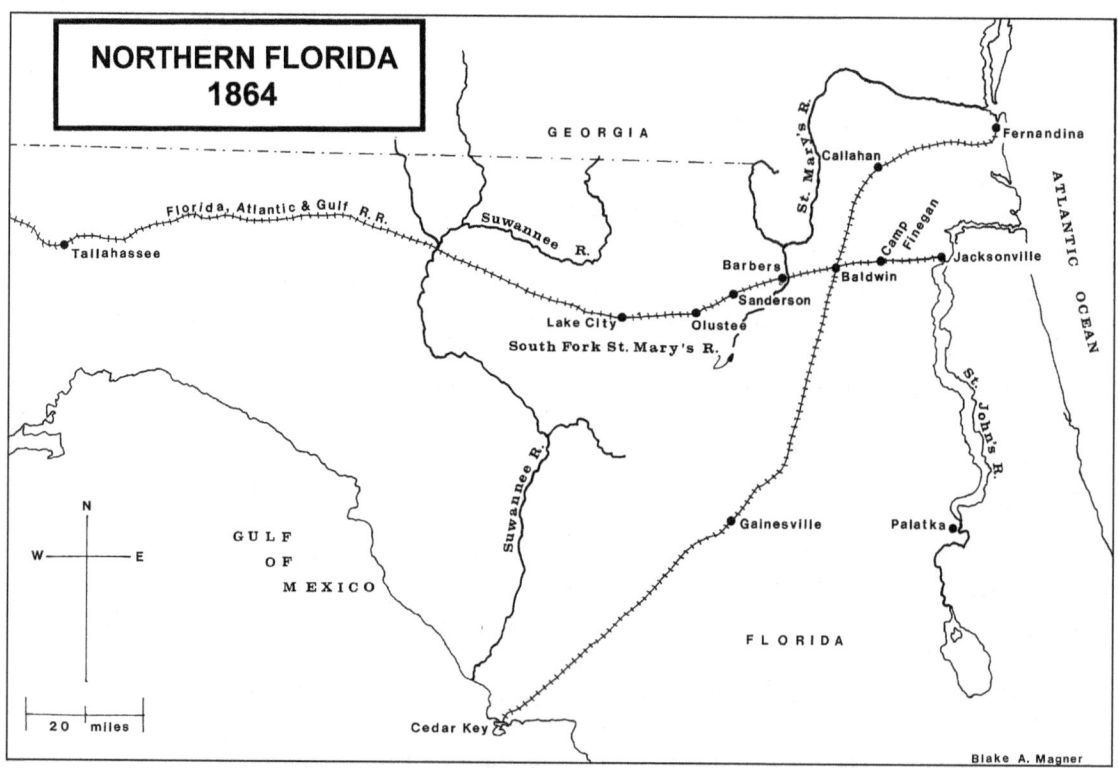

The revelers settled in for a brief night's rest at Camp Finegan and moved out the next morning at 8:00 a.m. The expedition continued westward along the line of the Florida, Atlantic & Gulf Railroad toward the rail junction at Baldwin, twelve miles beyond Finegan. The Union cavalry had seized this key crossing during its furious all-night ride while the 115th and the other foot soldiers dozed with bellies full. The configuration of Florida's 1864 transportation network gave strategic significance to Baldwin. The network consisted of two railroads: the Florida, Atlantic & Gulf running west from Jacksonville toward Tallahassee, and the Florida Railroad, which ran south and west from the Atlantic coast (at Fernandina on the Florida-Georgia border) through Gainesville and on to Cedar Key on the Gulf of Mexico. At Baldwin the lines intersected one another; whoever controlled the crossing gained a commanding foothold on both railroads.[12]

Colonel Henry's cavalry did not tarry at Baldwin but struck out immediately for the next strategic goal, a rail and road crossing of the south branch of the St. Mary's River, near Barber's Plantation. Here they met the first determined Confederate resistance and suffered the loss of three troopers killed and ten wounded before the rebels withdrew. The horsemen kept moving, occupying the small town of Sanderson, ten miles beyond Barber's, on February 10.[13]

The federal infantry trailed along, spending a night at Baldwin and one at Barber's before reaching Sanderson the day following the cavalry. Despite the country being roadless and wooded the troops found easy marching across the grassy forest floor. "Our march into the interior was rapid and very successful," concluded James Reid. Dr. Macfarlane proclaimed the forest the most beautiful he had ever seen:

> The great Georgia pines raising their straight, seamless shafts high in the air, then branching off into lofty domes and arches above our heads. The sod was strong beneath our feet; no underbrush to impede or anything to obstruct the vision except the trunks themselves. We could gallop our horses and draw our cannon and wagons wherever we pleased. At the streams and swamps the pines gave place to giant cypress trees, their strange looking, gnarly knees fantastically protruding from the soil and the beautiful Spanish moss hanging in festoons from the lofty branches.

The 115th led the infantry advance into Barber's, site of the cavalry skirmish. Here the scene took a more grisly aspect as the column passed by the fresh graves of fallen comrades. The infantrymen also found swords and other equipment discarded by the retreating enemy.[14]

Sanderson marked the end of the swift advance, four days and forty-five miles into rebel territory. Rain came in torrents and after one soggy night at Sanderson the infantry about-faced and returned to Barber's. A day later on February 13, the cavalry rejoined them. The horsemen had advanced nearly to the railroad crossing of the Suwannee River, an early objective of the campaign. The end of forward progress and the concentration at Barber's were ordered by General Seymour, who explained himself in a lengthy dispatch to General Gillmore, now on the scene in Florida. Seymour called the notion that Florida desired readmission a delusion, and he concluded that many more men than the expedition had available would be needed to support further movement. He cited their accomplishments to date and opined that failing now would be "a sad termination to a project brilliant thus far." He reminded Gillmore that he had to answer to his superiors "in case of mishap." In other words, after three days of spirited, energetic advance against an unprepared and outmanned foe, Seymour suddenly advised stopping and holding.[15]

The like-minded Gillmore quickly concurred, ordering Seymour to reign in his advanced troops and concentrate his forces without delay. Barber's remained the Union base of operations for the next week, a week that proved a generous and well-used gift of time bestowed by the federals on Florida's Confederate defenders.[16]

On February 13 Gillmore wrote the War Department of his intention to dig in and hold the area around Jacksonville while loyal men opened commerce in the area's natural resources. He assured his superiors that he intended the occupation to be permanent and recommended that the Port of Jacksonville be declared open. Enterprising businessmen wasted no time cashing in on the situation. As a February 18 report in the *New York Times* described, "Jacksonville is beginning to assume quite a business aspect. Traders have succeeded in obtaining permits to land their goods, and it is stated that a party contemplates opening a large hotel." Gillmore shortly returned to Hilton Head, leaving instructions for his field commander, General Seymour, that he should attempt no further advance.[17]

While ensconced at Barber's, General Seymour sent cavalry contingents on raids to Gainesville, where forty-nine federal troopers destroyed some rebel supplies and recruited thirty-three new black soldiers, and to Callahan Station on the Florida-Georgia border. The 115th went along on the Callahan sortie as infantry support together with three companies of the 40th Massachusetts Cavalry and one small cannon.[18]

In the New Yorkers' camp the story circulated that the cavalry commander had personally selected them to accompany his troopers as "it was his observation that the 115th were the greatest marchers of the entire force." True or not, the transmission of such a story on the camp grapevine enhanced the regiment's pride in its soldierly qualities. The regiment would need all its marching skills on this three day trek across seventy miles of wild country.[19]

The raiders set out in a northerly direction at 7:00 a.m. on February 14, trudging until dark then camping in desolate woods. Starting at daybreak the next day, they marched until 3:00 p.m. when some captured livestock became lunch. The colonel and his staff prepared to enjoy a fat goose but when his cook briefly left the bird unguarded, as recalled Surgeon Macfarlane, "some sacrilegious monster stole the goose." This brought a laugh from Dr. Macfarlane, but Colonel Sammons, not one to be deprived of his creature comforts so lightly, raged, "Damn the man that stole the goose and damn the man who thinks it a joke."[20]

The cavalry advance encountered only minor harassment from southern pickets and outdistanced the infantry. On the second day out the horsemen reached Callahan, where they drove off a handful of Confederates and wrecked two ferry boats and the telegraph office. The troopers declared the mission successful and turned back. When word reached the trailing foot soldiers of the 115th, they too turned about and headed back toward Barber's. The regiment marched until 8:00 p.m. that night, then camped in the rain.

The cavalry rejoined them as they continued southward all the next day, the third of the seemingly pointless journey. The day was highlighted by Lieutenant DeGraff's capture of a man he called a bushwacker: a fully-armed, out-of-uniform fellow he found hiding in some shrubs. DeGraff turned the captive over to the adjutant but kept the man's Colt revolver and mailed it home. At one point a small creek delayed the march, the soldiers needing to cross a log bridge single file. Private Charles Spiegel of Company C lost his footing and plunged neck deep into the fast-moving stream to the amusement of his unsympathetic comrades who christened him Gunboat Spiegel.[21]

With the captured livestock mostly consumed and their three-day supply of rations long since devoured, the weary contingent was down to hardtack and coffee that night. Roused from a brief bivouac at 2:00 a.m, an all-night march brought the exhausted raiders back to Barber's at 7:00 a.m. on February 17, exactly 72 hours after their departure. One cynic later described the objective of the mission as the capture of "whatever they might find," with its spoils amounting to "one pony, seven bushels of sweet potatoes, and one or two Florida hogs of the kind that need to have knots tied in their tails to prevent their getting through cracks."[22]

By this time, as Corporal Reid pointed out, "we had been marching almost continually since our entrance into Florida. Nearly every man was suffering from scalded and blistered feet, and not a few were tortured by cramps." The regiment, along with the rest of the Union army in northern Florida, now enjoyed a three day rest at Barber's. When next they marched, it would be into one of the most fiercely fought small battles of the Civil War.[23]

On the expedition's arrival in Florida, Seymour had rushed his men to take Baldwin. He wanted more than simple possession of that strategic rail junction; the Union commander had hoped to move quickly enough to seize a locomotive and train cars for his army to use on the captured rail lines. The Unionists did secure several freight cars but found no locomotives, a situation which led to some creative hauling operations by seventeen men of the 115th New York who drew the job of moving supplies for the Union forces in northern Florida. At their disposal were twenty miles of railroad, three rail cars, six mules, and their own raw energy and ingenuity. Their mission was to haul goods from the port at Jacksonville to the 6,000 federal troops around Baldwin and Barber's.

The squad of impromptu teamsters, led by Corporal John Reardon, hitched the mules to the empty railroad cars and set out for the depot at Jacksonville feeling they had drawn some easy duty. But within the first two miles they discovered a serious problem. Although the terrain was very flat, even shallow downgrades set the cars rolling dangerously toward the mules. "This must be remedied or we will ruin our motive power," cracked Reardon. To protect the animals the men devised brakes by cutting holes in the floors of the cars and inserting shafts of wood to lever between frames and wheels. The improvisation worked well and a single man could control a car easily.

Before long they found more trouble, this time involving several shallow trestles over swampy ground. These structures did not have solid decks, and the mules could not get across as a man could by stepping from crosstie to crosstie. The soldiers solved this dilemma by reversing roles with the mules, the mules riding in the cars and the soldiers pushing the strange train across by hand. But this solution proved inadequate on the first return trip from Jacksonville when after dark in a violent rain storm, it became impossible to see the bridges ahead and to know when to jump out and reverse roles. One poor fellow had to be assigned to walk ahead of the train with a candle, protecting the flame from the rain with a tin cup and shouting out warnings when he approached a trestle.

Reardon's freighting detachment overcame each obstacle and made many round trips on the railroad between February 10 and 27, carrying food, mail, ammunition, and wounded soldiers. The work became a bit easier on February 21 when a steam locomotive finally materialized. Owing to the poor condition of the track the train could not exceed ten miles per hour, and the old engine needed constant maintenance. Even so, the steam engine cut the twenty mile trip between Baldwin and Jacksonville down to two hours from a previous best time of five. "Our present motive power is faster than original," wrote Reardon. "But the mules were more reliable."

The transport duty was not without rewards. At two plantations along the railroad, the crew availed themselves of a generous supply of fresh food. The crew also discovered some hidden cases of liquor at one of the plantations. "Of course the liquor was taken, it being a necessary ingredient with quinine in this section to guard against fever," rationalized Reardon. On a grimmer note, during one stop in Jacksonville the men went into the public square to see a gallows from which hung a black soldier of the 55th Massachusetts, executed for "improper conduct toward a white woman." Reardon called it a horrible sight.

The unique railroad duty became one of Corporal Reardon's fond memories of soldiering. His reminiscences, literally penned on his deathbed with his wartime diaries at hand, contain more detail on these days than any others. He wrote that he could never recall the experience without a feeling of pleasure, and that he felt fortunate in the choice of men assigned to his detachment. "Each man performed his duty conscientiously and faithfully, no bickering, no envy, each vying with the other in his effort to do our work satisfactorily, and succeeded. Our labor was trying and at times dangerous, but we went through."[24]

The transport assignment provided Reardon and his men with more than fond memories. It protected them from the carnage of the Battle of Olustee. While this lucky group of seventeen hauled supplies, half of their regiment became casualties in the Florida pine woods.

It was on February 12 that General Gillmore endorsed Truman Seymour's conclusion that the expedition could accomplish no more and that Union forces should stop and secure their foothold in northeastern Florida. On February 15 Gillmore sailed back to Hilton Head assured that offensive operations had concluded and the long term occupation had begun. Then, on the 17th, Seymour penned another dispatch to Gillmore which caught him quite by surprise. The dispatch announced Seymour's intention to sever his supply line and strike out again toward the Suwannee River railroad bridge with most of his force. On receiving word of Seymour's perplexing reversal, Gillmore immediately wrote back to point out the contradictions between Seymour's latest letter and his earlier one and to restate his desire to hold and occupy the Jacksonville region.

Gillmore dispatched his chief of staff to personally deliver his urgent missive to Seymour and to stop Seymour's intended move. But the high-level messenger was too late; when he arrived at Jacksonville, he learned that Seymour's army had not only moved out but had already engaged in battle. Seymour later rationalized his actions: "The instant I could accumulate provisions enough to sally out, in pursuit of the original aim and end of the expedition—the destroying [of] communications by the Suwannee—that moment I advanced."[25]

Seymour judged that moment to have arrived on February 19. That evening he ordered his forces to prepare for an early forward movement the next morning. Eight regiments of infantry, the cavalry contingent, and artillerymen with a total of sixteen guns made ready—5,500 men in all. The soldiers received issues of several days' rations and sixty rounds of ammunition. During the night the temperature dropped and water froze in canteens, but the morning dawned clear and sunny and the air warmed swiftly. "Little did we think when we left Barber's on the morning of the 20th," mused one of the 115th, "that before night we would engage in a hard and bloody battle."[26]

The cavalry led the column, riding westward at 6:00 a.m., followed soon afterwards by Colonel J.R. Hawley's brigade of 1,500 infantrymen of the 7th Connecticut, 7th New Hampshire, and 8th U.S. Colored Troops. Barton's Brigade, 1,800 strong including 578 Upstate New Yorkers of the 115th, marched at 7:00 a.m. Artillery units accompanied the horsemen and each of the first two brigades of infantry. Colonel James Montgomery's brigade formed a rear guard, his 54th Massachusetts and 1st North Carolina regiments, both composed of black troops, moving out at 8:30 a.m.[27]

Moving rapidly as though expecting the same absence of resistance that had thus far marked their movements through Florida, the cavalry quickly outdistanced the rest of the force. Seymour took none of the precautions customary when advancing toward enemy forces, such as sending out forward skirmishers and flankers or moving at a cautious pace. Perhaps he had been lulled into a false confidence like James Clark who wrote that "our march had been so triumphant through Florida that we began to think the rebels would offer no serious resistance." Seymour certainly should have known better than a volunteer foot soldier like Clark, but he did a very poor job gathering advance information and he remained unaware of an ongoing Confederate buildup in his front. He then compounded his intelligence failure by discrediting reports from his own scouts that a strong southern force awaited him. As Clark later noted, the enemy "had quietly and secretly drawn all their forces from Georgia, South Carolina, and Florida, had concentrated at Olustee, eighteen miles from Barber's, and were waiting our advance."[28]

The rebels had indeed scrambled forces from a wide area to stop the Union encroachment in northern Florida. On February 11 when the federal cavalry first turned back from its advance toward the Suwannee, the southerners numbered just 600. By February 13 as Seymour ceased his aggressive drive and began to concentrate his troops at Barber's, the Confederate force still numbered only 2,250. The following week proved decisive as the rebels made productive use of the gift of time allowed them by the federal leaders. While the Yankee invaders settled in as an occupying army, Confederate numbers continued to rise. By the time Seymour had his abrupt change of heart and determined to renew the offensive, the strength of his enemy reached 5,200 men, nearly equal to his own.

Irish born Brigadier General Joseph Finegan commanded the Confederate force, men from Georgia and Florida who he organized into two brigades under Brigadier General Alfred H. Colquitt and Colonel George P. Harrison, Jr. Finegan chose to make a stand at a place called Olustee Station, where the railroad track and parallel roads funneled through a narrow strip of dry ground between a large lake known as Ocean Pond and extensive swamps a mile to the south. During the week's respite that the federals so obligingly bestowed upon them, the rebels erected a line of earthworks straddling the roadways and stretching across the entire width of dry ground from Ocean Pond to the swamps. If the invaders attempted any further advance along the rail line, they would be forced to move straight into the rebel's prepared position with its ever increasing number of defenders.[29]

When the Union force left Barber's on that fateful February 20, its immediate objective was to destroy the railroad bridge across the Suwannee River about fifty miles beyond Olustee. As the Confederates anticipated, the northerners' path led straight into their fixed position. In midafternoon the federal cavalry advance met resistance from the rebel's forward skirmishers, and the riders halted to wait for the infantry. At this point they were several miles west of Sanderson and four miles short of the Confederates' Olustee line. When Hawley's brigade of infantrymen arrived, his 7th Connecticut advanced against the rebel skirmish line. The southerners fell back fighting to a point where the highway crossed the railroad and several more gray infantry units waited. General Finegan intended these troops to lightly engage the federals and draw them back to the earthworks at Olustee. But as additional federals came up and joined the developing scrap, more Confederate units poured out of their works to reinforce their forward line. The open pinewoods surrounding this crossing, about two miles east of the Confederate's prepared entrenchments, became the accidental collision point for the two armies. This site was about to witness "nearly four hours of the pluckiest fighting of modern times."[30]

From the outset things went poorly for the Yankees. Artillery batteries moved too far in advance of the infantry and suffered badly. The 7th Connecticut, fighting on its own against increasing odds, ran low on ammunition and fell back. Seymour then threw in the rest of Hawley's Brigade, the 7th New Hampshire and 8th U.S. Colored Troops. General Seymour was directing his troop movements personally and not doing well. He stumbled into battle without warning or plan. Then he compounded his error by feeding his forces piecemeal into the fight, thus assuring his enemy the numerical advantage at the point of contact throughout the day. Like the 7th Connecticut before them, the 7th New Hampshire and 8th U.S.C.T. faced an unequal battle and fared poorly. Seymour now turned to Colonel Barton's New York brigade, the next unit in the federal column. As described by Corporal Reid, "It was at this critical time that urgent orders reached Barton's Brigade to come to the front as soon as possible."[31]

Receiving these orders, Barton formed his three regiments into battle line and commanded them to advance. "Battalion, forward! Guide center; double quick; march!" thundered Colonel Sammons to his 115th. The regiment covered the mile of distance to the front at a fast pace but the soldiers had already marched sixteen miles that day. Reid wrote that the rushed movement to the battlefront put "a great strain on our vitality.... But for the excitement of the moment many no doubt would have dropped from exhaustion." Reid and his mates soon proved they possessed remarkable reserves of vitality.[32]

Barton's Brigade advanced in its battle lines, *en echelon*, with the 47th New York at the

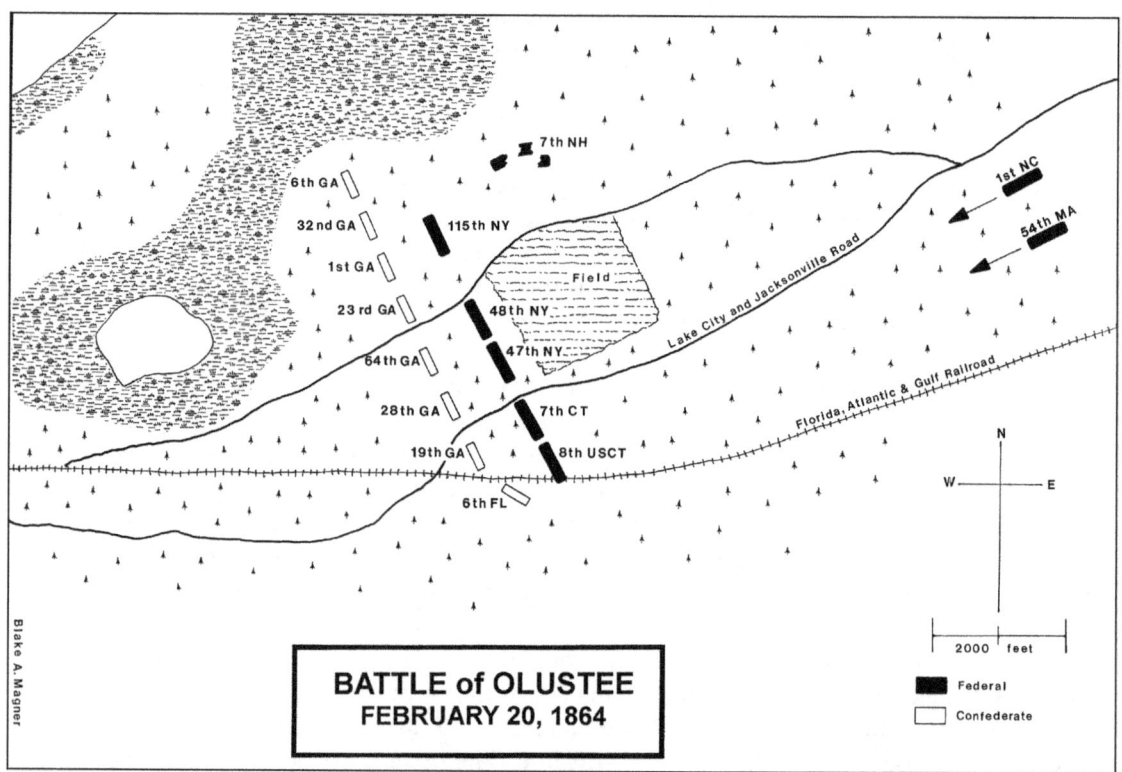

BATTLE of OLUSTEE
FEBRUARY 20, 1864

left front, the 48th New York in the center, and the 115th on the right. Nearing the position formerly held by the shattered 7th New Hampshire, the 115th put its recent parade drills to use by maneuvering to close a gap between it and the 48th. Now formed into a continuous line, Barton's units moved forward a short distance before halting to open fire on "the hateful columns of southern gray" plainly visible through the thin pines. The New Yorkers had come under heavy fire while moving to the front and perfecting their line, but maintained good order despite many casualties.[33]

The brigade "at once became hotly engaged," Colonel Barton reported. Advancing into "a perfect roar of musketry and artillery," some men of the 115th steeled themselves with shouts of "Harpers Ferry" and thoughts of vengeance. "We were immediately under a galling fire which we returned in kind. We were unable to drive them or advance further but we held the field for 2½ hours," remembered DeGraff. Just under 600 men of the 115th endured the face-to-face shootout, both sides blazing away at a rapid clip with men falling constantly. Barton's Brigade formed the major portion of the Union line during these hours, the crest of the Battle of Olustee. The remnant of the 8th U.S.C.T. held the federal left, and part of the 7th Connecticut re-formed and came up between the 8th and the left of Barton's Brigade. The 7th New Hampshire had dissolved and disappeared rearward. Artillery batteries struggled to hold positions in front of the blueclad line of infantry. The 115th, as the rightmost regiment in Barton's Brigade, held the extreme right of the Union line.[34]

"The battle now raged with unexampled fury. Men were falling here and there in great numbers," as one of the regiment described. In another's words, "the balls were flying thicker and thicker, the 115th was growing smaller and smaller, and the boys were falling faster and

This path at the Olustee Battlefield Historic State Park in Florida runs along the front line held by the 115th at the height of the battle (photograph by author).

faster, but they kept closing up to their battle flag." The 115th stood firm, remaining in line in the open woods and exchanging fire. A correspondent from the *New York Tribune* who accompanied the expedition wrote, "Desperate assaults on the Union right failed to drive in the brave 115th, holding the extremity of the line." The 115th was "praised by everybody for the brave stand which we made, but we paid for it dearly," according to Nicholas DeGraff. "It was just like leading our men up to slaughter," concluded Private Benjamin Northrup of Company H.[35]

The Confederates "fired rapidly and with deadly aim," wrote Reid. The 115th returned a rapid fire of its own, the regiment fully engulfed in its first pitched battle. James Clark described the scene:

> It was now a continuous roar on both sides, and for three long hours the swift tide of battle surged with cruel fury. There was no lull in the rattle of musketry—no calm and serene moment of security. The leaden messengers of death hailed down in increasing torrents. Grape and canister swept by with hideous music, and shell after shell tore through our ranks and burst amid heaps of our wounded heroes.

Reid noted the numbers falling among his regiment, but took solace in his belief that equal damage was being inflicted on the enemy. "How could it be otherwise? Muskets were being rapidly loaded by skillful hands and deliberately fired by cool, calculating veterans, and so the battle went on." Indeed, the Confederates opposing Barton's Brigade lost over 500 men. The 32nd Georgia, which held the gray line directly opposite the 115th New York, suffered more casualties than any other Confederate unit at Olustee.[36]

Lieutenant DeGraff suffered fever and ague during the previous week and was calling on the regimental surgeon when the sounds of skirmishing first reached the 115th. DeGraff and Dr. Macfarlane immediately set out to catch up with the regiment, the sick young soldier anxious to accompany his comrades into a fight and the surgeon needing to be there to attend to any casualties. Macfarlane dismounted and gave his horse to the infirm DeGraff. The lieutenant reached his Company D as it formed into battle line and found himself "at once in the midst of the conflict." DeGraff felt fortunate to escape unhurt from the battle, during which he felt strangely calm. He later wrote his father that in the heat of the fight he "did not realize any danger; it seemed I had no thought of the consequences." He described how one man was shot in the face as DeGraff helped him unload his cartridge box, and how another, Sergeant Levi Lingenfelter, took a ball through the head and fell dead at his side. "I knew he was dead, he died instantly, but it did not seem like death," wrote DeGraff, trying to explain the unexpected composure that embraced him during the battle.[37]

Like DeGraff, Benjamin Northrup expressed surprise at emerging unhurt. "I do not see how I escaped, for I was in the front all the time, and our company carried the flag, and of course we were fired into the most. It was hard to see our boys falling all around us, but we stood our ground."[38]

In the front line with Company C, James Reid stood between the "talkative, jovial" Private James A. Hanna and the "silent combatant" Corporal Sidney T. Cornell. Cornell, at twenty-five, was the eldest among these three Saratoga County natives. Reid observed that the two men beside him both acted as calm as if participating in drill and "neither showed the least concern for his personal safety, although the leaden messengers were thinning our ranks at a fearful rate." On Reid's right Cornell silently loaded, fired, and reloaded—noticeable because each time he was ready to fire he dropped onto his left knee, raised his rifle to his left shoulder, and carefully drew a bead on an unlucky rebel before pulling the trigger. On Reid's left Private Hanna chattered throughout the fight, voicing opinions on what the men ought to do as if he commanded the unit. At one point a riderless horse appeared in front of the enemy line. It fell suddenly then attempted several times to rise. "That horse is wounded and is in my way," said Hanna. "I'll put him out of his misery." Hanna aimed and fired and the horse dropped.

As Cornell stood to reload, a bullet struck him in the right side. It spun him completely around and he fell backwards toward the enemy. He was taken a short distance to the rear but died as he fought, without uttering a word. Within five minutes "the dull thud of the bullet was again heard." This ball hit Hanna above the left hip and passed through his body, shattering his cartridge box and scattering its contents. Reid bent to question the fallen Hanna about his wound but received only a smile in response from the dying twenty-two-year old. Charles Jenkins and John Duckett promptly stepped forward to replace Cornell and Hanna in the front rank. Both were hit inside of ten minutes. Jenkins stood his ground despite a painful shot in the leg. Duckett took a ball in the knee and hobbled to the rear.[39]

Lieutenant Clark described how the two tallest men in his company, Private Philip Link of Halfmoon and Corporal Charles Mulliken of Stillwater, were both killed by balls through the head. "If they had not been so tall perhaps they might both have been alive today." Clark reported that Mulliken, the twenty-four-year old son of the village blacksmith, was the first to die, shot as the regiment entered the fight. Private Link, a forty-two-year old, white-haired miller, received his fatal bullet at the front line. "Uncle Philip turned black in the face, threw up his hands and fell forward."[40]

Teenaged James Wilson, son of a widowed mother, fired all of the sixty rounds in his cartridge box then grabbed more from a dead comrade. Clark described what happened next:

> Leveling his gun for the sixty-first time, and seeing a mass of the enemy moving upon us, he said to Sergeant [Alfred] Gould in his usual pleasant way, 'Which way shall I aim this time, Alf?' He took good aim, but never fired, for he fell among the slain, and one of the bright lights of our campfire and weary marches had gone out forever.[41]

Clark himself escaped injury as his comrades fell all around him for nearly three hours and began to feel bullet proof. Eventually a stinging sensation in his right side shattered this illusion. He remained in line a short while after being hit but soon grew faint and headed for the rear after reporting his condition to Company Captain Solomon Smith. He came upon a surgeon working among a group of twenty wounded men. As he approached the group a shell burst in their midst sending mangled remains flying in all directions. Turning away in horror, Clark located his own regiment's Surgeon Macfarlane "surrounded by fifty wounded, his sleeves rolled up, his arms crimsoned with blood." He left the overburdened Macfarlane to his grisly work and joined the growing stream of walking wounded hurriedly retracing the route toward Barber's.[42]

Dr. Macfarlane busied himself with the wounded and could discern little about the progress of the battle although he could see columns forming behind him, preparing to enter the contest, and he could see men falling on all sides. At one point a cannon shot toppled a tree onto his open-air surgery, but it inflicted no further injuries. Macfarlane had established his aid station very near the front, as did Dr. Adolph Majer, the expedition's chief medical officer. Majer recorded the wounded soldiers coming "first in single drops, then trickling, after a while in a steady stream, increasing from a single row to a double and treble, and finally into a mass." Stray shots felled so many pines at his field hospital that Majer relocated a mile farther to the rear.[43]

As the regiments of Barton's Brigade approached the sounds of battle, a presentiment of doom overtook the 115th's Lieutenant William Tompkins. He removed a few sheets from his pocket and told the man beside him, "Here are some papers that I wish were in safekeeping; matters will not go well with me today." Just then he heard the orders to form battle lines and moved forward. As one of his comrades related his story, "whatever torture of mind Tompkins endured was not noticeable in his actions. There was no display of fear, but on the contrary he went here and there along the line cheering and encouraging the men, performing bravely his duties until death. He was hit squarely in the forehead and fell without a groan."[44]

Early in the battle a bullet hit Company A's Captain Garrett Van Derveer in the thigh. The captain refused to leave his men though they urged him to seek treatment. Instead he pushed the point of his sword into the ground to support himself and remained at the front shouting support to his men. His stubborn courage cost him his life when another ball entered his breast, striking just inside his left shoulder and exiting near his spine. Attendants carried him from the field in a blanket and rushed him to the rear.

Van Derveer was transported to Hilton Head for care but died there four days later. He left a young widow and a baby son, born three weeks after the 115th left for war, whom he had seen but once. Under the final record in the captain's diary, a brief entry in a different handwriting registers the dates and places of his wounding and death and adds the words "He died for his country." General Seymour noted that he held the captain in high esteem and called his death "one of the great

Captain Garrett Van Derveer of Company A was mortally wounded at Olustee (Lance Ingmire Collection).

misfortunes of the day." Colonel Sammons had recently recommended Van Derveer to become the 115th's lieutenant colonel, to replace George Batcheller who had departed the regiment amidst the internal wrangling at Hilton Head.[45]

Captain William Smith of Company K, who had become the first officer of the regiment to be wounded back at Maryland Heights, was luckier this day. He remained unhurt though his clothing was pierced several times. One ball struck Smith's blanket which he had rolled up and slung over his shoulder, passing through the fabric fourteen times before halting short of Smith's flesh. The Confederates also dealt Major Ezra Walrath a close call, one of their bullets cutting away his shoulder strap as "with the imperturbable cheerfulness and the cool courage which distinguished him, he moved along the line cheering and encouraging his soldiers."[46]

Colonel Sammons stayed at the front with his troops, riding up and down the line, always in the thickest of the fight. "He fought his regiment splendidly," one of his men recorded, "and his voice could be heard encouraging on the men amid the rattle of musketry and booming of cannon." General Seymour wrote that Sammons "behaved like one of the heroes of old and has won my respect forever." Mounted and exposed, the colonel's ample form offered an appealing target for enemy sharpshooters. Ultimately a rebel bullet found him and shattered the bones in his right foot. Sammons fell from his horse, injuring his head and leaving the vision in his right eye permanently impaired. But he remounted and stayed with his men throughout the action.[47]

One of the Union brigade commanders called the Battle of Olustee "a fair, square stand-up fight in pine woods," an apt description of the struggle between Barton's New York brigade and its foe. The opposing lines held their positions and shot it out at the deadly rifle range of 100 to 200 yards. But resources on hand eventually began to tilt in favor of

Colonel Sammons's hat, sword, and epaulets (Collection of the Montgomery County Department of History and Archives, Fonda, New York).

the southerners. While Barton's regiments held the front line, the Confederates facing them secured new supplies of ammunition brought forward from a rail car in their rear. Near the same time more rebel infantry arrived from the earthworks at Olustee Station, reinforcing and extending the line opposing Barton's men. The leftmost southern units, the 6th and 32nd Georgia, stretched beyond the Union right and moved forward a short distance, thus bringing a deadly flank fire against the 115th New York. The strengthened Confederates advanced along other portions of their front as well, and the northerners began to give ground, "for it was impossible," explained Private Northrup, "to stand the bullets and shells which they fired at us." Barton's Brigade had fought one hour or more on their original line.[48]

In its initial retrograde movement the Union line fell back about twenty-five yards. Over the next one to two hours—time estimates of the participants vary substantially—the northerners repeated this rearward move several times. The 115th and the rest of the line pulled back stubbornly and deliberately—facing the enemy and loading and firing. The movements brought the regiment into an open field where it continued to suffer heavily. Just as the 115th began to move back a ball pierced the side of Robert Fox of Company C, and he found himself lying between the lines with the bullets of both sides flying overhead. He crawled to a large tree, propped himself on the side facing his regiment and held up a hand "as though beseeching us to be careful and not hit him. It was a sorrowful sight." Fox later died a prisoner.[49]

A severely wounded Corporal Daniel Grant also fell into enemy hands and went to the infamous Andersonville, Georgia prison camp. Grant left home at age eighteen to enlist. Unknown to Grant, his discharge from service awaited him when he went into the fight at Olustee. It had been secured because his two brothers had recently died from disease, leaving his widowed mother alone on the family farm. He returned to the regiment after ten months of imprisonment "a living skeleton," and remained with the 115th until the war's end.[50]

By the time they began to give ground the men of Barton's regiments had little ammunition left, despite raiding the cartridge boxes of their fallen comrades. They were bolstered for a time by the arrival of Montgomery's all-black brigade, including the 54th Massachusetts. The 54th moved past Barton's Brigade and temporarily recovered some cannon that had been abandoned to the rebels. As the 54th passed by, some men of the 115th joined with them in their advance despite being short of ammunition. Montgomery's 1st North Carolina then moved up between the 47th and 48th New York. For a time Montgomery's regiments held the Union front, fighting bravely as the other units withdrew. Like the federal forces Seymour threw into the fight earlier, these regiments were outnumbered and suffered egregious losses. As Corporal Reid wrote, "the 54th kept good the famous record they made at Fort Wagner."[51]

With darkness falling and their ammunition expended Colonel Barton, at Seymour's direction, ordered his regiments to withdraw. Barton dispatched Lieutenant Frank Barnum of the 115th—then serving as brigade aide-de-camp—to transmit the retreat order to Colonel Sammons. Instead of immediately relaying the order to his men, Sammons rode along the line of the 115th to explain the need to fall back. He sought to ensure an orderly withdrawal and avoid panic. The delay did not please Barton and he twice more sent Barnum riding back to the 115th to hurry Sammons along. As DeGraff related, "this exasperated Colonel. S. and he shouted with the roar of battle around him, 'Give my compliments to General Barton and tell him to go to hell! I will fall back with my regiment when I am ready to do so.'" For a time the regiment stood alone but eventually the feisty Sammons and his men left the field, with shouts of defiance and faces turned to the enemy.[52]

The federal troops withdrew deliberately. As the on-the-scene reporter from the *New York Times* wrote, "The retreat was conducted leisurely and orderly. There was no confusion, no panic, nothing that indicated hurry." Part of the 7th Connecticut deployed as a rear guard, forming a skirmish line one-half mile in length to counter any pursuit by the victorious rebels. The cavalry brigade shared this role with the Connecticut men, each line alternately falling back behind the other. But the spent Confederates failed to mount any pursuit. "The enemy had been too badly punished; he was unable to follow up his advantage," concluded Dr. Macfarlane.

Attaining a safe distance, the northerners formed their brigades into parallel columns. The weary march did not stop until they had covered the sixteen miles back to Barber's where at 2:30 a.m. the troops filed into the same camps from which they had embarked the previous dawn. Some of the 115th found their campfires from the previous night still burning. Some made coffee; others sank immediately into an exhausted sleep. DeGraff summarized his regiment's experience of February 20, 1864, as "making a march of 32 miles and 2½ hours hard fighting without rest and nothing to eat but dry hard bread and swamp water to drink. This is soldiering in earnest. But it is too bad we got whipped."[53]

Dr. Macfarlane described the retreat as "weird and exciting in the extreme." It started with a crush of wagons, guns, horses and men seeking their place in line, "then the rapid march through those dark, gloomy woods, no one allowed to speak above a whisper, to make the slightest noise, or even to scratch a match," all blended with apprehension of pursuit and attack. Macfarlane gave his horse to a badly wounded man and walked to Barber's, but instead of resting there he worked until daylight dressing wounds.[54]

The retreating federals left forty severely injured men behind under the care of the surgeon of the 48th New York, among them the tragic Daniel Grant. These men, as one of their retreating comrades wrote, "were badly wounded and could not stir and they were left to the tender mercies of the enemy." Cavalrymen gave up their mounts to transport eighty other injured men out of harm's way. Hundreds more crowded onto every available ambulance, wagon, and gun carriage for a ride to safety. Others struggled rearward under their own power, including men with serious upper body wounds. These men dreaded capture and cruel confinement as prisoners of war, and tapped deep reserves of strength to carry them through the long night's trek to Barber's. They discovered, as Macfarlane wrote, that "fear is a terrible spur to endurance."[55]

James Clark, one of these walking wounded, observed that not all of them made it. "Some lay down along the road and declared that they could go no farther. Others were fast bleeding to death, and some fell down exhausted to die." Clark moved along with the miserable stream of wounded making its way eastward away from the battlefield. "We all concluded that it would be better to die walking or even crawling towards freedom, than to starve to death in rebel dungeons." Clark's group got help when some Massachusetts cavalrymen happened by and placed thirty wounded on their horses, Clark among them. But after carrying him a mile Clark's mount died and he finished his trek on foot. When he reached Barber's at 3:00 a.m. the lieutenant sat on a cracker box by a campfire and dropped into sleep.[56]

Also among the flood of wounded was remarkable sixty-four-year old Private James Gardner. A veteran of the War of 1812, Gardner enlisted in the 115th along with his son James, the youngest of his ten children. "Five feet 11 inches high without boots [and] straight as a yard of pump water," according to his son, the elder Gardner took bullets in the leg and chest during the battle, then walked back twelve miles before being picked up by an ambulance. He lingered for four weeks but died of his wounds at Hilton Head.[57]

As the 115th withdrew Joseph Abeel and James Reid discovered one of their Company C mates, Charles Nathaniel Baker, crawling toward the rear. Baker, a twenty-six-year old Saratoga County man known as Than, had fired twenty rounds before a rebel bullet passed through his foot. He hobbled back a short distance, sheltered himself behind a large pine, and cut the shoe away from his wounded foot. From there he moved toward the rear on hands and knees until the other Company C men found him. Using their two rifles spanned between them as a support, Abeel and Reid tried to help Baker stay with the retreating federals. But Baker's wounded extremity dragged through the shrub growth, bringing him bitter pain, and his hopping along between Abeel and Reid caused them to stumble repeatedly. The slowly retreating federal rear guard was gaining on them, and they tried to speed things by carrying Baker alternately on their backs and in a blanket. Despite such efforts, the rear guard caught up with them and advised them that the enemy was close by and that they should abandon the wounded soldier or be left behind. Private Baker agreed and urged Reid and Abeel to leave him saying, "Boys, you have done all you could for me, it is better for one to be taken prisoner than for all three."

Giving Baker a blanket and a canteen, the good Samaritans regretfully moved on. But glancing back they saw Baker again crawling away on hands and knees. Unwilling to abandon their struggling comrade, they returned to him. Baker once more urged them to move on without him, but at that moment good fortune arrived in the form of Lieutenant Francis Francisco of Company K. Francisco had missed the action, serving behind the lines as acting regimental quartermaster. However, he seized the first opportunity to ride toward the front. He observed the struggle of the three 115th men and joined them, helped Baker onto his saddle, and rode with him back into the darkness. At the site of the field hospital he left Baker with some other severely wounded men who had been left behind and told him to wait there for conveyances that would be sent back for the injured men. Baker had grave misgivings about any potential rescue.

When no one had come by midnight, Baker started eastward again, crawling at first, then fashioning crutches out of some discarded barrel staves. Painfully, the persistent soldier covered several miles by daybreak when he came upon a small boy with a slightly wounded horse. Seizing the horse from the boy, Baker's hopes for deliverance soared. But as he started to climb onto the horse he heard a shout. "If you mount that horse you are a dead Yank," bellowed a southern voice, and Baker became the prisoner of a squad of rebel cavalry. His ordeal continued that noon when his captors placed him in a wagon and drove him back to the battlefield. There they gathered a load of discarded muskets, pitching them into the wagon with Baker, several times causing him agonizing pain by striking his wrecked foot. Unfortunately Baker's sorrows had only begun—he would suffer the hellish captivity of Andersonville. But unlike twenty-eight other soldiers from the 115th who perished there, the determined Baker survived, rejoining his regiment a year later under quite remarkable circumstances.[58]

John Reardon and his detail of freight haulers were three miles out of Jacksonville when at 11:00 p.m. the night of February 20, urgent orders reached them to hurry their train back to assist with the evacuation of wounded. They arrived at Baldwin at 9:00 a.m. on February 21, just as the first casualties of the battle began to pour in from the west. Reardon left a vivid account:

> First came the officers of different regiments, some on horseback, some in ambulances or any kind of vehicle, with limbs shattered and blood dried on their garments showing evidence of very serious wounds. Then came the wrecks of artillery limbers and boxes covered with wounded too weak to walk. The artillery carriages show the effect of serious work, broken spokes and rims and bodies filled and scarred with minie balls. Poor horses suffered as well as the men, blood can be seen flowing from bodies and limbs, but they make no complaint. Following the artillery comes the wounded in large numbers, who could walk or must walk to escape capture as the ambulances, supply wagons, etc. filled with those first wounded. In one instance I helped a man on the car who has walked from Olustee here. He is suffering from a shot through the body. The poor fellow lived but a few days. The first of my company I saw coming was Lieutenant I.E. Smith, his face [so] begrimed with powder and smoke that I scarcely recognized him. He is suffering from a wound in the shoulder. He says the regiment suffered badly but conducted themselves nobly. We worked hard to get all the wounded present on board.

Lieutenant Clark was one of those fortunate enough to get a place on the cars going back to Jacksonville. As many as seventy men crowded onto each flatcar. They had to hold on to one another to keep from falling off, and the suffering continued on the slow mule-drawn ride.[59]

The federal force, reduced by the 1,861 casualties incurred at Olustee, abandoned Barber's and retired to Baldwin on February 22 and then to Jacksonville on the 25th. The army was back where it had started. The Confederates re-occupied Barber's and Baldwin as soon as these places were vacated by the northerners but made no move to attack.[60]

Captain Isaac E. Smith was among the 115th's 188 wounded in action at Olustee on February 20, 1864. Smith was a farmer in Minden in Montgomery County before the war and joined the 115th as a sergeant at age 21 (New York State Military Museum).

Truman Seymour came under severe criticism after the battle, both for commencing the offensive against his superior's wishes and for the way in which he conducted his forces during the fighting. The critics included not only General Gillmore and the newspapers, but also many of Seymour's own soldiers. An officer with the 8th U.S.C.T. railed that "Seymour might better have been in his grave than there." The discreet Lieutenant DeGraff chose to blame the War Department for assigning an incompetent commander to the expedition. All were aware that Seymour had faced similar recriminations for his role in the futile and costly Union assault on Fort Wagner in June 1863. The Union field commander indeed performed badly at Olustee. His lack of reconnaissance led to an unforeseen and unprepared collision with a strong enemy. Seymour personally placed artillery batteries in harm's way, too far in front of their infantry support. Most grievous of all, instead of consolidating his force for attack he fed his units piecemeal into the fight.[61]

Seymour claimed indifference to the criticism but took pains to defend himself. In a postmortem written to New York State Adjutant General John T. Sprague a month after the battle, Seymour said he "disapproved the whole affair in Florida in the most positive manner.... But I was ordered here and here I came." He asserted that though nothing was in writing, Gillmore had agreed that Florida could not be held unless the federal force took the crossing over the Suwannee River. Therefore, Seymour argued, when he moved on February 20 he was simply complying with the wishes of his commander. He blamed Gillmore for the failure to procure a locomotive and the resulting inability to supply an advanced force, which, Seymour now claimed, had caused him to stop short of the Suwannee during the first few days of the expedition.

Seymour's rationalizations included the claim that his advance had actually been providential. He reasoned that if he had remained at Barber's and the rebels had struck him first, the entire federal command would have been destroyed. Seymour made the improbable assertion that "it was very lucky that I attacked that afternoon of the 20th—had I waited until next morning, we should have been whipped beyond endurance." The letter concluded with bravado. "It was a mistake to come down here at all, but that's no fault of mine. And I doubtless made a mistake in trying to whip Mr. Reb but it is an error I am likely to commit whenever the chance is offered and I have such troops to do it with as I had on that day."[62]

General Seymour's time with the Department of the South soon ended. He returned to the Army of the Potomac where, within three months of the Battle of Olustee, he became a prisoner. Exchanged after several months in captivity, he ended the war as a division commander in Virginia.[63]

The fight at Olustee cost the 115th New York 296 casualties: 62 men dead, 188 wounded, and 46 missing. This amounted to 51% of the 578 men engaged. These are egregious numbers by any Civil War standard, but particularly for a static, stand-up battle such as that fought by Barton's Brigade at Olustee. While the American Civil War produced countless extremes of courage and carnage, it was not common for troops to endure this degree of punishment without breaking or seeking cover.[64]

The Battle of Olustee which cost the 115th so dearly is little known, essentially lost to history, and understandably so. The numbers engaged, around 5,000 on each side, were relatively small compared to most Civil War battles. In terms of strategic significance, Olustee had little impact on the course of the war or even on subsequent events in Florida. In human terms however, Olustee stands as one of the bloodiest fights of the entire war. DeGraff noted that "men that have been in the worst battles of the war say they never saw a sharper engagement or a heavier loss for the time we were engaged." Oliver W. Norton, an officer with the 8th U.S.C.T. who had witnessed the major eastern battles of the war's first three years while serving with the 83rd Pennsylvania in the Army of the Potomac, said that at Olustee he faced "the most destructive fire I ever knew."[65]

Data support the testimony of these witnesses. The figures below depict the Union's costliest battles of the war, ranked by percentage of killed and wounded among troops engaged.

Heaviest Union Losses of the Civil War[66]

Wilderness/Spotsylvania	29.6%
Port Hudson	26.7%
Olustee	26.5%
Stones River	22.3%
Cedar Mountain	21.9%
Fort Wagner	21.4%
Gettysburg	21.2%
Chickamauga	19.6%

Olustee ranks ahead of such epochal cataclysms as Gettysburg and Chickamauga. Its standing on the list is behind Wilderness/Spotsylvania and Port Hudson, but the nature of these fights were very different from Olustee. The figures for Wilderness/Spotsylvania include aggregate casualties for two weeks of struggle, while at Port Hudson the horrible toll resulted from repeated frontal assaults on an impregnable position. For stand-up, face-to-face fighting, Olustee ranks as the war's deadliest. And the 115th New York, with its fifty-one percent loss, contributed more than its share to the grim statistics.

The story of Barton's Brigade at Olustee is evocative of a similar vignette from Civil War history, one which has received considerable renown among modern historians. On the eve of the Second Battle of Bull Run, a Union brigade of one Indiana and three Wisconsin regiments had a chance encounter with the Confederate "Stonewall Brigade," fighters named in honor of their original commander, Stonewall Jackson. The unique band of Westerners in the Army of the

Private William Lake, wounded in action at Olustee. Lake enlisted at Canajoharie at age 19 (New York State Military Museum).

Potomac came to be called the Iron Brigade, and remains one of the most famous combat units produced by the Civil War. In gathering darkness on August 28, 1862 these two brigades were the principal antagonists in a musket fight at close range at the Brawner Farm at Gainesville, Virginia.

Prior to that evening only one of the Iron Brigade regiments had ever been in action: the 2nd Wisconsin at First Bull Run. Prior to Olustee only the 48th New York of Barton's Brigade had seen significant action—at Fort Wagner. Brawner Farm, like Olustee, was a toe-to-toe fight. In each case the opposing forces maintained their lines for a long couple of hours and exchanged fire. In both instances the Union regiments stood to it, taking and returning ghastly punishment until external circumstance put an end to the fighting, darkness at Brawner Farm and the void in ammunition at Olustee.[67]

Also in each case the northerners stood until many hundreds of their mates had been shot down. The Iron Brigade suffered 725 casualties among its 1,937 men engaged at Brawner Farm, or 37%. Barton's Brigade lost 824 men at Olustee, 46% of its 1,800. The Iron Brigade and its courageous maiden fight at Brawner Farm enjoy enduring fame 140 years later. The 115th New York and Barton's Brigade at Olustee remain obscure, a bloody sideshow of the War Between the States.[68]

The men of the 115th New York took justifiable pride in the performance of their regiment and their brigade at Olustee. As their commanding officers' reports and newspaper accounts throughout the North acknowledged their action, the shock of battle and the grieving for lost comrades gave way to the elation of achievement. In his official report General Seymour wrote, "The conduct of Colonel Barton's brigade was glorious, and I cannot too highly commend the pertinacity with which it held to its work." Less formally in his letter to Adjutant General Sprague, Seymour wrote that Barton's Brigade bore the brunt of the battle. He described the brigade's action and its losses and concluded, "Do you know better fighting than that? If so tell me of it, for I never saw anything finer than the steadiness of these fellows on that pleasant sunshiny afternoon on that wooded plain of Olustee."[69]

The *New York Times* reported, "There can be no doubt concerning the fighting qualities of Barton's Brigade. On this occasion they fought like tigers." And the *New York Herald* declared that Barton's Brigade "never did better, and that to their firmness and endurance, their pluck and steadiness, we owe the safety of our entire force."[70]

Within the ranks of the 115th such recognition gave great satisfaction. As one soldier wrote, "naturally every bosom of its membership swelled with pride and gratification." Despite their grievous losses morale remained high. Captain Shaw bragged that "had all the forces fought like the 115th a glorious victory would have been the result." Most importantly, the regiment now felt that it had erased any stigma attaching to the misfortunes of its first eighteen months in service. As Corporal Reid phrased it, the 115th had "emerged from every vestige of the humiliation of the Harpers Ferry surrender and subsequent arrest." In its initial test of full-scale war the 115th had, in one member's words, "closed up and stood the shock like a mountain of adamant."[71]

8

Bottled on Bermuda Hundred

"Nothing has been accomplished"

In the weeks following the Battle of Olustee the Union force settled in around Jacksonville. Wary of Confederate attack they erected earthworks, but there was no attempt by the Confederates to dislodge them from their foothold in northeastern Florida. For the moment the 115th enjoyed spring-like weather and a leisurely camp routine.

While the men savored the rest, complaints arose about camp accommodations. The 115th's tents, last seen at Hilton Head, still had not caught up with the regiment, leaving the men without shelter. Nor did the soldiers have much success in scavenging material to create shelter. What they managed to slap together looked like pigsties according to DeGraff, who worried that they might grow accustomed to such untidy quarters. "I am afraid some of us will be like the Irishman's cow that lived without eating but died just as she was getting used to it."[1]

The post-battle idyll at Jacksonville ended when Colonel Barton received orders to seize and hold Palatka, Florida, using a force that included the three regiments of his brigade, plus the 3rd Rhode Island Artillery, half of the 55th Massachusetts Infantry, and a company of engineers. These units could be spared from Jacksonville because numerous reinforcements had recently augmented federal strength in Florida. Palatka was located near the navigational limit of the St. John's River, about fifty miles south of Jacksonville. Its seizure would be in keeping with the northern command's earlier plan for the occupation of northeastern Florida, i.e., holding enough territory around Jacksonville to bring the region's economic resources under Union control.[2]

Barton's expedition departed Jacksonville the evening of March 9, 1864, and docked at Palatka at sunrise the next morning. Companies B and D of the 115th quickly jumped ashore and scattered through town, reconnoitering on behalf of the northerners. They discovered three civilian families but no armed rebels. The rest of the invaders disembarked uneventfully and began the occupation of Palatka.

John Reardon estimated that Palatka had a population of 300 before the war but its residents had deserted the village before the Yankee occupation. "Buildings generally are frame, some good, majority otherwise," noted Reardon. "The court house is small, two small churches, one Catholic the other Episcopal, one small hotel." Barton had orders to surround the town with field works and, as Corporal Reid recalled, "the task of fortifying this place was at once commenced and, by energetic work day and night, soon presented quite a stronghold." The 115th set up another rough camp, still without tents, and soon suffered from the elements. "We encamped outside town on low land, in fact the land about here is all low," grumbled Reardon. "Weather is rainy and our camp is soon flooded."[3]

Major Ezra Leroy Walrath commanded the 115th at this time, as he had since Colonel Sammons's wounding at Olustee. Sammons had returned to Hilton Head for treatment of his combat injuries and then went home to New York for further medical attention and recovery. The lieutenant colonelcy of the regiment remained vacant because Sammons's nominee for the post, Captain Van Derveer, died of his Olustee wounds on February 24. As a result, command of the regiment remained with Major Walrath. A native of Madison County, New York, Walrath had prior experience in leading an infantry regiment, though the experience was brief and tarnished.[4]

At the outbreak of the war Walrath was colonel of a Syracuse militia unit that promptly mustered into the federal volunteer service as the 12th New York Infantry. On July 18, 1861, Walrath led the 12th into action at Blackburn's Ford, Virginia, a prelude to the First Battle of Bull Run. During a brief skirmish one of Walrath's subordinates ordered a premature retreat and the 12th fled the field in panic. Colonel Walrath attempted to rally his men, as did Colonel Israel Richardson, their brigade commander and Walrath's immediate superior. Afterwards Richardson accused Walrath and his regiment of cowardice. In turn, the men of the 12th New York blamed Richardson for sending them to slaughter due to a jealous rage he harbored against Walrath, the jealousy stemming from Walrath's too-close friendship with Colonel Richardson's wife.[5]

Soon afterwards Walrath resigned his commission with the 12th. A year later he enlisted in the fledgling 115th New York, mustering in as captain of Company I and advancing to major of the regiment during the upheavals at Hilton Head. He lobbied for appointment to the position of lieutenant colonel, vacated when George Batcheller resigned his commission, but lost out when Colonel Sammons nominated Van Derveer to become his second-in-command. This promotion continued to elude Walrath after Van Derveer's death, as Sammons already had yet another man in mind for lieutenant colonel when he headed north to recuperate. But through the rest of the 115th's stint in Florida, and quite often during the remainder of the war, Major Walrath commanded the regiment.[6]

On March 20, 1864, Nicholas DeGraff wrote his family that, "We are

Ezra Walrath joined the 115th as a captain after prior service as colonel of the 12th New York. He became the regiment's major in late 1863 and frequently commanded the 115th later in the war. A native of Madison County, New York, he was a jewelry maker in Syracuse when the war began (New York State Military Museum).

having rather easy times now." He assured them that the regiment faced no imminent danger of attack and waxed eloquent about the weather and the place at which he found himself:

> The day is one of the most pleasant that could be imagined. The sun is shining warm with a cool breeze. We are in the midst of spring. The trees and shrubbery are all leafing out. Orange and peach trees are in full bloom and their fragrance scents the air. The mockingbird and others are filling the air with their music and it seems to me that if there is a place on earth where erring man should be contented with his lot it is such a land as this.

He went on to compare Palatka favorably with some of the familiar towns near his Mohawk Valley home. He wrote about church services, homes, gardens, wildlife, and at great length about the good fishing. He concluded that Palatka in better times "must have been a little piece of paradise all by itself."

The mood of DeGraff's letter darkened as his thoughts turned back one month to the struggle at Olustee. He wished never to see another day like it and expressed concern over the fate of wounded mates who fell into the hands of the enemy. He related that Chaplain Clemens had returned to Hilton Head to superintend the exhumation of the remains of Captain Van Derveer, which were to be returned to his Fultonville home for reburial. DeGraff complained about the vulgarity common among Union troops and advised his younger brother never to be like the many foolish soldiers who felt "'tis manly to be wicked."[7]

The federals posted at Palatka did not rely solely on their fortifications to defend against enemy incursions. They manned two rings of picket posts around the village, an outer line of mounted men and an inner line of foot soldiers. Things remained quiet for the first week at Palatka, but the peace broke on the afternoon of March 16 when rebel cavalry attacked one of the picket posts and captured two soldiers of the 115th. The attack proved the first of several hit-and-run raids by rebel horsemen around the works at Palatka.[8]

In late March Colonel Barton learned the location of a nearby Confederate cavalry post reputed to be a staging point for such rebel sorties. He ordered Solomon Smith, captain of the 115th's Company H, to lead a detail of men to eliminate the outpost. Before sunrise on April 1 Captain Smith ordered his company into line. He told his men of the proposed raid against the enemy position, known as Fort Gates, and asked for twenty-five volunteers to accompany him. The desired number promptly stepped forward, and by sunrise they breakfasted, packed, and joined Captain Smith and a local citizen guide aboard a small tugboat.

With its engine muffled for quiet and the infantrymen hidden from view, the tug steamed thirty miles up the St. John's River toward Fort Gates. Upstream from Palatka the river narrowed to no more than a stone's throw in width, carving a winding route amidst lakes and swamps teeming with alligators. The tug negotiated this maze of waterways and landed its passengers on the riverbank, still undetected. Captain Smith and his volunteers crept stealthily into the woods in single file at twelve foot intervals. A three mile trek took the raiders "alternately through swamps with water to our waists, and over little knolls which were fairly baking under the heat of the tropical sun." Reaching Fort Gates, they found the alleged Confederate stronghold to be a house surrounded by a thick hedge and a board fence. They had yet to see any rebels, nor had they been seen.

The Company H men quietly fanned out along the hedge and surrounded the house on three sides, the fourth being fronted by water. Wordlessly the men crawled through the dense vegetation to the board fence. Private Benjamin Thackrah, near the center of the line,

On April 1, 1864, twenty-five volunteers from the 115th raided a Confederate cavalry station known as Fort Gates near Palatka, Florida, capturing ten rebels after silently approaching through surrounding swamps. The action resulted in the only Medal of Honor awarded to a member of the 115th (*Deeds of Valor*).

stood and peered over the fence, only to find himself looking down the gun barrel of a rebel soldier. At the same moment the two 115th men nearest Thackrah also poked their heads above the fence. The startled Confederate did not shoot the equally startled Thackrah, but turned and darted for the house. The whole 115th squad then leaped over the fence yelling at the top of their lungs. The attackers closed around the house and Captain Smith called for the rebels inside to surrender. Several southern voices quickly answered, "We give in." Not a shot had been fired.

Eight Confederates, members of the 5th Georgia Cavalry, submitted peacefully. Given the date, April 1, some of their elated captors could not refrain from crying, "April fools." To this one of the prisoners responded, "I thought the hull Yankee army was comin' and I reckon we are April fooled right smart." Another of the Georgians still held in his hand a letter he had been writing when the Yankees appeared. The New Yorkers got a good laugh from the last words the man had written before his capture: "All is quiet along our lines."

Questioning the captives, Smith learned of two additional enemy soldiers posted nearby. A few of Smith's men swiftly surprised and bagged them, and the triumphant expedition returned to Palatka that night with a haul of ten rebels and fifteen horses. The affair prompted General John Hatch, who by then had succeeded Truman Seymour as federal commander, to issue a proclamation distributed throughout Union-held Florida. In it Hatch urged all the men under his command to emulate the "energy, intrepidity, and skill" shown in "the successful accomplishment of a daring and difficult expedition by a detachment of 25 men from the 115th New York Volunteers."[9]

The bloodless capture of this small Confederate post in the Florida wilderness rates as a significant event in the career of the 115th New York, for it resulted in the only Congressional Medal of Honor ever awarded to a member of the regiment. The recipient was twenty-year old, Scottish-born Private Thackrah. He received the medal by his own post-war initiative; nearly twenty-four years after the raid Thackrah wrote to Washington requesting the honor. At first denied, he persisted, secured influential help, and finally got the medal.

Thackrah initiated his quest on January 16, 1888, when he mailed a letter from his Amsterdam home to the U.S. Secretary of War. In it Thackrah transcribed General Hatch's proclamation, which described and acclaimed the Fort Gates raid. He related that he was one of the volunteers who conducted the raid, then stated the purpose of his letter: "My reason for drawing your attention to this matter is to ascertain from you if I am entitled to a Medal of Honor for said service." Several weeks later he received a terse denial.

Thackrah tried again a year later when he enlisted help from Solomon Smith, his former captain and leader of the expedition. Smith resubmitted Thackrah's application with a cover letter stating that Thackrah "served with distinguished bravery as a volunteer member of the detachment." The ex-captain added a lukewarm endorsement: "If consistent with the rules and regulations of your department, I most respectfully request that you will bestow a Medal of Honor on Private Thackrah." George Batcheller, former lieutenant colonel of the 115th then serving as Assistant Secretary of the United States Treasury, was also induced to get involved. Batcheller forwarded copies of both Smith's letter and Thackrah's statement to the War Department, along with a very brief note. Batcheller made no personal comments nor any recommendation; he merely asked the Secretary of War to give Thackrah's application his careful consideration. The War Department quickly rejected the application, reasoning that Thackrah's "service on that occasion was not of such a character as distinguished him above his comrades."

The following year, 1890, Thackrah tried once more, this time preparing an expanded account of the Fort Gates expedition, and securing help from his congressman. The revised account still did little to single out any personal actions by Thackrah during the raid—he simply served as one man among the detachment. The congressman dutifully forwarded his constituent's application, but added no comment or endorsement whatsoever. Within a week the War Department again disapproved.

What happened next cannot be determined from the written record, but it is clear that somewhere in Washington some influential conversations must have taken place. The record shows only that, four days after issuing its third rejection of Thackrah's request, the same War Department office that had just disapproved the application forwarded it to the commanding general of the army. The nation's top military officer immediately recommended, without comment, that Thackrah receive the nation's top military honor. A day later the Secretary of War concurred. Private Thackrah got his Congressional Medal of Honor in May, 1890.[10]

On April 6, 1864, the 115th's tents finally caught up with them at Palatka. The men spent the next two days constructing platforms on which to set the tents, raising them above the wet ground and the sand fleas. But as had happened frequently before, no sooner had the regiment gotten comfortably settled in a new camp than orders arrived to move on. By mid–April the Flying Infantry was back in Virginia.[11]

The man responsible for the 115th's abrupt departure from Florida was Ulysses S. Grant who had been named General-in-Chief of the Armies of the United States by President Lincoln in March. Grant believed the way to vanquish the Confederacy was to destroy its military, not to occupy its remote territory. In order to bring maximum force to bear against Confederate armed forces, Grant began to concentrate troops at several key points, massing Union strength for his planned spring offensives. The 115th New York and the rest of Barton's Brigade were heading for one of these staging areas to join the new Army of the James under General Benjamin F. Butler.[12]

Grant's plan for the spring campaign called for simultaneous advances by Union armies on five fronts, from Louisiana to Virginia. Major offensives were to be conducted by the Army of the Potomac in northern Virginia and by William T. Sherman's army in Georgia and these would be supported with thrusts by smaller forces in Louisiana, in Virginia's Shenandoah Valley, and toward Richmond from the southeast by Butler's Army of the James. Grant reasoned that keeping the Confederacy's diminishing resources occupied on several fronts would enable the Union war machine to grind it into submission, either by defeat in battle or by simple attrition. The coordinated advances would also force an end to the southerners' practice of rushing troops from one threatened theater to another. Such coordination of effort, long advocated by President Lincoln, had eluded the beleaguered chief executive through nearly three years of war and a succession of Union commanders. Lincoln was delighted as Grant briefed him on his strategy. Noting how the simultaneous moves would support one another he exclaimed, "Oh, yes! I see that. As we say out West, if a man can't skin he must hold a leg while somebody else does."[13]

Barton's Brigade evacuated Palatka on April 14, and after a brief stop at Hilton Head, set sail for Virginia on April 17. On board the steamer *Northern Light* one of the regiment penned his adieu, "Goodbye, Hilton Head and the South. May I never see you more." This time the men knew their destination and had some idea of the nature of the campaign ahead. As DeGraff interpreted their assignment, "We have got to help take Richmond after all."

Through one day in the Atlantic, the sea held calm and men began to believe they could endure this voyage without seasickness. But on the second day at sea a major storm struck and seasickness felled all but the heartiest. Corporal Joseph Abeel and a few of his Company C mates had eaten some sardines before the gale and came to regret it. Decades later the mere mention of sardines still nauseated Abeel. Relief finally came to the stricken soldiers as the *Northern Light* entered the more tranquil waters of Chesapeake Bay on April 20.[14]

The 115th New York went ashore at Gloucester Point, Virginia, on the York River opposite Yorktown. They found the hills beside the river cloaked in a sea of white, the tents of the burgeoning Army of the James. Here the regiment helped unload ships arriving to supply the army for the coming campaign and drilled for many long hours. After a week of bustle around the camps, two events came as harbingers of active operations. First when the soldiers' comfortable but bulky frame tents were exchanged for more mobile shelter halves; and second, when General Butler conducted a grand review of his troops on April 30.

While the 115th was camped at Gloucester Point a call went out for volunteers to serve in the navy. In spite of their rough sea voyages, and perhaps because of their recent experiences with infantry campaigning in Florida and the imminent prospect of more of the same, forty-two men from the regiment opted to become sailors. Thirty-nine of them were substitutes according to Private Dallas Paul of Corinth, a musician in Company G. In another curious event at Gloucester, the men were made to draw a ration of extra clothing, blankets and shoes, for which payment was drawn from their government clothing allowances. They found this inconsistent with ongoing preparations for active campaigning, which included efforts to reduce baggage. Knowing something of General Butler's shady reputation, the soldiers speculated as to whether their commander shared in the profits on these articles. Before long much of this material littered the hot, dusty roads of Virginia.[15]

A fourth regiment joined Barton's Brigade at Gloucester—the 76th Pennsylvania, veterans who had suffered heavily on the walls of Fort Wagner. As Butler organized the Army of the James, Barton's Brigade became part of General John W. Turner's Division of the Tenth Army Corps. In Civil War military organization, both North and South, several regiments formed a brigade, several brigades a division, several divisions a corps, and several corps an army. Butler's army was comprised of a cavalry corps and two infantry corps—the Eighteenth Corps under General William F. Smith and the Tenth Corps, comprised of 18,000 troops drawn mainly from the Department of the South and commanded by Quincy Gillmore. By the time all of these units arrived, that sea of tents around Gloucester and Yorktown would house a total of 38,000 men.[16]

The commander of the Army of the James was known more for his political background than his military prowess. A prominent criminal lawyer and state legislator in Massachusetts, Benjamin Butler gained notoriety in 1860 when as a delegate to the Democratic Party convention he voted on fifty-seven consecutive ballots to nominate Jefferson Davis for President of the United States. A brigadier general in the state militia, Butler took command of a Massachusetts regiment at the outbreak of the war. He saw only minor action before becoming the Union commandant of occupied New Orleans, where he achieved further notoriety for alleged corruption and became vilified throughout the South as "Beast" Butler for an order perceived to insult southern women. He had little prior experience leading an active campaign when he took command of the Army of the James. The men of the

115th New York soon grasped that their association with Butler represented another stroke of ill fortune for the regiment.[17]

Butler's role in Grant's grand strategy was to move against Richmond from the southeast while the Army of the Potomac, with which Grant would travel, moved toward the Confederate capital from the north. Grant expected Lee's Army of Northern Virginia to defend Richmond by challenging the movement of the Army of the Potomac. Butler's threat below the city would keep the rebels from reinforcing Lee with troops from the Richmond defenses or perhaps force Lee to diminish his strength by detaching troops to face Butler. The Army of the James was to advance up its namesake river toward Richmond, its movements synchronized with those of the Army of the Potomac. Grant also ordered Butler to hold the ground around his James River landing areas in order to provide an avenue by which Butler's force could later join with the Army of the Potomac. Butler assured General Grant that he foresaw no trouble with investing Richmond and linking up with the Army of the Potomac within ten days.[18]

The grand offensive commenced on May 4. Thirty-three thousand men of the Army of the James boarded transports which carried them down the York River into Chesapeake Bay then turned past Fortress Monroe to ascend the James River. The "monster fleet with its iron clads, gunboats, transports, schooners, tugs, ... literally jammed" the James, recalled Corporal Reid. Over 200 vessels of every description filled the view in all directions. After winding sixty miles up the historic river, the flotilla discharged its passengers in a slow, laborious process throughout the night of May 5–6. The 115th disembarked at Bermuda Hundred Landing at 8:00 a.m. on May 6.[19]

Bermuda Hundred Landing was located on the James a couple of miles above its confluence with the Appomattox River. It stood at the eastern end of the Bermuda Hundred peninsula, an area between the Appomattox River on the south and some broad, sweeping curves of the James River to the east and north. At the base of the peninsula—its western end—four miles separated the James from the Appomattox. Across this base and in accordance with his mandate from General Grant, Butler immediately began erecting defensive fortifications. He had effected a deep and alarming penetration into rebel Virginia, and he meant to hold onto it. Unfortunately Butler expended greater effort in building these works than in threatening Richmond, and squandered a grand opportunity to deal the Confederacy a decisive setback.

Later in the morning of May 6, the 115th joined the columns moving westward from the landing area. They marched at a rapid clip but halted frequently in the searing heat. Before long the soldiers began to lighten their loads by discarding excess clothes, shoes, and blankets, including the newly purchased items. Enough blankets lined the road to carpet the day's entire seven-mile line of march according to the regiment's more cynical observers. James Clark saw one local native who had collected a full wagon load of new shoes. As the coming of evening brought cooling relief, the regiment stopped and made camp in a large cornfield.[20]

This campsite was just two miles from the base of the Bermuda Hundred peninsula where Butler's earthworks were being erected. Just beyond the works lay the vital turnpike and railroad which linked Richmond with Petersburg, Virginia, an important industrial center through which ran most of Richmond's railroad access to the remainder of the Confederacy. The two cities and the critical roads between them lay within the grasp of Butler's anxious army. As the 33,000 Union troops landed along the James, only 5,000 rebels defended Richmond, and just 1,300 stood at Petersburg. But to the everlasting chagrin of

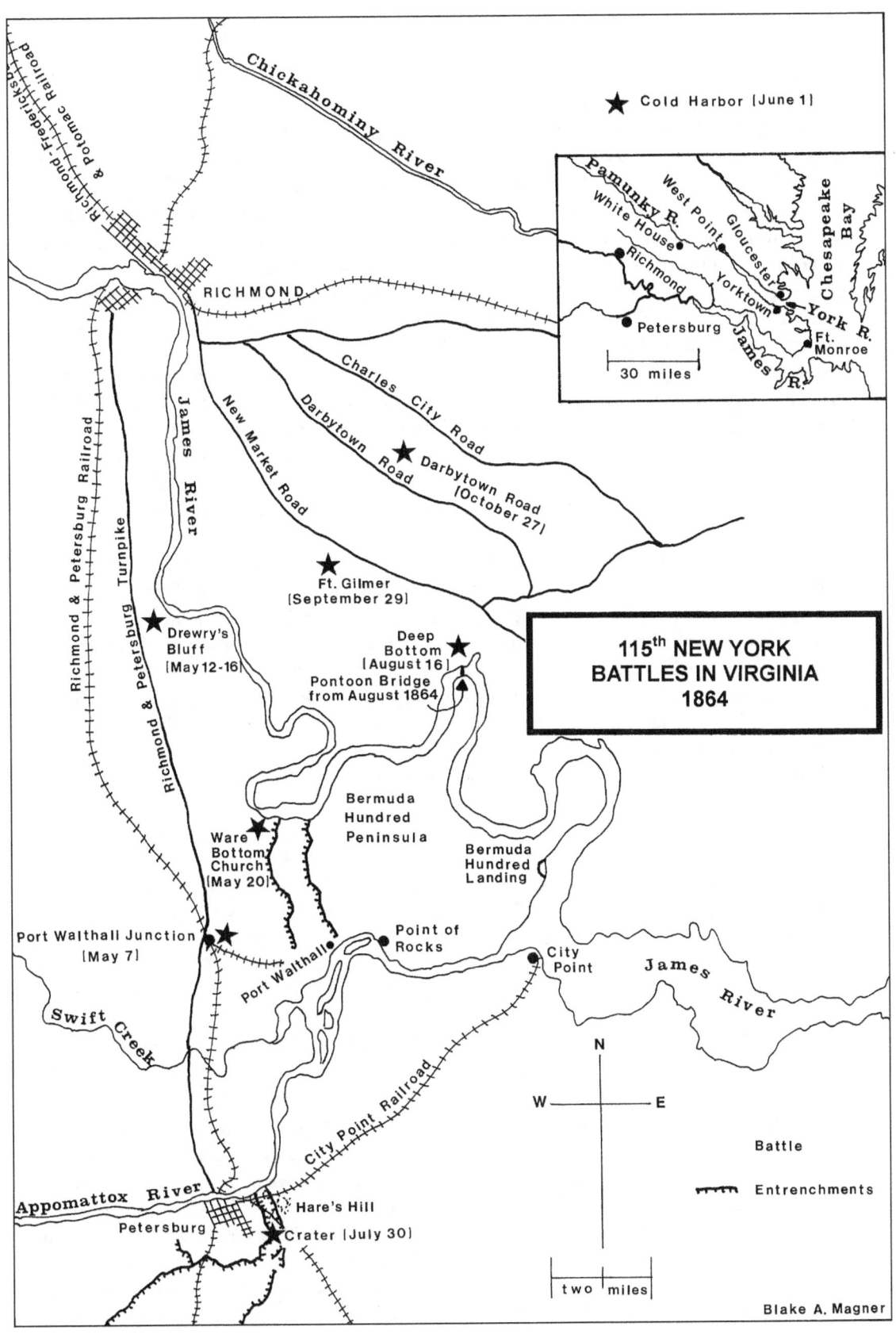

his men, instead of a determined drive against a vulnerable enemy, Butler made only modest, indecisive thrusts beyond the growing Bermuda Hundred entrenchments.[21]

In the late afternoon of May 6 Butler launched one brigade of 2,700 men at the railroad. Just 600 hastily assembled rebels opposed them, but this meager resistance and the approach of evening induced Union leaders to order their men back to their camps. One of these soldiers grumbled that he would have preferred more rifles in the front and fewer spades in the rear. The next day Butler again tried to break the railroad but once more committed only a small percentage of his forces to the effort—five brigades, a total of 8,000 men. Butler let his corps commanders select the units that would go on the mission, but he instructed them to take the best troops under the best brigade commanders. Barton's Brigade was among the units chosen, an honor which cost them dearly.[22]

Early on May 7 the 115th left camp and joined the long blue column tramping down the Old Stage Road toward the railroad. They had marched but a couple of miles before the sound of gunfire reached their ears as the lead federal units brushed with Confederate pickets. "We hear the skirmishers in advance assuring us from the continuous rattle of musketry that the enemy are wide awake and prepared," noted John Reardon. Since the brief contest of the previous afternoon, rebel strength in the area had increased to about 2,500 men.

The rebels had established a line along the Richmond & Petersburg Railroad that covered both the railroad mainline and a branch line which ran eastward to Port Walthall on the Appomattox River. The Old Stage Road intersected the branch line immediately east of its turnout from the mainline, a point known as Port Walthall Junction. Three federal brigades pushed aside the enemy pickets, moved down the road, and faced the Confederates along the tracks on both sides of the junction. A fourth Union brigade, that of Colonel Harris Plaisted, left the Old Stage Road and struck the railroad mainline undetected about a half-mile north of Port Walthall Junction. The 100th New York of Plaisted's brigade became engaged with the Confederates while his other regiments began destroying the tracks.[23]

Barton's Brigade moved in next. Attempting to strike the railroad between Plaisted's Brigade and the three brigades on the Union left, it moved off Old Stage Road and through woods described by Colonel Barton as almost impenetrable. The ground proved so difficult that skirmishers sent forward from Barton's lead unit, the 48th New York, were lost and not seen again all day. Barton's Brigade maneuvered from marching column into line of battle then closed in on the railroad and the waiting Confederates. The 48th New York formed the brigade's right and the 115th its left with the 47th New York and 76th Pennsylvania in between.[24]

After the tiring passage through the difficult terrain, the 115th formed into battle line and advanced across an open field, scattering some lingering enemy pickets. Reaching the edge of a bluff, they found an open valley spread before them. The railroad was cut into the side of the hill that formed the far side of the valley, 300 yards distant. "Our appearance on the brow of the hill was quickly observed by the enemy who occupied a commanding position on a corresponding hillside across the railroad," Reid remembered, "and a section of artillery immediately opened fire on us." The initial rebel fire fell short, striking the bluff below the regiment, but the Confederate gunners soon found the range and their bursting shells brought the day's first casualties to the 115th.[25]

A single well-aimed cannon shot killed two men and wounded two others. One of its large fragments tore off the shoulder of Sergeant Charles Brice of Company G, a twenty-

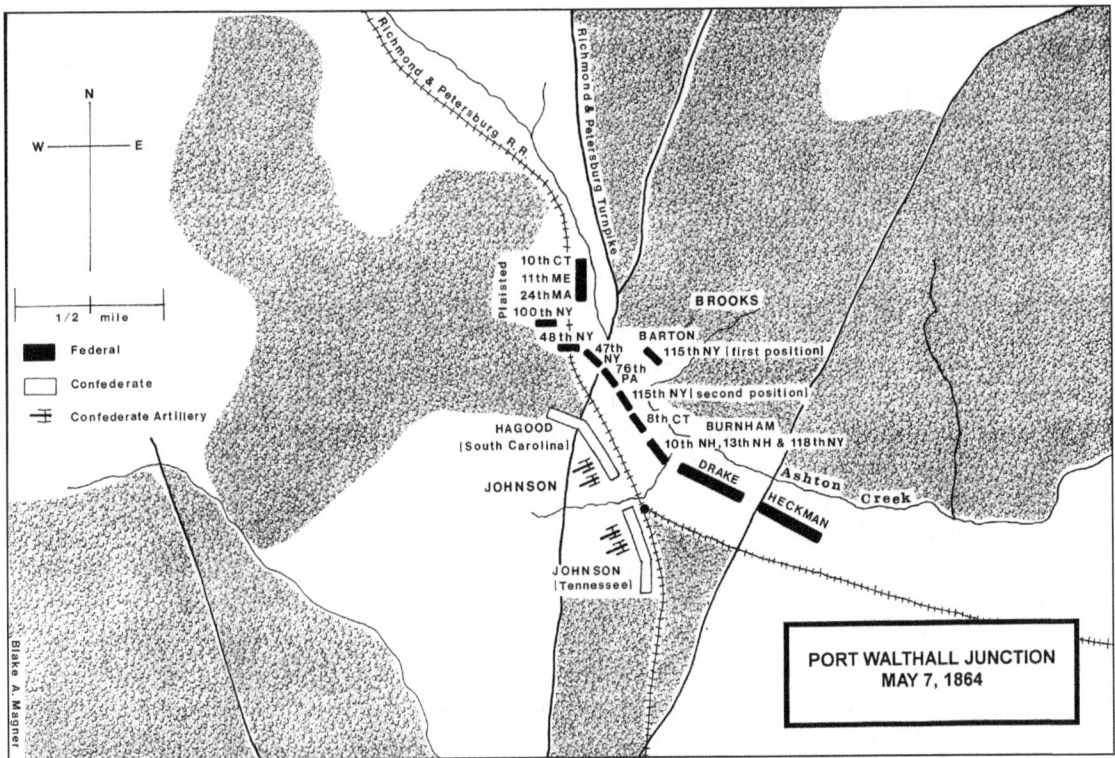

two-year old Saratoga County man, killing him instantly. Another passed through the knee of Private James Wager, one of the youngest and best liked men of Company C. An unfamiliar army surgeon hastily amputated Wager's leg but the twenty-year old private died four weeks later. One of Wager's Company C mates later stated that "it is fair to be supposed that had Surgeon Macfarlane attended him at first he might be with us today." Yet another piece of the same shell tore the sole off George Luffman's boot. The shot failed to keep Luffman out of the ensuing battle, but he complained loudly of losing his boot, one of a brand new pair recently sent him from home.[26]

Although Macfarlane did not operate on the luckless Private Wager, the 115th's surgeon was present at the rear attending wounded. Macfarlane described how surgeons from all the federal units gathered to establish a field hospital, dividing among themselves the various duties necessary to care for the casualties. Some of the doctors reviewed the incoming wounded and assigned priorities to their needs, some performed surgery, and others gave post surgical care. "A perfect division of labor is established, involving the least possible neglect of the wounded," wrote Macfarlane. "Every surgeon is busy with his particular duty and knows nothing of the battle waged about him."[27]

Along the regiment's line at the crest of the bluff, Major Walrath sat mounted among his men when a cannonball killed his horse. "The shot passed through my horse's shoulder, striking him on the left side under my left leg and passed out just over my right leg on his right side," the major reported matter-of-factly. Walrath tumbled to the ground but amazed his troops by springing to his feet and resuming command as if nothing had happened.[28]

The 115th held its position on the bluff for thirty minutes exchanging long-range fire with the enemy across the curving valley. Meanwhile federal units to their right worked at tearing up the railroad. "Our position was an exposed and dangerous one, and really it produced an anxiety for an order to go forward," averred Corporal Reid. A charge by rebel infantry against the 48th New York finally prompted the desired movement. "They came with their usual barbarous yell, and their dirty stars and bars led the advance," recalled a disdainful Sergeant Clark. The 115th raced to counter this enemy attack on their comrades. "Every man rushed forward," said Reid, "giving vent to that terrible roar that characterizes a Union charge. Down the hill that splendid line rushed amid a shower of bullets."[29]

Reaching the base of the hill, the regiment started across a wheatfield in the valley bottom. Nearing the far side of the valley, they discovered that the rebel line extended far beyond their own left flank so the New Yorkers halted behind a bush lined ditch. Secured behind this low hedgerow, prone or on their knees while firing their guns through the cover of the brush, the New Yorkers engaged the enemy. "Here we gave them a sharp fire and received a terrible fire in return," remembered DeGraff. A short distance ahead the southerners enjoyed a position on higher ground along a track bed cut into the side slope of the far hillside. "The rebels now began to blaze away furiously," recalled Clark.[30]

Company C Private George Van Steenberg knelt, watching to see the effect of one of his shots, when he spied a Confederate officer riding along the rebel line. Unable to reload fast enough to draw a bead on this inviting target, Van Steenberg called to George Luffman who stood beside him still chafing over the loss of his new boot. "Luff, Luff, shoot the son of a bitch on the white horse. My gun ain't loaded," cried Van Steenberg. Luffman aimed and fired. The result of his shot is unknown, but the Confederate general commanding the rebel forces at Port Walthall Junction later lamented the number of officers lost that day. A short while afterwards, as the 115th withdrew from the field, Van Steenberg took a ball in the abdomen, resulting in his death the next day.[31]

John Reardon, in line with Company E, knelt astride the legs of a man lying in front of him and fired over the prone man's head. Reardon noticed blood trickling down the face of the soldier lying to their right and called attention to it. The man wiped away the blood but discovered that it was not his own. "That man is dead," he told Reardon, referring to the soldier Reardon straddled. He had been shot in the head, his blood spurting onto his neighbor. Just then a ball struck Reardon. It pierced his coat and shirt, dealt a hammer-like blow to his wrist, and knocked the rifle from his hands. The shot stunned but did not seriously wound him.[32]

Private Christopher Keenholt, one of the older men in the regiment at forty-six, was shot in the leg. Doctors at the field hospital and later at an army hospital at Hampton, Virginia, advised the private that only amputation could save his life. Keenholt steadfastly refused surgery not wanting to "stump around on one leg and be a government pensioner" for the rest of his life. "If I must die," said Keenholt, an avid hunter and trapper, "let the tail go with the hide." He had his way and died at Hampton on June 17. Perhaps Keenholt's fatalistic decision was influenced by news of the death of his son. Just a few days after the elder Keenholt suffered his wounding at Port Walthall Junction, the younger Keenholt was killed while in battle with the 77th New York at Spotsylvania Court House. Lieutenants Thomas Wayne and Nicholas DeGraff of Company D were luckier. A bullet broke off the hilt of Wayne's sword and two balls passed through his coat, but none of these missiles scathed him. DeGraff too escaped injury though a ball dented a brass button on his coat sleeve.[33]

The 115th held their position and continued the close range fight with the rebels for a half hour. To their right the other units of Barton's Brigade also engaged the enemy, but of the three Union brigades on their left only a single regiment—the 8th Connecticut which adjoined the 115th—did any significant fighting. As the modest goal for this federal foray was to destroy the railroad and deny its use to the Confederates, these brigades remained content to hold the rebels opposite them in place while Plaisted's Brigade tore up the tracks.[34]

After destroying several hundred yards of track, Colonel Plaisted unexpectedly withdrew his brigade, an action that became a subject of later controversy between him and his superior. His action exposed Barton's Brigade to the full attention of the enemy at that end of the field, and the units forming Barton's right began to pull back. The 115th, its right now exposed and its left under pressure, soon followed suit.[35]

Major Walrath huddled with his officers. They agreed that at a predetermined signal the men would be sent off on their own to extricate themselves from their predicament, then rally at the top of the bluff at the spot where Walrath's horse was killed. As the withdrawing New Yorkers left the shelter of their hedgerow they came under intense fire. "Then was when we catched it," explained DeGraff. An old field dense with second growth timber adjoined the wheatfield in which the 115th fought and rather than head straight back through the open field, many of the men opted to take a less exposed route through the trees. But a high rail fence separated the two fields and as the soldiers scaled it they became inviting targets for rebel bullets. "The rebs could get a good sight of us, and many of our boys received wounds or death at this point," remembered Sergeant Peter Keck. The heaviest losses of the day took place at this fence, forty men hit there in five minutes by Clark's estimate.[36]

Keck, the 115th's Color Sergeant, had charged down the bluff less than an hour before, conspicuously carrying the regimental flag out ahead of the line of battle. As he withdrew the colors over the fence, a bullet cut through the flagstaff and lodged in his hip. "Hang on to the flag, boys, hang on to the flag," Keck shouted as he fell. Others grabbed and waved the precious banner as Keck made his painful way back to the rendezvous point. The wound proved the second of four that Keck would suffer wielding the flag of the 115th. "Peter seemed to have a faculty for getting in the way of rebel lead," concluded one of Keck's officers.[37]

As John Reardon raced for the fence, Sergeant Orrin Brown ran alongside him. Reardon would never forget the scene:

> As we approached it [the fence] the snapping and crackling of the bullets through the leaves and branches, and the lively patter on the logs in the fence, and occasionally the near explosion of a shell, made the situation one not readily forgotten. Brown and I reached the fence together and mounted the same panel. I dropped on the opposite side as quickly as possible. Not so with Brown. He was struck while on the fence and fell backward. I knew he was hit; I could tell by the dull sound.

Reardon crawled along the far side of the fence and reached through to Brown, but could not arouse him nor get him through the fence. Reardon then made his way back through the thick brush of the fallow field where, he recalled, "the bullets and shells were flying thick and fast about me." When he reached the bluff top a little later, an unexpected sight greeted him. "Lo and behold! There is my friend Brown whom they had shot off the fence." Brown had remained unconscious only briefly. The enemy bullet inflicted a bloody flesh wound across his face and knocked him out but did no serious harm. He had awakened soon after Reardon left him and scampered away.[38]

Sergeant Raymond Fonda met death at the fearful fence. Along the battlefront moments earlier he had inspired his company with his bravery, calmly standing while most of the regiment stayed low. "Fonda seemed to know no fear," wrote an admiring comrade, "and passed along the regimental line regardless of the exposure his erect figure begot." Private Van Steenberg's mortal wound also came at the bloody fence.

Seeing the carnage ahead as he approached the fence line, DeGraff fled alone obliquely up the hill. He heard bullets striking the ground near him but ran on to the shelter of the woods on top of the bluff, out of breath but safe. Reid also eschewed the fence and headed straight back toward the bluff. Halfway up he tired and slowed his pace, the "salty perspiration nearly scalding" his eyes. At that point he recalled the admonition given him by one of his neighbors back home, a War of 1812 veteran, to "be careful and not get shot in the back as blood on the back of that uniform would be a tell tale." With this thought the idea struck Reid that he should turn about and run backwards, but he quickly dispensed with that notion. Instead he zigzagged toward a large tree at the top of the hill. He leapt behind it, caught his breath a moment, fired one parting shot at the enemy, and rejoined his regiment.

Reid and the others reassembled as planned and made their way back to the defensive lines at Bermuda Hundred. By

Color Bearer Peter J. Keck of Oppenheim, Fulton County, in a post-war photograph. Keck was wounded in action four times while carrying the flag of the 115th (courtesy Mrs. Evelyn Frasier).

8:00 p.m. that evening, "weary and sullen," they reached the camp they had left at first light that morning.[39]

The encounter at Port Walthall Junction or, as the men of the 115th New York inscribed it on their flag, the Battle of Chesterfield Heights, cost the regiment nine dead and sixty wounded plus a generous measure of frustration. The troops of the 115th, indeed all the rank and file of the Army of the James, observed the power of Union arms and yearned to try that power against Richmond. The soldiers also had a sense of the relative weakness of the Confederate forces facing them. But instead of a determined advance in full strength, their leaders sent out small segments of the army piecemeal while determinedly erecting defensive fortifications. Topping the list of gripes was the abandonment of the tenuous toehold gained along the vital railroad at Port Walthall Junction. Looking back on the May 7 fight there, Sergeant Reardon saw useless sacrifice as the only accomplishment. "What were we sent out there for?" he wondered. The men in the camps at Bermuda Hundred started asking one another the irksome question, "How long will it take to get to Richmond if you advance two miles every day and come back to your starting point every night?"[40]

The soldiers of Barton's Brigade had particular reason to be bitter. They had fought virtually alone while thousands of blue clad soldiers in the other federal units never joined the fray. Five Union brigades moved against the Richmond & Petersburg Railroad that day, a total of nineteen regiments. But the only units to seriously engage the enemy were the four regiments of Barton's Brigade plus the 8th Connecticut, which fought at the left of the 115th, and the 100th New York of Plaisted's Brigade, which fought next to Barton's 48th New York. In suffering 196 casualties including 69 from the 115th, Barton's Brigade accounted for 59% of the 332 Union troop losses on May 7. (The 8th Connecticut suffered 72 casualties and the 100th New York 27.) The 8,000 federals outnumbered the rebels by over three-to-one but wasted their advantage. They inflicted only 184 losses on the southerners, did a little damage to the railroad, then went away. It took the Confederates a mere six hours to repair the tracks.[41]

Twenty-year old Whitney Lee of Ephratah, Fulton County, wounded in action at Port Walthall Junction, an action also called Chesterfield Heights (New York State Military Museum).

The baffling pattern repeated itself on May 9 and 10 when parts of Butler's army made modest, temporary excursions beyond the lines, halting when the rebels engaged them and then returning to the Bermuda Hundred camps. The 115th did not participate. On the 9th of May the regiment worked on the entrenchments. On the 10th they remained inside the works until mid afternoon listening to the sounds of combat. At 2:00 p.m. they moved toward the fighting but by that time the engagement had ended and the federal combatants were abandoning the field and returning to the security of their earthworks.

The 115th landed the task of fighting fires that erupted in the woods near the scene of the May 10 skirmishing. Confederate and Union leaders agreed to a two hour truce to rescue the wounded from the advancing fires, but it proved too late for some of the unfortunate men, and the scene became horrific. Sergeant Clark recalled that "the very air was freighted with the awful perfume of roasted men." The regiment succeeded in squelching the fires, spent the night on the scene, and returned to camp early the next day.[42]

The Army of the James spent Wednesday, May 11 resting and perfecting fortifications. The enemy devoted that day to moving 11,000 men up the Richmond-Petersburg Turnpike toward the Confederate capital. In the days since the Army of the James had landed these rebel troops scrambled from lower Virginia and North Carolina to meet the emergency. General Butler obliged them by keeping most of his forces inside the Bermuda Hundred lines and leaving the turnpike open to uncontested use by the southerners. When Butler finally made his movement against Richmond, these thousands of enemy fighters would be waiting for him.[43]

That night Butler issued orders for the long awaited movement. Early the next morning, May 12, the Eighteenth Corps, strengthened by General Turner's Division of the Tenth Corps (including Barton's Brigade) passed through the entrenchments and swung north toward Richmond. The remaining two divisions of the Tenth Corps supported the movement by guarding against any rebel threat from the south. As the men marched out of their camps and beyond their laboriously constructed earthworks, they still believed their mission to be the conquest of Richmond. But General Butler did not see it that way. He considered his mission to be a demonstration to threaten the Confederate capital and prevent any of its defenders from reinforcing Lee in his struggle against Grant and the Army of the Potomac. Sergeant Reardon was not alone in his opinion that General Grant made "the greatest mistake of his career" when he retained Butler to command the Army of the James.[44]

With a strong array of skirmishers to the front the federal units faced northward and formed into battle lines that extended one and one-half miles in width—from the Richmond-Petersburg Turnpike on its left, to the James River on the right—and moved out. From the moment the troops left their fortifications, rebel skirmishers stubbornly contested their advance. Hindered by rough terrain, torrential rains, and the enemy, the broad line moved sluggishly. Five miles out the advance halted when faced by a strong force of rebels along Proctor's Creek. A call went back for troops to come up and extend the left of the Union line beyond the flank of the enemy. By the time this help arrived the day had waned and the troops dug in for the night.[45]

The day's movement had taken the troops through the field of an earlier fight, and the sight of dead and burned bodies again greeted the men of the 115th. One of the unfortunates stood out in Reardon's memory. His clothing had burned off, but his body showed little sign of fire. Reardon described him as "young, fine looking, and of athletic build." The New Yorkers presumed him to be a rebel as they found a cake of cornbread beside him, but they could not be certain. They wrapped the dead soldier in a blanket and buried him in "another unknown grave containing a mother's darling."[46]

When Union troops anxiously probed toward the Confederate lines the next morning, they discovered that the rebels had fallen back during the night. The ponderous federal advance resumed with the next two days following the same pattern as the previous day: thousands of men in blue pushing forward in a driving rain behind a wide front of skirmishers who arduously rolled back their tenacious rebel counterparts. The 115th held a position near the center of the Union line, the various companies rotating duty as skirmishers. DeGraff's

Company D took this job on May 14. "We were driving them slowly but they gave us a sharp fire all day," he recalled. "We had to keep behind the trees or we would have been immediately shot down. Six men of my company were wounded, several in the regiment were killed, but we popped over a good many of the rebs in return."[47]

One evening during the torpid advance toward Richmond DeGraff received a letter from his mother. "We were having a fight and my regiment was laying under cover of a wood, the bullets whistling around us," DeGraff wrote his sister, describing his situation when the letter arrived. "I could not help but cry when I read mother's note. It was so good and in such a time it was doubly welcome and gave me more courage. I began to feel as though I was not born to be shot." The young lieutenant survived the day and the campaign unscathed.[48]

As the northerners resumed their movement on the morning of May 14, they discovered that the enemy had withdrawn into the formidable fortifications that ringed Richmond. "We sighted their main defensive works, full of graybacks," remembered DeGraff. These defenses were anchored on the James River at Drewry's Bluff five miles south of the city. The men of the 115th spotted these works from a point about two miles distant as they emerged from woods into a broad area where all the trees had been felled. To obstruct the invaders' approach the rebels had cut down the trees and left them jumbled on the ground. This so-called "slashing" provided fine cover for Confederate skirmishers who could be detected "only by the blue puffs of smoke from their guns."[49]

Samuel Clemens of Oppenhein in Fulton County, killed in action at Drewry's Bluff, Virginia, May 14, 1864 (courtesy Mr. Wayne Montana).

Deciding against a frontal assault through the slashing, the commanders of the Army of the James halted their advance. The army's position remained static on Sunday, May 15, though skirmishing between the lines continued. Rebel artillery also disturbed the Sabbath, firing from safely within their works and raining shells on the federal positions. One shot brought a scare to Private William H. Borden of Company B when he went to the brigade commissary to secure food for his regiment. "One shell kill the mule I had for carrying my grub to eat and came within about ten feet of where I stood," wrote Borden. "I see it when it was coming and it struck the ground twice before it hit the mule, but did not explode or if it had it would probably kill all of us."[50]

Corporal Reid looked into the slashing later that day and saw a man's body about sixty feet beyond the 115th's position. "I could see only a leg and that wore the Union blue." Reid and a man from Company F crept out to investigate. The corpse proved to be that of a young

Confederate. "Although in life an enemy, there was a sadness of the scene that brought regrets of his death," recalled Reid. Finding no gun or other equipment near the man, they concluded that he had been shot elsewhere "and started alone to the rear, only to bleed to death in this lonely place." They searched for identification but found none; the dead youth possessed only a small, battered watch. Reid's companion wanted to return the watch to the deceased's pocket, but Reid advised him to keep it rather than leave it to be snatched by some other scavenger. "It would simply be an exchange for the blue pants, the property probably of some dead Union soldier," he rationalized. Afterwards Reid never met his companion of that day without asking, "What time is it?" But in later years Corporal Reid regretted the incident, calling it "the nearest I ever came to robbing the dead."[51]

General Butler planned to renew the offensive on May 16, but the Confederates beat him to the punch. He had squandered numerous opportunities with his lethargic actions in the ten days since his landing at Bermuda Hundred. Now the enemy decisively seized all initiative away from him. The rebels poured out of the Drewry's Bluff lines and assaulted the Union positions in what proved the denouement of the ill-fated Bermuda Hundred campaign.[52]

While the rest of Barton's Brigade saw heavy action in the Battle of Drewry's Bluff, the 115th saw little. Barton's other three regiments held a frontline position at the Union center as the rebels pressed their dawn attack. The 115th was stationed behind them in reserve. About an hour into the struggle, the regiment was sent to reinforce the small rear guard protecting the Army of the James from rebel incursion from the direction of Petersburg. As the battle raged at Drewry's Bluff, the 115th peeled away from its reserve position, passing through a rain of shells and bullets. Seven men were hit, but their mates marched on in a disciplined line.[53]

The regiment hurriedly marched several miles south to the familiar ground of Chesterfield Heights. There they joined General Adelbert Ames, who with only four regiments faced two full brigades of Confederates bent on attacking the rear of the Union lines engaged at Drewry's Bluff. To mask the federals' relative weakness Ames had all of his troops deploy as skirmishers, hoping to hoodwink the enemy into concluding that he had a strong main line farther back. Whether because of this ruse or the innate caution of rebel commander William H.C. Whiting, the desired result was achieved. The rebels made only feeble efforts at further advance. On this occasion it was the southerners who wasted opportunity. Reid judged that "our insignificant numbers could have been easily brushed away by the large force confronting us had the commanding general of the enemy been energetic." The adversaries at Chesterfield Heights exchanged only desultory skirmish fire throughout the day.[54]

After a battle that claimed 4,000 Union and 3,000 Confederate casualties, Butler's army retreated across the eight miles over which they had so listlessly advanced during the previous four days. As a bitter Sergeant Reardon decried, "Butler, having let the opportunity slip and being unable to get a stay of the proceedings, returned with his shattered columns behind the works at Bermuda Hundred." The 115th wearily returned to its camp after a sojourn over the bleak and sodden Virginia landscape which cost the regiment thirty-one new casualties. "We marched back to the entrenchments and laid down on the ground entirely exhausted," wrote James Clark. "It seemed as though every bone in our bodies would break."[55]

On the following day, May 17, the Confederates established a strong position opposite the Army of the James's Bermuda Hundred lines, pinning General Butler and his Yankees inside. "His army, therefore, though in a position of great security, was as completely shut off from further operations against Richmond as if it had been in a bottle strongly corked," assessed General Grant, introducing the phrase that remains the standard description of Butler's futile campaign. "It required but a comparatively small force of the enemy to hold it there."[56]

Visions of glory faded, the soldiers of the Army of the James rested in camps they had not expected to see again. The men in the ranks, well aware of the opportunities lost and the wretched leadership that lost them, gave vent to their disappointment. "It has been some sorrowful times," wrote Private Borden of the days since his regiment first landed at Bermuda Hundred. Corporal Reid noted that the army now sat in the same positions it held upon its arrival ten days earlier, and complained that decisive action should have been taken against Richmond or Petersburg back then, as the cities had lain vulnerable and void of troops. In his estimation, "probably but few better opportunities were presented during the war for the accomplishment of great results." Sergeant Reardon grieved for the thousands lost without positive result. "It is ten days since we landed here. It is not encouraging to look back and see that nothing has been accomplished."[57]

Blue and gray faced one another across the opposing lines at Bermuda Hundred for the remainder of the war. The federals indeed were bottled up and posed no further threat to the Confederate capital. But though unable to advance beyond the entrenchments across the neck of the Bermuda Hundred peninsula, Union forces controlled the lower Appomattox and James Rivers. The 115th New York crossed and re-crossed these rivers many times over the next six months, leaving the dreary security of Bermuda Hundred for more of the bloody battlefields of Virginia.

9

Cold Harbor

"The boys felt ugly"

The regiment found important news awaiting when they returned to their Bermuda Hundred camp. Noted Corporal Reid, "A surprise was in store for the 115th on its return to the entrenchments, as we learned that a strange officer was to assume the position of lieutenant colonel of the regiment." The officer proved to be forty-one-year old Nathan J. Johnson. A native of Granville in Washington County, New York, Johnson left his law practice in the fall of 1861 to help recruit a company for the 93rd New York Infantry and became its captain. Colonel Sammons recommended Johnson for lieutenant colonel of the 115th when his first choice for the position, Captain Garret Van Derveer, died from wounds suffered at Olustee. With Colonel Sammons still absent due to his own Olustee wounds, the appointment of a new second-in-command held an added significance: the lieutenant colonel would immediately become the regiment's ranking officer and take charge.[1]

Many in the regiment disapproved of the new appointment. Not only was Johnson a stranger to the 115th, but he supplanted Major Walrath, who "had proved himself a brave and competent officer, and who for nearly three months had commanded the regiment to the satisfaction of the men ... and to our minds was clearly entitled to fill the vacancy of Lieutenant Colonel." Johnson's physical appearance did nothing to reassure the skeptics as he cut anything but a striking martial figure. When he arrived to take command, Johnson was assigned the only horse then available, an old, skinny animal on which he placed an elegant saddle and bridle that he had received as gifts from friends back home. Dressing the decrepit horse in the fancy new tack gave a comic air to what should have been a dignified moment. Instead the regiment's new leader, according to Nicholas DeGraff, "presented a ludicrous appearance." Certainly not the image Johnson intended.[2]

Although a stranger and an odd looking one at that, Johnson still managed to make a favorable impression on his first day leading the regiment, May 20, 1864. His opportunity came when rebels vigorously attacked the federal picket lines in front of the Tenth Corps, sending the Union advance guard reeling back toward its main entrenchments. As the Yankee pickets faltered, the 115th got the order to move out of the defenses and mount a counterattack to stop the approaching Confederates. Johnson led his men to the front where they formed for battle and awaited the order to charge. "The bullets flew around us pretty fast, and we lay flat on the ground to avoid them," remembered Lieutenant Clark.

As the men dropped for cover Lieutenant Colonel Johnson surprised them as he boldly rode to the front to view the situation and report the 115th's arrival to the officer in charge on the forward line. The regiment watched and remarked on their new leader's cool movement into this vulnerable position. DeGraff recalled the sight of Johnson:

Lieutenant Colonel Nathan J. Johnson joined the 115th on May 20, 1864, after prior service as a captain in the 93rd New York. He frequently commanded the regiment during Colonel Sammons's convalescences, but was fond of his liquor (Lance Ingmire Collection).

> mounted on his magnificently equipped steed and fully exposed to the rebel sharp shooters. A minute later we heard the thud of a bullet and the horse settled back and fell sprawling against the incline stone dead, the shot having pierced his breast. Our new fledged and heroic Colonel then, to the amusement of his command, stood, still exposed, and finishing his report to the officer, indifferently returned to the regiment, directing his orderly to remove the equipment from the animal and take it back to camp.³

In spite of the brave show of their new leader, the men of the 115th, severely diminished in number by this time, looked toward the front and saw little hope of success for the coming charge. Reid termed the planned move a rash undertaking. Expecting the worst, the men gave one another messages to relay to their families should they fall, and promised each other that no wounded comrades would be left on the field. The soldiers found the time spent awaiting orders to go into battle to be "moments of anxiety to the most hardened veteran, and really more trying to the courage than the actual movements in the charge." But a welcome reprieve came soon after Johnson's de-horsing when General Adelbert Ames, commander of the division that the 115th had moved out to reinforce, appeared on the scene to direct the proposed counterattack. Looking upon the much reduced band of New Yorkers, Ames asked, "What regiment is that?"

"The 115th New York," answered several of the men.

"Why," said a surprised Ames, "you are only a good sized color guard!"

Ames declared that "such a small body of men" was unsuited for the job at hand and redeployed the 115th as skirmishers. He then ordered the 97th Pennsylvania and the 13th Indiana to make the planned counterattack. These units charged gallantly but were decimated by rifle and artillery fire and fell back. The 115th remained engaged on the skirmish line until dark but held a sheltered position in a shallow ravine and suffered no casualties. The day's action, sometimes referred to as the Battle of Ware Bottom Church, added 1,500 names to the casualty lists and gave the Confederates improved positions as they entrenched opposite the Yankee lines.⁴

After dark the men of the regiment could hear a brass band playing behind the enemy lines. They also heard artillery moving along the Richmond-Petersburg Turnpike. At 2:00

a.m. another regiment relieved the 115th at the front. The tired troops returned to camp and "were quickly at rest in the arms of Morpheus, dreaming of home and Mother."[5]

The good impression that Nathan Johnson made on his first day under fire with the 115th was short-lived. When DeGraff later recorded the story of Johnson's May 20 actions, he felt compelled to add a postscript: "From our later experience with him I conclude he was at the time well reinforced with commissary whiskey." In fact, the regiment's new lieutenant colonel faced charges of drunkenness on duty that very first day. Captain Solomon Smith of Company H formally submitted a complaint against his commander, listing as witnesses eleven men of the 115th and four men of the 40th Massachusetts, most of whom were officers. Smith charged Johnson with being "so much under the influence of intoxicating drink as to render him totally unfit for duty." He also complained that Johnson argued loudly with the officer who delivered the order to get the 115th under arms and to the front, calling the order "a God damned humbug." Finally, Smith alleged that Johnson used "harsh, profane, disrespectful, and abusive language" within hearing of the troops, denouncing the commander of the 40th Massachusetts for retreating prematurely and shouting, "What in hell and damnation have you fallen back for, Colonel?"

Colonel Barton placed Johnson under arrest on May 24. "As the charges are of a very grave character and preferred by a perfectly responsible officer," Barton wrote to the division adjutant, "I have deemed it my duty to place Colonel Johnson in arrest and would respectfully recommend that he be at once tried by General Court Martial." Johnson appealed for release, vehemently denying the charges and calling them "false in every particular, except as to charging the 40th Mass. Regt. with falling back." He claimed that the accusations stemmed from prejudice against him as a newcomer to his regiment. "The charges against me will in the examination thereof be found to be false & malicious, occasioned by ill will because I was appointed Lieutenant Colonel of the regiment on the application of the Colonel, S. Sammons, outside of said regiment."

Despite Johnson's plea and Barton's request for an immediate court martial, Johnson remained untried and under arrest for two months. Then in late July, shortly after Colonel Sammons returned to the regiment, the charges were dropped by General Turner and the incident closed quietly.[6]

Perhaps hostility toward a "strange officer," an unknown outsider from another regiment who leaped to regimental command, played a part in this affair, which marked the second instance of subordinate officers of the 115th raising charges against their leader. Perhaps it was the anti–Sammons cabal rearing up again. Even so, it is surely possible that Johnson was indeed drinking, as later experience would show. This would not be the last time Lieutenant Colonel Johnson would stand accused of drunkenness on duty.

The 115th spent ten days at Bermuda Hundred following the Drewry's Bluff debacle—days of picket duty, skirmishing, strengthening fortifications, building roads, cutting wood and killing time. Corporal Reid described this period as "considerable picket firing, several artillery duels, and a vast amount of pick and shovel labor." On May 26 orders came to prepare to move. The regiment and the rest of Barton's Brigade were to be attached to the Eighteenth Corps, commanded by General William F. Smith, and sent to fight alongside the Army of the Potomac. They were about to get a taste of the epic struggle then raging between Ulysses S. Grant and Robert E. Lee.[7]

The confrontation between the two great commanders began when Grant sent the

Army of the Potomac across the Rapidan River on May 4, 1864, the same day Benjamin Butler launched his Army of the James toward Bermuda Hundred. Grant and Lee battled through the Wilderness, Spotsylvania, North Anna and lesser known points in a continuous encounter that produced a shocking 62,000 casualties in its first three weeks. By the end of the month the Army of the Potomac found itself east of Richmond, approaching a crossroads hamlet called Cold Harbor, with Lee's Army of Northern Virginia racing toward the same point, aiming to block Grant's way to the Confederate capital.[8]

Meanwhile Butler and his forces sat bottled up at Bermuda Hundred, contributing little to the Union cause. "Sufficient time had elapsed," wrote Corporal Reid, "to convince General Grant that the Army of the James was not performing its part in the united advance on the Confederate capital." As a result, the May bloodbaths having brought no dampening in Grant's resolve to remorselessly grind into the Confederates, the Union General-in-Chief made the logical decision to take a significant portion of the idle troops from Butler and move them to the support of the Army of the Potomac. Grant determined that Butler needed only 10,000 men to hold his strong position at Bermuda Hundred and so ordered the expanded Eighteenth Corps, with 16,000 infantrymen, sixteen pieces of artillery, and a squadron of cavalry, to head for Cold Harbor.[9]

On the afternoon of May 26, orders to get ready to march gave the 115th the first intimation of their change in status. The men prepared to move but faced another case of hurry-up-and-wait as the march did not get under way for more than twenty-four hours. They finally stepped out at 6:00 p.m. in the evening of May 27 but then marched just four miles toward the James River and bivouacked. This short jaunt proved the first leg of a circuitous 155 mile journey to Cold Harbor, a point only fifteen straight-line miles from the federal camps at Bermuda Hundred. The direct route was unavailable because the rebels held the north bank of the James River opposite Bermuda Hundred. Long voyages continued to be the lot of the Flying Infantry.

The pattern repeated on the following day when the troops waited in readiness throughout the morning and afternoon but did not resume the march until 6:00 p.m. This time they walked all night to City Point, Virginia where the 115th, the 47th New York, and the 76th Pennsylvania boarded the steamer *DeMolay*. The *DeMolay* joined a transport fleet that sailed down the James River to Fortress Monroe, then into Chesapeake Bay, up the York River and into its tributary Pamunkey River. The troops disembarked at White House Landing on the Pamunkey at 4:30 a.m. on the morning of May 31. Richmond lay just twenty-five miles to the west.

The men rested until late afternoon, then marched toward Cold Harbor and the Army of the Potomac, and one of the 115th's longest, most memorable days.[10]

As the Eighteenth Corps made its roundabout way to Cold Harbor via White House Landing, the Army of the Potomac approached from the northwest. Grant made Cold Harbor his next objective because of its location astride key roads leading to both his source of supply at White House Landing and to potential crossing points on the James River below the Richmond defenses. Union cavalry under General Philip Sheridan reached Cold Harbor on May 31, the first elements of the Army of the Potomac to do so, and found that Confederates had beaten them to the spot and were fast digging in. General Lee had also noted the importance of Cold Harbor, surmised that it would be Grant's next objective, and determined to get there first. His fast-moving veterans won the race to Cold Harbor, but Sheridan wrested the position from Lee's lead units. Sheridan's men modified the enemy earthworks to face back toward the rebels, then anxiously awaited the arrival of federal infantry during the restless night of May 31-June 1.[11]

As June 1 dawned a couple of uncoordinated Confederate attacks failed to dislodge Sheridan's outnumbered troopers. At 10:00 a.m. Grant's Sixth Corps reached Cold Harbor after an exhausting all-night march and relieved the cavalrymen: the main body of the Army of the Potomac had begun to arrive. Meanwhile the Eighteenth Corps was nowhere to be found. It had set out from White House Landing—about thirteen miles from Cold Harbor—at 5:00 p.m. the previous day. But faulty orders from Grant's staff sent them to the wrong place. Directives that corps commander General Smith received in triplicate instructed him to rush his corps toward New Castle, Virginia, instead of Cold Harbor.[12]

The Eighteenth Corps had endured a hurried march through most of the night, refreshed only by a three hour pause between 3:00 and 6:00 a.m. "The troops are quite exhausted, our load is heavy, consisting of one hundred rounds of ammunition, three days rations, knapsack and arms. The night is dark and roads dusty," remembered Sergeant Reardon. The men were unaware, of course, that their weary tramp headed them in the wrong direction.

A staff officer from Grant's headquarters caught up with Smith at New Castle early on June 1 and gave him revised instructions. Smith halted his columns and set about the thorny task of about-facing thousands of troops and sending them grumbling back along the same miles of road over which they had just advanced. "Near daylight the mistake in our orders was discovered," recorded Private Archibald McGlachlin of Company E. "We halted for a few moments, and thinking we had reached our destination the men began to prepare for breakfast, when the long roll rang out, the drums beat, and in a moment we were whisking away toward Cold Harbor."[13]

As McGlachlin and the rest of the Eighteenth Corps hurriedly reversed direction, the hardened veterans of the Army of the Potomac's Sixth Corps moved into place at Cold Harbor. Meanwhile tens of thousands more soldiers, northern and southern, sped toward the same isolated hamlet. As orders issued to General Smith advised, "The enemy have not long been in position about Cold Harbor, and it is of great importance to dislodge and, if possible, to rout him before he can intrench himself." Smith was to lead his Eighteenth Corps up onto the right of the Sixth Corps and join it in an attack on the rebels.[14]

It took several hours to cover the twelve miles from New Castle to Cold Harbor. "The day was very hot and water extremely scarce," wrote McGlachlin. "The dust enveloped us like a dense fog. Many times when ascending a hill or knoll, looking back over that weary dust covered line, we saw men carried out and laid under the friendly shade of a tree, suffering the painful agonies of sunstroke and physical exhaustion.... After covering our weary night march and making in all over 30 miles we touched elbows with the Sixth Corps." General Smith's corps had started its movement at White House on May 31 just thirteen miles from Cold Harbor, marched fifteen miles to New Castle and then turned about and trudged twelve more miles from New Castle to Cold Harbor. The mistaken orders had more than doubled the required marching distance. Clark described his regiment's condition when they finally reached Cold Harbor as "badly used up.... A large number of the men lay along the dusty road and under the burning rays of the southern sun, utterly unable to move; yet in that condition they took a glorious part in one of our great battles."[15]

The Eighteenth Corps formed into battle lines immediately upon their midafternoon arrival. Soon a barrage of artillery signaled a prelude to the assault. As Reardon wrote his sister the next day, "Our artillery was quickly got into position and commenced a vigorous shelling of the enemy. The cannonading from about 30 pieces was continuous and terrific for an hour." General Charles Devens's Division of the Eighteenth Corps, to which Barton's Brigade and the 115th belonged, took position on the Corps' left, adjoining the Sixth Corps veterans. Another of Devens's brigades, five regiments from Indiana, Maine, and New York under Colonel Jeremiah Drake, arrived ahead of Barton's Brigade and sprang to the attack first, at 5:00 p.m, June 1, 1864. Altogether 30,000 men of the Sixth and Eighteenth Corps advanced against the waiting Confederates.[16]

Drake's brigade drove the rebel skirmishers back to their entrenchments but as his brigade of onrushing blue clad troops closed on the southerners' position, rebel fire killed Drake and thwarted the advance of his men. They stopped and lay down, pinned in a position about a half mile from their starting point. Relief soon arrived for Drake's men when, as the *New York Times* reported, "Barton's Brigade here threw itself into the breach."[17]

The 115th charged forward with a long, loud cheer. The regiment first passed through a narrow woods, managing to maintain their alignment "as though formed for dress parade." Emerging from the timber, they faced open fields nearly a thousand yards across with a line of enemy trenches at the woodline on the far side. "Every man seemed to comprehend at a glance the desperate work before us, and with a wild cheer we struck double-quick," recalled Archibald McGlachlin. "Some ran faster than others and soon our line was going forward in a broken and irregular manner." A bullet passed through McGlachlin's foot as he left the woods and he crawled to a large tree from which he had a good view of his charging comrades. "The 115th still went forward in a zig-zag manner," he continued. "I expected every moment to see the colors stop and the regiment reform, but well for them all perhaps, they could not be restrained."[18]

John Reardon also recalled emerging from the woods into the open fields. "We started on a double-quick and commenced cheering and continued to cheer the whole way," he wrote. "Many fell crossing the cornfields. On we pushed, the enemy pouring into us a heavy fire of musketry and shell." As the 115th and Barton's other regiments reached the point where Drake's earlier attack had bogged down, some of Drake's troops passed through to the rear. Others joined Barton's men as they rushed onward toward the rebel lines.[19]

"The boys felt ugly," according to Lieutenant James Clark, "and were determined to make a big fight, and to reach the enemy's works." Dashing toward the woodline at the far side of the field, they saw the rebels retreating before them. "We struck into the woods over logs and brush," wrote Reardon, referring to slashings strewn in front of their trenches by the defensive-minded Confederates, "and so great was the excitement that I never saw the enemy earthworks until we come within ten feet of them. The enemy had now stopped firing and were running. Some were shot down. Others more wise threw down their arms and surrendered." The *Times* reported that the men of Barton's Brigade assaulted the enemy line "with a fierce hurrah, dashing unshrinkingly into the rifle pits over entanglements and pitfalls, taking 250 prisoners."[20]

The wounded Private McGlachlin, from his seat at the base of a sheltering tree, watched his comrades overcome the rebels. He was sure that the 115th was the first Eighteenth Corps unit to breach the Confederate line and surmised that their mad dash across the wide field aided them more than maintaining a disciplined alignment would have. "For once luck and chance beat discipline," he concluded. "On they sped, the colors well to the front, and before I realized what was passing they disappeared over the works. In utter dismay nearly 200 Confederates threw down their arms and surrendered—a larger number of men than our regiment had in the battle."[21]

Albert Dunning of Company C "mounted the works of the enemy and, grabbing a Johnnie by the collar of his coat, literally yanked him over the works and hurled him sprawling to the rear," recorded James Reid. Other triumphant 115th men loudly demanded that their beaten foes surrender. Corporal Reid said that this "seemed to paralyze the Johnnies and large numbers threw down their guns." Reardon saw some war-weary Confederates jump from their works to give themselves up and heard them yell to their captors, "Give the rebels hell, boys, I'm glad to get out of this." He contended that the prisoners did not need much guarding, "as they felt rejoiced to think they were done soldiering." Nicholas DeGraff witnessed another Confederate, less anxious to end his military career, shield himself by hoisting a wounded Yankee onto his back "and make for the rear, all speed."[22]

Claims about the number of prisoners taken vary, but the *Times* estimate of 250, a number also cited by Corporal Reid, cannot be far wrong. Barton's other units shared a hand in bagging rebels but, given the convergence of accounts of McGlachlin and others on this point, it is indeed possible that the number of prisoners captured by the regiment was greater than the 125 men of the 115th engaged in the fight that day.[23]

Confederates not disposed to surrender fled back to their main line of entrenchments. The works taken by the 115th and other units of the Sixth and Eighteenth Corps had been Confederate exterior lines. Some men of the brigade advanced beyond the captured works, but heavy fire from the more formidable Confederate main lines forced their return. Lieutenant DeGraff closed his account of June 1 thus: "Night came on apace and we lay where we were all night, aiding the reble and Union wounded as much as we could. Many grievously wounded made the night hideous with their groans and shrieks."[24]

In a long-savored respite from their usually dreadful fortunes, circumstance blessed the 115th on June 1, 1864, rewarding the regiment with a memorable success. Though proud of their accomplishment, the regiment's veterans did not fail to acknowledge the part that pure good luck played in their small triumph. They realized that they had taken an enemy position that was a weak point in the Confederate lines not defended as strongly as other sectors. Moreover, adjacent terrain protected them from the enfilading musketry and shellfire which exacted more severe losses in Barton's other units. While the 115th had just a handful of men wounded and none killed, the other three regiments of Barton's Brigade—the 47th and 48th New York and the 76th Pennsylvania—suffered heavily.

Nonetheless the men of the 115th found great satisfaction in their action on June 1. "The 115th, usually unfortunate in assignments to positions on such occasions, were particularly fortunate on this occasion, and although their loss was trifling their success was most brilliant and gratifying," asserted James Reid. The proud New Yorkers were well aware that the enemy they had defeated in their sector of battle were hardened veterans of Lee's storied Army of Northern Virginia—rebels who had, just moments before Barton's Brigade and the 115th dashed onto the scene, stood firm and repulsed Drake's initial Union assault. "It was a great day for the 115th," concluded Reid.[25]

Several men of the 115th sensed that a particular intensity gripped the regiment at Cold Harbor. Captain Fred Mosher of Company C recalled feeling an "insensibility to danger; I never felt that but once, and that was when we made the charge at Cold Harbor. After taking the first line of works I felt as though we could go through the entire Confederacy." Perhaps the added spark stemmed from pent up frustration following the recently concluded Bermuda Hundred campaign; the troops realized the opportunities botched during that unhappy episode and knew how poorly the Army of the James had been led. Or as Reid reasoned when he recalled the fervor of June 1, perhaps the forced marches suffered en route to Cold Harbor "maddened the boys" as they went into the charge. And the exhilaration of the enemy fleeing before them would have intensified whatever extra motivation the men had carried onto the battlefield. Certainly the rush of victory colored the men's recollections. As Clark simply said, "The boys felt ugly."[26]

While Barton's Brigade and adjoining units of the Sixth and Eighteenth Corps seized portions of the rebels' forward works, their success was not duplicated elsewhere on the Union assault line. With darkness approaching, the federals dug in all along the front. Meanwhile more units of the Army of the Potomac arrived and filed into line around Cold Harbor. The June 1 attack was but a preliminary; Grant planned a massive frontal assault for the next day.

The 115th spent the night of June 1–2 in the line of works it had captured, trying to gain some rest amid periodic skirmishing. Grant issued orders for a renewal of the assault on the morning of June 2, then delayed it until dawn of June 3. When finally relieved around midday on June 2, the 115th moved to the rear and cooked breakfast. The Eighteenth Corps spent June 2 "strengthening the position and making ready for the next conflict."[27]

Fred Mosher joined the 115th from Ballston at age 22. He served throughout the war without injury, as lieutenant and captain in Company C (Lance Ingmire Collection).

As Union forces established positions on June 2, a wide gap developed between the right of the Eighteenth Corps and the left of the Army of the Potomac's Fifth Corps. This

Contemporary sketch of the Union lines at Cold Harbor on June 1, 1864 (*Battles and Leaders*).

made it essential, according to General Smith, "to throw back the right flank of the [Eighteenth] corps to hold the open plain and to prevent that flank from being turned. This necessity put the division on the right quite out of the battle." Here fortune once more smiled on the 115th. Smith assigned Devens's Division to guard the right flank, indeed taking it out of the battle and sparing it from partaking in Grant's bloody, futile offensive.[28]

At dawn on June 3, 40,000 blue clad men charged Confederate lines which by then had been strengthened and reinforced. By 7:30 a.m. the fight was over, the Union repulsed all along the lines, 7,000 of them shot down. The 115th suffered a few losses that morning as it lay between contending artillery batteries, but even that position proved a safe haven compared to the hell entered by their 40,000 comrades along the four mile front. "The assault cost us heavily and probably without benefit to compensate," Grant later admitted. "I have always regretted that the last assault at Cold Harbor was ever made." The boys of the 115th never regretted missing it.[29]

For nine days following the bloodletting of June 3, Blue and Gray faced each other across the opposing lines at Cold Harbor. The 115th spent most of this time at the front in the trenches. Skirmishing and shelling were nearly continuous. "The Rebles works are not more than a stones throw from ours, and there we lay and watch each other," wrote DeGraff. "If our fellows see one of their heads you will hear the rifle crack, and the same with them." The 115th came under fire each day, suffering casualties in small, daily doses as illustrated throughout the veterans' recollections:

> June 4: There is continued dulsatory [sic] firing at some [point] on the lines all the time but few casualties ... though Company E had one of their men killed by a stray bullet as he lay asleep in camp.
> June 5: Heavy firing day and night. Two killed and two wounded during the day.
> June 6: Company C had two wounded on the 6th, Lewis Bertrand and Mark Cockran, both wounded in the head; the former went to the hospital, but Cockran considered his wound too slight and remained with the company.
> June 6: Heavy and continuous skirmishing during the entire day.... One man mortally wounded in the 115th.
> June 7: Considerable firing by sharpshooters during the morning. Our coffee is brought up by the cooks but is cold and worthless.
> June 9: Firing by sharpshooters is brisk. We remain in the trenches all day.
> June 10: The usual amount of skirmishing and artillery firing. Loss small.[30]

One afternoon a rebel sharpshooter killed Henry Goodrich as he moved along the trench lines carrying coffee to his mates in Company E. "The ball passed through his brain causing instant death," recalled one of his fellows. "We lay him beneath the cold ground as the sun is sinking in the far west. He was a brave and true soldier and within all a true Christian, morally strong, a good example, and beloved by his comrades." Henry's loss must have been a cruel blow to his younger brother Menzo Goodrich who had come of age and joined the regiment just five months earlier, in January 1864.[31]

The night following Mark Cockran's slight wound to the head he dreamed of being wounded in the right arm. The next morning he recounted the dream to some of his camp mates while drinking coffee, complaining that the arm felt numb and weak. That day a number of defective shells fired by a Union battery located behind the 115th exploded prematurely, raining shrapnel upon the regiment. Notified of the problem, the battery's commander replied that his orders were to continue firing and that the infantrymen should lie low. "That was not very consoling for our boys. They were between the fire of both friends and foes, with the greater danger from the friends," wrote Reid. One man was killed and another wounded before a fragment of defective Union shell tore through Cockran's right arm, making his premonition a reality. He underwent a field amputation of part of his arm but suffered terribly for nine months at a convalescent hospital in Washington. Surgeons finally discovered that Cockran's shoulder had also been damaged and removed the remainder of his arm up to its socket.[32]

Union regiments shared frontline duties, usually spending a day or night at the front, then being relieved and returning to camps at the rear on a daily cycle. On one occasion, as the 115th's chroniclers were quick to note, relief did not appear and the regiment spent forty-eight straight hours in the trenches. Both sides continually strengthened their positions, the New Yorkers contributing their share to the efforts, "using the shovel more than the musket." The 115th toiled and fought with shovel and musket among the Virginia trenches for the next six months.[33]

There was an occasional respite from the tedium of work and the ever present menace of cannons and rifles. On June 7 the armies declared a two hour truce in order to retrieve and bury the decomposing bodies still lying between the lines. Even though orders regarding the truce forbade contact with the enemy, the opposing soldiers were quick to ignore the directive and seek each other out. As soon as the white flags appeared, noted DeGraff, "firing instantly ceased and we all got up to take a look at each other." Sergeant Reardon found it "a strange sight to see men who a moment before were doing everything in their power to kill each other now standing in peace beholding one another with wonder." Some Company E men watched one rebel, "a remarkably lank giant of a fellow," slowly emerge from his works, "taking some time to get the kinks out of his frame." His slow rise and "extreme length" caused one of the 115th's wags to exclaim, "My God, is that fellow never going to stop coming up?"[34]

During the cease-fire a Union brass band moved to the front and struck up *Yankee Doodle*, raising howls from the Confederates, but then followed with *Dixie*, "which pleased the rebels amazingly." For a brief interlude mortal enemies traded rousing cheers and loud hoots as the band played regional favorites from North and South. Lieutenant DeGraff recalled that the impromptu concert "caused a good deal of merriment, both sides laughing heartily and shouting applause." DeGraff enjoyed this byplay but noted that the fun was short-lived: "After the truce firing instantly began again."[35]

Another day a small cavalry escort rode through camp parading a civilian who was seated backwards on a mule and adorned with sandwich signs reading "Libeler of the Press." The man, a reporter named Edward Cropsey from the *Philadelphia Inquirer*, had incurred the considerable wrath of General George G. Meade by writing that Meade, commander of the Army of the Potomac, wanted to retreat following the Battle of the Wilderness, only to be countermanded by Grant. The baseless story had its roots in camp rumor and was, needless to say, humiliating to Meade. Drumming out the offending reporter in such mortifying fashion was designed to serve as a warning to the rest of the press corps.[36]

James Clark noted a squad of Confederate prisoners wearing blue uniforms. To an inquiry about why they opted for the blue, the captured rebels replied that when they wore it among southern civilians, "the ladies think we have killed a Yankee and have on his clothes, so they wave handkerchiefs at us to show their respect for the deed." Perhaps the more naive among the well-supplied northerners accepted this macabre boast; most knew that the ill-clad Confederates needed to supply themselves from any available source, including dead Yankees.[37]

The soldiers' usual diet consisted of hardtack and salt pork often grown soft and mushy after long stays in the soldiers' haversacks during hot weather. On June 8 a fresh ration of pork and bacon arrived and found a ready welcome: "How glad the soldiers were! Its weight in pure gold would be no object."[38]

Visiting between regiments also provided diversion during the occasional quiet periods. A day after the fight of June 3, John Reardon went to find out if his brother Edmund had survived. Edmund served with the 2nd New York Heavy Artillery which was in line with the Second Corps a couple of miles left of the 115th. "I walked there between fear and doubt as to whether I would see him or not," Reardon recalled, but he soon rejoiced to find Edmund in good health. "After a pleasant visit of two hours I returned to my regiment." A week later on a quiet day that found most of the 115th washing their clothes, Edmund and some friends from the 2nd Heavy paid a call on the 115th.[39]

Lieutenant DeGraff turned twenty-two on June 9, a birth date he shared with his mother. He wrote and told her that he celebrated their mutual birthday by "laying in the front line of rifle pits wondering if you thought of me at home." DeGraff knew very well that his family had him in their thoughts; he had received his mother's most recent letter just a day earlier. "Your letters encourage me very much," his note continued. "Sometimes everybody wears a long face here and then a word of cheer from home is like a ray of sunlight on a stormy day." A day later the young lieutenant found that another relation had him in mind as well when Captain Alonzo DeGraff of the 14th New York Heavy Artillery came calling. A couple of nights afterwards Nick returned the visit, having dinner with Alonzo at the Ninth Corps camp of the 14th Heavy.

In his letter DeGraff speculated that Grant was "maturing some plan," and guessed that he would take the army south of the James—a prediction that soon proved accurate. He voiced the faith which the troops placed in their commander but tempered his statement of trust with a caution and a prayer. "We have all got great confidence in Grant's movements, but it is not very consoling when we think of the men which he loses.... God grant that the flow of blood may be stayed."[40]

Soon after the defeat of his June 3 offensive at Cold Harbor, Grant acknowledged the impossibility of dislodging Lee from his defenses and getting between Lee and Richmond. He resolved to take the army to the south side of the James River, seize the key Confederate industrial and transportation hub at Petersburg, and threaten Richmond from the south. The ambitious move would involve taking more than 100,000 men and all the trappings and supplies of a great army across forty miles of rugged terrain, including a broad, tidal river. To further complicate this daunting scenario, Grant wished to keep the move hidden from the Confederates for as long as possible, enabling his troops to take Petersburg before Lee could shift his strained resources to its defense. Preparations for the massive military migration proceeded stealthily as the two armies maintained their brutal standoff around Cold Harbor.[41]

The plan called for the Army of the Potomac to move overland and cross the James while the Eighteenth Corps returned to Bermuda Hundred using the same circuitous route via White House Landing by which it had approached Cold Harbor two weeks earlier (but eliminating the irksome detour through New Castle). Great pains were to be taken to disengage covertly from the vigilant Confederates, including maintaining activity along the picket lines and leapfrogging corps to mask the main movements. As Corporal Reid summarized: "Orders were promulgated minutely covering the movement of corps, batteries, trains, &c., with final orders that after dark on the 12th the movement should begin."[42]

The 115th did its part in the effort to fool the Confederates by leaving Company H behind in the picket line while the rest of the regiment pulled out on the evening of June 12. Company H stayed in place overnight digging trenches and firing at the enemy, then silently left the works the next morning. The ruse succeeded; at a distance of several miles the troops could hear the rebels still shooting at the abandoned federal positions. Indeed, the deception worked remarkably well all along the Union lines, leaving General Lee uncertain of his enemy's intentions and whereabouts.[43]

The 115th's return journey from Cold Harbor to Bermuda Hundred proved as frustrating as the approach. After a nightlong march to White House, the 115th waited through one full day and half of another before boarding a river transport and setting off down the Pamunkey. Their vessel, a crowded cattle boat called the *Salvor*, then ran aground just one mile from the dock and remained stuck in the mud for several hours. Finally freed by the rising tide, the *Salvor* made good time running the troops down the Pamunkey to the York, passing Fortress Monroe and steaming up the James.[44]

Clear sailing for the 115th and the balance of the Eighteenth Corps ended abruptly on the evening of June 15. A pontoon bridge hastily thrown into place to carry part of the Army of the Potomac across the James impeded further sailing up the river. Disembarking on the south bank, the Eighteenth Corps bivouacked for the night, then proceeded afoot twenty miles to City Point the next morning. The veterans remembered this march as one of the toughest of its experience, dust and heat being the main antagonists. Lieutenant Clark left a vivid description:

> The yellow clay, hardened by the sun and ground to powder by the tramp of a great army, rose up in thick, black columns and settled upon us, filling our eyes, and causing our eyeballs to roll with pain. The rays of the sun beat down upon us with searching power; our lips cracked open for want of water.... Our feet were blistered and sore as boils, and every step we took caused an agony of pain.... But 'tis sweet to suffer for one's country. 'Tis glorious to be tortured for the sacred cause of freedom.[45]

From City Point the regiment sailed up the Appomattox River to Point of Rocks, then marched to the familiar lines at Bermuda Hundred. On the morning of June 17 the men pitched their tents very near their former campsite. They had returned to their old camp and their old commander, General Butler, the brigade having been re-assigned to the Tenth Corps while en route back to Bermuda Hundred.[46]

The fighting around Cold Harbor cost federal forces over 14,000 casualties, including 3,020 in the temporarily expanded Eighteenth Corps. Barton's Brigade lost 224. The 115th New York paid a comparatively light toll for its brief taste of soldiering in the mainstream of the great national conflict, just four dead and fourteen wounded. "Looking over the past twenty days and all what our Reg't has been through," DeGraff wrote his father on June 19, "my heart raises in thankfulness to God for sparing us as he has from the general slaughter." Nonetheless the brutal, continuous warfare in the trenches alongside the Army of the Potomac proved an eye-opener for the New Yorkers. "We thought we knew what soldiering was," wrote Captain McKittrick, reflecting on his regiment's time at Cold Harbor, "but have come to the conclusion that our experience heretofore was mere child's play."[47]

10

War in Trench and Crater
"What a fearful thunder"

The complex shift of Union forces from Cold Harbor to the south side of the James River came off with barely a hitch, a rare triumph of military efficiency. Just below the river was the northerners' next objective, the vital railroad and industrial center of Petersburg. Only 2,200 Confederates under the command of a frantic General Pierre Gustave Toutant Beauregard were present to defend the city. General Lee and the Army of Northern Virginia remained near Richmond, uncertain of their enemy's intentions. But Grant and his lieutenants never managed to coordinate their forces and attack in sufficient strength to overcome Petersburg's sparse defenders. Piecemeal, unsustained attacks by arriving federal units failed to take the city. Grant's remarkable movement brought Petersburg within his grasp, but the prize eluded him.

In a desperate maneuver to defend Petersburg, Beauregard ordered the southern troops manning the Bermuda Hundred lines to abandon their position and move into Petersburg's defensive perimeter on June 15. The next morning General Butler discovered that the Confederates who had kept him bottled up at Bermuda Hundred had departed and that the lines opposite him stood nearly empty. He recognized the opportunity to take the turnpike and railroad linking Richmond and Petersburg and thereby block the passage of Lee's troops before they could rush to relieve Petersburg. When Grant got word of the situation at Bermuda Hundred, he too sensed opportunity and he sent most of the Sixth Corps there to aid Butler.

The leader of the Army of the James may have recognized the opportunity, but he failed to seize it. He lost several hours before sending a small force to occupy and destroy the Richmond & Petersburg Railroad. Then, over the next two days, the dilatory Butler sent too few troops to exploit the situation, failed to use all available force at the point of attack, and bickered ridiculously with Sixth Corps commander Horatio Wright. Meanwhile rebel troops continued to pour south from the Richmond area intent on forcing their way through Butler's weak toehold on the railroad to the relief of Petersburg.[1]

Such was the strategic situation when the 115th New York arrived back at Bermuda Hundred from Cold Harbor on the morning of June 17. This was a full day after General Butler discovered that the opposing rebels had withdrawn from their lines across the neck of the peninsula, but he still had not moved out in force nor completed his preparations for doing so. At 11:00 p.m. that night Butler finally readied an attack, and orders came for Barton's Brigade to move to the front. The 115th and Barton's other regiments marched south about a mile, passed over the earthworks, fixed bayonets, then crawled silently into a position very close to the unsuspecting southerners. Sixth Corps units passed behind the brigade and went into line farther to the right.[2]

The 115th New York lay still in the front line, rebel pickets visible in the moonlight. Two more lines of northerners lay behind the 115th, spaced twenty feet apart. Colonel Barton approached Major Walrath and whispered orders, the attack imminent. "We lie down, the moon shines bright, everything still," recorded John Reardon. Suddenly the Confederates opened fire. The Union approach had been discovered, the element of surprise lost. DeGraff said a prayer; he and his mates knew by now what front-rank troops could expect from a charge such as they were about to make. "We lay under high nervous tension awaiting the final command to go." But the good fortune of recent days remained with the 115th and the movement was abandoned. At 3:30 a.m. the relieved soldiers trod back to their camps.[3]

By that time rebels were again in place in strength opposite the Bermuda Hundred lines. They had discerned enemy plans and reacted, and the Yankee attack had been called off, much to the relief of the 115th and other troops. Two days had passed since the initial Confederate withdrawal from these lines, but poor Union leadership squandered this window of opportunity. The men in the ranks fully realized the shoddy performances of their commanders. Years later James Reid recounted the whole, sad tale and voiced his emphatic disapproval:

> Thus it will be seen that the great opportunity offered the Union forces of seriously interfering with the reinforcing of Beauregard at Petersburg by Lee's army was rendered nugatory by the vacillating methods of the immediate field commanders. The chance had passed and again the Bermuda line was hermetically sealed.[4]

Similar scenes unfolded all along the Bermuda Hundred and Petersburg fronts, the Union frittering away its initial advantage with rebels arriving hourly. The Confederates held. On the Bermuda Hundred front and in newly forming lines around the east side of Petersburg, the opposing troops dug in. The chance to take the city by storm had escaped the federals, and General Grant resigned himself and his forces to a long haul before Petersburg. The War Between the States in eastern Virginia took on a new complexion: static, siege warfare.

After the abortive action on the night of their arrival, June 17–18, the 115th spent three restful days in the Bermuda Hundred camp, then suddenly packed up and moved to a new camp at the extreme left of the Bermuda Hundred line near the Appomattox River. The move came as federal troops remaining at Bermuda Hundred spread out to cover sections of the lines vacated by other Tenth Corps units (which had gone off on a mission to establish a bridgehead across the James River) and by the Eighteenth Corps (which crossed the Appomattox to make another futile stab at Petersburg). The regiment set up camp on high ground in a pine grove and served frontline duty in a section of earthworks overlooking the Appomattox and the spires of Petersburg, a setting they regarded as relatively pleasant.[5]

The soldiers could also see the smoke and hear the din of battle raging along the Petersburg front to their south, but for the 115th things remained not only quiet but downright congenial. "Soldiers on both sides are friendly on this front," reported DeGraff. "Hello,

Johnny," the men called across the lines, offering an informal enlisted man's truce which the southerners readily accepted. "Firing ceases and we meet between the lines, half way, and often engage in friendly conversation and agree that no firing continue all day." The 115th exchanged goods and greetings with rebels of the 43rd Alabama. "So the time passed off finely compared to days when we are trying to kill each other," wrote Sergeant Reardon. He traded a rebel lieutenant coffee and sugar for a Richmond newspaper and recorded that the Alabamians "remarked that they wished we could always meet in peace and hoped the war would soon end." No doubt the New Yorkers shared the sentiment.[6]

That afternoon, June 22, President Lincoln rode along the Bermuda Hundred lines on a tour of inspection with General Butler. The entourage passed through the camp of the 115th. Soldiers from other units along the route recorded greeting the president with enthusiastic cheers, but the 115th New York stood silently as he went by, perhaps because he passed close among them and they could discern his serious mien. "There was no demonstration, all standing in their tracks, hats off at respectful attention," recalled DeGraff. "I was awe struck as I observed his pale face and care worn look, plainly showing the great physical and mental strain he was enduring."[7]

The regiment's first day in its new locale had proven eventful—friendly commerce with the enemy and a visit from their nation's commander-in-chief. Assuming their stay would be lengthy, the men also found time to improve their campsite. But they should have known better. "We retired for the night," wrote Corporal Reid, "in blissful ignorance of the orders that were on the way to pack up." Sure enough, late the next day those orders arrived, and the Flying Infantry moved on once more. They stepped out at 7:00 p.m., crossed the Appomattox River on a pontoon bridge at Point of Rocks, and marched twelve miles to a point on the Petersburg lines at Hare's Hill.[8]

The move resulted from orders for General John Turner's Tenth Corps Division, to which Barton's Brigade and the 115th were again assigned, to reinforce the Eighteenth Corps, still jousting with the rebels for position on Petersburg's northern perimeter. This prompted a grumble from Captain Kneeskern: "I have got tired [of] being lent out to the 18th Corps." Operations by the Eighteenth Corps soon sputtered. In a dismal twist, having suddenly departed comfortable environs the men had expected to occupy at length, the 115th New York ended up in a desolate and dangerous position at Hare's Hill. The regiment remained there for several weeks.[9]

The 115th arrived at their new location a couple of hours before dawn on June 24, relieving a Pennsylvania regiment of the Ninth Corps. The Pennsylvanians warned the New Yorkers to keep low at daylight, for their line lay perilously close to the Confederate works opposite. Military fortifications were not built in straight lines but turned to and fro at angles, providing their defenders with a crossfire against attacking troops. By this time the opposing lines snaked for miles around Petersburg. The peculiar turns in the lines and the terrain at Hare's Hill brought the opposing works closer together there than at most points. The right of the 115th was at the base of the hill and its left at the crest, its sector of the line running diagonally up the side of the hill and drawing closer to the enemy as it neared the hilltop. The Union line again angled toward the rear as it descended the hill's far side, thus forming a salient at the crest of Hare's Hill. A salient in the rebel line stood on an opposite rise of ground with a shallow ravine separating the foes where the two salients pointed angrily at one another.[10]

As the sun rose that morning the men of the 115th were roused by the crack of bullets. The growing daylight revealed to them the strongly built Union earthworks, faced with logs and topped by sandbags arranged to provide loopholes every few feet—openings that served as observation and firing points. Though anxious for a view of their surroundings, the newly arrived New Yorkers heeded the warning of the departed Pennsylvanians and only allowed themselves quick peeks at the enemy, gained by jumping up for a glance through the loopholes. What they saw were the equally formidable works of the enemy looming close by, punctuated by puffs of blue smoke from shots fired by watchful Confederate sharpshooters at careless Yankees. During the day a single shot by a rebel riflemen killed both twenty-six-year old Jacob Brown of the 115th's Company B and a soldier of the 48th New York. "The ball passed through both of their heads and killed them on the spot," recorded Captain Kneeskern.[11]

As daylight exposed the regiment's new surroundings, it also uncovered a scene even more alarming than the proximity of strong fortifications manned by a determined enemy. As Reid related, "There was another sight revealed to us that caused the blood to chill in the veins and our conversations to be hushed into whispers." Strewn across the no-man's-land between the lines were numerous bodies of federal dead, casualties of the early Union assaults against the Confederate defenses. Most were probably members of the First Maine Heavy Artillery which on June 18 had suffered 632 men killed and wounded in a frontal assault at the rebel works opposite Hare's Hill. DeGraff depicted the corpses as "all black and bloated and decomposing, having lain a week in the hot sun and scorching weather." Kneeskern cracked callously on the "good, healthy old smell" they emitted. Many wondered what these slain, untended comrades might portend for them.[12]

The regiment seemed destined to test their fate that same evening when Barton's Brigade formed in battle line just behind the federal works at Hare's Hill. The closeness of the opposing salients at Hare's Hill did not fail to gain the notice of the generals, and during the day the men of the 115th looked on as a rebel infantry attack just south of Hare's Hill was turned back. That enemy sortie had been aimed at breeching a lower point in the Union line and then rolling up the line to Hare's Hill. Now, federal brass intended to push the rebels off their hilltop salient opposite Hare's Hill. Corps commander General William Smith noted his desire "to take the hill in front of my left, which will save me from much annoyance if I succeed."[13]

As the 115th formed on Hare's Hill, word passed that they were to assault the rebel salient. The soldiers whispered prayers and exchanged messages for loved ones, and the regimental flag bearer exhorted his comrades to protect the colors—conversations that "harrowed the feelings," according to Corporal Reid. Word passed that the officer commanding a neighboring brigade had boasted that, with sufficient artillery support, he could take the Confederate position with little difficulty. Hearing this, one of Barton's wits asked, "Why in hell don't he take his own brigade if he is so anxious to charge?"

Captain William McKittrick stood silent a couple of paces in front of his Company C, sword point resting on the ground at his feet. His men noted his unusually contemplative demeanor. Finally the respected Mexican War veteran turned and addressed them in a strong, even voice:

> Boys, when we get the order to charge let us go forward at the utmost speed. Don't stop to fire, but have every gun loaded and ready to fire the instant we reach their works. Our success depends on the effect we can produce at their line.

The next command to be heard however was not to move forward, but to the rear. The planned assault was canceled. The 115th dropped back to another line of works 200 yards to the rear and bivouacked for the night. General Smith later explained that he had postponed the attack when he discovered that he had fewer men in line than expected—2,800 rather than 3,500.[14]

Incredibly, the same scenario played out again the following night. The 115th moved to the front with its division and the men steeled themselves for deadly work ahead, only to have the attack orders ultimately countermanded. This time Smith shelved his plans due to a report from his chief engineer regarding the great strength of the enemy position. He postponed the assault indefinitely, concluding that "the loss of life would probably not be proportioned to the results gained."[15]

But the indefinite postponement lasted just five days. On June 30 orders once more came to prepare to assault the enemy lines, with Colonel Barton and his brigade again scheduled to lead the way. The 115th New York moved out in late afternoon. Barton thoughtlessly deployed his men for battle in full view of the vigilant rebels. He had them cross over the breastworks on open ground, forgoing the potential concealment provided by a thick grove of trees fronting the works nearby. His error brought a stream of Confederates out of their lines to counterattack. The fight cost the division 210 killed and wounded before the rebels were beaten back. The 115th suffered just one man wounded because the enemy focused their charge not on Barton's Brigade, by then in line and ready, but on the other brigades of Turner's Division which were still deploying to support Barton. Meanwhile Confederate reinforcements moved toward the threatened point. This turn of events brought yet another eleventh hour cancellation of Union assault plans and Barton's Brigade and the other federal troops again fell back. The northerners made no subsequent effort to pierce the rebel defenses in this area.[16]

Blame for the debacle centered on Colonel William Barton. An irate General Turner immediately relieved Barton of command, accusing him of "gross carelessness and inattention in moving his column over the parapet in full view of the enemy's line, and therefore disclosing his movement when it was possible for him to have moved it under cover of the woods where he was ordered to go, and where the dictates of common sense should have directed him." The 115th had served its last with Colonel Barton who resigned from the army shortly after losing his command. He worked in the theater business until his death in New York City in 1891.[17]

The routine into which the troops settled consisted of rotation between the front lines and the rear on forty-eight hour cycles. Digging and guarding were the primary duties at the front. Just digging was the primary duty at the rear and the soldiers worked continuously to improve their fortifications. "Our brigade commenced energetically at this work and soon had the salient an impregnable fortress," bragged Reid. The men also applied their picks and shovels to other components of the defense network, including mortar batteries, covered ways, and rifle pits.[18]

Covered ways were excavations that protected men moving about between lines of trenches, both sides having laid miles of secondary trench lines. Such ways also ran between the main earthworks and rifle pits used by soldiers serving on picket duty in the no-man's-land beyond the works. The covered ways zigzagged across their route so as never to run perpendicular to the enemy's works and thus denying enemy riflemen a direct line of fire against men moving through the ways. Reid helpfully described the pattern as "somewhat like the tacking of a sailing vessel." Even after this precaution these excavated passages were vulnerable at the points where they changed direction, so the angles were covered with roofs of logs and earth to protect against enemy fire.[19]

Soldiers took turns serving as pickets, or advanced guards. Stationed 250 to 300 feet beyond the main earthworks, the pickets sheltered in rifle pits spaced about fifty feet apart. These outposts were simply square holes dug into the ground with the excavated dirt piled up toward the enemy in a protective berm, often with sandbags placed on top of the berm for extra security. A typical pit could hold six men. In front of Hare's Hill the line of pits formed a semicircle, conforming to the base of the hill. Most of the rifle pits were in place before the 115th arrived at Hare's Hill, so the New Yorkers worked at constructing covered ways connecting the pits with the main works, thereby protecting their movement as they scampered out to the pits for picket duty every two days. With alert enemy sharpshooters always on duty during the day, this work could only proceed at night. "It's death to expose oneself even for one moment," noted DeGraff.[20]

Officers enjoyed the privilege of building bombproofs for their quarters. These were constructed in the rear of the trenches by digging a square hole and covering it with heavy timbers topped by a layer of two to three feet of soil. When DeGraff wrote his sister describing the bombproofs he told a story about the night following their completion. A heavy rain fell after the officers retired that night and by midnight most of them had been driven out of their new warrens by deepening pools of water. DeGraff had fortunately situated himself on a high spot on the floor of his bombproof and slept through the night, waking with only his feet under water. The officers enjoyed a laugh over the incident.[21]

One night Company D and a company from another regiment drew the assignment of protecting a party of soldiers detailed to construct some new works out in the no-man's-land between the lines. The task brought them very near the enemy and, worse, placed them within the loathsome field of decaying corpses. This night duty so near the enemy and among the foul bodies of dead compatriots unnerved some of the men. Lieutenant DeGraff, who outranked all others in the party and thus commanded it, recalled that "the men were almost panic stricken, causing me the difficulty to establish them on the line as required." But DeGraff persevered and got his men formed into a picket line. Moving from one end of his line toward the other, he passed a soldier who appeared to be asleep. Grasping the man by the shoulder, he "was shocked to find it was one of the slain men." Recoiling and stumbling in the dark, he "stepped on the stomach of another corpse, startled at [the] report of escaping gas from his swollen and distorted body."

DeGraff diverted some of the work party from the trench excavation and had them throw a layer of dirt over the bodies. "It proved to be a poor job," he admitted, "but was best could be done under the circumstances." As day broke DeGraff's pickets and the work party took shelter in the newly constructed rifle pits. Rebel batteries began shelling them when dawn revealed the new construction and Union gunners responded in kind from within their lines. Although Lieutenant DeGraff had performed his duty manfully in an appallingly horrid situation the experience caught up with him. "Owing to the unusual and nerve racking labor of the night I found myself quite shaken up and at 10 a.m. felt sick. Had high fever all day." He got permission to return to camp where a good rest restored his composure.[22]

Vidette duty took men out beyond the rifle pits where they served as the army's early warning system, their job to stay alert and sound an alarm should the enemy approach. This assignment fell one evening to Private Edwin Rhodes of Company C. The cloudy night allowed only a faint glow of moonlight as Rhodes crept out to locate the man he was to relieve. Finding him apparently asleep he bent and whispered, "Come, my man, I am to relieve you." The fellow failed to stir so Rhodes, angry at the thought of a soldier asleep at an important post, pressed his foot into the prone man's shoulder to awaken him. To Rhodes's horror his boot sank into the man's flesh and the stench that arose from the putrefying body made it quite clear that this man was beyond waking.[23]

Work parties from the 115th took on the job of burying such fallen comrades. These parties split into two squads, one assigned to bury the dead, the other armed with rifles to protect the burial detail. They dug shallow trenches beside the slain, rolled in the bodies, and covered them with a shallow layer of dirt. "A few inches of earth constituted the last rites," wrote John Reardon. "Not a drum was heard nor a funeral note."[24]

The longer the thousands of men of the two armies remained in their trenches, the filthier their earthen homes became. After several weeks of such existence pure squalor prevailed. On July 15 Captain Kneeskern assured a friend at home that "if you could see the Boys you wood see a lot of dirty Raget lousy worn out Souldiers." Lice drew the chief complaints. "The most filthy of all pests that annoy a soldier are body-lice or gray-backs, commonly termed. The trenches were literally alive with them," wrote James Reid. During their periods at the rear the troops attempted to wash these tiny beasts out of their clothing, "but the banks of the little streams where we did our laundry work rivaled the trenches as abiding ground of the obnoxious pest."[25]

Other creatures shared the soldiers' quarters as well. Dr. Macfarlane constructed a den for himself by digging a hole six feet deep and four feet wide in the side of a ravine. He made it as comfortable as possible by stringing together and hanging a twine hammock for his bed. The surgeon found his warren to be good protection against enemy shells, but admitted that "sometimes I had to dispute the possession of my home with the snakes, toads, and lizards. They seemed to enjoy its cool, quiet shade."[26]

Dry weather prevailed around Petersburg, but when it did rain the soldiers got wet and stayed wet. Sergeant Reardon recorded one particularly uncomfortable night the regiment spent at the front:

> Night has been rainy and cold. We are compelled to take it without protection as we cannot have tents up. Water is four inches deep in the trenches where we are lying on the ground. In this situation we find ourselves 1:00 a.m., soaked, wet and cold. We move around to keep warm for fear of colds.

Despite the lice, mud, and other travails, Reid reported that "notwithstanding all the unfavorable conditions that beset us the health of the regiment continued fairly good."[27]

Of course dangers more menacing than insects, reptiles, and the elements attended life in the trenches. Remembered Corporal Reid, "Musket firing was incessantly carried on by the enemy with daily losses in killed and wounded that made a frightful aggregation before we left the lines." That aggregation would number ten dead, 25 wounded, and two missing from the 115th during their weeks in the siege lines. "'Tis death to stick your head above the work," DeGraff informed his mother and sister. He grew upset by men who, in spite of the well-known hazards, recklessly ventured into danger. He related the story of one of the regiment's cooks who, having delivered a meal to soldiers in the trench, foolishly peeked over the works for a look at the enemy, only to be instantly shot dead by a rebel sharpshooter. "Nobody pities him, 'tis his own fault," concluded an exasperated DeGraff. On that same day two men in DeGraff's Company D, Bill Nutt and John Hansow, were wounded by stray bullets.[28]

Just a few days after the killing of the cook, another of DeGraff's men brought tragedy upon himself by his own imprudence. Private William Glover hankered for a smoke and called out from his rifle pit to ask a friend in the next pit to throw him some tobacco. The friend's toss fell short and the pouch landed some twenty feet from Glover. DeGraff estimated that Glover looked out at that pouch and longed for his smoke for a full hour before he decided to risk jumping out after it. When he finally made his rush toward the seductive tobacco, a quick and watchful rebel sharpshooter fired a bullet that shattered Glover's left thighbone and lodged in his knee. Glover, who five months earlier had been wounded at Olustee and crawled off the field on hands and knees, scrambled back to the pit. He lay in pain all day, his mates unable to take him back into the lines until darkness brought greater safety. They recalled that Glover remained cheerful despite his suffering. Doctors amputated his leg but he died eighteen days later.[29]

At that time Lieutenant DeGraff commanded Company D in place of the absent Captain Sidney Lingenfelter. Lingenfelter earned distinction as one of the only men for whom DeGraff voiced distaste. DeGraff identified him as a principal conspirator in the anti–Sammons cabal and called him the greatest coward in the regiment. Lingenfelter left Petersburg for home on June 29, ostensibly due to illness. DeGraff had another explanation: "Our weak kneed Captain Lingenfelter, who was overcome with fright and heat, which we charitably called sunstroke, has gone home on leave to recuperate." On July 20 DeGraff received a letter from Lingenfelter advising that while en route back to the regiment the captain had again taken ill and would be delayed at the hospital at Fortress Monroe. DeGraff doubted Lingenfelter's excuse and added a cynical postscript: "Poor fellow must have heard a cannon and had another sunstroke."[30]

Several soldiers manned each rifle pit when their company served its turn on picket duty. Orders required that at least one man at each post be on constant watch through a loophole. Enemy riflemen readily sent pinpoint shots into these apertures, and peering through one for more than an instant could be fatal. At least three soldiers from the 115th met death in this way. One such misfortune took place in DeGraff's company. The lieutenant took a broad interpretation of the standing orders and advised his men not to look steadily through the loopholes but to jump and look then duck back down again. A passing line officer took note of this one day and insisted that the vigil must be continuous. "A few minutes later the watch was instantly killed by a Reble bullet which passed through the look hole," a rueful DeGraff reported. "He was one of [the] best and finest young men. I then returned to my former plan and we had no more fatalities."[31]

A similar fate befell Albert Dunning of Company C, the twenty-two-year old private remembered for pitching rebel prisoners over their own works at Cold Harbor. Following a quiet night on picket, some cooks delivered morning coffee to rifle pits which they could safely access through covered ways. Dunning and some of his mates lay in a neighboring pit that did not enjoy such secure access. "If you want some coffee, come and get it," the cooks called to them, never expecting any fool to hazard a try. Private Dunning took this call as a challenge to his manhood and dashed from one pit to the other. He filled his canteens with precious coffee and again made the 150 foot dash, surprisingly unmolested. Moments later however the impetuous Dunning ventured too near a loophole and a Confederate marksman sent a fatal ball into his forehead. Comrades covered the dead boy with a blanket and spent a morose day on picket with his corpse before the safety of darkness allowed stretcher bearers to haul away the remains.

Chaplain Clemens presided at the burial of the popular Dunning that same night. "I can assure you it was the most solemn scene I ever beheld," lamented Captain McKittrick, who called Dunning "one of the best soldiers in the regiment, brave as a lion." The captain faced the duty of forwarding the grim tidings to Dunning's family. "But what will his poor mother say when she hears the sad news?" McKittrick asked in a letter he wrote to his own family. "I will have to write her today, and oh, how I dread it, for what consolation can I offer her? To be sure, I can say he died for his country, but I know that will be but little to offer, for her whole affections were centered on him, her only boy."[32]

Where the line of earthworks receded from the salient on Hare's Hill the increasing distance from the enemy line afforded a bit of added security, but one still needed to use caution. Part of the 115th stood watch in this sector one day when two men of the 13th Indiana came walking along. The New York boys warned them against exposing themselves to rebel fire, "but they seemed to take pride in such recklessness." A single rebel bullet soon tore through a lower leg of each man. As one Hoosier began limping, his still feisty companion bellowed, "Don't limp, you damned fool, and let that rebel son of a bitch know he winged you." Reaching cover, the men crouched behind the works and examined their wounds. Though the bullet had struck bone on one man, resulting afterwards in amputation, the wounded Hoosiers stayed cheerful and congratulated one another on the prospect of a furlough. The 115th would come to know the 13th Indiana well in coming months. Archibald McGlachlin later wrote that "for downright, tenacious, unadulterated bulldog fighting, the 13th Ind. had no superior in the army."[33]

Rank provided no immunity from rebel bullets, as Major General John Turner learned one morning. DeGraff was on duty in the main works when he saw Turner walking toward him for a look around. The soldiers studied their earthworks well and knew the vulnerable points to avoid. As Turner approached DeGraff's position in the works he stepped through a row of bushes and emerged at a point known to the men as a hot spot. DeGraff wanted to shout a caution but his anxiety about the safety of his division commander could not overcome his reluctance to address an officer of such lofty station. Two minie balls promptly whizzed past Turner, giving him all the warning he needed. The general quickly retreated and returned to his tent.[34]

Sergeant Reardon drew the task of filling out the periodic muster rolls for his company. Seeking a quiet place to carry out his clerical duty, he spent two days in a small house behind the lines. He shared his shelter with brothers Francis and Chauncy Snyder, both of Company D. Owing to their ages (forty-six and forty-seven) the Snyder brothers escaped much of the harder duty that befell the 115th, and they had settled themselves comfortably into the house. As a frontline soldier Reardon was greatly amused when a rebel shell sliced through the chimney and gable end of their abode, trashing the place and shattering the Snyders' notions of security. "Well," chuckled Reardon, "I have never seen two more forlorn looking specimens of humanity during my service than the old men."[35]

As mentioned earlier, Chauncy Snyder's son, Chauncy, Jr., died of fever at Camp Douglas in November 1862. Another son, Alfred, had turned seventeen and joined the 115th in April 1864. One afternoon Alfred and thirty other men of the regiment formed a work detail constructing a mortar emplacement. Bullets began to whistle among the laborers. "Suddenly," James Clark wrote, "I heard a shout which chilled my blood." He turned to see young Alfred with a wound in his side "from which the blood poured in a great crimson stream." Snyder called farewell to his friends, who sprang to his side as he began to fall and lowered him gently to the ground. A summons went to the elder Snyder, but Alfred died before his father reached him. On approaching his fallen son, "the old man burst into tears and sobbed as though his heart would break."[36]

Describing the Fourth of July 1864, Nicholas DeGraff wrote: "Independence Day. Our disloyal brothers across our front are observing it by an all night fusillade of muskets and artillery." The federals responded at sunrise when "the national colors of the entire Union army were planted on our breastworks, where they floated in all their glory in full view of the enemy." The northerners also provided some fireworks of their own, hurling shells into Petersburg's streets at the rate of one a minute.[37]

A greater celebration followed the next day courtesy of a shipment of goods from the U.S. Sanitary Commission. The Commission, an organization formed by civilian volunteers, provided Union soldiers, particularly convalescents, with comforts unavailable through the military. Delicacies such as condensed milk, tea, and canned meats and vegetables, plus prized items like stationery, tobacco, and soap delighted the soldiers. Deliveries continued regularly, including on July 7 when each man in the 115th received a heartily relished drink of lemonade. "The Sanitary Commission is proving a great blessing to the army," wrote a grateful DeGraff. "God bless the givers."[38]

Another arrival cheered the regiment in early July—the surprise return of Philip Alback of Company C, missing since Olustee. Alback had strayed from the Union columns retreating from the battle and been captured by the enemy. While still in Florida he escaped from his captors, but although befriended and aided by courageous blacks, he was again collared by the Confederates and consigned to Andersonville. En route to the infamous Georgia prison camp, Private Alback jumped from a train in another attempt at freedom but was once more tracked down. After several weeks at Andersonville the persistent Alback bolted from a wood-gathering detail outside the compound, then traveled stealthily northward for three weeks before finding his way to General William T. Sherman's Union army, then fighting its way from Chattanooga to Atlanta. After reuniting with his regiment in Virginia, Alback described his Andersonville experience to his comrades and declared he would prefer a bayonet through his chest to a second imprisonment.[39]

James Reid later recounted an experience that came vividly to mind whenever he looked back on the 115th's time at Petersburg. It occurred on a moonlit night when the twenty-year old Corporal Reid led five privates out to the rifle pits for picket duty. The enemy spotted their movement toward the pits and, as Reid told it, "were especially lavish with their compliments and we, in turn, were kept busy dodging, squatting, and rolling here and there on the ground" to avoid their bullets. All made it safely to the pit. Reid, the youngest soldier in the party, commanded the detail though none of the privates hailed from his own company. He needed one man to go on to a smaller pit 50 feet farther in front for vidette duty. Calling for a volunteer and getting none, Reid turned and addressed himself to the nearest man and asked if he would go.

"I am moon-blind," replied the man, explaining his refusal to climb out of the rifle pit and again expose himself to rebel muskets.

"Moon-blind?" said Reid. "What is the nature of such blindness?"

"Caused by the moon shining in my face while sleeping, and now I can't see by moonlight."

"Will you go?" asked Reid, turning to a second man.

"I am moon-blind," replied number two.

"Is th-a-a-t s-o-o?" responded the corporal, and he turned to the third man and asked, "Well, how is it with you?"

"I am also moon-blind," replied number three, as did numbers four and five.

Reid had meanwhile drawn his bayonet and in the bitterest voice he could muster dressed down his reluctant party: "I have heard of all other kinds of beats, but this is the first time I have had the pleasure of the company of five full-grown moon-blind beats, and I am proud that neither of you disgraces the company I belong to." Reid then insisted that not one, but two of the reluctant privates must go out as videttes, and told all five he would put them on record for refusing orders. To this the first man, the original moon-blind soldier, responded, "I suppose I am the only moon-blind man in the lot, but I'll go for one." Reid excused him and ordered the second and third men to perform the detail and out they went.

After spending that night and the next day on picket with them Corporal Reid judged the five moon-blind beats to be good soldiers, and he never followed through with his threat to put them on report. He later concluded that they had merely been testing a younger man's mettle, and that the younger man had proven his stuff.[40]

Nearly two years earlier on Maryland Heights, Captain William Smith of Company K earned the distinction of becoming the first officer of the 115th to be wounded. In mid–July 1864 he became the second officer of the regiment charged with drunkenness on duty. Lieutenant Colonel William Coan of the 48th New York, who had succeeded Colonel Barton as brigade commander, accused Smith of intoxication, neglect of duty, and disobedience of orders when Smith, then serving as brigade officer of the day, failed to get the brigade's pickets out to their stations on time. A court-martial convened within several days, the trial taking place in a tent with its sides rolled up for relief from the Virginia heat.

The tent was located near the quarters of Smith's friend Dr. Macfarlane, who described Smith as one of the bravest men in the regiment. Macfarlane acknowledged that Smith disobeyed orders, but said that Smith did so to protect his men from a reckless movement. Dr. Macfarlane remembered that the trial was going badly for Smith when a rebel cannonball came to his rescue by striking a tent pole and leveling the tent. After that, according to the surgeon, "the court adjourned precipitately and fled to cover, while the Captain did not stir from his cracker box and laughed at his flying accusers." In contradiction to Macfarlane's recollection, in fact Smith was cashiered by the court-martial and dismissed from the service August 19, 1864. However his dismissal was later revoked and the governor of New York recommissioned him as captain in the 115th in March 1865.[41]

Colonel Sammons rejoined his regiment in the Petersburg siege lines on July 18, recuperated from the wounds he suffered in Florida five months earlier. Shortly after his sundown arrival he took time to write and let his family know that he had safely reached his destination. He recounted the final leg of his journey, the eight miles between City Point and the camp of the 115th. "The whole distance is filled up with troops," he wrote. "The movement of necessary troops, transportation wagons, ambulances, orderlies, &c. creates one vast cloud of dust which is easily discernible many miles distant." He described the situation around Petersburg and the death of Private John Hogan of Company A, recently killed by a sharpshooter, and concluded with an admonition that his two daughters must write frequently, "as I shall no doubt feel very lonely here."[42]

Sammons may have anticipated loneliness because of the controversy that accompanied his return. Due to the dismissal of Colonel Barton, Sammons now outranked all other officers in the brigade. Under prevailing army protocol this gave him command of the brigade. General Turner however preferred that control of the brigade remain in the hands of Lieutenant Colonel Coan of the 48th New York. As a result Turner left Sammons in limbo for ten days instead of reinstating him at the head of the 115th. The colonel's subsequent letters home offer no clues whether or not he aspired to lead the brigade or felt at all perturbed by Turner's failure to entrust him with the position. His status during this time puzzled his men, one of whom wrote, "for some cause unknown to us common mortals he did not at once take command of the regiment."[43]

Turner resolved the issue by swapping the 115th New York and the 97th Pennsylvania between two of the brigades within his division. The 97th moved to Coan's Brigade and the 115th joined the 4th New Hampshire, 9th Maine, 13th Indiana, and 169th New York in a brigade commanded by Colonel Louis Bell of the 4th New Hampshire, whose commission was senior to Sammons's.[44]

While Sammons's return created one command problem, it resolved a second. Since late May Lieutenant Colonel Nathan Johnson had remained under arrest while Major Ezra Walrath led the 115th. Johnson's release during that period would have again placed him at the head of the regiment, an outcome likely viewed as undesirable by the higher authorities. With Colonel Sammons's return, Johnson could be released to assume a place as the 115th's second-in-command. Johnson's liberation, Sammons's reinstatement, and the 115th's assignment to Bell's Brigade all took place simultaneously on July 28 although Johnson did not immediately rejoin the regiment.

That night the regiment moved to the left to join its new brigade which held a position in the lines just south of Hare's Hill. The 115th once again sported a full complement of officers, but the apparent stability proved short-lived. Rebel bullets would shatter the arrangement exactly two days later.[45]

Beginning in early July a story circulated among the troops that a mine was being dug to reach under the Confederate lines and then to be filled with gunpowder and detonated. As the month passed with no such marvelous occurrence, the rumors lost all credibility, written off as so much camp gossip. Late in July however the reports proved accurate. The scheme had been hatched by Colonel Henry Pleasants of the 48th Pennsylvania Infantry within a week of the stabilization of the siege lines around Petersburg. Pleasants had enjoyed a successful career as a mining engineer in the Pennsylvania coal fields prior to the war, and many coal miners served in the ranks of his regiment. He noted a location where only 100 yards separated Union and Confederate lines and there was a small ravine just behind the Union works that could conceal a mine entrance. He believed he and his men could construct a tunnel from that point to the rebel works and submitted his plan to his chain of command for approval.[46]

Digging actually began on June 25 and the main shaft, 510 feet long, was finished by July 17. The Pennsylvanians then extended side galleries left and right from the main tunnel directly under the Confederate earthworks and filled them with four tons of powder. The work was completed and ready for detonation by July 28.[47]

As work on the mine progressed, the numerous skeptics among federal commanders became more convinced of its feasibility. They readied a plan to assault and take Petersburg using the breach in the rebel works expected to be created by the mine explosion. Following the detonation federal artillery would pound the presumably surprised and discouraged rebels around the blast site. Infantry of the Ninth Corps, to which Pleasants' 48th Pennsylvania belonged, would pour through the leveled rebel fortifications, with some units then moving left and some right to roll up the Confederate lines, and others advancing straight ahead into Petersburg. Additional units would back up the Ninth Corps advance. To reduce the number of troops General Lee could rally to resist the main attack at the mine, General Grant also sent forces north of the James on a feint toward Richmond.[48]

On July 29 Colonel Pleasants received orders to fire the mine at 3:30 a.m. the next morning. That day, in addition to the usual picket duty, the soldiers of the 115th New York kept busy wielding picks and shovels laboring on a mortar battery, building more bombproofs, and adding traverses to the earthworks. Orders reached them in the late afternoon to turn in their tools and be ready to march that evening. Troops of the Second Corps took over the New Yorkers' place in the lines near 10:00 p.m., and the 115th, together with all the troops of Turner's Division, marched a couple of miles to their south and filed into line with the Ninth Corps about midnight.[49]

Word about the mine and the nature of their assignment quickly passed among the men. Despite the unique plan and the prospect of battle, the veteran soldiers lay down and went to sleep. "They were all sleeping soundly, sleeping as if they did not know that at daybreak they were to charge the enemy and that for many of them it was to be their last sleep on earth," recalled Surgeon Macfarlane. "The men had become used to the near presence of death." An acquaintance of Macfarlane, a fellow surgeon, joined him and they discussed the rumors afloat about a tunnel stretching to the enemy line and the planned explosion and assault. "We ridiculed the idea," Macfarlane remembered, "and he asked me if ever I heard anything so absurd."[50]

The men of the 115th were aroused at 3:00 a.m., anticipating the scheduled 3:30 detonation. They drank coffee and snacked on whatever fare they had hauled with them in their haversacks. "Everything was ready and waiting in hushed suspense." Yet 3:30 passed, and 4:00, and 4:30, and things remained hushed. Two brave Pennsylvanians re-entered the mine to investigate, discovering that all three of the fuses that were to touch off the huge explosion had gone out at a splice. Outside, commanders and men alike grew increasingly anxious at the delay, fearing that encroaching daylight would reveal the massed troops to the rebels. The Pennsylvania miners relit the fuses and this time the spark traced the fuses all the way to the powder. In moments came a sight that none would ever forget.[51]

The 115th's line rested on a slight elevation and by this time enough daylight had gathered to reveal to their view the "doomed fort." Finally, shortly before 5:00 a.m., the ground began to shake and the mine exploded. "Then came the heavy smothered sound of the explosion and the tremendous upheaval of that vast amount of earth and debris," recalled James Reid. Another onlooker from the 115th wrote, "It was grand and terrific. Oh, the sight begs description. The earth was thrown into the air a distance of 150 feet. Pieces of artillery and human beings were intermingled with huge sticks of timber and boulders of clay as large as a tent. Down they came, many of the men going into the earth and were buried alive." Lieutenant James Clark waxed more dramatic in his description: "The earth quakes! The very heavens above us are obscured from view. A dense, black column of smoke arises; the conflict has opened. A rebel fort has been blown in pieces, a regiment of traitors hurried into eternity in a moment's time." The unprecedented blast had the exact effect anticipated. It blew open a crater 200 feet wide and 25 feet deep, entombing nearly 300 unfortunate South Carolinians and clearing the enemy off several hundred yards of their lines.[52]

"Almost simultaneously with the explosion the artillery opened," recorded Reid. DeGraff recalled the big guns bellowing "with a tremendous shrieking of shells sent after the panic stricken Rebles." Fifty-four mortars and 110 cannon spewed lead on the rebels, attempting to saturate two miles of their lines adjacent to the crater. Wrote Clark, "Union cannon hail shell and grape into the ranks of the foe who are rushing in wild consternation from their works. What a fearful thunder."[53]

Within minutes of the eruption of the mine and the accompanying barrage of artillery, Ninth Corps forces poured out of their covered ways and dashed uncontested into the crater. "We hear a cheer," recounted Clark. "Thank God it is not the low, savage howl of the rebels, but the full, honest, hearty cheer of the Union boys; and it tells us they are making a charge." The mine explosion had wreaked considerable havoc in the Confederate works; the crashing artillery had augmented its effects, and now thousands of blue clad men sprang forward as planned. "Everything seemed to be going in our favor," sensed DeGraff. A wave of optimism flooded the regiment amid reports of success by the Ninth Corps and speculation that the 115th and Bell's Brigade would not be needed to join the fight. "Never before was I so elated," Dr. Macfarlane remembered, "for I felt sure Petersburg would be ours before night and the war would come to an end."[54]

But such optimism was short-lived. Except for the momentary delay with the fuses, the scheme for constructing and detonating the mine had succeeded beyond most expectations. The artillery had opened as per plan and the Ninth Corps advanced on cue, but this would prove the high point of the Union effort. As the infantry joined the fray, federal fortunes soured rapidly. Instead of using the crater as an avenue for further advance as called for in the grand design, the infantrymen paused in wonderment and confusion and dissolved into rescue parties assisting half-buried Confederates. Only small groups climbed to the lip of the crater, stopping there to dig in.[55]

Later inquiry revealed a series of poor judgments that left the Ninth Corps troops unsure of their mission as they entered the maelstrom of the crater. Ninth Corps commander Ambrose Burnside had, while work on the tunnel proceeded, selected and trained a newly recruited division of black troops to assume the lead role in the assault. At the last moment on the day before the attack, Grant and Meade instructed Burnside that he should use veteran white troops to spearhead the action. A frustrated Burnside then resorted to drawing lots to choose which of his white divisions should assume that dubious honor. Fate bestowed the short straw on a division led by a besotted general who spent the battle drinking in a bombproof. In the actual assault officers leading brigades, regiments, and companies into the crater had no firm grasp of their assignments and no field commander to lead them. One captain later recounted that every officer in the crater, from colonels to second lieutenants, was barking orders of some kind, usually contradictory.[56]

The crowded bedlam at the crater made it difficult for additional troops to move in as scheduled. Meanwhile increasing numbers of Confederates rallied and moved to the threatened sector. These rebels as well as quick reacting batteries of their artillery, subjected Yankees around the crater to deadly crossfire of spiraling volume. As more northerners including the 115th New York poured across the lines, they met both obstructing masses of their own troops and ever increasing resistance from the enemy.[57]

A short while after the Ninth Corps troops advanced on the crater, General Turner's Tenth Corps Division formed into battle line at the front of the Union works. The 115th held the extreme left of the division line, nearest the crater. For an hour the New Yorkers looked on from this position. Under the smoke of battle they could see the area between them and the crater thickly strewn with dead and wounded compatriots.

They watched as an all black division of Ninth Corps troops attacked the Confederate lines around the crater. These raw Colored Troops were entering battle for the first time. "We watch them eagerly," recalled one of the 115th. "Noble fellows! Grandly they cross the field." Under heavy fire some bogged down near the crater while others drew particular attention among the 115th by moving to the right and seizing a well-defended trench line from some stubborn rebels.[58]

Meanwhile General Turner moved forward for a personal reconnaissance of the ongoing battle. Advancing to the crater, he saw Union troops huddled in confused masses within the crater or very near it. Turner was the only Union division commander to see the inside of the fateful crater that day. Indeed, the want of such leadership on a broader scale helped turn the entire episode into one of the North's grandest debacles of the Civil War.[59]

General Turner returned to his command and ordered Colonel Bell to lead his brigade to the rebel line just taken by the black units. Commands of "Forward, hundred and fifteenth!" soon rang along the line. Color Sergeant Charles Fellows leaped out of the trench, then turned and urged his mates to follow. He waved his banner and "dashed toward the rebel works through a fearful storm of grape and canister." The regiment followed in an energetic rush giving the Union yell. Their advance brought them past the crater and up toward the line held by the black troops. One of the 115th, who identified himself only as "N" in a letter he sent to the newspaper in his Mohawk Valley hometown, described the scene:

Contemporary sketch of the Union advance at the Crater, July 30, 1864 (*Battles and Leaders*).

We were soon ordered to advance, and we did so, passing the demolished fortification on [our] left and over some of its debris, under the most galling and murderous charges of grape and canister that the oldest veteran ever saw. The ground in front of us was plowed up on almost every foot of it, and as the grape and canister struck it, the appearance put one in mind of a body of water when it rains, the drops striking and rising up little pyramids on the surface. How we ever passed through that terrible storm without being annihilated it is impossible to say, but we did.

The 115th came up on the near side of the trench captured and held by the Colored Troops. There they halted and lay down to protect themselves from the shower of lead passing overhead."[60]

The Ninth Corps soldiers crouched within the captured rebel trench, and the 115th New York lay behind it. The enemy kept it hot for all of them with a continuous fire of artillery and musketry. Luckily the rebel cannons stood on an elevation higher than that held by the New Yorkers and their black comrades, and the cannon muzzles could not be depressed sufficiently to fire into the mass of Union attackers. Some Confederates attempted to shovel down the top of their own breastwork to enable them to lower their gun barrels, but these enterprising southerners were stopped by well-directed rifle shots from the federals. The rebel artillery continued to fire but "succeeded only in a further mutilization of the dead that lay in great numbers near the crater."[61]

Rebel riflemen added their persistent fire to that of the big guns. Private Harry Thorne of Company C recalled the perils of the position the 115th had taken: "If we showed our heads over the works there was great danger of getting a ramrod or bullet through it, and perhaps

Henry C. (Harry) Thorne enlisted at Edinburgh in Saratoga County and remained uninjured, except for sunstroke, through three years as a private in Company C (Lance Ingmire Collection).

both, as the rebs were not particular if they fired one or both." Thorne lay next to Private Smith Harlow, who could not resist taking frequent peeks over the works, drawing enemy fire to the great discomfiture of Thorne and others nearby. Thorne warned Harlow, "If you don't keep your head out of sight you will get hit plum in the mouth." In short order "nearly the whole brigade were startled by the tremendous howl of Smith Harlow." The incautious private had indeed been shot in the jaw. Others wounded in this line included Benjamin Thackrah, in the thigh, and Almon Stone in the neck. All three survived.[62]

DeGraff noted the time as 9:45 a.m. when the black troops charged out of their captured earthworks to attack the next line of rebels. "They started forward in good shape with loud cheers," he remembered. The boys of the 115th quickly jumped into the shelter of the vacated trench. The Ninth Corps men "had not gone far before they wavered, then halted." They had collided with a brigade of Virginians who, shortly after the mine blast, had rushed toward the sound of battle. These hard charging Confederate veterans were infuriated to find themselves facing black soldiers and, with a chorus of rebel yells, routed them and sent them fleeing back toward the trench they had left shortly before.[63]

"Then began a scene such as I never wish to witness again," wrote DeGraff. "All the Negroes in front of us got panic struck and came back into our lines like a mighty torrent." "The Negroes immediately turned and fled, reaching our lines in the utmost disorder and fright, tumbling, rolling, and falling over the walls upon our men," recorded N. As they hurled themselves among Bell's Brigade, the bayonets of the panicked men wounded some of the soldiers massed in the trench. Cooler heads vainly tried to restore order. "Our officers, in conjunction with the officers of the colored troops, shouted, threatened, pushed back, kicked, struck with their swords, drew their pistols, and exhausted every imaginable effort to stay the overwhelming tide of blackness as it surged on and over us, followed by a stronger tide of furious rebels, but failed."[64]

All organization broke down as the terror-stricken Ninth Corps troops passed into and through the works held by Bell's Brigade. According to Lieutenant DeGraff, "they literally ran us down [and] it would be impossible to form our broken line, after the Negroes had gone, in time to meet the advancing Rebles." The black men's fear soon spread among their white comrades. As the enemy continued to pour enfilading fire from right and left into the trench and the oncoming Virginians rushed ever nearer, white troops began to follow black in a headlong withdrawal. "In less time than it takes to tell it, our line was broken and a stampede to the rear began," admitted Reid. "I ran as fast as my legs would carry me," DeGraff confessed. "When once I did get started to go back, every Reg't was mixed up Niggars and whites all flying as if for their lives. The bullets flew thick as hail around me. Men were getting hit on every side of me."[65]

Not everyone panicked and fled in the pell mell retreat, as several of the 115th made sure to point out. A number of the regiment stayed on to face the oncoming Virginians, including Colonel Sammons as well as Sergeant Fellows and the regiment's other flag bearers. Southerners soon passed beyond the left flank of the 115th near the crater, but Fellows defiantly kept his standard planted on the captured works until Confederates began to reach for it and orders came to fall back.[66]

One of the rebels took deliberate aim at Colonel Sammons and shot him in the hip. "It is almost a miracle that he was not killed, as the rebel was not more than eight feet from him when he fired," wrote one of Sammons's men. "Had the aim been surer one of the bravest officers in the service of our country would have fallen to rise no more." The colonel made it back to the Union lines with his men but not before twice being felled by the percussion of rebel shells. Sammons, having resumed command of his regiment just two days earlier, entered battle for the second time and suffered his second gunshot wound. The painful hip injury ended his military career, and Lieutenant Colonel Johnson, released from arrest just two days earlier, again assumed command of the 115th.[67]

"The whole line now fell back to our own front line and the day was lost," lamented DeGraff. The rebels did not pursue beyond their recaptured line and the small role of the 115th New York in the Battle of the Crater came to a close. The regiment had suffered twenty-five casualties: four dead, sixteen wounded, and five missing.[68]

"After the repulse the scene inside of our lines was indescribable," remembered DeGraff. "Stragglers everywhere, dead and wounded everywhere ... officers rampant everywhere rallying their men." As the tumult sorted out, cooks from the 115th managed to bring kettles of coffee to their tired comrades. One grateful soldier later stated that he forgot many details of his experiences that day, "but the opportune arrival of that coffee carries a lasting remembrance." Another drank his coffee and ate rations from his haversack amidst the bodies of several men, one of whom had been disemboweled by a shell. This man too never forgot that coffee break, calling it "the most sickening and horrible luncheon I ever participated in."[69]

By early afternoon the Confederates had reclaimed all of their breached defenses, including the ruined works at the crater. Bell's Brigade remained in wary readiness on the Union front for three more hours then went to the rear, with the exception of five "much incensed" companies of the 115th New York who remained on duty another twenty-four hours before being relieved.[70]

James Reid called the disorderly flight from the captured works near the crater "a terrible humiliation on our brigade." He blamed the panic in their sector on the retreating black soldiers, as did all of his comrades in the 115th, as well as Colonel Bell and General Turner in their official reports. It is true that on this day the raw Colored Troops had fled in precipitate panic, but the recriminations brought down upon them were magnified because of their race. Everything the blacks did came under special scrutiny, and any failures were instinctively associated with their being black. Such portrayals, of course, present an uneven picture. The history of the Civil War is replete with instances of shameful panic and epic gallantry among troops of both races.[71]

The soldiers placed the overall blame for the day's lost battle—the Crater Tragedy as Corporal Reid termed it—squarely on the Union high command where it belonged. "The affair was badly managed," wrote an officer of the regiment several days afterwards. "There did not appear to be anybody to give orders. It was confusion from beginning to end." Another soldier of the 115th concluded, "Never since the first gun was fired in the present war did a battle open with better promise of success for our army than in this battle. But as if we were always doomed to reverse, we did not make use of the advantage. The men were in high spirits and confident of a grand success, if only led on."[72]

11

Decoying at Deep Bottom
"We were mowed down like grass"

Early on July 31, 1864, the morning following the debacle at the Battle of the Crater, the 115th fell in with thousands of Union troops marching north toward the Appomattox River. "The roads were black with troops as far as the eye could reach and dense clouds of dust swept over the country like a tornado," remembered Lieutenant James Clark. The very hot day followed a stretch of arid weather that left most wells and streams bone-dry and made the march an extreme hardship. Few men could keep up with their companies and many straggled behind. Sunstroke felled scores and attempts to transport the stricken overburdened all available ambulances and wagons. The hazard was real, no mere soldier's dodge—three men died.

The scorched troops reached the Appomattox in the afternoon. "Although the water was the color of mud and as hot as though heated on a stove, yet the soldiers made for it as though struggling for dear life, and hundreds drank down the sickening liquid," recalled Clark. After a frolic in the murky Appomattox, the column re-formed and crossed the river on the Point of Rocks pontoon bridge, arriving at the familiar Bermuda Hundred lines before dark. The return to the campgrounds they had left in June felt almost like a homecoming to the men after their weeks in the Petersburg trenches. "But it seemed strange not to hear the usual picket firing and the stray bullet wizzing here and there, as there has not been an hour for the last 37 days in which we have not been under fire," recorded Nicholas DeGraff.[1]

Northern and southern troops manning the Bermuda Hundred lines maintained an informal truce. The soldiers' cease-fire and the a lack of offensive thrusts by either side kept things quiet. The deadly adversaries sat and talked together at a brook running between the lines and kept up a lively commerce in newspapers, coffee, and tobacco. "For several days the most perfect harmony prevailed between Blue and Grey," declared Clark. Men of the 115th became acquainted with the 3rd Virginia Infantry, a unit of Confederate General George Pickett's seasoned division. One day the Virginians left a sign at the brook that read, "Friends at the spring, enemies in battle." Corporal Reid later wrote, "These sentiments were literally carried out in both particulars. For more than a month on the Petersburg lines we had been under fire continually, creating a frightful casualty list, but now we were fraternizing with a foe equally as hostile—Pickett's veterans of Gettysburg fame."[2]

Given the respite of a few quiet days, the regiment set up a new camp and erected a log chapel for Chaplain Clemens. The peace held for nearly two weeks before marching orders signaled its finish early on August 13 and the 115th packed up and struck its tents. The troops then waited all afternoon and evening before finally moving out at 11:00 p.m. Through the night the column marched down the Bermuda Hundred peninsula, reaching the tip of Jones Neck on the James River at daybreak. A pontoon bridge crossed the river from Jones Neck to Deep Bottom on the northern shore where Union forces held a few acres of ground. Richmond stood only ten miles northwest of Deep Bottom, and the Confederate capital's defenders lay entrenched around the federal bridgehead.[3]

The 115th New York was en route to take part in General Grant's second offensive north of the James. The first had occurred as counterpoint to the Union attack at the crater just two weeks earlier. This second push by Grant across the James was prompted by his desire to prevent Lee from reinforcing General Jubal Early in the Shenandoah Valley. Early's command had wreaked havoc by advancing to within sight of Washington, D.C., and burning Chambersburg, Pennsylvania. Grant responded by consolidating an army under General Philip Sheridan and sending it to destroy Early. Lee, in turn, drew men from the stalemate around Richmond and Petersburg to send reinforcements to Early. Grant launched his August 1864 attack across the James to force Lee to return those troops to Richmond or, at minimum, to stop him from sending additional men to the Shenandoah.[4]

The Union offensive was led by General Winfield Scott Hancock with forces consisting of his own Second Corps and the Tenth Corps, now under the command of Major General David B. Birney. Birney replaced Quincy Gillmore after Gillmore's ouster following the failed initial Union attacks on Petersburg in June. The Tenth Corps contingent included two infantry divisions, the first led by Brigadier General Alfred Terry, and the second, to which the 115th belonged, under Brigadier General William Birney, elder brother of the corps commander. Terry's Tenth Corps division marched across the pontoon bridge around midnight and engaged rebel skirmishers at 5:00 a.m. on Friday, August 14. The Second Corps, in a ploy meant to deceive the enemy, marched to City Point then boarded transports and steamed several miles down the James toward the Chesapeake, only to double back and disembark at Deep Bottom.

Seven Confederate brigades, approximately 7,000 men, guarded entrenched lines facing the Deep Bottom bridgehead. Their position ran northward along Bailey's Creek from Deep Bottom to Fussell's Mill and westward from Deep Bottom along Fourmile Creek and New Market Heights. Terry's Tenth Corps division advanced from the pontoon bridge and assailed the rebels along Fourmile Creek. Later in the morning the Second Corps shuffled off the transport ships and moved to Terry's right, engaging the southern lines stretching toward Fussell's Mill.[5]

As this fighting got under way, the 115th and the rest of William Birney's Tenth Corps division crossed the James River. The Deep Bottom pontoon bridge consisted of a series of flat-bottomed thirty-one foot long boats anchored parallel to one another across the river. Planks spanning their gunwales formed a continuous deck from shore to shore. Reid accurately termed it a floating roadway. The men of the regiment could not resist the fun of causing the bridge to sway by marching across in cadence, in spite of officers' entreaties to stop. Once on the northern bank the 115th's brigade moved into position on the left of the Tenth Corps line. About half of the 115th deployed as skirmishers. In midafternoon the 115th was ordered to the right and marched some distance before the order was countermanded and

Pontoon bridge across the James River between Bermuda Hundred and Deep Bottom, used several times by the 115th New York (Massachusetts Commandery, Military Order of the Loyal Legion, U.S. Army Military History Institute).

the New Yorkers returned to their original position. Similar frustrating marches and countermarches would mark the next three excessively hot days.[6]

Assorted federal attacks on August 14—none of which involved the 115th—failed to dislodge the rebels. General Hancock then devised a plan to extract the Tenth Corps from its position on the Union left and march it several miles around behind the entire Second Corps to surprise and envelop the weaker Confederate left flank near Fussell's Mill. The ambitious flanking maneuver was to take place during the night with the assault to take place the next morning, August 15. As a result the 115th roused from slumber at 11:00 p.m. on August 14 and marched into the wooded darkness.[7]

The weary trek continued until 1:30 a.m. "We didn't know where we were, and in fact didn't care, and dropping down were soon asleep," recalled Reid. At 5:00 a.m. a rainstorm wakened Reid for the day. Dr. Macfarlane complained about an interrupted night's sleep, but noted that he had grown accustomed to open air catnaps: "I would wind myself in my blanket and lie down anywhere, almost under my horse's feet. I don't know but I can sleep as soundly in the middle of the road with my canteen for a pillow, as I ever did in the widest and softest of beds."

The march toward the Union right resumed at 8:00 a.m. The sun came out and turned the day hot and sultry and sunstroke felled many, including Private Harry Thorne, who staggered and fell to the ground unconscious before friends could help him. "We all remember the day as one of suffering and exhaustion," recalled a comrade. Seemingly aimless and endless marching compounded the agony. The timetable for the flanking maneuver proved hopelessly optimistic as officers struggled to lead their drained men over rugged and unfamiliar terrain in the searing heat. Much of the day passed before the Tenth Corps got into position. Its assault on the Confederate left was postponed until the morning of August 16.[8]

The soldiers of the Tenth Corps rose and readied for battle at 3:00 a.m. on Tuesday August 16, a day that was to grow even hotter than the previous scorching days. General Terry's four brigades advanced first, leading the way through a dense forest of oak and pine. After driving rebel skirmishers out of one deep ravine, the advancing federals encountered an entrenched rebel line on the opposite crest of a second ravine. The rebels had felled trees for fifty yards in front of their thinly manned works, creating a tangled slashing that slowed the Yankees as they descended into the ravine then climbed the opposite slope toward the southerners. But the blue troops hacked through and routed the outnumbered Confederates from their trenches after hand-to-hand fighting. The triumphant Union troops drove on for several hundred yards, ultimately halted by stiffening Confederate resistance and another steep walled ravine running obliquely northwest from the second ravine.

At the apex of that assault, the troops in the center of the Union line advanced beyond those on their left and right, forming a semicircular salient bulging into the rebel line. Federal units on the left could not advance due to both the sheer terrain and enemy resistance near the confluence of the second ravine and the oblique ravine. On the right, the Union line bent back to anchor on the trenches at the second ravine. The northerners held this salient for thirty minutes. Meanwhile several brigades of Confederate reinforcements converged in response to the emergency. Then with General Lee himself on the field, the southerners advanced and enveloped the salient of Yankees. Pressed in a deadly crossfire, the Union men retreated to the captured rebel works at the second ravine.[9]

As this action took place General William Birney's Tenth Corps division arrived at the first ravine, nearly a half mile behind the captured rebel works at the second ravine. Bell's Brigade of the 13th Indiana, 9th Maine, 4th New Hampshire, and 115th New York led the division.[10] The musketry to their front grew heavy and captured Confederates began streaming through to the rear. One of the prisoners abruptly stopped and called out "Captain Smith!" With outstretched hand he approached Captain Solomon Smith of Company H. The regiment watched as "the captain grasped the extended hand and they shook cordially." The friendly Confederate had been taken captive the previous April by Smith and his volunteer detail at Fort Gates near Palatka, Florida. Since then the Georgian had been exchanged and returned to Confederate service. As the brief conversation ended, the prisoner warned Smith, "Look out, Captain, that is a dangerous place in there."[11]

Due to the absence of Colonel Bell, Colonel Francis Osborn of the 24th Massachusetts commanded the brigade on this day. As Osborn ordered his regiments into battle line he suddenly raised a hand to his neck and reeled in his saddle, struck by a stray bullet from the front. As the senior officer remaining in the brigade, the 115th's Major Walrath assumed command. He immediately sped the brigade toward battle, not even allowing the troops time to shed their knapsacks. As Walrath ordered his men to double quick, word spread that their help was needed up front to hold a captured line of works. "And right gallantly did the 115th respond," bragged DeGraff. "We took the run for about a half mile through dense woods."

The regiment rushed through the forest to the steep second ravine and into the slashing in front of the captured rebel trench line. Several dead Union soldiers stood within the slashing, their lifeless bodies held upright by the webbed foliage. These men were fatalities of the earlier advance by Terry's Division that dislodged the enemy from their works. The 115th passed the standing corpses and worked their way up the slope through the snarled vegetation to the

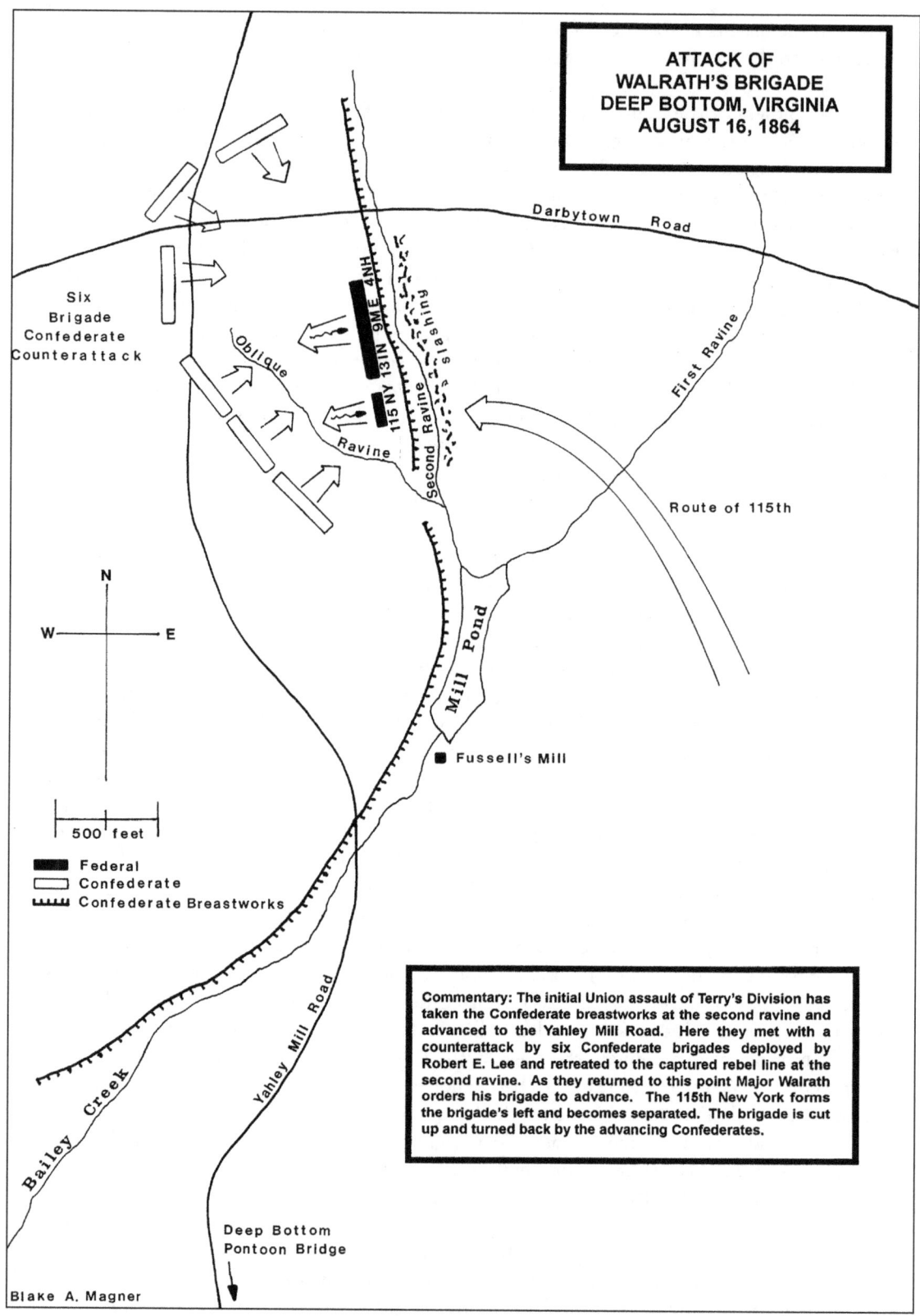

captured works, winded and disorganized from the dash through the thick woods and across the tangled ravine, carrying full packs in the midday heat. As they stopped and reorganized, northern troops retreating from the murderous Confederate counter-offensive streamed toward the same position from the opposite direction. "The troops in front were coming back in confusion and passed through our column in haste to the rear," remembered Reid.[12]

There would be no rest for Walrath's fatigued brigade. Division commander William Birney immediately ordered Walrath to take his lone brigade forward into the maelstrom of enemy troops that had just dispatched the four brigades of Terry's initial assault force. Birney's directive proved costly, the task futile. "We are subjected to another official blunder to our undoing," moaned Lieutenant DeGraff, blasting Birney for sending "troops already exhausted on a fool charge for a forlorn hope." Declared Reid: "It was a reckless order at all events, and appeared to have been made without even a slight investigation of what was to be accomplished."[13]

Nonetheless the 175 men of the 115th sprang over the works with a cheer and charged across a cornfield. "They opened on us as soon as we were in sight, a withering fire from every point. We moved forward on the double quick. Men falling on every side," recalled Sergeant Reardon. The 115th held the left flank of the brigade line and somehow became separated from the other regiments. Confederates fired into the New Yorkers' front and both flanks from the edge of the oblique ravine which curled around the far edge of the cornfield. "Our loss in crossing the field is heavy," continued Reardon. "I think I never saw or heard the firing more rapid or continuous. The bullets passed in and around us like hail. They cut the ground and corn stubble something terrible. The woods seemed to be full of rebels." Seventy-three men of the 115th were shot down, sixteen fatally. "We were mowed down like grass," wrote DeGraff.[14]

The regiment pushed on for several hundred yards, crossing the open field to some trees edging the oblique ravine. Here they halted and the men sidled to the right and over a fence to find shelter in a more thickly wooded area. As at Port Walthall Junction the previous May, the unit suffered many casualties in scaling a fence in an exposed position. "After getting over the fence, the regiment was very much broken up as they reached the woods," recalled Lieutenant Charles L. Clark, commanding Company E. Clark then directed his men to rally on the colors, another unfortunate order since the vicinity of the 115th's flags may have been the hottest spot on the field.

Color Sergeant Peter Keck, recently recovered from a wound suffered while crossing the fence at Port Walthall Junction, had carried the flag across the cornfield without mishap, but just as Clark issued his order, Keck took a ball in the right knee. He found Lieutenant Clark and reported his wound. Clark told him to give the flag to one of the corporals and head for the rear. Keck relinquished the prized banner to Corporal James Himes, but Himes soon suffered a fatal bullet in his chest. Corporal Abbot Musgrove next grabbed the flag, only to fall when a bullet "crashed through his brain." Himes and Musgrove both hailed from Cohoes, New York, and were still teenagers when they enlisted in the 115th.[15]

Facing fire from three sides, the regiment's battle line now bent in a semicircle. The beleaguered men could not hold on. "Our position soon became too hot and without support we must abandon the ground," explained Reardon. The men moved farther right into the trees and headed back to their starting point, the captured rebel trench at the second ravine. The 115th fled the field leaving the ground covered with dead and wounded while the rebels continued "firing and yelling like Indians." Wrote Captain McKittrick of Company C, "I think if we had stayed at the front much longer we would all have been captured." The regiment conducted their retreat in good order, the men careful to note that there was no evidence of panic. They were defeated but not dispirited, some men even voicing their disdain for the rebels by singing *We'll Rally Round the Flag, Boys* as they fell back.[16]

By the time the 115th returned to it, the second ravine had become a very hot place. Rebel forces had recaptured the works on the Union right and commenced an enfilading fire on the New Yorkers from that direction. This fire caused the regiment to retreat briefly from the works and move toward the rear and southward away from the rebel enfilade. But the regiment soon moved forward again into the works only to discover a new threat from the other direction—the left end of the line had also been recaptured by the advancing enemy. "We had not been there but a little while," recorded McKittrick, "when the left of the line gave way." Fortunately just as the 115th began to take fire from rebels pouring into the works on its left, help arrived on its right in the form of the 9th U.S. Colored Troops. "They came in finely and deployed to our right and stopped the fire from that direction," recalled McKittrick, "but we were still getting it from the left. The Rebs advanced their line so that they got a raking fire along our whole line."[17]

Moments later orders came to withdraw. "It was an order easy to give but not so easy to accomplish," continued McKittrick, "for we had to pass through the slashing again, and every man had to get out of it the best way he could, and of course as soon as we started the Rebs opened fire heavier than ever." The survivors worked their way back and the 115th rejoined its brigade at the point they had started from that morning.[18]

In the 115th's fight near Fussell's Mill, part of the battle that history now calls Strawberry Plains or Second Deep Bottom, 42% of the soldiers of the regiment became casualties—16 dead, 35 wounded and 22 missing out of approximately 175 men who entered the cornfield. Major Walrath headed the list, his tenure as brigade commander cut short by a shell fragment that entered his side during the advance. Captain Solomon Smith, whose Confederate acquaintance had warned him of the danger ahead, had his left elbow shattered by a rebel bullet. Smith's arm was amputated and he was lost to the 115th, returning home to Clifton Park in Saratoga County. Lieutenant Francis Francisco, a twenty-nine-year old from Wells in Hamilton County, was killed while leading Company K into the fight and later buried nearby under a flag of truce.[19]

Lieutenant John Van De Sande of Fort Plain, mortally wounded at Deep Bottom, August 16, 1864 (New York State Military Museum).

A Confederate minie ball pierced the temple of First Lieutenant John Van De Sande, a lawyer from Fort Plain in Montgomery County. Sent to Fortress Monroe for treatment, he clung to life for over two weeks. His father and brother traveled to his side and were with him when he died on September 3, but Van De Sande never regained consciousness, never passed a final word with his grieving family.[20]

Sergeant Frank Conover of Company D

was killed as the regiment crossed the cornfield. His younger brother Seely, a corporal in Company B, rushed to his side. Unable to revive his lifeless sibling, Seely pushed on only to be shot during the retreat and captured by the enemy. Later exchanged, he lay in a U.S. Army hospital in Annapolis and recounted memories of his brother in an anguished letter to a friend at home:

> I awake in the still hours of night and lay thinking of times agone. Will I ever forget them? Ah no, they are too deeply graven on my soul as with a pen of iron.... The last I saw of Frank was ... with the missiles of death hurtling and hissing around us. Ah! too well I remember his face, as calm as in life but oh so limp as I shook and called him by name. Frank! Frank! shall I never see you more?[21]

Corporal Seely Conover was shot and captured at Deep Bottom after running to the side of his brother, Frank, who was killed in the same action. He later served as mayor of Amsterdam, New York (Lance Ingmire Collection).

The oppressive heat also served to thin the ranks of the Union attackers, sunstroke felling many, including James Reid, John Reardon, and Nicholas DeGraff. All were assisted to safety. DeGraff awoke in a rear area where he saw a burial party at work. They had gathered fifty bodies and dug a long trench in which the slain were laid side by side and covered with blankets. One man among the dead wore an "excellent pair of high top new boots." The men of the burial detail knew that Chaplain Clemens, who was there working among them, needed new footwear, and so removed the unlucky soldier's boots and gave them to the cleric. DeGraff later went to the field hospital and walked among the rows of wounded men, searching for members of his company. Amidst the surgeons hard at work amputating limbs he again came across Chaplain Clemens, who was using a barn lantern to search among the wounded for those who had died. A detail of men stood by waiting to carry them away for burial. DeGraff called it "a scene never to be forgotten."[22]

Dr. Macfarlane recorded one additional casualty of the 115th's participation at Second Deep Bottom. In an August 22 letter home Macfarlane enclosed a piece of the regimental flag that had been torn off during the action. "There is nothing left of the old flag now but tatters," he wrote. "It will hardly hold together to be unrolled. The flagstaff has been shot in two several times and in the last battle on the 16th two corporals were shot dead and a sergeant wounded while carrying it."[23]

The August 16 fight at Deep Bottom would stand as another bitter defeat for the regiment although the men were satisfied that they had performed their duty well. James Reid felt that "probably no better fighting was done in any campaign than the fearless charges on the 16th." The soldiers blamed defeat on their leaders, chiefly division commander William Birney, for recklessly sending Walrath's Brigade on "a fool charge." That night an angry DeGraff wrote in his diary, "'Tis the old story. The generals know nothing about what is going on on the front. They send us forward. After that we must take care of ourselves. At

12 noon we had their breastwork, had driven them into their second line. At 3 p.m. we were whipped at all points." Still fuming two days later, DeGraff penned a letter to his father. "But what good does it do to fight well and to have the best men killed because they go the farthest to the front?" he asked. "Father, isn't it time I was getting discouraged? The 115th has been the victim of Blundering Generals in five different engagements. A regiment never was composed of better men, but every time we are ordered into some Reble nest and are repulsed."[24]

The lieutenant's frustration is understandable. In two years of service the regiment in which he took such pride had suffered surrender at Harpers Ferry, imprisonment at Chicago, the ignominy of the Camp Douglas fire, and an idle year in the south. It had been in several pitched battles, each time on the offensive and each time performing well. And each time, its side had been defeated. At Olustee the 115th lost half its men through Truman Seymour's foolish piecemeal tactics. The regiment endured abysmal leadership at Bermuda Hundred and again at the Battle of the Crater. At Cold Harbor they scored a breakthrough against the enemy but, unsupported, were forced to withdraw. Now they had been chased from the field at Deep Bottom with barely 100 healthy men remaining with the unit.

In spite of everything, DeGraff stayed hopeful. "But I will cheer up hoping that this is the last.... I hope and trust that fighting for the 115th is over for this summer." But Deep Bottom would not be the regiment's last fighting nor its last disappointment. The 115th would eventually have its day of glory, but it would come far from Virginia and not before the regiment took part in two more fruitless, costly offensives north of the James.[25]

Little action took place on August 17, both sides content to dig in and lick their wounds. On August 18 Lieutenant Colonel Nathan Johnson rejoined the 115th. He had been under arrest since May for drunkenness on duty, but the charges against him had been quietly dropped on July 28. In May, Johnson's arrest had come only four days after he joined the 115th as its lieutenant colonel. This time he stayed with the regiment less than one day—on the very night he returned to the regiment, Johnson would once again find himself under arrest for drunkenness on duty.[26]

As the highest ranking among the officers of the four regiments of the brigade, Johnson assumed brigade command when he arrived on August 18. The events leading to his re-arrest started at 1:00 p.m. that day when he led the brigade out of the Union main line to take its turn at manning a picket line 200 yards to the front. Peace and quiet prevailed at the front until 5:30 p.m. when the sound of officers barking orders disturbed the silence. Calls of "close up on the right; steady on the left; forward guide center" came from so near that many thought they must be coming from Union officers, but oddly the voices came from farther toward the front. Rebel troops suddenly darting out of the brushy woods cleared up any doubts. The 115th and several other surprised northern regiments abandoned their rifle pits and bolted back to their main line, leaving behind several killed and captured. Johnson suffered a flesh wound in his arm but was among the wounded men who scampered back to the earthworks.[27]

The surprise rebel infantry assault on the Union position north of Fussell's Mill was made in conjunction with cavalry attacks farther north, part of a Confederate attempt to drive the Yankees back to the James. The rebel plan failed as the federals regrouped and repulsed the southerners after a thirty minute fight. Shortly after things quieted down, an agitated Lieutenant Colonel Johnson began the series of actions that led some to suppose him to be intoxicated and to seek his re-arrest.[28]

Johnson was enraged to have his brigade driven so hastily from the picket line. He accused Captain William Shaw of allowing the 115th New York "to fall back altogether too soon and not holding it at the picket line as he ought, but running away from it disgracefully." A fuming Johnson resolved that his brigade should reoccupy the lost ground, telling another officer that "he would reestablish that picket line if he was killed in doing it." The lieutenant colonel's ire soared further when black troops of the 9th U.S.C.T., which held the line to the right of Johnson's brigade, advanced scouts beyond the works and into the rifle pits from which Johnson's men had just fled. Johnson raged that "no damned niggers should reestablish his picket line."[29]

After receiving conflicting reports as to whether the enemy still occupied the picket line, Johnson decided to go see for himself. Taking just one soldier along, he crept through the forest to within 250 yards of the rebel main line. The lone man with him, Private John Reed of Company G of the 115th, later said he never expected to get back alive but was determined to go just as far as his commander. Reed reported seeing the bodies of two men of the 115th killed in that afternoon's Confederate attack, but he and Johnson saw no rebels. They returned to the Union position with the lieutenant colonel fully committed to leading his brigade back out to its old picket line.[30]

Many officers under Johnson's command thought his plan reckless. Rarely did any good come of infantry operations in darkness. "None of us liked the idea," wrote one of the 115th's company commanders. "We stood ten chances of being gobbled up to one of getting out safe." Unable to dissuade Johnson, the 115th's Captain Shaw and Captain Billings Brastow of the 9th Maine sent a report back to General Birney that Johnson was drunk and unfit to command. Birney sent an aide to find and arrest Johnson.[31]

Meanwhile the undeterred Johnson led his men forward into the darkness. But, perplexingly, he halted the advance and returned to the works, only to turn around again and lead the troops back out. Johnson later claimed that he made these moves pursuant to orders from Birney; others saw them as evidence that he was drunk. When the brigade reached the left of the old line Johnson personally placed troops into positions in the rifle pits. Suddenly a voice calling "Halt! Who goes there?" accosted Johnson. His answer "Friends of the Union," brought forth a demand for his surrender. Realizing they had bumped into Confederates in their old line, Johnson's nervous men turned and ran. "There was a break and rush for camp each one for himself, the Johnnies sending a volley of bullets after us," recalled Lieutenant DeGraff. As the men stumbled back into their main works a seething Johnson cursed them as cowards. Moments later an officer approached the scene looking for Johnson. When Johnson identified himself the officer told him, "Consider yourself under arrest by order of General Birney."[32]

A court martial convened twelve days later to try Johnson on the charge of drunkenness on duty. The prosecution called six witnesses. Three of them, including the 115th's Captain Shaw, testified that they concluded Johnson to be drunk because of the crude manner in which he spoke to the officers of the Colored Troops and the way he ordered his brigade back and forth over the works. Only one prosecution witness—the division staff officer who arrested Johnson—claimed any physical evidence to confirm Johnson's intoxication, stating that he smelled liquor on Johnson's breath. The other two witnesses disagreed, testifying that they did not consider Johnson drunk on August 18.

The court martial acquitted Johnson and returned him to duty with the 115th New York on September 4, 1864. The lieutenant colonel may have acted foolishly on August 18 (Corporal Reid considered him "rash and prone to attempt plans that periled his command"), and he may indeed have downed a drink or two (Lieutenant DeGraff concluded that day that "Johnson had sampled his whiskey"), but the accusations that he was intoxicated were clearly unsubstantiated. Johnson showed a mean spirit and a distinct bias toward the black troops, and he let concern over his own reputation lead him to act imprudently. On the other hand, his units, including the 115th, certainly deserved Johnson's displeasure by allowing the appearance of the enemy to spook them so easily.[33]

After Johnson's arrest on August 18 the 115th was moved a mile to the rear, then another mile to the right (or north) to support the Union cavalry, which the Confederates had also attacked that day. Fifteen unlucky men went out on picket duty while the rest of the regiment stacked arms and slept, bivouacked in a farm field. The next morning Corporal Reid counted the regiment's muskets, tallying but seventy-five. Adding the men on picket, he realized that the 115th had only ninety men available for duty. Officers later assembled the regiment for an inspection. Reid noted wryly that it did not take much time to complete their review.[34]

After two quiet days Union forces abandoned their positions north of the James. The 115th re-crossed the pontoons at Deep Bottom, marched back up the Bermuda Hundred peninsula, and returned to its old camp near the Bermuda Hundred earthworks on August 21. In the eight day excursion to Deep Bottom the regiment lost over half of its remaining men. "What Gen'l Grant and the country has gained by the campaign it would be hard to conjecture," moaned DeGraff. Grant might explain that, although the federals won no battlefield victories at Deep Bottom, they did halt the flow of Confederate reinforcements to the Shenandoah Valley, as he intended. In addition, while the Second and Tenth Corps occupied Lee north of the James, Grant launched an initiative south of Petersburg, successfully extending the Union siege lines and cutting the Weldon Railroad, an important link between Petersburg, Richmond and the rest of the Confederacy.

But DeGraff and thousands of other common foot soldiers knew nothing of that. "I can't help but grumble," continued DeGraff. "Every thing goes wrong. All our moves are failures." The Second Deep Bottom campaign cost the Union 2,900 casualties, including nearly 1,700 in the Tenth Corps. The Confederacy counted about 1,500 total losses.[35]

12

Fort Gilmer and Darbytown Road
"It looked like suicide"

After leaving Deep Bottom the 115th spent a mercifully uneventful week on the Bermuda Hundred lines before returning with the Tenth Corps to the trenches of Petersburg. At Petersburg the regiment took a position just north of Hare's Hill, where it had spent several tough weeks in June and July. The men resumed the routine of three days manning the trenches alternating with three days at their camp a half mile to the rear. Artillery duels and sharpshooter action punctuated the monotony, but for the most part soldiers' truces prevailed and casualties were few.[1]

The men enjoyed regular delivery of newspapers and kept up to date on national events. They read with concern of war weariness among the people of the North and of vocal Peace Democrats, labeled by their opponents as Copperheads, who wanted to brand the war a failure and negotiate peace with the South. Copperhead influence reached its zenith in August 1864 when the Democratic Party nominated George B. McClellan to run against Abraham Lincoln in the fall presidential election. Almost universally the men of the 115th and other Union units wanted to see the war through to final victory. In spite of the hardships of a gruesome struggle whose end was not yet in sight, the soldiers had no desire for a negotiated peace settlement and did not support the election of the former commander of the Army of the Potomac. "I acknowledge I am tired of the war," wrote Captain McKittrick, "but I am not tired enough to accept a dishonorable peace." James Reid averred that ninety percent of the army shared his captain's sentiments since they volunteered to assure "that treason and rebellion should not succeed." They wanted to finish the job.[2]

Lieutenant DeGraff wholeheartedly agreed. "God is indeed blessing us and giving success to our arms," he assured his mother in a September letter. "All we want now is for the country to heartily and unitedly support our Army and the Rebles will never have another victory. Oh, how I hate those men who talk of peace when there can be no peace as long as there is a Reble in arms. McClellan and his minions seem to be sworn to bring the country to grief, but God grant that they may be overthrown in their devilish schemes. I am going to vote for Abraham Lincoln, believing that he is the man for the times."[3]

As the troops mulled over national politics, danger still lurked along the front lines.

In spite of the informal cease-fires and frequent trading between Blue and Gray, both sides needed to be watchful of specially equipped sharpshooters and their dreaded brand of warfare. One day DeGraff's company was harassed by a particularly bothersome rebel rifleman who concealed himself behind a large tree. DeGraff hailed down a passing Union sharpshooter and asked the man for his help in silencing the Confederate sniper. The man obliged, setting up his heavy gun and waiting for his rebel counterpart to reveal himself. The 115th men anxiously shared his vigil. "Finally he fired and then deliberately again loaded and placed his gun in position." The sight of two Confederate stretcher bearers running to the rebel sniper's nest confirmed the success of the initial shot. Then the Union marksman drew another bead and shot down one of the stretcher bearers. The other ran off and the two wounded rebels lay in place until dark. "That ended the sharpshooting at that point for some time."

DeGraff wondered how the enemy sharpshooter had been so effective in picking off victims while keeping himself so well concealed. He later found out. After the war's close when the 115th passed through Petersburg on their way home, he returned to the site and investigated. He "found that they had bolted two pieces of tree trunks together with iron plates with a hole for the rifle through the iron plate, thus making it quite safe for them to be constantly on the watch. We were slow that we did not use the same device."[4]

On September 3 several of the New Yorkers went to a neighboring Union camp to witness a military execution. They found three regiments drawn up in lines around three sides of a gallows. The condemned man, in iron shackles and escorted by a chaplain, marched clumsily past the assemblage. Behind him followed six men bearing his roughhewn wooden coffin, a guard of twenty-five infantrymen, and a squad of cavalry with drawn sabers. The provost marshall read the court findings that convicted the man of murdering a soldier of his own company. The prisoner then climbed a ladder onto the deck of the gallows where he and the chaplain knelt in prayer for five minutes. The marshall placed the noose around the man's neck and a hood over his head and left him alone on the platform. "The scene is now most affecting, when we realize that a human being [is] up there with the cap drawn, shutting out the light, left to his thoughts, far from home and friends," wrote John Reardon who saw the condemned soldier swoon during his final moments. At a signal from the marshall the hangman pulled the rope, "landing the ill-fated man into eternity."[5]

On September 9 bands played, cannon boomed, and troops cheered when news arrived of General Sherman's conquest of Atlanta. A similar scene erupted just twelve days later, when word came that General Sheridan had defeated the rebels at Winchester in the Shenandoah Valley. Southern soldiers retaliated in kind when a daring raid behind federal lines by Confederate cavalry netted a herd of 2,500 cattle for the jubilant rebels. "Beef, beef! Get your Yankee beef!" they jeered at the bluecoats across the lines. The haul from the Beefsteak Raid could not feed them all however, and hungry southerners began drifting into Union lines, deserting their cause as all but lost.[6]

Federal soldiers enjoyed an old Unionist Virginia lady who occasionally approached the troops to ask about the war's progress. During one such visit one of the men told her that he had bad news. "La-me, do tell," demanded the woman.

"The rebs have dammed up the Mississippi and are going to drown the world," replied the wag.

The startled woman went off and repeated the story to her pastor who tried to soothe her by reminding her of the Bible's promise that the Lord would never again destroy the world by flood.

"The Lord has got nothing to do with it," she retorted. "It's them darned rebs."[7]

"There is no change in our situation here," DeGraff informed his sister on September 22. "Times are getting rather dull if anything. There is so much sameness in this duty in the trenches." If the young lieutenant was bored and looking for change he did not have long to wait. Just three days later the 115th picked up camp and moved a couple of miles to the rear. At the new campsite they received issues of rations and ammunition, and spent a "hustling time cleaning up arms, accouterments and clothing." From these activities the veterans correctly surmised a new campaign in the offing, and on the morning of September 28 orders came to move out. As the regiment prepared to march Captain McKittrick took a moment to send home a note about the coming move. "Where are we going? No one knows, but there are a hundred rumors in regard to it," he wrote. The soldiers soon learned that they were headed back into action across the James River as General Grant began a new offensive. McKittrick's brief letter was his last; he was killed in action the following day.[8]

From Petersburg the 115th trekked toward Point of Rocks and crossed the Appomattox River. The entire Tenth Corps snaked its way along a few choked roads and progress was very slow. "It seemed to us that every wagon in the whole army were blocking the roads ahead of us," groaned DeGraff, who claimed that the march took four times longer than it should have. The regiment continued the sluggish tramp throughout the night, traversing the Bermuda Hundred peninsula and crossing the James River to Deep Bottom at 4:00 a.m. The men caught a one hour rest then stripped for battle, leaving a pile of knapsacks under a few guards. The regiment moved out at dawn and skirmishing began at once.[9]

The major objective of Grant's third offensive north of the James was to support Sheridan's ongoing campaign in the Shenandoah Valley, a campaign by which Grant aimed to subdue the long contested valley once and for all. By moving forces above the James to threaten Richmond, Grant intended to prevent Lee from stripping troops away from the Richmond lines and sending them to help defend the Shenandoah. Wrote Grant, "On the 28th of September, to retain Lee in his position, I sent ... the 18th Corps and Birney with the 10th Corps to make an advance on Richmond, to threaten it."[10]

While Grant's primary objective involved Sheridan's Valley campaign, he expected his lieutenants to recognize and seize any opportunity to strike Richmond. As federal forces extended the Union siege lines to the south and west of Petersburg throughout the summer, Grant knew that Lee's defense lines were stretched ever longer and thinner. So in hopes of decisive victory in the Shenandoah and to exploit any potential opportunity against the thinly held rebel lines east of Richmond, the 115th New York and 26,000 other blue clad troops again clattered across the pontoon bridges over the James.[11]

The Eighteenth Corps crossed the river upstream from Deep Bottom at Aiken's Landing, a point several miles closer to the Confederate's main Richmond defense line. This line was a formidable system of forts, moats, and earthworks that the rebels had labored to perfect since 1862. Nonetheless Eighteenth Corps units were able to drive the enemy from portions of the Richmond line around Fort Harrison before being halted by stiffening rebel resistance. The Tenth Corps, with an attached division of U.S. Colored Troops from the Eighteenth Corps, drove the southerners from New Market Heights in some hard fighting, with the black regiments doing most of the bloody work. This enabled Foster's Division of the Tenth Corps, which had not been engaged at New Market Heights, to lead an advance four miles up New Market Road, bringing it opposite the Richmond defenses north of Fort Harrison. After Second Deep Bottom, Brigadier General Robert Foster replaced William Birney in command of this division, which contained Bell's Brigade and the 115th New York.[12]

Enemy rearguard actions slowed Foster's advance, but the northerners routed rebel pickets from two advance lines of earthworks during the morning. At noon Confederate troops with two pieces of artillery posted near Laurel Hill Church obstructed the Yankee approach. "Their artillery was trained on the pike which they raked effectively, exploding their shells in our midst, killing and wounding many," recalled Sergeant Reardon. A reporter from the *New York Herald* who traveled with the Tenth Corps called it "one of the most furious storms of shells that it has ever been my lot to witness."[13]

General Foster personally moved forward into the storm of lead to reconnoiter the situation, then swiftly ordered his three brigades to attack the pesky battery and its Gray infantry support. The rebels beat a hasty retreat into the main Richmond defense lines, just three-quarters of a mile distant, leaving behind some dead soldiers and a stock of artillery ammunition and equipment.[14]

The Richmond lines, specifically a moated fortress at one of its salients known as Fort Gilmer, glared at the Union troops across the open ground. The fort stood to the left of the New Market Road, and Foster formed his troops to confront it. As it faced Fort Gilmer, Foster's battle line stood along the road, gaining some shelter behind the roadway's embankment. General Foster examined his line and, to his chagrin, found only about 1,400 men representing his division's fourteen regiments. He blamed straggling and shirking for the turnout being several hundred men lower than it should have been. "Many of these men fell out in the darkness between Petersburg and Deep Bottom and others fell out at the time of the formation to charge the battery, the thick undergrowth favoring their retiring," concluded Foster.[15]

None of the chroniclers of the 115th mention any straggling or shirking by members of their regiment, but it had been a long overnight march and only about sixty of the New Yorkers took part in the coming assault on Fort Gilmer. Undoubtedly a number of men of the 115th fell behind exhausted or, unwilling to go farther, skulked into the forest as had so many of their Yankee comrades on this difficult day. Those who straggled or shunned their duty evaded a dangerous task: over half of those men of the 115th who pressed on and joined the charge against the imposing fort were soon shot down.[16]

Those of Foster's troops present with their units stood dutifully in their battle line along New Market Road and gazed warily at Fort Gilmer. "We now formed ourselves in sight of what looked to be a line of works of the strongest kind. They instantly began shelling us with great violence," wrote DeGraff. At 1:25 p.m. a messenger from corps headquarters advised Foster that he was expected to charge and capture the menacing works before him. Foster relayed the unwelcome order to his units. "What was our astonishment and terror when we received orders that we would charge those forts," continued DeGraff. "It looked like suicide to attempt it."[17]

The five regiments of Bell's Brigade formed the left of Foster's battle line. Three ravines creased the ground between them and the walls of Fort Gilmer, each filled with a jumble of downed timber. Several hundred yards to their right, the Richmond defenses ran perpendicular to the face of Fort Gilmer which the northerners were about to attack, enabling rebel guns posted there to gain an enfilading fire on Foster's line. The earthen walls of the fort stood 15 feet high and were fronted by two lines of abatis and a moat ten feet deep. DeGraff had good reason to call the proposed assault suicide.[18]

In spite of their fear or perhaps because of it, the men of the 115th began to shout as they climbed out of the highway cut and started toward Fort Gilmer. "At the command 'Go,' with a great cheer and continued cheering we went out at a run," recalled DeGraff. "On, on we went tearing through the underbrush and fallen trees, shot and shell screeching round our heads and the line getting thinner all the time, many getting hit, others falling down exhausted." At each ravine men paused in fear and fatigue and became targets for the enfilading artillery from their right. And at each ravine some men decided that they had gone far enough and stayed behind when the thinning line advanced. A small remnant reached the last ravine, beyond which an open farm field stretched to Fort Gilmer's moat. DeGraff admitted that he could not rally many of his company to enter this field. Nonetheless he and a few other stalwarts pushed on. "But we were doomed to disappointment and disaster."[19]

As the Union attackers neared Fort Gilmer, southern infantrymen defending its walls added a fierce musketry to the blizzard of artillery lead tearing apart the Yankee lines. Several hundred rebels from the works on the northerners' right scrambled to the attack point and added their rifles to the chorus. "As soon as we got near enough to their works for their musketry they poured into us a cutting fire, killing and wounding nearly everyone who was in the advance, repulsing and scattering us to the winds," wrote DeGraff. "I did not think when we started we would take the line of works, but I did not imagine such terrible slaughter." Even those stouthearted men who went with DeGraff on the final rush across the field

Modern view of Fort Gilmer, near Richmond, Virginia, showing the moat and remains of the north-facing wall of the earthen fort. On September 29, 1864, the 115th participated in a hopeless assault on the face of Fort Gilmer, with just a handful of men advancing as near as the field on the left, where Captain McKittrick was killed (photograph by author).

to Fort Gilmer could not pierce the deadly storm. They took shelter behind a small cabin in the field and hoped that reinforcements would join them. But they and a brave few from other regiments were on their own. As a dejected DeGraff summed up, "Our line was shattered, broken, and scattered and the day was lost."[20]

Fort Gilmer proved "almost utterly unassailable," reported the *New York Herald* correspondent. "The assault, though brilliant in its character and executed with heroic determination and bravery, was thus unsuccessful." The surviving men of the 115th and the other regiments made their way back to New Market Road. Jeering rebels stood atop their earthworks to fire parting shots and derision at the withdrawing Union men.[21]

Parties of federals went back under the protection of skirmishers to retrieve the wounded, but not all could be recovered, particularly those who had advanced the closest to Fort Gilmer. "Much to our regret and sorrow our dead and wounded fell into the hands of the Reble horde," wrote DeGraff, who was the only officer of the 115th to escape unscathed. "I thank God that I am yet among the living. He is very merciful to me. I went through it all without getting a scratch." Most were not so blessed. Of the 60 or so of the 115th who assaulted Fort Gilmer, 33 became casualties—five dead, 24 wounded, and four missing in action—over 50% of the soldiers who made the assault.[22]

McKITTRICK.

Captain McKittrick died during the advance. The commander of Company C fell as he climbed out of the second ravine, bent over double by a shell that killed him instantly.

Captain William McKittrick and his pistol. McKittrick was killed by an artillery shell during the assault on Fort Gilmer. The Ballston native had been a cavalryman in the Mexican war (Lance Ingmire Collection).

His body was left behind in the retreat and not recovered. McKittrick, who as a teenage cavalryman saw extensive action in the Mexican War, had led his company into all of the 115th's battles of the last two years. One of his men, Sergeant William Jennings, sent the mournful news to the homefront in a letter to the *Ballston Journal*: "Company C has lost its head and chief, one whose counsels and care were ever employed in behalf of those who like himself had left their homes and friends to fight the battles of their country." Major Walrath said he loved McKittrick as a brother and left this eulogy:

> When the hateful missile struck him to the earth the army lost one of its best soldiers, his family and friends one never to be forgotten and whose memory will be kept green and fresh in the hearts of his fellow comrades.[23]

One of McKittrick's Company C men, Lewis Bertrand, pressed on toward Fort Gilmer after seeing McKittrick fall. The thirty-four-year old private from the Town of Galway in Saratoga County, described as reclusive by his comrades, had just returned to the regiment after recovering from a head wound suffered at Cold Harbor. He was one of the brave few who made the closest advance on Fort Gilmer. "He and others pressed on to the point of repulse when Bertrand was seen to fall, shot through the head, killing him instantly. His body was also left on the field," recalled comrade James Reid.[24]

Sergeant Charles Spiegel, christened Gunboat Spiegel by his comrades in Florida, saw Bertrand fall and ran to his side. Spiegel lifted Bertrand's head in a futile attempt to aid him and took a rebel ball through the chest for his effort. Leaving Bertrand, Spiegel crawled to the shelter of a nearby stump. Just then a mounted Confederate officer emerged from the fort, swinging his sword to rally his troops for a counter charge. The alert and angry Spiegel took action. "My gun was loaded and I wanted some revenge for my wounds." Laying his rifle across the stump, he took aim and killed the officer's horse. Spiegel had the satisfaction of seeing the dismounted rebel run back into the fort. The twenty-nine-year old sergeant recovered, but his service with the 115th was ended.[25]

Sergeant Charles Kline of Company D, a farmer from Amsterdam, also went with the dauntless few who climbed out of the last ravine and rushed toward Fort Gilmer. The intrepid Kline even pushed forward when Lieutenant DeGraff and the other Company D men paused behind the sheltering cabin. A comrade who watched him from the cabin refuge marveled at Kline's "wonderful heroism." But within moments a bullet smashed into his left elbow and brought him to a stop. The southerners shouted for Kline to surrender, but he turned and ran for the ravine. Field surgeons later amputated the sergeant's lower arm but gangrene set in and Kline underwent two more operations, each reducing the length of his arm but saving his life.[26]

Leading the 115th again proved hazardous duty, as did carrying its flags. A shot from Fort Gilmer fractured the scapular bone in Lieutenant Colonel Nathan Johnson's right shoulder. The wound sent Johnson home for several weeks to recover. Arrests for drunkenness had shortened Johnson's first stay with the regiment to four days and his second stay to less than one full day. Now—twenty-five days since his acquittal on the second charge—a Confederate bullet sent him packing once more. Johnson would not rejoin the 115th until January 1865.[27]

A bullet pierced Sergeant Charles Fellows's right leg as he carried the 115th's battle flag toward Fort Gilmer, and he became one of the unfortunates to be left to the enemy. After he lay in pain and thirst throughout the night Confederates took Fellows captive and their surgeons amputated his wrecked limb. The rebels freed Fellows after the surgery and he was taken to a U.S. Army hospital in Annapolis, but it proved too late. The color bearer died on November 11, 1864, with his wife and father at his side. They returned his remains to his Mechanicville home, where an overflow crowd attended the twenty-six-year old's funeral during a heavy early season snowstorm. A banner hanging above the church pulpit read:

> He gave up his life, his country to save
> And claimed for the sacrifice only a grave.[28]

After pulling back from Fort Gilmer and regrouping along the New Market Road, Foster's Division withdrew to a position in one of the Confederate trench lines it had taken during the morning advance. Another Tenth Corps division assaulted the Richmond defense line later in the afternoon of September 29 while the 115th and the rest of Foster's units rested along New Market Road. This attack struck the rebel lines between Fort Gilmer and Fort Harrison and was bloodily repulsed. With it the Union advance came to an end and the federals dug in. Tenth Corps soldiers built new works to connect the captured rebel advance lines with Fort Harrison, where the Eighteenth Corps still held a portion of the main Richmond defense line.[29]

While the northerners spent the night of September 29–30 digging, the southerners, with General Lee himself on the scene and intent on retaking Fort Harrison, spent the night scrambling reinforcements. By afternoon on the 30th Lee had assembled eight brigades and was ready to take the offensive. Rebel soldiers poured out of their lines and made several charges on Fort Harrison, but each was repulsed by the Union Eighteenth Corps.[30]

Following the fighting of September 29–30, Grant decided to hold on to the positions gained north of the James where his troops posed an imminent threat to the rebel capital, just six miles away. This time there would be no withdrawal back across the river.[31]

The soldiers of the 115th and their Union comrades of the Tenth and Eighteenth Corps worked through October strengthening the new siege lines east of Richmond. On occasion Blue and Gray battled along the front but, to the disappointment of no one, the 115th did not participate. As DeGraff explained to his sister, "This is the first time this summer that we have been within hearing distance of a battle without having a hand in before it was over." Later in the month, hours of drilling replaced some of the hours of manual labor.[32]

Deserters poured in from the rebel lines each night. "It is a sight to see them coming every day, one, two, three at a time," reported Reardon. Reid spoke with some of these men before they were whisked away to headquarters for questioning. He recorded that they all felt their cause was lost and the end of the war was near. One fleeing Confederate even "kneeled reverently and thanked God that he was under the stars and stripes once more."[33]

During this period many new recruits joined the Union force, mostly conscripted men or substitutes, who accepted $300 to serve in place of the conscripts. Few such men joined the 115th. DeGraff theorized that they avoided the regiment because it did so much fighting. Reid reported two new soldiers in Company C, including Samuel B. Cornell, whose brother Sidney had been killed fighting beside Reid at Olustee, and Heinrite Gorr, a forty-four-year old German from Troy, New York, considered by Reid to be "of doubtful material for a soldier." When word spread that he had brought a supply of tobacco with him, Gorr quickly made numerous friends among his new comrades. They all seemed badly in need of tobacco and his supply dwindled rapidly. Finally Gorr started using his broken English to claim that the tobacco was very dry. To illustrate his point, he would spray spittle into his tobacco box "in about the manner that a Chinaman sprinkles clothes." As a result Gorr lost a few friends but held on to more of his tobacco.[34]

Near the end of October Grant went on the offensive once more. This time his declared objective was to seize and hold the Southside Railroad southwest of Petersburg. Beyond this military objective, the general sought a battlefield victory just before Election Day to help boost his commander-in-chief's re-election prospects. His plan called for troops from the Army of the Potomac to move out of their Petersburg lines on October 27. At the same time, in order to assure that the Confederates could not move reinforcements from their defenses north of the James to the threatened point below Petersburg, General Butler's Army of the James was to make a simultaneous advance, striking the rebel lines east of Richmond.[35]

Butler issued orders to his corps commanders on the day before the proposed attack. Grant wanted the Army of the James to make only a demonstration toward Richmond to hold enemy troops in their positions, but Butler devised a more ambitious plan for his forces. Since the previous federal offensive that had included the assault on Fort Gilmer, the Tenth and Eighteenth Corps, which made up the Army of the James, had constructed and held the Union siege lines east of the Confederate capital. The Tenth Corps held the right, or northern end of the federal line, and the Eighteenth Corps held the left, anchored on the James River. Butler directed the Tenth Corps to advance, drive in the enemy skirmish lines, and threaten their main works. While the Tenth Corps made this feint toward Richmond, the Eighteenth Corps, leaving behind a minimal force to hold its sector of the siege lines, was to swing around behind the Tenth Corps and strike the rebel left flank northeast of Richmond. Butler's intelligence showed this flank to be weakly defended. The general instructed that should his forces penetrate this flank, they were to enter Richmond. A cynical Corporal Reid later called this directive Butler's "fond hope that by some good fortune the enemy would make some blunder that would allow our forces to slip in and capture Richmond."[36]

For the 115th New York the new offensive began at 5:00 a.m. on October 27, 1864, when the regiment fell into line and marched out of camp. By this date, thanks to new recruits and the return to the regiment of veterans recovered from earlier wounds, the 115th numbered about 224 men. The unit still served in Bell's Brigade of Foster's Division of the Tenth Corps. The corps' 8,500 troops moved to the north a couple of miles, then formed into battle lines near Darbytown Road. Lieutenant DeGraff reveled in the scene:

> [We] formed our lines for an advance just as the sun was rising beautifully in the east. We formed in three lines of battle, one behind the other. Oh, it was a grand and imposing sight, colors waving in the breeze, bayonets glistening in the morning sunshine, and then the conviction that soon, perhaps in minutes, we would be in the deadly strife.

With skirmishers to the front, the blue lines advanced 300 yards and drove rebel pickets from a line of rifle pits. The northerners halted at this line and, amid skirmishing and maneuvering to avoid artillery fire, held the position throughout the morning.[37]

At noon the 115th was ordered to the front as skirmishers. They joined the 13th Indiana in the line of rifle pits which had just been wrested from the Confederates. From this position the men exchanged fire with rebel riflemen sheltered in a belt of timber. "The Rebles were in a woods close in our front shooting from behind trees," recalled DeGraff. "We did not advance but kept up a steady fire into the woods until about 4:30 p.m." According to Reid, the men fired up to 100 rounds apiece during the four hour battle and the enemy responded in kind, all to no apparent effect. "Our shoulders were actually lamed by the recoil of our guns.... Certainly the regiment never expended ammunition so foolishly, unless the noise we made counts for success. The enemy were doing us but little harm and I doubt if we did them more."[38]

At the right end of the 115th's line stood the small house of a Virginia family. In spite of warnings of pending combat the residents refused to leave, instead taking refuge under the building during the fighting. Their home became a hot spot as Union soldiers took positions in and around it during the long afternoon scuffle. Later as fighting subsided, the 115th's Dr. Macfarlane checked on the family and found them badly frightened. The mother, the only woman Macfarlane ever saw wounded in battle, had suffered a severe leg wound.[39]

Sergeant Jennings took a bullet in the right hand during the skirmish. Reid and his friend James Dunk watched as the usually ramrod straight Jennings stooped low and made his way down the line, tightly holding his right hand in his left. In spite of his wound, Jennings regained his military bearing when Captain Fred Mosher accosted him. "Are you wounded, Jennings?" demanded Mosher. Dunk and Reid laughed out loud when they saw Jennings react. He jumped to attention, snapped his wounded hand to his brow in salute, and barked, "A slight wound to the hand, sir."[40]

Colonel Bell received orders to advance his brigade, chase the rebels back into their main entrenchments, and if possible storm their works. At 4:30 p.m. he sent the 115th New York and 13th Indiana forward. The 9th Maine, 900 strong after extensive recruiting, followed a distance behind them in a second battle line. "We started forward with a cheer, firing as we went," recalled DeGraff. Moving at a rapid step, the Blue soldiers closed on the Confederates in the trees. "Our line advanced through the woods, driving the rebels, who made the sternest resistance," reported the *New York Herald's* correspondent, "but the cool, determined courage of our men swept everything before them."[41]

Reaching the far edge of the timber, the northerners could see strong rebel earthworks across sixty yards of slashing. As they emerged from the trees, the rebels opened on them with musketry and grapeshot from a six-gun battery. At the same moment musket fire poured into the 115th from the rear, shocking and confusing the men and causing additional casualties. "We could not stand a front and rear fire both at once and began to fly back," admitted DeGraff.

The New Yorkers soon discovered that the shots from behind had come from the ranks of the 9th Maine. Corporal Reid later theorized that the many raw recruits among the Mainers were spooked by a rain of branches and splinters which fell on them as gunfire raked the tree canopy above them, and by the whizzing and screeching of minie balls and grapeshot. "They were mostly new men and got excited, thought we were Johnnys and so blazed away," allowed DeGraff. In any case, the 9th Maine's fire put the 115th in motion. Part of the regiment peeled off to the left and rear, and the rest to the right and rear.[42]

Bell's Brigade managed to regroup rapidly, the 115th and the other regiments again taking position in the captured rebel rifle pits, or "gopher holes," as Colonel Bell called them. Soon afterwards the federal lines withdrew under orders and moved a short distance farther to the rear. Here the 115th spent a rainy, though quiet night on picket duty. Through the long day the regiment had suffered only twenty casualties including five dead, but many of these came at the hands of the 9th Maine. Lieutenant James Clark judged these friendly fire casualties to be "far worse than being killed or maimed by the enemy."[43]

While the 115th and the Tenth Corps made their noisy display in front of the rebel defenses on October 27, the Eighteenth Corps looped around the Tenth Corps as planned and struck the Confederate left. But the rebels were not fooled. They anticipated the move against their flank, mustered reinforcements, and easily turned back the attackers. Butler's hope of taking Richmond had misfired, but his Army of the James kept thousands of southern troops occupied as General Grant intended. Even so, the simultaneous federal thrust south of Petersburg also failed, Confederates turning back elements of the Union Second, Fifth and Ninth Corps near Hatcher's Run. The Southside Railroad stayed open to the Confederates, and federal hopes for an election eve victory were dashed. The siege of Petersburg and Richmond would continue through the winter of 1864–65.[44]

After a sodden night on picket duty at Darbytown Road the 115th returned to its camp near Fort Gilmer. For several days the federals maintained a state of high alert, fearing a Confederate counteroffensive. Nicholas DeGraff reported the troops' "enthusiasm at low ebb." Their demonstration had cost 1,600 casualties and gained nothing.[45]

Excitement over the national elections permeated the camps in October and early November as Election Day drew near. The soldiers actually began voting in mid–October when ballots were distributed to the troops. They voted for local, state, and presidential candidates by filling in the ballots and mailing them to their home districts to be tallied on Election Day, November 8. Most troops still shared the sentiment that they must re-elect Lincoln and spurn the Peace Democrats in order to validate the war's sacrifices. As Sergeant Jennings stated in a letter to the *Ballston Journal*: "The soldiers of all political creeds are a unit so far as the restoration of the Union is concerned, that the blood of their comrades shall not be shed in vain." Lieutenant DeGraff saw the choice between Lincoln and McClellan as the monumental decision of "whether our government and constitution is able to sustain itself free and independent as our fathers handed it to us, or whether the slimy heel of the Reble traitor shall tread under foot the glorious Stars and Stripes of a misled republic."[46]

The twenty-two-year old DeGraff, voting in a national election for the first time, recorded, "I proudly registered my vote for our able and heroic President Abraham Lincoln. He is getting the votes of all loyal and patriotic men." DeGraff joined a solid majority. Lincoln won with 55% of the popular vote nationwide, but the incumbent president captured a resounding 80% of ballots cast by Union soldiers. This ratio held true in the 115th New York, where Company B gave 27 votes to Lincoln and 3 to McClellan, and Companies C, D, and E backed Lincoln 21 to 7, 14 to 6, and 33 to 7, respectively. "The Union and flag are safe," declared DeGraff. General Grant considered the President's decisive win and, equally important, the orderly manner in which the nation conducted the hotly contested wartime election, worth more than a battlefield victory.[47]

On November 2 orders to construct winter quarters brought a predictable reaction, as Reid recorded: "The 115th from past experience in building winter quarters, had a presentiment that such an idea meant a move for them." The men went to work constructing cabins but events soon proved the regiment's skeptics correct—the 115th did not even spend the rest of the month in these quarters let alone the rest of the winter.[48]

Following a couple of quiet weeks split between picket duty at the front and leisure in the new winter huts, the predicted move became reality, and its timing could not have been worse. The order arrived on November 23, Thanksgiving Eve, as DeGraff complained. "On the forenoon of the 23rd I came off of picket. Found everything all quiet and snug in camp. Everyone anticipating a good time on the morrow, Thanksgiving Day, as we were expecting those turkeys, etc. But what was our surprise about 4 p.m. on receiving orders to be ready to march early in the morning, taking everything with us." The 115th marched away at 8:00 a.m. Thanksgiving morning, watching forlornly as another regiment immediately appropriated their huts. They crossed the James and returned to the Bermuda Hundred front where, on Thanksgiving night, the men bivouacked on the cold ground. "It came exceedingly tough to pitch our little shelter tents again upon the ground with the remembrance that other troops were enjoying the cozy winter quarters we had built by so much labor," wrote one disgruntled New Yorker. A belated turkey dinner the next day provided some consolation.[49]

The 115th made the march to Bermuda Hundred alone, unaccompanied by any other units. The regiment was temporarily attached to an unfamiliar brigade garrisoning the Bermuda Hundred lines. After three days of picket duty and cold bivouacs, the regiment moved to a camp a half mile in the rear. This time the 115th benefitted from another unit's misfortune instead of the other way around, as the New Yorkers took over the newly completed winter camp of the 205th Pennsylvania which had been reassigned to the Army of the Potomac and sent to Petersburg. Still, there would be no comfortable winter's respite for the 115th. After enjoying the Pennsylvanian's huts for just one week, the regiment was off again.[50]

During the short stay at Bermuda Hundred, the 115th alternated on picket duty with black units of the Eighteenth Corps. Whenever the black troops appeared at the front, things heated up as the Confederates immediately opened fire. "The rebels resent the appearance of the colored troops whenever they come on the line," explained Reardon. "There is no visiting or exchange of papers and friendly chat. Then nothing but war. They use every means to annoy and make life unpleasant for the colored men." By contrast, when the 115th appeared on the picket line the rebels sought truce. The New Yorkers happily obliged, exchanging newspapers, swapping northern coffee for southern tobacco, and visiting with their adversaries. Confederates told the 115th that they found it insulting to be opposed by former slaves, and declared "they will fire on every black soldier they see anywhere and at anytime."[51]

On December 5 the regiment marched back down the Bermuda Hundred peninsula and across the James where they rejoined Bell's Brigade and received news. The Army of the James had been reorganized, eliminating the Tenth and Eighteenth Corps. The white troops of both corps now comprised the new Twenty-Fourth Corps. All of the black units from the former Tenth Corps and Eighteenth Corps were consolidated as the Twenty-Fifth Corps. Bell's Brigade remained intact and the units comprising its division did not change, but a new man now commanded the division, Brigadier General Adelbert Ames, a West Pointer from Maine. "The 10th Corps were very much displeased to lose their old corps number," wrote Corporal Reid, "but derived some satisfaction that our divisions were kept intact in the new corps."[52]

More news came the next day: the 115th and Ames's Division were about to join a long awaited expedition against Wilmington, North Carolina. The men re-crossed the James on December 7 and the next morning they marched to Bermuda Hundred Landing, boarded transport ships, and set sail for Fortress Monroe.[53]

13

Two Calls on Fort Fisher
"Win or die"

By late 1864 the demise of the Confederacy seemed imminent. In eastern Virginia Lee's forces stretched to the breaking point around Richmond and Petersburg. High rates of desertion from the poorly supplied ranks of the proud Army of Northern Virginia clearly indicated that hundreds of cold, hungry veterans had resigned themselves to defeat. In the Shenandoah Valley, the autumn scorched earth campaign of General Philip Sheridan had devastated the land and finished the valley's role as a critical source of supply to rebel armies. General William T. Sherman followed up his capture of Atlanta by marching across Georgia to the sea, where he seized Savannah and offered it to President Lincoln as a Christmas present. Sherman moved as he pleased, for the Confederates could no longer mount any effective resistance in the war's southeastern theater. And—as significant as any battlefield triumph—Lincoln's clear election victory signaled the end of any hope in the seceded states for a negotiated peace.

Along the Atlantic and Gulf coasts the Union's naval blockade, together with federal armies occupying key coastal areas, added to the litany of Confederate woes. By late 1864 nearly all of the long southern coastline was sealed by the Union navy. There remained however one glaring exception which stuck prominently in the craws of the U.S. Navy and federal leaders in Washington, D.C.: the blockade had never been able to seal the mouth of the Cape Fear River, access to the port of Wilmington, North Carolina. In December 1864, Wilmington was the only Confederate port still accessible to blockade runners bringing in vital shipments of guns and other equipment from European suppliers.

Wilmington lay twenty miles up the Cape Fear River from the Atlantic, and the unique geography around the mouth of the river had protected the city from the U.S. Navy through nearly four years of war. The Cape Fear actually entered the sea at two points divided by a large island. Between the two inlets impassable shoals protruded twenty-five miles from the island into the ocean, enlarging the sailing distance between the inlets to nearly fifty miles. Blockade vessels could not effectively patrol the entire area.

The Cape Fear River flows southward from Wilmington, forming an acute angle with the Atlantic coastline, an ever narrowing peninsula of land laying between river and sea. Near the tip of this peninsula stood massive Fort Fisher, its guns commanding the coast, the river, and the northern inlet between the Atlantic and the Cape Fear.

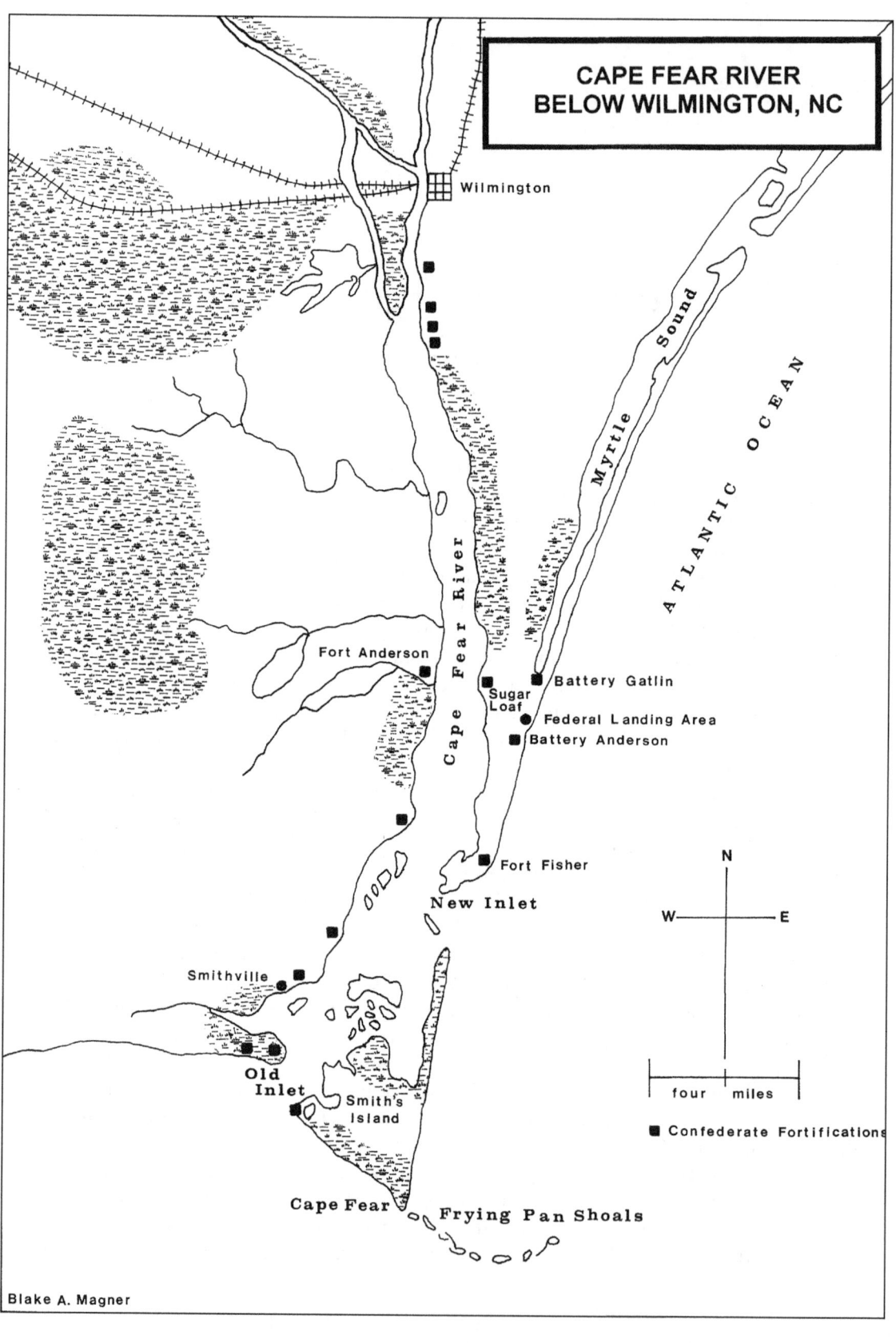

The fort, together with numerous batteries at both Cape Fear inlets and several points along the river between the coast and Wilmington, protected the port from federal encroachment.[1]

Navy officials had lobbied for a joint army and navy expedition against Fort Fisher since 1862, but War Department priorities remained elsewhere. During the summer of 1864 however, after the fall of Mobile Bay in Alabama sealed the last open rebel port on the Gulf of Mexico, the importance of Wilmington to the Confederacy became more pronounced, and administration officials in Washington turned a more sympathetic ear to the Wilmington enterprise. President Lincoln and Secretary of War Edwin Stanton came to favor the expedition, and they turned to General Grant for his judgment.[2]

Grant reluctantly endorsed the project and committed a few thousand men from the Army of the James to undertake it. He named General Godfrey Weitzel, Chief Engineer of the Army of the James, to lead the army's portion of the joint operation. Weitzel immediately sailed southward to reconnoiter the area around Fort Fisher, and he and the naval commander, Admiral David Dixon Porter, began preparations for the expedition. But Weitzel did not get to lead the army force into the campaign because his commanding officer, General Benjamin Butler, pulled rank and announced that he would personally lead the army's portion of the venture—much to that army's misfortune.[3]

Porter gathered a fleet of fifty-seven navy warships to move against Fort Fisher and Wilmington, including ironclads, steamers, and sailing ships. Altogether the amalgam of vessels mounted 619 guns of all sizes. Butler's 6,500 troops, mostly infantry but including some artillery and cavalrymen, occupied an additional twenty-five ships—the transport fleet—which also carried twenty days' rations for the army, 300 rounds of artillery ammunition per gun, 100 rounds of rifle ammunition per infantryman, plus hundreds of picks, shovels, axes, mules, and horses. The naval fleet needed to put into Beaufort, North Carolina, for supplies so the transport fleet, in order to time its rendezvous properly with the navy, sailed around Chesapeake Bay for a day and a half before putting to sea on the afternoon of December 14. The two fleets were scheduled to converge off the Atlantic coast near Fort Fisher the next day.[4]

By the time the transport fleet sailed into the Atlantic, the men of the 115th New York had already been on board the steamer *Haze* for six days, most of that time spent at anchor off Fortress Monroe. The soldiers did not know their expedition's destination as they weathered those long eventless days. Corporal Reid described the *Haze* as "a short, tubby vessel which rolled and pitched on fairly smooth water, and more so according to roughness." The regiment lodged in a lower hold, squeezed into quarters so tight that some men had to bunk atop the ship's coal supply. Reid likened the 115th's situation to "the Middle Ages in a Congo slave ship." Putting to sea finally relieved the monotony and the elements cooperated: "The weather was exceedingly fine, the sea smooth, and, but for the cramped, incommodious quarters, the voyage would have been delightful."[5]

When the men awoke on December 15 they found the fleet bearing southwest. The flotilla held this course until 10:00 p.m. when the ships anchored for the night twenty miles off shore and eighteen miles north of Fort Fisher. General Butler sailed ahead to a prearranged rendezvous point a bit farther south, where he discovered that the navy had not yet arrived. Butler and his men fumed and sailed in circles for three more days before the tardy warships appeared.[6]

The soldiers decried the "vexatious delays" as patience wore thin and the air below deck grew ever fouler. "We are getting heartily sick of life in our present situation, to be huddled together like cattle, not a particle of the most necessary accommodation furnished," complained Sergeant Reardon. "The hold of the vessel in which we are crowded, filthy before we entered, is in a horrible condition of foulness.... To get a whiff of the air at the hatch as it escapes is on a par with sewer gas."[7]

Regimental Surgeon Carrington Macfarlane gained some relief from the tedium when he found a supply of fish hooks in the officers' quarters and crafted fishing lines by waxing and twisting together some sewing thread. He baited his hooks with pork and, as he tossed a line over the side, discovered that he was providing entertainment for the whole bored regiment. "Three hundred spectators looking on and laughing at me, but not one of them was more surprised than I myself when I drew in my line and found on it four fish.... After that someone was always fishing."[8]

Dishearteningly, the arrival of the navy on the night of December 17 did not bring an end to the shipboard confinement as the soldiers had hoped. The run of pleasant weather ended, replaced by a gale that scattered the transports and made a landing impossible. The next day the rough seas persisted and General Butler ordered the transport fleet to sail for Beaufort where the ships regrouped and resupplied with coal and water. Crowning the misery, when the fleet reached Beaufort Butler would not allow the soldiers, who had been squeezed on the malodorous ships for twelve long days, to go ashore. He feared that the men would leak word of the expedition's purpose.

The cramped troopship spent most of the next four days at sea off Beaufort, where rough weather heaved them about and made the soldiers miserable. John Reardon recorded that it was impossible to stand on the deck of the storm-tossed ship and that life below deck was wretched. On December 22 he wrote, "Had a very bad night. Sleep under the circumstances is not to be thought of, down in a stuffy, hot, ill-odored hole. It is a wonder some of the weaker ones did not die." Mercifully the storm finally relented and later that day the transports landed at Beaufort for more coal and water. On Christmas Eve they again sped south toward Fort Fisher.[9]

General Butler devised and championed a plan to fill an old ship with gunpowder, move it as close as possible to Fort Fisher, and reduce the fort to rubble by detonating the huge floating bomb. Many scoffed, but others including Admiral Porter agreed that the scheme might work. Porter chose the aging, 295-ton shallow draft steamship *Louisiana* for the task. He stripped her of all unnecessary fixtures and added framing on her deck to maximize the amount of powder she could hold. Sailors stuffed 215 tons of powder into the old vessel.

The navy had borne the stormy weather while at sea near Fort Fisher. Then, without waiting for the return of Butler and the transport fleet from Beaufort, Porter ordered the *Louisiana* to approach the beach near the fort during the night of December 23–24. A volunteer crew managed to get her within 300 yards of the fort without being detected, then lit fuses and hurriedly rowed away to a waiting escape vessel. The rest of Porter's fleet withdrew twelve miles offshore to avoid damage from the expected blast.

The *Louisiana* blew up at 1:46 a.m. Christmas Eve morning. Sailors lining the rails of their ships twelve miles away saw a glare on the horizon and heard a dull report. When they expectantly steamed toward shore at daybreak, they were disappointed to see Fort Fisher still standing "grim as ever, apparently uninjured," according to Captain Thomas Selfridge, commander aboard the *USS Huron*. The sound of the blast startled people in Wilmington and terrified a troop of teenaged North Carolina Junior Reserves camped on the beach near Fort Fisher, but the explosion had no impact at all on the fort.¹⁰

At daylight on December 24 the Union armada approached Fort Fisher and prepared for battle. Fifty-six warships anchored in four parallel lines three-quarters of a mile off the beach. Each ship was assigned a specified target area within the fort, and shortly after noon more than 600 guns opened on Fort Fisher. They bombed the fort for five hours, firing 10,000 shells at the rebel stronghold. By contrast the Confederates had only 3,600 shells on hand to serve their forty-four guns, and fired just 672 shots in response to the naval bombardment. The fort's 1,400-man garrison endured the attack in bombproof shelters while most of the federal fire landed harmlessly on Fort Fisher's sand walls and grounds. The spectacular barrage damaged only six rebel guns and seriously wounded just four southerners, one mortally.¹¹

The fortress could absorb such punishment because it was simply a well-designed pile of sand. Thousands of federal shells did little more than blanket the fort's outer embankment with craters. The fort was built in the shape of a huge number seven. The mile long upright of the seven, known as the sea face, was a mound of sand running parallel to the beach and containing several massive batteries that housed twenty-four heavy guns. At the southern tip of the sea face stood the largest of these batteries, the Mound Battery, a sixty foot man-made mountain of sand, which took the Confederates a year and a half to build using an incline railway and steam engine. The guns of the Mound Battery commanded the northern inlet from the Atlantic Ocean into the Cape Fear River.

A mile north of the Mound Battery, at the northern end of the sea face, stood another huge gun emplacement called the Northeast Bastion. From here the fortress turned perpendicular to the sea face and stretched east-to-west across the peninsula. Measuring nearly one-half mile from the sea to the Cape Fear River, this wall formed the top of the huge seven and was known as the land face. The sand walls of the land face stood twenty-three feet

U.S. Navy bombardment of Fort Fisher, North Carolina, in preparation for the infantry assault (*Battles and Leaders*).

Land face of Fort Fisher, whose sand walls stood 23 feet high. The high points are the perpendicular traverses, mounds of sand 30 feet high with bombproofs built within. Note the wooden palisade along the base of the walls. The 115th charged across the ground in this photograph during the victorious attack of January 15, 1865 (Massachusetts Commandery, Military Order of the Loyal Legion, U.S. Army Military History Institute).

high and were forty-eight feet thick at the base. Fifteen enormous traverses, mounds of sand thirty feet high and twenty-five feet thick, divided the land face into gun chambers housing twenty guns. The traverses ran perpendicular to the land face, extending thirty to forty feet from the wall into the interior of the fort. The bombproofs that so effectively protected rebel soldiers from the navy's shells were inside these huge traverses.

The southerners cleared the peninsula of vegetation for a half mile north of the fort's land face in order to create a field of fire against any ground assault. Along the exterior base of the land face they built a nine foot high palisade of sharpened logs that stretched from the sea to the river. The strength and proportions of Fort Fisher certainly impressed those who ventured south to capture her. "That height and size," concluded an officer of the 115th, "make one think as he looks at them of the work of the Titans." The rear of Fort Fisher stood essentially open to the Cape Fear River, but additional batteries and the shallow depth of the river combined to protect the fort from assault on the river side. The Union infantry, sailing toward Fort Fisher as the navy spewed its epic bombardment, would have to approach the rebel citadel at its imposing land face.[12]

The transport fleet steamed into sight of the fort shortly before the navy concluded its Christmas Eve onslaught. "The decks of our vessels were crowded with soldiers eager to see all that was to be seen and to hear all that was to be heard," recalled Reid. "These great frigates, gunboats, and monitors ... launch their broadsides in uninterrupted fire upon the works," wrote Dr. Macfarlane. "Soon the sea is spotted everywhere with the empty ammunition boxes." Covering acres of ocean as they flowed out to sea with the tide, these wooden chests, which the sailors tossed overboard after expending their contents, provided a memorable sight.[13]

After the warships concluded their day's work and retired, General Weitzel and another of General Butler's staff officers met with Admiral Porter to plan the next day's action. Butler was incensed about Porter exploding the powder ship before his arrival and refused to meet with the admiral personally. Porter assured Weitzel that the navy's guns had decimated Fort Fisher and that the infantry would have an easy time entering the fortress—claims which Weitzel wisely discounted.[14]

The meeting resulted in a plan that called for the navy to renew its bombardment and the army to land and assault the fort the following day. As both federal fleets retired for the evening the soldiers of the 115th repaired to the overcrowded, fetid quarters of the *Haze* for their seventeenth night on board. The prospect of going ashore in the morning, even for a Christmas Day attack on the awe-inspiring rebel fortress, must have seemed a welcome relief.

The next day, Christmas, the cannonade resumed. "With the first appearance of day the decks were again sought," wrote Corporal Reid. "Both of the great fleets were in sight, creating an imposing scene. Dispatch vessels were flying here and there and the signal corps were kept busy with their flag signals. About 10 a.m. the naval fleet advanced to position and half an hour later recommenced the bombardment." Fort Fisher's commander, Colonel William Lamb, noted ironically that it was "Christmas, the anniversary of the Prince of Peace," as the U.S. Navy armada renewed its savage assault. The warships again fired all day long, sending another 10,000 missiles toward the rebels.[15]

Later in the morning some of the warships peeled away and steamed northward to shell two detached rebel fortifications, Battery Anderson and Battery Gatlin, three and five miles north of Fort Fisher, respectively. Their task was to soften up the designated landing zone for the infantry. Meanwhile, the ships of the transport fleet moved within 800 yards of shore and began lowering surf boats. These craft, twenty-five feet long and rowed by crews of six or eight sailors, would shuttle the infantry to the beach. More such boats came over from the naval fleet to assist in landing the army regiments. Macfarlane described the scene: "Then from the men-of-war, skimming over the glassy water come myriads of little boats to our transports, the oarsmen armed with cutlasses and revolvers and our flag flying in the stern sheets of each."[16]

The anxious soldiers of the 115th crammed the deck of the *Haze* and lined her railings. Then, "over the rail and down the rope ladders the boys scrambled," recorded Reid, "full of hilarity and enthusiasm at the novel idea of debarkation, and eager with delight to leave the pent-up quarters which for seventeen days had been our abode." The transfer from ship to boat required caution. "The ocean is rough, swells running high, and any mishap might overturn or crush the small boats, with almost a certain loss of life, the soldiers being loaded down with gun and big supply of ammunition, blanket or overcoat." The New Yorkers handled it well and the boats were "soon filled to their gunwales with armed troops who were rowed as near the shore as possible."

As the launches pulled away from the ships the soldiers realized their Christmas Day landing would be, as Reid noted, "no holiday affair." The din of crashing surf reached the soldiers' ears, and they looked toward shore and saw five foot waves rumbling onto the beach. Nearing shore, the oarsmen turned the sterns of their craft toward the beach, then struggled to maintain positions close enough to allow the infantrymen to stay dry as they debarked, but in deep enough water to avoid their boats being grounded and swamped by the surf. Reid saw this happen to two boats that preceded his. The sailors instructed the infantrymen to wait for a wave to spend its force on the shore, then leap over the stern as it receded and hustle ashore before the next wave caught them from behind.

Reid and one comrade led the way out of their launch. "As the water rolled under our boat the stern was raised away up, the beach was clear, and we jumped out on the hard sand." They timed it perfectly and landed dry-shod, earning bravos from the oarsmen. Others "did not calculate so well and got a wetting." Surgeon Macfarlane did poorly: he and his companions got soaked and tumbled ashore by a wave. Many of the troops suffered similar mishaps.[17]

Colonel Louis Bell's Brigade—still made up of the 13th Indiana, 4th New Hampshire, and the 115th and 169th New York—comprised the Third Brigade of Brigadier General Ames's Division. Ames's First Brigade, under General N. Martin Curtis of the 142nd New York, had been the first to land. Curtis's Brigade quickly forced the surrender of Battery Anderson, situated on the beach just south of the landing zone. A small force of rebels from Battery Gatlin, located nearly two miles north of the landing zone, rushed into the adjoining woods and opened musketry fire on the Yankees as they filtered onto the beach. Sergeant Reardon noted that the 115th felt this fire just as they began landing, "so as the saying goes we are between the devil and the deep sea."[18]

Union gunboats sprayed shells into the woods that hid the rebels. "The roar of the big guns, the bursting of shells in the tree tops with limbs flying in every direction must have made the position of the enemy a little like a Hades," recalled Reardon. Union infantry also engaged the Confederates and within thirty minutes things quieted as the rebels retreated northward into a line which crossed the peninsula from Battery Gatlin to Sugar Loaf Battery on the east bank of the Cape Fear River. The 2,200 soldiers of Ames's Division completed their adventurous landing without further opposition.[19]

Curtis's First Brigade then led the advance southward down the peninsula toward Fort Fisher, encountering no more resistance. Skirmishers cut the telegraph lines connecting the fort with Wilmington and took up positions seventy-five paces from the fort's palisade. The 115th New York and the rest of Bell's Brigade moved into line in support of Curtis's men and awaited the order to strike. Meanwhile the navy continued to bomb the fort. Some stray shells actually killed and wounded a number of federal infantrymen.[20]

The Union troops confronting Fort Fisher's land face noted that its guns stayed completely silent and that not a single rebel could be seen. Lieutenant William Walling of the 142nd New York boldly ventured onto the fort's wall and snatched a Confederate flag that had been felled by a navy shell—an act that earned him the Medal of Honor. General Curtis was certain he could easily take the fort and issued an order to bring up reserves to assist his skirmishers in an attack. But just then word arrived from General Butler that there would be no attack; the troops were to withdraw. Curtis and his men were dumbstruck, as were the men of the 115th. "This sudden change of plan is not only a surprise but a mystery to the troops," wrote Reardon, who said that the sudden turn of events brought to the soldiers' minds a couplet:

> As we are so soon done for
> It's a wonder what we begun for.

The ground troops grudgingly about-faced and headed back up the peninsula.[21]

Night had fallen by the time the bewildered foot soldiers got back to the landing area.

"Since landing the wind had risen, the sea was rough and becoming more so," remembered James Reid. "The night was dark and rainy, and with the high rolling surf breaking on the shore, made conditions of embarkation seem a perilous undertaking." This time the men made little pretense of trying to stay dry, wading out to the launches through the roiling salt water. Reid's boat pulled alongside the *Haze* at 11:00 p.m., and the New Yorkers struggled out of the landing craft and up the sides of the bounding ship. Despite the hazards only one man drowned among the troops returning from shore.[22]

The 115th, cold and wet when they reached ship, "were pleased to get to the shelter and warmth of even the suffocating atmosphere of our quarters in the *Haze*." They were luckier than some: roughening seas prevented many of their comrades from returning to their transports and 700 men spent a miserable, soggy Christmas night on the beach. The foul weather continued through December 26, keeping the last of these infantrymen beached until the following day. They finally got aboard their transports on December 27, and the fleet steamed away from Fort Fisher.[23]

Butler's decision to scuttle the Fort Fisher expedition and return to Virginia sparked headline generating controversy, including hearings by the U.S. Congress Joint Committee on the Conduct of the War. The furor resulted in Butler's removal from command, although Butler may actually have made a wise decision not to attack on Christmas night. Only 2,200 of his 6,500 troops were ashore; he had credible intelligence about a large division of Confederate troops approaching from Wilmington; and the fort had suffered only minimal damage from the naval bombardment. But Grant's orders to Butler stated that if the initial federal assault failed to take Fort Fisher, Butler should entrench his troops. Grant expected them to work with the navy to besiege and capture the fort and the other rebel fortifications protecting Wilmington. Butler defied this directive by returning to Virginia, and Grant sacked him; he had bungled his last campaign.[24]

After a three day journey the 115th New York finally disembarked from the *Haze* for good at 2:00 p.m. on December 30, 1864, on the north bank of the James River at Deep Bottom, Virginia. Except for the abortive landing that brought them ashore for a few hours on Christmas afternoon, the regiment had been aboard the miserable ship for twenty-two days. "We never suffered more," concluded Corporal Reid. The New Yorkers reached their old campground in the Richmond siege lines at dark on the cold and rainy night but found it occupied by other troops and slept nearby in the mud.

Before heading up the James, the *Haze* had spent some time anchored off Fortress Monroe where the 115th received a shipment of mail that included welcome letters from home. The mail apprized many of the soldiers that Christmas packages were en route, but that delightful prospect would fall victim to the continuing reign of bad luck over the 115th, as the men soon learned. After the trials of the fruitless Fort Fisher expedition and a dismal night in the mud at the Richmond trenches, the men suffered the depressing discovery that the Christmas packages sent from home had been lost or stolen. The holiday shipments, plus other personal baggage the soldiers could not carry along on the abortive North Carolina campaign, had been stored in their Virginia camp to await the men's return; but when the men eagerly entered the site on December 31 they found the camp looted.

The demoralized regiment spent a chilled, wet, entirely disagreeable New Year's Eve in a woodlot. Their outlook brightened a bit on New Year's Day of 1865 when several regiments were detailed to help the 115th cut timber and set up a new camp and by day's end the men had constructed tent platforms, covered them with pine boughs, and started campfires. Wrote Corporal Reid, "We had all worked like beavers in the construction of our camp, taking every opportunity we could get for washing clothes and freeing our persons of the vermin"—the lice which had plagued their weeks aboard the *Haze*. But true to form, as soon as the regiment began to grow comfortable in a fresh camp, orders came to vacate. At 9:00 a.m. January 3rd the 115th was commanded to get ready to move out in two hours. They were heading back to Fort Fisher.[25]

General Grant and other federal officials could not tolerate the failure to take Wilmington and wasted little time appointing a new army commander and ordering the fleets back to North Carolina. In addition, since General Sherman had marched across Georgia and seized Savannah in late December, Grant had further strategic motivation for capturing Wilmington: he wished to turn it into a port that would support Sherman's upcoming campaign through the Carolinas, rather than allow it to remain in Confederate hands as a threat to Sherman's rear. To lead the land forces for the second Wilmington campaign Grant chose a man familiar to the 115th New York, former Tenth Corps commander Major General Alfred H. Terry. Terry's force consisted of all the troops that comprised the first expedition plus several additional units, a total of 8,900 men. Admiral Porter again commanded the naval force, this time fifty-nine warships with 627 guns.[26]

The 115th crossed the familiar pontoon bridge at Deep Bottom for a final time on January 3. They spent a snowy night bivouacked near Bermuda Hundred Landing and on January 4 boarded the steamship *DeMolay*, the same vessel that had run them aground in the Pamunkey River en route to Cold Harbor on May 30, seven months earlier. Then the regiment sailed away from Virginia, not to return during the war. They suffered through another crowded, storm-tossed sea voyage, arriving off Fort Fisher during the night of January 12–13, 1865.[27]

Gazing out from Fort Fisher, rebel Colonel Lamb noted the twinkling of lights that indicated the return of the federal fleets and quickly relayed the news to Wilmington over the restored telegraph lines. The fort itself remained intact with its full complement of armament. Its garrison had been increased, but still measured only a woefully inadequate total of 1,900 men from North Carolina, South Carolina, and Georgia.[28]

Offshore the Union force readied for action as daylight approached. Navy gunboats laid down a curtain of shellfire to chase the enemy from the landing zone. The northern infantrymen left their transports and repeated the perilous beach landing in a high surf, making the largest amphibious landing of American troops until D-Day in Normandy in 1944. Other than some men getting a soaking and ruining their rations and gunpowder, no casualties occurred.[29]

General Terry immediately ordered earthworks dug across the peninsula from the Atlantic to the Cape Fear River in order to protect his rear should any rebel troops approach from Wilmington. He assigned all of his landing force to man the quickly dug fortification, with the exception of Ames's Division. Terry intended to use Ames's 3,300 troops, among whom were Bell's Brigade and the 115th New York, to make the attack on Fort Fisher. The soldiers completed the rearguard earthwork by the morning of January 14. Ames's Division then advanced into positions nearer Fort Fisher while General Terry met with Admiral Porter to plot a strategy for taking the rebel bastion the next day. Thankfully for the Union soldiers, this time around the army and navy acted like allies instead of rivals.[30]

As the army went ashore and prepared for its mission, the navy repeated its epic bombardment of Fort Fisher. The barrage commenced as the infantry made its landing, and

Union infantry made amphibious landings on the beach north of Fort Fisher on December 25, 1864, and again on January 14, 1865 (*Harper's Weekly*).

continued round-the-clock for over forty-eight hours. The navy's cannonade proved far more effective than it had in December. After his prior try at Fort Fisher, Admiral Porter shed the notion that his guns could level the great sand citadel and instead made the fort's cannons his target. He had his warships anchor closer to shore than they had three weeks earlier and concentrate their fire on the rebels' land face batteries in an attempt to eliminate the guns confronting the infantry. And instead of retiring all his ships after dark, the admiral kept his ironclads in place overnight, maintaining a steady shellfire that prevented the Confederates from using this time to make repairs. The strategy worked: although a day and a half of bombardment did no meaningful damage to Fort Fisher's great walls, it disabled most of the rebels' land face guns.[31]

Lieutenant Colonel Nathan Johnson, recovered from the shoulder wound he suffered at Fort Gilmer in September, returned to command the 115th on its second excursion to Fort Fisher. He noted that the navy continued to shell the fort "right smart" as the infantry got into position to attack during the evening of January 14. But at sunset when he turned his binoculars toward the Confederate stronghold, he was discouraged that he "could not discover that any portion of it had been knocked down but that it still loomed up against the evening sky with all its formidable proportions and gigantic strength."

The next morning, January 15, 1865, the troops of Ames's Division started to close in on Fort Fisher. The 115th New York "began to prepare for work and got ready to move and about 12 o'clock we got orders to advance which we did, the navy firing away as if the Dogs of War did delight to bark & bite in the meantime," related Johnson. "We moved up to within ¾ of a mile of the fort and then laid us down to rest and await the cessation of the bombardment." The three brigades of Ames's Division formed in three lines facing the west

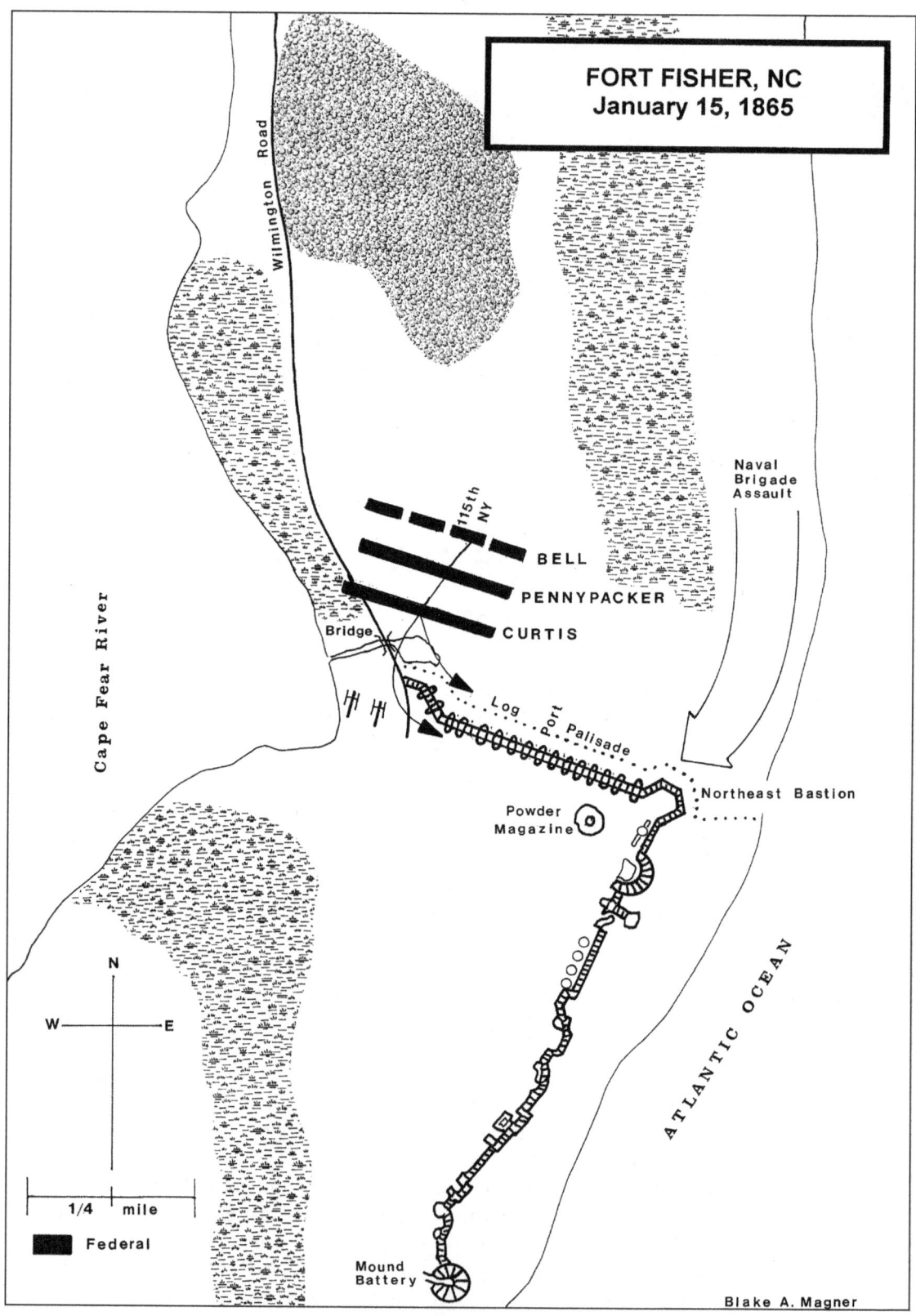

end of the fort's land face, the end nearest the Cape Fear River. The 115th formed in the third line with the rest of Bell's Brigade.[32]

The northerners made several advances that brought General Curtis's First Brigade within 200 yards of the fort, with Colonel Bell's Third Brigade less than 400 yards behind them and Colonel Galusha Pennypacker's Second Brigade in between. In addition 100 sharpshooters, mostly from Bell's 13th Indiana, dug in just 175 yards from the fort intending to pick off any rebels who mounted the parapet walls to confront the federal assault. A few brave Confederates dashed out to fire on the attackers despite the shellfire and the sharpshooters, and inflicted some casualties in all three brigades.[33]

Nearer the beach about 2,000 marines and sailors from the ships' crews had landed that morning and faced Fort Fisher's Northeast Bastion. Admiral Porter was determined that the navy share in the glory of conquering the mighty Confederate fortress, and these men had responded to the admiral's call for volunteers to participate in the storming of the fort. The so-called boarding party consisted of men from dozens of ships. These brave mariners were terribly out of their element in the coming action, charging a strong position armed only with revolvers and cutlasses.[34]

As these army and navy forces faced their objective, they had to admire the sharp work of the naval gunners. The great sand walls of the fort still stood intact as Johnson had noted in his surveillance the previous evening, but the warships had succeeded in destroying their intended targets. Only one of the heavy guns that lined the fort's land face remained serviceable, and the log palisade was peppered with gaps. Most rebel troops remained hidden away in their bombproofs. Finally at 3:25 p.m. steam whistles sounded from the navy ships, a pre-arranged cue to ensure a coordinated, simultaneous ground attack by the army and navy contingents on shore. At the signal the navy cannons redirected their furor toward Fort Fisher's sea face, and U.S. soldiers, sailors, and marines rushed the fort.[35]

The ill-suited naval boarding party sprang to the attack. Johnson witnessed their movement from the 115th's position in the third line of infantry. "We were about to charge when we saw the Marines advancing on the fort with pistols and cutlasses. Great Caesar's Ghost! Didn't we look with some amazement at such a performance? Pistols and cutlasses to storm the strongest work in America with!" Rebel Colonel Lamb reported that fewer than 1,200 healthy men remained available to him when the Yankee ground attack began. The southerners poured out of their bombproofs and into position atop the fort's walls. Five hundred of them defended the Northeast Bastion against the charging seamen.

The boarding party advanced with great dash and courage and came out with great losses. Within thirty minutes nearly 300 of them lay dead or wounded, the rest pinned down in front of the fort or dashing headlong up the beach in retreat. Johnson recorded that before the 115th got halfway to the fort, "the Marines were running back, terribly cut up and defeated." They had failed to board Fort Fisher.[36]

As Colonel Lamb and his men at the Northeast Bastion raised triumphant cheers at the withdrawal of the sailors and marines, they looked to their left and saw Union flags atop the western end of Fort Fisher's land face. At once they raced over to help the 600 Confederates defending that sector against the onrushing federal infantry. As planned, Curtis's First Brigade of four New York regiments had charged toward that corner of the fort upon hearing the signal whistles from the warships offshore. Rebel musketry from the land face walls had not been enough to deter these seasoned foot soldiers from their advance, but rebel field artillery, stationed at a gate at the west end of the fort where the Wilmington Road entered it, caused the lines to veer to their left. The federals slogged across a marshy slough then through the log palisade, its gaps widened by courageous volunteer axe-men known as pioneers. With the help of the sharpshooters' covering fire, Curtis's four regiments slowly worked their way up the grass-covered sand slope of the land face wall and drove the rebel defenders out of the first battery. They had achieved a lodgement on the fort's great wall.[37]

Twenty-year old Colonel Galusha Pennypacker's Second Brigade followed closely behind. Pennypacker's command included the 47th and 48th New York and the 76th, 97th, and 203rd Pennsylvania. These units caught up to the rear of Curtis's Brigade while hundreds of Curtis's men were still struggling across the marshy ground and squeezing through the gaps in the palisade. Units intermingled and Pennypacker's troops joined Curtis's in driving the rebels out of the first two traverses. Parts of Pennypacker's Second Brigade also moved against the Confederate artillery positioned in front of the riverside gate at the land face's west end. These northerners suffered many losses as the rebel gunners stood to their task until many were downed and their position overrun.[38]

Two men of the 115th New York assisted in driving away these rebel artillerists. Corporal Albon Hanner, a twenty-eight-year old from Northampton, and Private George Kinnicut, a thirty-one-year old recruit from Schenectady who had joined the regiment four months earlier, volunteered to serve on a detail to pick off the rebel cannoneers from the cover of a small building outside the fort. Kinnicut was wounded, but Hanner remained in action while four others were slain beside him.[39]

Fighting now concentrated around the third traverse. The blue clad troops of Ames's first two brigades faced a counterattack by Colonel Lamb and the 500 southerners who had just repelled the sailors and marines at the Northeast Bastion. At this point Colonel Bell received word to lead his Third Brigade into the melee and he ordered his four regiments forward. Then, as Bell started across the bridge that carried the Wilmington Road over the slough, a rebel ball pierced his chest. Lieutenant Hugh Sanford of Company D of the 115th, assigned as an aide to the colonel, was at his side and heard the bullet strike his commander. The stricken Bell watched his troops advance on the fort for a time before being carried to the rear. He died the next day.[40]

The fall of their commander did not slow the men of the Third Brigade who were not far behind the first two brigades, in either space or time. Johnson reported that the Third Brigade entered the fort "conjointly with a portion of the First Brigade." Captain Fred Mosher recalled the 115th bogging down in the slough and veering toward the bridge. Most of the bridge deck had been torn up, so Mosher and many others crossed on the stringers. Rebel riflemen on the fort's wall greeted them with heavy fire, as did the Confederate artillery at the gate which had not yet been silenced. Once across the bridge, some poured through the riverside gate and others ran up the fort's sandy outer parapet wall. Soon these men of New York, New Hampshire, and Indiana joined hundreds of northerners from the first two brigades in the close struggle with rebel defenders on the traverses, "all vying with each other," wrote the grandiloquent Johnson, "in the noble emulation of who should be first in the grand achievements of that memorable day."[41]

The 13th Indiana and 115th New York were the first of Bell's units to advance. Sergeant Peter Keck rushed into Fort Fisher and up the first traverse where he hurriedly planted the 115th's flag. From there he began a footrace with the color bearer of the 13th Indiana as they ran side-by-side trying to be first to raise their regiment's standard on the next traverse. Early in the fight Keck took a gunshot in the right breast, the fourth wound he suffered while carrying the regimental flag, but he stayed in action throughout the battle.[42]

The 115th separated into two wings on reaching the fort. Johnson led one over the successive traverses of Fort Fisher's land face walls. As they fought their way to the seventh traverse, the other contingent followed Major Walrath into the fort and along the interior base of the land face, staying even with their comrades on the traverses. "All organization at this time was completely broken," wrote Captain Mosher. "Every man was his own commander and realized he must win or die."[43]

The struggle for Fort Fisher focused on the massive traverses, each presenting a new defensive position from which the Confederates could resist further Yankee advance. Close-quarter fighting marked the top of each successive traverse as the bravest among the Union attackers mounted the crests and grappled with rebel defenders in the growing darkness. Piles of dead and wounded men tumbled down the sand slopes and hindered movement. "The fighting now is on in earnest hand to hand, our infantry pushing the enemy from traverse to traverse," recorded John Reardon. Meanwhile other federals among the disorganized mob of troops made their way along the outer wall of the land face or through the fort's inner grounds. Shortly after sunset, with half the land face in Union hands and the tired attackers beginning to falter, General Terry ordered a reserve brigade into the fight. These fresh men spearheaded a renewed rush against the diminished and fatigued Confederates.[44]

Stephen Olney, a Saratoga Springs man, led Company D into the fort. A lieutenant from Company F, Olney had taken temporary command of Company D in place of Nicholas DeGraff, who remained in Virginia on detached duty. This assignment cost Olney his life when a rebel shot him as he advanced around one of the traverses. Another Company D man promptly shot and killed Olney's assailant. Though others experienced close calls, the twenty-seven-year old Lieutenant Olney was the lone officer of the 115th to die in the battle. Lieutenant Colonel Johnson had two near misses — one when an exploding shell leveled but did not harm him, and another when a soldier of the regiment was shot down as Johnson stood next to him giving orders. Similar fortune blessed Captain Mosher when a rebel bullet loosened one of his shoulder straps but did not cut his skin.[45]

The bloody combat lasted several hours. Inexorably, Union numbers prevailed. "We kept on struggling, bleeding, dying. We kept on until victory crowned our labors," related the dramatic Nathan Johnson. By 10:00 p.m. rebel resistance broke down. "It was now dark, and after going traverse to traverse and more or less hand to hand encounters, the firing all at once seemed to cease, and soon after word came that the enemy had surrendered," wrote Captain Mosher. As Johnson said a few days later: "We fought for seven long, bloody, terrible hours until at 10:00 p.m. the rebs caved in & Ft. Fisher passed into Union hands."[46]

"The scene which followed upon the surrender was brilliant beyond description," reported *Harper's Weekly*, a nationally circulated tabloid. "The hearty cheer from the captured fort was echoed from the entire fleet. From every vessel rockets were thrown up into the air, filling the sky with brightness."[47]

No one could have appreciated these victory fireworks more than the men of the 115th New York. After two and a half frustrating and ill-starred years of service, after a dismaying succession of murderous battles that began eleven months earlier at Olustee, the regiment had finally prevailed over the rebels. "We were excited and elated beyond measure," wrote Macfarlane. Johnson expressed awe at the accomplishment: "When we had obtained possession of the fort we were surprised at what we had done. It is the strongest and largest work in America if not the world." Sergeant Reardon called it a glorious victory. He described

The Navy fleet launches a fireworks display to celebrate the capture of Fort Fisher late on January 15, 1865 (*Harper's Weekly*).

the troops as "so elated they almost forgot about sleeping, and after the prisoners are safely marched out and put under guard near the fort, the boys spent most of the time until morning roaming about examining every bombproof or any other structure in search of goods."[48]

It cannot be determined with precision how many men of the 115th actually took part in the storming of Fort Fisher. A large part of the regiment remained on picket duty near the landing zone and fifty men of the regiment had remained in Virginia to work in hospital and ambulance details and other detached duties. The 115th suffered only seventeen casualties during the fight. The limited number of men engaged would account for this low figure, as would the regiment's position in the third line of the infantry assault. Altogether, the victory cost the Union attackers 664 casualties. Around 500 rebels were killed or wounded and 1,400 became prisoners.[49]

The 115th suffered over 600 battlefield casualties during the disheartening string of combat setbacks they endured between Olustee, Florida in February 1864 and Darbytown Road, Virginia eight months later. Now they finally tasted victory with a relatively small toll of two men dead and fifteen wounded. But the hard luck New Yorkers would not get to savor this bit of irony. Their win over the rebels did not signal an end to their run of dogged misfortune. Deep within the bowels of Fort Fisher lay the source of the greatest tragedy yet to befall the 115th. Wrote Reardon: "After all is quiet in the night our brigade stacked arms in the fort and those who wished lay down to sleep, some never to arise in this world."[50]

A large underground chamber within the Northeast Bastion contained Fort Fisher's main powder magazine which still held 13,000 pounds of gunpowder. The 115th and 169th New York and the 4th New Hampshire unwittingly chose the ground above the immense magazine as their bivouac after the battle. At 8:00 a.m. the next morning as these troops lay asleep in what James Clark later called the fancied security of Fort Fisher, the below-ground chamber exploded.[51]

Earlier in the morning soldiers from the 115th who had remained on picket duty near the landing zone received orders to rejoin their regiment. About a mile and a half above the fort they passed the captured rebel troops. James Reid described how "nearing the fort the evidences of the great conflict were to be seen on every hand." He viewed the shattered palisades and noted that "hardly a square yard of what was once the smooth, grassy slope of the fort but what was furrowed by the naval fire." Ascending the fort's land face wall, Reid and his mates were sombered by the sight of numerous corpses from both armies among the broken guns and other debris of battle.[52]

As Reid and Reardon and the other 115th men returning from picket duty approached Fort Fisher, their regiment's calamity unfolded. Reardon witnessed the event from a distance of several hundred feet:

> About 8 a.m. all who are awake are startled by a terrific explosion in the fort. A tremor of the earth was the first intimation I saw or felt of the catastrophe. On looking up we saw a great cloud of dust, timbers, etc. flying in every direction. There was not the concussion and roar there would have been had the soil been of clay or some other compact material. The fort is built of sand and the magazine covered with this soil and, instead of flying up and out in more or less large pieces, it seemed to rise up and spread like a huge wave covering everything for some distance.[53]

Captain Mosher luckily was astir when the magazine blew. He and Major Walrath had shared a blanket during the night. "The following morning we arose, got some water and were making our toilet when the explosion occurred," recalled Mosher. "At that instant, I stood with my cap in my left hand combing my hair with the other, my back to the magazine. The earth seemed to shake and move like a wave." The blast hurled Mosher and Walrath outward and showered them with timbers and debris. Others were not so lucky. As Lieutenant Colonel Johnson wrote, "Some were actually blown to atoms. We found a leg here and an arm there and entrails in another place. It was an awful sight." Dr. Macfarlane sadly recounted the explosion "killing and burying many a brave man who had passed unharmed through the previous day's fighting."[54]

Corporal Reid crested the land face wall some time after the blast and spotted Private Amos Brown, cook for Company C. He clambered down the inner slope toward Brown. "I hastily descended and asked him where our regiment was," Reid related. "With tears in his eyes and quivering voice he replied, 'They are all buried by the explosion of the magazine.'" By the time Reid arrived rescue operations had begun.[55]

The *New York Tribune* reported that "almost the whole three regiments were buried alive, to a greater or lesser depth, by the falling debris of earth, shot, shell, timbers." One to ten feet of sand and rubble covered "everything and everybody near the place." Survivors at once scrambled to save their trapped comrades. Privates Jeremiah Coy and Waldo Young had just arisen when the earth enveloped them. Young was buried with only his face exposed, his leg broken by the body of another man. Though painfully injured himself, Coy found Young and began to dig him out but passed out after a few moments. Others soon rescued both men. James Getman, a twenty-year old musician from Nelliston, New York, was buried with only his left hand exposed. By wiggling that hand he attracted the attention of Corporal Fred Meyer of nearby Ephratah and was saved. Getman emerged with only one of his shoes, the other lost in the rubble.[56]

Sergeant Henry Heaton and Corporal Jadua Countryman had wearily bedded down together after the defeat of the Confederates. When Heaton arose to get breakfast the next morning he awakened Countryman, but Countryman opted for some extra sleep and stayed behind. After the explosion Heaton attempted to lead a group of rescuers to find Countryman. "He tried to guide us to the spot as near as possible, but this was practically guesswork owing to the changed condition of the grounds," wrote Reardon, who joined the rescue party. They never found Countryman. "From his position, which was certainly a dangerous one, he must have gotten the full force of the explosion and might have been thrown into the ocean, distant not more than thirty rods," surmised Reardon. Dr. Macfarlane especially mourned the death of Countryman, who served as his hospital steward.[57]

The frantic effort to unearth the survivors and

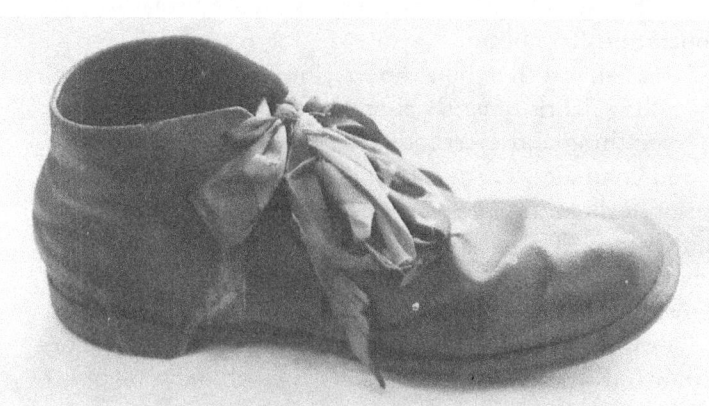

Private James Getman, one of the 115th's musicians, was buried in debris by the magazine explosion at Fort Fisher. Getman was saved but lost one of his shoes. He and his descendants saved its mate, which is now on display at the Reaney Library in St. Johnsville, New York (Margaret Reaney Memorial Library, St. Johnsville, New York).

the grim work of recovering the dead continued throughout the day. "Those on the flat not deeply covered were soon released. Those under two or more feet of earth are buried alive to be found later," remembered one man of the 115th. Work continued until the afternoon of January 17 when the dead were reburied in a mass grave along with many of those killed in taking the fort on the 15th.[58]

Horrified Union troops initially blamed the magazine explosion on the enemy. But suspicion soon centered on federal soldiers seen exploring the captured fort, including the powder magazines, with lit torches and candles in hand. Dr. Macfarlane later named a thirty-seven-year old private from Company G as the culprit: "The explosion was caused by a good-for-nothing Frenchman, Martin Delacateur, a member of the 115th regiment, who was seen to enter the magazine in a search for whiskey, carrying a lighted candle." After the blast Delacateur, a native of Saratoga Springs, was never seen again. He was one of three members of the 115th who remained unaccounted for after rescue and recovery operations ceased, the three presumed vaporized or hurled into the Atlantic. Altogether the regiment suffered eleven killed and forty-one wounded by the explosion.[59]

Corporal Fred Meyer served with the 115th throughout the war without injury. After the Fort Fisher magazine explosion, Meyer saved his friend James Getman when he spotted Getman's wiggling hand sticking up from the rubble (New York State Military Museum).

On January 21 the Army convened a formal board of inquiry to investigate the cause of the calamity. The witness list included Lieutenant Colonel Johnson, Major Walrath, and Captain Mosher. Walrath and Mosher were among several who testified that they had seen federal soldiers, sailors, and marines entering the magazines and bombproofs in search of plunder. Walrath stated that these men "would light matches inside and let them burn to see what was in the magazine." No one mentioned Private Delacateur nor any other individual by name. The board quickly pinned the blame for the disaster on these anonymous scavengers. It also faulted a luckless officer of the 13th Indiana who General Ames had ordered to place guards at all entry ways to magazines and bombproofs. The officer had found and placed guards at thirty-one such entrances, but unfortunately, by the time of the explosion he had not yet worked his way to the main rebel magazine where the blast occurred.[60]

One of the flags of the 115th New York also fell victim to the tragic magazine explosion. Already tattered and torn from two and a half years of campaigning, the regiment's New York State flag now lay shredded beyond usefulness. Corporal Reid noted the loss of the cherished banner:

> This flag, with Old Glory, was a sacred emblem to every member of the regiment, presented to us by the ladies at Fonda, saved from the surrender at Harpers Ferry, borne aloft by those heroic bearers Keck and Fellows, they had been the rallying point on many hard contested fields. Underneath their very folds wounds and death had come to more than a score of color bearers and their guards; pierced by the enemy's missiles until they were surely the rags of the principles they represented.

Reid lamented that now that the flag had witnessed victory, it would be separated from the regiment's other sacred emblem, its United States flag. Someone proposed that each man of the regiment should have a piece of the ruined state flag and the remaining cloth was cut up and parceled among the men. Major Walrath presided over the distribution. To honor the memory of Captain Garret Van Derveer, who suffered a mortal wound at Olustee, the major sent a piece of the flag to Van Derveer's young widow.[61]

After the battle General Ames ordered the Third Brigade to garrison Fort Fisher. Colonel Bell's death, plus an injury suffered by the colonel of the 169th New York in the powder blast, left the 115th's Lieutenant Colonel Johnson as senior officer and therefore commander of the brigade. In a January 30 letter to an acquaintance back home Johnson jokingly called himself "the first Union Commander of Fort Fisher, N.C."[62]

Troops of the 115th helped care for the wounded and bury the dead on January 17, then began setting up camp within the fort's grounds. "In a surprisingly short time we were comfortably housed, each tent having its fireplace and chimney," wrote Reid. Notable within the camp was half of a fifteen inch naval shell, which served the New Yorkers as a wash basin, although the heavy shell was a great inconvenience to empty.[63]

Confederate blockade runners, unaware that Fort Fisher had succumbed to the enemy, continued to arrive. At least five such ships anchored and were captured while the 115th garrisoned the fort. The men particularly enjoyed one arrival when they watched the ship set anchor and lower a boat and saw her captain rowed ashore expecting to report to the Confederate commander. As one of the 115th's officers described the event, "He was politely informed that he was a prisoner and that his ship and cargo would be presented to Uncle Sam."[64]

The regiment spent a quiet three weeks at camp within Fort Fisher. But the soldiers knew they had work ahead when General Grant came to the fort in late January. He surprised the men when he did not pause to make even a cursory inspection of the famous Confederate fortress. The Union war leader was all business, wasting no time relishing or recognizing his troops' victory. Grant spent two days conferring with officers and poring over maps, planning the next campaign. The men who took Fort Fisher would soon be in motion again.[65]

14

Peace and Home Again

"Great rejoicing! Our fighting is ended"

When General Grant traveled to Fort Fisher, he brought with him Major General John McAllister Schofield, commander of the Union Twenty-Third Corps. At Nashville, Tennessee, in mid–December, Schofield and his corps were instrumental in a federal victory that ended large scale Confederate military resistance outside Virginia. Following the Union victory in Tennessee and Sherman's successes in Georgia, the northern high command crafted a strategy for an 1865 campaign to defeat the rebels in the east. Part of the plan involved bringing Schofield and his 21,000 men to the Atlantic coast.

The Union scheme for concluding the war in 1865 called for Sherman to drive northward from Savannah through the Carolinas into Virginia. If Grant had not defeated or chased Lee from Richmond and Petersburg by that time, surely a united effort by Sherman's westerners and the Army of the Potomac would finish the job. Toward this strategic objective, Sherman's initial task was to move on Goldsboro, North Carolina, an inland city linked by railroad to the seaports at New Bern and Wilmington. These rail lines from the coast would then serve as supply lines for Sherman's push into Virginia.

While Sherman drove his 60,000 veterans over the 425 miles between Savannah and Goldsboro, Schofield was to move out of Fort Fisher, seize Wilmington, secure the rail line between Wilmington and Goldsboro, and unite his force with Sherman's for the final push to victory. Schofield, an 1853 West Point graduate born in western New York and raised in Illinois, took command of the newly created Department of North Carolina which consisted of his own Twenty-Third Corps plus the 8,000 men who had triumphed over Fort Fisher under General Terry. Schofield's men began arriving at Fort Fisher on February 7, 1865.[1]

Nicholas DeGraff got his first look at Fort Fisher on February 6, three weeks after his regiment participated in the Union victory there. He was awed by the formidable fort and impressed that his comrades had taken it. "The troops engaged in its capture are deserving of all praise. Though I can claim none of the honor I am proud of my Regiment, the gallant 115th N.Y." The previous October DeGraff had been promoted to first lieutenant and given command of the Bermuda Hundred ambulance service. He and several dozen other men of the 115th had been pulled away from the regiment to work in the ambulance corps, an assignment they relished. "What great luck," DeGraff exclaimed in a letter to his sister. "Why I could hardly feel better if I had suddenly fell heir to a fortune."

In Virginia, DeGraff supervised eleven ambulances, each assigned a driver and two stretcher bearers. His staff also included a cook, an orderly, five sergeants and thirty horses. His camp stood a half mile behind the Bermuda Hundred earthworks and occupied three acres which held neat cabins for his men plus a log-sided stable with a canvas roof for the horses. DeGraff had his own saddle horse, acquired a pet cat, and met a "pretty secesh girl." Best of all, there was little combat and the ambulances were not very busy.

Unfortunately this interlude was darkened by DeGraff's anxiety to get home to see his father, who had become gravely ill. His repeated attempts to get a furlough were denied by division and corps staff. In January he wrote his sister of yet another failure to obtain leave and vented his frustration. "I declare my patience is almost gone. A man might about as well be sentenced to the penitentiary for three years as to offer his services to the Government." DeGraff kept trying but never did get his furlough, and he never again saw his father, who died on March 26, 1865.[2]

In the weeks after the federal seizure of Fort Fisher Confederate forces still held a defensive line five miles north of the fort. This line ran from Sugar Loaf Battery on the east bank of the Cape Fear River to Myrtle Sound, a long, narrow north-south inlet separated from the Atlantic Ocean by a thin strip of beach. On the west bank of the river, opposite Sugar Loaf, the rebels held Fort Anderson, a strong earthen battery. From Fort Anderson the southerners' line extended a short distance westerly where it anchored on impassable swampland. In order to take Wilmington, Schofield and his force would need to drive the Confederates from this line.[3]

On February 11 Schofield began the offensive. He sent Terry's 8,000 troops, now known as Terry's Provisional Corps, to attack the rebel Sugar Loaf-Myrtle Sound line. At 4:00 a.m. on a cold and frosty morning the camp of the 115th and their brigade, still within the comfortable confines of Fort Fisher, came astir. At 6:00 a.m. the brigade's five regiments—13th Indiana, 9th Maine, 4th New Hampshire, 115th New York, and 169th New York—marched out of the fort and joined the other brigades of Ames's Division, who stood massed and waiting for them along the beach north of the fort. A slow all-day march brought Terry's men within rifle range of the rebel line where they dug in and bivouacked for the night.[4]

To avoid a costly frontal assault on the prepared rebels and instead surprise and outflank them at the eastern end of their line, Union leadership adopted a plan devised by their Chief Engineer, Lieutenant Colonel Cyrus Comstock. The rebel line anchored on Myrtle Sound and left the thin strip of beach between the east shore of Myrtle Sound and the Atlantic undefended. Under Comstock's plan, navy ships would transport a supply of pontoon boats to a point on shore north of the Confederate position where the infantry, moving up the beach under cover of darkness, would meet them. The foot soldiers would use the pontoon boats to cross Myrtle Sound, then assault the southerners from the rear. The weather however did not cooperate. Heavy winds and high seas on February 12 and 13 combined, as Schofield reported, "to render the execution of this plan impossible." Meanwhile the 115th spent the two days in a chilly bivouac.[5]

During the night of February 14–15 the northerners tried a different tactic. They attempted to haul the pontoon boats up the beach on mule-drawn wagons. With the wagons went the infantry assault troops, the 115th New York among the first wave. The movement was sluggish, hindered by heavy surf and deep, loose sand. The mule teams struggled with the heavy loads of pontoons and the infantry had to stop occasionally and wait for the wagons to catch up. When it became clear that the column could not achieve its objective before daylight, orders came to abandon the move. DeGraff summed up the wasted night's effort: "Our Brigade taking the lead, marched up the beach past the Reble works. Moving cautiously and quietly went about five miles, and then as quietly about-faced and marched back, arriving at our camp at 5 a.m. Rain pouring in torrents. Lay in bivouac all day. What next?"[6]

Unable to implement the pontoon-aided flanking strategy by land or sea, General Schofield turned his attention to the west side of the Cape Fear River. On February 17 the 115th got orders to move at sunset, struck their tents, and prepared to leave their camp opposite the Confederate Sugar Loaf line. Night fell with no further orders, so they set the tents back up and turned in, but by 10:00 p.m. orders had them on the move again. The men marched south and arrived at the tip of the peninsula below Fort Fisher at dawn. There the troops boarded a ship which took them across the Cape Fear River to the dilapidated village of Smithville, North Carolina. After a brief respite there, the regiment was on the road again, marching northward another ten miles before nightfall and stopping just south of Fort Anderson.[7]

Joined by additional units of the Twenty-Third Corps which had just completed their long journey from Tennessee, the Union force faced Fort Anderson along the west bank of the Cape Fear. General Schofield again spared his soldiers the perils of a frontal assault. Leaving two brigades opposite the fort to occupy the enemy's attention, he sent most of his troops, the 115th among them, on a long march around the swamps that protected Fort Anderson's western flank. Meanwhile navy gunboats on the Cape Fear River rained thousands of shells on Fort Anderson and its small garrison. When rebel scouts detected the Union flanking movement, the Confederates hurriedly abandoned the fort. "The enemy were too weak to oppose such a force as now rapidly approached, and wisely withdrew." That night, with no casualties more serious than sore feet, the New Yorkers camped inside Fort Anderson.[8]

The next day, February 20, 1865, the 115th New York re-crossed the Cape Fear River and joined Terry's Corps in pursuit of Confederate units who had abandoned their Sugar Loaf line after learning of Fort Anderson's fall. "The enemy were easily forced back without the expenditure of much ammunition," wrote Reid. "In this manner the advance was continued until the enemy were forced into the defensive works of Wilmington." There, among previously prepared artillery positions three miles below the city, the outmanned southerners dug in. The 115th New York and their brigade unslung knapsacks, readied their muskets, and awaited orders to assault the rebel line.[9]

As they lay in line waiting to charge, some men of the regiment were haunted by the specter of the day in Florida, a year to the day earlier, when over half of the 115th, nearly 300 men, fell victim to rebel bullets. Wrote one enlisted man, "the coincidence of dates ... produced a general reluctance on the part of our regiment for charging the enemy that day, and we hoped for some postponement or abandonment of the idea." They got their wish when General Ames decided against the attack. Ames's decision was a good one, for the following night in the face of impossible odds, the rebels evacuated Wilmington. The 115th marched into the city on February 22 having suffered not a single battle casualty since leaving Fort Fisher.[10]

Scores of Wilmington's citizens, mainly old men, women, and children, came out of their homes to watch the Union conquerors file in. In contrast to the open hostility that had greeted the northerners in Virginia, ladies waved handkerchiefs in greeting and some houses flew the stars and stripes. Wilmington's black residents, whom John Reardon estimated to be three-quarters of the population, turned out in force and gave the federals a raucous greeting. "Our reception by them was wildly enthusiastic," remembered Macfarlane. "The Negroes were absolutely crazy with delight. They shouted, they sang, they prayed." Women cried and hugged the soldiers. "They were on every corner with armfuls of tobacco, bags of peanuts, pails of water to give us to drink, etc., etc. They could not give us enough," wrote DeGraff. Military bands played patriotic tunes and navy gunboats capped the noisy celebration by firing artillery salvos that rattled buildings.[11]

The 115th had a very brief stay in Wilmington. The regiment entered the city at 11:00 a.m., enjoyed the cacophonous welcome, and marched out three hours later in pursuit of the fleeing rebels. Along with Ames's entire division, the New Yorkers advanced nine miles to Northeast Station, where the rail line toward Goldsboro crossed the northeast branch of the Cape Fear River. There the pursuers caught up with the retreating Confederates as they attempted to burn the 300 foot railroad bridge spanning the river. Union artillery and musketry chased the southerners from the rail bridge, but the rebels had already broken up a pontoon bridge nearby.[12]

Ames's Division set up camp at Northeast Station where they spent the following week, a week made extraordinary by the arrival of thousands of federal soldiers released from Confederate prison camps. With southern forces recoiling from Union advances in Georgia and the Carolinas and facing shortages of supplies, Confederate commanders decided to release prisoners of war held in various camps around the region. In doing so they transferred the burden of caring for them to the Yankees, "thus relieving us and embarrassing the enemy," as one highly placed Confederate officer explained. A contingent of rebel officers returned to Wilmington under a flag of truce on February 24 to negotiate the return of the prisoners. The men would be released on parole, i.e., returned to the custody of their own army but sworn not to rejoin the fight against the Confederacy. As it turned out, precious few of these unfortunate men were in any condition to return to battle.[13]

The Union troops at Northeast Station gathered food, clothing, and medical supplies for the returning prisoners, and quickly rebuilt the pontoon bridge across the river. To ensure that "the welcome from their long captivity should be appropriately observed," they constructed an arched portal at one end of the bridge and decorated it with American flags. On February 26 the first 2,000 prisoners debarked from rail cars on the far side of the river and started across the pontoons. With military bands playing *Home, Sweet Home*, the 115th and other federal regiments lined the riverbanks to greet them, "not even dreaming of the sights of wretchedness that were to follow."[14]

The awaiting troops were horrified at the sight of their returning comrades, emaciated and dressed in tatters, many with barely enough strength to walk across the bridge. Macfarlane described the refugees as "the most abject, pitiful mass of humanity the mind could conceive, their faces vacant, cadaverous and staring, and their minds gone to the verge of dementia." DeGraff detailed the spectacle in a letter to his sister:

> The poor fellows tried to cheer, but it was faint. They had hardly the strength to walk and carry their rags and filth. It was affecting to hear them fervently thank God we are under the old flag once more, another hurrah for the stars and stripes. They had their feet tied up in rags of all kinds, anything to cover their nakedness. It was a heartrending scene.[15]

Two thousand more of the former prisoners arrived the next day in a condition just as bad as the earlier group. DeGraff stood near General Ames as he watched them stagger in and saw tears in the general's eyes and heard him remark, "Horrible! Someone will have to answer for this cruelty." Nearly 10,000 miserable returnees arrived at Northeast Station during the week that the 115th spent there. The troops that greeted their arrival reacted with shock, anger, and compassion. Many of the prisoners died despite all urgent efforts to care for them, but most were sent north and recovered.[16]

Several joyous reunions took place as the prisoners poured in. During one of the daily arrivals John Reardon stood near the bridge, hoping for the return of captured members of his own regiment. After a while two ragged men Reardon did not recognize stopped and called to him. It took Reardon a moment to identify them as Privates Fisher Van Epps and Orville Snell of his own Company B, both of whom had been taken by the enemy at Deep Bottom on August 16, 1864. Reardon estimated that Snell had been reduced from a robust 170 pounds to a weight of no more than 100 pounds. When Reardon later penned a memoir of his army experience he reported that both Snell and Van Epps got home and lived for several years, but both suffered health problems for the remainder of their lives.[17]

In what may have been the most remarkable reunion scene of all, Private Charles Nathaniel Baker stepped off the pontoon bridge right into the midst of his own Company C where the first to greet him were James Reid and Joseph Abeel, the two men who had vainly tried to assist the wounded Baker off of the battlefield at Olustee exactly one year and one week earlier. Reid described the delivery of Baker straight into the arms of himself and Abeel as a scene of "almost complete earthly happiness." Typhoid fever put Baker into the army hospital at Annapolis for four months, but he recovered and returned home to Galway, Saratoga County, where he lived until his death in 1892.[18]

The final shipment of prisoners of war consisted of several hundred Union officers who came in on March 1. Officers had been held separately from enlisted men and enjoyed much better treatment from their southern captors. These men had intact clothing and the strength to celebrate their deliverance with several choruses of patriotic songs.[19]

The liberated captives went from Northeast Station to Wilmington, where Union physicians treated them. Dr. Macfarlane was among a staff of eighteen surgeons separated from their regiments and assigned to care for the returnees. "We made room for them in the churches, town hall, warehouses and lofts of the city. These soon became one vast hospital," he recorded. As if these men had not suffered enough, an epidemic of typhoid fever broke out. Macfarlane called the disease "terribly malignant." It killed not only many of the returned captives, but some of the healthy men assigned to care for them as well, including six doctors. Macfarlane had the unenviable duty of requisitioning coffins for deceased soldiers; he needed them at the rate of twenty to thirty every day. This work continued for three weeks. "I did not have the fever," Macfarlane wrote, "but when my work with them was done and the prisoners all sent north, I had to go to bed as a result of mental and physical exhaustion."[20]

On March 2 the 115th marched back to Wilmington and established a camp near the city, where the regiment spent two restful, uneventful weeks. "We had but little to do and were becoming quite lazy," summed up James Reid. John Reardon, promoted to second lieutenant in Company B while the 115th was at Northeast Station, took time to work on company muster rolls and made several trips to a theater in Wilmington. On a Sunday evening he dropped in on one of the city's churches where he heard the minister deliver a highly patriotic sermon. "It chanced to be a colored preacher and congregation," and from the shocked expression of those in attendance Reardon gathered that Wilmington's recently liberated black population was unaccustomed to hearing such themes openly espoused among blacks. "Many of his remarks were such that I think it would have been unsafe for him to have expressed three weeks previous in the same pulpit. I formed my conclusion from the manner they were received by the congregation, especially the elder ones. No doubt they felt that the words used would have been looked upon as high treason." Unfortunately, Reardon did not record the contents of the sermon.[21]

The lazy stay at Wilmington ended on March 15 when the 115th with the rest of Ames's Division headed north toward a junction with Sherman's hard marching troops. Sherman and his 60,000 men had set out from Savannah on February 1. By February 18 they had taken Columbia and Charleston, South Carolina, and on March 11 occupied Fayetteville, North Carolina—an advance of nearly 400 miles in just over five weeks. Sherman then left Fayetteville for the final push to Goldsboro on March 15, the same day Ames's forces left Wilmington.[22]

The 115th marched for six days, covering eighty-six miles along the railroad toward Goldsboro. The regiment finally stopped and set up a camp on the rainy afternoon of March 21. All that afternoon and evening the men could hear the sounds of battle off to the west of the camp. It was the third and last day of the fighting that had raged around Bentonville, North Carolina, as an outnumbered Confederate force under General Joseph Johnston vainly tried to stop Sherman's advance. As the 115th huddled in sodden tents several miles away and listened, the battle concluded with Johnston retreating northward.[23]

The next day the regiment strained for a look at the celebrated General Sherman when he came to Terry's headquarters, and on March 23 they watched closely as two corps of Sherman's soldiers marched by their camp. "Learning of the approach of a portion of the famous Shermanites, curiosity led several of us to the road to see them pass," recorded Reid. The New Yorkers wanted to get a look at the men who had fought their way through Chickamauga and Chattanooga to Atlanta, then foraged their way through a wide swath of Georgia and Carolina. The Shermanites had become accustomed to operating beyond the reach of the friendly supply lines considered so indispensable by the Army of the Potomac and other federal armies in the eastern theater. They supplied their needs and often loosed a savage vengeance on the South by foraging, or bumming, over the countryside. The 115th's veterans found the westerners shabby and begrimed but noted the chickens and hams they carried and the variety of mules, horses, farm wagons and buggies transporting the men and their loot.[24]

At one point a halt in the march brought an Illinois regiment abreast of the camp of the 115th. The men of the two units sized one another up and began trading good-natured barbs. One of the Illinoisans asked why the New Yorkers had guards posted. "To keep Sherman's Bummers from foraging through our camp," rejoined a spokesman from the 115th. Noting the newer clothes on the easterners, an Illinois officer said, "Guess yer hain't been out long. New regiment?" The 115th played along with the insult, one New Yorker professing that they were indeed new. Corporal Reid relates the rest of the exchange:

> "Well how in thunderation did you get way up in this country?" asked the Illinoisan.
> "Walked, of course," was our reply.
> "Where from?" he queried.
> "FORT FISHER," we thundered.
> "F-o-r-t F-i-s-h-e-r?" he drawled. "Were you there when the fort was captured? Did you help Terry capture that fort?" And when he was informed that we belonged to Terry's Corps and helped in the capture of the fort ... he said, "Well now, fellers, I take it all back. Them new clothes and that camp guard led me to think you were a new regiment."

With that revelation the Illinoisans raised a cheer for the 115th, calling them bully boys, and they marched off with a parting boast that they were going to "drive Johnston up into Virginia with Lee and then lick the whole crowd."[25]

Even before merging with Sherman's troops, Terry's men—the 115th New York among them—had taken up bumming. In a letter written during the march from Wilmington, DeGraff wrote, "We take every bit of food for man or beast that we find. Also all horses, mules, cattle, sheep, hogs, &c. Regular Sherman style." In some cases the foraging Shermanites preceded the easterners to local prizes, often trailing a wake of devastation. Reardon, describing a foraging trek of his own, told of one farm where the westerners had taken absolutely everything, including the watch of a boy lying feverish in bed and a chicken cooking in a pot intended to provide broth for the sick boy. "It is pitiful to hear their story and see the condition. Sherman's bummers left them as they left thousands of others on their line of march, without a morsel to eat, without a horse, cow or ox to till the soil, and without the seed to plant of any description, even dig the potatoes up already planted. They must eventually starve as their neighbors cannot help them, all being in a similar condition for miles and miles." He tried to make amends for the acts of his western allies by taking the farmer to a mill run by Union soldiers and obtaining a supply of cornmeal for him.[26]

While denouncing the deeds of Sherman's men, Lieutenant Reardon rationalized his own bumming, noting that he foraged from prosperous citizens he judged to have "no love for a Union soldier." In his self-serving logic, Reardon reasoned that since these people "surely have not contributed a cent toward putting down the rebellion, we think it not more than just to make a small levy on their resources." He also eased his conscience by noting that instead of leaving their victims with nothing, "the boys are advised not to rob them entirely, but make a fair sort of division."[27]

DeGraff led an eight man foraging party beyond Union camps into the Carolina countryside on March 24. About three miles out a former slave on an abandoned plantation warned the party that a force of Confederate troops had been there earlier that morning. DeGraff's squad pushed on cautiously and soon saw a line of enemy skirmishers heading toward them. The rebels opened fire and the foragers hastily skedaddled back to their own lines. Union pickets engaged the advancing Confederates in a brief fight. "There was quite a fusillade. They fell back and it was all over," recalled DeGraff. Although the men had no way of knowing it, these were the last shots that the soldiers of the 115th New York would ever hear fired in anger.[28]

While the bulk of Sherman's army moved on and occupied Goldsboro, the 115th New York spent ten days serving as a railroad guard, spread out along the tracks between Goldsboro and Wilmington. Meanwhile General Sherman went to Virginia to meet with President Lincoln and General Grant to plot the final defeat of the Confederacy, returning on March 30. His force continued to rest and re-fit at Goldsboro until April 10 when it moved out in pursuit of Johnston.[29]

The 115th left its railroad guard duty behind on April 8 and trekked northward, joined by Sherman's men as they left Goldsboro on the tenth. The New Yorkers noted proudly that they had no trouble keeping up with "these great marchers." With Schofield's troops joining Sherman's, the Union force exceeded 80,000 men, and Johnston's Confederates retreated before them in the direction of Raleigh.[30]

As the 115th passed through a wooded area on the morning of April 12, its fifth straight day on the march, a strange commotion broke out a distance up the line ahead of them.

The procession halted as the loud shouting and cheering drew closer. "Like a wave these sounds rolled toward us through the several divisions, brigades, and regiments," recalled James Reid. "Our inquisitiveness was at its height long before the sequel of these strange proceedings reached us. In all expectancy we gaze forward." Soon they saw the infantry columns parting to make way for a solitary horseman galloping down the road, shouting as he came. When they could finally hear the man's words, the boys of the 115th instantly joined the wild celebration. The rider brought news of the surrender of General Lee to General Grant at Appomattox Court House in Virginia on April 9.

"Such hearty, roaring cheers as passed down the line until it died away in the distance, I never heard or expect to hear again," wrote Reardon. Visions of peace and home buoyed the soldiers, who knew well that Johnston could not resist them and that no other Confederate force could sustain the war. When the trek resumed, it felt entirely different. "The boys are light hearted, and marching seems but play." That night, recalled Reid, "Our camp fires burned more brightly, our food never tasted better, no grumbling, all were happy."[31]

The joyous scene was repeated just three days later when tossed hats and cheering soldiers heralded news of Johnston's surrender to Sherman. "Music by the bands, cheering, firing of guns and other demonstrations of joy were indulged to the fullest extent. As the boys grew tired they returned to camp to meet and congratulate each other on the fact that now our furlough would be a permanent one," wrote a jubilant 115th man. Lieutenant DeGraff sat and breathlessly penned a note home. "I have hardly been able to think for myself lately on account of the great events that are transpiring.... The troops are wild with joy and we all expect to be home before long. What a splendid termination of this long and bloody war. We have whipped them fairly and effectively."[32]

The whirlwind of momentous events continued. Just two short days later, national tragedy succeeded national triumph as the troops in North Carolina learned of Lincoln's assassination on April 14. "Universal sadness and sorrow" replaced the ecstasy of final victory among the army. Extra guards were stationed around Raleigh to keep angry soldiers from exacting vengeance by burning the city. "The assassination of our beloved President was a horrible deed and one of the blackest stains of the accursed rebellion," wrote DeGraff.[33]

Saddened but triumphant, the army settled in around Raleigh. They remained poised for battle because it took until late April for the terms of Johnston's surrender to be finalized. Sherman had exceeded his authority by negotiating a treaty with Johnston that ventured into civil matters such as the re-establishment of state governments and courts in the vanquished Confederacy, and Washington rejected the treaty. Johnston was forced to accept unconditional capitulation. "Great rejoicing! Our fighting is ended," penned an exultant DeGraff.[34]

Most of the federal units began heading northward soon after Johnston's final surrender. The victorious troops marched through Washington, D.C., in Grand Reviews on May 23 and 24, then went home. But the 115th New York was not with them. The regiment ended the war the same way it began the war, unlucky and apart from the mainstream. The New Yorkers remained stationed in occupied Raleigh.[35]

The 115th spent a relaxed and uneventful seven weeks guarding Raleigh after the other troops pulled out, a period which Dr. Macfarlane described as delightful ease. But the men yearned for home and rejoiced when word finally came that the regiment would muster out on June 17. Corporal Reid joyfully reported the "welcome orders for our departure home," but tempered his joy with some reflections on his regiment's "arduous service of almost three years, burying in southern soil nearly one-third of our original membership by reason of the ravages of war, and a much larger percentage to bear the scars of battle and diseased bodies for life." A total of 330 men of the 115th died during their service—82 killed in action, 57 mortally wounded in battle, and 191 dead of disease and other causes, including 10 killed in the Fort Fisher magazine explosion and 54 who perished far from home in Confederate prisons. The grim statistics also include 470 non-fatal battle wounds.[36]

A total of 1300 men served with the 115th New York—the original thousand who marched from Camp Mohawk to Fonda and headed off to war on August 29, 1862, plus 300 recruits later added to the ranks of the unit. Thirteen hundred citizen-soldiers marched, camped and fought with the 115th, and endured the war's ghastly toll of 800 dead and wounded.[37]

The eager men started homeward on June 19. Leaving the later recruits behind to finish out their terms of service with other units, 280 men boarded a train and headed north—280 men who had followed the flags of the 115th out of Camp Mohawk and through Virginia, Maryland, Illinois, South Carolina, Florida, and North Carolina for thirty-four months. The train trip ended sixteen miles short of Petersburg, Virginia, beyond which the tracks had been destroyed by Union troops during the siege. The regiment marched the sixteen miles into Petersburg "tired and hungry, but a happy and jolly party." They lingered a day in Petersburg where some traipsed over the old battlegrounds, sombered by skeletons of less fortunate soldiers that still littered parts of the former no-man's-land.[38]

A slow train ride brought the men

Corporals John Robert Watt of Saratoga County and Edward C. Buddle of Montgomery County were both among the 280 men who marched with the 115th throughout its Civil War odyssey (New York State Military Museum).

to the James River at City Point, where they waited while their ship unloaded a cargo of Confederate prisoners, freed from a prison camp in Maryland. "They were a strong, robust lot of men, showing no signs of ill treatment," noted Reid. "They were delighted because the war was closed and apparently as happy as we were in the thoughts of soon being home." Reid contrasted their condition with that of the emaciated Union soldiers the 115th saw released in North Carolina. The disembarking southerners and the northbound Yankees shared a meal at City Point, where "no discrimination was made between the Blue and Gray."

The 115th boarded the aptly named steamer *North Point* on the afternoon of June 23. The ship did not set sail until 3:00 a.m. when it finished taking on coal and other necessities. The slumbering men of the 115th were awakened when the crew of the *North Point* fired up her steam engines. This brought grumbles from some until one wise veteran loudly reminded his comrades of the purpose of those engines: "Every turn of those wheels, boys, brings us nearer home." That afternoon, as the regiment sailed out of Chesapeake Bay and into the Atlantic for the fourth and final time, James Reid happily noted that on this occasion their ship "pointed north, instead of south toward the angry waters of Hatteras."[39]

The *North Point* anchored in New York harbor at sunset on June 25. Surgeon Macfarlane had gone ahead while the regiment paused at Petersburg, and was already in New York. He brought with him the replacement United States flag which the 115th had received near the end of their service in North Carolina. While awaiting his comrades' arrival, the doctor recorded the names and dates of the regiment's battles in gold lettering on the stripes of its fresh American flag. Macfarlane and the newly inscribed banner greeted the veterans when they disembarked at the Battery in lower Manhattan on the morning of June 26.

The regiment paraded up Broadway under the new colors, "justly proud as the spectators tried to read the inscriptions." Beside the bright new U.S. colors, the men carried the remnants of their original national flag, "so tattered and torn, war-worn and bloodstained that they could not be unrolled from their flagstaffs." Macfarlane wrote that he and his comrades "were more proud of the old colors.... We knew all the storms of iron and lead they had passed through and, too, we knew all the brave men who died for the honor of carrying them."[40]

The men enjoyed dinner at the Eighth National Guard Armory then marched back to the Battery and boarded the Hudson River steamer *Thomas Way* for an overnight sail upriver to Albany. Cannon boomed a welcome to the regiment at New York's capital city the next morning, and a Citizen's Committee treated the men to breakfast at several Albany hotels. Local newspapers hailed the 115th's return, recounted their deeds, and praised them. The *Waterford Sentinel* concluded a lengthy history of the 115th with this tribute:

> The regiment has always conducted itself nobly in every battle in which it has been engaged, and its history reflects honor upon the counties which it represented. We gladly welcome home these and other returning heroes who have periled life and health, and have borne the hardships consequent upon the life of a soldier for the sake of their country, and may they live long to enjoy the benefit of their labor and see a united, prosperous, peaceful and happy country as the fruit of their sacrifice.[41]

One last vexation befell the 115th before the men were able to return to their homes and families. After the welcoming breakfast, the regiment marched to a campground outside Albany where they had to wait eight more days before the state's military bureaucracy managed to process their discharge and give them their final pay. Dr. Macfarlane complained about "a system of annoyance, extortion and delays that exasperated us beyond measure."

Part of the extortion he refers to may have been the government's offer to sell the soldiers their rifles for four dollars. "Magnanimous government," grumped Reid, who gloated that "not to my knowledge did Uncle Sam make a sale."[42]

The veterans did pretty much as they pleased during this final encampment; discipline was minimal. Friends and relatives came to the camp for long-awaited reunions and some of the soldiers managed to get home for a visit. The men received their final pay and discharges on July 3, 1865. "They then separated to their various homes," wrote ex–Lieutenant Clark, "and the 115th Regiment ceased to exist, except in the memory of a grateful people."[43]

15

Epilogue

"Your colors have been foremost in the fight"

In the years after the war the veterans of the 115th settled down to homes, careers, and families, but the bonds of their shared service beckoned them back together. They established the 115th New York Volunteer Infantry Veterans Association and started holding annual reunions in 1882. Each year they met at a different location in the regiment's recruiting area on a date as near as possible to August 29, the anniversary of the 115th's departure from Camp Mohawk. The meetings continued for over forty years, well beyond the time when the majority of the veterans had passed away.[1]

James Reid became a newspaper correspondent in Boston after the war, residing in Newton Center, Massachusetts. He served as historian for the 115th's Veterans Association and traveled back to the regiment's home grounds for the annual reunion for thirty-three consecutive years. Reid wrote a complete history of the 115th which appeared in weekly installments in the *Ballston Journal* between March 4, 1893 and June 6, 1896. His lengthy monograph provides a very detailed and personal regimental history in which he utilized correspondence with his former comrades as a supplement to his own diaries and recollections. He also made extensive use of just-published volumes of the War Department's *Official Records* and the 1884–1887 four-volume series *Battles and Leaders of the Civil War* to integrate the 115th's actions and travels into the war's broader context. It is surprising that Reid's valuable work, which he titled "The War Against Secessia," was never published in book form.

Reid lived in New York, Ohio, Iowa, Indiana and Illinois in the ten years following the Civil War, finally settling in Massachusetts where he stayed until his death in 1925 at the age of eighty-one.[2]

John Reardon returned to his home southwest of Fultonville on May 9, 1865, having left North Carolina ahead of the others of his regiment due to ill health. The 7:00 a.m. New York Central train from Albany and a rainy carriage ride brought him home to his surprised parents at 10:00 a.m. "My father has changed but little in three years of my absence, but not so with mother," he wrote in his final diary entry. Reardon thought that his fifty-five-year old mother looked seventy. "Her hair was a light brown color and I cannot recall seeing any evidence of gray when I left home. Now it is almost white. The worry and anxiety that was hers during the absence of my brother and myself was strikingly marked in her features and actions." Reardon's brother Edmund returned on crutches two months later, and their mother died that autumn. "Her life was shortened I feel from the effect on her of our service in the war, though she had the satisfaction of seeing us both return home."[3]

Reardon moved a few miles up the Mohawk River Valley to the village of St. Johnsville after the war. There he raised a family, served as postmaster and town supervisor, and ran a meat market and a gristmill. For years his children urged him to write an account of his war experience based upon his two wartime diaries. The aging veteran finally took up the task when failing health confined him to his house during the winter of 1907–08. Each week his daughters forwarded his work to the local newspaper, and the story of Reardon's service with the 115th unfolded in the *St. Johnsville News* between February 8 and July 15, 1908.

The *News* published a letter to the editor from Reardon's daughter Susie Frances along with the June 10 installment. The letter related the story of her father's diaries and his five month struggle to transcribe and edit them as he lay on his deathbed. She also conveyed the sad news that Lieutenant Reardon had passed away on May 30— ironically the Decoration Day holiday that he had long cherished. But Susie Frances also advised readers that she and her sister would complete their father's work, as he had implored them to do during his last days. Their task was easy, for Reardon had taken his account through his regiment's January 1865 victory at Fort Fisher before he lost his race with death.[4]

Lieutenant James Clark also left the 115th early due to illness. He received his discharge from the army in December of 1864 and returned to his home in Clifton Park in Saratoga County where he began immediately to compose his history of the regiment. His book, which bears the grand title of *The Iron Hearted Regiment: Being an Account of the Battles, Marches and Gallant Deeds Performed by the 115th N.Y. Vols.*, was published in the early fall of 1865. It was among the earliest of many hundreds of regimental histories published by Union and Confederate veterans in the decades after the Civil War.[5]

The Iron Hearted Regiment provides a colorful account of the events witnessed by Clark and numerous profiles of his regimental colleagues, but it is not without some heavy doses of exaggeration. The book's publication is the earliest known use of the nickname *Iron Hearted Regiment* for the 115th New York. This appellation gained favor in later years among newspapermen and others writing about the 115th, and it is often used today. But its use by the veterans themselves in their postwar writings is virtually nonexistent, despite its being a title that any soldier would clearly be proud to claim. The name is likely a marketing contrivance by Clark or his editor; it is not a name that the regiment carried out of the war with them. Nonetheless, while Clark's comrades did not adopt the flattering nickname he bestowed upon them, he did provide them with the volume that served for decades as the unit's only published history.

Colonel Simeon Sammons never returned to the 115th after his wounding at the Battle of the Crater on July 30, 1864. Sammons led his regiment into battle twice, at Olustee and the Crater, and was shot both times. After the Crater he spent several weeks in hospitals at Fortress Monroe and Annapolis, then went home for further treatment and convalescence. But a very slow recovery from the painful hip wound ended the colonel's days as a soldier. He resigned his commission in early January 1865 while the regiment made its second excursion to North Carolina. Sammons bade farewell to his men in an emotional message which he had printed and forwarded to them in Carolina. Sammons thanked the men for their "kind and generous confidence" and praised them:

> Your record, thus far, is one you may be truly proud of. In the numerous engagements in which you have borne a part no disgrace has stained your reputation—no dishonor attaches to your good name; and on many a hard fought battlefield your colors have been foremost in the fight, and they have never been desecrated by rebel hands. You have endured hardships, toil and privation with fortitude and without a murmur, and by your discipline and soldierly bearing won encomiums even from unwilling lips.

The colonel paid homage to the dead and wounded of the 115th and beseeched an overruling Providence to see the men through the war and return them with safety and honor to their homes and families. He closed with an explanation of his decision to leave the regiment: "I had cherished hopes of being able to remain until the expiration of your term of service. My wound and failing health compelled me to resign."

Sammons's farewell message evoked two similarly emotional responses from his soldiers: a letter from the enlisted men of the 115th and a resolution prepared by the regiment's officers. The enlisted men's letter expressed their gratitude and admiration:

> In you we recognize our champion and deliverer from the cloud that overhung our early history, and to your unceasing efforts we owe much of our present prosperity. In the camp, by your zealous and persevering labors you developed the latent talent of the Reg't and brought it to a high standard of military efficiency, so necessary on the field of battle. And when called upon to meet the foe, you proved yourself a worthy leader, whom we were willing to follow, proud to own, and were honored in belonging to your command and, in after engagements, to maintain the honor of 'Colonel Sammons's Reg't' was our highest ambition. You will ever be held dear in the hearts of your men as a commander, a leader, and a friend.

The men wished Sammons health and happiness and told him that they hoped to soon accomplish their mission and join him back in their native state.

Not to be outdone, two days after the enlisted men sent their passionate adieu to Colonel Sammons, the regiment's officers gathered and appointed a committee to "draft resolutions expressive of the feelings of the meeting." Major Ezra Walrath chaired the committee, whose members were Captains William Shaw, John Kneeskern, William Smith and Egbert Savage, and Lieutenant Martin McMartin, all of whom served among the 115th's original cast of officers. The proclamation by the officer's committee was more formal but just as gracious as the men's. It expressed their esteem for Sammons and lavished flowery praise on their former commander. The officers acknowledged "the necessity which impelled" Sammons's resignation, wished him good health, and bemoaned that they had "lost a brave, generous, kind & genial companion in arms, [and] the country has lost one of its most gallant and devoted Officers & Soldiers."[6]

Colonel Sammons did not retire completely from public service. Even before his resignation from the army he had been elected to represent Montgomery County in the New York State Legislature. He was a delegate to the Democratic National Convention in 1868, and in 1870 he began a two year term as Harbor Master of New York. Mainly he stuck to his farm outside Fonda where he welcomed his friends, especially fellow veterans. He died in 1881 at age sixty-nine. In 1899 many veterans of the 115th gathered at the family ceme-

Many veterans of the 115th gathered at the Sammons family cemetery in 1899 when this monument was dedicated to their late colonel (photograph by author).

tery on the Sammons farm to help dedicate a monument to the colonel's memory; the simple stone obelisk honors him still.[7]

Nicholas DeGraff's brother John met him in Albany when the 115th returned in late June 1865, and together they journeyed back to the family farm that Nicholas had not seen since July 1862. He noted that after his three years' travels with the 115th the distance between the well-known towns of his youth seemed shorter than before. At the farm he found all much he had left it except for his "dear father's empty chair."[8]

DeGraff was still just twenty-three-years old at the war's close. He left the farm and moved to nearby Amsterdam, where he lived for the rest of his life, raised a family, and became a businessman. His service with the 115th New York remained a strong focal point of his remaining sixty-three years. He was very active in veteran's affairs, and he assembled a complete record of his military career. To do so, he preserved the letters he had written home to his family and the pocket diaries he had kept during his army service and used them to write a lengthy memoir of his Civil War experience.

DeGraff ran a shoe store and other businesses in Amsterdam after his army career, and became well-known and respected around town. Fitting his station, he always dressed nat-

Post-war portrait of George Blackwood and his wife Abigail. George enlisted in the 115th from the Saratoga County town of Corinth at age 30 along with his 18-year-old brother William. George was wounded at Cold Harbor and left festering on the field for three days, later attributing his survival to maggots entering his wound and preventing gangrene. William was wounded at Olustee, Florida on February 20, 1864, was captured and died on July 28 at the infamous Confederate prison camp at Andersonville, Georgia (Lance Ingmire Collection).

tily in suit, vest, spats, and fedora, unless gardening or woodworking. A skilled carpenter, he crafted wagons and sleighs for his grandsons.[9]

DeGraff remained involved in veterans affairs throughout his life. In addition to being an officer in the 115th New York Veterans Association for most of its long existence, he was a member of the local post of the Grand Army of the Republic, the national organization for Union veterans of the Civil War. No one provided more service to the veterans of the 115th than DeGraff, who received a gold badge at the regiment's 45th reunion in 1925 in recognition of his thirty-six years as the Association's secretary and treasurer. It was DeGraff who kept the roster and mailing list, sent the annual invitations, and collected the $1.00 annual dues. The roster showed that the men of the 115th had dispersed throughout the U.S. in the decades after their service, and each year more and more letters came back to DeGraff from far and wide noting a former comrade's inability to attend that year's reunion or advising that yet another of the 115th had passed on. DeGraff closed the 1925 reunion, held on the 63rd anniversary of the regiment's muster, with a note that provides a fitting epitaph for the 115th:

> Rejoicing with comrades of our other wars in the stability of our government and the happiness of our people, under the favor and blessing of Almighty God, we rest from the great work that we did in reclaiming our brothers of the southland from their error of secession and restoring the flag to its sovereign place at the head of a united people, which grows in magnitude and importance as the years multiply, and we, as we so rapidly are approaching the last roll call, are justified in feeling that the whole people approve and applaud the heroic achievements of the Boys in Blue of the greatest of Civil Wars.[10]

Afterword

"Riding a white horse and carrying the U.S. flag"

In the early part of the 20th century Nicholas DeGraff's daughter, Laura DeGraff Bennett, traveled frequently from her home in Ontario, Canada, to her native Amsterdam, New York for lengthy visits with her family. She packed up her young sons Norman and William, bid goodbye to her husband and his Toronto paper box factory, and entrained for Grandpa DeGraff's home in Amsterdam. Many decades had passed since her father had left the family farm at Tribes Hill and joined the 115th New York Volunteers at Camp Mohawk, but he remained robust and active. Each fair day he would walk his grandsons down the steep hill from his home into the city. Folks along the way greeted them with wishes of "Good morning, Major DeGraff."

These treks often included a visit to the local firehouse, and Grandpa seemed to know just when to arrive, for the boys always got to watch the company fire drill. They thrilled to the firemen sliding down the brass pole, harnessing the draught horses, and revving up the big wagon-borne steam powered pumper. Afterwards when the teams returned to their stalls, cubes of sugar emerged from Grandpa's pockets, which the boys eagerly fed the horses. Every so often the walk to town included a stop to purchase live oysters, for which Grandpa had developed a taste at Annapolis, Yorktown, and Hilton Head. The old veteran could still lug the five gallon wooden barrels of this favored delicacy back up the hill on one shoulder.

"As I picture Grandpa he was inclined to be serious, very strong and sturdy, and his stature was as straight as an old soldier's could be," remembered William Bennett, who was born in 1910 when his grandfather was already sixty-seven-years old. When Bill and his older brother Norman visited, Grandpa erected a tent and flagpole on his front lawn and taught the boys a proper salute. Perhaps foremost among the boys' memories is Grandpa leading the Civil War veteran contingent in local parades. Three-quarters of a century later Bill Bennett clearly recalled his grandfather on such occasions proudly "riding a white horse and carrying the U.S. flag."

Gradually there were fewer and fewer veterans marching with him in the parades, but DeGraff stayed active until he died in his sleep in 1928 at the age of eighty-six. His widow died one week later.

Nicholas DeGraff had led his grandsons on lengthy hikes through fields and woods, reminiscent of treks he had made long before with fellow soldiers at Hilton Head. On these

Nicholas DeGraff as a 22-year old lieutenant in the 115th and as an 85-year old in Amsterdam, New York.

treks he told his grandsons about the life cycles of frogs, mosquitos and other creatures. These walks in woods and fields with his grandfather stirred in Bill Bennett a lifelong interest in the natural world. He later traveled the world as a naturalist, interrupted by service in France and Germany in World War II, before settling down to a Florida retirement.

Mr. Bennett inherited his grandfather's Civil War letters, diaries and other keepsakes, as well as his voluminous handwritten memoir. When he retired to Florida he entrusted these family heirlooms to public archives, enabling the author to track him down from a yellowed address label in the DeGraff Collection at the Montgomery County Department of History and Archives. We maintained a lively correspondence for several years and I was very pleased to have Bill refer to the Silo's as his "Family in the North," and to read his enthusiastic reactions to news of my children's progress in school and sports, as well as our many family vacation trips.

He also reacted enthusiastically to each chapter of the story of the 115th as I forwarded the freshly completed drafts to him at the rate of two or three per year. Soon after I triumphantly sent him the final chapter I received a note advising of his death, which occurred a month short of his eighty-ninth birthday and just before I had mailed him that final chapter in the 115th's saga.

Acknowledging that his passing was at hand, Mr. Bennett himself had prepared the announcement of his own death. As his grandfather had done so many times in his letters home from an inhuman warfront, Bill found a heartening message in a doleful circumstance, and in his farewell letter he endowed himself with a simple and joyous epitaph: "I have enjoyed a very adventurous and an unusually happy life and have few regrets and a lot to be thankful for."

I am eternally grateful to Bill Bennett. This story of the 115th would be dry indeed had Bill not freely shared the rich letters and diaries and memoir of his beloved Grandpa DeGraff, and it may never have been completed without the incentive of his interest and friendship.

Appendix A: Chronology of the 115th New York

1862

July 1	President Lincoln calls for 300,000 new recruits.
July 5	New York State Governor Morgan appoints committee to organize an infantry regiment from the 15th Senatorial District: Fulton, Hamilton, Montgomery, and Saratoga Counties.
July 17	Committee meets at the Fonda Hotel, Fonda, New York, to commence organizing and recruiting. It unanimously recommends Simeon Sammons for appointment as colonel.
July 18–August 19	Recruiting underway in the towns and villages of the 15th Senatorial District.
August 19–29	Regiment assembles and trains at Camp Mohawk near Fonda, New York.
August 27	Regiment officially musters into federal service; is designated as 115th New York Volunteer Infantry.
August 29	115th breaks camp; boards train at Fonda; is greeted by governor at Albany; arrives in New York City.
August 30–September 1	Travel from New York City to Sandy Hook, Maryland.
September 1–3	Regiment divided into four contingents along railroad line between Winchester and Harpers Ferry, Virginia.
September 3	Regroup at Charles Town, Virginia; retreat to Bolivar Heights, just west of Harpers Ferry.
September 3–15	In camp at Bolivar Heights.
September 13	Advance to Maryland Heights; skirmish with enemy; retreat to Bolivar Heights.
September 15	Harpers Ferry surrendered to Confederates. Confederates parole all captured federal troops pending official exchanges of prisoners.
September 16–21	March from Harpers Ferry to Annapolis, Maryland.
September 21–25	At Camp Parole in Annapolis.
September 25–29	Travel by rail from Annapolis to Chicago, Illinois.
September 30–November 20	Interned as paroled prisoners of war at Camp Douglas in Chicago.
November 20	Depart Camp Douglas; barracks burns down as regiment leaves.
November 20–23	Travel by rail from Chicago to Washington, D.C.
November 22–26	Board of Inquiry at Camp Douglas investigates barracks fire; finds 115th guilty of arson.
November 24	Sightseeing in Washington, D.C.; march through city to Arlington, Virginia.
November 24–December 12	At Camp Chase in Arlington; build winter quarters.
December 1	Regiment learns of its official exchange; they are no longer paroled prisoners of war.

December 12	Move to Camp Vermont in Alexandria, Virginia.
December 12–26	At Camp Vermont; build winter quarters.
December 26–28	Sail to Yorktown, Virginia.
December 28–January 22, 1863	In camp at Yorktown.

1863

January 7	Seventy-five men from 115th go on raid to West Point, Virginia.
January 22–26	Sail from Yorktown to Hilton Head, South Carolina.
January 26–June 28	At Hilton Head.
January 30	Men learn they have been convicted of burning down their Camp Douglas barracks.
February 9	Colonel Sammons goes to Washington, D.C., to defend regiment.
March 17	Regiment learns of its exoneration by the U.S. War Department.
June 4	Companies B and E participate in the raiding and burning of Bluffton, South Carolina.
June 28	Regiment moves to Beaufort, Port Royal Island, South Carolina.
June 28–October 7	At Beaufort, South Carolina.
August 29–September 10	Colonel Sammons faces court martial for conduct unbecoming an officer and other charges brought by his own subordinates. He is cleared of all charges.
October 7–19	On picket duty at Port Royal Ferry.
October 19–December 1	At Beaufort, South Carolina.
December 1–19	On picket duty at Port Royal Ferry.
December 19	Return to Beaufort.
December 20–21	Sail to Hilton Head.
December 21–February 5, 1864	At Hilton Head.
December 22	Join the 47th and 48th New York in a brigade commanded by Colonel William Barton of the 48th.

1864

February 5–7	Sail from Hilton Head to Jacksonville, Florida.
February 8–12	Begin Florida Campaign of 1864; advance westward from Jacksonville into interior Florida.
February 12–14	At Barber's Plantation, Florida.
February 14–17	Raid to Callahan Station, Florida, near Georgia border; 70 mile round trip on foot.
February 17–20	At Barber's Plantation.
February 20	Battle of Olustee, Florida. 115th suffers 296 casualties (51%) in its first major combat.
February 20–22	Retreat to Baldwin, Florida.
February 22–25	At Baldwin.
February 25	Withdraw to Jacksonville.
February 25–March 9	At Jacksonville.
March 9	Sail up St. John's River to Palatka, Florida.
March 9–April 14	Occupy Palatka.
April 1	Twenty-five volunteers from 115th conduct raid on Confederate Fort Gates; take ten rebels prisoner. Private Benjamin Thackrah earns Medal of Honor.
April 14–21	Sail to Yorktown, Virginia, via Jacksonville, Hilton Head, and Fortress Monroe.
April 21–May 4	In camp at Gloucester Point, Virginia; attached to Army of the James under General Benjamin Butler.
May 4–May 6	Sail from Gloucester to Bermuda Hundred, Virginia.
May 6–May 12	At Bermuda Hundred.

May 7	Battle of Port Walthall Junction, or Chesterfield Heights, Virginia: 69 casualties; return to Bermuda Hundred.
May 12–May 16	Advance on Richmond; Battle of Drewrys Bluff: 31 casualties.
May 16	Withdraw to Bermuda Hundred.
May 16–27	At Bermuda Hundred.
May 20	Lieutenant Colonel Nathan Johnson joins 115th. Battle of Ware Bottom Church: no casualties in 115th. Johnson accused of drunkenness on duty.
May 27–June 1	Travel to Cold Harbor via the James, York, and Pamunkey Rivers and a march from White House Landing via New Castle.
June 1	Assault on Confederate lines at Cold Harbor; 115th takes a line of trenches and 200+ prisoners.
June 1–12	In trenches at Cold Harbor: 18 casualties in the June 1 assault and subsequent trench duty.
June 12–17	Return to Bermuda Hundred.
June 17–23	In camps at Bermuda Hundred.
June 22	President Lincoln passes through camp of 115th.
June 23	Move to camp at Hare's Hill in Petersburg, Virginia, siege lines.
June 23–July 29	In trenches and camp at Hare's Hill.
July 30	Battle of the Crater: 25 casualties.
July 31	March from the Crater to Bermuda Hundred.
July 31–August 13	At Bermuda Hundred.
August 13–14	March to Deep Bottom, Virginia, on north side of James River.
August 14–21	At Deep Bottom.
August 16	Battle of Second Deep Bottom or Strawberry Plains: 73 casualties.
August 18	Lieutenant Colonel Johnson again arrested for drunkenness on duty.
August 21	Return to Bermuda Hundred.
August 21–28	At Bermuda Hundred.
August 28–September 25	In Petersburg siege lines north of Hare's Hill.
September 25–28	At temporary camp at rear of Petersburg lines preparing for campaign.
September 28	March across James River to Deep Bottom.
September 29	Assault on Fort Gilmer: 33 casualties.
September 30–November 24	In siege lines east of Richmond, Virginia.
October 27	115th in engagement at Darbytown Road, Battle of Chaffin's Farm, Virginia: 20 casualties; regiment hit by fire of 9th Maine.
November 24	Thanksgiving Day march to Bermuda Hundred.
November 24–December 5	At Bermuda Hundred.
December 5–7	Return to Richmond siege lines across James River.
December 7	Re-cross James River.
December 8	March to Bermuda Hundred Landing.
December 9	Board steamer *Haze*.
December 9–25	Aboard *Haze*. Travel to Fort Fisher, North Carolina, via Fortress Monroe, Potomac River, and two stops at Beaufort, North Carolina.
December 25	Amphibious landing and aborted assault at Fort Fisher, North Carolina.
December 25–30	Sail on *Haze* from Fort Fisher, North Carolina, to Deep Bottom, Virginia.
December 30–January 3, 1865	In camp behind Richmond siege lines.

1865

January 3	March to Bermuda Hundred Landing.
January 4–14	Sail back to Fort Fisher.
January 14	Second amphibious landing at Fort Fisher.
January 15	Assault and capture of Fort Fisher: 17 casualties.
January 16	Fort Fisher powder magazine explodes beneath the bivouac of the 115th: 11 dead and 41 wounded.

January 16–February 11	In camp within Fort Fisher.
February 11–17	Operations against Confederate Sugar Loaf-Myrtle Sound line north of Fort Fisher.
February 18–19	Advance on Fort Anderson on west side of Cape Fear River.
February 20–21	Advance on Wilmington, North Carolina.
February 22	Enter Wilmington after Confederate evacuation; march to Northeast Station, North Carolina, in pursuit of rebels.
February 22–March 2	At Northeast Station; greet and assist thousands of prisoners of war released by Confederates.
March 2–15	Occupy Wilmington, North Carolina.
March 15–April 14	Campaign from Wilmington to Raleigh, North Carolina.
April 12	Learn of Lee's surrender to Grant at Appomattox, Virginia.
April 14–June 19	Occupy Raleigh.
April 26	Confederate General Joseph Johnston surrenders to General William T. Sherman. War is over for 115th.
June 19–25	Travel from Raleigh to New York City.
June 26	Parade through New York City.
June 27	Sail to Albany, New York.
June 27–July 3	At Albany.
July 3	115th discharged from service.

Appendix B: Regimental Roster

This roster is a reproduction of the regimental roster produced in 1903 by the New York State Adjutant General.[1] As such, the spelling of soldier names and place names is highly variable and there is considerable inconsistency in recording place names. For example, Saratoga Springs is frequently listed as Saratoga Spa; there are numerous spellings for the Saratoga County town of Charlton; and the May 7, 1864, battle at Port Walthall Junction, Virginia, is also shown as Chesterfield Heights, Chester Heights, or Chester Station, Virginia, for those soldiers whose roster entries include casualties in that action.

Users are referred to the Chronology for accurately matching casualty entries in the roster with the battlefield engagements of the 115th, and those seeking fuller and more reliable information on individual soldiers are referred to the service and pension records available from the National Archives and Records Administration (www.archives.gov).

ABBOTT, FRANK.—Age 25 years. Enrolled, August 4, 1862, at Johnstown to serve three years; mustered in as first lieutenant, Co. E, August 20, 1862; discharged, November 19, 1862, at Chicago, Ill. Commissioned first lieutenant, September 10, 1862, with rank from August 20, 1862, original.

ABEAL, HAMILTON.—Age, 17 years. Enlisted, March 28, 1864, at Milton, to serve three years; mustered in as private, Co. I, April 19, 1864; transferred to Co. H, Forty-seventh Infantry, June 17, 1865; also borne as Abeel.

ABEEL, JOSEPH C.—Age, 22 years. Enlisted, August 1, 1862, at Northumberland, to serve three years; mustered in as corporal, Co. C, August 11, 1862; captured in action, September 15, and paroled September 16, 1862, at Harper's Ferry, Va.; promoted sergeant no date; mustered out with company, June 17, 1865, at Raleigh, N.C.

ABEL, J. LOREN.—Age, 22 years. Enlisted, August 11, 1862, at Stillwater, to serve three years; mustered in as wagoner, Co. H, August 14, 1862; captured in action, September 15, and paroled September 16, 1862, at Harper's Ferry, Va.; promoted corporal, no date; died of typhoid fever, July 3, 1863, at hospital, Hilton Head, S.C.

ABRAMS, ALBERT M.—Age, 21 years. Enlisted, August 9, 1862, at Wells, to serve three years; mustered in as private, Co. K, August 16, 1862, captured in action, September 15, and paroled September 16, 1862, at Harper's Ferry, Va.; promoted corporal, no date; mustered out with company, June 17, 1865, at Raleigh, N.C.

ACKERT, ALVERGREEN.—Age, 15 years. Enlisted at Mohawk, to serve three years, and mustered in as musician, Co. A, August 7, 1862; captured in action September 15, and paroled September 16, 1862, at Harper's Ferry, Va.; killed in action, January 16, 1865, at Fort Fisher, N.C.; also borne as Ackhert and Ackart.

ACKLEY, GEORGE H.—Age, 18 years. Enlisted, August 22, 1862, at Johnstown, to serve three years; mustered in as private, Co. K, August 23, 1862; captured in action, September 15, and paroled, September 16, 1862, at Harper's Ferry, Va.; again captured, March 17, 1864, at Pilatka, Fla.; exchanged and returned to company, April 20, 1865; mustered out with company, June 17, 1865, at Raleigh, N.C.

ACKLEY, OSCAR L.—Age, 18 years. Enlisted, July 22, 1862, at Halfmoon, to serve three years; mustered in as private, Co. H, August 8, 1862; captured in action, September 15, and paroled, September 16, 1862, at Harper's Ferry, Va.; killed in action, February 20, 1864, at Olustee, Fla.

ACKLEY, SENECA.—Age, 43 years. Enlisted, August 8, 1862, at Greenfield, to serve three years; mustered in as private, Co. C, August 11, 1862; captured in action, September 15, and paroled, September 16, 1862, at Harper's Ferry, Va.; transferred to Veteran Reserve Corps, no date; discharged, June 29, 1865, at Albany, N.Y., as of Co. G, Eleventh Regiment, Veteran Reserve Corps.

ADAMS, HENRY.—Age, 37 years. Enlisted, August 4, 1862, at Saratoga Spa, to serve three years; mustered in as corporal, Co. F, August 12, 1862; captured in action, September 15 and paroled, September 16, 1862, at Harper's Ferry, Va.; promoted sergeant, no date; wounded in action, February 20, 1864, at Olustee, Fla.; discharged for wounds, December, 1864.

ADCOCK, THOMAS H.—Age, 22 years. Enlisted, August 5, 1862, at Northumberland, to serve three years; mustered in as private, Co. F, August 12, 1862; captured in action, September 15, and paroled, September 16, 1862, at Harper's Ferry, Va.; wounded and captured in action, February 20, 1864, at Olustee, Fla.; no further record.

AHR, MICHAEL.—Age, 25 years. Enlisted, August 9, 1862, at Moreau, to serve three years; mustered in as private, Co. G, August 18, 1862; captured in action, September 15, and paroled, September 16, 1862, at Harper's Ferry, Va.; promoted corporal, May 22, 1865; mustered out with company, June 17, 1865, at Raleigh, N.C.

ALBACK, PHILIP.—Age, 27 years. Enlisted at Albany, to serve three years, and mustered in as private, Co. C, October 28, 1863; captured in action, February 20, 1864, at Olustee, Fla.; escaped from Andersonville, Ga., July 18, 1864; mustered out, June 15, 1865, at Raleigh, N.C.

ALBRIGHT, HENRY.—Age, 21 years. Enlisted, July 28, 1862, at Minden, to serve three years; mustered in as private, Co. B, August 14 1862; captured in action, September 15, and paroled, September 16, 1862 at Harper's Ferry, Va.; deserted, October 5, 1862 at Chicago, Ill.

ALBRIGHT, JACOB.—Age, 27 years. Enlisted, August 9, 1862, at Charleston, to serve three years; mustered in as private, Co. D, August 15, 1862; captured in action, September 15, and paroled, September 16, 1862, at Harper's Ferry, Va.; mustered out with detachment, June 23, 1865, at Albany, N.Y.; also borne as Allbright.

ALEXANDER, GEORGE.—Age, 19 years. Enlisted, December 16, 1963, at Clifton Park, to serve three years; mustered in as private, Co. H., December 17, 1863; killed in action, October 27, 1864, in front of Richmond, Va.

ALEXANDER, JOEL S.—Age, 21 years. Enlisted, August 8, 1862, at Charlton, to serve three years; mustered in as private, Co. I, August 15, 1862; captured in action, September 15, and paroled, September 16, 1862, at Harper's Ferry, Va.; promoted sergeant, no date; killed in action, February 20, 1864, at Olustee, Fla.

ALEXANDER, OSCAR.—Age, 18 years. Enlisted, August 7, 1862, at Charlton, to serve three years; mustered in as private, Co. I, August 20, 1862; captured in action, September 15, and paroled, September 16, 1862, at Harper's Ferry, Va.; promoted corporal, no date; wounded in action, February 20, 1864, at Olustee, Fla.; mustered out, June 7, 1865, at Balfour Hospital, Norfolk, Va.

ALEXANDER, WILLIAM H.—Age, 22 years. Enlisted, August 12, 1862, at Ballston, to serve three years; mustered in as private, Co. I, August 20, 1862; captured in action, September 15, and paroled, September 16, 1862, at Harper's Ferry, Va.; wounded in action, October 1, 1864, at Chaffin's Farm, Va.; absent since and at muster-out of company.

ALGER, GEORGE.—Age, 18 years. Enlisted at Schenectady, to serve three years, and mustered in as private, Co. A, July 27, 1864; mustered out, September 2, 1865, at Albany, N.Y.; also borne as Algar.

ALGER, WILLIAM L.—Age, 25 years. Enlisted, August 13, 1862, at Canajoharie, to serve three years; mustered in as private, Co. B, August 14, 1862; captured in action, September 15, and paroled, September 16, 1862, at Harper's Ferry, Va.; wounded in action, February 20, 1864, at Olustee, Fla.; pro–Corps [sic], January 1, 1865, as William S.

ALGYER, DAVID.—Age, 17 years. Enlisted at Albany, to serve three years, and mustered in as private, Co. A, April 4, 1865; transferred to Co. A, Forty-seventh Infantry, June 17, 1865.

ALLEN, ALFRED.—Age, 22 years. Enlisted at Johnstown, to serve three years, and mustered in as private, Co. E, August 13, 1862; captured in action, September 15, and paroled, September 16, 1862, at Harper's Ferry, Va.; wounded in action, October 1, 1864, at Chaffin's Farm, Va.; mustered out with company, June 17, 1865, at Raleigh, N.C.

ALLEN, ALONZO.—Age, 23 years. Enlisted, August 2, 1862, at Milton, to serve three years; mustered in as corporal, Co. C, August 8, 1862; captured in action, September 15, and paroled, September 16, 1862, at Harper's Ferry, Va.; wounded in action, February 20, 1864, at Olustee, Fla.; promoted sergeant, May 1, 1865; mustered out with company, June 17, 1865, at Raleigh, N.C.

ALLEN. JOSEPH.—Age, 32 years. Enlisted, July 23, 1862, at Glen, to serve three years; mustered in as musician, Co. A, July 25, 1862; captured in action, September 15, and paroled, September 16, 1862, at Harper's Ferry, Va.; promoted corporal, no date; sergeant, March 1, 1865; mustered out, June 15, 1865, at Smithville, N.C.

ALLEN, SAMUEL.—Age, 40 years. Enlisted, August 11, 1862 at Clifton Park, to serve three years; mustered in as private. Co. H, August 14, 1862; captured in action, September 15, and paroled, September 16, 1862, at Harpers Ferry, Va.; discharged, July 4, 1863.

ALPAUGH, WILBER.—Age, 18 years. Enlisted, August 7, 1862, at Canajoharie, to serve three years; mustered in as private, Co. B, August 20, 1862; captured in action, September 15, and paroled, September 16, 1862, at Harper's Ferry, Va.; wounded in action, February 20, 1864, at Olustee, Fla.; mustered out, July 7, 1865, at Lovell Hospital, Portsmouth Grove, R.I.

AMBRIDGE, NELSON.—Age, 22 years. Enlisted at Palatine, to serve three years, and mustered in as private, Co. A, August 5, 1862; captured in action, September 15, and paroled, September 16, 1862, at Harper's Ferry, Va.; deserted, December 25, 1862, at Alexandria, Va.

AMSTEAD, JACOB.—Age, 20 years. Enlisted at Poughkeepsie, to serve three years, and mustered in as private, Co. K, October 24, 1863; missing in action, August 18, 1864, at Deep Bottom, Va.; also borne as John W. Almstead; no further record.

ANDERSON, DAVID.—Age, 23 years. Enlisted, August 19, 1862, at Broadalbin, to serve three years; mustered in as private. Co. K, August 20, 1862; captured in action, September 15, and paroled, September 16, 1862, at Harper's Ferry, Va.; deserted, September 18, 1862, at Frederick, Md.

ANDERSON, JOHN.—Age, 43 years. Enlisted, August 11, 1862, at Clifton Park, to serve three years; mustered in as private, Co. H. August 14, 1862; captured in action, September 15, and paroled, September 6, 1862, at Harper's Ferry, Va.; wounded in Action, June 15, 1864, at Petersburg, Va., and October 1, 1864, at Chaffin's farm, Va.; descriptive list sent to Albany, N.Y., May 22, 1865; no further record.

ANDREWS, FREDERICK W.—Age, 25 years. Enlisted, August 9, 1862 at Corinth, to serve three years; mustered in as private, Co. F, August 19, 1862; captured in action, September 15, and paroled, September 16, 1862, at Harper's Ferry, Va.; died, May 2, 1863 in hospital at David's Island, New York Harbor.

ANDREWS, SYLVESTER.—Age, 21 years. Enlisted, July 17, 1862, at Saratoga Springs, to serve three years; mustered in as private, Co. G, July 31, 1862; captured in action, September 15, and paroled, September 16, 1862, at Harper's Ferry, Va.; died of typhoid fever, July 23, 1863, in hospital at Beaufort, S.C.

ARGERSINGER, JESSE.—Age, 19 years. Enlisted at Ephratah, to serve one year, and mustered in as private, Co. E, August 8, 1864; wounded in action, October 1, 1864, at Chaffins Farm, Va.; mustered out with company, June 17, 1865, at Raleigh, N.C.

ASHMAN, JOHN J.—Age, 21 years. Enrolled, August 13, 1862, at Ballston, to serve three years; mustered in as private, Co. I, August 26, 1862; promoted first sergeant, no date; mustered in as first lieutenant, Co. A, January 8, 1865; mustered out with company, June 17, 1865, at Raleigh, N.C. Commissioned first lieutenant, May 17, 1865, with rank from January 7, 1865, vice J. W. Davis discharged.

ASPENBILER, VALENTINE.—Age, 39 years. Enlisted at Tarrytown to serve three years, and mustered in as private, Co. E. October 29, 1863; deserted, March 13, 1864.

AVERY, ISAIAH.—Age, 20 years. Enlisted at Brooklyn, to serve three years, and mustered in as private, Co. F, March 6, 1865; deserted, April 10, 1865, at Faison's Depot, N.C.

AUMACK, JAMES S.—Age, 30 years. Enlisted at Glen, to serve three years, and mustered in as corporal, Co. A, July 30, 1862; captured in action, September 15, and paroled, September 16, 1862, at Harper's Ferry, Va.; promoted sergeant, no date; wounded in action, February 20, 1864, at Olustee, Fla.; killed in action, August 18, 1864, at Deep Bottom, Va.

AUSTIN, JAMES H.—Age, 19 years. Enlisted, August 12, 1862, at Johnstown, to serve three years; mustered in as private, Co. E, August 13, 1862; captured in action, September 15, and paroled, September 16, 1862, at Harper's Ferry, Va.; mustered out with company, June 17, 1865, at Raleigh, N.C.

BABCOCK, HARVEY W.—Age, 23 years. Enlisted August 3, 1862, at Canajoharie, to serve three years; mustered in as private, Co. I, August 4, 1862; captured in action, September 15, and paroled, September 16, 1862, at Harper's Ferry, Va.; deserted, September 18, 1862, at Frederick, Md.

BAILEY, LEWIS S.—Age, 19 years. Enrolled, August 8,1862, at Greenfield, to serve three years; mustered in as corporal, Co. F, August 12, 1862; promoted sergeant and first sergeant, no dates; wounded in action, February 20, 1864, at Olustee, Fla.; mustered in as second lieutenant, June 8, 1865; mustered out with company, June 17, 1865, at Raleigh, N.C. Commissioned second lieutenant, May 17, 1865, with rank from February 1, 1865, vice C. Kline promoted.

BAILEY, WILLIAM.—Age, 23 years. Enlisted at New York City, to serve three years, and mustered in as private, Co. K, November 14, 1863; wounded in. action, February 20, 1864, at Olustee, Fla.; transferred to the Navy, April 27, 1864.

BAISLEY, DAVID.—Age, 18 years. Enlisted at Brooklyn, to serve one year, and mustered in as private, Co. G, March 6, 1865; mustered out July 21, 1865, at New York City; also borne as Daniel.

BAKER, BENJAMIN A.—Age 24 years. Enlisted, August 20, 1862, at Mayfield, to serve three years; mustered in as private, Co. E, August 21, 1862; captured in action, September 15, and paroled, September 16, 1862, at Harper's Ferry, Va.; died of smallpox January 11, 1863, at hospital, Washington, D.C.

BAKER, CHARLES N.—Age 25 years. Enlisted, August 8, 1862, at Greenfield, to serve three years; mustered in as private, Co. C, August 11, 1862; captured in action September 15, and paroled, September 16, 1862 at Harpers Ferry, Va.; wounded and captured in action, February 20, 1864, at Olustee, Fla.; paroled, February 26, 1865, at Goldsboro, N.C.; mustered out, July 21, 1865, at hospital, Annapolis, Md.

BAKER, DARIUS.—Age. 29 years. Enlisted, August 12, 1862, at Mayfield, to serve three years; mustered in as private, Co. E, August 15, 1862; captured in action, September 15, and paroled, September 16, 1862, at Harper's Ferry, Va.; deserted, December 17, 1862.

BAKER, ISAAC.—Age, 37 years. Enlisted at Greenfield, to serve three years, and mustered in as private, Co. C, August 11, 1862; captured in action, September 15, and paroled, September 16, 1862, at Harper's Ferry, Va.; discharged, October 5, 1863.

BAKER, ROBERT.—Age, 20 years. Enlisted at Troy, to serve three years, and mustered in as private, Co. A, May 20, 1864; captured in action, August 18, 1864, at Deep Bottom, Va.; died, November 29, 1864, at Salisbury, N.C.

BAKER, WILLIAM H.—Age, 21 years. Enlisted, July 26, 1862, at Florida, to serve three years; mustered in as corporal, Co. D, August 2, 1862; captured in action, September 15, and paroled, September 16, 1862, at Harper's Ferry, Va.; returned to ranks, no date; mustered out with company, June 17, 1865, at Raleigh, N.C.

BALL, JUSTIN.—Age, 27 years. Enlisted at Albany, to serve three years, and mustered in as private, Co. H, February 27, 1865; mustered out with detachment, June 8, 1865, at New Berne, N.C.

BALLOU, CYRUS N.—Age, 36 years. Enrolled at Mohawk, to serve three years, and mustered in as first sergeant, Co. A, August 8,1.862; wounded in action, February 20, 1864, at Olustee, Fla.; mustered in as second lieutenant, Co. F, February 24, 1864; transferred to Co. A, May 2, 1864; wounded and captured in action, August 16, 1864, at Deep Bottom, Va.; paroled, no date; mustered in as captain, April 6, 1865; mustered out with company, June 17, 1865, at Raleigh, N.C. Commissioned second lieutenant, April 7, 1864, with rank from February 24, 1864, vice J.W. Davis promoted; captain, April 6, 1865, with rank from January 21, 1865, vice S. P. Smith discharged.

BANTA, MARCUS.—Age, 28 years. Enlisted, August 12, 1862, at Broadalbin, to serve three years; mustered in as private, Co. K, August 16, 1862; no further record.

BARBER, VERNUM.—Age, 26 years. Enlisted, August 9, 1862, at Galway, to serve three years; mustered in as private, Co. C, August 14, 1862; captured in action, September 15, and paroled, September 16, 1862, at Harper's Ferry, Va.; died of disease, December 7, 1862, at hospital, Washington, D.C., as Vernon.

BARCLAY, HENRY.—Age, 29 years. Enlisted, August 14, 1862, at Johnstown, to serve three years; mustered in as private, Co. E, August 15, 1862; captured in action, September 15, and paroled, September 16, 1862, at Harper's Ferry, Va.; deserted, October 8, 1862.

BARKER, FRANKLIN H.—Age, 21 years. Enlisted, August 14, 1862, at Johnstown, to serve three years; mustered in as private, Co. E, August 15, 1862; captured in action, September 15, and paroled, September 16, 1862, at Harper's Ferry, Va.; wounded in action, February 20, 1864, at Olustee, Fla.; mustered out, July 15, 1865, at Albany, N.Y., while in hospital at Troy, N.Y.

BARROW, FREDERICK N.—Age, 40 years. Enrolled, July 19, 1862, at Halfmoon, to serve three years; mustered in as first lieutenant, Co. H, August 20, 1862; discharged, February 3, 1863. Commissioned first lieutenant, September 10, 1862, with rank from August 20, 1862, original.

BARROW, RODERICK F.—Age, 19 years. Enlisted at Charleston, to serve three years, and mustered in as private, Co. D, August 15, 1862; captured in action, September 15. and paroled, September 16, 1862, at Harper's Ferry, Va.; killed in action, February 20, 1864, at Olustee, Fla.

BARNES, WALTER D.—Age, 23 years. Enlisted, August 9, 1862, at Moreau, to serve three years; mustered in as private, Co. F, August 19, 1862; captured in action, September 15, and paroled, September 16, 1862, at Harper's Ferry, Va.; promoted corporal, no date; wounded and captured in action, February 20, 1864, at Olustee, Fla.; died, October 23, 1864, at Andersonville, Ga.

BARNEY, DANIEL W.—Age, 26 years. Enlisted, August 8, 1862, at Edinburgh, to serve three years; mustered in as wagoner, Co. C, August 14, 1862; captured in action, September 15, and paroled, September 16, 1862, at Harper's Ferry, Va.; mustered out with company, June 17, 1865, at Raleigh, N.C.

BARNUM, FRANCIS D.—Age, 22 years. Enrolled at Charlton, to serve three years, and mustered in as second lieutenant, Co. I, August 20, 1862; as first lieutenant, January 27, 1864; as captain, February 1, 1865; transferred to Co. K, Forty-seventh Infantry, June 17, 1865. Commissioned second lieutenant, September 10, 1862, with rank from August 20, 1862, original; first lieutenant, April 22,. 1864, with rank from January 27, 1864, vice D. M. Kittle promoted; captain, May 17, 1865, with rank from February 1, 1865, vice D. M. Kittle discharged.

BARRETT, AARON B.—Age, 18 years. Enlisted, August 12, 1862, at Wells. to serve three years; mustered in as private, Co. K, August 16, 1862; captured in action, September 15, and paroled, September 16, 1862, at Harper's Ferry, Va.; promoted. corporal, no date; wounded in action, August 18, 1864, at Deep Bottom, Va.; mustered out with company, June 17, 1865, at Raleigh, N.C.

BARRETT, WILLIAM.—Age, 18 years. Enlisted, August 8, 1862, at Milton, to serve three years; mustered in as private Co. C, August 11, 1862; captured in action, September 15, and paroled, September 16, 1862, at Harper's Ferry, Va.; mustered out with company, June 17, 1865, at Raleigh, N.C.

BARRY, W1LLIAM.—Age, 20 years. Enlisted at Schenectady, to serve three years, and mustered in as private, Co. H, April 21, 1864; killed in action, June 12, 1864, at Cold Harbor, Va.; also borne as Charles Berry.

BARTLETT, AMASA.—Age, 21 years. Enlisted, August 12, 1862, at Saratoga Springs, to serve three years; mustered in as private, Co. G, August 19, 1862; captured in action, September 15, and paroled, September 16, 1862, at Harper's Ferry, Va.; promoted corporal, no date; killed in action, February 20, 1864, at Olustee, Fla.

BATCHELLER, GEORGE S.—Age, 26 years. Enrolled at Fonda, to serve three years, and mustered in as lieutenant-colonel, August 27, 1862; discharged, November 13, 1863. Commissioned lieutenant-colonel, August 30, 1862, with rank from August 27, 1862, original.

BAYARD, AUGUSTUS W.—Age, 19 years. Enlisted, August 5, 1862, at Halfmoon, to serve three years; mustered in as private, Co. H, August 7, 1862; captured in action, September 15, and paroled, September 16, 1862, at Harper's Ferry, Va.; promoted corporal, April 28, 1865; mustered out with detachment, June 23, 1865, at Albany, N.Y.

BEAM, PETER H.—Private, Co. H, Forty-eighth Infantry; transferred to Co. I, this regiment, January 3, 1864; to Co. H, Forty-seventh Infantry, June 17, 1865.

BECK, THEODORE.—Age, 24 years. Enlisted, March 7, 1865, at New York City, to serve three years; mustered in as private, Co. I, March 27, 1865; mustered out, May 31, 1865, at Foster Hospital, New Berne, N.C.

BECKER, HENRY T.—Age, 18 years. Enlisted, August 4, 1862, at Canajoharie, to serve three years; mustered in as private, Co. B, August 6, 1862; captured in action, September 15, and paroled, September 16, 1862, at Harper's Ferry, Va.; died of consumption, July 12, 1863, at Hilton Head, S.C., as Henry S. Boker.

BECKER, JOHN J.—Age, 18 years. Enlisted, August 13, 1862, at Canajoharie, to serve three years; mustered in as private, Co. B, August 14, 1862; captured in action, September 15 and paroled, September 16, 1862, at Harper's Ferry, Va.; wounded in action, July 18, 1864, at Petersburg, Va.; absent since and at muster-out of company.

BELLIS, JAMES.—Age, 22 years. Enlisted, August 6, 1862, at St. Johnsville, to serve three years; mustered in as private, Co. B, August 12, 1862; captured in action, September 15, and paroled, September 16, 1862, at Harper's Ferry, Va.; wounded in action, February 20, 1864, at Olustee, Fla.; mustered out, May 23 1865, at Jarvis Hospital, Baltimore, Md.

BELLOWS, GEORGE H.—Age, 21 years. Enlisted, July 25, 1862, at Root, to serve three years; mustered in as wagoner, Co. A, July 26, 1862; captured in action, September 15, and paroled, September 16, 1862, at Harper's Ferry, Va.; grade changed to private, no date; wounded in action, February 20, 1864, and died of his wounds, March 11, 1864, at Olustee, Fla.

BEMIS, WILLARD E.—Age, 21 years. Enlisted, August 5, 1862, at Amsterdam, to serve three years; mustered in as private, Co. D, August 6, 1862; captured in action, September 15, and paroled, September 16, 1862, at Harper's Ferry, Va.; discharged for disability, January 21, 1863, at Yorktown, Va.; also borne as Bemus.

BEMUS, CHARLES E.—Age, 18 years. Enlisted, August 12, 1862, at Saratoga. Springs, to serve three years; mustered in as private, Co. G August 19, 1862; captured in action, September 15, and paroled, September 16, 1862, at Harper's Ferry, Va.; wounded in action, February 20, 1864, at Olustee, Fla.; mustered out with detachment, May 27, 1865, at Foster Hospital, New Berne, N.C., as Bemis.

BEMUS, MYRON L.—Age, 23 years. Enlisted, August 5, 1862, at Amsterdam, to serve three years; mustered in as private, Co. D, August 6, 1862; captured in action, September 15, and paroled, September 16, 1862, at Harper's Ferry, Va.; wounded in action, September 29, 1864, at Chaffin's Farm, Va.; died of his wounds, October 11, 1864, at hospital, Annapolis, Md.

BENKER, HENRY.—Age, 32 years. Enlisted at Brooklyn, to serve three years, and mustered in as private, Co. F, August 31, 1863; wounded and captured in action, February 20, 1864, at Olustee, Fla.; paroled, no date; transferred to Co. C, Forty-seventh Infantry, June 17, 1865; also borne as Benkil.

BENNETT, ELIJAH.—Age, 32 years. Enlisted, August 6, 1862, at Day, to serve three years; mustered in as private, Co. C, August 14, 1862; captured in action, September 15, and paroled, September 16, 1862, at Harper's Ferry, Va.; deserted, October 8, 1862, at Chicago, Ill.

BENNETT, HUGH.—Age, 23 years. Enlisted at Albany, to serve three years, and mustered in as private, Co. F, October 28, 1863; wounded in action, February 20, 1864, at Olustee, Fla.; transferred to the Navy, April 27, 1864.

BENSON, JOSEPH B.—Age, 32 years. Enlisted, August 6, 1862, at North Hampton, to serve three years; mustered in as musician, Co. E, August 16, 1862; captured in action, September 15, and paroled, September 16, 1862, at Harper's Ferry, Va.; died, September 4, 1863, at hospital, Beaufort, S.C.

BENSON, PRESERVED A.—Age, 24 years. Enlisted, August 5, 1862, at Edinburg, to serve three years; mustered in as private, Co. C, August 8, 1862; captured in action, September 15, and paroled, September 16, 1862, at Harper's Ferry, Va.; mustered out, June 13, 1865, at Smithville, N.C.

BENSON, WESSON.—Age, 21 years. Enlisted, August 5, 1862, at Edinburgh, to serve three years; mustered in as private, Co. C, August 14, 1862; captured in action, September 15, and paroled, September 16, 1862, at Harper's Ferry, Va.; wounded and captured in action, February 20, 1864, at Olustee, Fla.; died of his wounds, March 26, 1864, at Lake City, Fla., while a prisoner of war.

BERGE, WILLIAM.—Age, 25 years. Enlisted at Goshen, to serve three years, and mustered in as private, Co. A, February 25, 1865; transferred to Co. A, Forty-seventh Infantry, June 17, 1865.

BERTRAND, LEWIS.—Age, 32 years. Enlisted August 5, 1862, at Galway, to serve three years; mustered in as private, Co. C, August 12, 1862; captured in action, September 15, and paroled, September 16, 1862, at Harper's Ferry, Va.; killed in action, September 29 1864, at Chaffin's Farm, Va.

BESAN, DAVID.—Age, 18 years. Enlisted in Seventeenth Congressional District, to serve one year, and mustered in as private, unassigned, February 24, 1865; mustered out, August 14, 1865, at Hart's Island, New York Harbor.

BESE, JOSEPH.—Age, 40 years. Enlisted at Glen, to serve three years, and mustered in as private, Co. A, July 2, 1862; captured in action, September 15, and paroled, September 16, 1862, at Harper's Ferry, Va.; discharged for disability, August 28, 1863, at Beaufort, S.C., as Bize.

BETTS, CHARLES H.—Age, 22 years. Enlisted, August 5, 1862, at Halfmoon, to serve three years; mustered in as private, Co. H, August 7, 1862; no further record.

BETTS, FRANK.—Age,—years. Enlisted at Fonda, to serve three years, and mustered in as musician, Co. I, August 26, 1862; captured in action, September 15, and paroled, September 16, 1862, at Harper's Ferry, Va.; deserted, September 18, 1862, at Frederick, Md.

BETTS, RICHARD A.—Age, 44 years. Enlisted, July 31, 1862, at Saratoga Springs, to serve three years; mustered in as private, Co. F, August 12, 1862; captured in action, September 15, and paroled, September 16, 1862, at Harper's Ferry, Va.; transferred to Veteran Reserve Corps, September 16, 1863.

BEUTLER, LOUIS.—Age, 31 years. Enlisted at Brooklyn, to serve one year, and mustered in as private, Co. K, February 22, 1965; transferred to Co. I, Forty-seventh Infantry, June 17, 1865; also borne as Lewis Butler.

BICKMAN, WILLIAM.—Age, 35 years. Enlisted at Brooklyn, to serve three years, and mustered in as private, Co. C, September 2, 1863; killed, January 16, 1865, by explosion of magazine, at Fort Fisher, N.C.; also borne as Bachman.

BIEBER, WILLIAM.—Age, 20 years. Enlisted at New York City, to serve three years, and mustered in as private, Co. G, August 25, 1863; transferred to Co. D, Forty-seventh Infantry, June 17, 1865.

BILLINGTON, HENRY.—Age, 40 years. Enlisted, August 5, 1862, at Canajoharie, to serve three years; mustered in as private, Co. I, August 16, 1862; captured in action, September 15, and paroled, September 16, 1862, at Harper's Ferry, Va.; wounded in action, August 18, 1864, at Deep Bottom, Va.; died of his wounds, September 29, 1864, at hospital, Beverly, N.J.

BILLINGTON, HENRY I.—Age, 36 years. Enlisted, August 13, 1862, at Ephratah, to serve three years; mustered in as private, Co. E, August 15, 1862; captured in action, September 15, and paroled, September 16, 1862, at Harper's Ferry, Va.; wounded in action, May 14, 1864, at Drewry's Bluff, Va.; mustered out, July 6, 1865, at Lovell Hospital, Portsmouth Grove, R.I.

BIRS, MICHAEL.—Age 23 years. Enlisted, July 23, 1862, at Mohawk, to serve three years; mustered in as private, Co. A, July 24, 1862; captured in action, September 15, and paroled, September 16, 1862, at Harper's Ferry, Va.; killed in action, May 7, 1864, at Port Walthall Junction, Va.

BISHOP, CHARLES J.—Age, 24 years. Enlisted, August 14, 1862, at Mayfield, to serve three years; mustered in as private, Co. E, August 15, 1862; captured in action, September 15, and paroled, September 16, 1862, at Harper's Ferry, Va.; mustered out with company, June 17, 1865, at Raleigh, N.C.

BISSONETT, JOHN B.—Age, 19 years. Enlisted at Schenectady, to serve three years, and mustered in as private, Co. B, February 24, 1865; transferred to Co. A, Forty-seventh Infantry, June 17, 1865.

BLACKMER, STEPHEN R.—Age, 18 years. Enlisted at Malta, to serve three years, and mustered in as private, Co. C, August 11, 1862; captured in action, September 15, and paroled, September 16, 1862, at Harper's Ferry, Va.; wounded in action, May 14, 1864, at Drewry's Bluff, Va.; transferred to Co. D, Tenth Regiment, Veteran Reserve Corps, no date; mustered out with detachment, June 28, 1865, at Washington, D.C.; also borne as Blackmar.

BLACKWOOD, GEORGE N.—Age, 30 years. Enlisted, August 11, 1862, at Saratoga Springs, to serve three years; mustered in as private, Co. G, August 19, 1862; captured in action, September 15, and paroled, September 16, 1862, at Harper's Ferry, Va.; absent, wounded and missing, since February 20, 1864, at Olustee, Fla.; no further record.

BLACKWOOD, WILLIAM H.—Age, 18 years. Enlisted, August 12, 1862, at Saratoga Springs, to serve three years; mustered in as private, Co. G, August 19, 1862; captured in action, September 15, and paroled, September 16, 1862, at Harper's Ferry, Va.; wounded and captured in action, February 20, 1864, at Olustee, Fla.; died at Andersonville, Ga., July 28, 1864.

BLOWERS, GEORGE W.—Age, 21 years. Enlisted, July 23, 1862, at Mayfield, to serve three years; mustered in as private, Co. A, July 24, 1862; captured in action, September 15, and paroled, September 16, 1862, at Harper's Ferry, Va.; wounded in action, February 20, 1864, at Olustee, Fla.; mustered out with company, June 17, 1865, at Raleigh, N.C.

BLOWERS, REUBEN.—Age, 30 years. Enlisted at Mohawk, to serve three years, and mustered in as private, Co. A, July 28, 1862; captured in action, September 15, and paroled, September 16, 1862, at Harper's Ferry, Va.; mustered out with company, June 17, 1865, at Raleigh, N.C.

BLOWERS, SILAS B.—Age, 21 years. Enlisted, August 7, 1862, at Saratoga Springs, to serve three years; mustered in as private, Co. G, August 19, 1862; captured in action, September 15, and paroled, September 16, 1862, at Harper's Ferry, Va.; mustered out with company, June 17, 1865, at Raleigh, N.C.

BOARDWELL, SID.—Age, 42 years. Enlisted at Schenectady, to serve three years, and mustered in as private, Co. H, April 21, 1864; wounded in action, June 15, 1864, in front of Petersburg, Va.; transferred to Co. F, Forth-seventh Infantry, June 17, 1865.

BOHLING, HENRY.—Age, 21 years. Enlisted at Tarrytown, to serve one year, and mustered in as private Co. H, March 4, 1865; mustered out, July 6, 1865, at New York City.

BOHME, HERMAN.—Age, 27 years. Enlisted at Tarrytown, to serve three years, and mustered in as private, Co. B, October 27, 1863; transferred to Co. B, Forty-seventh Infantry, June 17, 1865.

BOLSTER, JAMES.—Age, 26 years. Enlisted at Oppenheim, to serve three years, and mustered in as private, Co, E. August 15, 1862; captured in action, September 15, and paroled, September 16, 1862, at Harper's Ferry, Va.; died of fever, July 26, 1863, at hospital, Beaufort, S.C.

BOND, JOHN D.—Age, 24 years. Enlisted at Glen, to serve three years, and mustered in as private, Co. A, August 9, 1862; captured in action, September 15, and paroled, September 16, 1862, at Harper's Ferry, Va.; died of chronic diarrhea, May 20, 1865, at Fortress Monroe, Va.

BORASA, CHARLES.—Age, 23 years. Enlisted at Brooklyn, to serve three years, and mustered in as private, Co. G, March 6, 1865; deserted, April 7, 1865, at Magnolia, N.C.

BORDEN, JR., WILLIAM H.—Age, 19 years. Enlisted, August 13, 1862, at Canajoharie, to serve three years; mustered in as private, Co. B, August 14, 1862, captured in action, September 15, and paroled, September 16, 1862, at Harper's Ferry, Va.; mustered out with company, June 17, 1865, at Raleigh, N.C., as Burden.

BORDWELL, JOHN.—Age, 18 years. Enlisted at Schenectady, to serve three years, and mustered in as private, Co. H, April 21, 1864; transferred to Co. F, Forty-seventh Infantry, June 17, 1865; also borne as Boardwell.

BOURDRON, CHARLES.—Age, 19 years. Enlisted at Parishville, to serve one year, and mustered in as private, Co. E, February 23, 1865; transferred to Co. D, Forty-seventh Infantry, June 17, 1865; also borne as Bourdrous.

BOVEE, JEREMIAH W.—Age, 22 years. Enlisted, August 9, 1862, at Canajoharie, to serve three years; mustered in as sergeant, Co. I, August 16, 1862; captured in action, September 15, and paroled, September 16, 1862, at Harper's Ferry, Va.; promoted first sergeant, no date; deserted on expiration of furlough, June 12, 1863.

BOWIE, DAVID.—Age, 21 years. Enlisted, July 28,

1862, at Minden, to serve three years; mustered in as private, Co. B, August 14, 1862; captured in action, September 15, 1862, at Harper's Ferry, Va.; paroled, September 16, 1862; died of typhoid fever, August 14, 1863, at Beaufort, S.C.; prior service in Third U.S. Artillery.

BOWMAN, JOSEPH.—Age, 33 years. Enlisted at Ninth Congressional District, to serve three years, and mustered in as private, Co. E, August 28, 1863; killed in action, February 20, 1864, at Olustee, Fla.

BOWMAN, THERON.—Age, 21 years. Enlisted, August 12, 1862, at Mayfield, to serve three years; mustered in as private, Co. E, August 15, 1862; captured in action, September 15, and paroled, September 16, 1862, at Harper's Ferry, Va.; died of typhoid fever, June 27, 1863, at hospital, Hilton Head, S.C.

BOYCE, SCHUYLER.—Age, 42 years. Enlisted, August 11, 1862, at Saratoga Springs, to serve three years; mustered in as private, Co. G, August 19, 1862; captured in action, September 15, and paroled, September 16 1862, at Harper's Ferry, Va.; discharged for disability, March 29, 1865, at Albany, N.Y.

BOYD, WILLIAM.—Age, 18 years. Enlisted, July 28, 1862, at Amsterdam, to serve three years; mustered in as private, Co. D, July 30, 1862; captured in action, September 15, and paroled, September 16, 1862, at Harper's Ferry, Va.; discharged for disability, May 19, 1863, at Hilton Head, S.C.

BOYER, WILLIAM.—Age, 18 years. Enlisted at Brooklyn, to serve one year, and mustered in as private, Co. K, February 22, 1865; transferred to Co. H, Forty-seventh Infantry, June 17, 1865.

BRADT, CHARLES H.—Age, 21 years. Enlisted at Johnstown, to serve three years, and mustered in as private, Co. K, August 25, 1862; captured in action, September 15, and paroled, September 16, 1862, at Harper's Ferry, Va.; promoted first sergeant, no date; killed in action, February 20, 1864, at Olustee, Fla.

BRADT, EDWARD.—Age, 26 years. Enlisted, August 6, 1862, at Caroga, to serve three years; mustered in as private, Co. K, August 12, 1862; captured in action, September 15, and paroled, September 16, 1862, at Harper's Ferry, Va.; discharged, October 29, 1863, at Albany, N.Y.; also borne as Bratt.

BRADT, JOHN L.—Age, 41 years. Enlisted, August 12, 1862, at Albany, to serve three years; mustered in as private, Co. E, August 15, 1862; captured in action, September 15, and paroled, September 16, 1862, at Harper's Ferry, Va.; mustered out with company, June 17, 1865, at Raleigh, N.C.; also borne as Bratt.

BRADT, LORENZO E.—Age, 21 years. Enlisted, August 6, 1862, at Caroga, to serve three years; mustered in as corporal, Co. K, August 12, 1862; captured in action, September 15, and paroled, September 16, 1862, at Harper's Ferry, Va.; promoted sergeant, no date; wounded in action, February 20, 1864, at Olustee, Fla.; transferred to Co. I, Second Regiment, Veteran Reserve Corps, no date; discharged, July 3, 1865, at Camp Carrington, Indianapolis, Ind.; also borne as Bratt.

BRADT, PETER.—Age, 22 years. Enlisted, August 6, 1862, at Caroga, to serve three years; mustered in as private, Co. K, August 12, 1862; captured in action, September 15, and paroled, September 16, 1862, at Harper's Ferry, Va.; discharged, January 22, 1863, at Yorktown, Va.; also borne as Bratt.

BRADY, JOHN.—Age, 19 years. Enlisted at Tarrytown, to serve three years, and mustered in as private, Co. G, October 29, 1863; transferred to the Navy, April 27, 1864.

BRAISTED, JR., THOMAS H.—Age, 23 years. Enlisted at New York City, to serve three years, and mustered in as private, Co. H, August 28, 1863; discharged for disability, April 5, 1865.

BRAND, JOHN C.—Age, 32 years. Enlisted, August 12, 1862 at Charlestown, to serve three years; mustered in as sergeant, Co. D, August 15, 1862; mustered out with company, June 17, 1865, at Raleigh, N.C. Commissioned, not mustered, second lieutenant, May 17, 1865, with rank from February 1, 1865, vice J. M. Hill promoted.

BRANDT, CONRAD.—Age, 32 years. Enlisted at Brooklyn, to serve one year, and mustered in as private, Co. C, February 28, 1865; transferred to Co. C, Forty-seventh Infantry, June 17, 1865.

BRENNAN, ANDREW.—Age, 21 years. Enlisted at Tompkinsville, to serve one year, and mustered in as private, Co. H, February 27, 1865; transferred to Co. K, Forty-seventh Infantry, June 17, 1865.

BREWER, DAVID R.—Age, 28 years. Enlisted, August 13, 1862, at Florida, to serve three years; mustered in as private Co. D, August 15, 1862; captured in action, September 15, and paroled, September 16, 1862, at Harper's Ferry, Va.; wounded and captured in action, August 16, 1864, at Deep Bottom, Va.;. paroled, no date; discharged for disability, May 18, 1865, at hospital, Troy, N.Y.

BREWER, RICHARD.—Age, 21 years. Enlisted, July 28, 1862, at Saratoga Springs, to serve three years; mustered in as private, Co. C, July 31, 1862; captured in action, September 15, and paroled, September 16, 1862, at Harper's Ferry, Va.; mustered out with company, June 17, 1805, at Raleigh, N.C.

BRICE, CHARLES.—Age, 21 years. Enlisted, August 9, 1862 at Moreau, to serve three years; mustered in as private, Co. G, August 18, 1862; captured in action, September 15, and paroled, September 16, 1862, at Harper's Ferry, Va.; promoted corporal, no date; sergeant, November 20, 1863; killed in action,, May 7, 1864, at Chester Heights, Va.; as Charles B.

BRICE, JOHN.—Age, 17 years. Enlisted at Schenectady, to serve three years, and mustered in as private, Co. K, March 30, 1865; transferred to Co. I, Forty-seventh Infantry, June 17, 1865; also borne as Bryce.

BRICE, THOMAS E.—Age, 20 years. Enlisted, August 9, 1862, at Moreau, to serve three years; mustered in as private, Co. G, August 18, 1862; captured in action, September 15, and paroled, September 16, 1862, at Harper's Ferry, Va.; promoted corporal, no date; transferred to Co. B, Tenth Regiment, Veteran Reserve Corps, December 23, 1863; mustered out with detachment, June 27, 1865, at Washington, D.C.

BRIGGS, JOHN H.—Age, 32 years. Enlisted, August 5, 1862, at Milton, to serve three years; mustered in as private, Co. G, August 8, 1862; captured in action, September 15, and paroled, September 16, 1862, at Harper's Ferry, Va.; wounded in action, August 16, 1864, at Deep Bottom, Va.; mustered out, June 10, 1865, at Albany, N.Y., while in hospital, Troy, N.Y.

BRISBIN, ANDREW.—Age, 24 years. Enlisted,

August 2, 1862, at Wilton, to serve three years; mustered in as sergeant, Co. F, August 12, 1862; captured in action, September 15, and paroled, September 16, 1862, at Harper's Ferry, Va.; returned to ranks, no date; discharged for disability, March 12, 1863.

BRISBIN, LORIN.—Age, 35 years. Enlisted, August 7, 1862, at Wilton, to serve three years; mustered in as private, Co. F, August 12, 1802; captured in action, September 15, and paroled, September 16, 1862, at Harper's Ferry, Va.; discharged for disability, March 3, 1863, at Hilton Head, S.C.

BRITTON, JAMES.—Age, 19 years. Enlisted, August 12, 1862, at Charleston, to serve three years; mustered in as private, Co. D, August 16, 1862; captured in action, September 15, and paroled, September 16, 1862, at Harper's Ferry, Va.; mustered out with company, June 17, 1865, at Raleigh, N.C., as James H.

BROCKWAY, GEORGE E.—Age, 18 years. Enlisted, August 5, 1862, at Halfmoon, to serve three years; mustered in as private, Co. H, August 14, 1862; captured in action, September 15, and paroled, September 16, 1862, at Harper's Ferry, Va.; appointed musician, no date; mustered out with company, June 17, 1865, at Raleigh, N.C.

BROOKS, ARCHIBALD F.—Age, 21 years. Enlisted, August 11, 1862, at Corinth, to serve three years; mustered in as private, Co. F, August 19, 1862; captured in action, September 15, and paroled, September 16, 1862, at Harper's Ferry, Va.; died of fever, December 22, 1862, at hospital, Chicago, Ill.

BROOKS, ELI.—Age, 21 years. Enlisted, August 11, 1862, at North Hampton, to serve three years; mustered in as private, Co. E, August 15, 1862; captured in action, September 15, and paroled, September 16, 1862, at Harper's Ferry, Va.; wounded in action, January 15, 1865, at Fort Fisher, N.C.; mustered out with company, June 17, 1865, at Raleigh, N.C.

BROOKS, GEORGE.—Age, 35 years. Enlisted, August 14, 1862, at Corinth, to serve 3 years; mustered in. as private, Co. G, August 19, 1862; captured in action, September 15, and paroled, September 16, 1862, at Harper's Ferry, Va.; discharged for disability, July 25, 1863, at New York City, as George B.

BROOKS, HENRY A.—Age, 36 years. Enlisted at Goshen, to serve three years, and mustered in as private, Co. A, October 7, 1863; wounded in action, May 14, 1864, at Proctor's Creek, Va.; died of his wounds, June 24, 1864, at Fort Monroe, Va.

BROOKS, JAMES B.—Age, 26 years. Enlisted, August 7, 1862, at North Hampton, to serve three years; mustered in as private, Co. E, August 15, 1862; captured in action, September 15 and paroled, September 16, 1862, at Harper's Ferry, Va. wounded in action, February 20, 1864, at Olustee, Fla.; died of injuries, January 17, 1865, at Regimental Hospital, Fort Fisher, N.C.

BROPHY, TIMOTHY.—Age, 25 years. Enlisted, August 10, 1862, at Saratoga Springs, to serve three years; mustered in. as private, Co. G, August 19, 1862; captured in action, September 15, and paroled, September 16, 1862, at Harper's Ferry, Va.; discharged for disability, March 7, 1863, at Alexandria, Va.

BROUGHAM, GEORGE C.—Age, 22 years. Enlisted at Brooklyn, to serve three years, and mustered in as private, Co. F, August 31, 1863; wounded in action, February 20, 1864, at Olustee, Fla.; transferred to the Navy, April 27, 1864.

BROUGHTON, EBENEZER C.—Age, 27 years. Enlisted, August 5, 1862, at Halfmoon, to serve three years; mustered in as private, Co. H, August 7, 1862; captured in action, September 15, and paroled, September 16, 1862, at Harper's Ferry, Va.; deserted, September 17, 1862, at Frederick, Md.

BROWER, ABRAHAM.—Age, 18 years. Enlisted, July 26, 1862, at Amsterdam, to serve three years; mustered in as private, Co. D, July 30, 1862; captured in action, September 15, and paroled, September 16, 1862, at Harper's Ferry, Va.; mustered out, June 6, 1865, at Albany, N.Y., as Abram.

BROWER, FRANCIS.—Age, 37 years. Enlisted, July 28, 1862, at Corinth, to serve three years; mustered in as private, Co. F, August 12, 1862; captured in action, September 15, and paroled, September 16, 1862, at Harper's Ferry, Va.; discharged for disability, December 12, 1862, at Chicago, Ill., as Brewer.

BROWER, JOHN M.—Age, 44 years. Enlisted, July 31, 1862, at Halfmoon, to serve three years; mustered in as private, Co. H, August 6, 1862; captured in action, September 15, and paroled, September 16, 1862, at Harper's Ferry, Va.; deserted, October 16, 1862, at Chicago, Ill., as John W.

BROWN, AMOS O.—Age, 19 years. Enlisted, August 8, 1862, at Edinburgh, to serve three years; mustered in as private, Co. C, August 15, 1862; captured in action, September 15, and paroled, September 16, 1862, at Harper's Ferry, Va.; mustered out with company, June 17, 1865, at Raleigh, N.C.

BROWN, CHARLES.—Age, 23 years. Enlisted at Tarrytown, to serve three years, and mustered in as private, Go. F, August 25, 1863; transferred to the Navy, April 27, 1864.

BROWN, GEORGE.—Age, 22 years. Enlisted at New York City, to serve three years, and mustered in as private, Go. H, August 28, 1863; transferred to Co. B, First New York Volunteer Engineers, for promotion to second lieutenant, March 24, 1865.

BROWN, GEORGE.—Age, 26 years. Enlisted at Andes, to serve three years, and mustered in as private, Co D, February 25, 1865; transferred to Co. B, Forty-seventh Infantry, June 17, 1865.

BROWN, GEORGE C.—Age, 24 years. Enlisted at Jamaica, to serve three years, and mustered in as private, Co. F, October 30, 1863; wounded in action, May 14, 1864, at Drewry's Bluff, Va.; deserted on expiration of furlough, November 30, 1864, at hospital, Washington, D.C.

BROWN, JACOB B.—Age, 24 years. Enlisted, August 19, 1862, at St. Johnsville, to serve three years; mustered in as private, Co. B, August 20, 1862; captured in action, September 15, and paroled, September 16, 1862, at Harper's Ferry, Va.; wounded in action, February 20, 1864, at Olustee, Fla.; killed in action, June 24, 1864, at Petersburg, Va.

BROWN, JAMES S.—Age, 30 years. Enlisted, August 13, 1862, at Canajoharie, to serve three years; mustered in as private, Co. B, August 14, 1862; captured in action, September 15, and paroled, September 16, 1862, at Harper's Ferry, Va.; wounded in action,

January 16, 1865, at Fort Fisher, N.C.; mustered out, May 26, 1865, at McDougal Hospital, New York Harbor.

BROWN, JOHN.—Age, 28 years. Enlisted at Fonda, to serve three years, and mustered in as private, Co. A, August 8, 1862; captured in action, September 15, and paroled, September 16, 1862, at Harper's Ferry, Va.; promoted sergeant, no date; deserted on expiration of furlough, June 1, 1863, at New York City.

BROWN, JOHN.—Age, 18 years. Enlisted at Brooklyn, to serve three years, and mustered in as private, Co. C, February 28, 865; transferred to Co. A, Forty-seventh Infantry, June 17, 1865.

BROWN, JOHN.—Age, 31 years. Enlisted, August 4, 1862, at Canajoharie, to serve three years; not mustered in as private, Co. I; deserted, August 20, 1862, at Fonda, N.Y.

BROWN, LAYMAN.—Age, 37 years. Enlisted, August 23, 1862, at Minden, to serve three years; mustered in as private, Co. H, August 25, 1862; no further record.

BROWN, ORREN H.—Age, 20 years. Enlisted, August 5, 1862, at St. Johnsville, to serve three years; mustered in as private, Co. B, August 12, 1862; captured in action, September 15, and paroled, September 16, 1862, at Harper's Ferry, Va.; promoted corporal, October 11, 1862; sergeant, January 1, 1864; wounded in action, May 7, 1864, at Chester Heights, Va.; mustered out with company, June 17, 1865, at Raleigh, N.C.

BROWN, WILLIAM.—Age, 21 years. Enlisted at Jamaica, to serve three years, and mustered in as private, Co. F, October 30, 1863; wounded in action, February 20, 1864, at Olustee, Fla.; transferred to the Navy, April 27, 1864.

BROWN, JR., WILLIAM.—Age, 21 years. Enlisted at Jamaica, to serve three years, and mustered in as private, Co. F, October 30, 1863; transferred to the Navy, April 27, 1864.

BRUNSWICK, WILLIAM.—Age, 30 years. Enlisted at Tarrytown, to serve three years, and mustered in as private, Co. H, October 29, 1863; wounded in action, February 20, 1864, at Olustee, Fla.; transferred to Co. K, Forty-seventh Infantry, June 17, 1865.

BRYANT, WILLIAM G.—Age, 18 years. Enlisted, July 18, 1862, at Saratoga Springs, to serve three years; mustered in as musician, Co. G, July 31, 1862; captured in action, September 15, and paroled, September 16, 1862, at Harper's Ferry, Va.; grade changed to private, no date; wounded in action, February 20, 1864, at Olustee, Fla.; mustered out with company, June 17, 1865, at Raleigh, N.C.; also borne as N. B. Bryant.

BUCHANAN, ARCHIBALD.—Age, 44 years. Enlisted, August 5, 1862, at Broadalbin, to serve three years; mustered in as sergeant, Co. K, August 16, 1862; captured in action, September 15, and paroled, September 16, 1862, at Harper's Ferry, Va.; returned to ranks, no date; transferred to Veteran Reserve Corps, October 20, 1864.

BUCK, GEORGE B.—Age, 18 years. Enlisted at Schenectady, to serve three years, and mustered in as private, Co. G, March 3, 1865; transferred to Co. E, Forty-seventy Infantry, June 17, 1865.

BUCKLEY, PATRICK.—Age, 25 years. Enlisted at Goshen, to serve one year, and mustered in as private, Co. F, February 21, 1865; transferred to Co. C, Forty-seventh Infantry, June 17, 1865.

BUDDLE, EDWARD C.—Age, 30 years. Enlisted, August 5, 1862, at Canajoharie, to serve three years; mustered in as corporal, Co. B, August 12, 1862; captured in action, September 15, and paroled, September 16, 1862, at Harper's Ferry, Va.; again captured and paroled, no dates; mustered out, June 22, 1865, at Albany, N.Y.; also borne as Budle.

BUEL, GEORGE W.—Age, 24 years. Enlisted, August 11, 1862, at Oppenhern, to serve three years; mustered in as private, Co. E, August 15, 1862; captured in action, September 15, and paroled, September 16, 1862, at Harper's Ferry, Va.; again captured in action, February 20, 1864, at Olustee, Fla.; died, August 15, 1864, at Andersonville, Ga.

BUELL, HIRAM.—Age, 23 years. Enlisted at Tarrytown, to serve three years, and mustered in as private, Co. K, October 20, 1863; deserted to the enemy, November 18, 1863, from Ladies Island, S.C.

BULLOCK, JOSEPH H.—Age, 22 years. Enlisted, August 6, 1862, at Halfmoon, to serve three years; mustered in as private, Co. H, August 7, 1862; captured in action, September 15, and paroled, September 16, 1862, at Harper's Ferry, Va.; mustered out with company, June 17, 1865, at Raleigh, N.C.

BUMP, MILLINGHAM.—Age, 18 years. Enlisted at Mohawk, to serve three years, and mustered in as private, Co. K, August 12, 1862; captured in action, September 15, and paroled, September 16, 1862, at Harper's Ferry, Va.; discharged, May 27, 1863, at Hilton Head, S.C.

BUNZEY, HARVEY.—Age, 29 years. Enlisted, August 9, 1862, at Charleston, to serve three years; mustered in as private, Co. D, August 15, 1862; captured in action, September 15, and paroled, September 16, 1862, at Harper's Ferry, Va.; mustered out with company, June 17, 1865, at Raleigh, N.C.

BURBEE, CASSIUS M.—Age, 21 years. Enlisted, August 12, 1862, at Saratoga Springs, to serve three years; mustered in as private, Co. F, August 14, 1862; captured in action, September 15, and paroled, September 16, 1862, at Harper's Ferry, Va.; died of fever, July 25, 1863, at hospital, Hilton Head, S.C.

BURBLY, MILO E.—Age, 21 years. Enlisted, August 5, 1862, at Milton, to serve three years; mustered in as private, Co. C, August 8, 1862; captured in action, September 15, and paroled, September 16, 1862, at Harper's Ferry, Va.; wounded in action, August 16, 1864, at Deep Bottom, Va.; absent since and at Troy, N.Y. at muster-out of company; also borne as Barbed.

BURDICK, LEWIS A.—Age, 21 years. Enlisted, August 2, 1862, at Northumberland, to serve three years; mustered in as private, Co. F, August 12, 1862; captured in action, September 15, and paroled, September 16, 1862, at Harper's Ferry, Va.; wounded in action, February 20, 1864, at Olustee, Fla.; mustered out, May 17, 1865, at David's Island, New York Harbor.

BURGES, EDMUND.—Age, 32 years. Enlisted, August 7, 1862, at Northampton, to serve three years; mustered in as private, Co. E, August 15, 1862; captured in action, September 15, and paroled, September 16, 1862, at Harper's Ferry, Va.; mustered out with company, June 17, 1865, at Raleigh, N.C.

BURK, ELI.—Age, 42 years. Enlisted at New York City, to serve one year, and mustered in as private, Co. I, March 7, 1865; transferred to Co. H, Forty-seventh Infantry, June 17, 1865.

BURKE, DANIEL.—Age, 40 years. Enlisted, July 28, 1862, at Mohawk, to serve three years; mustered in as private, Co. A, July 29, 1862; captured in action, September 15, and paroled, September 16, 1862, at Harper's Ferry, Va.; mustered out, June 6, 1865, at New Berne, N.C.

BURKE, GEORGE W.—Age, 27 years. Enlisted, August 9, 1862, at St. Johnsville, to serve three years; mustered in as private, Co. B, August 12, 1862; captured in action, September 15, and paroled, September 16, 1862, at Harper's Ferry, Va.; sentenced by general court martial to serve twelve months without pay from June 3, 1865; absent in confinement at muster-out of company.

BURKE, ROBERT E.—Age, 26 years. Enlisted, August 19, 1862, at St. Johnsville, to serve three years; mustered in as private, Co. B, August 20, 1862; captured in action, September 15, and paroled, September 16, 1862, at Harper's Ferry, Va.; mustered out with detachment, June 3, 1865, at hospital, Washington, D.C., as Burker.

BURNETT, RICHARD.—Age, 37 years. Enlisted at Goshen, to serve three years, and mustered in as private, unassigned, February 28, 1865; mustered out with detachment, June 9, 1865, at Washington, D.C., while in Sickel Hospital, Alexandria, Va.

BURNHAM, JOHN R.—Age, 19 years. Enlisted, August 4, 1862, at Wilton, to serve three years; mustered in as private, Co. F, August 12, 1862; captured in action, September 15, and paroled, September 16, 1862, at Harper's Ferry, Va.; wounded in action, February 20, 1864, at Olustee, Fla.; mustered out with company, June 17, 1865, at Raleigh, N.C.

BURPEE, CHARLES.—Age, 20 years. Enlisted, August 7, 1862, at Greenfield, to serve three years; mustered in as private, Co. F, August 12, 1862; captured in action, September 15, and paroled, September 16, 1862, at Harper's Ferry, Va.; promoted sergeant, no date; mustered out with company, June 17, 1865, at Raleigh, N.C.

BURNS, HUGH.—Age, 37 years. Enlisted at Brooklyn, to serve one year, and mustered in as private, Co. C, February 28, 1865; transferred to Co. C, Forty-seventh Infantry, June 17, 1865.

BURNS, JAMES.—Age, 21 years. Enlisted at Tarrytown, to serve three years, and mustered in as private, Co. E, August 25, 1863; transferred to Co. D, Forty-seventh Infantry, June 17, 1865.

BURNS, JOHN.—Age, 23 years. Enlisted, August 6, 1862, at St. Johnsville, to serve three years; mustered in as private, Co. B, August 12, 1862; captured in action, September 15, and paroled, September 16, 1862, at Harper's Ferry, Va.; mustered out with company, June 17, 1865, at Raleigh, N.C.

BURNS, LEONARD.—Age, 26 years. Enlisted, August 13, 1852, at Florida, to serve three years; mustered in as private, Co. B, August 15, 1862; captured in action, September 15, and paroled, September 16, 1862, at Harper's Ferry, Va.; mustered out with company, June 17, 1865, at Raleigh, N.C.

BURNS, MICHAEL.—Age, 25 years. Enlisted at Ninth Congressional District, to serve three years, and mustered in as private, Co. E, August 28, 1863; discharged, October 22, 1864, Washington, D.C.

BURNS, PETER.—Age, 25 years. Enlisted at Johnstown, to serve three years, and mustered in as private, Co. E, August 13, 1862; captured in action, September 15, and paroled, September 16, 1862, at Harper's Ferry, Va.; deserted, October 12, 1862.

BURR, SAMUEL.—Age, 23 years. Enlisted, August 5, 1862, at Broadalbin, to serve three years; mustered in as corporal, Co. K, August 12, 1862; captured in action, September 15, and paroled, September 16, 1862, at Harper's Ferry, Va.; promoted sergeant, no date; absent at Albany, N.Y., at muster-out of company.

BURTON, WINSLOW.—Age, 36 years. Enlisted, August 9, 1862, at Charleston, to serve three years; mustered in as private, Co. D, August 15, 1862; captured in action, September 15, and paroled, September 16, 1862, at Harper's Ferry, Va.; died of chronic diarrhea, October 28, 1864, at hospital, New York Harbor.

BUSHY, ALBERT G.—Age, 18 years. Enlisted at Root, to serve three years, and mustered in as private, Co. H, March 2, 1865; mustered out, September 5, 1865, at Albany, N.Y., as Bushey.

BUTLER, LAURENCE.—Age, 19 years. Enlisted at Albany, to serve three years, and mustered in as private, Co. F, October 28, 1863; mustered out, July 6, 1865, at McDougall Hospital, New York Harbor, as Lawrence Buckley.

BUTLER, PETER.—Age, 23 years. Enlisted, August 13, 1862, at Day, to serve three years; mustered in as private, Co. C, August 14, 1862; captured in action, September 15, and paroled, September 16, 1862, at Harper's Ferry, Va.; killed in action, February 20, 1864, at Olustee, Fla.

BUTLER, PETER.—Age, 44 years. Enlisted, August 13, 1862, at Clifton Park, to serve three years; mustered in as private, Co. H, August 14, 1862; captured in action, September 15, and paroled, September 16, 1862, at Harper's Ferry, Va.; wounded in action, September 30, 1864, at Chaffin's Farm, Va.; promoted corporal, May 1, 1865; mustered out with company, June 17, 1865, at Raleigh, N.C.

BUTLER, SYLVESTER.—Age, 18 years. Enlisted at Schenectady, to serve three years, and mustered in as private, Co. H, January 15, 1864; transferred to Co. F, Forty-seventh Infantry, June 17, 1865.

BUYCE, ORRA.—Age, 23 years. Enlisted, August 12, 1862, at Wells, to serve three years; mustered in as corporal, Co. K, August 16, 1862; captured in action, September 15, and paroled, September 16, 1862, at Harper's Ferry, Va.; discharged for disability, April 17, 1863.

BYER, HENRY.—Age, 22 years. Enlisted, July 28, 1862, at Minden, to serve three years; mustered in as private, Co. B, August 13, 1862; captured in action, September 15, and paroled, September 16, 1862, at Harper's Ferry, Va.; deserted, September 28, 1962, in the State of Ohio; also borne as Heinrich Beier.

CADY, DANIEL.—Age, 24 years. Enlisted, August 12, 1862, at Edinburgh, to serve three years; mustered in as private, Co. F, August 19, 1862; captured in action, September 15, and paroled, September 16, 1862, at Harper's Ferry, Va.; mustered out with company, June 17, 1865, at Raleigh, N.C.

CAGARUN, JAMES.—Age, 18 years. Enlisted at Schenectady, to serve three years, and mustered in as private, Co. G, March 4, 1865; transferred to Co. E, Forty-seventh Infantry, June 17, 1865; also borne as Cogovan.

CAIN, DAVID.—Age, 21 years. Enlisted at Goshen, to serve three years, and mustered in as private, Co. A, October 18, 1863; wounded in action, June 2, 1864, at Cold Harbor, Va.; transferred to Co. A, Forty-seventh Infantry, June 17, 1865.

CALDWELL, JAMES P.—Age, 28 years. Enlisted at Mohawk, to serve three years, and mustered in as private, Co. A, July 28, 1862; captured in action, September 15, and paroled, September 16, 1862, at Harper's Ferry, Va.; wounded in action, July 30, 1864, at Petersburg, Va.; discharged for disability, May 23, 1865.

CAMPBELL, DELEVAN.—Age, 27 years. Enlisted, December 1863, at Palatine, to serve three years; mustered in as private, Co. I, January 2, 1864; transferred to Co. B, Forty-seventh infantry, June 17, 1863.

CAMPBELL, FRANCIS.—Age, 31 years. Enlisted at Brooklyn, to serve three years, and mustered in as private, Co. H, September 2, 1863; wounded in action, February 20, 1864, at Olustee, Fla.; transferred to the Navy, April 27, 1864.

CAMPBELL, HENRY C.—Age, 18 years. Enlisted, August 11, 1862, at Greenfield, to serve three years; mustered in as private, Co. F, August 19, 1862; captured in action, September 15, and paroled, September 16, 1862, at Harper's Ferry, Va.; wounded in action, August 16, 1864, at Deep Bottom, Va.; died of his wounds, October 1, 1864, at hospital, David's Island, New York Harbor.

CANFIELD, AUGUSTUS C.—Age, 28 years. Enlisted, August 15, 1862, at Oppenheim, to serve three years; mustered in as private, Co. B, August 16, 1862; captured in action, September 15, and paroled, September 16, 1862, at Harper's Ferry, Va.; wounded in action, February 20, 1864, at Olustee, Fla., and May 14, 1864, at Drewry's Bluff, Va.; mustered out, June 10, 1865, at Emory Hospital, Washington, D.C.

CANNON, PATRICK.—Age, 22 years. Enlisted at Milton, to serve three years, and mustered in as private, Co. C, August 11, 1862; captured in action, September 15, and paroled, September 16, 1862, at Harper's Ferry, Va.; discharged for insanity, October 25, 1863, at Washington, D.C.

CARMICHAEL, JAMES M.—Age, 34 years. Enlisted at Johnstown, to serve three years, and mustered in as wagoner, Co. K, August 23, 1862; captured in action September 15, and paroled, September 16, 1862, at Harper's Ferry, Va.; mustered out with company, June 17, 1865, at Raleigh, N.C.

CARPENTER, JOSEPH.—Age, 18 years. Enlisted at Glen, to serve one year, and mustered in as private, Co. K, September 7, 1864; mustered out with company, June 17, 1865, at Raleigh, N.C.

CARPENTER, TRUMAN.—Age, 25 years. Enlisted, August 8, 1862, at Greenfield, to serve three years; mustered in as private, Co. F; captured in action, September 15, and paroled, September 16, 1862, at Harper's Ferry, Va.; detached to Battery B, Eleventh U. S. Light Artillery, from May 14, 1863, until mustered out, June 13, 1865, at Richmond, Va.

CARR, GEORGE.—Age, 18 years. Enlisted, August 5, 1862, at Stillwater, to serve three years; mustered in as private, Co. H, August 7, 1862; captured in action, September 15, and paroled, September 16, 1862, at Harper's Ferry, Va.; wounded in action, February 20, 1864, at Olustee, Fla.; mustered out with company, June 17, 1865, at Raleigh, N.C., as Carre.

CARROLL, EUGENE 24.—Age, 32 years. Enlisted, August 9, 1862, at Milton, to serve three years; mustered in as private, Co. C, August 11, 1862; captured in action, September 15, and paroled, September 16, 1862, at Harper's Ferry, Va.; deserted, October 16, 1862, at Chicago, Ill.

CARROLL, JOHN.—Age, 21 years. Enlisted at Tarrytown, to serve three years, and mustered in as private, Co. K, October 28, 1862; discharged, January 30, 1864.

CARSON, ELISHA.—Age, 44 years. Enlisted at Glen, to serve three years, and mustered in as private, Co. A, July 30, 1982; captured in action, September 15, and paroled, September 16, 1862, at Harper's Ferry, Va.; captured in action, February 20, 1864, at Olustee, Fla.; died, August 22, 1864, at Andersonville, Ga.

CARSTON, HENRY.—Age, 18 years. Enlisted at Brooklyn, to serve three years, and mustered in as private, Co. I, March 11, 1865; transferred to Co. H. Forty-seventh Infantry, June 17, 1865; also borne as Carsten.

CARVER, MARTIN.—Age, 21 years. Enlisted, August 9, 1862, at Canajoharie, to serve three years; mustered in as private, Co. I, August 16, 1862; captured in action, September 15, and paroled, September 16, 1862, at Harper's Ferry, Va.; wounded in action, February 20, 1864, at Olustee, Fla.; promoted sergeant, no date; mustered out with company, June 17, 1865, at Raleigh, N.C.

CASEY, JOHN.—Age, 21 years. Enlisted at Schenectady, to three years, and mustered in as private, Co. H, February 23, 1865; transferred to Co. K, Forty-seventh Infantry, June 17, 1865.

CASS, HENRY W.—Age, 33 years. Enlisted, August 6, 1862, it Corinth, to serve three years; mustered in as first sergeant, Co. F, August 19, 1862; discharged, August 31, 1863, for promotion to first lieutenant in Thirty-fourth Infantry, U. S. Colored Troops; also borne as Henry M. Commissioned, not mustered, second lieutenant, November 25, 1863, with rank from October 24, 1863, vice S.H. Olney promoted.

CASSIDY, GEORGE.—Age, 23 years. Enlisted, August 4, 1862, at Florida, to serve three years; mustered in as private, Co. D, August 15, 1862; captured in action, September 15, and paroled, September 16, 1862, at Harper's Ferry, Va.; died of typhoid fever, July 8, 1863, at hospital, Hilton Head, S.C.

CASSIDY, JAMES.—Age, 25 years. Enlisted at Brooklyn, to serve three years, and mustered in as private, Co. F, March 6, 1865; transferred to Co. F, Forty-seventh Infantry, June 17, 1865.

CASTLER, ALFRED J.—Age, 18 years. Enlisted, August 11, 1862, at Glen, to serve three years; mustered in as private, Co. A, August 15, 1862; captured in action, September 15, and paroled, September 16, 1862, at Harper's Ferry, Va.; wounded in action, February 20, 1864, at Olustee, Fla.; wounded and captured in action, August 16, 1864, at Deep Bottom, Va.; paroled and promoted corporal, no date; discharged for wounds, June 29, 1865, as Kesler; also borne as Cosler.

CARERT, NICHOLAS.—Age, 44 years. Enlisted, August 7, 1862, at Charlton, to serve three years; mustered in as wagoner, Co. I, August 18, 1862; captured in action, September 15, and paroled, September 16, 1862, at Harper's Ferry, Va.; grade changed to private, no date; died, October 29, 1863, at hospital, Beaufort, S.C.

CHASE, GEORGE L.—Age, 18 years. Enlisted at Schenectady, to serve three years, and mustered in as private, Co. C, February 25, 1865; transferred to Co. B, Forty-seventh Infantry, June 17, 1865.

CHATFIELD, HOWARD.—Age, 28 years. Enlisted at Goshen, to serve one year, and mustered in as private, Co. F, February 21, 1865; transferred to Co., B, Forty-seventh Infantry, June 17, 1865; also borne as Edward.

CHRIST, PHILIP.—Age, 24 years. Enlisted at Brooklyn, to serve one year, and mustered in as private, Co. C, February 28, 1865; transferred to Co. B, Forty-seventh Infantry, June 17, 1865.

CHRISTENON, VOLDENEORE.—Age, 18 years. Enlisted at New York City, to serve three years, and mustered in as private, Co. 1, August 24, 1863; transferred to Co.—, Forty-seventh Infantry, June 17, 1865.

CHRISTIE, HARVEY C.—Age, 27 years. Enlisted, August 12, 1862, at Mayfield, to serve three years; mustered in as private, Co. E, August 26, 1862; captured in action, September 15, and paroled, September 16, 1862, at Harper's Ferry, Va.; promoted sergeant, February 1, 1863; commissary sergeant, March 1, 1863; died, August 2, 1863, in U.S. Hospital, S.C.

CHRISTY, PHILIP S.—Age, 36 years. Enlisted, August 5, 1862, at Milton, to serve three years; mustered in as private, Co. C, August 8, 1862; captured in action, September 15, and paroled, September 16, 1862, at Harper's Ferry, Va.; wounded and captured in action, February 20, 1864, at Olustee, Fla.; died, while a prisoner of war, no date.

CHURCH, LUTHER.—Age, 18 years. Enlisted, August 11, 1862, at Moreau, to serve three years; mustered in as private, Co. G, August 18, 1862; captured in action, September 15, and paroled, September 16, 1862, at Harper's Ferry, Va.; wounded in action, February 20, 1864, at Olustee, Fla.; mustered out, June 3, 1865, at hospital, Fort Monroe, Va., as Luther C.

CLAFLIN, ANDREW M.—Age, 24 years. Enlisted at Amsterdam, to serve three years, and mustered in as private, Co. D, August 9, 1862; captured in action, September 15, and paroled, September 16, 1862, at Harper's Ferry, Va.; discharged for disability, May 19, 1863, at Hilton Head, S.C.; again enlisted for one year, and mustered in, March 23, 1865, and transferred to Co. C, Forty-seventh Infantry, June 17, 1365.

CLAPSON, CHARLES.—Age, 23 years. Enlisted, July 24, 1862, at Glen, to serve three years; mustered in as private, Co. A, July 25, 1862; captured in action, September 15, and paroled, September 16, 1862, at Harper's Ferry, Va.; promoted corporal, no date; accidentally wounded, May 26, 1863, and died of his wounds, June 16, 1863, at Hilton Head, S.C.

CLARK, ANDREW.—Age, 19 years. Enlisted, July 30, 1862, at Amsterdam, to serve three years; mustered in as private, Co. D, August 2, 1862; captured in action, September 15, and paroled, September 16, 1862, at Harper's Ferry, Va.; died of typhoid fever, June 28, 1863, at Hilton Head, S.C.

CLARK, CHARLES L.—Age, 34 years. Enrolled at Johnstown, to serve three years, and mustered in as sergeant, Co. E, August 11, 1862; as second lieutenant, November 17, 1864; as first lieutenant, April 29, 1865; mustered out with company, June 17, 1865, at Raleigh, N.C. Commissioned second lieutenant, November 19, 1864, with rank from November 17, 1864, vice A. C. Slocum promoted; first lieutenant, May 17, 1865, with rank from April 29, 1865, vice D. H. Graves promoted.

CLARK, HENRY.—Age, 18 years. Enlisted at Clifton Park, to serve three years, and mustered in as musician, Co. H, August 8, 1862; captured in action, September 15, and paroled, September 16, 1862, at Harper's Ferry, Va.; mustered out with company, June 17, 1865, at Raleigh, N.C.

CLARK, JAMES H.—Age, 21 years. Enrolled, July 26, 1862, at Clifton Park, to serve three years; mustered in as private, Co. H, August 1, 1862; promoted first sergeant, August 20, 1862; mustered in as second lieutenant, February 7, 1863; as first lieutenant, January 27, 1864; wounded in action, February 20, 1864, at Olustee, Fla.; discharged for disability, December 29, 1864. Commissioned second lieutenant, May 13, 1863, with rank from February 6, 1863, vice A. G. Noxon promoted; first lieutenant, April 22, 1864, with rank from January 27, 1864, vice A. G. Noxon resigned.

CLARK, JOHN R.—Age, 26 years. Enlisted at Broadalbin, to serve three years, and mustered in as private, Co. K, August 25, 1862; captured in action, September 15, and paroled, September 16, 1862, at Harper's Ferry, Va.; promoted sergeant, no date; wounded and captured in action, May 7, 1864, at Chester Heights, Va., and died of his wounds, August 11, 1864, in Poplar Lawn Hospital, at Petersburg, Va.

CLARK, JR., JOHN W.—Age, 20 years. Enlisted, August 9, 1862, at Galway, to serve three years; mustered in as private, Co. C, August 14, 1862; captured in action, September 15, and paroled, September 16, 1862, at Harper's Ferry, Va.; promoted corporal, no date; wounded in action, August 16, 1864, at Deep Bottom, Va., and died of his wounds, no date.

CLARK, NATHANIEL.—Age, 19 years. Enlisted at Malta, to serve three years, and mustered in as private, Co. C, August 11, 1862; captured in action, September 15, and paroled, September 16, 1862, at Harper's Ferry, Va.; transferred to 105th Co. Second Battalion, Veteran Reserve Corps, May 30, 1864; discharged, August 26, 1865, at McClellan Hospital, Philadelphia, Pa.

CLARK, NOAH B.—Age, 21 years. Enlisted, August 7, 1862, at Wilton, to serve three years; mustered in as private, Co. F, August 14, 1862; captured in action, September 15, and paroled, September 16, 1862, at Harper's Ferry, Va.; wounded in action, February 20, 1864, at Olustee, Fla.; promoted corporal, May 1, 1865; mustered out with company, June 17, 1865, at Raleigh, N.C.

CLARK, THOMAS.—Age, 26 years. Enlisted, August 15, 1862, at Minden, to serve three years; mustered in as private, Co. I, August 18, 1862; captured in action, September 15, and paroled, September 16, 1862, at Harper's Ferry, Va.; mustered out with company, June 17, 1865, at Raleigh, N.C.

CLARK, THOMAS.—Age, 27 years. Enlisted at Eighteenth Congressional District, to serve three years; mustered in as private Co. C, February 27, 1865; transferred to Co. B, Forty-seventh Infantry, June 17, 1865.

CLARK, WILBUR M.—Age, 26 years. Enlisted, August 8, 1862, at Saratoga Springs, to serve three years; mustered in as wagoner, Co. G, August 18, 1862; captured in action, September 15, and paroled, September 16, 1862, at Harper's Ferry, Va.; transferred to the Navy, April 27, 1864.

CLARK, WILLIAM.—Age, 20 years. Enlisted at Ninth Congressional District, to serve three years, and mustered in as private, Co. D, August 28, 1863; wounded in action, February 20, 1864, at Olustee, Fla.; transferred to Co. C, Forty-seventh Infantry, June 17, 1865.

CLARK, WILLIAM H.—Age, 21 years. Enlisted at Poughkeepsie, to serve three years, and mustered in as private, Co. F, October 28, 1863; wounded in action, February 20, 1864, at Olustee, Fla.: transferred to Co. K, Forty-seventh Infantry, June 17, 1865.

CLEMANS, SYLVESTER W.—Age, 44 years. Enrolled at Halfmoon, to serve three years; mustered in as private Co. H, August 18, 1862; as chaplain, October 29, 1862; discharged, September 13, 1864; also borne as Clements. Commissioned chaplain, September 10, 1862, with rank from August 20. 1862, original.

CLEMANS, WILLIAM S.—Age, 18 years. Enlisted, July 25, 1862, at Halfmoon, to serve three years; mustered in as private Co. H, August 6, 1862; captured in action, September 15. and paroled, September 16, 1862, at Harper's Ferry, Va.; mustered out with company, June 17, 1865, at Raleigh, N.C.

CLEMONS, SAMUEL.—Age, 23 years. Enlisted, August 14, 1862, at Oppenheim, to serve three years; mustered in as private, Co. E, August 15, 1862; captured in action, September 15, and paroled, September 16, 1862, at Harper's Ferry, Va.; killed in action, May 14, 1864, at Drewry's Bluff, Va., as Clemens.

CLOBRIDGE, SELDEN C.—Age, 21 years. Enrolled, August 8, 1862, at Saratoga Springs, to serve three years; mustered in as corporal, Co. G, August 18, 1862; captured in action, September 15, and paroled, September 16, 1862, at Harper's Ferry, Va.; promoted sergeant, January 18, 1864; wounded in action, February 20, 1864, at Olustee, Fla.; mustered in as first lieutenant, Co. C, May 17, 1865; discharged for disability, July 18, 1865, at Ira Harris Hospital, Albany, N.Y.; also borne as Colbridge. Commissioned first lieutenant, May 17, 1865, with rank from April 29, 1865, vice I. E. Smith promoted.

CLOTHER, ASA J.—Age, 25 years. Enlisted, July 26, 1862, at Saratoga Springs, to serve three years; mustered in as corporal, Co. F, August 12, 1862; captured in action, September 15, and paroled, September 16, 1862, at Harper's Ferry, Va.; returned to ranks, no date; mustered out with company, June 17, 1865, at Raleigh, N.C.

CLUTE, HENRY.—Age, 36 years. Enlisted at Day, to serve three years, and mustered in as private, Co. C, August 14, 1862; captured in action, September 15, and paroled, September 16, 1862, at Harper's Ferry, Va.; killed, January 16, 1865, by explosion of magazine at Fort Fisher, N.C.; also borne as Chute.

COCHRAN, MARK.—Age, 32 years. Enlisted at Milton, to serve three years, and mustered in as private, Co. C, August 8, 1862; captured in action, September 15, and paroled, September 16, 1862, at Harper's Ferry, Va.; wounded in action, February 20, 1864. at Olustee, Fla.; absent in hospital at Troy, N.Y., since and at muster out of company; also borne as Cockran.

COFFREY, JOHN.—Age, 21 years. Enlisted at Brooklyn, to serve three years, and mustered in as private, Co. G, September 3, 1863; wounded in action, February 20, 1864, at Olustee, Fla.; transferred. to Co. E, Forty-seventh Infantry, June 17, 1865; also borne as Caffrey.

COLE, CHESTLETON C.—Age, 30 years. Enlisted, July 24, 1862, at Glen, to serve three years; mustered in as sergeant, Co. A, July 25, 1862; captured in action, September 15, and paroled, September 16, 1862, at Harper's Ferry, Va.; returned to ranks, no date; wounded in action, May 14, 1864, at Drewry's Bluff, Va.; mustered out with company, June 17, 1865, at Raleigh, N.C.

COLE, FRANCIS.—Age, 18 years. Enlisted at Johnstown, to serve three years, and mustered in as private, Co. K, August 21, 1862; captured in action, September 15, and paroled, September 16, 1862, at Harper's Ferry, Va.; died, October 31, 1862, at Chicago, Ill.

COLE, GEORGE D.—Age, 21 years. Enlisted, August 9, 1862, at Halfmoon, to serve three years; mustered in as private, Co. H, August 14, 1862; captured in action, September 15, and paroled, September 16, 1862, at Harper's Ferry, Va.; wounded and captured in action, February 20, 1864, at Olustee, Fla.; paroled, October 18, 1864; mustered out with detachment, May 27, 1865, at Foster Hospital, New Berne, N.C.

COLE, JAMES W.—Age, 26 years. Enlisted, August 6, 1862, at Milton, to serve three years; mustered in as private, Co. C, August 8, 1862; captured in action, September 15, and paroled, September 16, 1862, at Harper's Ferry, Va.; discharged for disability, January 22, 1863, at Yorktown, Va.

COLE, JOHN.—Age, 31 years. Enlisted, August 8, 1862, at Caroga, to serve three years; mustered in as private, Co. K, August 12, 1862; captured in action, September 15, and paroled, September 16, 1862, at Harper's Ferry, Va.; promoted corporal, no date; wounded in action, February 20, 1864, at Olustee, Fla.; discharged, April 3, 1865.

COLE, JOSEPH.—Age, 22 years. Enlisted at Albany, to serve three years, and mustered in as private, Co. K, October 29, 1863; transferred to the Navy, April 27, 1864.

COLE, MELVIN W.—Age, 20 years. Enlisted, August 15, 1862, at Broadalbin, to serve three years; mustered in as musician, Co. K, August 16, 1862; captured in action, September 15, and paroled, September 16, 1862, at Harper's Ferry, Va.; promoted principal musician, October 31, 1863; mustered out, May 15, 1865, at Wilmington, N.C.

COLE, RUFUS A.—Age, 25 years. Enlisted, September 5, 1864, at Ephratah, to serve one year; mustered in as private, Co. E, September 6, 1864; mustered out with company, June 17, 1865, at Raleigh, N.C.

COLEMAN, EZRA.—Age, 34 years. Enlisted, August 7, 1862, at St. Johnsville, to serve three years; mustered in as private, Co. I, August 12, 1862; captured in action, September 15, and paroled, September 16, 1862, at Harper's Ferry, Va.; wounded in action, October 27, 1864, at Darbytown Road, Va.; died of his wounds, December 11, 1864, at hospital, Fort Monroe, Va.

COLGROVE, PHILIP V.—Age, 19 years. Enlisted, August 14, 1862, at Charleston, to serve three years; mustered in as private Co. D, August 15, 1862; captured in action, September 15, and paroled, September 16, 1862, at Harper's Ferry, Va.; discharged for disability, about December 15, 1862, at Chicago, Ill.

COLGROVE, WILLIAM E.—Age, 35 years. Enlisted, August 12, 1862, at Charlton, to serve three years; mustered in as private, Co. D, August 15, 1862; captured in action, September 15, and paroled, September 16, 1862, at Harper's Ferry, Va.; again captured in action, August 16, 1864, at Deep Bottom, Va.; died, December 3, 1864, at Salisbury, N.C.

COLLIER, AUGUSTUS.—Age, 21 years. Enrolled, August 11, 1862, at St. Johnsville, to serve three years; mustered in as corporal, Co. B, August 13, 1862; promoted first sergeant, no date; mustered in as second lieutenant, December 2, 1864; as first lieutenant. February 23, 1865; mustered out with company, June 17, 1865, at Raleigh, N.C., as John Augustus Collier. Commissioned second lieutenant, November 19, 1864, with rank from November 17, 1864, vice I. B. Smith promoted; first lieutenant and adjutant, not mustered, May 17, 1865, with rank from February 23, 1865, vice H. S. Sanford promoted.

COLLINS, ARCHIBALD.—Age, 44 years. Enlisted at Canajoharie, to serve three years, and mustered in as private, Co. I, December 19, 1863; died, September 19, 1864, at Base Hospital, Point of Rocks, Va.

COLLINS, DAVID S.—Age, 29 years. Enlisted, August 4, 1862, at St. Johnsville, to serve three years; mustered in as private Co. B, August 13, 1862; captured in action, September 15, and paroled, September 16, 1862, at Harper's Ferry, Va.; discharged for disability, November 1, 1862, as David L.

COLLINS, EUGENE.—Age, 18 years. Enlisted at Day, to serve one year, and mustered in as private, Co. B, April 6, 1865; transferred to Co. B, Forty-seventh Infantry, June 17, 1865.

COLLINS, HIRAM L.—Age, 22 years Enlisted, August 4, 1862, at Saratoga Springs, to serve three years; mustered in as private, Co F, August 12, 1862; captured in action, September 5, and paroled, September 16, 1862, at Harper's Ferry, Va.; killed in action, February 20, 1864, at Olustee, Fla.

COLLINS JOHN.—Age 19 years.—Enlisted, July 28, 1862, at Saratoga Springs; captured in action, September 15, and paroled, September 16, 1862, at Harper's Ferry, Va.; appointed wagoner, no date; deserted, January 4, 1863.

COLLOPY, PATRICK.—Age, 23 years. Enlisted, August 2, 1862, at Saratoga Springs, to serve three years; mustered in as corporal, Co. G, August 18, 1862; promoted sergeant, no date; killed in action, February 20, 1864, at Olustee, Fla.; also borne as Colophy.

COLONEY, ISAAC.—Age, 28 years. Enlisted, August 14, 1862, at Oppenheim, to serve three years; mustered in as corporal, Co. E, August 15, 1862; captured in action, September 15, and paroled, September 16, 1862, at Harper's Ferry, Va.; deserted, October 8, 1862.

COLONY, JR., GEORGE.—Age, 18 years. Enlisted, August 2, 1862, at Galway, to serve three years; mustered in as private, Co. C, August 14, 1862; captured in action, September 15, and paroled, September 16, 1862, at Harper's Ferry, Va.; died of typhoid fever, July 8, 1863, at hospital, Hilton Head, S.C.

CONKLIN, CHESTER.—Age, 37 years. Enlisted at Schenectady, to serve one year, and mustered in as private, Co. A, August 13, 1864; mustered out with company, June 17, 1865, at Raleigh, N.C.

CONNOLY, THOMAS.—Age, 19 years. Enlisted at Brooklyn, to serve three years, and mustered in as private, Co. H, September 2, 1863; wounded and captured in action, February 20, 1864, at Olustee, Fla.; paroled, no date; transferred to Co. F, Forty-seventh Infantry, June 17, 1865.

CONOVER, FRANK M.—Age, 25 years. Enlisted, August 11, 1862, at Charleston, to serve three years; mustered in as private, Co. D, August 15, 1862; captured in action, September 15, and paroled, September 16, 1862, at Harper's Ferry, Va.; promoted sergeant, no date; killed in action, August 16, 1864, at Deep Bottom, Va.

CONOVER, SEELY.—Age, 21 years. Enlisted, August 7, 1862, at Canajoharie, to serve three years; mustered in as private, Company B, August 11, 1862; captured in action, September 15, and paroled, September 16, 1862, at Harper's Ferry, Va.; promoted corporal, October 11, 1862; wounded and captured in action, August 16, 1864, at Deep Bottom, Va.; exchanged, November 25, 1864, and returned to duty, March 14, 1865; mustered out with company, June 17, 1865, at Raleigh, N.C.

COOK, NORMAN.—Age 19 years. Enlisted, August 5, 1862, at Minden, to serve three years; mustered in as private, Co. B, August 13, 1862; captured in action, September 15, and paroled, September 16, 1862, at Harper's Ferry, Va.; wounded in action, February 20, 1864, at Olustee, Fla.; promoted corporal, March 1, 1865; mustered out with company, June 17, 1861, at Raleigh, N.C.

COOL, HENRY J.—Age, 43 years. Enlisted, August 11, 1862, at Oppenheim, to serve three years; mustered in as private, Co. E. August 15, 1862; captured in action, September 15, and paroled, September 16, 1862, at Harper's Ferry, Va.; discharged for disability, May 13, 1864, at David's Island, New York Harbor.

COOL, HERMAN.—Age, 31 years. Enlisted, August 14, 1862, at Johnstown, to serve three years; mustered in as private, Co. E, August 15, 1862; captured in action, September 15, and paroled, September 16, 1862, at Harper's Ferry, Va.; died of fever, January 3, 1865, at hospital, Fort Monroe, Va.

COOL, JESSE.—Age, 30 years. Enlisted, September 3, 1864, at Ephratah, to serve one year; mustered in as private, Co. B, September 6, 1864; wounded in action, January 15, 1865, at Fort. Fisher, N.C.; absent, sick in hospital at Troy, N.Y., at muster-out of Company.

COOL, NORMAN M.—Age, 18 years. Enlisted at Oppenheim, to serve three years, and mustered in as private, Co. K, August 21, 1862; captured in action, September 15, and paroled, September 16, 1862, at Harper's Ferry, Va.; deserted, October 11, 1862, at Chicago, Ill.

CORL, JAMES 11.—Age, 21 years. Enlisted, August 11, 1862, at Charlton, to serve three years; mustered in as private, Co. I, August 15, 1862; captured in action, September 15, and paroled, September 16, 1862, at Harper's Ferry, Va.; wounded in action, July 8, 1864, near Petersburg, Va.; died of his wounds, July 14, 1864, at hospital, Virginia.

CORLEW, HIRAM.—Age, 19 years. Enlisted at Schenectady, to serve one year, and mustered in as private, Co. A, August 13, 1864; mustered out with company, June 17, 1865, at Raleigh, N.C.

CORLEW, ROSWELL.—Age, 43 years. Enlisted at Schenectady, to serve one year, and mustered in as private, Co. A, August 13, 1864; died of diarrhea, March 21, 1865, at hospital, Wilmington, N.C.

CORNELL, JAMES P.—Age, 27 years. Enlisted at St. Johnsville, to serve three years, and mustered in as private, Co. I, April 14, 1864; transferred to Co. H, Forty-seventh Infantry, June 17, 1865; also borne as James C. and Jonathan P. Cornal.

CORNELL, SAMUEL.—Age, 28 years. Enlisted, December 18, 1863, at Broadalbin, to serve three years; mustered in as private, Co. C, January 25, 1864; transferred to Co. B, Forty-seventh Infantry, June 17, 1865; also borne as Samuel B.

CORNELL, SIDNEY T.—Age, 24 years. Enlisted at Clifton Park, to serve three years, and mustered in as corporal, Co. C, August 14, 1862; captured in action, September 15, and paroled, September 16, 1862, at Harper's Ferry, Va.; killed in action, February 20, 1864, at Olustee, Fla.

COSTELLO, MICHAEL.—Age, 21 years. Enlisted, August 10, 1862, at Saratoga Springs, to serve three years; mustered in as private, Co. G, August 18, 1862; captured in action, September 15, and paroled, September 16, 1862, at Harper's Ferry, Va.; wounded in action, February 20, 1864, at Olustee, Fla.; promoted corporal, May 22, 1865; mustered out with company, June 17, 1865, at Raleigh, N.C.

COSTELLOW, THOMAS.—Age, 24 years. Enlisted, July 26, 1862, at Saratoga Springs, to serve three years; mustered in as private, Co. G, August 9, 1862; captured in action, September 15, and paroled, September 16, 1862, at Harper's Ferry, Va.; discharged for disability, June 6, 1863, at New Berne, N.C., as Costello.

COUGHLAN, WILLIAM.—Age, 42 years. Enlisted at Brooklyn, to serve three years, and mustered in as private, Co. G, September 3, 1863; transferred to Co. G, Forty-seventh Infantry, June 17, 1865.

COULTER, JAMES.—Age, 29 years. Enlisted at Tarrytown, to serve three years, and mustered in as private, Go. K, October 30, 1863; transferred to the Navy, April 27, 1864.

COUNTRYMAN, JADUA.—Age, 18 years. Enlisted, July 30, 1862, at St. Johnsville, to serve three years; mustered in as corporal, Co. B, August 6, 1862; captured in action, September 15, and paroled, September 16, 1862, at Harper's Ferry, Va.; killed, January 16, 1865, by explosion of magazine, at Fort Fisher, N.C.

COUNTRYMAN, JAMES M.—Age, 22 years. Enlisted at Rosendale, to serve three years, and. mustered in as private, Co. D, September 8, 1863; wounded in action, February 20, 1864, at Olustee, Fla.; died of chronic diarrhea, April 4, 1865, at Fort Monroe, Va.

COWAN, ROBERT F.—Age, 33 years. Enlisted at Buffalo, to serve three years, and mustered in as private, Co. F, May 5, 1864; transferred to Co. K, Forty-seventh Infantry, June 17, 1865.

COWEN, PATRICK H.—Age, 43 years. Enrolled at Fonda, to serve three years, and mustered in as captain, Co. G, August 20, 1862; as major, August 30, 1862; discharged, June 27, 1863, at Port Royal, S.C. Commissioned captain, August 21, 1862, with rank from August 20, 1862, original; major, August 30, 1862, with rank from same date, original.

COWLES, EDWARD.—Age, 18 years. Enlisted, August 9, 1862, at Wells, to serve three years; mustered in as corporal, Co. K, August 16, 1862; captured in action, September 15, and paroled, September 16, 1862, at Harper's Ferry, Va.; promoted sergeant, no date; wounded in action, February 20, 1864, at Olustee, Fla.; killed in action, June 3, 1864, at Cold Harbor, Va.

COY, JEREMIAH.—Age, 33 years. Enlisted, August 8, 1862, at Greenfield, to serve three years; mustered in as private, Co. C, August 11, 1862; captured in action, September 15, and paroled, September 16, 1862, at Harper's Ferry, Va.; wounded in action, January 15, 1865, at Fort Fisher, N.C.; mustered out with detachment, June 9, 1865, at New Berne, N.C.

COYLER, JAMES.—Age, 18 years. Enlisted, August 6, 1862, at Milton, to serve three years; mustered in as private, Co. C, August 11, 1862; captured in action, September 15, and paroled, September 16, 1862, at Harper's Ferry, Va.; deserted, September 25, 1862, at Baltimore, Md., as Cuyler.

COYN, JOHN.—Age, 19 years. Enlisted at Schenectady, to serve three years, and mustered in as private, Co. H, April 28, 1864; transferred to Co. F, Forty-seventh Infantry, June 17, 1865.

COZZENS, CHARLES D.—Age, 18 years. Enlisted, August 8, 1862, at Edinburg, to serve three years; mustered in as private, Co. C, August 14, 1862; captured in action, September 15, and paroled, September 16, 1862, at Harper's Ferry, Va.; wounded in action, February 20, 1864, at Olustee, Fla.; captured, May 16, 1864, near Hatchers, Va.; mustered out subsequent to August 8, 1865.

CRAIG, THOMAS.—Age, 25 years. Enlisted at Tarrytown, to. serve three years, and mustered in as private, Co. E, October 27, 1863; wounded in action, February 20, 1864, at Olustee,. Fla.; transferred to the Navy, April 27, 1864.

CRANDALL, ENOS.—Age, 21 years. Enlisted, August 11, 1862, at Saratoga Springs, to serve three years; mustered in as private, Co. G, August 19, 1862; captured in action, September 15, and paroled, September 16, 1862, at Harper's Ferry, Va.; transferred to Veteran Reserve Corps, July 11, 1863.

CRANDALL, GEORGE.—Age, 22 years. Enlisted, July 29, 1862, at Charlton, to serve three years; mustered in as private, Co. I, August 26, 1862; deserted, August 27, 1862, at Fonda, N.Y.

CRANDALL, PAUL.—Age, 24 years. Enlisted, August 11, 1862, at Saratoga Springs, to serve three years;

mustered in as private, Co. G, August 18, 1862; captured in action, September 15, and paroled, September 16, 1862, at Harper's Ferry, Va.; died of typhoid fever, July 6, 1863, at hospital, Hilton Head, S.C.; also borne as Crandell.

CRANDALL, RUSSELL.—Age, 21 years. Enlisted at Albany, to serve three years, and mustered in as private, Co. I, October 30, 1863; wounded and captured in action, February 20, 1864, at Olustee, Fla.; died, July 6, 1864, at Andersonville, Ga.

CRANKER, ALEXANDER.—Age, 31 years. Enlisted, August 20, 1862, at Root, to serve three years; mustered in as private, Co. I, August 26, 1862; captured in action, September 15, and paroled, September 16, 1862, at Harper's Ferry, Va.; transferred to Forty-eighth Company, Second Battalion, and to Co. K, Seventh Regiment, Veteran Reserve Corps, no dates; mustered out with detachment, June 29, 1865, at Washington, D.C.; also borne as Cranken.

CRATAR, ALMONTE D.—Age, 19 years. Enlisted, August 11, 1862, at Galway, to serve three years; mustered in as private, Co. C, August 12, 1862; captured in action, September 15, and paroled, September 16, 1862, at Harper's Ferry, Va.; wounded in action, May 16, 1864, at Drewry's Bluff, Va.; absent since and in hospital, at Newark, N. J., at muster-out of company.

CROAK, JOHN.—Age, 20 years. Enlisted, August 7, 1862, at Saratoga Spa, to serve three years, mustered in as private, Co. F, August 12, 1862; captured in action, September 15, and paroled, September 16, 1862, at Harper's Ferry, Va.; wounded in action, February 20, 1864, at Olustee, Fla., and August 16, 1864, at Deep Bottom, Va.; discharged for wounds, December 8, 1864; also borne as Croate.

CROMELL, FREDERICK.—Age, 25 years. Enlisted at Tarrytown, to serve three years, and mustered in as private, Co. A, October 27, 1863; killed in action February 20, 1864, at Olustee, Fla.; also borne as Cromwell.

CROUCH, JARED J.—Age, 31 years. Enlisted, August 12, 1862, at Milton, to serve three years; mustered in as corporal, Co. I, August 20, 1862; captured in action September 15, and paroled, September 16, 1862, at Harper's Ferry, Va.; discharged for disability, no date; also borne as Jared L.

CROSBY, JOHN M.—Age, 32 years. Enlisted, July 23, 1862, at Fonda, to serve three years; mustered in as private, Co. I, August 2, 1862; captured in action, September 15, and paroled, September 16, 1862, at Harper's Ferry, Va.; deserted, September 25, 1862, at Baltimore, Md., as John W.

CROSS, GEORGE H.—Age, 27 years. Enlisted at Amsterdam, to serve one year, and mustered in as private, Co. D, March 25, 1865; transferred to Co. B, Forty-seventh Infantry, June 17, 1865.

CROSS, ORREN.—Age, 36 years. Enlisted at Johnstown, to serve three years, and mustered in as private, Co. E, August 15, 1862; captured in action, September 15, and paroled, September 16, 1862, at Harper's Ferry, Va.; deserted, November 21, 1862.

CROW, FRANK.—Age, 19 years. Enlisted, August 14, 1862, at Mohawk, to serve three years; mustered in as private, Co. D, August 15, 1862; captured in action, September 15, and paroled, September 16, 1862, at Harper's Ferry, Va.; again captured in action, May 16, 1864, at Drewry's Bluff, Va.; died of scorbutus, October 21, 1864, at Andersonville, Ga.

CROWDEN, WILLIAM.—Age, 24 years. Enlisted at Mohawk, to serve three years, and mustered in as private, Co. A, August 8, 1862; captured in action, September 15, and paroled, September 16, 1862, at Harper's Ferry, Va.; deserted, February, 1863, at Fort Monroe, Va.

CROUSE, LEONARD I.—Age, 23 years. Enlisted, August 12, 1862, at St. Johnsville, to serve three years; mustered in as private, Co. B, August 13, 1862; captured in action, September 15, and paroled, September 16, 1862, at Harper's Ferry, Va.; mustered out with company, June 17, 1865, at Raleigh, N.C., as Leonard J.

CRUISE, GEORGE.—Age, 40 years. Enlisted, August 7, 1862, at Milton, to serve three years; mustered in as private, Co. C, August 8, 1862; captured in action, September 15, and paroled, September 16, 1862, at Harper's' Ferry, Va.; mustered out, June 6, 1865, at New Berne, N.C.

CUDNEY, JOHN.—Age, 18 years. Enlisted, July 26, 1862, at Clifton Park, to serve three years; mustered in as private, Co. H, August 8, 1862; captured in action, September 15, and paroled, September 16, 1862, at Harper's Ferry, Va.; wounded; in action, February 20, 1864, at Olustee, Fla.; mustered out with company, June 17, 1865, at Raleigh, N.C.

CUNNING, WILLIAMSON.—Age, 22 years. Enlisted, August 5, 1862, at Amsterdam, to serve three years; mustered in as private, Co. D, August 6, 1862; captured in action, September 15, and paroled, September 16, 1862, at Harper's Ferry, Va.; mustered out with company, June 17, 1865, at Raleigh, N.C.

CUNNINGHAM, WILLIAM.—Age, 21 years. Enlisted at New York City, to serve three years, and mustered in as private, Co. K, March 8, 1865; transferred to Co. H, Forty-seventh Infantry, June 17, 1865.

CURREEN, GEORGE H.—Age, 27 years. Enrolled, August 4, 1862, at Milton, to serve three years; mustered in as sergeant, Co. C, August 11, 1862; promoted first sergeant, August 26, 1862; wounded in action, February 20, 1864, at Olustee, Fla.; mustered in as second lieutenant, February 21, 1864; as first lieutenant, June 11, 1864; wounded in action, July 30, 1864, before Petersburg, Va.; discharged for disability, December 2, 1864. Commissioned second lieutenant, April 13, 1864, with rank from February 20, 1864, vice W. Tompkins, killed in action, first lieutenant, July 8, 1861, with rank from June 11, 1864, vice F. Mosher promoted.

CURRY, EDWARD.—Age, 43 years. Enlisted, August 3, 1862, at Saratoga Springs, to serve three years; mustered in as private, Co. G, August 6, 1862; captured in action, September 15, and paroled, September 16, 1862, at Harper's Ferry, Va.; mustered out with company, June 17, 1865, at Raleigh, N.C.

CURRY, THOMAS.—Age, 38 years. Enlisted at Goshen, to serve one year, and mustered in as private, Co. A, February 5, 1865; transferred to Co. A, Forty-seventh Infantry, June 17, 1865, at Raleigh, N.C.; also borne as Corry.

CUTTENDEN, DAVID H.—Age, 18 years. Enlisted, August 4, 1862, at Galway, to serve three years; mustered in as musician, Co. C, August 12, 1862; captured in action, September 15, and paroled, September 16, 1862, at Harper's Ferry, Va.; mustered out with company, June 17, 1865, at Raleigh, N.C.

DAKE, JOHN WESLEY.—Age, 21 years. Enlisted, August 21, 1862, at Milton, to serve three years; mustered in as private, Co. I, August 22, 1862; captured in action, September 15, and paroled, September 16, 1862, at Harper's Ferry, Va.; promoted corporal, no date; wounded in action, February 20, 1864, at Olustee, Fla.; mustered out, June 5, 1865, at New Berne, N.C. as Wesley J. Date.

DALRYMPLE, DAVID H.—Age, 29 years. Enlisted at Stratford, to serve three years, and mustered in as private, Co. E, August 16, 1862; captured in action, September 15, and paroled, September 16, 1862, at Harper's Ferry, Va.; wounded in action, February 20, 1864, at Olustee, Fla.; mustered out, June 2, 1865, at hospital, New Berne, N.C.

DALY, JOHN.—Age, 26 years. Enlisted at New York City, to serve three years, and mustered in as private, Co. B, August 25, 1863; wounded in action, February 20, 1864, at Olustee, Fla.; transferred to the Navy, April 27, 1864.

DAVENPORT, ADDISON L.—Age, 20 years. Enlisted, August 9, 1862, at Edinburgh, to serve three years; mustered in as corporal, Co. C, August 14, 1862; captured in action, September 15, and paroled, September 16, 1862, at Harper's Ferry, Va.; returned to ranks, no date; mustered out, June 16, 1865, at Smithville, N.C.

DAVIS, ABRAM L.—Age, 29 years. Enlisted, August 11, 1862, at Moreau, to serve three years; mustered in as private, Co. G, August 18, 1862; captured in action, September 15, and paroled, September 16, 1862, at Harper's Ferry, Va.; wounded in action, February 20, 1864, at Olustee, Fla.; mustered out with company, June 17, 1865, at Raleigh, N.C.

DAVIS, JOHN W.—Age,—years. Enrolled, August 13, 1862, at Fonda, to serve three years; mustered in as second lieutenant, Co. A, August 20, 1862; wounded and captured in action, February 20, 1864, at Olustee, Fla.; mustered in as first lieutenant, to date April 14, 1864; paroled, January, 1865; discharged for wounds, January 7, 1865. Commissioned second lieutenant, September 10, 1862, with rank from August 20, 1862 original; first lieutenant, April 7, 1864, with rank from February 24, 1864, vice W. Ferguson promoted.

DAVIS, STEPHEN.—Age, 23 years. Enlisted, August 4, 1862, at Milton, to serve three years; mustered in as private, Co. C, August 11, 1862; captured in action, September 15, paroled September 16, 1862 at Harper's Ferry, Va.; mustered out with detachment, June 5, 1865, at Fort Monroe, Va.

DAY, JOHN M.—Age, 19 years. Enlisted at Tompkins, to serve three years, and mustered in as private, Co. E, February 28, 1865, transferred to Co. D, Forty-seventh Infantry, June 17, 1865; also borne as John W.

DEAN, ALFRED I.—Age, 40 years. Enlisted at Wilton, to serve three years, and mustered in as private, Co. F, July 24, 1862; died, May, 1865, at hospital, Fort Monroe, Va.

DEAN, JR., ELIJAH.—Age, 28 years. Enlisted, August 14, 1862, at Saratoga Springs, to serve three years; mustered in as private, Co. G, August 22, 1862; captured in action, September 15, and paroled, September 16, 1862, at Harper's Ferry, Va.; discharged for disability, November 17, 1863, at hospital, Fort Columbus, New York Harbor, as Elisha.

DEAN, JR., JAMES M.—Age, 26 years. Enlisted at Ephratah, to serve three years, and mustered in as private, Co. A, July 25, 1862; captured in action, September 15, and paroled, September 16, 1862, at Harper's Ferry, Va.; died of typhoid fever, June 6, 1863, at hospital, Hilton Head, S.C.

DECKER, STEPHEN.—Age, 44 years. Enlisted, August 9. 1862, at Moreau, to serve three years; mustered in as private, Co. G, August 19, 1862; captured in action, September 15, and paroled, September 16, 1862, at Harper's Ferry, Va.; wounded and captured in action, August 18, 1864, at Deep Bottom, Va.; reported died while a prisoner of war; no further record.

DEGRAFF, CHARLES H.—Age 20 years. Enlisted at Halfmoon, to serve three years, and mustered in as private, Co. H, July 21, 1862; captured in action, September 15, and paroled, September 16, 1862, at Harper's Ferry, Va.; wounded and captured in action, February 20,1864 at Olustee, Fla.; died, August 18, 1864, at Andersonville, Ga., as De Graff.

DE GRAFF, JAMES.—Age, 21 years. Enlisted at Palatine, to serve three years, and mustered in as private. Co. K, August 27, 1862; captured in action, September 15, and paroled, September 16, 1862, at Harper's Ferry, Va.; absent, sick at muster-out of company.

DE GRAFF, NICHOLAS.—Age, 20 years. Enrolled, July 23, 1862, at Amsterdam, to serve three years; mustered in as first sergeant. Co. D, July 30, 1862; as second lieutenant, February 19, 1863; wounded in action, May 7, 1864, at Chester Station, Va.; mustered in as first lieutenant, October 8, 1864; mustered out with company, June 17, 1865, at Raleigh, N.C. Commissioned second lieutenant, May 13, 1863, with rank from February 18, 1863, vice H. S. Sandford promoted; first lieutenant November 19, 1864. with rank from October 8, 1864, vice Thomas Wayne, promoted.

DE LACTURE, MARTIN.—Age, 35 years. Enlisted, July 30, 1862, at Saratoga. Springs, to serve three years; mustered in as private, Co. G, August 9, 1862; captured in action, September 15, paroled September 16, 1862 at Harper's Ferry, Va.; killed in action, January 16, 1865, at Fort Fisher, N.C., as De Lacature.

DELAINE, JAMES.—Age, 28 years. Enlisted at Kingston, to serve three years, and mustered in as private, Co. D, October 26, 1863; discharged, August 22, 1864, at Hilton Head, S.C.

DELAND, CHARLES B.—Age, 20 years. Enlisted, August 12, 1862, at Saratoga Springs, to serve three years; and mustered in as private, Co. G, August 19, 1862; captured in action, September 15, paroled September 16, 1862 at Harper's Ferry, Va.; died of disease, February 21, 1863, at hospital, Chicago, Ill.

DEMAREST, EDGAR D.—Age, 18 years. Enlisted, August 5, 1862, at Broadalbin, to serve three years; mustered in as private, Co. K, August 12, 1862; captured in action, September 15, and paroled, September 16, 1862, at Harper's Ferry, Va.; mustered out with company, June 17, 1865, at Raleigh, N.C., as Demorest; also borne as Demerest.

DEMING, EDGAR L.—Age, 20 years. Enlisted, August 8, 1862, at Day, to serve three years; mustered in as private, Co. C, August 14, 1862; captured in action, September 15, and paroled, September 16, 1862, at Harper's Ferry, Va.; promoted corporal, May 1, 1865; mustered out with company, June 17, 1865, at Raleigh, N.C., as Demming.

DEMORE, JOHN.—Age, 24 years. Enlisted at Amsterdam, to serve three years, and mustered in as private, Co. K, August 5, 1862; captured in action, September 15, and paroled, September 16, 1862, at Harper's Ferry, Va.; wounded in action, May 7, 1864, at Chester Station, Va.; mustered out, May 12, 1865 at Albany, N.Y.

DENEGER, CHARLES.—Age, 40 years. Enlisted, July 26, 1862, at Glen, to serve three years; mustered in as private, Co. A, July 28, 1862; captured in action, September 15, and paroled, September 16, 1862, at Harper's Ferry, Va.; killed by explosion of magazine, January 16, 1865, at Fort Fisher, N.C., as Denegar.

DENMARK, JOHN.—Age, 26 years. Enlisted, July 31, 1862, at St. Johnsville, to serve three years; mustered in as private, Co. B, August 12, 1862; captured in action, September 15, and paroled, September 16, 1862, at Harper's Ferry, Va.; died of typhoid pneumonia, April 15, 1863, Hilton Head, S.C., as Denemark.

DENSLER, GEORGE H.—Age, 31 years. Enlisted, August 5, 1862, at Palatine, to serve three years; mustered in as private Co. I, August 26, 1862; deserted, August 27, 1862, at Fonda, N.Y.

DENSMORE, SYLVANUS.—Age, 21 years. Enlisted, August 11, 1862, at Greenfield, to serve three years; mustered in as private, Co. G, August 19, 1862; captured in action, September 15, and paroled, September 16, 1862, at Harper's Ferry, Va.; promoted corporal, no date; wounded and captured, February 20, 1864, at Olustee, Fla.; died, June 22, 1864, at Andersonville, Ga., as Densimore.

DERRICK, LIVINGSTON.—Age, 18 years. Enlisted, August 7, 1862, at Canajoharie, to serve three years; mustered in as private, Co. I, August 8, 1862; captured in action, September 15, paroled September 16, 1862 at Harper's Ferry, Va.; transferred to Co. B, no date; wounded in action, August 16, 1864, at Deep Bottom, Va.; discharged, to date June 17, 1865; also borne as Derick.

DE VAN, CHARLES.—Age 19 years. Enlisted, August 15, 1862, at Palatine, to serve three years; mustered in as private, Co. A, August 16. 1862; captured in action, September 15, and paroled, September 16, 1862 at Harper's Ferry, Va.; killed in action, August 18, 1864, at Deep Bottom, Va.

DEVOE, CHARLES.—Age, 26 years. Enlisted, August 12, 1862, at Stillwater, to serve three years; mustered in as private, Co. H, August 14, 1862; captured in action, September 15, paroled September 16, 1862 at Harper's Ferry, Va.; discharged, June 30, 1863, at Albany, N.Y.

DEW, MICHAEL.—Age, 26 years. Enlisted at Minden, to serve three years, and mustered in as private, Co. H, August 25, 1862; no further record.

DEYO, JOHN.—Age, 21 years. Enlisted, July 25, 1862, at Saratoga Springs, to serve three years; mustered in as corporal, Co. G, July 31, 1862; captured in action, September 15, and paroled, September 16, 1862, at Harper's Ferry, Va.; wounded in action, May 7, 1864, at Chester Station, Va.; absent since and at muster-out of company.

DIBBLE, CHARLES R.—Age, 20 years. Enlisted, August 12, 1862, at Stratford, to serve three years; mustered in as private, Co. E, August 16, 1863; captured in action, September 15, and paroled, September 16, 1862, at Harper's Ferry, Va.; wounded in action, February 20, 1864, at Olustee, Fla.; promoted corporal, November 1, 1864; mustered out with company, June 17, 1865, at Raleigh, N.C.

DIEFENDORF, HENRY X.—Age,—years. Enrolled, August 20, 1862, at Fonda, to serve three years; mustered in as first lieutenant, Co. B, August 26, 1862; discharged, May 2, 1863; also borne as Henry R. Commissioned first lieutenant, September 10, 1862, with rank from August 20, 1862, original.

DILLINGHAM, AARON.—Age, 43 years. Enlisted, August 6, 1862, at Halfmoon, to serve three years; mustered in as private, Co. H, August 7, 1862; captured in action, September 15, and paroled, September 16, 1862, at Harper's Ferry, Va.; died, February 14, 1865, at hospital, Fort Monroe, Va.

DILLON, JAMES.—Age, 23 years. Enlisted at New York City, to serve three years, and mustered in as private, Co. D, February 28, 1865; transferred to Co. C, Forty-seventh Infantry, June 17, 1865.

DINEEN, HUMPHREY.—Age, 18 years. Enlisted at Brooklyn, to serve one year, and mustered in as private, Co. F, March 6, 1865; transferred to Co. F. Forty-seventh Infantry, June 17, 1865.

DINGMAN, PETER.—Age, 40 years. Enlisted, August 8, 1862, at Broadalbin, to serve three years; mustered in as private, Co. K, August 12, 1862; captured in action, September 15, and paroled, September 16, 1862, at Harper's Ferry, Va.; mustered out with company, June 17, 1863 at Raleigh, N.C.

DINGMAN, WILLIAM H.—Age, 19 years. Enlisted, August 9, 1862, at Broadalbin, to serve three years; mustered in as private, Co. K, August 16, 1862; captured in action, September 15, and paroled, September 16, 1862, at Harper's Ferry, Va.; discharged, February 8, 1864, at hospital, New York.

DINKHOFF, ADOLPH.—Age, 24 years. Enlisted at New York City, to serve three years, and mustered in as private, Co. C, August 26, 1863; wounded in action, February 20, 1864, at Olustee, Fla.; deserted, September 8, 1864, from hospital at Willets Point, New York Harbor; also borne as Denkoff and Donkhoff.

DISBROW, WILLIAM.—Age, 43 years. Enlisted, August 21, 1862, at Glen, to serve three years; mustered in as private, Co. I, August 26, 1862; captured in action, September 15, and paroled, September 16. 1862, at Harper's Ferry, Va.; wounded in action, February 20, 1864. at Olustee, Fla.; died, December 11, 1864, at hospital, Fort Monroe, Va.

DISHART, PETER.—Age, 40 years. Enlisted August 25, 1862, at Amsterdam, to serve three years and mustered in as private, Co. G; deserted, same date, at Fonda, N.Y.; also borne as Dischent.

DIX, HENRY A.—Age, 19 years. Enlisted at New York City, to serve three years, and mustered in as private, Co. A, August 24, 1863; discharged, May 27, 1864, at Gloucester Point to enlist in the Navy.

DODDS, SYLVENUS N.—Age, 34 years. Enlisted, August 11, 1862, at Amsterdam, to serve three years; mustered in as private, Co. D, August 12, 1862; captured in action, September 15, and paroled, September 16, 1862, at Harper's Ferry, Va.; killed, November 11, 1862, on railroad at Chicago, Ill., as Sylvanus N.

DONOGHUE, THOMAS.—Age, 27 years. Enlisted, July 23, 1862, at Halfmoon, to serve three years; mustered in as private, Co. H, August 1, 1862; captured in action, September 15, and paroled, September 16, 1862, at Harper's Ferry, Va.; mustered out, May 27, 1865, at hospital, Fort Monroe, Va.

DONOHUE, JOHN.—Age, 35 years. Enlisted, August 5, 1862, at Saratoga Spa to serve three years; mustered in as private, Co. F, August 12, 1862; captured in action September 15, and paroled, September 16, 1362, at Harper's Ferry, Va.; wounded in action, February 20, 1864, at Olustee, Fla.; promoted corporal, May 1, 1865; mustered out with company, June 17, 1865, at Raleigh, N.C.

DOOLEY, THOMAS.—Age, 23 years. Enlisted at Tarrytown, to serve three years, and mustered in as private, Co. E, October 28, 1863; wounded and captured in action, February 20, 1864, at Olustee, Fla.; died of fever, June 1, 1864, in Confederate hospital at Andersonville, Ga.

DORN, MICHAEL A.—Age, 35 years. Enlisted, August 11, 1862, at Caroga, to serve three years; mustered in as private, Co. K, August 12, 1862; captured in action, September 15, and paroled, September 16, 1862, at Harper's Ferry, Va.; wounded in action, February 20, 1864, at Olustee, Fla.; mustered out with company, June 17, 1865, at Raleigh, N.C.; also borne as Dorm.

DOWNY, TIMOTHY.—Age, 41 years. Enlisted at Amsterdam to serve three years, and mustered in as private, Co. G, and deserted, August 25, 1862, at Fonda, N.Y.

DOXTADER, PHILANDER.—Age, 28 years. Enlisted, August 14, 1862, at Stratford, to serve three years; mustered in as private, Co. E, August 15, 1862; captured in action, September 15, and paroled, September 16, 1862, at Harper's Ferry, Va.; wounded in action, August 16, 1864, at Deep Bottom, Va.; discharged, May 22, 1865, at hospital, Chester, Pa.

DOXTATER, DANIEL B.—Age 21 years. Enlisted August 14, 1862 at Johnstown to serve three years; mustered in as private, Co. E, August 15, 1862; captured in action, September 15, paroled September 16, 1862 at Harper's Ferry, Va.; wounded in action, February 20, 1864, at Olustee, Fla.; died, March 12, 1864 at hospital, Beaufort, S.C.; also borne as Doxtader.

DOYLE, HENRY.—Age, 29 years. Enlisted at Goshen to serve three years, and mustered in as private, Co. D, February 28, 1865; transferred to Co. C, Forty-seventh Infantry, June 17, 1865.

DRAKE, EZRA W.—Age, 27 years. Enlisted, August 12, 1862, at Greenfield, to serve three years; mustered in as private, Co. F, August 14, 1862; captured in action, September 15, and paroled, September 16, 1862, at Harper's Ferry, Va.; mustered out with company, June 17, 1865, at Raleigh, N.C.

DREGART, GEORGE.—Age, 30 years. Enlisted at Brooklyn, to serve one year, and mustered in as private, Co. H, February 28, 1865; transferred to Co. K, Forty-seventh Infantry, June 17, 1865; also borne as Degardt.

DRESCHER, ADOLPH.—Age, 21 years. Enlisted at Brooklyn, to serve three years, and mustered in as private, Co. C, February 28, 1865; transferred to Co. C, Forty-seventh Infantry, June 17, 1865.

DRISCOLL, WILLIAM.—Age, place, date of enlistment and muster-in as private, not stated; transferred to Co. K, Forty-seventh Infantry, June 17, 1865.

DRYNEN, MAURICE J.—Age, 35 years. Enlisted, August 9, 1862, at Edinburgh, to serve three years; mustered in as private, Co. C, August 14, 1862; captured in action September 15, and paroled, September 16, 1862, at Harper's Ferry, Va.; killed in action, October 27, 1864, at Darbytown Road, Va.; also borne as Drynan.

DUBOIS, JOHN W.—Age, 21 years. Enlisted, August 11, 1862, at Saratoga Springs, to serve three years; mustered in as private, Co. G, August 19, 1862; captured in action, September 15, and paroled, September 16, 1862, at Harper's Ferry, Va.; promoted corporal, no date; killed in action, June 27, 1864, at Petersburg, Va.; also borne as John M.

DUCKETT, JOHN.—Age, 27 years. Enlisted at Milton, to serve three years, and mustered in as private, Co. C, August 8, 1862; captured in action, September 15, and paroled, September 16, 1862, at Harper's Ferry, Va.; wounded in action, February 20, 1864 at Olustee, Fla.; mustered out with company, June 17,1865, at Raleigh, N.C.

DUCROZET, EUGENE.—Age, 30 years. Enlisted at Goshen, to serve three years, and mustered in as private, Co. D, February 11, 1865; transferred to Co. C, Forty-seventh Infantry, June 17, 1865.

DUEL, PETER.—Age, 30 years. Enlisted, August 11, 1862, at Corinth, to serve three years; mustered in as private, Co. F, August 19, 1862; captured in action, September 15, and paroled, September 16, 1862, at Harper's Ferry, Va.; died of fever, November 28, 1863, at hospital, Beaufort, S.C.

DUFFIN, JOHN.—Age, 21 years. Enlisted at Tarrytown, to serve three years, and mustered in as private, Co. G, March 6, 1865; transferred to Co.—, Forty-seventh Infantry, June 17, 1865.

DUFFY, MICHAEL.—Age, 28 years. Enlisted at Tarrytown, to serve three years, and mustered in as private, Co. G, March 3, 1865; transferred to Co. G, Forty-seventh Infantry, June 17, 1865; also borne as Duff.

DUFFY, PATRICK.—Age, 23 years. Enlisted at Brooklyn, to serve one year, and mustered in as private, Co. I, March 11, 1865; captured, April 14, 1865; paroled, April 30, 1865; transferred to Co. H, Forty-seventh Infantry, June 17, 1865.

DUGAN, JOHN.—Age, 20 years. Enlisted, August 11, 1862, at Waterford, to serve three years; mustered in as private, Co. H, August 18, 1862; captured in action, September 15, and paroled, September 16, 1862, at Harper's Ferry, Va.; promoted corporal, no date; died of typhoid fever, August 6, 1863, at hospital, Beaufort, S.C.

DUMMER, HENRY B.—Age, 29 years. Enlisted, August 5, 1862, at Waterford, to serve three years; mustered in as private, Co. H, August 18, 1862; captured in action, September 15, and paroled, September 16, 1862, at Harper's Ferry, Va.; wounded in action,

February 20, 1864, at Olustee, Fla.; mustered out with company, June 17, 1865, at Raleigh, N.C.

DUNBAR, CHARLES.—Age, 24 years. Enlisted at Mohawk, to serve three years, and mustered in as private, Co. D, August 25, 1862; captured in action, September 15, and paroled, September 16, 1862, at Harper's Ferry, Va.; discharged for disability, January 10, 1863, near Annapolis, Md.

DUNK, JAMES.—Age 18 years. Enlisted, August 2, 1862, at Milton, to serve three years; mustered in as private; Co. C, August 8, 1862; captured in action, September 15, and paroled, September 16, 1862, at Harper's Ferry, Va.; mustered out with company, June 17, 1865, at Raleigh, N.C.

DUNNING, ALBERT.—Age, 20 years. Enlisted, July 31, 1862, at Malta, to serve three years; mustered in as private, Co. C, August 11, 1862; captured in action, September 15, and paroled, September 16, at Harper's Ferry, Va.; killed, July 26, 1864, while on picket, before Petersburg, Va.

DUPLACEY, PETER.—Age, 25 years. Enlisted at Elizabeth, to serve one year, and mustered in as private, Co. E, February 28, 1865; transferred to Co. A, Forty-seventh Infantry, June 17, 1865.

DUSCIN, WILLIAM.—Age, 33 years. Enlisted at Jamaica, to serve three years, and mustered in as private, Co. K, October 30, 1863; transferred to Co. I, Forty-seventh Infantry, June 17, 1865; also borne as Dusien.

DUTCHER, JOHN.—Age, 21 years. Enlisted, July 23, 1862, at Mayfield, to serve three years; mustered in as private, Co. A, July 24, 1862; captured in action September 15, and paroled, September 16, 1862, at Harper's Ferry, Va.; wounded in action, February 20, 1864, at Olustee, Fla.; promoted corporal, April 1, 1865; mustered out with company, June 17, 1865, at Raleigh, N.C.

DWIGHT, JOHN W.—Age, 18 years. Enlisted at Brooklyn, to serve one year, and mustered in as private, Co. K, February 24, 1865; transferred to Co. H, Forty-seventh Infantry, June 17, 1865.

DYE, JOHN H.—Age, 18 years. Enlisted at Mayfield, to serve three years, and mustered in as private, Co. K, August 18, 1862; captured in action, September 15, and paroled, September 16, 1862, at Harper's Ferry, Va.; discharged, January 16, 1863, at Washington, D.C.; also borne as Day.

DYER, CHARLES.—Age, 33 years. Enlisted at Tarrytown, to serve three years, and mustered in as private, Co. E, October 28, 1863; wounded in action, February 20, 1864, at Olustee, Fla.; deserted, May 21, 1865.

DYER, EDWARD.—Age, 22 years. Enlisted at Eighteenth Congressional District, to serve three years, and mustered in as private, Co. A, March 25, 1864; deserted, June 20, 1864, at Bermuda Hundred, Va.

DYER, JAMES.—Age, 23 years. Enlisted, August 25, 1862, at Minden, to serve three years; mustered in as private, Co. I, August 26, 1862; deserted, August 27, 1862, at Fonda, N.Y.

EAGAN, RICHARD.—Age, 19 years. Enlisted at New York City, to serve three years, and mustered in as private, Co. I, March 7, 1865; transferred to Co. H, Forty-seventh Infantry, June 17, 1865.

EATON, ALBERT.—Age, 18 years. Enlisted at Brooklyn to serve one year, and mustered in as private, Co. F, March 6, 1865; transferred to Co. F, Forty-seventh Infantry, June 17, 1865.

EATON, ALFRED G.—Age, 22 years. Enlisted, August 9, 1862, at Charleston, to serve three years; mustered in as private, Co. D. August 15, 1862; captured in action, September 15, and paroled, September 16, 1862, at Harper's Ferry, Va.; discharged for disability, August 29, 1863, at Beaufort, S.C.

EATON, NICHOLAS H.—Age, 21 years. Enlisted, August 13, 1862 at Charleston, to serve three years; mustered in as private, Co. D, August 15, 1862; captured in action, September 15, and paroled, September 16, 1862, at Harper's Ferry, Va.; wounded in action, February 20, 1864, at Olustee, Fla.; promoted corporal, no date; mustered out, May 15, 1865, at hospital, Fort Monroe, Va.

EGAN, PATRICK.—Age, 23 years. Enlisted at Minden, to serve three years, and mustered in as private, Co. H, August 25 1862; no further record.

EIGHMY, JR., ALFRED.—Age, 23 years. Enlisted at Milton, to serve three years, and mustered in as private, Co. C, August 11, 1862; captured in action September 15, and paroled, September 16, 1862 at Harper's Ferry, Va.; mustered out with company, June 17, 1865, at Raleigh N.C.

EIGNBROADT, CHARLES.—Age, 25 years. Enlisted, August 8, 1862, at Palatine, to serve three years, mustered in as private, Co. A, August 9, 1862; captured in action, September 15, and paroled, September 16 1862 at Harper's Ferry, Va.; wounded in action, May 7, 1864 at Chester Heights, Va.; promoted corporal, March 1, 1865, mustered out with company June 17, 1865, at Raleigh, N.C.

ELDRED, JAMES M.—Age 21 years. Enlisted August 11, 1862, at North Hampton to serve three years; mustered in as private, Co. E, August 15, 1862; captured in action, September 15, and paroled, September 16 1862, at Harper's Ferry, Va.; discharged for disability, November 8, 1862, at Chicago, Ill.

ELLIS, SAMPSON.—Age, 22 years. Enlisted, July 23, 1862, at Saratoga Springs, to serve three years; mustered in as private Co. G, July 31, 1862; captured in action, September 15, and paroled September 16 1862 at Harper's Ferry, Va.; discharged for disability, June 22, 1863 at Yorktown, Va.; also borne as Elles.

EMPEROR, CHRISTOPHER.—Age, 21 years. Enlisted, August 1, 1862 at Ballston, to serve three years, mustered in as private Co. C, August 8, 1862; captured in action, September 15, paroled September 16, 1862 at Harper's Ferry, Va.; deserted, September 25, 1862 at Baltimore, Md.

EMPY, GUY.—Age 28 years. Enlisted at Norfolk, to serve three years, and mustered in as private Co. E, February 27, 1865; transferred to Co. E, Forty-seventh Infantry, June 17, 1865.

ENGLEBRATH, HENRY.—Age, 37 years. Enlisted at Brooklyn, to serve three years, and mustered in as private, Co. I, September 2, 1863; died, April 8, 1865 at hospital, Wilmington, N.C.

ENGLEHART, CARL.—Age, 30 years. Enlisted at Tarrytown, to serve three years, and mustered in as private, Co. H, October 30, 1863; transferred to Co. F, Forty-seventh Infantry, June 17, 1865.

ENGLISH, JAMES.—Age, 21. Enlisted August 12, 1862, at Florida to serve three years; mustered in as private, Co. D, August 13, 1862; captured in action, September 15, and paroled, September 16, 1862, at Harper's Ferry, Va.; discharged for disability, December 24, 1862, at Washington, D.C.; subsequent service in Fifth U. S. Infantry.

ENNEY, GEORGE.—Age, 28 years. Enlisted at Mohawk, to serve three years, and mustered in as private, Co. A, August 8, 1862; captured in action, September 15, and paroled, September 16, 1862, at Harper's Ferry, Va.; absent, sick at hospital, David's Island, New York Harbor, since March, 1865, and at muster-out of company.

ENNIS, WILLIAM R.—Age, 18 years. Enlisted at Schenectady, to serve three years, and mustered in as private, Co. G, March 4, 1865; transferred to Co. K, Forty-seventh Infantry; June 17, 1865.

ERKENBRACK, PHILIP.—Age, 29 years. Enlisted, August 11, 1862, at Caroga, to serve three years; mustered in as private, Co. K, August 12, 1862; captured in action, September 15, and paroled, September 16, 1862, at Harper's Ferry, Va.; wounded in action, February 20, 1864, at Olustee, Fla.; discharged, April 28, 1865.

ETER, EDWARD.—Age, 26 years. Enlisted at Schenectady, to serve three years, and mustered in as private, Co. G, March 2, 1865; transferred to Co. E, Forty-seventh Infantry, June 17, 1865; also borne as Etter.

EVANS, GEORGE M.—Age, 22 years. Enlisted, August 11, 1862, at Edinburgh, to serve three years; mustered in as private, Co. C, August 14, 1862; captured in action, September 15, and paroled, September 16, 1862, at Harper's Ferry, Va.; wounded and captured in action, August 16, 1864, at Deep Bottom, Va.; paroled, no date; mustered out, May 15, 1865, at West Building's Hospital, Baltimore, Md. as George W. Evans.

EVANS, OLIVER.—Age, 40 years. Enlisted, July 29, 1862, at Saratoga Springs, to serve three years; mustered in as private, Co. G, August 9, 1862; captured in action, September 15, and paroled, September 16, 1862, at Harper's Ferry, Va.; mustered out with company, June 17, 1865, at Raleigh, N.C. as Evens.

EVENS, ELANE F.—Age, 20 years. Enlisted, August 5, 1862, at Day, to serve three years; mustered in as private, Co. C, August 8, 1862; captured in action, September 15, and paroled, September 16, 1862, at Harper's Ferry, Va.; killed in action, February 20, 1864, at Olustee, Fla.

EVEREST, ALFRED C.—Age, 37 years. Enlisted at Schenectady, to serve one year, and mustered in as private, Co. E, September 3, 1864; mustered out with company, June 17, 1865, at Raleigh, N.C.

EVERTS, WILLIAM H.—Age 22 years. Enlisted, August 15, 1862, at Clifton Park, to serve three years; mustered in as private, Co. H., August 18, 1862; captured in action, September 15, and paroled, September 16, 1862, at Harper's Ferry, Va.; died November 1, 1862, at Clifton Park, N.Y., as Evarts.

FAGAN, JAMES.—Age, 24 years. Enlisted at Brooklyn, to serve three years, and mustered in as private, Co. G, September 3, 1863; transferred to the Navy, April 27, 1864.

FAGAN, JR., JOHN.—Age, 18 years. Enlisted, July 12, 1864, at New York Harbor, to serve three years; mustered in as private, Co. G, July 19, 1864; transferred to Co. G, Forty-seventh Infantry, June 17, 1865.

FAGAN, PATRICK.—Age, 20 years. Enlisted at Brooklyn, to serve three years, and mustered in as private, Co. K, February 21, 1865; deserted, May 1, 1865, at Raleigh, N.C.

FAILING, JR., ABRAM.—Age, 18 years. Enlisted, August 11, 1862, at St. Johnsville, to serve three years; mustered in as private, Co. B, August 12, 1862; captured in action, September 15, and paroled, September 16, 1862, at Harper's Ferry, Va.; wounded in action, February 20, 1864, at Olustee, Fla., and August 16, 1864, at Deep Bottom, Va.; mustered out with detachment, May 11, 1865, at Albany, N.Y., as Faling.

FAILLING, DAVID.—Age, 19 years. Enlisted, August 6, 1862, at Caroga, to serve three years; mustered in as private, Co. K, August 12, 1862; captured in action, September 15, and paroled, September 16, 1862, at Harper's Ferry, Va.; wounded in action, February 20, 1864, at Olustee, Fla.; mustered out with company, June 17, 1865, at Raleigh, N.C., as Failing.

FAILLING, EBENEZER.—Age, 44 years. Enlisted, August 6, 1862, at Caroga, to serve three years; mustered in as private Co. K, August 12, 1862; captured in action, September 15, and paroled, September 16, 1862, at Harper's Ferry, Va.; mustered out, May 28, 1865, at hospital, Fort Monroe, Va., as Failing.

FAIRCHILD, NELSON H.—Age, 21 years. Enlisted, August 11, 1862, at Johnstown, to serve three years; mustered in as private, Co. E, August 15, 1962; captured in action, September 15, and paroled, September 16, 1862, at Harper's Ferry, Va.; promoted non-commissioned officer, no date; returned to ranks, November 1, 1864; mustered out with detachment, June 3, 1865, at hospital, Washington, D.C.

FAIS, JOHN.—Age, 26 years. Enlisted at Tarrytown, to serve three years, and mustered in as private, Co. A, October 27, 1863; wounded and captured in action, February 20, 1864, at Olustee, Fla.; died of diarrhea, April 30, 1864, at Andersonville, Ga., also borne as Faus.

FARLEY, PATRICK.—Age, 25 years. Enlisted, at Tarrytown, to serve one year, and mustered in as private, Co. G, March 6, 1865; transferred to Co. G, Forty-seventh Infantry, June 17, 1865.

FARRAR, GEORGE H.—Age,—years. Enrolled at Saratoga Springs, to serve three years, and mustered in as second lieutenant, Co. G, August 26, 1862; promoted first lieutenant, October 31, 1862; discharged for disability, March 4, 1863. Commissioned second lieutenant, September 10, 1862, with rank from August 20, 1862, original; first lieutenant, October 31, 1862, with rank from August 30, 1862, vice E.B. Savage promoted.

FARREN, FRANCISCO.—Age, 29 years. Enlisted at New York City, to serve three years, and mustered in as private, Co. C, August 28, 1863; wounded in action, February 20, 1864, at Olustee, Fla.; transferred to the Navy, April 27, 1864; also borne as Favian.

FAULDS, ANDREW.—Age, 18 years. Enlisted at Albany, to serve one year, and mustered in as private, Co. A, April 7, 1865; transferred to Co. A, Forty-seventh Infantry, June 17, 1865.

FAULKNER, SIMEON.—Age, 31 years. Enlisted, July 23, 1862, at St. Johnsville, to serve three years; mustered in as private, Co. I, August 8, 1862; captured in action, September 15, and paroled, September 16, 1862, at Harper's Ferry, Va.; wounded in action, September 29, 1864, at Chaffins Farm, Va.; mustered out, May 29, 1865, at hospital, Fort Monroe, Va.; also borne as Simon.

FELLOWS, CHARLES B.—Age, 24 years. Enlisted, August 5, 1862, at Stillwater, to serve three years; mustered in as corporal, Co. H, August 7, 1862; captured in action, September 15, and paroled, September 16, 1862, at Harper's Ferry, Va.; wounded and captured in action, October 1, 1864, at Chaffins Farm, Va.; paroled and promoted sergeant, no dates; died, November 11, 1864, at hospital, Annapolis, Md.

FENKER, GEORGE.—Age, 20 years. Enlisted at New York City, to serve three years, and mustered in as private, Co. I, March 7, 1865; transferred to Co. H, Forty-seventh Infantry, June 17, 1865; also borne as Feaker.

FERGUSON, BENJAMIN.—Age, 30 years. Enlisted, August 12, 1862, at Mayfield, to serve three years; mustered in as private, Co. E, August 15, 1862; captured in action, September 15, and paroled, September 16, 1862, at Harper's Ferry, Va.; transferred to Co. A, Nineteenth Regiment, Veteran Reserve Corps, September 1, 1863; re-enlisted as a veteran, September 3, 1864; mustered out with detachment, November 15, 1865, at Elmira, N.Y., as Fergason; also borne as Furgeson.

FERGUSON, WILLETT.—Age, 32 years. Enrolled, August 13, 1862, at Fonda, to serve three years; mustered in as first lieutenant, Co. A, August 21, 1862; as captain, April 13, 1864; discharged for disability, to date, December 31, 1864. Commissioned first lieutenant, September 10, 1862, with rank from August 20, 1862, original; captain, March 23, 1864, with rank from February 24, 1864, vice Garret Vanderveer, deceased.

FILKINS, ABRAM.—Age, 39 years. Enlisted, August 11, 1862, at Halfmoon, to serve three years; mustered in as private, Co. H, August 14, 1862; captured in action, September 15, and paroled, September 16, 1862, at Harper's Ferry, Va.; absent, sick in hospital at Albany, N.Y., at muster-out of company.

FILKINS, JOHN W.—Age, 42 years. Enrolled, July 23, 1862, at Halfmoon, to serve three years; mustered in as sergeant, Co. H, August 7, 1862; promoted first sergeant, February 20, 1863; mustered in as second lieutenant, January 27, 1864; wounded in action, July 29, 1864, before Petersburg, Va.; discharged for wounds, November 4, 1864. Commissioned second lieutenant, April 22, 1864, with rank from January 27, 1864, vice James H. Clark promoted.

FILKINS, LOCY.—Age, 40 years. Enlisted, August 11, 1862, at Clifton Park, to serve three years; mustered in as private, Co. H, August 14, 1862; captured in action, September 15, and paroled, September 16, 1862, at Harper's Ferry, Va.; wounded in action, February 20, 1864, at Olustee, Fla.; mustered out with company, June 17, 1865, at Raleigh, N.C.

FILLDING, JAMES.—Age, 29 years. Enlisted at Brooklyn, to serve three years, and mustered in as private, Co. H, August 27, 1863; transferred to the Navy, April 27, 1864.

FIRTH, WILLIAM H.—Age, 25 years. Enlisted at Broadalbin, to serve one year, and mustered in as private, Co. D, March 23, 1865; transferred to Co. G, Forty-seventh Infantry, June 17, 1865.

FISHER, CHARLES S.—Age, 25 years. Enlisted, August 2, 1862, at Galway, to serve three years; mustered in as sergeant, Co. C, August 12, 1862; captured in action, September 15, and paroled, September 16, 1862, at Harper's Ferry, Va.; promoted first sergeant, July 21, 1864; killed in action, September 29, 1864, at Chaffins Farm, Va.

FISHER, CONRAD.—Age, 19 years. Enlisted at Brooklyn, to serve one year, and mustered in as private, Co. F, March 6, 1865; transferred to Co. F, Forty-seventh Infantry, June 17, 1865.

FISHER, GEORGE.—Age, 21 years. Enlisted at Goshen, to serve three years, and mustered in as private, Co. H, February 28, 1865; transferred to Co. K, Forty-seventh Infantry, June 17, 1865.

FITZGERALD, JOHN.—Age, 20 years. Enlisted at New York City, to serve three years, and mustered in as private, Co. F, August 28, 1863; transferred to the Navy, April 27, 1864.

FITZGERALD, JOHN.—Age, 17 years. Enlisted at Eighteenth Congressional District, to serve one year, and mustered in as private, Co. C, February 27, 1865, transferred to Co. C, Forty-seventh Infantry, June 17, 1865.

FITZGERALD, PATRICK.—Age, 19 years. Enlisted at Brooklyn, to serve three years, and mustered in as private, Co. K, February 23, 1865; transferred to Co. I, Forty-seventh Infantry, June 17, 1865.

FITZGERALD, THOMAS.—Age, 25 years. Enlisted at Goshen, to serve one year, and mustered in as private, Co. F, March 6, 1865; transferred to Co. K. Forty-seventh Infantry, June 17, 1865.

FITZGIBON, MICHAEL.—Age, 22 years. Enlisted, July 29, 1862, at Saratoga, to serve three years; mustered in as private, Co. F, August 12, 1862; captured in action, September 15, and paroled, September 16, 1862, at Harper's Ferry, Va.; deserted, November 8, 1862, at Chicago, Ill.

FLANAGAN, JOHN.—Age, 36 years. Enlisted at New York City, to serve three years, and mustered in as private, Co. A, February 27, 1865; transferred to Co. A, Forty-seventh Infantry, June 17, 1865.

FLANAGAN, MICHAEL.—Age, 39 years. Enlisted at Minden, to serve three years, and mustered in as private, Co. H, August 25, 1862; no further record.

FLEMMING, JAMES.—Age, 21 years. Enlisted at New York City, to serve three years, and mustered in as private, Co. A, February 27, 1865; transferred to Co. A, Forty-seventh Infantry, June 17, 1865.

FLINT, EDWARD E.—Age, 18 years. Enlisted, December 15, 1863, at Charleston, to serve three years; mustered in as private, Co. B, January 2, 1864; transferred to Co. B, Forty-seventh Infantry, June 17, 1865.

FLINT, MORGAN M.—Age, 18 years. Enlisted at Canajoharie, to serve three years, and mustered in as private, Co. I, August 8, 1862; captured in action September 15, and paroled, September 16, 1862, at Harper's Ferry, Va.; killed in action; May 20, 1864, at Drewry's Bluff, Va.

FLINT, WILLIAM E.—Age, 21 years. Enlisted, August 7, 1862, at Canajoharie, to serve three years; mustered in as private, Co. B, August 12, 1862; captured in action, September 15, and paroled, September 16, 1862, at Harper's Ferry, Va.; captured in action and supposed dead, February 20, 1864, at Olustee, Fla.

FLINT, WILLIAM H.—Age, 18 years. Enlisted, August 5, 1862, at Canajoharie, to serve three years; mustered in as private, Co. B, August 12, 1862; captured in action, September 15, and paroled, September 16, 1862, at Harper's Ferry, Va.; wounded in action, October 27, 1864, at Darbytown Road, Va.; mustered out, May 29, 1865, at Albany, N.Y.

FLOOD, ORANGE.—Age, 18 years. Enlisted at Schenectady, to serve three years, and mustered in as private, Co. G, March 3, 1865; transferred to Co. G, Forty-seventh Infantry, June 17, 1865.

FOLENSBEE, NATHAN F.—Age, 30 years. Enlisted, August 9, 1862, at Charleston, to serve three years; mustered in as private, Co. D, August 15, 1862; captured in action, September 15, and paroled, September 16, 1862, at Harper's Ferry, Va.; mustered out with company, June 17, 1865, at Raleigh, N.C.

FOLENSBEE, PETER A.—Age, 21 years. Enlisted, August 1, 1862, at Amsterdam, to serve three years; mustered in as private, Co. D, August 2, 1862; captured in action, September 15, and paroled, September 16, 1862, at Harper's Ferry, Va.; killed in action, February 20, 1864, at Olustee, Fla., as Folnsbee.

FOLMSBEE, PETER.—Age, 44 years. Enlisted, August 5, 1862, at Halfmoon, to serve three years; mustered in as private, Co. H, August 7, 1862; captured in action, September 15, and paroled, September 16. 1862, at Harper's Ferry, Va.; transferred to Co. C, Twelfth Regiment, Veteran Reserve Corps, April 28, 1864; mustered out with detachment, June 28, 1865, at Washington, D.C.

FONDA, E. RAYMOND.—Age, 24 years. Enlisted, July 21, 1862, at Halfmoon, to serve three years; mustered in as private, Co. H, August 1, 1862; captured in action, September 15, and paroled, September 16, 1862, at Harper's Ferry. Va.; promoted sergeant-major, October 16, 1862; wounded in action, May 7, 1864, at Chester Station, Va.; died of his wounds, July 22, 1864, in Ladies Home Hospital, New York City; prior service in First Vermont Volunteers.

FOOT, MELVILLE B.—Age, 22 years. Enlisted, August 6, 1862, at North Hampton, to serve three years; mustered in as sergeant, Co. E, August 15, 1862; captured in action, September 15, and paroled, September 16, 1862, at Harper's Ferry, Va.; mustered out with company, June 17, 1865, at Raleigh, N.C.

FORBES, EDWIN.—Age, 18 years. Enlisted at Lawrence, to serve one year, and mustered in as private, Co. E, February 24, 1865; transferred to Co. E, Forty-seventh Infantry, June 17, 1865, as Edward.

FORD, CHARLES.—Age, 23 years. Enlisted at Kingston, to serve three years, and mustered in as private, Co. I, February 26, 1865; deserted, April 15, 1865, at Duplins Cross Roads, Va.

FORD, WILLIAM.—Age, 24 years. Enlisted at New York City, to serve three years, and mustered in as private, Co. K, October 3, 1863; deserted, September 12, 1864, at Petersburg, Va.

FORREST, CHARLES.—Age, 19 years. Enlisted at Schenectady, to serve one year, and mustered in as private, Co. K, September 10, 1864; mustered out with company, June 17, 1865, at Raleigh, N.C.

FORT, JOHN L.—Age, 23 years. Enlisted, August 9, 1862, at Charlton, to serve three years; mustered in as private, Co. I,. August 18, 1862; captured in action, September 15, and paroled, September 16, 1862, at Harper's Ferry, Va.; promoted corporal, no date; captured in action, October 1, 1864, at Chaffins Farm, Va.; died, October 12, 1864, at Salisbury N.C.

FOSMYRE, DANIEL.—Age 24 years. Enlisted at Albany, to serve one year, and mustered in as private, Co. K, August 25, 1864; mustered out with company, June 17, 1865, at Raleigh, N.C.; also borne as Daniel A. Fosmire.

FOSTER, JR., GEORGE D.—Late adjutant, Ninety-seventh Infantry. Commissioned first lieutenant, not mustered, December 29, 1864, with rank front same date, vice G. H. Curreen discharged.

FOSTER, GEORGE F.—Age, 26 years. Enlisted, August 6, 1862, at Milton, to serve three years; mustered in as private, Co. C, August 5, 1862; captured in action, September 15, and paroled, September 16, 1862, at Harper's Ferry, Va.; promoted corporal, October 1, 1864; mustered out with company, June 17, 1865, at Raleigh, N.C.

FOSS, WILLIAM.—Age, 22 years. Enlisted, August 4, 1862, at Galway, to serve three years; mustered in as private, Co. C, August 12, 1862; captured in action, September 15, and paroled, September 16, 1862, at Harper's Ferry, Va.; mustered out with company, June 17, 1865, at Raleigh, N.C.; also borne as Fox.

FOURKELL, CONRAD.—Age, 18 years. Enlisted at Florida, to serve one year, and mustered in as private, Co. B, April 8, 1865; transferred to Co. C, Forty-seventh Infantry, June 17, 1865; also borne as Forkle.

FOURNIER, JOHN E.—Age, 18 years. Enlisted at Schenectady, to serve three years, and mustered in as private, Co. B, February 24, 1865; transferred to Co. B, Forty-seventh Infantry, June 17, 1865; also borne as John G.

FOWLER, AMBROSE.—Age, 19 years. Enlisted, August 11, 1862, at Halfmoon, to serve three years; mustered in as sergeant, Co. H, August 14, 1862; captured in action, September 15. and paroled, September 16, 1862, at Harper's Ferry, Va.; returned to ranks, no date; wounded in action, August 16, 1864, at Deep Bottom, Va.; mustered out with company, June 17, 1865, at Raleigh, N.C.

FOX, JAMES O.—Age, 23 years. Enlisted, August 11, 1862, at Broadalbin, to serve three years; mustered in as sergeant, Co. K, August 12, 1862; captured in action, September 15, and paroled, September 16, 1862, at Harper's Ferry, Va.; returned to ranks and promoted corporal, no date; wounded and captured, May 7, 1864, at Chester Station, Va.; died of his wounds, May 31, 1864, at Petersburg, Va.

FOX, ROBERT.—Age, 32 years. Enlisted, August 4, 1862, at Milton, to serve three years; mustered in as corporal, Co. C, August 8, 1862; captured in action, September 15, and paroled, September 16, 1862, at Harper's Ferry, Va.; wounded and captured in action,

February 20, 1864, at Olustee, Fla.; died, June, 1864, while a prisoner of war.

FOX, WILLIAM M.—Age, 29 years. Enlisted, August 14, 1862, at Broadalbin, to serve three years; mustered in as private, Co. K, August 23, 1862; captured in action, September 15, and paroled, September 16. 1862, at Harper's Ferry. Va.; discharged, August 29, 1863.

FRANCIS, RICHARD.—Age, 30 years. Enlisted at Brooklyn, to serve three years, and mustered in as private, Co. H, August 31, 1863; killed in action, February 20, 1864, at Olustee, Fla.

FRANCISCO, FRANCIS H.—Age, 27 years. Enrolled, August 13, 1862, at Wells, to serve three years; mustered in as second lieutenant, Co. K, August 21, 1862; as first lieutenant, May 23, 1863; killed in action, August 16, 1864, at Deep Bottom, Va. Commissioned second lieutenant, September 10, 1862, with rank from August 20, 1862, original; first lieutenant, November 13, 1863, with rank from May 22, 1863, vice R. Sexton resigned.

FRANK, JEAN.—Age, 24 years. Enlisted at Tarrytown, to serve one year, and mustered in as private, Co. K, March 8, 1865; mustered out with detachment, May 31, 1865, at Foster Hospital, New Berne. N.C.

FRAZIER, DANIEL.—Age, 29 years. Enlisted at Albany, to serve three years, and mustered in as private, Co. F, October 28, 1863; wounded in action, February 20, 1864, at Olustee, Fla.; transferred to Veteran Reserve Corps, January 1, 1865.

FREDENDALL, GEORGE.—Age, 19 years. Enlisted, August 11, 1862, at Florida, to serve three years; mustered in as private, Co. D, August 15, 1862; captured in action, September 15, and paroled, September 16, 1862, at Harper's Ferry, Va.; mustered out with company, June 17, 1865, at Raleigh, N.C.

FREDENDALL, JAMES.—Age, 22 years. Enlisted, August 4, 1862, at Florida, to serve three years; mustered in as private, Co. D, August 15, 1862; captured in action, September 15, and paroled, September 16, 1862, at Harper's Ferry, Va.; wounded in action, May 6, 1864, at Chester Station, Va.; promoted corporal, no date; mustered out with detachment, May 11, 1865, at Albany, N.Y.

FREDERICK, MARTIN.—Age, 21 years. Enlisted, August 11, 1862. at Caroga, to serve three rears; mustered in as private, Co. K, August 12, 1862; captured in action, September 15, and paroled, September 16, 1862, at Harper's Ferry, Va.; deserted, September 25, 1862, at Baltimore, Md.

FREDERICK, WILLIAM.—Age, 27 years. Enlisted at New York City, to serve three years, and mustered in as private, Co. I, August 26, 1863; wounded in action, February 20, 1864, at Olustee, Fla.; transferred to the Navy, April 25, 1864.

FREDERICK, WILLIAM L.—Age, 35 years. Enlisted at Mohawk, to serve three years, and mustered in as private, Co. K, August 19, 1862; captured in action, September 15, and paroled. September 16, 1862, at Harper's Ferry, Va.; discharged at hospital, New York City, no date.

FREEMAN, ANDREW J.—Age, 19 years. Enlisted, August 7, 1862, at Milton, to serve three years; mustered in as private, Co. C, August 11, 1862; captured in action, September 15, and paroled, September 16, 1862, at Harper's Ferry, Va.; wounded prior to August 2, 1864; absent in hospital at Albany, N.Y., and at muster-out of company.

FREEMAN, GEORGE.—Age, 25 years. Enlisted at Fonda, to serve three years and mustered in as private, Co. I, August 26, 1862; deserted August 28, 1862, at Fonda, N.Y.

FREEMAN, GEORGE.—Age, 28 years. Enlisted at Mohawk, to serve three years, and mustered in as private, Co. H, July 26, 1862; deserted, September 8, 1862, at Harper's Ferry, Va.

FRENCH, JOHN.—Age, 20 years. Enlisted, July 26, 1862, at Florida, to serve three years; mustered in as private, Co. D, August 2, 1862; captured in action, September 15, and paroled, September 16, 1862, at Harper's Ferry, Va.; died of typhoid fever, May 12, 1864, at Bermuda. Hundred, Va.

FRENCH, WALTON W.—Age, 26 years. Enrolled at Albany, to serve three years, and mustered in as captain, Co. F, August 20, 1862.; wounded in action, February 20, 1864, at Olustee, Fla.; discharged; for wounds, June 20, 1864. Commissioned captain, September 10, 1862, with rank from August 20, 1862, original.

FRICK, CHARLES.—Age, 36 years. Enlisted at Tarrytown, to serve one year, and mustered in as private, Co. G, March 6, 1865; transferred to Co. G, Forty-seventh Infantry, June 17, 1865; also borne as Friek.

FROMILLER, RUDOLPH.—Age, 18 years. Enlisted at Brooklyn, to serve one year, and mustered in as private, Co. C, February 28, 1865; transferred to Co. C, Forty-seventh Infantry June 17, 1865; also borne as Randolph.

FROST, JOSEPH H.—Age, 19 years. Enlisted at Goshen, to serve one year, and mustered in as private, Co. F, March 6, 1865; transferred to Co. F, Forty-seventh Infantry, June 17, 1863.

FRY, PETER.—Age, 23 years. Enlisted at Schenectady, to serve one year, and mustered in as private, Co. K, August 12, 1864; mustered out with company, June 17, 1865, at Raleigh, N.C.

FRYER, CHARLES.—Age, 20 years. Enlisted, August 14, 1862, at Saratoga Spa, to serve three years; mustered in as private, Co. F, August 19, 1862; captured in action, September 15, and paroled, September 16, 1862, at Harper's Ferry, Va.; died, June 5, 1865, on U. S. transport Spaulding.

FULLER, WILLIAM T.—Age, 26 years. Enlisted, August 13, 1862, at Northumberland, to serve three years; mustered in as private, Co. F, August 19, 1862; captured in action, September 15, and paroled, September 16, 1862, at Harper's Ferry, Va.; mustered out with company, June 17, 1865, at Raleigh, N.C.

FURRER, PAUL.—Age, 25 years. Enlisted at New York City, to serve three years, and mustered in as private, Co. A, February 27, 1865; transferred to Co. A, Forty-seventh Infantry, June 17, 1865; also borne as Furor.

GAGE, JAMES R.—Age, 23 years. Enlisted, August 11, 1862, at Caroga, to serve three years; mustered in as private, Co. K, August 12, 1862; captured in action, September 15, and paroled, September 16, 1862, at Harper's Ferry, Va.; promoted corporal, no date;

mustered out with company, June 17, 1865, at Raleigh, N.C.

GALLEGER, PATRICK.—Age, 24 years. Enlisted at Amsterdam, to serve three years; mustered in as private, Co. G, and deserted, August 25, 1862, at Fonda, N.Y.

GALLUSHA, DAVID.—Age, 29 years. Enlisted, August 11, 1862, at Northumberland, to serve three years; mustered in as private, Co. C, August 15, 1862; captured in action, September 15, and paroled, September 16, 1862, at Harper's Ferry, Va.; discharged for disability, December 31, 1862, at Mt. Pleasant Hospital, Washington, D.C.; also borne as Galusha.

GANBY, JOHN.—Age, 19 years. Enlisted at Poughkeepsie, to serve three years, and mustered in as private, Co. D, February 24, 1865; transferred to Co. D, Forty-seventh Infantry, June 17, 1865; also borne as Ganly.

GARDINER, ROBERT.—Age, 43 years. Enlisted at New York City, to serve three years, and mustered in as private, Co. K, February 1, 1865; promoted corporal, no date; transferred to Co. H, Forty-seventh Infantry, June 17, 1865.

GARDNER, ANTHONY.—Age, 22 years. Enlisted, July 30, 1862, at Canajoharie, to serve three years; mustered in as private, Co. I, August 26, 1862; deserted, August 27, 1862, at Fonda. N.Y.

GARDNER, JAMES.—Age, 19 years. Enlisted, August 7, 1862, at Canajoharie, to serve three years; mustered in as private, Co. I, August 16, 1862; captured in action, September 15, and paroled, September 16, 1862, at Harper's Ferry, Va.; mustered out, June 5, 1865, at Albany, N.Y. as Gardinier.

GARDNER, JAMES.—Age, 43 years. Enlisted at Palatine, to serve three years, and mustered in as private, Co. A, August 7, 1862; captured in action, September 15, and paroled, September 16, 1862, at Harper's Ferry, Va.; wounded in action, February 20, 1864, at Olustee, Fla.; died of his wounds, March 19, 1864.

GARDNER, WILLIAM.—Age, 22 years. Enlisted at Palatine, to serve three years, and mustered in as private, Co. A, August 18, 1862; captured in action, September 15, and paroled, September 16, 1862, at Harper's Ferry, Va.; deserted, October 1, 1862, at Chicago, Ill.; returned under president's proclamation, March 28, 1865; transferred to Co. A, Forty-seventh Infantry, June 17, 1865.

GARLOCK, AARON.—Age, 21 years. Enlisted at Minden, to serve three years, and mustered in as private, Co. B, August 13, 1862; captured in action, September 15, and paroled, September 16, 1862 at Harper's Ferry, Va.; promoted corporal, September 1, 1864; sergeant, March 1, 1863; mustered out with company, June 17 1865 at Raleigh, N.C.

GARNER, ELIJAH H.—Age, 19 years. Enlisted, August 11, 1862, at Saratoga Spa, to serve three years; mustered in as private, Co. F, August 14, 1862; captured in action, September 15, and paroled, September 16, 1862, at Harper's Ferry, Va.; wounded in action, February 20, 1864, at Olustee, Fla.; promoted corporal, no date; mustered out with company, June 17, 1865, at Raleigh, N.C.

GAUL, FREDERICK.—Age, 27 years. Enlisted at Tarrytown, to serve three years, and mustered in as private, Co. G, October 28, 1863; transferred to Co. F, Forty-seventh Infantry, June 17, 1863.

GAVAN, WILLIAM.—Age, 26 years. Enlisted at Brooklyn, to serve three years, and mustered in as private, Co. H., February 23, 1865; transferred to Co. K. Forty-seventh Infantry, June 17, 1865.

GETMAN, JAMES H.—Age, 18 years. Enlisted, August 9, 1862, at Ephratah, to serve three years; mustered in as private, Co. E, August 16, 1862; captured in action, September 15, and paroled, September 16, 1862, at Harper's Ferry, Va.; appointed musician, no date; wounded in action, October 27, 1864, at Darbytown Road, Va., and January 15, 1865, at Fort Fisher, N. C; mustered out, May 15, 1865, at Albany, N.Y.

GETMAN, JOSHUA.—Age, 26 years. Enlisted, August 9, 1862, at Ephratah, to serve three years; mustered in as private, Co. E, August 15, 1862; captured in action, September 15, and paroled, September 16, 1862, at Harper's Ferry, Va.; wounded while on picket before Petersburg, Va., no date; July 30, 1864, at mine explosion, Petersburg, Va., and in action, October 27, 1864, at Darbytown Road, Va.; mustered out, June 3, 1865, at Albany N.Y.

GILBERT, JOHN A.—Age, 21 years. Enlisted, August 9, 1862, at Saratoga Springs, to serve three years; mustered in as private, Co. G, August 19, 1862; captured in action, September 15, and paroled, September 16, 1862, at Harper's Ferry, Va.; wounded in action, September 29, 1864, near Richmond, Va.; mustered out, May 28, 1865, at hospital, Fort Monroe, Va.

GILDAY, DANIEL.—Age, 23 years. Enlisted, August 13, 1862, at Minden, to serve three years; mustered in as private, Co. B, August 14, 1862; captured in action, September 15, and paroled, September 16, 1862, at Harper's Ferry, Va.; again captured in action, February 20, 1864, at Olustee, Fla.; casualty list reports him as dead; no further record.

GILES, JOHN.—Age, 41 years. Enlisted at New York City, to serve three years, and mustered in as private, Co. K, February 27, 1865; transferred to Co. H, Forty-seventh Infantry, June 17, 1865.

GILLESPIE, JAMES K.—Age, 36 years. Enlisted, August 8, 1862, at Milton, to serve three years; mustered in as sergeant, Co. C, August 9, 1862; wounded and captured in action and paroled, September 16, 1862, at Harper's Ferry, Va.; returned to ranks, no date; absent, sick in General Hospital, Wilmington, N.C. at muster-out of company.

GILLINS, JOHN.—Age, 22 years. Enlisted, August 1, 1862, at Amsterdam, to serve three years; mustered in as private, Co. D, August 2, 1862; captured in action, September 15, and paroled, September 16, 1862, at Harper's Ferry, Va.; wounded and captured in action, February 20, 1864, at Olustee, Fla.; paroled February 23, 1865, at Wilmington, N.C.; mustered out, June 15, 1865, at hospital, Division No. 2, Annapolis, Md., as Gillens.

GITTINGS, JAMES H.—Age, 19 years. Enlisted, August 11, 1862, at Waterford, to serve three years; mustered in as private, Co. H, August 18, 1862; captured in action, September 16, and paroled, September 16, 1862, at Harper's Ferry, Va.; promoted corporal, no date; wounded and captured in action, February 20,

1864 at Olustee, Fla.; died, August 25, 1864 at Andersonville, Ga., as Gettings.

GLADWIN, HAROLD.—Age, 18 years. Enlisted at Brooklyn, to serve one year, and mustered in as private, Co. C, February 28, 1865; transferred to Co. C, Forty-seventh Infantry, June 17, 1865.

GLEN, OSWALD.—Age, 18 years. Enlisted at Schenectady, to serve one year, and mustered in as private, Co. E, September 5, 1864; absent, sick at McDougall Hospital, New York Harbor, at muster-out of company.

GLOVER, WILLIAM E.—Age, 32 years. Enlisted, August 11, 1862, at Amsterdam, to serve three years; mustered in as private, Co. D, August 12, 1862; captured in action, September 15, and paroled, September 16 1862, at Harper's Ferry, Va.; wounded in action, February 20, 1864, at Olustee, Fla.; died, July 24, 1864, at hospital, Point of Rocks, Va., of wounds received in front of Petersburg, Va.

GOLDSMITH, MAX.—Age 25 years. Enlisted at Tompkinsville, to serve one year, and mustered in as private, Co. G, March 6, 1865; deserted, May 8, 1865, at Raleigh, N.C.

GONGLASS, LOUIS.—Age. 20 years. Enlisted at Tarrytown, to serve three years, and mustered in as private, Co. B, February 27, 1865; transferred to Co. B, Forty-seventh Infantry, June 17, 1865.

GOODBREAD, ALBERT.—Age, 16 years. Enlisted at Schenectady, to serve one year, and mustered in as private, Co. E, September 1, 1864; mustered out with company, June 17, 1865, at Raleigh, N.C.

GOODBREAD, CHAUNCEY.—Age, 21 years. Enlisted at Palatine, to serve three years, and mustered in as private, Co. I, August 2, 1862; captured in action, September 15, and paroled, September 16, 1862, at Harper's Ferry, Va.; mustered out with company, June 17, 1865, at Raleigh, N.C.

GOODBREAD, DANIEL T.—Age, 27 years. Enlisted, August 1, 1862, at Palatine, to serve three years; mustered in as private, Co. A, August 2, 1862; captured in action, September 15, and paroled, September 16, 1862, at Harper's Ferry, Va.; discharged for disability, March 23, 1863, at Albany, N.Y.

GOODEMOOT, DANIEL.—Age, 23 years. Enlisted, July 26, 1862, at Amsterdam, to serve three years; mustered in as private, Co. D, July 30, 1862; captured in action, September 15, and paroled, September 16, 1862, at Harper's Ferry, Va.; deserted October 4, 1862, at Chicago, Ill.; also borne as Goodamoot.

GOODRICH, FRED S.—Age, 26 years. Enlisted July 21, 1862 at Halfmoon to serve three years; mustered in as private Co. H, August 7, 1862; transferred to and promoted second lieutenant, Thirty-third United States Colored Troops, in 1864, as Frederick P. Commissioned not mustered first lieutenant June 7, 1865, with rank from same date, vice J. H. Clark resigned.

GOODRICH, HENRY.—Age, 24 years. Enlisted, August 11, 1862, at Canajoharie, to serve three years; mustered in as private, Co. B, August 13, 1862; captured in action, September 15, and paroled, September 16, 1862, at Harper's Ferry, Va.; killed, June 3, 1864, in the trenches at Cold Harbor, Va.

GOODRICH, LEWIS A.—Age, 20 years. Enlisted at Canajoharie, to serve three years, and mustered in as private, Co. B, August 13, 1862; captured in action, September 15, and paroled, September 16, 1862, at Harper's Ferry, Va.; wounded in action August 18, 1864, at Deep Bottom, Va.; mustered out June 28, 1865 at Smithville, N.C.

GOODRICH, MENZO D.—Age, 20 years. Enlisted, December 21, 1863, at Canajoharie, to serve three years; mustered in as private, Co. B, January 4, 1864; mustered out, June 7, 1865, at Norfolk, Va.

GOODSELL, LEWIS.—Age, 18 years. Enlisted at Goshen, to serve one year, and mustered in as private, Co. F, March 6, 1865; transferred to Co. F, Forty-seventh Infantry, June 17, 1865.

GORDON, SCHUYLER.—Age, 19 years. Enlisted, August 9, 1862, at Charleston, to serve three years; mustered in as corporal, Co. D, August 16, 1862; captured in action, September 15, and paroled, September 16, 1862, at Harper's Ferry, Va.; promoted sergeant, no date; wounded in action, August 14, 1864, at Strawberry Plains, Va.; mustered out with detachment, May 18, 1865, at White Hall Hospital, Philadelphia, Pa.

GORHAM, WILLIAM H.—Age, 25 years. Enlisted, July 21, 1862, at Halfmoon, to serve three years; mustered in as private, Co. H, August 7, 1862; captured in action, September 15, and paroled, September 16, 1862, at Harper's Ferry, Va.; promoted sergeant, no date; mustered out with company. June 17, 1865, at Raleigh, N.C.

GORR, HENRY.—Age, 44 years. Enlisted at Troy, to serve one year, and mustered in as private, Co. C, August 8, 1864; mustered out with detachment, June 9, 1865, at New Berne, N.C.

GOSSELIN, ZOTIQUE.—Age, 19 years. Enlisted at Schenectady, to serve three years and mustered in as private, Co. G, March 2, 1865; transferred to Co. G, Forty-seventh Infantry, June 17, 1865; also borne as Zatigue.

GOULD, ALFRED.—Age, 23 years. Enlisted, July 21, 1862, at Halfmoon, to serve three years; mustered in as sergeant, Co. H, August 1, 1862; captured in action, September 15, and paroled, September 16, 1862, at Harper's Ferry, Va.; mustered out with company, June 17, 1865, at Raleigh, N.C.

GOUSCHE, GUSTAVE.—Age, 25 years. Enlisted at Tompkinsville, to serve one year, and mustered in as private, Co. G, March 6, 1865; transferred to Co. F, Forty-seventh Infantry, June 17, 1865.

GOW, JOHN.—Age, 44 years. Enlisted at Mohawk, to serve three years, and mustered in as private, Co. A, August 6, 1862; captured in action, September 15, and paroled, September 16, 1862, at Harper's Ferry, Va.; died of remittent fever, July 8, 1863, at Hospital No. 3, Beaufort, S.C.

GRACY, JOHN.—Age, 45 years. Enlisted, October 21, 1863, at Poughkeepsie, to serve three years; mustered in as private, Co. F, October 31, 1863¹ wounded in action, February 20, 1864, at Olustee, Fla.; mustered out, June 6, 1865, at New Berne, N.C., as Gracey; also borne as Geary.

GRADWELL, RICHARD.—Age, 44 years. Enlisted at Tarrytown, to serve one year, and mustered in as private, Co. G, February 21, 1865; transferred to Co. G, Forty-seventh Infantry, June 17, 1865.

GRANNIS, JOHN D.—Age, 18 years. Enlisted at Goshen, to serve three years, and mustered in as private, Co. A, October 8, 1863; mustered out, June 17, 1865, at hospital, Fort Monroe, Va.

GRANT, CHARLES.—Age, 29 years. Enlisted at Brooklyn, to serve three years, and mustered in as private, Co. K, September 2, 1863; transferred to Navy, April 27, 1864.

GRANT, DANIEL.—Age, 18 years. Enlisted, July 31, 1862, at Amsterdam, to serve three years; mustered in as corporal, Co. D, August 2, 1862; captured in action, September 15, and paroled, September 16, 1862, at Harper's Ferry, Va.; wounded in action February 20, 1864 at Olustee, Fla.; returned to ranks, no date; discharged, April 30, 1965, at Raleigh, N.C.

GRAVES, DAVID H.—Age, 21 years. Enrolled, July 22, 1862, at Saratoga Springs, to serve three years; mustered in as sergeant, Co. G, July 31, 1862; promoted first sergeant, August 26. 1862; mustered in as second lieutenant, August 29, 1862, as first lieutenant, March 5, 1863; wounded in action, February 20, 1864, at Olustee, Fla., and at Petersburg, Va., in 1864; mustered in as captain, April 29, 1863; transferred to Co. B, Forty-seventh Infantry, June 17, 1865. Commissioned second lieutenant, October 31, 1862, with rank from August 30, 1862, vice G. H. Farrar promoted; first lieutenant, May 13, 1863, with rank from March 4, 1863, vice G. H. Farrar resigned: captain, June 17, 1865, with rank from April 29, 1865, vice F. B. Savage promoted.

GRAY, ANDREW.—Age, 25 years. Enlisted, August 25, 1862 at Minden to serve three years; mustered in as private, Co I, August 26, 1862; deserted, August 27, 1862, at Fonda, N.Y.

GRAY, LUMAN.—Age, 21 years. Enlisted, August 7, 1862, at Corinth, to serve three years; mustered in as private, Co. G August 19, 1862; captured in, action, September 15, and paroled, September 16, 1862, at Harper's Ferry, Va.; deserted December 25, 1862, at Pittsburgh, Pa.; also borne as Numan Grey.

GRAY, ROBERT.—Age, 37 years. Enlisted, July 28, 1862, at Minden, to serve three years; mustered in as private, Co. B, August 13, 1862; captured in action, September 15, and paroled, September 16, 1862, at Harper's Ferry, Va.; deserted, September 28, 1862, in the State of Ohio.

GREEN, FRANCIS.—Age, 22 years. Enlisted at Schenectady, to serve three years, and mustered in as private, Co. G, March 2, 1865; transferred to Co. G, Forty-seventh Infantry, June 17 1865.

GREEN, JAMES.—Age, 21 years. Enlisted, August 13, 1862, at Minden, to serve three years; mustered in as private Co. B, August 15, 1862; captured in action, September 15, and paroled, September 16, 1862, at Harper's Ferry, Va.; promoted corporal, January 6, 1864; wounded and captured in action, February 20, 1864, at Olustee, Fla.; paroled, no date; mustered out, May 22, 1865, at hospital, Annapolis, Md.

GREEN, LODOWICK S.—Age, 27 years. Enlisted, August 6, 1862, at Saratoga Spa, to serve three years; mustered in as private, Co. F, August 12, 1862; captured in action, September 15, and paroled, September 16, 1862, at Harper's Ferry, Va.; mustered out with company, June 17, 1865, at Raleigh, N.C.

GREER, JOHN.—Age, 22 years. Enlisted, August 5, 1862, at Milton, to serve three years; mustered in as private, Co. C, August 8, 1862; captured in action. September 15, and paroled, September 16, 1862, at Harper's Ferry, Va.; mustered out with company, June 17, 1865, at Raleigh, N.C.

GREGORY, THOMAS.—Age, 20 years. Enlisted at New York City, to serve three years, and mustered in as private, Co. D, October 28, 1863; transferred to Co. B, Forty-seventh Infantry, June 17, 1865.

GREY, JAMES.—Age, 33 years. Enlisted at Goshen, to serve three years, and mustered in as private, Co. F, October 28, 1863; wounded in action, February 20, 1864, at Olustee, Fla.; transferred to the Navy, April 27, 1864.

GRIPPEN, SIDNEY C.—Age, 18 years. Enlisted at Schenectady, to serve three years, and mustered in as private, Co. F, February 24, 1865; transferred to Co. K, Forty-seventh Infantry, June 17, 1865; also borne as Griffin.

GROESBECK, HARLEY.—Age, 18 years. Enlisted, August 7, 1862, at Milton, to serve three years; mustered in as private, Co. C, August 9, 1862; captured in action, September 15, and paroled, September 16, 1862, at Harper's Ferry, Va.; mustered out, June 25, 1865, at Smithville, N.C., as Harsley Groesbeck.

GROFF, DRULLA.—Age, 22 years. Enlisted, August 14, 1862, at Wells, to serve three years; mustered in as private, Co. K, August 16, 1862; captured in action, September 15, and paroled, September 16, 1862, at Harper's Ferry, Va.; wounded and captured in action, August 16, 1861, at Deep Bottom, Va.; paroled, no date; absent, sick, at Baltimore, Md., at muster-out of company as Dwella.

GROSS, CHARLES.—Age, 32 years. Enlisted, July 29, 1862, at Glen, to serve three years; mustered in as sergeant, Co. A, July 30, 1862; captured in action, September 15, and paroled, September 16, 1862, at Harper's Ferry, Va.; wounded in action, June 4, 1864, at Cold Harbor, Va.; died of his wounds, July 4, 1864, at Washington, D.C.

GROVES, GEORGE C.—Age, 27 years. Enlisted at Johnstown, to serve three years, and mustered in as private, Co. E, August 13, 1862; captured in action, September 15, and paroled, September 16, 1862, at Harper's Ferry, Va.; mustered out, June 6, 1863, at New Berne, N.C.; also borne as Graves.

HAGADONE, HARMON.—Age, 39 years. Enlisted, August 8, 1862, at Saratoga Springs, to serve three years; mustered in as corporal, Co. G, August 19, 1862; captured in action, September 15, and paroled, September 16, 1862, at Harper's Ferry, Va.; returned to ranks, October 13, 1862; wounded and captured in action, February 20, 1864, at Olustee, Fla.; paroled, December, 1864; mustered out with detachment, May 27, 1865, at Foster Hospital, New Berne N.C., as Hagadon; also borne as Hagedorn.

HAGADORNE, JOHN W.—Age 20 years. Enlisted December 31, 1863 at Canajoharie, to serve three years; mustered in as private, Co. I, January 4, 1864; transferred to Co. H, Forty-seventh Infantry, June 17, 1865.

HAGEDORN, GEORGE N.—Age, 18 years. Enlisted, August 12, 1862, at Saratoga Springs, to serve three years; mustered in as private, Co. G, August 19, 1862; captured in action, September 15, and paroled,

September 16, 1862, at Harper's Ferry, Va.; discharged for disability, December 14, 1863, at New York City, as George H. Hagadorn; also borne as Hagerdon and Hagidone.

HAIGHT, GRIFFIN.—Age, 18 years. Enlisted, July 31, 1862, at Saratoga Spa, to serve three years; mustered in as private Co. F, August 12, 1862; captured in action, September 15, and paroled, September 16, 1862, at Harper's Ferry, Va.; transferred to Veteran Reserve Corps. July 15, 1863.

HAIGHT, JOSEPH W.—Age, 44 years. Enlisted July 31, 1862, at Saratoga Springs to serve three years; mustered in as private, Co. G, August 5, 1862; captured in action, September 15, and paroled, September 16, 1862, at Harper's Ferry, Va.; transferred to Veteran Reserve Corps, March 8, 1864; also borne as Height.

HAINES, JACOB L.—Age, 32 years. Enrolled, August 12, 1862, at Mayfield, to serve three years; mustered in as first sergeant, Co. E, August 15, 1862; as first lieutenant, October 22, 1862; discharged, April 6, 1864, at Palatka, Fla.; prior service as first sergeant, Co. F, Seventh Cavalry. Commissioned first lieutenant, November 24, 1862, with rank from October 21, 1862, vice R. McDonald discharged.

HAIRE, THOMAS.—Age, 33 years. Enlisted at New York City, to serve three years, and mustered in as private, Co. G, October 30, 1863; wounded and missing in action, August 18, 1864, at Deep Bottom, Va.; no further record.

HALE, JOHN H.—Age, 18 years. Enlisted, August 14, 1862, at Johnstown, to serve three years; mustered in as musician, Co. E, August 16, 1862; captured in action, September 15, and paroled, September 16, 1862, at Harper's Ferry, Va.; again captured in action, August 16, 1864, at Deep Bottom, Va.; paroled, no date; mustered out with company, June 17, 1865, at Raleigh, N.C.

HALL, ABNER.—Age, 21 years. Enlisted, August 5, 1862, at Amsterdam, to serve three years; mustered in as private, Co. D, August 6, 1862; captured in action, September 15, and paroled, September 16, 1862, at Harper's Ferry, Va.; deserted, October 4, 1862, at Chicago, Ill.; apprehended December 5, 1863; transferred to Co. D, Forty-seventh Infantry, June 17, 1865.

HALL, ARCHIBALD.—Age 22 years. Enlisted at Schenectady, to serve three years; and mustered in as private, Co. D, August 22, 1864; transferred to Co. D, Forty-seventh Infantry, June 17, 1865.

HALL, CORNELIUS V.—Age, 22 years. Enlisted, August 12, 1862, at Mayfield, to serve three years, mustered in as private, Co. E, August 16, 1862; captured in action, September 15, and paroled, September 16, 1862, at Harper's Ferry, Va.; promoted corporal, August 31, 1863; wounded in action, February 20, 1864, at Olustee, Fla.; mustered out with company, June 17, 1865, at Raleigh, N.C.

HALL, JOHN.—Age, 23 years. Enlisted, August 11, 1862, at Johnstown, to serve three years; mustered in as private, Co. E, August 15, 1862; captured in action, September 15, and paroled, September 16, 1862, at Harper's Ferry, Va.; transferred to Veteran Reserve Corps, July 20, 1863.

HALPIN, JOHN.—Age, 18 years. Enlisted, August 11, 1862, at Waterford to serve three years; mustered in as private, Co. H, August 18, 1862; captured in action, September 15, and paroled, September 16, 1862, at Harper's Ferry, Va.; mustered out June 23, 1865, at Smithville, N.C.

HAM, EDGAR.—Age, 18 years. Enlisted, August 13, 1862, at Wilton, to serve three years; mustered in as private, Co. F, August 19, 1862; captured in action, September 15, and paroled, September 16, 1862, at Harper's Ferry, Va.; wounded in action, May 7, 1864, at Chester Station, Va.; mustered out with company, June 17, 1865, at Raleigh, N.C.; also borne as Ham.

HAMBLIN, AUGUSTUS A.—Age, 29 years. Enlisted at Amsterdam, to serve three years, and mustered in as private, Co. D, August 15, 1862; also borne as Gustavus A.; no further record.

HAMMOND, BENJAMIN.—Age, 19 years. Enlisted, August 9, 1862, at Broadalbin, to serve three years; mustered in as private, Co. K, August 12, 1862; captured in action, September 15, and paroled, September 16, 1862, at Harper's Ferry, Va.; promoted corporal, no date; absent, sick, at muster-out of company.

HANAHAN, PETER.—Age, 23 years. Enlisted at Johnstown, to serve three years, and mustered in as private, Co. K, August 25, 1862; captured in action, September 15, and paroled, September 16, 1862, at Harper's Ferry, Va.; deserted, April 8, 1864, at Annapolis, Md., as Hanmahan; also borne as Hanrahan.

HANDY, DAVID.—Age, 33 years. Enlisted, August 12, 1862, at St. Johnsville, to serve three years; mustered in as private, Co. B, August 14, 1862; captured in action, September 15, and paroled, September 16, 1862, at Harper's Ferry, Va.; discharged for disability, August 29, 1863.

HANLY, JOHN.—Age, 23 years. Enlisted at Brooklyn, to serve one year, and mustered in as private, Co. H, February 28, 1865; mustered out with detachment, June 8, 1865, at New Berne, N.C., as Hanley.

HANNA, JAMES A.—Age, 21 years. Enlisted at Milton, to serve three years, and mustered in as private, Co. C, August 11, 1862; captured in action, September 15, and paroled, September 16, 1862, at Harper's Ferry, Va.; killed in action, February 20, 1864, at Olustee, Fla.

HANNER, ALBON.—Age, 26 years. Enlisted, August 13, 1862, at Northampton, to serve three years; mustered in as private, Co. E, August 15, 1862; captured in action, September 15, and paroled, September 16, 1862, at Harper's Ferry, Va.; wounded in action, June, 1864, at Petersburg, Va.; promoted sergeant, February 8, 1865; mustered out with company, June 11, 1865, at Raleigh, N.C.

HANSEL, ANDREW.—Age, 19 years. Enlisted at Goshen, to serve one year, and mustered in as private, Co. F, March 6, 1865; transferred to Co. F, Forty-seventh Infantry, June 17, 1865.

HANSON, ABRAM.—Age, 21 years. Enlisted, August 5, 1862, at Minden, to serve three years; mustered in as private, Co. B, August 12, 1862; captured in action, September 15, and paroled, September 16, 1862, at Harper's Ferry, Va.; mustered out with company, June 17, 1865, at Raleigh, N.C.

HANSON, ABRAM D.—Age, 28 years. Enlisted at Amsterdam, to serve three years, and mustered in as private, Co. D, December 7, 1863; transferred to Co. A, no date; mustered out, June 9, 1865.

HANSON, JOHN.—Age, 21 years. Enlisted, August 4, 1862, at Amsterdam, to serve three years; mustered in as private, Co. D, August 9, 1862; captured in action, September 15, and paroled, September 16, 1862, at Harper's Ferry, Va.; mustered out with company, June 17, 1865, at Raleigh, N.C. as Hansow.

HANSON, STEPHEN C.—Age, 22 years. Enlisted at Stillwater, to serve three years, and mustered in as private, Co. H, August 16, 1862; captured in action, September 15, and paroled, September 16, 1862, at Harper's Ferry, Va.; transferred to Veteran Reserve Corps, no date; also borne as Harrison.

HANSON, WILLIAM.—Age, 18 years. Enlisted at Schenectady, to serve three years, and mustered in as private, Co. D, December 7, 1863; captured, March 31, 1865, near Magnolia, N.C.; paroled, no date; transferred to Co. B, Forty-seventh Infantry, June 17, 1865.

HANVEY, PATRICK.—Age, 22 years. Enlisted, August 15, 1862, at Minden, to serve three years; mustered in as private, Co. I, August 16, 1862; captured in action, September 15, and paroled, September 16, 1862, at Harper's Perry, Va.; deserted, October 12, 1862, at Chicago, Ill.

HARDELL, ADAM.—Age, 27 years. Enlisted at Brooklyn, to serve one year, and mustered in as private, Go. K, February 21, 1865; died, June 8, 1865, at Post Hospital, Raleigh, N.C.

HARDEN, PETER.—Age, 22 years. Enlisted in Eighteenth Congressional District, to serve three years, and mustered in as private, Co. C, April 25, 1864; mustered out, August 11, 1865, at New York City.

HARDY, JOHN.—Age, 20 years. Enlisted, August 9, 1862, at Saratoga Spa, to serve three years; mustered in as private Co. F, August 19, 1862; captured in action, September 15, and paroled, September 16, 1862, at Harper's Ferry, Va.; wounded in action, February 20, 1864, at Olustee, Fla.; mustered out with company, June 17, 1865, at Raleigh, N.C.

HARLOW, JAMES.—Age, 22 years. Enlisted at Albany, to serve one year, and mustered in as private, Co. F, May 30, 1864; mustered out with company, June 17, 1865, at Raleigh, N.C.

HARLOW, JOB J.—Age, 21 years. Enlisted, August 6, 1862, at Fort Plain, to serve three years; mustered in as private, Co. B, August 12, 1862; wounded in action, December, 1862, at Fredericksburg, Va. [sic]; promoted commissary sergeant, August 17, 1863; mustered out with regiment, June 17, 1865, at Raleigh, N.C.

HARLOW, SMITH.—Age, 18 years. Enlisted, August 8, 1862, at Milton, to serve three years; mustered in as private, Co. C, August 13, 1862; captured in action, September 15, and paroled, September 16, 1862, at Harper's Ferry, Va.; wounded in action, June, 1864, at Petersburg, Va.; discharged for wounds, January 5, 1865.

HARRINGTON, PHILIP.—Age, 39 years. Enlisted at Amsterdam, to serve three years, and mustered in as private, Co. A, April 14, 1864; mustered out, May 27. 1865, at hospital, Fort Monroe, Va.

HARRIS, SEYMOUR.—Age, 27 years. Enlisted, July 30, 1862, at Milton, to serve three years; mustered in as private, Co. C, August 8, 1862; captured in action, September 15, and paroled, September 16, 1862, at Harper's Ferry, Va.; deserted, December 26, 1862, at Alexandria, Va.

HARRISON, GEORGE B.—Age, 27 years. Enlisted, August 7, 1862, at North Hampton, to serve three years; mustered in as private, Co. E, August 15, 1862; captured in action, September 15, and paroled, September 16, 1862, at Harper's Ferry, Va.; promoted corporal, November 1, 1864; captured in action, January 15, 1865, at Fort Fisher, N.C.; paroled, no date; absent, sick in hospital, Albany N Y., at muster-out of company.

HARROWER, ISAAC.—Age, 22 years. Enlisted, July 30, 1862, at Amsterdam, to serve three years, mustered in as private, Co. D, August 11, 1862; captured in action, September 15, and paroled, September 16, 1862, at Harper's Ferry, Va.; died of chronic diarrhea, August 7, 1864, at hospital, Fort Monroe, Va.

HARROWER, JOHN B.—Age, 25 years. Enlisted, July 30, 1862, at Amsterdam, to serve three years; mustered in as private, Co. D, August 11, 1862; captured in action, September 15, and paroled, September 16, 1862, at Harpers Ferry, Va.; promoted corporal, November 18, 1862; returned to ranks, no date; discharged for disability, April 3, 1865, at Fort Schuyler, New York Harbor.

HART, HENRY C.—Age, 22 years. Enlisted, July 23, 1862, at Amsterdam; to serve three years; mustered in as private, Co. D, July 31, 1862; captured in action, September 15, and paroled, September 16, 1862, at Harper's Ferry, Va.; mustered out, June 8, 1865, at hospital, Fort Monroe, Va.

HART, JOHN.—Age, 22 years. Enlisted at Minden, to serve three years, and mustered in as private, Co. H, August 25, 1862; no further record.

HART, PHILANDER A.—Age, 23 years. Enlisted at Albany, to serve one year, and mustered in as private, Co. K, August 25, 1864; mustered out with company, June 17, 1865, at Raleigh, N.C.

HARTT, GEORGE.—Age, 40 years. Enlisted, July 27, 1862, at Glen, to serve three years; mustered in as private, Co. A, July 28, 1862; captured in action, September 15, and paroled, September 16, 1862, at Harper's Ferry, Va.; wounded and captured in action, February 20, 1864, at Olustee, Fla.; paroled and sent to Annapolis, Md., no dates; also borne as Hart; no further record.

HASSELL, HENRICH.—Age, 30 years. Enlisted at Brooklyn, to serve three years, and mustered in as private, Co. H, September 1, 1863; wounded in action, August 16, 1864, at Deep Bottom, Va.; transferred to Co. K, Forty-seventh Infantry, June 17, 1865; also borne as Henry Hessell.

HAYLOCK, HENRY.—Age, 23 years. Enlisted, August 13, 1862, at Halfmoon, to serve three years; mustered in as corporal, Co. H, August 14, 1862; captured in action, September 15, and paroled, September 16, 1862, at Harper's Ferry, Va.; discharged, July 4, 1863.

HAYNER, WESLEY.—Age, 26 years. Enlisted, August 11, 1862, at Clifton Park, to serve three years; mustered in as sergeant, Co. H, August 11, 1862; captured in action, September 15, and paroled, September 16, 1862, at Harper's Ferry, Va.; wounded in action, February 20, 1864, at Olustee, Fla.; discharged for disability, May 15, 1865, at hospital, Albany, N.Y., as Haynor.

HEATON, HENRY W.—Age, 21 years. Enrolled, August 2, 1862, at Charlton, to serve three years;

mustered in as corporal, Co. I, August 9, 1862; promoted sergeant-major, September 1, 1864; wounded in action, January 15, 1865, at Fort Fisher, N.C.; mustered in as second lieutenant, Co. C, April 1, 1865; mustered out with company, June 17, 1865, at Raleigh, N.C. Commissioned second lieutenant, May 17, 1865, with rank from February 1, 1865, vice J. W. Filkins discharged.

HEAVEY, THOMAS.—Age, 44 years. Enlisted at Amsterdam, to serve three years, and mustered in as private, Co. D, August 2, 1862; captured in action, September 15, and paroled, September 16, 1862, at Harper's Ferry, Va.; wounded in action, February 20, 1864, at Olustee, Fla.; mustered out, June 12, 1865, at McDougall Hospital, New York Harbor, as Havey.

HEDDES, FERDINAND.—Age, 25 years. Enlisted, August 30, 1863, at Tarrytown, to serve three years; mustered in as private, Co. K, October 30, 1863; discharged, July 29, 1864, at hospital, Philadelphia, Pa.

HEENAN, DENNIS.—Age, 30 years. Enlisted, July 30, 1862, at Saratoga Springs, to serve three years; mustered in as private, Co. G, August 5, 1862; deserted, August 30, 1862, at New York City, as Dennis C.; also borne as Henan.

HEISELMAN, LEONARD.—Age, 39 years. Enlisted at Brooklyn, to serve one year, and mustered in as private, Co. F, March 6, 1865; transferred to Co. F, Forty-seventh Infantry, June 17, 1865; also borne as Hieselman.

HEISSER, HENRY.—Age, 43 years. Enlisted at Glen, to serve three years, and mustered in as private, Co. A, July 25, 1862; captured in action, September 15, and paroled, September 16, 1862, at Harper's Ferry, Va.; wounded in action, June 30, 1864, in front of Petersburg, Va.; died of his wounds, July 28, 1864, at Hammond Hospital, Point Lookout, Md.; also borne as Haesar and Haiser.

HENDERSON, HUGH.—Age, 28 years. Enlisted at Poughkeepsie, to serve three years, and mustered in as private, Co. K, October 7, 1863; transferred to Co. H, Forty-seventh Infantry, June 17, 1865.

HENDRICKSON, ANTHONY.—Age, 28 years. Enlisted at New York City, to serve three years, and mustered in as private, Co. D, August 28, 1863; transferred to the Navy, May 2, 1864.

HENEGHAN, THOMAS.—Age, 21 years. Enlisted at Schenectady, to serve three years, and mustered in as private, Co. H, April 26, 1864; died of typhoid fever, September 2, 1864, at hospital, Fort Monroe, Va.

HENRY, THOMAS JAMES.—Age, 33 years. Enlisted, July 23, 1862, at Mohawk, to serve three years; mustered in as private. Co. A, July 24, 1862; captured in action, September 15, and paroled, September 16, 1862, at Harper's Ferry, Va.; wounded in action, February 20, 1864, at Olustee, Fla.; captured in action, August 16, 1864, at Deep Bottom, Va.; paroled, no date; mustered out with company, June 17, 1865, at Raleigh, N.C., as Thomas Henry, Jr.

HERMANCE, ALONZO.—Age, 19 years. Enlisted, August 2, 1862, at Galway, to serve three years; mustered in as private, Co. C, August 14, 1862; captured in action, September 15, and paroled, September 16, 1862, at Harper's Ferry, Va.; wounded in action, February 20, 1864, at Olustee, Fla.; mustered out with company, June 17, 1865, at Raleigh, N.C.

HERNAN, PATRICK.—Age, 44 years. Enlisted at New York City, to serve three years, and mustered in as private, Co. E, August 25, 1863; wounded in action, February 20, 1864, at Olustee, Fla.; deserted, March 13, 1864; also borne as Patrick Herman.

HERNE, JOHN A.—Second lieutenant, Co. B, Forty-third Infantry. Commissioned, not mustered, first lieutenant, December 10, 1864, with rank from same date, vice J. H. Clark discharged.

HERRICK, JOSEPH M.—Age, 19 years. Enlisted, August 5, 1862, at Edinburgh, to serve three years; mustered in as private, Co. C, August 8, 1862; captured in action, September 15, and paroled, September 16, 1862, at Harper's Ferry, Va.; wounded in action, August 16, 1864, at Deep Bottom, Va.; promoted corporal, no date; mustered out, June 26, 1865, at Albany, N.Y.

HERRITH, GEORGE.—Age, 28 years. Enlisted at Brooklyn, to serve three years, and mustered in as private, Co. A, February 23, 1865; transferred to Co. A, Forty-seventh Infantry, June 17, 1865.

HESS, WILLIAM S.—Age, 19 years. Enlisted at St. Johnsville, to serve three years, and mustered in as private, Co. B, August 11, 1862; captured in action, September 15, and paroled, September 16, 1862, at Harper's Ferry, Va.; mustered out with company, June 17, 1865. at Raleigh, N.C.

HEWIT, ELISHA.—Age, 27 years. Enlisted, August 6, 1862, at Saratoga Springs, to serve three years; mustered in as private, Co. G, August 9, 1862; captured in action, September 15, and paroled, September 16, 1862, at Harper's Ferry, Va.; discharged for disability, April 14, 1868, at New York City, as Hewett.

HICKEY, GEORGE J.—Age, 20 years. Enlisted, August 7, 1862, at Canajoharie to serve three years; mustered in as private, Co. B, August 12, 1862; captured in action, September 15, and paroled, September 16, 1862, at Harper's Ferry, Va.; wounded in action, June 4, 1864, at Cold Harbor, Va.; mustered out with detachment, May 11, 1865, at Albany, N.Y.

HICKEY, THOMAS.—Age, 20 years. Enlisted at Schenectady, to serve three years, and mustered in as private, Co. G, March 3, 1865; transferred to Co. E, Forty-seventh Infantry, June 17, 1865.

HICKOK, AMBROSE C.—Age, 21 years. Enlisted, August 6, 1862, at Corinth, to serve three years; mustered in as private, Co. F, August 19, 1862; captured in action, September 15, and paroled, September 16, 1862, at Harper's Ferry, Va.; promoted corporal, February 4, 1863; sergeant, April 29, 1864; transferred to Veteran Reserve Corps, September 16, 1864; mustered out with detachment, June 28, 1865, at Washington, D.C., as of Co. E, Fourteenth Regiment, Veteran Reserve Corps.

HICKS, DARWIN R.—Age, 21 years. Enlisted, July 30, 1862, at St. Johnsville, to serve three years; mustered in as musician, Co. B, August 2, 1862; captured in action, September 15, and paroled, September 16, 1862, at Harper's Ferry, Va.; mustered out with company, June 17, 1865, at Raleigh, N.C.

HICKS, JAMES W.—Age, 18 years. Enlisted at Halfmoon, to serve three years, and mustered in as private, Co. H, August 14, 1862; captured in action, September 15, and paroled, September 16, 1862, at Harper's

Ferry, Va.; died, February 2, 1863, at General Hospital; also borne as James H.

HIGGINS, JOHN W.—Age, 27 years. Enlisted, August 6, 1862, at St. Johnsville, to serve three years; mustered in as private, Co. B, August 7, 1862; captured in action, September 15, and paroled, September 16, 1862, at Harper's Ferry, Va.: mustered out June 17, 1865 at Wilmington, N.C.

HIGGINS, LAURENCE.—Age, 18 years. Enlisted, August 11, 1862, at Waterford, to serve three years; mustered in as private, Co. H, August 18, 1862; captured in action, September 15, and paroled, September 16, 1862, at Harper's Ferry, Va.; died, November 18, 1862, at hospital, Chicago, Ill., as Lawrence; also borne as Higins.

HILL, JAMES M.—Age, 26 years. Enrolled August 5, 1862, at Broadalbin, to serve three years; mustered in as sergeant, Co. K, August 12, 1862; promoted first sergeant, no date; mustered in as second lieutenant, May 23, 1863; transferred to Co. E, Forty-seventh Infantry, June 17, 1865, at Raleigh, N.C. Commissioned second lieutenant, November 25, 1863, with rank from May 22, 1863, vice F. H. Francisco promoted; first lieutenant, not mustered, May 17, 1863, with rank from February 1, 1865, vice F. D. Barnum promoted.

HILL, JOHN.—Age, 23 years. Enlisted, August 14, 1862, at Greenfield, to serve three years; mustered in as private, Co. G, August 18, 1862; captured in action. September 15, and paroled, September 16, 1862, at Harper's Ferry, Va.; promoted corporal, May 22, 1865; mustered out with company, June 17, 1865, at Raleigh, N.C.

HILL JOSIAH.—Age, 27 years. Enlisted, August 14, 1862, at Greenfield, to serve three years; mustered in as corporal, Co. G, August 18, 1862; captured in action, September 15, and paroled, September 16, 1862, at Harper's Ferry, Va.; deserted, September 30, 1862, at Chicago, Ill.

HILL, ORREN.—Age, 23 years. Enlisted, August 1, 1862, at Milton, to serve three years; mustered in as private, Co. C, August 11, 1862; captured in action, September 15, and paroled, September 16, 1862, at Harper's Ferry, Va.; mustered out with company, June 17, 1865, at Raleigh, N.C.

HILLABRANT, ALBERT.—Age, 22 years. Enlisted, August 11, 1862, at Johnstown, to serve three years; mustered in as private, Co. E, August 15, 1862; captured in action, September 15, and paroled, September 16, 1862, at Harper's Ferry, Va.; mustered out with company, June 17, 1865, at Raleigh, N.C.; also borne as Helibrant.

HILLE, WILLIAM.—Age, 18 years. Enlisted, August 6, 1862, at Caroga, to serve three years; mustered in as private, Co. K, August 12, 1862; captured in action, September 15, and paroled, September 16, 1862, at Harper's Ferry, Va.; absent, sick in hospital, Davids Island, New York Harbor, at muster-out of company; also borne as Hillie.

HILTON, HENRY.—Age, 25 years. Enlisted, August 9, 1862, at Charlton to serve three years; mustered in as corporal, Co. D, August 15, 1862; captured in action, September 15, and paroled, September 16, 1862, at Harper's Ferry, Va.; discharged for disability, January 1, 1863, near Alexandria, Va.

HILTON, JOHN.—Age, 21 years. Enlisted, August 11, 1862, at Johnstown, to serve three years; mustered in as private, Co. E, August 18, 1862; captured in action, September 15, and paroled, September 16, 1862, at Harper's Ferry, Va.; mustered out with detachment, June 23, 1865, at Albany, N.Y.

HILTON, WILLIAM.—Age, 18 years. Enlisted at Glen, to serve three years, and mustered in as private, Co. A, July 30, 1862; captured in action, September 15, and paroled, September 16, 1862, at Harper's Ferry, Va.; promoted sergeant, no date; mustered out with company, June 17, 1865, at Raleigh, N.C.

HIMES, JAMES K. P.—Age, 18 years. Enlisted, July 22, 1862, at Halfmoon, to serve three years; mustered in as private, Co. H, August 1, 1862; captured in action, September 15, and paroled, September 16, 1862, at Harper's Ferry, Va.; wounded in action, February 20, 1864, at Olustee, Fla.; promoted corporal, no date; killed in action, August 16, 1864. at Deep Bottom, Va.

HINCKLE, FRANCIS.—Age, 19 years. Enlisted at New York City, to serve three years, and mustered in as private, Co. A, February 27, 1865; transferred to Co. A, Forty-seventh Infantry, June 17, 1865; also borne as Hinkle.

HINCKLEY, ADOLPHUS W.—Age, 34 years. Enlisted at New York City, to serve three years, and mustered in as private, Co. A, February 27, 1865; transferred to Co. A, Forty-seventh Infantry, June 17, 1865; also borne as Hinkley.

HINMAN, BENJAMIN.—Age 18 years. Enlisted at Brooklyn, to serve one year, and mustered in as private, Co. H, February 28, 1865; transferred to Co. K, Forty-seventh Infantry, June 17, 1865; also borne as Hineman.

HINNAN, ALBERT.—Age, 21 years. Enlisted, August 6, 1862. at Amsterdam, to serve three years; mustered in as private, Co. D, August 11, 1862; captured in action, September 15, and paroled, September 16, 1862, at Harper's Ferry, Va.; mustered out with company, June 17, 1865, at Raleigh, N.C., as Inman.

HOAG, GEORGE T.—Age, 19 years. Enlisted at Halfmoon, to serve three years, and mustered in as corporal, Co. H, August 8, 1862; promoted first sergeant, no date; wounded in action, January 15, 1865, at Fort Fisher, N.C.; mustered out with company, June 17, 1863, at Raleigh, N.C. Commissioned, not mustered, second lieutenant, June 27, 1865, with rank from April 29, 1863, vice C. L. Clark promoted.

HODGES, TIMOTHY.—Age, 38 years. Enlisted, August 9, 1862, at Moreau, to serve three years; mustered in as corporal, Co. F, August 19, 1862; captured in action, September 15, and paroled, September 16, 1862, at Harper's Ferry, Va.; discharged for disability, April 24, 1863.

HODGES, WILLIAM.—Age, 18 years. Enlisted at Brooklyn, to serve one year, and mustered in as private, Co. K, February 23, 1865; transferred to Co. I, Forty-seventh Infantry, June 17, 1865.

HOFFMAN, CHARLES W.—Age, 18 years. Enlisted, August 1, 1864, at Schenectady, to serve three years; mustered in as private, Co. I, August 4, 1864; transferred to Co. H, Forty-seventh Infantry, June 17, 1865.

HOFFMAN, GERMANUS.—Age, 28 years. Enlisted

at Tarrytown, to serve three years, and mustered in as private, Co. G, October 28, 1863; wounded in action, no date; discharged for wounds, May 1, 1864.

HOGAN, JOHN.—Age, 26 years. Enlisted at Mohawk, to serve three years, and mustered in as private, Co. A, July 26, 1862; captured in action, September 15, and paroled, September 16, 1862, at Harper's Ferry, Va.; wounded in action, February 20, 1864, at Olustee, Fla.; killed in action, July 13, 1864, in front of Petersburg, Va.

HOGAN, JOHN A.—Age, 21 years. Enlisted, August 11, 1862, at Waterford, to serve three years; mustered in as corporal, Co. H, August 18, 1862; captured in action, September 15, and paroled, September 16, 1862, at Harper's Ferry, Va.; deserted, October 16, 1862, at Chicago, Ill.

HOGG, PETER.—Age, 22 years. Enlisted at Goshen, to serve three years, and mustered in as private, Co. G, March 6, 1865; mustered out, July 27, 1865, at Lovell Hospital, Portsmouth Grove, R. I.

HOLDEN, JOHN.—Age, 38 years. Enlisted at New York City, to serve three years, and mustered in as private, Co. D, August 28, 1863; transferred to Co. B, Forty-seventh Infantry, June 17, 1865.

HOLLETT, JAMES F.—Age, 28 years. Enlisted at Johnstown, to serve three years, and mustered in as private, Co. E, August 13, 1862; captured in action, September 15, and paroled, September 16, 1862, at Harper's Ferry, Va.; promoted corporal, February 11, 1863; mustered out with company, June 17, 1865, at Raleigh, N.C., as Hollett.

HOLLETT, JOHN H.—Age, 27 years. Enlisted at Schenectady, to serve one year, and mustered in as private, Co. E, September 5, 1864; promoted corporal, no date; wounded in action, February 20, 1864, at Olustee, Fla.; returned to ranks, no date; mustered out with company, June 17, 1865, at Raleigh, N.C.

HOLLIDAY, WILLIAM R.—Age, 38 years. Enlisted at Johnstown, to serve three years, and mustered in as private, Co. E, August 11, 1862; captured in action, September 15, and paroled, September 16, 1862, at Harper's Ferry, Va.; discharged for disability, January 22, 1863, at Yorktown, Va.

HOLZNER, JOHN.—Age, 40 years. Enlisted at Glen, to serve three years, and mustered in as private, Co. A, August 6, 1862; captured in action, September 15, and paroled, September 16, 1862, at Harper's Ferry, Va.; died of sunstroke, July 31, 1864, at Deep Bottom, Va., as Halzner.

HOMKEY, WILLIAM.—Age, 21 years. Enlisted at St. Johnsville, to serve three years, and mustered in as private, Co. B, August 5, 1862; captured in action, September 15, and paroled, September 16, 1862, at Harper's Ferry, Va.; wounded in action, January 15, 1865, at Fort Fisher, N.C.; mustered out, June 25, 1865, at hospital, Fort Monroe, Va.; also borne as Hompkey.

HONEYWELL, GRANDES G.—Age, 19 years. Enlisted, August 12, 1862, at Broadalbin, to serve three years; mustered in as private, Co. K, August 10, 1862; captured in action, September 15, and paroled, September 16, 1862, at Harper's Ferry, Va.; mustered out with company, June 17, 1865, at Raleigh, N.C., as Grodus G.; also borne as Grote Honeywell.

HONEYWELL, WILLIAM H.—Age, 22 years. Enlisted, August 12, 1862, at Broadalbin, to serve three years; mustered in as private, Co. K, August 16, 1862; captured in action, September 15, and paroled, September 16, 1862, at Harper's Ferry, Va.; deserted, September 20, 1862, at Chicago, Ill.

HOPKINS, DAVID A.—Age, 29 years. Enlisted, August 7, 1862, at Greenfield, to serve three years; mustered in as private, Co. F, August 12, 1862; captured in action, September and paroled, September 16, 1862, at Harper's Ferry, Va.; deserted, November 22, 1862, at Cleveland, O.

HORAN, JOHN T.—Age, 21 years. Enlisted at Brooklyn, to serve one year, and mustered in as private, Co. H, February 28, 1865; promoted corporal, May 1, 1865; transferred to Co. G, Forty-seventh Infantry, June 17, 1865.

HORNING, JOHN.—Age, 33 years. Enlisted at Mohawk, to serve three years, and mustered in as private, Co. A, July 25, 1862; captured in action, September 15, and paroled, September 16, 1862, at Harper's Ferry, Va.; deserted, October 16, 1862, at Chicago, Ill.

HORNING, SILAS W.—Age, 18 years. Enlisted, July 24, 1862, at Glen, to serve three years; mustered in as corporal, Co. A, July 25, 1862; captured in action, September 15, and paroled, September 16, 1862, at Harper's Ferry, Va.; wounded in action, August 18, 1864, at Deep Bottom, Va.; discharged for disability, September 22, 1864, at David's Island, New York Harbor.

HORTON, THOMAS R.—Age, 40 years. Enrolled at Fonda, to serve three years, and mustered in as first lieutenant and adjutant, July 19, 1862; discharged for disability, February 18, 1863. Commissioned first lieutenant and adjutant, September 10, 1862, with rank from July 19, 1862, original.

HOSE, HENRY.—Age, 18 years. Enlisted, July 31, 1862, at St. Johnsville, to serve three years; mustered in as private, Co. B, October 28, 1862; wounded in action, February 20, 1864, at Olustee, Fla.; mustered out with company, June 17, 1865, at Raleigh, N.C.

HOSLEY, EMERY W.—Age, 19 years. Enlisted, August 5, 1862, at Edinburgh, to serve three years; mustered hi as private, Co. C, August 8, 1862; captured in action, September 15, and paroled, September 16, 1862, at Harper's Ferry, Va.; died of fever, October 23, 1862, at General Hospital.

HOUGHTALING, GEORGE A.—Age, 22 years. Enlisted, July 28, 1862, at Halfmoon, to serve three years; mustered in as private, Co. H, August 1, 1862; captured in action, September 15, and paroled, September 16, 1862, at Harper's Ferry, Va.; wounded in action, February 20, 1864, at Olustee, Fla.; captured in action, August 16, 1864, at Deep Bottom, Va.; paroled, no date; absent, in Cottage Green Barracks, Md., at muster out of company.

HOUGHTON, JOHN H.—Age, 21 years. Enlisted, August 12, 1862, at Saratoga Springs, to serve three years, mustered in as private, Co. G, August 19, 1862; captured in action, September 15, and paroled, September 16, 1862, at Harper's Ferry, Va.; killed in action, May 14, 1864, at Proctor's Creek, Va.

HOUSE, JAMES I.—Age, 34 years. Enlisted, August 12, 1862, at Waterford, to serve three years; mustered in as private, Co. H, August 18, 1862; captured in action, September 15, and paroled, September 16, 1862, at Harper's Ferry, Va.; died, November 4, 1862, at hospital, Chicago, Ill.

HOUSINGER, BAKER.—Age, 41 years. Enlisted, August 12, 1862, at Waterford, to serve three years; mustered in as private, Co. H, August 18, 1862; captured in action, September 15, and paroled, September 16, 1862, at Harper's Ferry, Va.; discharged for disability, at Beaufort, S.C., no date.

HOWARD, GEORGE.—Age, 36 years. Enlisted at Brooklyn, to serve one year, and mustered in as private, Co. H, February 28, 1865; mustered out with detachment, June 8, 1865, at New Borne, N.C.

HOWE, WENDELL B.—Age, 19 years. Enlisted, August 8, 1862, at Day, to serve three years; mustered in as private, Co. C, August 14, 1862; captured in action, September 15, and paroled, September 16, 1862, at Harper's Ferry, Va.; wounded in action, February 20, 1864, at Olustee, Fla.; killed in action, July 22, 1864, before Petersburg, Va.

HOWLAND, JAMES.—Age, 18 years. Enlisted at Schenectady, to serve three years, and mustered in as private, Co. H, April 15, 1864; transferred to Co. K, Forty-seventh Infantry, June 17, 1865.

HOYLE, NATHAN.—Age, 29 years. Enlisted, June 23, 1864 at New York Harbor, to serve three years; mustered in as private, Co. G, July 12, 1864; wounded, July, 1864, before Petersburg, Va.; transferred to Co. F, Forty-seventh Infantry, June17, 1865; also borne as Nathan W.

HOYT, GEORGE.—Age, 21 years. Enlisted, August 4, 1862, at Canajoharie, to serve three years; mustered in as private, Co. B, August 11, 1862; captured in action, September 15, and paroled, September 16, 1862, at Harper's Ferry, Va.; wounded in action, February 20, 1864, at Olustee, Fla.; absent since and at muster-out of company; also borne as Hoit.

HOYT, JAMES A.—Age, 21 years. Enlisted, August 6, 1862, at Charlton, to serve three years; mustered in as corporal, Co. I, August 7, 1862; captured in action, September 15, and paroled, September 16, 1862, at Harper's Ferry, Va.; discharged for disability, no date.

HUBBARD, JOHN A.—Age, 20 years. Enlisted at Mohawk, to serve three years, and mustered in as corporal, Co. A, August 12, 1862; wounded and captured in action, September 15, and paroled, September 16, 1862, at Harper's Ferry, Va.; discharged for disability, December 30, 1862, at Baltimore, Md.

HUBIS, NARCIA.—Age, 39 rears. Enlisted at Tarrytown, to serve three years, and mustered in as private, Co. B, October 29, 1863; wounded in action, February 20, 1864, at Olustee, Fla., and May 16, 1864, at Drewry's Bluff, Va.; mustered out, June 25, 1865, at hospital, Fort Monroe, Va., as Narcia H. Ribas.

HUGHES, JAMES.—Age, 20 years. Enlisted at Kingston, to serve one year, and mustered in as private, Co. G, March 6, 1865; deserted, April 7, 1805, at Magnolia, N.C.

HULSAVER, CHRISTOPHER.—Age, 20 years. Enlisted at Troy, to serve three years, and mustered in as private, Co. B, January 14, 1865; transferred to Co. B, Forty-seventh Infantry, June 17, 1865; also borne as Christopher C. Hulsifer.

HUMPHREY, MINOR R.—Age, 19 years. Enlisted, August 12, 1862, at Charleston, to serve three years; mustered in as private, Co. D, August 15, 1862; captured in action, September 15, and paroled, September 16, 1862 at Harper's Ferry, Va.; discharged, June 25, 1863, as Mynor J.; also borne as Minan I.

HUNGERFORD, SAMUEL L.—Age, 18 years. Enlisted, August 6, 1862, at Minden, to serve three years; mustered in as private, Co. B, August 11, 1862; captured in action, September 15, and paroled, September 16, 1862, at Harper's Ferry, Va.; discharged for disability, November 11, 1863.

HUNT, MICHAEL.—Age, 19 years. Enlisted at Schenectady, to serve three years, and mustered in as private, Co. G, March 4, 1865; deserted, April 7, 1865, at Magnolia, N.C.

HUNTER, JAMES.—Age, 24 years. Enlisted at Albany, to serve three years, and mustered in as private, Co. K, October 29, 1863; wounded in action, February 20, 1864, at Olustee, Fla.; discharged, July 30, 1864, at hospital, Beaufort, S.C.

HUNTER, JOHN.—Age, 27 years. Enlisted at Albany, to serve three years, and mustered in as private, Co. F, October 28, 1863; transferred to the Navy, April 27, 1864.

HUNTER, JOHN J.—Age, 23 years. Enlisted, August 6, 1862, at Galway, to serve three years; mustered in as private, Co. C, August 12, 1862; captured in action, September 15, and paroled, September 16, 1862, at Harper's Ferry, Va.; mustered out while in Sickel hospital. Alexandria. Va., August 12, 1865, at Washington, D.C.

HURD, JR., SAMUEL.—Age, 25 years. Enlisted, August 6, 1862, at Caroga, to serve three years; mustered in as musician, Co. K, August 12, 1862; captured in action, September 15, and paroled, September 16, 1862, at Harper's Ferry, Va.; mustered out with company, June 17, 1865, at Raleigh, N.C.

HURLEY, JAMES.—Age, 21 years. Enlisted at Goshen, to serve three years, and mustered in as private, Co. F, October 7, 1863; wounded in action, May 16, 1864, at Drewry's Bluff, Va.; transferred to Co. K, Forty-seventh Infantry, June 17, 1865.

HUTCHINGS, WILLIAM L.—Age, 18 years. Enlisted at Schenectady, to serve one year, and mustered in as private, Co. B, April 6, 1865; transferred to Co. C, Forty-seventh Infantry, June 17, 1865.

HUTCHINSON, JOHN W.—Age, 25 years. Enlisted, August 8 1862, at Edinburgh, to serve three years; mustered in as private, Co. C, August 14, 1862; captured in action, September 15, and paroled, September 16, 1862, at Harper's Ferry, Va.; died of fever, August 30, 1863, at Regimental Hospital, Beaufort, S.C.

HUTCHKINS, FREDERICK.—Age, 35 years. Enlisted August 11, 1862, at Amsterdam, to serve three years; mustered in as private, Co. D, August 13, 1862; captured in action, September 15, and paroled, September 16, 1862, at Harper's Ferry, Va., discharged, February 13, 1865, at Elmira, N.Y., as Frederick A. Hutchins.

HUTTERMARKS, BENJAMIN.—Age, 23 years. Enlisted at Schenectady, to serve one year, and mustered in as private, Co. F, September 13, 1864; mustered out with company, June 17, 1865, at Raleigh, N.C.

HYDE, BENJAMIN B.—Age, 44 years. Enlisted, August 1, 1862, at Saratoga Springs, to serve three years; mustered in as private, Co. G, August 5, 1862; captured in action, September 15, and paroled, September 16, 1862, at Harper's Ferry, Va.; discharged for disability, October 21, 1862, at Chicago, Ill.

IDE, DANIEL B.—Age, 30 years. Enlisted, August 7, 1862, at Corinth, to serve three years; mustered in as corporal, Co. F, August 19, 1862; captured in action, September 15, and paroled, September 16, 1862, at Harper's Ferry, Va.; discharged for disability, November 7, 1862, at Chicago, Ill.

IDE, GILBERT C.—Age, 21 years. Enlisted, August 7, 1862, at Corinth, to serve three years; mustered in as private, Co. F, August 19, 1862; captured in action, September 15, and paroled, September 16, 1862, at Harper's Ferry, Va.; promoted corporal, January 20, 1863; sergeant, November 1, 1864; mustered out, June 23, 1865, at Albany, N.Y.

IDE, NATHAN M.—Age, 25 years. Enlisted, August 2, 1862, at Corinth, to serve three years; mustered in as sergeant, Co. F, August 12, 1862; captured in action, September 15, and paroled, September 10, 1862, at Harper's Ferry, Va.; killed in action, October 27, 1864, at Darbytown Road, Va.

INGERSON, HIRAM H.—Age, 27 years. Enrolled, July 19, 1862, at Fonda, to serve three years; mustered in as assistant surgeon, August 19, 1862; discharged for disability, October 25, 1863. Commissioned assistant surgeon, September 10, 1862, with rank from July 19, 1862, original.

IRISH, ISAAC V.—Age, 43 years. Enlisted, August 13, 1862, at Halfmoon, to serve three years; mustered in as private, Co. H, August 14, 1862; captured in action, September 15, and paroled, September 16, 1862, at Harper's Ferry, Va.; absent, sick in hospital, near Troy, N.Y., at muster-out of company.

JACKSON, MARTIN.—Age, 21 years. Enlisted at Tarrytown, to serve three years, and mustered in as private, Co. K, October 30, 1863; transferred to the Navy, April 27, 1864.

JACOBY, JAMES R.—Age, 31 years. Enlisted, August 6, 1862, at Ephratah, to serve three years; mustered in as private, Co. E August 7, 1862; wounded and captured in action, September 15, and paroled, September 16, 1862, at Harper's Ferry, Va.; wounded in action August 16, 1864, at Deep Bottom, Va., and January 15, 1865, at Fort Fisher, N.C.; mustered out, June 7, 1865, at hospital, Fort Monroe, Va.

JAMES, JOHN F.—Age, 32 years. Enlisted, August 13, 1862, at Northampton, to serve three years; mustered in as private, Co. E, August 15, 1862; captured in action, September 15, and paroled, September 16, 1862, at Harper's Ferry, Va.; deserted, October 2, 1862.

JEANDREAW, PETER.—Age, 21 years. Enlisted at Albany to serve three years, and mustered in as private Co. F, October 28, 1863; killed in action, February 20, 1864 at Olustee, Fla.; also borne as Jeandreau.

JENKINS, CHARLES W.—Age, 18 years. Enlisted, August 8, 1862, at Edinburgh, to serve three years; mustered in as private, Co. C, August 14, 1862; captured in action, September 15, and paroled, September 16, 1862, at Harper's Ferry, Va.; wounded in action, May 7, 1864, at Chester Station, Va.; promoted corporal, May 1, 1865; mustered out with company, June 17, 1865, at Raleigh, N.C.

JENNINGS, MICHAEL.—Age, 26 years. Enlisted, July 30, 1862, at Saratoga Springs, to serve three years; mustered in as private, Co. G, August 19, 1862; captured in action, September 15, and paroled, September 16, 1862, at Harper's Ferry, Va.; deserted, January 7, 1863, from Hospital, at New York City.

JENNINGS, WILLIAM J.—Age, 39 years. Enlisted, August 7, 1862, at Milton, to serve three years; mustered in as sergeant, Co. C, August 8, 1862; wounded in action, October 27, 1864, at Darbytown Road, Va.; mustered out, June 24, 1865, at hospital, Fort Monroe, Va. Commissioned, not mustered, second lieutenant, December 9, 1864, with rank from November 4, 1864, vice G. H. Curreen promoted.

JERMAIN, JAMES.—Age, 23 years. Enlisted, August 11, 1862, at Milton, to serve three years; mustered in as private, Co. I, August 12, 1862; captured in action, September 15, and paroled, September 16, 1862, at Harper's Ferry, Va.; wounded and captured in action, February 20, 1864, at Olustee, Fla.; died, August 27, 1864, at Andersonville, Ga.

JEWELL, GEORGE W.—Age, 37 years. Enlisted, August 8, 1862, at Caroga, to serve three years; mustered in as private, Co. K, August 26, 1862; captured in action, September 15, and paroled, September 16, 1862, at Harper's Ferry, Va.; wounded in action, May 14, 1864, at Drewry's Bluff, Va.; absent since and at muster out of company.

JOHNS, JOSEPH.—Age, 22 years. Enlisted at Tarrytown, to serve three years, and mustered in as private, Co. D, October 27, 1863; wounded in action, February 20, 1864, at Olustee, Fla.; transferred to the Navy, May 2, 1864.

JOHNSON, AARON.—Age, 18 years. Enlisted, August 11, 1862, at Johnstown, to serve three years; mustered in as private, Co. E, August 19, 1862; captured in action, September 15, and paroled, September 16, 1862, at Harper's Ferry, Va.; wounded in action, February 20, 1864, at Olustee, Fla.; mustered out with company, June 17, 1865, at Raleigh, N.C.

JOHNSON, CHARLES W.—Age, 31 years. Enlisted at Brooklyn, to serve three years, and mustered in as private, Co. K, September 1, 1863; wounded in action, February 20, 1864, at Olustee, Fla.; mustered out, May 27, 1865, at Norfolk, Va.

JOHNSON, DAVID E.—Age, 24 years. Enlisted, July 21, 1862, at Saratoga Springs, to serve three years; mustered in as sergeant, Co. G, July 31, 1862; captured in action, September 15, and paroled, September 16, 1862, at Harper's Ferry, Va.; discharged for disability, January 20, 1863, at Annapolis, Md.

JOHNSON, ENOCH P.—Age, 20 years. Enlisted, August 3, 1862, at Saratoga Springs, to serve three years; mustered in as private, Co. G, August 5, 1862; captured in action, September 15, and paroled, September 16, 1862, at Harper's Ferry, Va.; wounded in action, February 20, 1864, at Olustee, Fla.; transferred to the Navy, April 27, 1864.

JOHNSON, HENRY.—Age, 42 years. Enlisted at Tarrytown, to serve three years, and mustered in as private, Co. I, October 30, 1863; wounded and captured in action, February 20, 1864, at Olustee, Fla.; died, August 17, 1864. at Andersonville, Ga.

JOHNSON, JR., JEPTHA.—Age, 18 years. Enlisted, July 24, 1862, at Saratoga Springs, to serve three years; mustered in as private, Co. G, July 31, 1862; captured in action, September 15, and paroled, September 16, 1862, at Harper's Ferry, Va.; wounded in action, February 20, 1864, at Olustee, Fla.; mustered out, June 6, 1865, at Albany, N.Y.

JOHNSON, LEWIS.—Age, 18 years. Enlisted in Eighteenth Congressional District, to serve three years, and mustered in as private, Co. C, February 27, 1865; transferred to Co. C, Forty-seventh Infantry, June 17, 1865; also borne as Johnston.

JOHNSON, NATHAN J.—Captain Co. I, Ninety-third Infantry; mustered in as lieutenant-colonel, this regiment, April 15, 1864; wounded in action, August 18, 1864, at Deep Bottom, Va.; October 1, 1864. at Chaffin's Farm, Va.; January 15, 1865, at Fort Fisher, N.C.; mustered in as colonel April 29, 1865; mustered out June 17, 1865, with regiment at Raleigh, N.C. Commissioned lieutenant colonel, March 30, 1864, with rank from November 13, 1863, vice G. S. Batcheller honorably discharged; colonel, June 17, 1865, with rank from April 29, 1865, vice S. Sammons discharged.

JOHNSON, SANDERS.—Age 23 years. Enlisted at Ephratah to serve three years, and mustered in as private, Co. E, August 18, 1862; captured in action, September 15, and paroled, September 16, 1862, at Harper's Ferry, Va.; wounded in action, August 16, 1864, at Deep Bottom, Va.; died of his wounds August 26, 1864, at hospital, Annapolis, Md.

JOHNSON, STEPHEN A.—Age, 23 years. Enlisted, August 14, 1862, at Northampton, to serve three years; mustered in as private, Co. E, August 16, 1862; captured in action, September 15, and paroled, September 16, 1862, at Harper's Ferry, Va.; wounded in action, June 3, 1864, and died of his wounds June 5, 1864, at Cold Harbor, Va.

JOHNSON, THOMAS.—Age, 20 years. Enlisted at Albany, to serve three years, and mustered in as private, Co. F, October 28, 1863; transferred to Co. K, Forty-seventh Infantry, June 17, 1865; also borne as Johnston.

JONES, CHARLES.—Age, 24 years. Enlisted at Jamaica, to serve three years, and mustered in as private, Co. I, February 13, 1865; transferred to Co. H, Forty-seventh Infantry, June 17, 1865.

JONES, DAVID W.—Age, 18 years. Enlisted, August 6, 1862, at Edinburgh, to serve three years; mustered in as private, Co. C, August 8, 1862; captured in action, September 15, and paroled, September 16, 1862, at Harper's Ferry, Va.; wounded and captured in action, August 16, 1864, at Deep Bottom, Va.; no further record.

JONES, GEORGE.—Age, 23 years. Enlisted at New York City, to serve three years, and mustered in as private, Co. G, March 6, 1863; deserted, May 2, 1865, at Raleigh, N.C.

JONES, GEORGE S.—Age, 18 years. Enlisted at Mohawk, to serve three years, and mustered in as private, Co. K, August 26, 1862; captured in action, September 15 and paroled September 16, 1862, at Harper's Ferry, Va.; discharged, December 26, 1862, at Washington, D.C.

JONES, HENRY F.—Age, 21 years. Enlisted, August 8, 1862, at Greenfield, to serve three years; mustered in as private, Co. C, August 11, 1862; captured in action, September 15, and paroled, September 16, 1862, at Harper's Ferry, Va.; wounded in action, February 20, 1864, at Olustee, Fla.; discharged, May 12, 1865, at Albany, N.Y.

JONES, ISAAC.—Age, 23 years. Enlisted at New York City, to serve three years, and mustered in as private, Co. I, August 25, 1863; died at hospital, Hilton Head, S.C., no date.

JONES, LEWIS.—Age, 22 years. Enlisted, August 8, 1862, at Greenfield, to serve three years; mustered in as private, Co. C, August 11, 1862; captured in action, September 15, and paroled, September 16, 1862, at Harper's Ferry, Va.; wounded in action, February 20, 1864, at Olustee, Fla.; died of his wounds, at hospital, Albany, N.Y., no date.

JONES, WILLIAM.—Age, 31 years. Enlisted at Schenectady, to serve three years, and mustered in as private, Co. G, March 3, 1865; deserted, May 3, 1865, at Raleigh, N.C.

JORDON, BERNARD.—Age, 36 years. Enlisted at Albany, to serve three years, and mustered in as private, Co. B, March 30, 1865; transferred to Co. C, Forty-seventh Infantry, June 17, 1865; also borne as Jordan.

JOYCE, PATRICK.—Age, 23 years. Enlisted, August 6, 1862, at Palatine, to serve three years; mustered in as private, Co. A, August 7, 1862; captured in action, September 15, and paroled, September 16, 1862, at Harper's Ferry, Va.; wounded in action, July, 1864, at Petersburg, Va.; transferred to Co. G, Tenth Regiment, Veteran Reserve Corps, January 16, 1865; mustered out with detachment, June 28, 1865, at Washington, D.C.

KABENGGACKER, FRANZ.—Age, 29 years. Enlisted at New York City, to serve three years, and mustered in as private, Co. D, February 21, 1865; transferred to Co. B, Forty-seventh Infantry, June 17, 1865; also borne as Kabbanggacker.

KAISER, JOHN.—Age, 40 years. Enlisted in Ninth Congressional District, to serve three years, and mustered in as private, Co. A, August 27, 1863; killed in action, September 27, 1864, at Chaffin's Farm, Va.

KAITEN, JOHN.—Age, 18 years. Enlisted in Eighteenth Congressional District, to serve three years, and mustered in as private, Co. C, February 25, 1865; transferred to Co. F, Forty-seventh Infantry, June 17, 1865.

KANE, HENRY.—Age, 42 years. Enlisted, August 5, 1862, at Palatine, to serve three years; mustered in as private, Co. I, August 26, 1862; captured in action, September 15, and paroled September 16, 1862, at Harper's Ferry, Va.; mustered out, May 27, 1865, at Foster Hospital, New Berne, N.C.

KANE, WILLIAM H.—Age, 21 years. Enlisted, August 12, 1862, at Malta to serve three years; mustered in as corporal, Co. I, August 14, 1862; captured in action, September 15, and paroled, September 16, 1862, at Harper's Ferry, Va.; wounded in action, August 16, 1864 at Deep Bottom, Va. died of his wounds, September 16, 1864, at hospital, Beverly, N.J.

KECK, ANDREW.—Age, 29 years. Enlisted at Oppenheim, to serve three years, and mustered in as private, Co. F, August 15, 1862; wounded and captured in action, September 15, and paroled, September 16, 1862, at Harper's Ferry, Va.; mustered. out with detachment, May 11, 1865, at Albany, N.Y.

KECK, PETER J.—Age, 23 years. Enlisted, August 14, 1862, at Oppenheim, to serve three years; mustered in as corporal, Co. E, August 15, 1862; captured September 15 and paroled September 16, 1862, at Harper's Ferry, Va.; promoted sergeant, December 1, 1863; wounded in action at Olustee, Fla., February 20, 1864; at Chesterfield Heights, May 7, 1864; at Deep Bottom, Va., August 16, 1804, and Fort Fisher, N.C., January 15, 1865; mustered out with company, June 17, 1865, at Raleigh, N.C. Commissioned, not mustered, first lieutenant, June 17, 1865, with rank from April 29, 1865, vice J. A. Herne not mustered.

KECK, WILLIAM H. H.—Age, 22 years. Enlisted, August 14, 1862, at Oppenheim, to serve three years; mustered in as private, Co. E, August 16, 1862; captured in action, September 15, and paroled, September 16, 1862, at Harper's Ferry, Va.; discharged for disability, February 12, 1863, at Fairfax, Va.

KEENHOLTS, CHRISTOPHER F.—Age, 44 years. Enlisted at Milton, to serve three years, and mustered in as private, Co. C, August 8, 1862; captured in action, September 15, and paroled, September 16, 1862, at Harper's Ferry, Va.; wounded in action, May 7, 1864, at Chester Station, Va.; died of his wounds, June 17, 1864, at hospital, Hampton, Va.

KEIDERLING, HENRY.—Age, 37 years. Enlisted, August 20, 1862, at Glen, to serve three years; mustered in as private, Co. A, August 22, 1862; captured in action, September 15, and paroled, September 16, 1862, at Harper's Ferry, Va.; absent on furlough since May 5, 1865, and at muster-out of company, as Keyderling.

KEIM, FREDERICK.—Age 33 years. Enlisted at Tarrytown, to serve three years, and mustered in as private, Co. F, August 25, 1863; wounded and captured in action, February 20, 1864, at Olustee, Fla.; transferred to Co. K, Forty-seventh Infantry, June 17, 1865; also borne as Kevin.

KEINER, FREDERICK W.—Age, 25 years. Enlisted at Palatine, to serve three years, and mustered in as private, Co. I, August 21, 1862; captured in action, September 15, and paroled, September 16, 1862, at Harper's Ferry, Va.; promoted corporal, no date; mustered out with company, June 17, 1865, at Raleigh, N.C.

KELLEY, PATRICK.—Age, 42 years. Enlisted, August 9, 1862, at Clifton Park, to serve three years; mustered in as private, Co. H, August 14, 1862; captured in action, September 15, and paroled, September 16, 1862, at Harper's Ferry, Va.; discharged, August 29, 1863.

KELLEY, R. B.—Age, 20 years. Enlisted August 15, 1862, at Ballston, to serve three years; mustered in as private Co. I, August 26, 1862; captured in action, September 15, and, paroled, September 16, 1862, at Harper's Ferry, Va.; wounded in action, February 20, 1864, at Olustee, Fla., mustered out with company, June 17, 1865, at Raleigh, as Robert B. Kelly.

KELLOGG, CHARLES F.—Age, 21 years. Enlisted, August 11,1862, at Charleston, to serve three years; mustered in as private, Co. D, August 15, 1862; captured in action, September 15, and paroled, September 16, 1862, at Harper's Ferry, Va.; died of fever, December 16, 1802, at Alexandria, Va.

KELLOGG, WILLIAM H.—Age, 24 years. Enlisted, August 11, 1862, at Charleston, to serve three years; mustered in as private, Co. H, August 15, 1862; transferred to Co. D, no date; captured in action, September 15, and paroled, September 16, 1862, at Harper's Ferry, Va.; wounded in action, February 20, 1864, at Olustee, Fla.; promoted corporal, no date; mustered out with company, June 17, 1863, at Raleigh, N.C., as Kelly.

KELLY, JOHN.—Age, 22 years. Enlisted, August 4, 1862, at Canajoharie, to serve three years; mustered in as private Co. I, August 14, 1862; captured in action, September 15, and paroled, September 16, 1862, at Harper's Ferry, Va.; deserted, October 31, 1862, at Chicago, Ill.

KELLY, MICHAEL.—Age, 42 years. Enlisted at Brooklyn, to serve three years, and mustered in as private, Co. G, August 31, 1863; wounded in action, June 24, 1864, before Petersburg, Va.; died, August 29, 1864, at hospital, Fort Monroe, Va.

KEMP, OSCAR.—Age 21 years. Enlisted at Milton, to serve three years, and mustered in as private, Co. C, August 11, 1862; captured in action, September 15, and paroled, September 16, 1862, at Harper's Ferry, Va.; mustered out, May 30, 1865, at hospital, Petersburg, Va.

KENDALL, DANIEL W.—Age, 18 years. Enlisted, August 9, 1862, at Saratoga Springs, to serve three years; mustered in as corporal, Co. G, August 19, 1862; captured in action, September 15, and paroled, September 16, 1862, at Harper's Ferry, Va.; discharged for disability, April 9, 1863, at Albany, N.Y.

KENNEDY, HUGH.—Age, 23 years. Enlisted at Tarrytown, to serve three years, and mustered in as private, Co. F, August 25, 1863; wounded in action, February 20, 1864, at Olustee, Fla.; transferred to the Navy, April 27, 1864.

KENNEDY, JOHN.—Age, 23 years. Enlisted, July 22, 1862, at Saratoga Springs, to serve three years; mustered in as private, Co. G, July 31, 1862; captured in action, September 15, and paroled, September 16, 1862, at Harper's Ferry, Va.; transferred to Co. K, Tenth Regiment, Veteran Reserve Corps, October 22, 1863; re-transferred to this company and regiment, February 6, 1864; wounded in action, May 7, 1864, at Chester Station, Va.; discharged for wounds, at Washington, D.C., no date.

KENNICUTT, JACOB.—Age, 22 years. Enlisted at Schenectady, to serve one year, and mustered in as private, Co. D, September 3, 1864; absent, sick in hospital, at Fort Monroe, Va., at muster-out of company; also borne as Philip.

KEOCHNER, THEODORE.—Age, 24 years. Enlisted at Troy, to serve three years, and, mustered in as private, Co. A, May 18, 1864; captured in action., August 16, 1864, at Deep Bottom, Va.; paroled, no date; mustered out, June 29, 1865, at Wilmington, N.C.

KEYDERLING, JOHN.—Age, 32 years. Enlisted at Glen to serve three years, and mustered in as private, Co. A, July 25, 1862; captured in action, September 15, paroled September 16, 1862 at Harper's Ferry, Va.;

mustered out June 6, 1865, at hospital, Fort Monroe, Va., as Kaiser.

KEYSER, JOHN.—Private, Co. K, Forty-eighth Infantry; transferred to Co. D, this regiment, January 3, 1864; mustered out, June 8, 1865, at hospital, Fort Monroe, Va., as Kaiser.

KILCOIN, MICHAEL.—Age, 20 years. Enlisted at Schenectady, to serve three years, and mustered in as private, Co. H, April 19, 1864; discharged, April 23, 1865.

KILMER, CORNELIUS.—Age, 19 years. Enlisted at Kingston, to serve one year, and mustered in as private, Co. I, February 25, 1863; transferred to Co. H, Forty-seventh Infantry, June 17, 1865.

KILMER, MARTIN V. B.—Age, 24 years. Enlisted at Kingston, to serve three years, and mustered in as private, Co. I, February 28, 1865; transferred to Co. H, Forty-seventh Infantry, June 17, 1865.

KING, SAMUEL.—Age, 21 years. Enlisted, August 16, 1862, at Providence, to serve three years; mustered in as private, Co. I, August 18, 1862; captured in action, September 15, and paroled September 16, 1862, at Harper's Ferry, Va.; wounded in action, February 20, 1864, at Olustee, Fla.; mustered out with detachment, May 12, 1865, at Albany, N.Y.

KINNEY, PATRICK.—Age, 18 years. Enlisted at New York City, to serve two years, and mustered in as private, Co. C, February 27, 1865; transferred to Co. E, Forty-seventh Infantry, June 17, 1865; also borne as Kenny.

KINNICUTT, GEORGE W.—Age, 29 years. Enlisted at Schenectady, to serve one year, and mustered in as private, Co. E, September 3, 1864; wounded in action, January 15, 1865, at Fort Fisher, N.C.; mustered out, May 26, 1865, at Albany,

KINNICUTT, PHILIP.—Age, 19 years. Enlisted at Schenectady, to serve one year, and mustered in as private, Co. E, September 3, 1864; wounded in action, September 29, 1864, at Chaffin's Farm, Va.; absent since, and at muster out of company.

KINSLER, JACOB.—Age, 44 years. Enlisted, at Goshen, to serve one year, and mustered in as private, Co. F, February 21, 1865; mustered out, May 27, 1865, at hospital, New Berne, N, C.

KIRK, HENRY V.—Age, 23 years. Enlisted, July 29, 1862, at Mohawk, to serve three years; mustered in as private, Co. I, August 26, 1862; captured in action, September 15, and paroled September 16, 1862, at Harper's Ferry, Va.; promoted sergeant, no date; mustered out with company, June 17, 1865, at Raleigh, N.C.

KIRKHAM, AMBROSE W.—Age, 29 years. Enlisted, August 14, 1862, at Glen, to serve three years; mustered in as private, Co. A, August 18, 1862; captured in action, September 15, and paroled, September 16, 1862, at Harper's Ferry, Va.; wounded and captured in action, February 20, 1864, at Olustee, Fla.; paroled, no date; discharged for disability, May 20, 1865, at Chester, Pa.

KIRKWOOD, STEPHEN.—Age, 26 years. Enlisted, August 8, 1862 at Mayfield to serve three years; mustered in as private, Co. E, August 15, 1862; captured in action September 15, and paroled September 16, 1862, at Harper's Ferry, Va.; mustered out with company, June 17, 1865, at Raleigh, N.C.

KIRSH, FRANCIS.—Age, 23 years. Enlisted at Palatine, to serve three years, and mustered in as private, Co. K, August 22, 1862; captured in action, September 15, and paroled, September 16, 1862, at Harper's Ferry, Va.; died of fever, June 21, 1863, at Hilton Head, S.C.

KITTLE, DAVID M.—Age, 27 years. Enrolled at Fonda, to serve three years, and mustered in as first lieutenant, Co. I, August 26, 1862; as captain, January 27, 1864; wounded in action, at Chesterfield Heights, May 7, 1864; discharged for disability, October 22, 1864. Commissioned first lieutenant, September 10, 1862, with rank from August 20, 1862, original; captain, April 22, 1864, with rank from January 27, 1864, vice E. L. Walrath promoted.

KITTS, ROBERT.—Age, 22 years. Enlisted, July 29, 1862, at Canajoharie, to serve three years; mustered in as private, Co. B, August 2, 1862; captured in action, September 15, and paroled, September 16, 1862, at Harper's Ferry, Va.; discharged for disability, August 29, 1863.

KLEE, CHARLES.—Age, 42 years. Enlisted at Brooklyn, to serve three years, mustered in as private, Co. K, February 22, 1865; mustered out with detachment, May 31, 1865, at Poster Hospital, New Borne, N.C.

KLINE, CHARLES.—Age, 22 years. Enrolled, July 24, 1862, at Amsterdam, to serve three years; mustered in as sergeant, Co. D, July 30, 1862; promoted first sergeant, no date; wounded in action, September 29, 1864, at Chaffin's Farm, Va.; mustered in as second lieutenant, November 19, 1864; mustered out with company, June 17, 1865, at Raleigh, N.C. Commissioned second lieutenant, November 19, 1864, with rank from October 8, 1864, vice N. De Graft promoted; first lieutenant, not mustered, May 17, 1865, with rank from February 1, 1865, vice S. H. Olney resigned.

KLINE, GEORGE.—Age, 20 years. Enlisted, July 26, 1862, at Amsterdam, to serve three years; mustered in as private, Co.. D, July 30, 1862; captured in action September 15, and paroled, September 16, 1862, at Harper's Ferry, Va.; promoted corporal, no date; wounded in action, February 20, 1864, at Olustee, Fla., and August 16, 1864, at Deep Bottom, Va.; promoted sergeant, no date; mustered out with company, June 17, 1865, at Raleigh, N.C.

KNATCH, THEODORE.—Age, 27 years. Enlisted at New York City, to serve one year, and mustered in as private, Co. A February 27, 1865; transferred to Co. A, Forty-seventh Infantry, June 17, 1865; also borne as Kuatch.

KNEESKERN, JOHN P.—Age, __ years. Enrolled, August 20, 1862, at Fonda, to serve three years; mustered in as captain, Co. B, August 21, 1862; wounded in action, January 15, 1865, at Fort Fisher, N.C.; mustered out with company, June 17, 1865, at Raleigh, N.C. Commissioned captain, September 10, 1862, with rank from August 20, 1862, original.

KNIGHT, RANSOM.—Age, 33 years. Enlisted, August 13, 1862, at Ballston, to serve three years; mustered in as private, Co. I, August 15, 1862; captured in action, September 15, and paroled, September 16, 1862, at Harper's Ferry, Va.; died, April 20, 1865, at hospital, Wilmington, N.C., as Rensselaer Knight.

KOEHLER, JOHN ADAM.—Age, 25 years. Enlisted, August 6, 1862, at Minden, to serve three years; mustered in as private, Co. B, August 7, 1862; captured in action, September 15, and paroled September 16, 1862, at Harper's Ferry, Va.; wounded in action, October 27, 1864, at Darbytown Road, Va.; mustered out, May 27, 1865, at hospital, Fort Monroe, Va.; also borne as Kolhner.

KONIGS, JULIUS B.—Age, 19 years. Enlisted at Brooklyn, to serve three years, and mustered in as private, Co. A, October 2, 1863; discharged, November 23, 1864, for promotion to first lieutenant in Seventeenth U. S. Colored Troops.

KORBAR, JOHN.—Age, 30 years. Enlisted at Tarrytown, to serve three years, and mustered in as private, Co. G, October 28, 1863; killed in action, February 20, 1864, at Olustee, Fla.

KORSCHEFSKY, ALEXANDER.—Age, 44 years. Enlisted, August 19, 1862, at Canajoharie, to serve three years; mustered in as private, Co. I, August 20, 1862; captured in action, September 15, and paroled, September 16, 1862, at Harper's Ferry, Va.; died, July, 1864, at hospital, New York City; also borne as Kershuskey.

KROUSE, THEODORE.—Age, 22 years. Enlisted at Tarrytown, to serve three years, and mustered in as private, Co. A, October 27, 1863; discharged for disability, February 5, 1864.

LACY, JOHN.—Age, 19 years. Enlisted at Tarrytown, to serve one year, and mustered in as private, Co. G, March 6, 1865; transferred to Co. G, Forty-seventh Infantry, June 17, 1865.

LADAN, BERNARD.—Age, 18 years. Enlisted at Brooklyn, to serve one year, and mustered in as private, Co. F, March 6, 1865; transferred to Co. F, Forty-seventh Infantry, June 17, 1865.

LAINEGER, ALEXANDER.—Age, 30 years. Enlisted August 20, 1862 at Glen to serve three years; mustered in as private, Co. A, August 22, 1862; captured in action, September 15, and paroled, September 16, 1862, at Harper's Ferry, Va.; wounded in action, June 18, 1864, at Petersburg, Va.; discharged for disability, April 3, 1865, at Rochester, N.Y., as Lanegar; also borne as Lenegar.

LAINEGER SOLOMON.—Age, 32 years. Enlisted, August 20, 1862, at Glen, to serve three years; mustered in as private, Co. A, August 22, 1862; captured in action, September 15, and paroled, September 16, 1862, at Harper's Ferry, Va.; wounded, June, 1864, at Bermuda Hundred, Va.; discharged for disability, November 5, 1864, at Elmira, N.Y., as Lanegar; also borne as Lenegar.

LAKE, JOSHUA.—Age, 25 years. Enlisted, August 11, 1862, at Johnstown, to serve three years; mustered in as private, Co. E, August 13, 1862; captured in action, September 15, and paroled, September 16, 1862, at Harper's Ferry, Va.; wounded in action, January 15, 1865, at Fort Fisher, N.C.; mustered out with company, June 17, 1865, at Raleigh, N.C.

LAKE, WILLIAM W.—Age, 19 years. Enlisted at Canajoharie, to serve three years, and mustered in as private, Co. B, August 13, 1862; captured in action, September 15, and paroled, September 16, 1862, at Harper's Ferry, Va.; wounded in action, February 20, 1864, at Olustee, Fla.; absent, wounded, since May 14, 1865, and at muster-out of company.

LAMB, CHARLES.—Age, 39 years. Enlisted, August 6, 1862, at Caroga, to serve three years; mustered in as private, Co. K, August 12, 1862; captured in action, September 15, and paroled, September 16, 1862, at Harper's Ferry, Va.; wounded in action, January 16, 1865, at Fort Fisher, N.C.; died of his wounds, January 21, 1865.

LAMB, FRANKLIN E.—Age, 18 years. Enlisted, August 11, 1862, at Caroga, to serve three years; mustered in as private, Co. K, August 12, 1862; captured in action, September 15, and paroled, September 16, 1862, at Harper's Ferry, Va.; wounded and captured in action, August 16, 1864, at Deep Bottom, Va.; paroled, no date; mustered out, July 10, 1865, at Lovel Hospital, Portsmouth Grove, R.I.

LAMPMAN, PETER B.—Age, 33 years. Enlisted at St. Johnsville, to serve three years, and mustered in as private, Co. B, August 6, 1862; captured in action, September 15, and paroled, September 16, 1862, at Harper's Ferry, Va.; transferred to Veteran Reserve Corps, January 31, 1864; discharged with detachment as corporal, July 3, 1865, at Lytle Barracks, Cincinnati, Ohio, as of Co. I, Sixth Regiment Veteran Reserve Corps.

LAMPMAN, WILLIAM H.—Age, 18 years. Enlisted at St. Johnsville, to serve three years, and mustered in as private, Co. B, August 8, 1862; captured in action, September 15, and paroled, September 16, 1862, at Harper's Ferry, Va.; mustered out with company, June 17, 1865, at Raleigh, N.C.

LANCASTER, JOSEPH.—Age, 20 years. Enlisted at Goshen, to serve three years, and mustered in as private, Co. A, October 7, 1863; wounded in action, February 20, 1864, at Olustee, Fla., and August 16, 1864, at Deep Bottom, Va.; transferred to Co. A, Forty-seventh Infantry, June 17, 1865.

LANDT, WILLIAM N.—Age, 29 years. Enlisted, August 11, 1862, at Glen, to serve three years; mustered in as private, Co. A, October 28, 1862; died in the winter of 1864-65, at General Hospital.

LANEGAR, ABRAM H.—Age, 25 years. Enlisted at Glen, to serve three years, and mustered in as private, Co. A, July 26, 1862; captured in action, September 15, and paroled, September 16, 1862, at Harper's Ferry, Va.; deserted, September 26, 1862, at Harrisburg, Pa.

LANEGAR, IRA.—Age, 22 years. Enlisted, August 15, 1862, at Glen to serve three years; mustered in as private, Co. A, August 16, 1862; captured in action, September 15, and paroled, September 16, 1862, at Harper's Ferry, Va.; deserted, September 26, 1862 at Harrisburg, Pa.

LANEGAR, JACOB.—Age, 17 years. Enlisted at Schenectady to serve one year, and mustered in as private, Co. A, September 7, 1864, mustered out, June 22, 1865, at Jarvis Hospital, Baltimore, Md.; also borne as Lenager.

LANEGAR, JOHN A.—Age, 24 years. Enlisted at Glen, to serve three years, and mustered in as private, Co. A, July 29, 1862; captured in action, September 15, and paroled, September 16, 1862, at Harper's Ferry, Va.; killed in action, February 20, 1864, at Olustee, Fla.

LANEGAR, PETER.—Age 41 years. Enlisted at Glen, to serve three years, and mustered in as private, Co. A, July 28, 1862; captured in action, September 15, and paroled, September 16, 1862, at Harper's Ferry, Va.; killed, January 16, 1865, by explosion of magazine at Fort Fisher, N.C.

LANG, WILLIAM.—Age, 25 years. Enlisted at Tarrytown, to serve three years, and mustered in as private, Co. G, October 28, 1863; deserted, March 12, 1864, at Palatka, Fla.

LAPIUS, JOHN H.—Age, 19 years. Enlisted, August 2, 1862, at Clifton Park, to serve three years; mustered in as private, Co. H, August 6, 1862; captured in action, September 15, and paroled, September 16, 1862, at Harper's Ferry, Va.; promoted corporal, May 1, 1865; mustered out with company, June 17, 1865, at Raleigh, N.C.

LAPPE, CHARLES G.—Age, 36 years. Enlisted at Minden to serve three years, and mustered in as private, Co B, August 11, 1862; captured in action, September 15, and paroled September 16, 1862, at Harper's Ferry, Va.; wounded in action, August 16, 1864, at Deep Bottom, Va.; mustered out, June 21, 1865, at Elmira, N.Y.

LAROSE, JOSEPH.—Age, 33 years. Enlisted, August 11, 1862, at Saratoga Springs, to serve three years; mustered in as private, Co. G, August 18, 1862; captured in action, September 15, and paroled, September 16, 1862, at Harper's Ferry, Va.; discharged for disability, May 9, 1863, at Hilton Head, S.C., as Laross.

LARRIE, JOHN.—Age, 31 years. Enlisted at Brooklyn, to serve three years, and mustered in as private, Co. K, September 2, 1863; wounded, no date; mustered out, May 18, 1865, at McDougall hospital, New York Harbor.

LASCH, GOTTLIEB.—Age, 23 years. Enlisted at New York City, to serve three years, and mustered in as private, Co. G, August 28, 1863; wounded, August, 1864; discharged, to date, December 15, 1864; also borne as Losch.

LASHER, AMENZO.—Age, 21 years. Enlisted, August 5, 1862 at Palatine, to serve three years; mustered in as private, Co. A, August 26, 1862; captured in action, September 15, and paroled, September 16, 1862, at Harper's Ferry, Va.; deserted, December 26, 1862, at Alexandria, Va.

LASHER, JOHN.—Age, 20 years. Enlisted at Palatine, to serve three years, and mustered in as private, Co. A, August 18, 1862.; captured in action, September 15, and paroled, September 16, 1862, at Harper's Ferry, Va.; wounded and captured in action, February 20, 1864, at Olustee, Fla.; paroled, no date; absent in General Hospital, Chestnut Hill, Philadelphia, Pa., at muster-out of company.

LASHER, PETER.—Age, 40 years. Enlisted, August 16, 1862, at Providence, to serve three years; mustered in as private, Co. I, August 18, 1862; captured in action, September 15, and paroled, September 16, 1862, at Harper's Ferry, Va.; died, September 28, 1864, at General Hospital, City Point, Va.

LASHER, WILLIAM J.—Age, 21 years. Enlisted, July 30, 1862, at St. Johnsville, to serve three years; mustered in as first sergeant, Co. B, August 11, 1862; captured in action, September 15, and paroled, September 16, 1862, at Harper's Ferry, Va.; discharged for disability, May 9, 1863.

LAYTON, NATHAN.—Age, 23 years. Enlisted at Palatine, to serve three years, and mustered in as private, Co. K, August 26, 1862; captured in action, September 15, and paroled, September 16, 1862, at Harper's Ferry, Va.; mustered out, May 18, 1865, as Nathan J.

LEE, ALEXANDER.—Age, 18 years. Enlisted, August 12, 1862, at Saratoga Springs, to serve three years; mustered in as private, Co. G, August 18, 1862; captured in action, September 15, and paroled, September 16, 1862, at Harper's Ferry, Va.; wounded in action, February 20, 1864, at Olustee, Fla.; promoted corporal, March 1, 1864; mustered out with company, June 17, 1863, at Raleigh, N.C., as Alexander A.

LEE, ELI D. M.—Age, 22 years. Enlisted at Ephratah, to serve three years, and mustered in as private, Co. E, August 7, 1862; captured in action, September 15, and paroled, September 16, 1862, at Harper's Ferry, Va.; promoted corporal, December 1, 1862; wounded and captured in action, August 16, 1864, at Deep Bottom, Va.; paroled, no date; mustered out with detachment, May 23, 1865, at Mower Hospital, Philadelphia, Pa.

LEE, JAMES A.—Age, 18 years. Enlisted, August 9, 1862, at Saratoga Springs, to serve three years; mustered in as private, Co. G, August 18, 1862; captured in action, September 15, and paroled, September 16, 1862, at Harper's Ferry, Va.; mustered out with company, June 17, 1865, at Raleigh, N.C.

LEE, JOHN E.—Age, 18 years. Enlisted at Rome, to serve three years, and mustered in as private, Co. E, January 11, 1864; mustered out, June 7, 1865, at Satterlee Hospital, Philadelphia, Pa.

LEE, WHITNEY A.—Age, 18 years. Enlisted at Ephratah, to serve three years, and mustered in as private, Co. A; July 30, 1862; captured in action, September 15, and paroled, September 16, 1862, at Harper's Ferry, Va.; wounded in action, May 7, 1864, at Chester Heights, Va.; discharged for disability, June 15, 1865.

LEE, WILLIAM.—Age, 20 years. Enlisted at Albany, to serve three years, and mustered in as private, Co. F, October 28, 1863; wounded in action, February 20, 1864, at Olustee, Fla. transferred to the Navy, April 27, 1864.

LENART, JOSEPH.—Age, 33 years. Enlisted at New York City, to serve three years, and mustered in as private, Co. D, February 28, 1865; transferred to Co. B, Forty-seventh Infantry, June 17, 1865; also borne as Joseph Leonard.

LEPPER, THOMAS.—Age 20 years. Enlisted, July 23, 1862 at Amsterdam, to serve three years; mustered in as private, Co. D, August 1, 1862; captured in action, September 15, and paroled, September 16, 1862, at Harper's Ferry, Va.; wounded in action, February 20, 1864, at Olustee, Fla.; mustered out with company, June 17, 1865, at Raleigh, N.C.

LEROY, FRANCIS.—Age, 32 years. Enlisted, August 6, 1862, at Saratoga Spa, to serve three years; mustered in as private, Co. F, August 12, 1862; promoted corporal, no date; captured in action, September 15, and paroled, September 16, 1862, at Harper's Ferry, Va.; deserted, October 29, 1862, at Chicago,. Ill.

LEVERE, LOUIS.—Age, 20 years. Enlisted at Brooklyn to serve three years, and mustered in as private, Co. K, February 21, 1865; transferred to Co. I, Forty-seventh Infantry, June 17, 1865; also borne as Lievere and Lieure.

LEVINESS, JAMES.—Age, 21 years. Enlisted at Brooklyn to serve three years, and mustered in as private, Co. G, September 2, 1863; wounded in action, February 20, 1864, at Olustee, Fla.; wounded and missing in action July 7, 1864 at Chester Heights, Va.; no further record.

LEWIS, BENJAMIN.—Age 25 years. Enlisted at New York City, to serve three years, and mustered in as private, Co. D, February 28, 1865; transferred to, Co. D, Forty-seventh Infantry, June 17, 1865.

LEWIS, JOHN.—Age, 37 years. Enlisted at Palatine, to serve three years, and mustered in as private, Co. A, August 15, 1862; captured in action, September 15, and paroled, September 16, 1862, at Harper's Ferry, Va.; mustered out with company, June 17, 1865, at Raleigh. N.C.

LEWIS, NICHOLAS B.—Age, 27 years. Enlisted, August 11, 1862, at Canajoharie, to serve three years; mustered in as private, Co. I, August 16, 1862; no further record.

LIEBY, FREDERICK.—Age, 24 years. Enlisted at Brooklyn, to serve three years and mustered in as private, Co. G, March 11, 1865; transferred to Co. E, Forty-seventh infantry, June 17, 1865; also borne as Libby.

LIGHTHALL, OLIVER.—Age, 28 years. Enlisted, August 11, 1862, at Root, to serve three years; mustered in as private, Co. A, August 12, 1862; captured in action, September 15, and paroled September 16, 1862, at Harper's Ferry, Va.; wounded in action, May 7, 1864, at Chester Heights, Va.; promoted corporal, no date; sergeant, April 1, 1865; mustered out with company, June 17, 1865, at Raleigh, N.C.

LIMER, FRANK.—Age, 27 years. Enlisted, August 11, 1862, at Caroga, to serve three years; mustered in as private, Co. K, August 12, 1862; captured in action, September 15, and paroled September 16, 1862, at Harper's Ferry, Va.; promoted corporal, no date; mustered out with company, June 17, 1865, at Raleigh, N.C., as Lymer.

LINCOLN, SIDNEY.—Age, 20 years. Enlisted, August 8, 1862, at Greenfield, to serve three years; mustered in as private, Co. C, August 11, 1862; captured in action, September 15, and paroled September 16, 1862, at Harper's Ferry, Va.; wounded in action, February 20, 1864, at Olustee, Fla.; died of his wounds, February 22, 1864, at hospital, Jackson, Fla.; also borne as Sidney D.

LINGENFELTER, LEVI.—Age, 22 years. Enlisted, July 23, 1862, at Amsterdam, to serve three years; mustered in as corporal, Co. D, July 30, 1862; captured in action, September 15, and paroled, September 16, 1862, at Harper's Ferry, Va.; promoted sergeant, no date; killed in action, February 20, 1864, at Olustee, Fla.

LINGENFELTER, SIDNEY D.—Enrolled at Amsterdam, to serve three years, and mustered in as captain, Co. D, August 20, 1862; discharged for disability, October 8, 1864. Commissioned captain, September 10, 1862, with rank from August 20, 1862, original.

LINGHAM, JAMES.—Age, 38 years. Enlisted at Albany, to serve three years, and mustered in as private, Co. F, October 28, 1863; wounded in action, February 20, 1864, at Olustee, Fla.; transferred to the Navy, April 27, 1864.

LINK, PHILIP.—Age, 40 years. Enlisted, August 7, 1862, at Halfmoon, to serve three years; mustered in as private, Co. H, August 14, 1862; captured in action, September 15, and paroled September 16, 1862, at Harper's Ferry, Va.; killed in action, February 20, 1864, at Olustee, Fla.

LINTNER, JOHN P.—Age, 21 years. Enlisted at Minden, to serve three years, and mustered in as private, Co. B, August 13, 1862; captured in action, September 15, and paroled, September 16, 1862, at Harper's Ferry, Va.; wounded in action, no date; died of his wounds, August 1, 1864, at New York Harbor.

LITTEL, JAMES.—Age, 21 years. Enlisted, August 7, 1862, at Amsterdam, to serve three years; mustered in as private, Co. D, August 8, 1862; captured in action, September 15, and paroled, September 16, 1862, at Harper's Ferry, Va.; absent sick, in General Hospital, at muster-out of company; also borne as Little.

LITTEL, WILLIAM.—Age, 21 years. Enlisted, August 7, 1862, at Amsterdam, to serve three years; mustered in as private, Co. D, August 11, 1862; captured in action, September 15, and paroled, September 16, 1862, at Harper's Ferry, Va.; promoted corporal, no date; mustered out with company, June 17, 1865, at Raleigh, N.C.; also borne as Little.

LITTLE, SIMON P.—Age, 19 years. Enlisted, August, 1862, at Stratford, to serve three years; mustered in as private, Co. F, August 16, 1862; captured in action, September 15, and paroled, September 16, 1862, at Harper's Ferry, Va.; wounded a action, February 20, 1864, at Olustee, Fla., and October 27, 1864 at Darbytown Road, Va.; absent, wounded in Grant Hospital, Willets Point, N.Y., at muster-out of company.

LITZ, ANDREW.—Age, 44 years. Enlisted, August 21, 1864, at Schenectady, to serve one year, and mustered in as private, Co. E, August 26, 1864; died, May 8, 1865, at hospital, Smithville, N.C.

LOCKWOOD, OSCAR.—Age, 18 years. Enlisted, July 24, 1862, at Amsterdam, to serve three years; mustered in as private, Co. D, July 30, 1862; captured in action, September 15, and paroled, September 16, 1862, at Harper's Ferry, Va.; mustered out with company, June 17, 1865, at Raleigh, N.C.

LOOK, WILLIAM B.—Age, 37 years. Enlisted, July 23, 1862, at Halfmoon, to serve three years; mustered in as private, Co. H, August 1, 1862; captured in action, September 15, and paroled September 16, 1862, at Harper's Ferry, Va.; discharged, February 25, 1865, at General Hospital, near Troy, N.Y.

LOOP, HAVILLAH J.—Age, 18 years. Enlisted, August 9, 1862, at Corinth, to serve three years; mustered in as private, Co. F, August 25, 1862; captured in action, September 15, and paroled, September 16, 1862, at Harper's Ferry. Va.; again captured in action, May 7, 1864, at Chester Heights, Va.;. paroled, no date; mustered out while in General Hospital, Troy, N.Y., June 12, 1865, at Albany, N.Y.; also borne as Loap.

LOPER, LUTHER M.—Age, 25 years. Enlisted, August 6, 1862, at Saratoga. Springs, to serve three years; mustered in as sergeant, Co. G, August 18, 1862; promoted first sergeant, November 20, 1863; wounded in action, February 20, 1864, at Olustee, Fla., and October 1, 1864, at Chaffin's Farm, Va.; mustered out with company, June 17, 1865, at Raleigh, N.C. Commissioned first lieutenant, not mustered, May 17, 1865, with rank from February 1, 1865, vice F. H. Francisco, deceased.

LOUCKS, MOSES.—Age, 23 years. Enlisted, August 13, 1862 at Ephratah, to serve three years; mustered in as private, Co. F, August 26, 1862; captured in action, September 15, and paroled, September 16, 1862, at Harper's Ferry, Va.; wounded in action, September 29, 1864, at Chaffin's Farm, Va.; absent since and at muster-out of company.

LOUCKS, WILLIAM H.—Age, 23 years. Enlisted, August 13, 1862, at Ephratah, to serve three years; mustered in as private, Co. F, August 15, 1862; captured in action, September 15, and paroled, September 16, 1862, at Harper's Ferry, Va.; died of fever, July 3, 1863, at General Hospital, Beaufort, S.C.

LOVEJOY, GEORGE D.—Age, 24 years. Enlisted, August 5, 1862 at Northumberland, to serve three years; mustered in as private, Co. F, August 12, 1862; captured in action, September 16, 1862, at Harper's Ferry, Va.; deserted, November 29, 1862, on expiration of furlough; subsequent service in Fifth United States Cavalry.

LOVELAND, TRUMAN M.—Age, 21 years. Enlisted, August 12, 1862 at Ballston, to serve three years; mustered in as private, Co. I, August 18, 1862; captured in action, September 15, and paroled, September 16, 1862, at Harper's Ferry, Va.; appointed musician, no date; mustered out with company, June 17, 1865, at Raleigh, N.Y.

LOWELL, MORTIMER D.—Age, 21 years. Enlisted at Glen, to serve three years, and mustered in as private, Co. A, August 8, 1862; captured in action, September 15, and paroled, September 16, 1862, at Harper's Ferry, Va.; mustered out, June 5, 1865, at Fort Monroe, Va.

LUCK, GEORGE H.—Age, 22 years. Enlisted, August 13, 1862, at Northampton, to serve three years; mustered in as private, Co. E, August 15, 1862; captured in action, September 15, and paroled, September 16, 1862, at Harper's Ferry, Va.; wounded, no date; absent since and at muster-out of company.

LUDWIG, ROBERT.—Age, 34 years. Enlisted at New York City, to serve three years, and mustered in as private, Co. D, February 28, 1865; transferred to Co. D, Forty-seventh Infantry, June 17, 1865.

LUFFMAN, GEORGE W.—Age, 19 years. Enlisted, August 1, 1862 at Milton, to serve three years; mustered in as private, Co. C, August 8, 1862; captured in action, September 15, and paroled, September 16, 1862, at Harper's Ferry, Va.; died of diarrhea, March 2, 1863, in Base Hospital, near Fort Fisher, N.C.

LUFT, HOWARD.—Age, 18 years. Enlisted at Kingston, to serve one year, and mustered in as private, Co. H, March 1, 1865; transferred to Co. I, Forty-seventh Infantry, July 17, 1865.

LUSK, HIRAM.—Age, 21 years. Enlisted, July 23, 1862, at Mayfield, to serve three years; mustered in as private, Co. A, July 24, 1862.; captured in action, September 15, and paroled, September 16, 1862, at Harper's Ferry, Va.; absent, sick in hospital, Fort Schuyler, N.Y., since January, 1864, and at muster-out of company.

LUSK, SAMUEL H.—.Age, 23 years. Enlisted at Palatine, to serve three years, and mustered in as private, Co. A, August 15, 1862; captured in action, September 15, and paroled, September 16, 1862, at Harper's Ferry, Va.; wounded in action, February 20, 1864, at Olustee, Fla.; discharged for disability in 1864.

LYFORD, NORMAN W.—Age, 21 years. Enlisted at Broadalbin, to serve three years, and mustered in as private, Co. K August 26, 1862; captured in action, September 15, and paroled, September 16, 1862, at Harper's Ferry, Va.; missing in action, May 7, 1864, at Chester Heights, Va.; reported mortally wounded and died while en route to hospital, Fort Monroe, Va.

LYNN, JAMES.—Age, 22 years. Enlisted at New York City, to serve three years, and mustered in as private, Co. D, September 1, 1863; transferred to Co. D, Forty-seventh Infantry, June 17, 1865.

LYON, GEORGE B.—Age, 30 years, Enlisted, August 11, 1862, at Saratoga Springs, to serve three years; mustered in as corporal Co. G, August 19, 1862; captured in action, September 15 and paroled September 16, 1862, at Harper's Ferry, Va.; promoted sergeant, no date; wounded in action, February 20, 1864 at Olustee, Fla.; mustered out with company, June 17, 1865 at Raleigh, N.C.; also borne as Lyons.

LYONS, JAMES S.—Age, 28 years. Enlisted, August 8, 1862, at Greenfield to serve three years; mustered in as private, Co. C August 11, 1862; captured in action, September 15, and paroled, September 16, 1862, at Harper's Ferry, Va.; wounded in action, February 20, 1864, at Olustee, Fla.; mustered out with company, June 17, 1865, at Raleigh, N.C.

LYONS, JOHN.—Age, 24 years. Enlisted at New York City, to serve three years, and mustered in as private, Co. H, March, 7, 1865; deserted, April 5, 1865, at Leesburg, N.C.

LYONS, RICHARD S.—Age, 24 years. Enlisted at Brooklyn to serve three years, and mustered in as private, Co. G, August 31, 1862; promoted corporal, March 12, 1864; returned to ranks, February 9, 1865; transferred to Co. E, Forty-seventh Infantry, June 17, 1865.

MACK, PETER H.—Age, 18 years. Enlisted at Kingston, to serve three years, and mustered in as private, Co. H, March 6, 1865; transferred to Co. K, Forty-seventh Infantry, June 17, 1865; also borne as Peter H. Mark.

MADIGAN, SIMON.—Age, 30 years. Enlisted at Goshen, to serve three years, and mustered in as private, Co. A, February 25, 1865; transferred to Co. A, Forty-seventh Infantry, June 17, 1865.

MAGADIEN, LOUIS.—Age, 33 years. Enlisted at St. Johnsville, to serve three years, and mustered in as private, Co. B, July 30, 1862; captured in action, September 15, and paroled September 16, 1862, at Harper's Ferry, Va.; mustered out, May 28, 1865, at hospital, Fort Monroe, Va.

MAGANN, JAMES M.—Age, 19 years. Enlisted in

Eighteenth Congressional District, to serve three years, and mustered in as private, Co. E, April 15, 1864; transferred to Co. E, Forty-seventh Infantry, June 17, 1863; also borne as McGann.

MAGUIRE, MICHAEL.—Age, 27 years. Enlisted at New York City, to serve three years, and mustered in as private, Co. I, August 27, 1863; wounded in action, February 20, 1864, at Olustee, Fla.; transferred to the Navy, April 25, 1864; also borne as McGuire.

MAHAR, WILLIAM.—Age, 30 years. Enlisted, August 13, 1862, at Hadley, to serve three years; mustered in as private, Co. F, August 21, 1862; captured in action, September 15, and paroled, September 16, 1862, at Harper's Ferry, Va.; wounded in action, February 20, 1864, at Olustee, Fla.; absent on furlough since May 4, 1865, and at muster-out of company as Mayhan.

MAHONE, JOHN.—Age, 18 years. Enlisted at Brooklyn, to serve three years, and mustered in as private, Co. C, February 28, 1865; mustered out June 10, 1865, at hospital, Raleigh, N.C.

MAIER, JACOB.—Age, 30 years. Enlisted at Kingston, to serve three years, and mustered in as private, Co. I, March 6, 1865; transferred to Co. H, Forty-seventh Infantry, June 17, 1865, as Mair.

MALERY, LORENZO.—Age, 18 years. Enlisted, August 8, 1862, at Corinth, to serve three years; mustered in as private, Co. G, August 9, 1862; captured in action, September 15, and paroled, September 16, 1862, at Harper's Ferry, Va.; killed in action, January 16, 1865, at Fort Fisher, N.C.; also borne as Mallery.

MALLERY, HENRY W.—Age, 20, years. Enlisted, August 7, 1862, at Corinth to serve three years; mustered in as private, Co. F, August 19, 1862; captured in action, September 15, and paroled, September 16, 1862, at Harper's Ferry, Va.; captured in action, August 16, 1864, at Deep Bottom, Va.; exchanged, May, 1865; mustered out, June 5, 1865, at Fort Monroe, Va.

MALLERY, WILLIAM.—Age, 28 years. Enlisted at Brooklyn, to serve three years, and mustered in as private, Co. F, February 28, 1865; deserted, May 5, 1865, at Raleigh, N.C.

MALOMBY, MICHAEL.—Age, 21 years. Enlisted at Brooklyn, to serve three years, and mustered in as private, Co. H, September 1, 1863; transferred to Co. I, Forty-seventh Infantry, June 17, 1865.

MALONEY, MICHAEL.—Age, 23 years. Enlisted, July 28, 1862, at Minden, to serve three years; mustered in as private, Co. B, July 30, 1862; captured in action, September 15, and paroled, September 16, 1862, at Harper's Ferry, Va.; again captured in action, July 30, 1864, at Mine Explosion, Petersburg, Va.; escaped and returned to duty, April 22, 1865; mustered out with company, July 17, 1865, at Raleigh, N.C.

MALOY, JOHN.—Age, 18 years. Enlisted at Brooklyn, to serve three years, and mustered in as private, Co. K, February 21, 1865; transferred to Co. I. Forty-seventh Infantry, June 17, 1865.

MAMAUT, LOUIS.—Age, 32 years. Enlisted at Tarrytown. to serve three years, and mustered in as private, Co. F, August 25, 1863; transferred to the Navy, April 27, 1864.

MANCHESTER, JR., ISAAC.—Age, 25 years. Enlisted, August 7, 1862, at Broadalbin, to serve three years: mustered in as private, Co. K, August 12, 1862; captured in action, September 15, and paroled, September 16, 1862, at Harper's Ferry, Va.; discharged, February 27, 1865.

MANION, THOMAS.—Age, 26 years. Enlisted at Schenectady, to serve three years, and mustered in as private, Co. D, July 19, 1864; transferred to Co. D, Forty-seventh Infantry, June 17, 1865; also borne as Mannion.

MANN, DAVID L.—Age, 23 years. Enlisted at Johnstown, to serve three years; mustered in as private, Co. E, August 15, 1862; captured in action, September 15, and paroled, September 16, 1862, at Harper's Ferry, Va.; promoted corporal, no date; discharged for disability, September 25, 1863, at Beaufort, S.C.

MANNING, LEVI.—Age, 20 years. Enlisted, August 8, 1862, at Corinth, to serve three years; mustered in as private, Co. F, August 19, 1862; captured in action, September 15, and paroled, September 16, 1862, at Harper's Ferry, Va.; wounded in action, May 7, 1864, at Chester Station, Va.; promoted corporal, November 1, 1864; mustered out with company, June 17, 1865, at Raleigh, N.C; also borne as Henry Levi Manning.

MANTANEY, WILLIAM.—Age, 39 years. Enlisted at Schenectady, to serve one year, and mustered in as private, Co. E. August 31, 1864; killed in action, October 27, 1864, at Darbytown Road, Va.

MARCELLUS, CHARLES N.—Age, 22 years. Enrolled, August 8, 1862, at Broadalbin, to serve three years; mustered in as sergeant, Co. K, August 26, 1862; promoted first sergeant, no date; mustered in as second lieutenant, April 1, 1865; mustered out with company, June 17, 1865, at Raleigh, N.C. Commissioned second lieutenant, May 17, 1865, with rank from February 23, 1865, vice W. McIntosh promoted.

MARCH, ADOLPH.—Age, 40 years. Enlisted at Kingston, to serve one year, and mustered in as private, Co. I, March 6, 1865; transferred to Co. H, Forty-seventh Infantry, June 17, 1865; also borne as Marsh.

MARSELIS, CHARLES N.—Age, 19 years. Enlisted, August 8, 1862, at Broadalbin, to serve three years; mustered in as private, Co. K, August 12, 1862; captured in action, September 15, and paroled, September 16, 1862, at Harper's Ferry, Va.; promoted sergeant, no date; mustered out with company, June 17, 1865, at Raleigh, N.C.; also borne as Charles M. Marcellus.

MARSHAL, JAMES.—Age, 40 years. Enlisted at Tarrytown, to serve three years, and mustered in as private, Co. I, October 29, 1863; transferred to Co. H, Forty-seventh Infantry, June 17, 1865.

MARSHAL, SAMUEL.—Age, 26 years. Enlisted, July 24, 1862, at Amsterdam, to serve three years; mustered in as private, Co. D, July 30, 1862; captured in action, September 15, and paroled, September 16, 1862, at Harper's Ferry, Va.; deserted, November 6, 1862, at Chicago, Ill., as Marshall.

MARSHALL, JOHN.—Age, 40 years. Enlisted at Albany to serve three years, and mustered in as private, Co. F, October 28, 1863; discharged for disability, May 26, 1864.

MARTIN, FREDERICK.—Age, 24 years. Enlisted, August 9, 1862, at Ballston, to serve three years; mustered in as corporal, Co. I, August 13, 1862; no further record.

MARTIN, FREDERICK.—Age 24 years. Enlisted at

Ballston, to serve three years, and mustered in as private, Co. I, August 21, 1862; captured in action, September 15, and paroled, September 16, 1862, at Harper's Ferry, Va.; promoted corporal, no date; mustered out, June 7, 1865 at hospital, Fort Monroe, Va., as Fred A.

MARTIN, JOHN.—Age, 19 years. Enlisted, August 5, 1862, at Charlton, to serve three years; mustered in as private, Co. I, August 18, 1862; captured in action, September 15, and paroled, September 16, 1862, at Harper's Ferry, Va.; mustered out with detachment, May 12, 1865, at Albany, N.Y.

MARTIN, LEWIS.—Age, 43 years. Enlisted, August 2, 1862, at Palatine, to serve three years; mustered in as private, Co. A, August 5, 1862; captured in action, September 15, and paroled, September 16, 1862, at Harper's Ferry, Va.; deserted, November 16, 1862, at Chicago, Ill.

MARTIN, JR., LEWIS.—Age, 18 years. Enlisted at Palatine, to serve three years, and mustered in as private, Co. A, August 9, 1862; captured in action, September 15, and paroled, September 16, 1862, at Harper's Ferry, Va.; deserted, November 16, 1862, at Chicago, Ill.

MARTIN, THOMAS.—Age, 20 years. Enlisted at Kingston, to serve three years, and mustered in as private, Co. I, March 6, 1865; deserted, April 19, 1865, at Magnolia, N.C.

MARTON, WILLIAM H. H.—Age, 22 years. Enlisted, August 12, 1862, at Charleston, to serve three years; mustered in as private, Co. D, August 15, 1862; captured in action, September 15, and paroled, September 16, 1862, at Harper's Ferry, Va.; promoted corporal, no date; mustered out, May 25, 1865, at hospital, Fort Monroe, Va., as Martin.

MASON, JAMES J.—Age, 24 years. Enlisted at Eighteenth Congressional District, to serve three years, and mustered in as private, Co. C, April 24, 1864; deserted, August 28, 1864, at Bermuda Hundred, Va.

MASON, JOHN H.—Age, 30 years. Enlisted, August 7, 1862, at Day, to serve thee years; mustered in as corporal, Co. C, August 14, 1862; captured in action, September 15, and paroled, September 16, 1862, at Harper's Ferry, Va.; wounded in action, February 20, 1864, at Olustee, Fla.; mustered out with company, June 17, 1865, at Raleigh, N.C.

MATHEWS, GEORGE.—Age, 26 years. Enlisted at Tarrytown, to serve one year, and mustered in as private, Co. G, March 6, 1865; transferred to Co. G, Forty-seventh Infantry, June 17, 1865; also borne as Matthews.

MATOTT, VICTOR.—Age, 27 years. Enlisted, July 28, 1862, at Saratoga Springs, to serve three years; mustered in as private, Co. G, July 31, 1862; captured in action, September 15, and paroled, September 16, 1862, at Harper's Ferry, Va.; promoted corporal, November 20, 1863; sergeant, no date; died, May 22, 1865, at hospital, Portsmouth Grove, R. I., also borne as Matoll.

MAXFIELD, RICHARD.—Age, 21 years. Enlisted, July 28, 1862; at Minden, to serve three years; mustered in as private, Co. B, August 7, 1862; captured in action, September 15, and paroled, September 16, 1862, at Harper's Ferry, Va.; wounded and captured in action, February 20, 1864, at Olustee, Fla.; exchanged, November, 1864; absent, sick, at muster-out of company.

MAXON, GEORGE.—Age, 18 years. Enlisted at Canajoharie, to serve three years, and mustered in as private, Co. I, August 11, 1862; captured in action, September 15, and paroled, September 16, 1862, at Harper's Ferry, Va.; wounded and captured in action, May 7, 1864, at Chester Station, Va.; paroled, no date; mustered out with company, June 17, 1865, at Raleigh, N.C.

MAY, JUSTUS J.—Age, 19 years. Enlisted, August 12, 1862, at Saratoga Spa, to serve three years; mustered in as private, Co. F, August 20, 1862; captured in action, September 15, and paroled, September 16, 1862, at Harper's Ferry, Va.; discharged for disability, November 7, 1862, at Chicago, Ill.

MAYER, JOHN A.—Age, 42 years. Enlisted, August 5, 1862, at Bleecker, to serve three years; mustered in as private, Co. A, August 6, 1862; captured in action, September 15, and paroled, September 16, 1862, at Harper's Ferry, Va.; discharged for disability, July 25, 1863, at Central Park, N.Y.

McALLISTER, CORNELL.—Age, 19 years. Enlisted, August 12, 1862, at Mayfield, to serve three years; mustered in as private, Co. E, August 16, 1862; captured in action, September 15, and paroled, September 16, 1862, at Harper's Ferry, Va.; wounded in action, February 20, 1864, at Olustee, Fla., and August 16, 1864, at Deep Bottom, Va.; mustered out with company, June 17, 1865, at Raleigh, N.C.

McBRIDE, JOHN.—Age, 32 years. Enlisted at Brooklyn, to serve three years and mustered in as private, Co. H, September 2, 1863; wounded in action, May 16, 1864, at Drewry's Bluff, Va.; deserted on expiration of furlough, July 24, 1864, from hospital at Point Lookout, Md.

McBRIDE, THOMAS.—Age, 37 years. Enlisted at New York City, to serve three years, and mustered in as private, Co. K, March 11, 1865; transferred to Co. I, Forty-seventh Infantry, June 17, 1865.

McCANN, EDWARD.—Age, 31 years. Enlisted at Glen, to serve three years, and mustered in as private, Co. A, August 9, 1862; captured in action, September 15, and paroled, September 16, 1862, at Harper's Ferry, Va.; promoted corporal, September 18, 1862; mustered out, June 2, 1865, at Albany, N.Y.

McCARTHY, PHILIP.—Age, 21 years. Enlisted, July 29, 1862, at Florida, to serve three years; mustered in as private, Co. D, August 2, 1862; captured in action, September 15, and paroled, September 16, 1862, at Harper's Ferry, Va.; deserted, November 30, 1862, at Chicago, Ill.

McCARTY, JOHN.—Age. 23 years. Enlisted at Tarrytown, to serve three years, and mustered in as private, Co. I, October 30, 1863; transferred to the Navy, April 25, 1864.

McCOLLOM, JAMES.—Age, 24 years. Enlisted, August 4, 1862, at Florida, to serve three years; mustered in as private, Co. D, October 28, 1862; captured in action, September 15, and paroled, September 16, 1862, at Harper's Ferry, Va.; killed in action, August 16, 1864, at Deep Bottom, Va.

McCOLLOM, WILLIAM.—Age, 21 years. Enlisted,

July 24, 1862, at Amsterdam, to serve three years; mustered in as corporal, Co. D, July 30, 1862; captured in action, September 15 and paroled, September 16, 1862, at Harper's Ferry, Va. wounded in action, February 20, 1864, at Olustee, Fla.; mustered out with detachment, June 23, 1865, at Albany, N.Y.

McCOWATT, WALTER.—Age, 44 years. Enlisted, August 6, 1862, at Amsterdam, to serve three years; mustered in as private, Co. D, August 7, 1862; captured in action, September 15, and paroled, September 16, 1862, at Harper's Ferry, Va.; discharged for disability, November 4, 1862, at Chicago, Ill. as McCowett.

McCOY, JOHN.—Age, 28 years. Enlisted, August 15, 1862, at Canajoharie, to serve three years; mustered in as private, Co. I, August 16, 1862; captured in action, September 15, and paroled September 16, 1862, at Harper's Ferry, Va.; discharged for disability, no date; also borne as McKoy.

McDOUGAL, JOHN.—Age, 22 years. Enlisted at New York City, to serve three years, and mustered in as private, unassigned, February 27, 1865; mustered out, July 24, 1865, at Harts Island, New York Harbor.

McDONALD, PHILIP.—Age, 21 years. Enlisted at Saratoga Springs, to serve three years, and mustered in as private, Co. G, July 31, 1862; deserted, prior to August 26, 1862, at Fonda, N.Y.

MCDOWELL, JOHN H.—Age, 38 years. Enlisted at Goshen, to serve three years, and mustered in as private, Co. A, October 7, 1863; wounded and captured in action, February 20, 1864, at Olustee, Fla.; paroled, no date, transferred to Co. A, Forty-seventh Infantry, June 17, 1865; also, borne as McDonald.

McFARLANE, CARRINGTON.—Age, 27 years. Enrolled at Hilton Head, S.C., to serve five years, and mustered in as surgeon, September 10, 1863; mustered out with regiment, June 17, 1865, at Raleigh, N. C; prior service as assistant surgeon, Eighty-first Infantry. Commissioned surgeon, July 23, 1863, with rank from June 27, 1863, vice, R.E. Sutton resigned.

McGINNESS, MARCUS.—Age, 20 years. Enlisted at Amsterdam, to serve one year, and mustered in as private, Co. D, March 25, 1865; transferred to Co. C, Forty-seventh Infantry, June 17, 1865; also borne as Marcus B. McGinnis.

McGLACHLIN, ARCHIBALD.—Age, 19 years. Enlisted, August 11, 1862, at Johnstown, to serve three years; mustered in as private, Co. E, August 18, 1862; captured in action, September 15, and paroled, September 16, 1862, at Harper's Ferry, Va.; wounded in action, February 20, 1864, at Olustee, Fla.; transferred to Co. G, Nineteenth Regiment, Veteran Reserve Corps, January 24, 1865; mustered out with detachment, July 24 1865, at Buffalo, N.Y.; also borne as McGlochlin.

McGREGOR, ANDREW.—Age, 19 years. Enlisted at Brooklyn, to serve three years, and mustered in as private, Co. B, January 11, 1865; transferred to Co. B, Forty-seventh Infantry, June 17, 1865.

McGREIVY, THOMAS.—Age, 21 years. Enlisted at Minden, to serve three years, and mustered in as private, Co. B, August 13, 1862; captured in action, September 15, and paroled, September 16, 1862, at Harper's Ferry, Va.; deserted, October 24, 1862, at Chicago, Ill., as McGrievy; also borne as McGreevy.

McGUIRE, ANDREW.—Age, 22 years. Enlisted at Kingston, to serve three years, and mustered in as private, Co. F, October 27, 1863; wounded in action, February 20, 1864, at Olustee, Fla.; transferred to Co. C, Forty-seventh Infantry, June 17, 1865; also borne as James.

McGUIRE, BARNEY.—Age, 35 years. Enlisted, August 23, 1862 at Amsterdam, to serve three years; mustered in as private, Co. K. August 25, 1862; deserted August 27, 1862, at Fonda, N.Y.

McGUIRE, BARNEY.—Age, 43 years. Enlisted at Glen, to serve three years, and mustered in as private, Co. I, August 15, 1862; captured in action, September 15, and paroled, September 16, 1862, at Harper's Ferry, Va.; captured in action, August 16, 1864, at Deep Bottom, Va.; paroled, no date; died of chronic diarrhea at Parole Camp, Annapolis, Md., no date, as Bernard McGuire.

McHARG, JOHN.—Age, 44 years. Enlisted at Schenectady, to serve three years, and mustered in as private, Co. D, September 19, 1864; mustered out, May 18, 1865, at McDougall Hospital, New York Harbor.

McINTOSH, AARON.—Age, 37 years. Enlisted, July 29, 1862 at Amsterdam, to serve three years; mustered in as private, Co. D, July 30, 1862; captured in action, September 15, and paroled, September 16, 1862, at Harper's Ferry, Va.; discharged for disability, November 4, 1862, at Chicago, Ill.

McINTOSH, LEVI.—Age, 23 years. Enlisted, August 11, 1862, at Saratoga Springs, to serve three years; mustered in as private, Co. G, August 19, 1862; captured in action, September 15, and paroled, September 16, 1862, at Harper's Ferry, Va.; died, July 11, 1863, in hospital, at Hilton Head, S.C.; also borne as McIntoch.

McINTOSH, WALLACE.—Age, 24 years. Enrolled, August 13, 1862, at Milton, to serve three years; mustered in as private, Co. I, August 15, 1862; promoted sergeant, no, date; mustered in as second lieutenant, January 4, 1865; mustered out with company, June 17, 1865, at Raleigh, N.C. Commissioned second lieutenant, December 9, 1864, with rank from November 4, 1864, vice G. O. Smith discharged; first lieutenant, not mustered, May 17, 1865, with rank from February 23, 1865, vice A. C. Slocum promoted.

McKAY, WILLIAM W.—Age, 25 years. Enlisted, July 26, 1862, at Amsterdam, to serve three years; mustered in as sergeant, Co. D, July 30, 1862; captured in action, September 15, and paroled, September 16, 1862, at Harper's Ferry, Va.; returned to ranks, no date; mustered out with company, June 17, 1865, at Raleigh, N.C.

McKENNA, JOHN.—Age, 35 years. Enlisted at Brooklyn to serve one year, and mustered in as private, Co. C, February 28, 1865; transferred to Co. C, Forty-seventh Infantry, June 17, 1865.

McKENZIE, DONALD.—Age, 24 years. Enlisted at New York City to serve three years, and mustered in as private, Co. D, February 28, 1865; transferred to Co. C, Forty-seventh Infantry, June 17, 1865.

McKEON, FRANCIS.—Age, 25 years. Enlisted at Tarrytown, to serve three years, and mustered in as private, Co. H, October 29 1863; transferred to the Navy, April 27, 1864.

McKERCHER, JAMES.—Age, 21 years. Enlisted, August 6, 1862 at Amsterdam, to serve three years; mustered in as private, Co. D, August 7, 1862; captured in action, September 15, and paroled, September 16, 1862, at Harper's Ferry, Va.; discharged for disability, February 5, 1863, near Alexandria, Va.

McKITTRICK, WILLIAM H.—Enrolled at Fonda, to serve three years, and mustered in as captain, Co. C, August 26, 1862; killed in action, September 29, 1864, near Chaffin's Farm, Va. Commissioned captain, September 10, 1862, with rank from August 20, 1862, original.

McKNIGHT, JOHN S.—Age, 42 years. Enlisted, August 9, 1862, at Milton, to serve three years; mustered in as private, Co. I, August 12, 1862; captured in action, September 15, and paroled, September 16, 1862, at Harper's Ferry, Va.; transferred to Veteran Reserve Corps, no date.

McLAUGHLIN, HUGH.—Age, 27 years. Enlisted, August 14, 1862, at Johnstown, to serve three years; mustered in as private, Co. E, August 15, 1862; captured in action, September 15, and paroled, September 16, 1862, at Harper's Ferry, Va.; promoted corporal, no date; wounded in action, February 20, 1864, at Olustee, Fla.; discharged, October 25, 1864, at Washington, D.C.

McMAHAN, MICHAEL.—Age, 18 years. Enlisted, August 11, 1862, at Root, to serve three years; mustered in as private, Co. A, August 12, 1862; captured in action, September 15, paroled September 16, 1862 at Harper's Ferry, Va.; mustered out with detachment while at hospital, Point Lookout, Md., June 3, 1865, at Washington, D.C.; also borne as McMahon.

McMARTIN, DONALD.—Age, 37 years. Enlisted at Johnstown, to serve three years, and mustered in as private, Co. I, August 26, 1862; no further record.

McMARTIN, MARTIN.—Age,—years. Enrolled at Fonda, to serve three years, and mustered in as first lieutenant and quartermaster, July 19, 1862; mustered out with regiment, June 17, 1865, at Raleigh, N.C. Commissioned first lieutenant and quartermaster, September 10, 1862, with rank from July 19, 1862, original.

McMASTER, HENRY P.—Age, 29 years. Enlisted, August 6, 1862, at Caroga, to serve three years; mustered in as first sergeant, Co. K, August 12, 1862; captured in action, September 15, and paroled, September 16, 1862, at Harper's Ferry, Va.; discharged, October 25, 1862, at Chicago, Ill.

McMASTER, JOHN S.—Age, 19 years. Enlisted, August 14, 1862, at Florida, to serve three years; mustered in as private, Co. D, August 15, 1862; captured in action, September 15, and paroled, September 16, 1862, at Harper's Ferry, Va.; promoted corporal, no date; wounded in action, February 20, 1864, at Olustee, Fla., and August 16, 1864, at Deep Bottom, Va.; died of his wounds, September 4, 1864, at hospital, Fort Monroe, Va.

McMEHON, PATRICK.—Age, 21 years. Enlisted, July 31, 1862, at Minden, to serve three years; mustered in as private, Co. B, August 2, 1862; captured in action, September 15, and paroled, September 16, 1862, at Harper's Ferry, Va.; mustered out with company, June 17, 1865, at Raleigh, N.C., as McMahon.

McNAB, JAMES.—Age, 40 years. Enlisted, August 4, 1862, at Milton, to serve three years; mustered in as private, Co. C, August 8, 1862; captured in action, September 15, and paroled, September 16, 1862, at Harper's Ferry, Va.; mustered out with company, June 17, 1865, at Raleigh, N.C.

McNALLY, JAMES.—Age, 26 years. Enlisted, August 1, 1862, at Amsterdam, to serve three years; mustered in as private, Co. D, August 2, 1862; captured in action, September 15, and paroled, September 16, 1862, at Harper's Ferry, Va.; wounded in action, February 20, 1864 at Olustee, Fla.; absent, sick in hospital, Point Lookout, Md., at muster-out of company; also borne as McNelly.

McNAMARA, MICHAEL.—Age, 18 years. Enlisted at Tompkins, to serve three years, and mustered in as private, Co. E, February 24, 1865; transferred to Co. E, Forty-seventh Infantry, June 17, 1865; also borne as McNamery.

McOMBER, NEWTON S.—Age, 18 years. Enlisted, August 9, 1862, at Moreau, to serve three years; mustered in as private, Co. G, August 18, 1862; captured in action, September 15, and paroled September 16, 1862, at Harper's Ferry, Va.; absent, sick in hospital, at Fort Monroe, Va., since December, 1864, and at muster-out of company; also borne as Newton F.

MEAD, JOHN.—Age, 25 years. Enlisted at New York City, to serve three years, and mustered in as private, Co. I, August 28, 1863; transferred to the Navy, April 25, 1864.

MEAGHER, JOHN.—Age, 44 years. Enlisted at New York City to serve three years, and mustered in as private, Co. A, August 25, 1863; mustered out May 27, 1865, at hospital, Fort Monroe, Va.

MEIER, EHLER.—Age, 22 years. Enlisted at New York City to serve three years, and mustered in as private, Co. G, March 11, 1865; transferred to Co. E, Forty-seventh Infantry, June 17, 1865; also borne as Etta Mier.

MELESKI, JOSEPH.—Age, 42 years. Enlisted at Tarrytown, to serve three years, and mustered in as private, Co. E, September 1, 1863; mustered out, May 27, 1865, at Foster Hospital, New Berne, N. C; also borne as Muleski.

MENDER, JOSEPH.—Age, 21 years. Enlisted at Poughkeepsie, to serve three years, and mustered in as private, Co. K, October 23, 1863; transferred to Co. I, Forty-seventh Infantry, June 17, 1865.

MERRITT, JOHN.—Age. 44 years. Enlisted, August 6, 1862, at Corinth, to serve three years; mustered in as private, Co. F, August 19, 1862; captured in action, September 15, and paroled, September 16, 1862, at Harper's Ferry, Va.; wounded in action, February 20, 1864 at Olustee, Fla.; discharged for disability, March 1, 1865; also borne as Merrett.

MEYER, FREDERICK.—Age, 27 years. Enlisted, August 9, 1862, at Ephratah, to serve three years; mustered in as private, Co. E, August 16, 1862; promoted corporal, August 26, 1862; captured in action, September 15, and paroled, September 16, 1862, at Harper's Ferry, Va.; mustered out with company, June 17, 1865, at Raleigh, N.C., as Myers.

MILLER, CHARLES.—Age, 31 years. Enlisted at Brooklyn, to serve three years, and mustered in as private, Co. H, September 1, 1863; transferred to the Navy, April 27, 1864.

MILLER, CHARLES W.—Age, 25 years. Enlisted at Malta, to serve three years, and mustered in as corporal, Co. I, August 15, 1862; captured in action, September 15, and paroled, September 16, 1862, at Harper's Ferry, Va.; returned to ranks, no date; mustered out with company, June 17, 1865, at Raleigh, N.C.

MILLER, FERNANDO.—Age, 23 years. Enlisted, July 30 1862, at Milton, to serve three years; mustered in as private, Co. C, August 11, 1862; captured in action, September 15, and paroled, September 16, 1862, at Harper's Ferry, Va.; died of disease, September 22, 1863, in Regimental Hospital at Beaufort, S.C.; also borne as Ferdinand.

MILLER, GEORGE.—Age, 40 years. Enlisted at Minden, to serve three years, and mustered in as private, Co. B, July 23, 1862; captured in action, September 15, and paroled, September 16, 1862, at Harper's Ferry, Va.; died, December, 1864, while on furlough.

MILLER, JOHN.—Age, 35 years. Enlisted at New York City, to serve three years, and mustered in as private, Co. A, August 25, 1863; mustered out, May 31, 1865, at hospital, Fort Monroe, Va.

MILLER, JOHN H.—Age, 20 years. Enlisted, July 30, 1862, at St. Johnsville, to serve three years; mustered in as private, Co. B, August 11, 1862; captured in action, September 15, and paroled, September 16, 1862, at Harper's Ferry, Va.; wounded in action, August 16, 1864, at Deep Bottom, Va.; mustered out with company, June 17, 1865, at Raleigh, N.C.

MILLER, MELVIN.—Age, 26 years. Enlisted, August 14, 1862, at Ephratah, to serve three years; mustered in as private, Co. K, August 21, 1862; captured in action, September 15, and paroled, September 16, 1862, at Harper's Ferry, Va.; died of fever, March 5, 1865, at Johnstown, N.Y.

MILLER, MICHAEL.—Age, 31 years. Enlisted, August 20, 1862, at Glen, to serve three years; mustered in as private, Co. K, August 22, 1862; captured in action, September 15, and paroled, September 16, 1862, at Harper's Ferry, Va.; died of chronic diarrhea, January 19, 1864 at Beaufort, S.C.

MILLER, NORMAN.—Age, 22 years. Enlisted, July 30, 1862 at St. Johnsville, to serve three years; mustered in as private, Co. B, August 11, 1862; captured in action, September 15, and paroled, September 16, 1862 at Harper's Ferry, Va.; promoted corporal, no date; returned to ranks, September 1, 1864; mustered out, June 9, 1865, at hospital, Fort Monroe, Va.

MILLER, PETER.—Age, 27 years. Enlisted at Brooklyn, to serve one year and mustered in as private, Co. F, March 6, 1865; transferred to Co. F, Forty-seventh Infantry, June 17, 1865.

MILLER, THEODORE.—Age, place, date of enlistment and muster-in as private, Co. A, not stated; no description list received; dropped from the rolls and sent to Department Headquarters per special field order No. 67, Middle Division, Army of Mississippi; no further record.

MILLER, WILLIAM J.—Age, 22 years. Enlisted, August 7, 1862, at Minden, to serve three years; mustered in as private, Co. B, August 11, 1862; captured in action, September 15, and paroled, September 16, 1862, at Harper's Ferry, Va.; mustered out with company, June 17, 1865, at Raleigh, N.C.

MILLHAM, GEORGE.—Age, 37 years. Enlisted at Milton, to serve three years, and mustered in as private, Co. C, August 8, 1862; captured in action, September 15, and paroled, September 16, 1862, at Harper's Ferry, Va.; discharged for disability, January 25, 1864, at Hilton Head, S.C.

MILLS, WILLIAM.—Age, 24 years. Enlisted at Kingston, to serve one year, and mustered in as private, Co. H, March 2, 1865; promoted corporal, May 16, 1865; transferred to Co. K, Forty-seventh Infantry, June 17, 1865.

MINGAY, JAMES.—Age, 18 years. Enlisted, August 1, 1862, at Saratoga Spa, to serve three years; mustered in as sergeant, Co. F, August 12, 1862; captured in action, September 15, and paroled, September 16, 1862, at Harper's Ferry, Va.; discharged, December 16, 1863, to enlist as hospital steward, U. S. Army.

MOAK, CHARLES.—Age, 19 years. Enlisted, August 6, 1862, at Caroga, to serve three years; mustered in as private, Co. K, August 12, 1862; captured in action, September 15, and paroled, September 16, 1862, at Harper's Ferry, Va.; died of measles, January 2, 1863, at Washington, D.C.

MOAK, JOHN W.—Age, 18 years. Enlisted, August 13, 1862, at Minden, to serve three years; mustered in as private, Co. B, August 18, 1862; captured in action, September 15, and paroled, September 16, 1862, at Harper's Ferry, Va.; discharged for disability, August 29, 1863.

MOLONY, MICHAEL.—Age, 21 years. Enlisted at Amsterdam, to serve three years, and mustered in as private, Co. G, August 18, 1862; captured in action, September 15, and paroled, September 16, 1862, at Harper's Ferry, Va.; wounded in action, February 20, 1864, at Olustee, Fla.; mustered out with company, June 17, 1865, at Raleigh, N.C.; also borne as Maloney.

MONROE, ALEXANDER.—Age, 29 years. Enlisted, August 12, 1862, at Broadalbin, to serve three years; mustered in as private, Co. K, August 16, 1862; captured in action, September 15, and paroled, September 16, 1862, at Harper's Ferry, Va. died of chronic diarrhea, October 10, 1863; at Hilton Head, S.C.

MONTANEY, EDWARD S.—Age, 21 years. Enlisted, August 12, 1862, at Charleston, to serve three years; mustered in as corporal, Co. D August 15, 1862; captured in action, September 15, and paroled, September 16, 1862, at Harper's Ferry, Va.; discharged for disability, August 29, 1864, at New York Harbor, as Montanye.

MONTANEY, JAMES N.—Age, 24 years. Enlisted at Oppenheim to serve three years, and mustered in as private, Co. E, August 15, 1862; captured in action, September 15, paroled September 16, 1862 at Harper's Ferry, Va.; wounded in action, February 20, 1864, at Olustee, Fla.; mustered out with company, June 17, 1865, at Raleigh, N.C., as Mantaney; also borne as Matauny.

MOON, FRANK.—Age, 22 years. Enlisted July 23, 1862 at Amsterdam, to serve three years; mustered in as corporal, Co. D, July 30, 1862; captured in action, September 15, paroled September 16, 1862 at Harper's

Ferry, Va.; returned to ranks, no date; mustered out with company, June 17, 1865, at Raleigh, N.C.

MOONEY, WILLIAM.—Age, 27 years. Enlisted at Brooklyn, to serve three years, and mustered in as private, Co. I, September 1, 1863; deserted April 19, 1865, at Magnolia, N.C.

MOONEY, WILLIAM.—Age, 21 years. Enlisted at New York City, to serve three years and mustered in as private, Co. H, March 7, 1865; deserted April 5 1865, at Leesburg, N.C.

MORAN, THOMAS.—Age, 27 years. Enlisted at Tarrytown, to serve three years, and mustered in as private Co. G, March 6, 1865; transferred to Co. G, Forty-seventh Infantry, June 17, 1865.

MORRILL, FRANKLIN.—Age, 43 years. Enlisted, August 8, 1862 at Edinburgh, to serve three years; mustered in as sergeant, Co. C, August 14, 1862; captured in action, September 15, and paroled, September 16, 1862, at Harper's Ferry, Va.; mustered out with company, June 17, 1865, at Raleigh, N.C.

MORRIS, ANDREW.—Age, 18 years. Enlisted at Kingston, to serve one year, and mustered in as private, Co. H, March 1, 1865; transferred to Co. I, Forty-seventh Infantry, June 17, 1865.

MORRIS, JR., STEPHEN.—Age, 23 years. Enlisted at Glen, to serve three years, and mustered in as sergeant, Co. A, July 28, 1862; captured in action, September 15, and paroled, September 16, 1862, at Harper's Ferry, Va.; wounded in action, February 20, 1864, at Olustee, Fla.; died of his wounds, March 13, 1864, at Beaufort, S.C.; prior service in Twenty-fifth Militia.

MORRISON, GEORGE.—Age, 20 years. Enlisted in Eighteenth Congressional District, to serve three years, and mustered in as private, Co. C, April 22, 1864; deserted, May 27, 1864, near Hatchers, Va.

MORRISON, JOHN.—Age, 21 years. Enlisted at Brooklyn, to serve three years, and mustered in as private, Co. G, September 3, 1863; transferred to the Navy, April 27, 1864.

MORSEIN, JOHN.—Age, 21 years. Enlisted at Brooklyn, to serve three years, and mustered in as private, Co. A, September 13, 1863; wounded in action, February 20, 1864, at Olustee, Fla.; discharged for disability, at Mower Hospital, Chestnut Hill, Philadelphia, Pa., no date.

MOSHER, DANIEL.—Age, 39 years. Enlisted, August 9, 1862, at Amsterdam, to serve three years; mustered in as private, Co. D, August 12, 1862; captured in action, September 15, and paroled, September 16, 1862, at Harper's Ferry, Va.; transferred to Veteran Reserve Corps, July 9, 1863.

MOSHER, FREDERICK S.—Age, 22 years. Enrolled at Fonda, to serve three years, and mustered in as first lieutenant, Co. C, August 10, 1862; as captain, Co. F, June 11, 1864; transferred to Co. C, July 19, 1864; mustered out with company, June 17, 1865, at Raleigh, N.C.; also borne as Frederick G. Commissioned first lieutenant, September 10, 1862, with rank from August 20, 1862, original; captain, July 8, 1864, with rank from June 11, 1864, vice W. W. French discharged.

MOSHER, JOSEPH L.—Age, 27 years. Enlisted, August 11, 1862, at Canajoharie, to serve three years; mustered in as sergeant, Co. B, August 12, 1862; captured in action, September 15, and paroled, September 16, 1862, at Harper's Ferry, Va.; returned to ranks, no date; mustered out, with company, June 17, 1865, Raleigh, N.C.

MOSHER, ROBERT.—Age, 18 years. Enlisted at Brooklyn, to serve one year, and mustered in as private, Co. C, February 28, 1865; transferred to Co. B, Forty-seventh Infantry, June 17, 1865.

MOSHER, SIMON.—Age, 24 years. Enlisted, August 15, 1862, at Oppenheim, to serve three years; mustered in as private, Co. E, August 26, 1862; captured in action, September 15, and paroled, September 16, 1862, at Harper's Ferry, Va.; died of typhoid fever, August 3, 1863, at hospital, Beaufort, S.C.

MOULTRE, FRANK.—Age, 20 years. Enlisted at St. Johnsville, to serve three years, and mustered in as private, Co. A, April 14, 1864; captured in action, August 16, 1864, at Deep Bottom, Va.; escaped, April 1, 1865, at Richmond, Va.; mustered out with detachment, June 12, 1865, at Raleigh, N.C.; also borne as Molter.

MOUNT, LUCAS W.—Age, 23 years. Enlisted, August 13, 1862, at Canajoharie, to serve three years: mustered in as private, Co. B, August 15, 1862; captured in action, September 15, and paroled, September 16, 1862, at Harper's Ferry, Va.; promoted corporal, no date; wounded and captured in action, May 7, 1864, at Chester Station, Va.; died of his wounds, June 27, 1864, at Poplar Lawn Hospital, Petersburg, Va.

MOURER, WILLIAM.—Age, 19 years. Enlisted at New York City, to serve three years, and mustered in as private, Co. I, October 31, 1863; mustered out, October 4, 1865, to date June 17, 1865 at Albany, N.Y.

MOWERS, STEPHEN.—Age, 23 years. Enlisted, July 28, 1862, at Stratford, to serve three years; mustered in as private, Co. E, August 16, 1862; captured in action, September 15, paroled September 16, 1862 at Harper's Ferry, Va.; deserted November 16, 1863.

MOYER, JOHN F.—Age, 21 years. Enlisted, July 28, 1862, at Minden, to serve three years; mustered in as corporal, Co. B, August 2, 1862; captured in action, September 15, and paroled, September 16, 1862, at Harper's Ferry, Va.; returned to ranks, no date; wounded in action, February 20, 1864, at Olustee, Fla.; mustered out, June 13 1865, at Smithville, N.C.

MOYER, MORGAN W.—Age, 21 years. Enlisted at Minden, to serve three years, and mustered in as private, Co. B, August 13, 1862; captured in action, September 15, and paroled, September 16, 1862, at Harper's Ferry, Va.; discharged for disability, March 12, 1863.

MOYER, SYLVANUS.—Age, 44 years. Enlisted, August 4, 1862, at Canajoharie, to serve three years; mustered in as private, Co. I, August 14, 1862; captured in action, September 15, and paroled, September 16, 1862, at Harper's Ferry, Va.; killed in action, May 7, 1864, at Chester Heights, Va.

MULANEY, MICHAEL.—Age, place, date of enlistment and muster-in as private, Co. A, not stated; deserted on expiration of furlough, November 20, 1864, from hospital at Fortress Monroe, Va.

MULLER, FREDERICK.—Age, 24 years. Enlisted at New York City, to serve three years, and mustered in as private, Co. E, October 26, 1863; wounded in action, February 20, 1864, at Olustee, Fla.; transferred to Co. E, Forty-seventh Infantry, June 17, 1865; also borne as Mullen.

MULLIGAN, JOHN.—Age, 44 years. Enlisted at Halfmoon, to serve three years, and mustered in as private, Co. H, August 14, 1862; captured in action, September 15, and paroled, September 16, 1862, at Harper's Ferry, Va.; discharged, August 29, 1863.

MULLIKEN, CHARLES H.—Age, 22 years. Enlisted, August 4, 1862, at Stillwater, to serve three years; mustered in as private, Co. H, August 7, 1862; captured in action, September 15, and paroled, September 16, 1862, at Harper's Ferry, Va.; promoted corporal, no date; killed in action, February 20, 1864, at Olustee, Fla.; also borne as Milliken.

MURPHY, PATRICK.—Age, 19 years. Enlisted at Tarrytown, to serve one year, and mustered in as private, Co. G, February 22, 1865; transferred to Co. G, Forty-seventh Infantry, June 17, 1865.

MURPHY, PATRICK.—Age, 43 years. Enlisted at Brooklyn, to serve three years, and mustered in as private, Co. H, September 1, 1863; transferred to Co. I Forty-seventh Infantry, June 17, 1865.

MURRAY, HENRY.—Age, 18 years. Enlisted at Brooklyn, to serve one year, and mustered in as private, Co. F, March 6, 1865; transferred to Co. F, Forty-seventh Infantry, June 17, 1865; also borne as Murry.

MURREY, PATRICK.—Age, 24 years. Enlisted at Milton, to serve three years. and mustered in as private, Co. I, August 8, 1862; captured in action, September 15, and paroled, September 16, 1862, at Harper's Ferry, Va.; deserted, September 18, 1862, at Frederick, Md.; also borne as Murray.

MUSGROVE, ABBOTT C.—Age, 19 years. Enlisted, July 21, 1862, at Halfmoon, to serve three years; mustered in as corporal, Co. H, August 20, 1862; captured in action, September 15, and paroled, September 16, 1862, at Harper's Ferry, Va.; killed in action, August 16, 1864, at Deep Bottom, Va.

MUSSEY, ABRAM.—Age, 33 years. Enlisted, August 11, 1862, at Caroga, to serve three years; mustered in as private, Co. K, August 12, 1862; captured in action, September 15, and paroled, September 16, 1862, at Harper's Ferry, Va.; promoted sergeant, no date; mustered out with company, June 17, 1865 at Raleigh, N.C.; also borne as Massey.

MYER, AUGUST.—Age, 22 years. Enlisted at Tarrytown, to serve three years, and mustered in as private, Co. B, October 27, 1863; transferred to Co. A, Forty-seventh Infantry, June 17, 1865; also borne as Meyer.

MYER, GUS.—Age, 28 years. Enlisted at Brooklyn, to serve one year, and mustered in as private Co. K, February 28, 1865; transferred to Co. D, Forty-seventh infantry, June 17, 1865.

MYER, HENRY.—Age, 20 years. Enlisted at Brooklyn, to serve one year, and mustered in as private, Co. K, February 21, 1865; transferred to Co. D, Forty-seventh Infantry, June 17, 1865; also borne as Myers. Neink.

MYERS, LEVI.—Age, 35 years. Enlisted, August 8, 1862, at Edinburgh, to serve three years; mustered in as private, Co. C, August 14, 1862; captured in action, September 15, and paroled, September 16, 1862, at Harper's Ferry, Va.; wounded in action, February 20, 1864, at Olustee, Fla.; mustered out with company, June 17, 1865, at Raleigh, N.C.

MYRES, CORNELIUS.—Age, 25 years. Enlisted, August 11, 1862, at Wilton, to serve three years; mustered in as private, Co. F, August 14, 1862; captured in action, September 15, and paroled, September 16, 1862, at Harper's Ferry, Va.; discharged for disability, January 19, 1863.

MYRES, HANFORD.—Age, 19 years. Enlisted, August 11, 1862, at Wilton, to serve three years; mustered in as private, Co. F, August 14, 1862; captured in action, September 15, and paroled, September 16, 1862, at Harper's Ferry, Va.; wounded in action, February 20, 1864, at Olustee, Fla.; absent, in General Hospital, since and at muster out of company; also borne as Myers.

NAUGHTON, BARNEY.—Age, 36 years. Enlisted at Ephratah, to serve three years, and mustered in as private, Co. K, August 21, 1862; captured in action, September 15, and paroled, September 16, 1862, at Harper's Ferry, Va.; wounded in action, May 16, 1864, at Drewry's Bluff, Va.; mustered out with detachment, May 23, 1865, at Mower Hospital, Philadelphia, Pa., as Nauton.

NAUSBUM, HERMAN.—Age, 17 years. Enlisted at Tarrytown, to serve three years, and mustered in as private, Co. C, October 27, 1863; transferred to the Navy, April 27, 1864.

NEAR, BEEKMAN R.—Age, 26 years. Enlisted, August 21, 1862, at Ballston, to serve three years; mustered in as private, Co. I, August 23, 1862; promoted corporal, February, 1863; sergeant, November 1, 1864; first sergeant, no date; wounded in action, January 15, 1865, at Fort Fisher, N.C.; absent on furlough at muster-out of company. Commissioned second lieutenant, not mustered, May17, 1865, with rank from April 21, 1865, vice L. Sheffer killed in action.

NEAR, CHARLES.—Age, 42 years. Enlisted at Schenectady, to serve three years, and mustered in as private, Co. H, April 15, 1864; died, January 27, 1865, at hospital, Hampton, Va.

NEAR, CYRUS.—Age, 18 years. Enlisted, August 6, 1862, at Caroga, to serve three years; mustered in as private, Co. K, August 12, 1862; captured in action, September 15, and paroled, September 16, 1862, at Harper's Ferry, Va.; absent, at Albany, N.Y., awaiting discharge, at muster out of company; also borne as Cyrus W.

NEELEY, THOMAS.—Age, 33 years. Enlisted, July 25, 1862, at Glen, to serve three years; mustered in as private, Co. A, August 26, 1862; captured in action, September 15, and paroled, September 16, 1862, at Harper's Ferry, Va.; deserted, about September 27, 1862, at Harrisburg, Pa.

NEIMKE, HERMAN.—Age, 24 years. Enlisted at Brooklyn, to serve three years, and mustered in as private, Co. C, February 28, 1865; transferred to Co. C, Forty-seventh Infantry, June 17, 1865; also borne as Neink.

NELLIS, JOHN C.—Age, 20 years. Enlisted, August 9, 1862, at St. Johnsville, to serve three years; mustered in as private, Co. B, August 11, 1862; captured in action, September 15, and paroled. September 16, 1862, at Harper's Ferry, Va.; mustered out with detachment, June 23, 1865, at Albany, N.Y.

NELLIS, PETER.—Age, 24 years. Enlisted, August 12, 1862, at St. Johnsville, to serve three years; mustered in as private, Co. B, August 15, 1862; captured in action, September 15, and paroled, September 16, 1862. at Harper's Ferry, Va.; deserted, October 1, 1862, at Chicago, Ill.

NELLIS, STEPHEN B.—Age, 31 years. Enlisted, August 4, 1862, at Palatine, to serve three years; mustered in as corporal, Co. A, August 5, 1862; captured in action, September 15, and paroled, September 16, 1862, at Harper's Ferry, Va.; deserted, October 19, 1862, at Chicago, Ill.

NELSON, JOHN.—Age, 34 years. Enlisted at Brooklyn, to serve one year, and mustered in as private, Co. K, March 21, 1865; transferred to Co. D, Forty-seventh Infantry, June 17, 1865.

NELSON, MOSES B.—Age, 31 years. Enlisted at Goshen, to serve one year, and mustered in as private, Co. F, February 21, 1865; transferred to Co. K, Forty-seventh Infantry, June 17, 1865.

NELSON, WILLIAM.—Age, 22 years. Enlisted at Brooklyn, to serve one year, and mustered in as private, Co. G, September 1, 1863; transferred to the Navy, April 27, 1864.

NEWMAN, HENRY.—Age, 21 years. Enlisted at Tarrytown, to serve three years, and mustered in as private, Co. D, October 27, 1863; wounded in action, February 20, 1864, at Olustee, Fla.; transferred to Co. C, Forty-seventh Infantry, June 17, 1865.

NEWTON, WILLIAM E.—Age 22 years. Enlisted, August 5, 1862, at Saratoga Spa, to serve three years; mustered in as private, Co. F, August 12, 1862; captured in action, September 15, and paroled, September 16, 1862, at Harper's Ferry, Va.; killed in action, January 15, 1865, at Fort Fisher, N.C.

NIEDERLANDER, FRANK.—Age, 27 years. Enlisted, August 2, 1862, at Minden, to serve three years; mustered in as private, Co. B, August 11, 1862; captured in action, September 15, and paroled, September 16, 1862, at Harper's Ferry, Va.; captured in action, February 20, 1864, at Olustee, Fla.; reported dead on casualty list.

NOBLES, JOHN S.—Age, 30 years. Enlisted, July 30, 1862, at Milton, to serve three years; mustered in as private, Co. F, August 12, 1862; captured in action, September 15 and paroled, September 16, 1862, at Harper's Ferry. Va.; died of diarrhea, December 15, 1862, at Princeton, Ill., while on furlough.

NORKES, WILLIAM.—Age, 18 years. Enlisted at Schenectady, to serve three years, and mustered in as private, Co. G, March 4, 1865; mustered out, September 14, to date, June 17, 1865, at Albany, N.Y., as Nokes.

NORMAN, CHARLES.—Age, 20 years. Enlisted at Kingston to serve three years, and mustered in as private, Co. D, October 24, 1862; mustered out, July 22, 1865, at hospital, Fort Monroe, Va.

NORMAN, CHRISTOPHER.—Age 39 years. Enlisted at Schenectady, to serve three years, and mustered in as private, Co. G, March 6, 1865; deserted, April 7, 1865, at Magnolia, N.C.

NORRIS, JAMES.—Age, 38 years. Enlisted, August 11, 1862, at Galway, to serve three years; mustered in as private, Co. C, August 12 1862; captured in action, September 15, paroled September 16, 1862 at Harper's Ferry, Va.; discharged for disability, February 5, 1863, at Annapolis, Md.

NORRIS, WILLIAM.—Age, 30 years. Enlisted at Albany, to serve three years, and mustered in as private, Co. G, October 28, 1863; deserted, March 31, 1864, from hospital at New York Harbor.

NORTH, PATRICK.—Age, 31 years. Enlisted, August 7, 1862, at Canajoharie, to serve three years; mustered in as private, Co. I, August 16, 1862; captured in action, September 15, and paroled, September 16, 1862, at Harper's Ferry, Va.; mustered out with company, June 17, 1865, at Raleigh, N.C.

NORTHRUP, BENJAMIN K.—Age, 32 years. Enlisted, August 13, 1862, at Clifton Park, to serve three years; mustered in as private, Co. H, August 14, 1862; captured in action, September 15, paroled September 16, 1862 at Harper's Ferry, Va.; absent, sick in hospital, Fort Monroe, Va., at muster-out of company.

NOXON, ALFRED G.—Age, 18 years. Enrolled, July 14, 1862, at Halfmoon, to serve three years; mustered in as second lieutenant, Co. H, August 20, 1862: as first lieutenant, February 6, 1863; discharged, October 25, 1863. Commissioned second lieutenant, September 10, 1862, with rank from August 20, 1862, original; first lieutenant, May 13, 1863, with rank from February 6, 1863, vice F. N. Barlow resigned.

NUTT, JR., WILLIAM H.—Age, 27 years. Enlisted, July 23, 1862, at Amsterdam, to serve three years; mustered in as private, Co. D, July 30, 1862; captured in action, September 15, paroled September 16, 1862 at Harper's Ferry, Va.; wounded in action, August 16, 1864, at Deep Bottom, Va.; mustered out with company, June 17, 1865 at Raleigh, N.C.

OBE, JOHN.—Age, 30 years. Enlisted at Lisbon, to serve three years, and mustered in as private, Co. E, February 28, 1865; deserted, May 1, 1865.

OBE, JOSEPH.—Age, 19 years. Enlisted at Schenectady, to serve three years, and mustered in as private, Co. B, February 25, 1865; transferred to Co. B, Forty-seventh Infantry, June 17, 1865, also borne as Obie.

OLIVER, JOHN.—Age, 32 years. Enlisted at Tarrytown, to serve three years, and mustered in as private, Co. E, October 27, 1863; transferred to the Navy, April 27, 1864.

OLMSTEAD, CALEB B.—Age, 24 years. Enlisted, August 15, 1862, at Broadalbin, to serve three years; mustered in as sergeant, Co. K, August 16, 1862; captured in action, September 15, and paroled, September 16, 1862, at Harper's Ferry, Va.; returned to ranks and appointed musician, no date; mustered out, May 15, 1865, at Albany, N.Y.

OLMSTEAD, EDWARD.—Age, 27 years. Enlisted, August 14, 1862, at Malta, to serve three years; mustered in as private, Co. I, August 18, 1862; captured in action, September 15, and paroled, September 16, 1862, at Harper's Ferry, Va.; died, July 6, 1863, at hospital, New York City.

OLNEY, STEPHEN S.—Age, 25 years. Enrolled, August 20, 1862, at Saratoga Springs, to serve three years; mustered in as second lieutenant, Co. F, September 10, 1862; as first lieutenant, December 26, 1863; killed in action, January 15, 1865, at Fort Fisher, N.C. Commissioned second lieutenant, September 10, 1862, with rank from August 20, 1862 original; first lieutenant, November 25, 1863, with rank from October 24, 1863, vice D. H. Parker resigned.

OMAND, CHARLES.—Age, 20 years. Enlisted at Brooklyn, to serve three years, and mustered in as private, Co. D, September 1, 1863; wounded and captured in action, February, 20, 1864, at Olustee, Fla.; paroled, May 28, 1865; mustered out, June 12, 1865, at Raleigh, N.C.

ONDERKIRK, JACOB.—Age, 29 years. Enlisted, August 1, 1862, at Amsterdam, to serve three years; mustered in as private, Co. H, August 5, 1862; surrendered to the Thirty-second Infantry, to which he belonged, no date.

O'NEAL, HENRY.—Age, 19 years. Enlisted, August 8, 1862, at Root, to serve three years; mustered in as private, Co. A, August 12, 1862; wounded in action, February 20, 1864 at Olustee, Fla., and May 14, 1864 at Drewry's Bluff, Va.; absent in hospital, Point Lookout, Md., at muster-out of company.

O'NEIL, JOHN.—Age, 24 years. Enlisted at Tarrytown, to serve three years, and mustered in as private, Co. D, October 27, 1863; wounded in action, June 3, 1864, at Cold Harbor, Va.; transferred to Co. C, Forty-seventh Infantry, June 17, 1865; also borne as O'Niel.

ORSBORN, WILLIAM H.—Age, 29 years. Enlisted, August 5, 1862, at Saratoga, to serve three years; mustered in as private, Co. F, August 12 1862; captured in action, September 15, and paroled, September 16, 1862, at Harper's Ferry, Va.; discharged for disability, March 12, 1863, as Osborn.

OSBORN, AARON H.—Age, 19 years. Enlisted, July 30, 1862, at Saratoga Springs, to serve three years; mustered in as private, Co. F, August 12, 1862; captured in action, September 15, and paroled, September 16, 1862, at Harper's Ferry, Va.; wounded in action. October 27, 1864, at Darbytown Road, Va.; mustered out with company June 17, 1865, at Raleigh, N.C.

OSBORN, JOHN S.—Age, 18 years. Enlisted, July 31, 1862, at Northumberland, to serve three years; mustered in as private, Co. F, August 12, 1862; captured in action, September 15, and paroled, September 16, 1862, at Harper's Ferry, Va.; wounded in action, February 20, 1864, at Olustee, Fla.; transferred to Veteran Reserve corps, January 30, 1865, as Orsborn.

OSER, JOHN.—Age, 30 years. Enlisted at New York City, to serve three years, and mustered in as private, Co. G, March 7, 1865; transferred to Co. E, Forty-seventh Infantry, June 17, 1865; also borne as Osier.

OSTERBERGER, GEBHARD.—Age 37 years. Enlisted at Tarrytown, to serve one year, and mustered in as private, Co. G, March 6, 1865; transferred to Co. G, Forty-seventh Infantry, June 17, 1865; also borne as Ostenberger.

OSTERHOUT, DANIEL D.—Age, 21 years. Enlisted at Glen, to serve three years, and mustered in as private, Co. A, August 11, 1862; captured in action, September 15, paroled September 16, 1862 at Harper's Ferry, Va.; died of inflammation of bowels, May 6, 1863, at hospital, Beaufort, S.C.

OSTRANDER, GEORGE W.—Age, 22 years. Enlisted, August 12, 1862, at Stillwater, to serve three years; mustered in as private, Co. H, August 14, 1862; captured in action, September 15, and paroled September 16, 1862, at Harper's Ferry, Va.; promoted corporal, no date, mustered out with detachment, May 18, 1865, at White Hall Hospital, Philadelphia, Pa.

OSTRANDER, JOHN A.—Age, 18 years. Enlisted, August 14, 1862, at Charleston, to serve three years; mustered in as private, Co. D, August 15, 1862; captured in action, September 15, and paroled, September 16, 1862, at Harper's Ferry, Va.; discharged for disability, August 29, 1863, at Beaufort, S.C.

OTTO, ANTHONY.—Age, 19 years. Enlisted, August 6, 1862, at Canajoharie, to serve three years; mustered in as private, Co. B, August 12, 1862; captured in action, September 15, and paroled, September 16, 1862, at Harper's Ferry, Va.; promoted corporal, November 1, 1864; mustered out with company, June 17, 1865, at Raleigh, N.C.

OWENS, BENARD.—Age, 30 years. Enlisted at Tarrytown, to serve three years, and mustered in as private, Co. D. October 27, 1863; wounded in action, February 20, 1864, at Olustee, Fla.; mustered out, June 9, 1865, at New Berne, N.C.; also borne as Bernerd.

PADDLEFORD, CYRUS.—Age, 23 years. Enlisted, August 8, 1862, at Greenfield, to serve three years; mustered in as private, Co. C, August 11, 1862; captured in action, September 15, and paroled, September 16, 1862, at Harper's Ferry, Va.; mustered out with company, June 17, 1865, at Raleigh, N.C.

PARKE, JOHN.—Age, 18 years. Enlisted, August 7, 1862, at Broadalbin, to serve three years; mustered in as corporal, Co. K, August 12, 1862; captured in action, September 15, and paroled, September 16, 1862, at Harper's Ferry, Va.; died, October 26, 1863, at Beaufort, S.C.

PARKER, CHARLES L.—Age, 18 years. Enlisted, August 9, 1862, at Greenfield, to serve three years; mustered in as private, Co. F, August 14, 1862; captured in action, September 15, and paroled, September 16, 1862, at Harper's Ferry, Va.; wounded in action, June 15, 1864, at Petersburg, Va.; died of his wounds, August 23, 1864, at hospital, Fort Monroe, Va.

PARKER, JOHN DELOS.—Age, 21 years. Enrolled at Albany, to serve three years, and mustered in as first lieutenant, Co. F, August 20, 1862; discharged for disability, June 17, 1863. Commissioned first lieutenant, September 10, 1862, with rank from August 20, 1862, original.

PARKHURST, REUBEN.—Age, 22 years. Enlisted at Milton. to serve three years, and mustered in as private, Co. C, August 11, 1862; promoted hospital steward, January 1, 1865; mustered out with regiment, June 17, 1865 at Raleigh, N.C.

PARKMAN, FREDERICK E.—Age, 20 years. Enlisted, August 8, 1862, at Corinth, to serve three years; mustered in as private, Co. G, August 19, 1862; captured in action, September 15, and paroled, September 16, 1862, at Harper's Ferry, Va.; discharged for disability, February 4, 1863, at Chicago, Ill.

PARSON, HENRY.—Age, 18 years. Enlisted, December 22, 1863, at Charleston, to serve three years; mustered in as private, Co. B, January 2, 1864; transferred to Co. B, Forty-seventh Infantry, June 17, 1865.

PATTERSON JAMES.—Age, 27 years. Enlisted at

Schenectady, to serve three years, and mustered in as private, Co. D, March 2, 1865; transferred to Co. C, Forty-seventh Infantry, June 17, 1865; also borne as Paterson.

PAUL, AZARIAH.—Age, 18 years. Enlisted, August 9, 1862, at Wells, to serve three years; mustered in as private, Co. K, August 16, 1862; captured in action, September 15, and paroled, September 16, 1862, at Harper's Ferry, Va.; died of fever, June 21, 1863, at Hilton Head, S.C.

PAUL, DALLAS F.—Age, 18 years. Enlisted, August 6, 1862, at Corinth, to serve three years.; mustered in as musician, Co. G, August 20, 1862; captured in action, September 15, and paroled, September 16, 1862, at Harper's Ferry, Va.; mustered out with company, June 17, 1865, at Raleigh, N.C.

PEACOCK, DAVID K.—Age, 21 years. Enlisted, July 28, 1862, at Minden, to serve three years; mustered in as sergeant, Co. B, August 3, 1862; captured in action, September 15, and paroled, September 16, 1862, at Harper's Ferry, Va.; wounded in action, February 20, 1864, at Olustee, Fla.; mustered out with company, June 17, 1865, at Raleigh, N.C.

PEARSHALL, GEORGE H.—Age, 23 years. Enlisted, August 12, 1862 at Northumberland, to serve three years; mustered in as corporal, Co. F, August 19, 1862; deserted, August 28, 1862, at Fonda, N.Y.

PECK, WILLIAM A.—Age, 18 years. Enlisted at Broadalbin, to serve three years, and mustered in as private, Co. K, August 20, 1862; captured in action, September 15, and paroled, September 16, 1862, at Harper's Ferry, Va.; wounded in action, February 20, 1864, at Olustee, Fla.; mustered out with company, June 17, 1865, at Raleigh, N.C., as Peek.

PECK, WILLIAM H.—Age, 36 years. Enlisted, August 19, 1862, at Broadalbin, to serve three years; mustered in as private, Co. K, August 20, 1862; captured in action, September 15, and paroled, September 16, 1862, at Harper's Ferry, Va.; wounded in action, February 20, 1864, at Olustee, Fla.; mustered out with company, June 17, 1865, at Raleigh, N.C.

PECKHAM, ANDREW J.—Age, 28 years. Enlisted, August 12, 1862, at Greenfield, to serve three years; mustered in as private, Co. I, August 15, 1862; captured in action, September 15, and paroled, September 16, 1862, at Harper's Ferry, Va.; promoted corporal, no date; wounded in action, June 1, 1864, at Cold Harbor, Va.; died of his wounds, no date.

PEDRICK, WILLIAM.—Age, 25 years. Enlisted, August 6, 1862, at Caroga, to serve three years; mustered in as private, Co. K, August 12, 1862; captured in action, September 15, and paroled, September 16, 1862, at Harper's Ferry, Va.; promoted corporal, no date; wounded in action, February 20, 1864, at Olustee, Fla.; mustered out with company, June 17, 1865, at Raleigh, N.C.

PEELER, DANIEL.—Age, 35 years. Enlisted, August 21, 1862, at Palatine, to serve three years; mustered in as private, Co. I, August 23, 1862; captured in action, September 15, and paroled, September 16, 1862, at Harper's Ferry, Va.; wounded and captured in action, February 20, 1864, at Olustee, Fla.; died of typhoid fever, June 22, 1864, at Andersonville, Ga.

PEELER, JOHN H.—Age, 21 years. Enlisted at Palatine, to serve three years, and mustered in as private, Co. A August 5, 1862; captured in action, September 15, and paroled, September 16, 1862, at Harper's Ferry, Va.; promoted corporal, no date; wounded in action, May 14, 1864, at Drewry's Bluff, Va.; died of his wounds, May 19, 1864, at hospital, Hampton, Va.

PERKINS, HIRAM A.—Age, 18 years. Enlisted August 2, 1862, at Northumberland, to serve three years; mustered in as private, Co. I, August 12, 1862; captured in action September 15, and paroled, September 16, 1862, at Harper's Ferry, Va. wounded in action, February 20, 1864, at Olustee, Fla.; mustered out with company, June 17, 1865, at Raleigh N.C.

PERRY, JR., JOHN P.—Age, 22 years. Enrolled at Albany, to serve three years; mustered in as assistant surgeon January 20, 1863; discharged for disability, August 21, 1863. Commissioned assistant surgeon, January 17, 1863, with rank from same date, vice S. Peters resigned.

PERRY, THOMAS D.—Age, 22 years. Enlisted, August 12, 1862, at Mayfield, to serve three years; mustered in as private, Co. E, August 15, 1862; captured in action, September 15, and paroled, September 16, 1862, at Harper's Ferry, Va.; discharged for disability, January 12, 1863, at Chicago, Ill.

PETER, ALEXANDER.—Age, 24 years. Enlisted at Tarrytown, to serve three years, and mustered in as private, Co. K, October 30, 1863; deserted, November 1, 1864, at Chaffin's Farm, Va.

PETERS, LEWIS.—Age, place, date of enlistment and muster-in as private, Co. F, not stated; died, September 11, 1864, at hospital, Davids Island, New York Harbor.

PETERS, SAMUEL.—Age, __ years. Enrolled at Fonda, to serve three years; mustered in as assistant surgeon, August 20, 1862; discharged for disability, January 8, 1863; also borne as Samuel A. Commissioned assistant surgeon, September 10, 1862, with rank from August 20, 1862, original.

PETERSON, HENRY C.—Age, 22 years. Enlisted, July 26, 1862, at Clifton Park, to serve three years; mustered in as private, Co. H, August 1, 1862; captured in action, September 15, paroled September 16, 1862 at Harper's Ferry, Va.; transferred to Co. I, Sixth Regiment, Veteran Reserve Corps, October 11, 1864; promoted corporal, no date; mustered out with detachment, July 3, 1865, at Cincinnati, Ohio.

PETTIT, CHARLES.—Age, 30 years. Enlisted, August 5, 1862, at Milton, to serve three years; mustered in as private, Co. I, August 12, 1862; captured in action, September 15, and paroled, September 16, 1862, at Harper's Ferry, Va.; mustered out with detachment, June 8, 1865, at New Berne, N.C.

PETTIT, JOHN.—Age, 34 years. Enlisted at Canajoharie, to serve three years, and mustered in as private, Co. A, July 26, 1862; captured in action, September 15, and paroled, September 16, 1862, at Harper's Ferry, Va.; transferred to Co. I, October 1, 1862; discharged for disability, no date; also borne as Petit.

PETTIT, LEVI.—Age, 37 years. Enlisted at Broadalbin, to serve three years, and mustered in as private, Co. K, August 21, 1862; captured in action, September 15, and paroled, September 16, 1862, at Harper's Ferry Va.; killed in action, February 20, 1864, at Olustee, Fla.

PFIEFFER, EDWARD.—Age, 38 years. Enlisted at Brooklyn, to serve one year, and mustered in as private, Co. F, March 6, 1865; transferred to Co. F, Forty-seventh Infantry, June 17, 1865; also borne as Phiffer.

PHILLIPS, LEVI.—Age 18 years. Enlisted, August 14, 1862, at Oppenheim, to serve three years; mustered in as private, Co. E, August 16, 1862; captured in action, September 15, paroled September 16, 1862 at Harper's Ferry, Va.; wounded in action, February 20, 1864, at Olustee, Fla., and September 29, 1864, at Chaffin's Farm, Va.; Mustered out, June 3, 1865, at Trenton Barracks, Trenton, N. J.

PHILLIPS, THOMAS.—Age, 25 years. Enlisted at Goshen, to serve three years, and mustered in as private, Co. H, October 8, 1863; wounded in action, February 20, 1864, at Olustee, Fla.; transferred to the Navy, April 27, 1864.

PHOENIX, ALFRED.—Age, 18 years. Enlisted, August 5, 1862, at Halfmoon, to serve three years; mustered in as private, Co. H, August 7, 1862; captured in action, September 15, and paroled September 16, 1862, at Harper's Ferry, Va.; wounded in action, February 20, 1864, at Olustee, Fla.; absent, sick in hospital, at Fort Monroe, Va., at muster-out of company; also borne as Phenix.

PICONI, GALTAIN.—Age, 32 years. Enlisted at Jefferson, to serve three years, and mustered in as private Co. G, May 23, 1864; borne on muster-out roll as a deserter, no date or place.

PLACE, JOHN R.—Age, 29 years. Enlisted August 9, 1862 at Saratoga Springs, to serve three years and mustered in as private, Co. G, August 19, 1862; captured in action, September 15, and paroled, September 16, 1862, at Harper's Ferry, Va.; died, October 11, 1864, at hospital, Beverly, N. J.

PLANK, PHILIP.—Age, 44 years. Enlisted at Johnstown, to serve three years, and mustered in as private, Co. E, August 11, 1862; captured in action, September 15, and paroled, September 16, 1862, at Harper's Ferry, Va.; discharged for disability, January 12, 1865, at Albany, N.Y.

PLATT, JAMES H.—Age, 19 years. Enlisted, August 7, 1862, at North Hampton, to serve three years; mustered in as private, Co. E, August 21, 1862; captured in action, September 15, and paroled, September 16, 1862 at Harper's Ferry, Va.; died of fever, July 27, 1863, at Regimental Hospital, Beaufort, S.C.

PLUNKETT, JOHN.—Age, 43 years. Enlisted at Tarrytown, to serve three years, and mustered in as private, Co. H, October 1, 1863; discharged for disability, July 3, 1864, at Beaufort, S.C.

PORTER, CHARLES.—Age, 29 years. Enlisted at Schenectady, to serve one year, and mustered in as private, Co. G, August 4, 1864; mustered out, July 3, 1865, at Davids Island, New York Harbor.

POTTS, GEORGE H.—Age, 19 years. Enlisted, August 12, 1862 at Saratoga Spa, to serve three years; mustered in as musician, Co. F, August 19, 1862; captured in action, September 15, paroled September 16, 1862 at Harper's Ferry, Va.; discharged for disability, December 12, 1862.

POWELL, MARIUS.—Age 19 years. Enlisted, July 30, 1862, at St. Johnsville, to serve three years; mustered in as musician, Co. B, August 2, 1862; captured in action, September 15, paroled September 16, 1862 at Harper's Ferry, Va.; mustered out with company, June 17, 1865, at Raleigh, N.C.

POWELL, WILLIAM T.—Age, 30 years. Enlisted, August 4, 1862, at Waterford, to serve three years; mustered in as corporal, Co. H, August 18, 1862; captured in action, September 15, paroled September 16, 1862 at Harper's Ferry, Va.; discharged for disability, October 20, 1863.

POWLIS, DAVID.—Age, 23 years. Enlisted at Schenectady, to serve three years, and mustered in as private, Co. G, March 6, 1865; transferred to Co. G, Forty-seventh Infantry, June 7, 1865.

PRATT, WILLIAM H.—Age, 22 years. Enlisted at Goshen, to serve three years, and mustered in as private, Co. A, October 8, 1863; wounded in action, February 20, 1864, at Olustee, Fla.; promoted corporal, no date; discharged for disability, April 3, 1865.

PREMO, FRANK.—Age, 18 years. Enlisted at Ballston, to serve three years, and mustered in as private, Co. C, February 28, 1865; transferred to Co. C, Forty-seventh Infantry, June 17, 1865.

PRICE, ABRAM.—Age, 27 years. Enlisted, August 8, 1862, at Saratoga Springs, to serve three years; mustered in as private, Co. G, August 18, 1862; wounded in action, February 20, 1864, at Olustee, Fla.; died, April 11, 1865, at hospital, Magnolia, N.C., as Abram F.

PRICE, AUGUSTUS.—Age, 25 years. Enlisted, August 9, 1862, at Canajoharie, to serve three years; mustered in as private, Co. I, August 16, 1862; captured in action, September 15, paroled September 16, 1862 at Harper's Ferry, Va.; wounded in action February 20, 1864, at Olustee, Fla., and August 16, 1864, at Deep Bottom, Va.; promoted sergeant, no date; mustered out with company, June 17, 1865, at Raleigh, N.C.

PRICE, MARTIN.—Age, 21 years. Enlisted, July 30, 1862, at Canajoharie, to serve three years; mustered in as private, Co. I, August 16, 1862; captured in action, September 15, and paroled, September 16, 1862, at Harper's Ferry, Va.; discharged for disability, no date.

PRIMROSE, WALLACE.—Age, 22 years. Enlisted at Tarrytown, to serve three years, and mustered in as private, Co. B, February 27, 1865; transferred to Co. B, Forty-seventh Infantry, June 17, 1865.

PRYOR, ROBERT.—Age, 29 years. Enlisted, August 12, 1862, at Wilton, to serve three years; mustered in as private, Co. F, August 14, 1862; captured in action, September 15, and paroled, September 16, 1862, at Harper's Ferry, Va.; deserted, October 1, 1862, at Chicago, Ill.

PURDY, MORGAN L.—Age, 28 years. Enlisted, August 9, 1862, at Moreau, to serve three years; mustered in as private, Co. G, August 18, 1862; captured in action, September 15, and paroled, September 16, 1862, at Harper's Ferry, Va.; promoted corporal, no date; wounded in action, February 20, 1864, at Olustee, Fla.; discharged for disability, June 27, 1864, at Hilton Head, S.C.

PUTMAN, STEWART.—Age, 22 years. Enlisted at Johnstown, to serve three years; mustered in as private, Co. E, August 13, 1862; captured in action, September 15, and paroled, September 16, 1862, at Harper's Ferry, Va.; promoted corporal, November 1,

1862; wounded in action, February 20, 1864, at Olustee, Fla., and June 15, 1864, at Petersburg, Va.; mustered out with company, June 17, 1865, at Raleigh, N.C.

PUTNAM, GEORGE H.—Age, 26 years, Enlisted, August 9, 1862, at Moreau, to serve three years; mustered in as sergeant, Co. G, August 18, 1862; discharged for disability, October 20, 1862, at Chicago, Ill.

PUTZAR, FREDERICK.—Age, 31 years. Enlisted, August 5, 1862, at Galway, to serve three years; mustered in as private. Co. I, August 7, 1862; captured in action, September 15 and paroled, September 16, 1862, at Harper's Ferry, Va.; wounded in action, February 20, 1864, at Olustee, Fla.; promoted corporal, no date; captured in action, August 16, 1864, at Deep Bottom, Va.; reported died at Andersonville, Ga., no date.

QUILLET, REUBEN S.—Age, 38 years. Enlisted, July 31, 1862, at Amsterdam, to serve three years; mustered in as private, Co. G, August 6, 1862; captured in action, September 15, and paroled, September 16, 1862, at Harper's Ferry, Va.; promoted corporal, April 4, 1865; mustered out with detachment. June 24, 1865, at Albany, N.Y.

QUILTY, BARTHOLOMEW.—Age, 38 years. Enlisted, December 19, 1863, at Mohawk, to serve three years; mustered in as private, Co. A, December 29, 1863; wounded in action, January 15, 1865, at Fort Fisher, N.C.; transferred to Co. A, Forty-seventh Infantry, June 17, 1865; also borne as Quiltz.

QUINDLAND, THOMAS.—Age, 28 years. Enlisted at Brooklyn, to serve three years, and mustered in as private, Co. G, September 3, 1863; wounded in action, May 14, 1864, at Drewry's Bluff, Va.; transferred to Co. G, Eighteenth Regiment, Veteran Reserve Corps, April 12, 1865; mustered out, November 21, 1865, at Washington, D.C., as Quinlan.

QUINLAN, THOMAS.—Age, 23 years. Enlisted at New York City, to serve three years, and mustered in as private, Co. K, March 11, 1865; transferred to Co. D, Forty-seventh Infantry, June 17, 1865.

RADY, JOHN.—Age, 20 years. Enlisted at Brashear, to serve three years, and mustered in as private, Co. E, February 27, 1864; transferred to Co. E, Forty-seventh Infantry, June 17, 1865; also borne as Reddy.

RAFFERTY, JAMES H.—Age, 21 years. Enlisted at Kingston, to serve three years, and mustered in as private, Co. F, October 28, 1863; deserted, June 6, 1865, at Raleigh, N.C.

RAIDER, HENRY.—Age, 28 years. Enlisted at Tarrytown, to serve three years, and mustered in as private, Co. H, October 29, 1863; discharged, February 1, 1865, at hospital, Portsmouth Grove, R. I.

RATHMIRE, ABRAM.—Age, 35 years. Enlisted at Johnstown, to serve three years, and mustered in as private, Co. E, August 13, 1862; captured in action, September 15, and paroled, September 16, 1862, at Harper's Ferry, Va.; killed in action, February 20, 1864, at Olustee, Fla.

RAY, BENJAMIN.—Age, 24 years. Enlisted at Albany, to serve three years, and mustered in as private, Co. K, October 29, 1863; transferred to the Navy, April 27, 1864.

REAME, AUGUST.—Age, 18 years. Enlisted at Brooklyn, to serve one year, and mustered in as private, Co. C, February 28, 1865; transferred to Co. C, Forty-seventh Infantry, June 17, 1865.

REAMER, WILLIAM I.—Age, 18 years. Enlisted at Schenectady, to serve one year, and mustered in as private, Co. F, September 12, 1864; mustered out with company, June 17, 1865, at Raleigh, N.C.

REARDON, JOHN.—Age, 23 years. Enrolled, August 6, 1862, at St. Johnsville, to serve three years; mustered in as private, Co. B, August 12, 1862; promoted corporal, August 26, 1862; sergeant, May 9, 1863; wounded in action, May 7, 1864, at Chesterfield Heights, Va.; promoted first sergeant, December 7, 1864; mustered in as second lieutenant, February 23, 1863; mustered out with detachment, June 23, 1865, at Albany, N.Y. Commissioned second lieutenant, May 17, 1865, with rank from February 23, 1865, vice J. A. Collier appointed adjutant.

RECTOR, PIERSON.—Age, 25 years. Enrolled at Hilton Head, S.C., to serve three years, and mustered in as assistant surgeon, January 5, 1864; transferred to One Hundred and Twenty-seventh Infantry, February 17, 1864, to which he formerly belonged. Commissioned assistant surgeon December 14, 1863, with rank from August 22, 1863, vice J. S. Perry, Jr., resigned.

REDMOND, JOHN.—Age, 37 years. Enlisted, August 14, 1862, at Saratoga Springs, to serve three years; mustered in as private, Co. G, August 22, 1862; captured in action, September 15, paroled September 16, 1862 at Harper's Ferry, Va.; deserted, September 18, 1862, at Frederick, Md.

REED, JR., JOHN.—Age, 22 years. Enlisted, August 9, 1862, at Saratoga Springs, to serve three years; mustered in as private, Co. G, August 19, 1862; captured in action, September 15, paroled September 16, 1862 at Harper's Ferry, Va.; wounded in action, February 20, 1864, at Olustee, Fla.; promoted corporal, March 1, 1864; absent, wounded at hospital, Fortress Monroe, Va., since October, 1864, and at muster-out of company.

REES, THOMAS.—Age, 23 years. Enlisted at New York City, to serve three years, and mustered in as private, Co. I, August 25, 1863; wounded and captured in action, February 20, 1864, at Olustee, Fla.; died at Andersonville, Ga., no date.

REID, JAMES E.—Age, 18 years. Enlisted, August 5, 1862, at Milton, to serve three years; mustered in as private, Co. C, August 9, 1862; captured in action, September 15, and paroled, September 16, 1862, at Harper's Ferry, Va.; promoted corporal, no date; mustered out with company, June 17, 1865, at Raleigh, N.C., as Reed.

REINHART, PETER.—Age, 26 years. Enlisted at Tarrytown, to serve three years, and mustered in as private, Co. H, October 29, 1863; wounded in action, February 20, 1864, at Olustee, Fla.; killed in action, January 15, 1865, at Fort Fisher, N.C.

REKEE, ALFRED.—Age, 18 years. Enlisted at Schenectady, to serve three years, and mustered in as private, Co. B, February 24, 1865; transferred to Co. B, Forty-seventh Infantry, June 17, 1865; also borne as Reeked.

RENOLD, LEONARD.—Age, 26 years. Enlisted at Brooklyn, to serve three years, and mustered in as private, Co. C, February 21, 1865; transferred to Co.—, Forty-seventh Infantry, June 17, 1865.

REOBUS, JOHN.—Age, 38 years. Enlisted at Brooklyn, to serve one year, and mustered in as private, Co. K, February 21, 1865; transferred to Co. D, Forty-seventh Infantry, June 17, 1865; also borne as Rebus.

REY, DENNIS.—Age, 21 years. Enlisted at Minden, to serve three years, and mustered in as private, Co. H, August 23, 1862; no further record.

REYNOLDS, MILES.—Age, 27 years. Enlisted at Mayfield, to serve three years, and mustered in as private, Co. A, July 31, 1862; captured in action, September 15, and paroled, September 16, 1862, at Harper's Ferry, Va.; wounded in action, September 29, 1864, at Chaffin's Farm, Va.; mustered out, May 27, 1865, at hospital, Fort Monroe, Va., as Niles.

REYNOLDS, SIMEON.—Age, 24 years. Enlisted, July 23, 1862, at Fonda, to serve three years; mustered in as private, Co. F, August 26, 1862; transferred to Co. I, and deserted, August 27, 1862 at Fonda, N.Y.

REYNOLDS, WILLIAM.—Age, 21 years. Enlisted, July 24, 1862, at Mohawk, to serve three years; mustered in as private, Co. A, July 25, 1862; captured in action, September 15, paroled September 16, 1862 at Harper's Ferry, Va.; wounded in action, September 29, 1864 at Chaffin's Farm, Va.; absent since in hospital, Albany, N.Y. and at muster-out of company.

RHODES, CHARLES.—Age, 23 years. Enlisted, August 7, 1862, at Northampton, to serve three years; mustered in as private, Co. E, August 15, 1862; captured in action, September 15, and paroled, September 16, 1862, at Harper's Ferry, Va.; wounded and captured in action, February 20, 1864, at Olustee, Fla.; died, June 26, 1864, in Confederate Hospital, Petersburg, Va.; also borne as Rhoads.

RHODES, CHARLES W.—Age, 18 years. Enlisted, December 12, 1863, at Hope, to serve three years; mustered in as private, Co. E, December 16, 1863; transferred to Co. E, Forty-seventh Infantry, June 17 1865.

RHODES, EDWIN.—Age, 23 years. Enlisted, August 6, 1862, at Day, to serve three years; mustered in as private, Co. C, August 8, 1862; captured in action, September 15, and paroled, September 16, 1862, at Harper's Ferry, Va.; wounded in action, August 16, 1864, at Deep Bottom, Va.; promoted corporal, May 1, 1865; mustered out with company, June 17, 1865, at Raleigh, N.C.

RHODES, HIRAM.—Age, 22 years. Enlisted, August 13, 1862, at Northampton, to serve three years; mustered in as private, Co. E, August 15, 1862; captured in action, September 15, and paroled, September 16, 1862, at Harper's Ferry, Va.; mustered out with company, June 17, 1865, at Raleigh, N.C.

RHODES, JOHN A.—Age, 25 years. Enlisted, August 13, 1862 at Northampton, to serve three years; mustered in as private, Co. E, August 15, 1862; captured in action, September 15, and paroled, September 16, 1862, at Harper's Ferry, Va.; discharged December 8, 1864.

RICE, FRANCIS.—Age, 30 years. Enlisted, August 11, 1862, at Edinburgh, to serve three years; mustered in as private, Co. I, August 18, 1862; captured in action, September 15, and paroled, September 16, 1862, at Harper's Ferry, Va.; died, November 19, 1862, at hospital, Chicago, Ill.

RICE, GEORGE L.—Age, 28 years. Enlisted at Glen, to serve three years, and mustered in as private, Co. A, July 28, 1862; captured in action, September 15, and paroled, September 16, 1862, at Harper's Ferry, Va.; transferred to Veteran Reserve Corps, September 12, 1863.

RICE, MICHAEL.—Age, 33 years. Enlisted, August 9, 1862, at Edinburgh, to serve three years; mustered in as corporal, Co. C, August 14, 1862; captured in action, September 15, and paroled, September 16, 1862, at Harper's Ferry, Va.; wounded in action, no date; mustered out, June 13, 1865, at hospital Fort Monroe, Va.

RICE, WILLIAM D.—Age, 21 years. Enlisted, August 21, 1862, at Broadalbin, to serve three years; mustered in as private, Co. K, August 23, 1862; deserted, September 15, 1862, at Harper's Ferry, Va.

RICH, FRANK E.—Age, 18 years. Enlisted, August 15, 1862, at Root, to serve three years; mustered in as private, Co. I, August 20, 1862; captured in action, September 15, and paroled, September 16, 1862, at Harper's Ferry, Va.; mustered out with company, June 17, 1865, at Raleigh, N.C.

RICHARDS, JAMES.—Age, 18 years. Enlisted, August 8, 1862, at Halfmoon, to serve three years; mustered in as private, Co. H, August 26, 1862; captured in action, September 15, and paroled, September 16, 1862, at Harper's Ferry, Va.; died, July 2, 1863, at Provost Guard Hospital, Hilton Head, S.C.

RICHARDSON, HIRAM.—Age, 18 years. Enlisted, August 5, 1862, at Halfmoon, to serve three years; mustered in as private, Co. H, August 7, 1862; captured in action, September 15, and paroled, September 16, 1862, at Harper's Ferry, Va.; died November 8, 1862, at hospital, Chicago, Ill.

RICHARDSON, ISAAC.—Age, 32 years. Enlisted at Kingston, to serve three years, and mustered in as private, Co. F, October 30, 1863; wounded in action, May 7, 1864, at Chester Station, Va.; transferred to Co. K, Forty-seventh Infantry, June 17, 1865.

RIDER, ASA B.—Age, 23 years. Enlisted, August 9, 1862, at Charleston, to serve three years; mustered in as private, Co. D, August 15, 1862; captured in action, September 15, and paroled, September 16, 1862 at Harper's Ferry, Va.; died of fever, November 23, 1862, at Chicago, Ill.

RIDER, SAMUEL T.—Age, 24 years. Enlisted August 11, 1862, at Charleston, to serve three years; mustered in as private, Co. D, August 15, 1862; captured in action, September 15, paroled September 16, 1862 at Harper's Ferry, Va.; mustered out with company, June 17, 1865, at Raleigh, N.C.

RIGHTMOYER, JEREMIAH.—Age, 18 years. Enlisted, July 23, 1862, at Palatine, to serve three years; mustered in as private, Co. I, August 2, 1862; captured in action, September 15, and paroled, September 16, 1862, at Harper's Ferry, Va.; mustered out with company, June 17, 1865, at Raleigh, N.C.

RIGHTMOYER, PETER N.—Age, 19 years. Enlisted, July 29, 1862, at Palatine, to serve three years; mustered in as private, Co. I, August 2, 1862; captured in action, September 15, and paroled, September 16, 1862, at Harper's Ferry, Va.; wounded and captured in action, February 20, 1864, at Olustee, Fla.; paroled and discharged for disability, no dates.

RIPLEY, JOSHUA.—Age, 43 years. Enlisted, July 25, 1862, at Glen, to serve three years; mustered in as private, Co. A, July 28, 1862; grade changed to first class musician, August 25, 1862; promoted principal musician, July 1, 1863; mustered out with company, June 17, 1865, at Raleigh, N.C.

RISING, WILLIAM.—Age, 44 years. Enlisted, August 11, 1862, at Moreau, to serve three years; mustered in as private, Co. G, August 18, 1862; captured in action, September 15, and paroled, September 16, 1862, at Harper's Ferry, Va.; transferred to Veteran Reserve Corps, September 6, 1863.

RIST, JOHN.—Age, 23 years. Enlisted at Brooklyn, to serve one year, and mustered in as private, Co. I, March 11, 1865; transferred to Co. I, Forty-seventh Infantry, June 17, 1865; also borne as Riest.

RISTONE, JONATHAN.—Age, 22 years. Enlisted at New York City, to serve three years, and mustered in as private, Co. G, August 26, 1863; deserted, February 15, 1864, at Jacksonville, Fla.

ROACH, JAMES P.—Age, 19 years. Enlisted at Schenectady, to serve three years, and mustered in as private, Co. K, March 28, 1865; transferred to Co. K, Forty-seventh Infantry, June 17, 1865.

ROBINSON, JOHN.—Age, 23 years. Enlisted at Brooklyn, to serve three years, and mustered in as private, Co. G, September 2, 1863; transferred to the Navy, April 27, 1864.

ROBINSON, JOHN.—Age, 20 years. Enlisted at New York City, to serve three years, and mustered in as private, Co. A, August 25, 1863; wounded and captured in action, February 20, 1864, at Olustee, Fla.; died of diarrhea, August 22, 1864, at Andersonville, Ga.

ROBINSON, WILLIAM F.—Age, 19 years. Enlisted, August 14, 1862, at Amsterdam, to serve three years; mustered in as private, Co. D, August 16, 1862; captured in action, September 15, and paroled, September 16, 1862, at Harper's Ferry, Va.; mustered out with detachment, May 1, 1865, at Albany, N.Y.; also borne as Robison.

ROCKMYER, ABRAM.—Age, 43 years. Enlisted at Palatine, to serve three years, and mustered in as private, Co. K, August 23, 1862; captured in action, September 15, and paroled, September 16, 1862, at Harper's Ferry, Va.; died, March 14, 1865, at Fort Monroe, Va., as Rockmire; also borne as Rightmoyer.

RODRIGUE, JOSE.—Age, 21 years. Enlisted at Tarrytown, to serve three years, and mustered in as private, Co. B, February 27, 1865; deserted, April 1, 1865, at Duplin Roads, N.C.

ROGERS, FRANKLIN.—Age, 20 years. Enlisted at Schenectady, to serve one year, and mustered in as private, Co. F, September 8, 1864; mustered out with company, June 17, 1865, at Raleigh, N.C.

ROGERS, JOHN.—Age, 22 years. Enlisted at Goshen, to serve three years, and mustered in as private, Co. A, February 25, 1865; mustered out, June 10, 1865, at Raleigh, N.C.; also borne as Rodgers.

ROGERS, NICHOLAS G.—Age, 36 years. Enlisted at Amsterdam, to serve one year and mustered in as private, Co. D, March 25, 1865; transferred to Co. D, Forty-seventh Infantry, June 17, 1865.

ROLF, GEORGE.—Age, 21 years. Enlisted, August 18, 1862, at Canajoharie, to serve three years; mustered in as private, Co. I, August 20, 1862; captured in action, September 15, and paroled, September 16, 1862, at Harper's Ferry, Va., and deserted, same date, at Frederick, Md., as Ralph.

ROMP, FRANCIS.—Age, 23 years. Enlisted at Brooklyn, to serve one year, and mustered in as private, Co. K, February 21, 1865; transferred to Co. I, Forty-seventh Infantry, June 17, 1865.

RONALD, ALEXANDER.—Age, 18 years. Enlisted, August 9, 1862, at Wells, to serve three years; mustered in as private, Co. K, August 16, 1862; captured in action, September 15, and paroled, September 16, 1862, at Harper's Ferry, Va.; promoted corporal, no date; wounded in action, July 30, 1864, and died of his wounds, July 31, 1864, before Petersburg, Va.

ROSA, ELIJAH A.—Age, 20 years. Enlisted, August 11, 1862, at Broadalbin, to serve three years; mustered in as private, Co. K, August 12, 1862; captured in action, September 15, paroled September 16, 1862 at Harper's Ferry, Va.; discharged, July 20, 1863.

ROSA, LEWIS.—Age, 24 years. Enlisted, August 14, 1862, at Florida, to serve three years; mustered in as private, Co. D, August 15, 1862.; captured in action, September 15, and paroled, September 16, 1862, at Harper's Ferry, Va.,; mustered out with company, June 17, 1865, at Raleigh, N.C. as Rossa; also borne as Rosse.

ROWLEY, WILLIAM.—Age, 44 years. Enlisted, August 14, 1862, at Broadalbin, to serve three years; mustered in as private, Co. K, August 16, 1862; captured in action, September 15, and paroled, September 16, 1862, at Harper's Ferry, Va.; discharged, March 13, 1864.

RUPERT, NICHOLAS.—Age, 21 years. Enlisted, August 11, 1862, at Minden, to serve three years; mustered in as private, Co. B, August 12, 1862; captured in action, September 15, and paroled, September 16, 1862, at Harper's Ferry, Va.; captured in action, August 16, 1864, at Deep Bottom, Va., and reported killed.

RUSSELL, CORNELIUS H.—Age, 30 years. Enlisted at Goshen, to serve one year, and mustered in as private, Co. F, February 21, 1865; transferred to Co. H, Forty-seventh Infantry, June 17, 1865.

RUST, HENRY.—Age, 19 years. Enlisted, July 26, 1862, at Amsterdam, to serve three years; mustered in as private, Co. D, July 30, 1863; captured in action, September 15, and paroled, September 16, 1862, at Harper's Ferry, Va.; mustered out with company, June 17, 1865, at Raleigh, N.C.

RYAN, JOHN.—Age, 32 years. Enlisted at Minden, to serve three years, and mustered in as private, Co. H, August 25, 1862; no further record.

RYNEKER, JACOB.—Age, 20 years. Enlisted at New York City, to serve three yeans; and mustered in as private, Co. D, February 28, 1865; transferred to Company D, Forty-seventh Infantry, June 17, 1865.

RYNEX, JAMES W.—Age, 26 years. Enlisted at Schenectady, to serve one year, and mustered in as private, Co. D, August 16, 1864; mustered out with company, June 17, 1865, at Raleigh, N.C.

SALFELD, DAGUBERT.—Age, 21 years. Enlisted at Brooklyn, to serve three years, and mustered in as private, Co. C, September 2, 1863; transferred to Co. B, Forty-seventh Infantry, June 17, 1865; also borne as Saulfield.

SALISBURY, WILLIAM F.—Age, 21 years. Enlisted, August 8, 1862, at Saratoga Springs, to serve three years; mustered in as private, Co. G, August 18 1862; captured in action, September 15, and paroled, September 16, 1862, at Harper's Ferry, Va.; promoted corporal, no date, sergeant, March 1, 1864; wounded in action, September 29, 1864, at Chaffin's Farm, Va., and January 15, 1865, at Fort Fisher, N.C.; mustered out with company, June 17, 1865, at Raleigh, N.C.; also borne as William H.

SALTSMAN, ALBERD.—Age, 21 years. Enlisted, August 4, 1862 at Amsterdam, to serve three years, mustered in as private, Co. D, August 12, 1862; captured in action, September 15, paroled September 16, 1862 at Harper's Ferry, Va.; died of fever, November 15, 1862, at Chicago, Ill., as Alfred C.

SAMMONS, SIMEON.—Age,—years. Enrolled at Fonda to serve three years and mustered in as colonel, August 27, 1862; wounded in action, February 20, 1864, at Olustee, Fla., and at Petersburg, Va., July 30, 1864; discharged for disability, November 19, 1864. Commissioned colonel August 30, 1862, with rank from August 27, 1862 original.

SAMPSON, HENRY.—Age, 26 years. Enlisted at Halfmoon, to serve three years, and mustered in as private, Co. H, August 7, 1862; captured in action, September 15, paroled September 16, 1862 at Harper's Ferry, Va.; wounded in action, February 20, 1864, at Olustee, Fla.; transferred to the Navy, April 27, 1864.

SANER, CHARLES W.—Age, 31 years. Enlisted, August 11, 1862, at Johnstown, to serve three years; mustered in as private, Co. E, October 28, 1862; wounded, no date; transferred to Co. C, Forty-seventh Infantry, June 17, 1865.

SANFORD, HUGH S.—Age, 30 years. Enrolled at Amsterdam, to serve three years, and mustered in as second lieutenant, Co. D, August 20, 1862, as first lieutenant and adjutant, February 19, 1863; wounded in action, June 1, 1864, at Cold Harbor, Va.; mustered out, June 17, 1865, at Fonda, N.Y. Commissioned second lieutenant, September 10, 1862, with rank from August 20, 1862, original; first lieutenant and adjutant, April 14, 1863, with rank from February 18, 1863, vice T. R. Horton discharged; captain, May 17, 1865, with rank from February 23, 1865, vice T. Wayne discharged.

SAVAGE, EGBERT B.—Age, 22 years. Enrolled, August 20, 1862, at Saratoga Springs, to serve three years; mustered in as first lieutenant, Co. G, August 20, 1862; as captain, November 1, 1862; wounded in action, September 29, 1864, at Chaffin's Farm, Va.; transferred to Co. I, Forty-seventh Infantry, June 17, 1865. Commissioned first lieutenant, September 10, 1862, with rank from August 20, 1862, original; captain, October 31, 1862, with rank from August 30, 1862, vice P.H. Cowen, promoted; major not mustered, June 17, 1865, with rank from April 29, 1865, vice E.L. Walrath promoted.

SAVENHART, JACOB.—Age, 43 years. Enlisted at Palatine, to serve three years, and mustered in as private, Co. A, August 18, 1862; captured in action, September 15, and paroled, September 16, 1862, at Harper's Ferry, Va.; mustered out, to date May 15, 1865, at New York City, as Sabenhart.

SAWER, CHARLES W.—Age, 31 years. Enlisted, August 11, 1862, at Johnstown, to serve three years; mustered in as private, Co. E, October 28, 1862; mustered out with detachment, May 15, 1865, at Albany, N.Y.

SCHAFFER, PHILIP.—Age, 18 years. Enlisted, August 19, 1862, at Milton, to serve three years; mustered in as private, Co. I, August 22, 1862; captured in action, September 15, and paroled, September 16, 1862, at Harper's Ferry, Va.; discharged for disability, no date, as Shaffer.

SCHARFF, CHARLES.—Age, 18 years. Enlisted, August 6, 1862, at Canajoharie, to serve three years; mustered in as private, Co. I, August 16, 1862; captured in action, September 15, and paroled, September 16, 1862, at Harper's Ferry, Va.; wounded in action, February 20, 1864, at Olustee, Fla.; mustered out with company, June 17, 1865, at Raleigh, N.C., as Charles W.; also borne as Sharff.

SCHLOSBURGH, HARRIS.—Age, 21 years. Enlisted at Schenectady, to serve one year, and mustered in as private, Co. E, July 29, 1864; wounded, no date; mustered out, September 25, 1865, to date June 17, 1865; also borne as Slasburgh.

SCHRAM, DANIEL K.—Age, 41 years. Enlisted at St. Johnsville, to serve three years, and mustered in as private, Co. B, August 11, 1862; captured in action, September 15, and paroled, September 16, 1862, at Harper's Ferry, Va.; discharged for disability, September 8 1864.

SCHUYLER, CHARLES.—Age, 29 years. Enlisted, August 13, 1862, at Canajoharie, to serve three years; mustered in as private, Co. B, August 15, 1862: captured in action, September 15, and paroled, September 16, l862, at Harper's Ferry, Va.; mustered out with company, June 17, 1865, at Raleigh, N.C.

SCORSBY, WILLIAM H.—Age, 20 years. Enlisted at Stratford, to serve three years, and mustered in as private, Co. E, August 14, 1862; captured in action, September 15, and paroled, September 16, 1862, at Harper's Ferry, Va.; wounded in action, February 20, 1864, at Olustee, Fla., and August 16, 1864, at Deep Bottom, Va.; promoted corporal, November 1, 1864; mustered out with detachment, June 23, 1865, at Albany, N.Y.

SCOTT, BENJAMIN.—Age, 39 years. Enlisted, August 26, 1862 at Johnstown, to serve three years; mustered in as private, Co. E, October 31, 1862; mustered out, July 15, 1865, at Lovell Hospital, Portsmouth Grove, R. I.

SCOTT, IRA.—Age, 20 years. Enlisted, August 9, 1862, at Moreau, to serve three years; mustered in as private, Co. G, August 18, 1862; captured in action, September 15, and paroled, September 16, 1862, at Harper's Ferry, Va.; wounded in action, February 20, 1864, at Olustee, Fla.; promoted corporal, March 1, 1864; sergeant, May 22, 1865; mustered out with company, June 17, 1865, at Raleigh, N.C.

SCOTT, JOHN.—Age, 18 years. Enlisted in Eighteenth Congressional District, to serve three years, and mustered in as private, Co. E, June 13, 1864; died of fever, December 26, 1864, at hospital, Point of Rocks, Va.

SEAGRIST, HERMAN.—Age, 21 years. Enlisted at

Brooklyn, to serve one year, and mustered in as private, Co. K, February 21, 1865; transferred to Co. D, Forty-seventh Infantry, June 17, 1865.

SEAMAN, RICHARD.—Age, 18 years. Enlisted at Kingston, to serve one year, and mustered in as private, Co. I, February 28, 1865; transferred to Co. I, Forty-seventh Infantry, June 17, 1865.

SEAVER, JACOB.—Age, 38 years. Enlisted at Halfmoon, to serve three years, and mustered in as private, Co. H, August 14, 1862; captured in action, September 15, and paroled September 16, 1862, at Harper's Ferry, Va.; mustered out with company, June 17, 1865, at Raleigh, N.C.; also borne as Sever.

SECORE, DANIEL.—Age, 26 years. Enlisted at Tarrytown, to serve three years, and mustered in as private, Co. H, October 29, 1863; wounded in action, February 20, 1864, at Olustee, Fla.; transferred to Co. K, Forty-seventh Infantry, June 17, 1865.

SEELEY, HENRY.—Age, 27 years. Enlisted, August 9, 1862, at Broadalbin, to serve three years; mustered in as corporal, Co. K, August 12, 1862; captured in action, September 15, and paroled, September 16, 1862, at Harper's Ferry, Va.; returned to ranks, no date; died, June 19, 1863, at Hilton Head, S.C.; also borne as Luly.

SELLER, FREDERICK.—Age, 34 years. Enlisted at Bleecker, to serve three years, and mustered in as private, Co. A, July 29, 1862; captured in action, September 15, and paroled, September 16, 1862, at Harper's Ferry, Va.; wounded in action, May 15, 1864, at Drewry's Bluff, Va.; mustered out with company, June 17, 1865, at Raleigh, N.C.

SEXTON, RALPH.—Age, 37 years. Enrolled at Broadalbin, to serve three years, and mustered in as first lieutenant, Co. K, August 20, 1862; discharged for disability, May 22, 1863, at Hilton Head, S.C., as Saxton. Commissioned first lieutenant, September 10, 1862, with rank from August 20, 1862, original.

SEXTON, WARREN J.—Age, 28 years. Enlisted, August 15, 1862, at Caroga, to serve three years; mustered in as private, Co. K, August 16, 1862; captured in action, September 15, and paroled, September 16, 1862, at Harper's Ferry, Va.; promoted corporal, no date; deserted, August 27, 1863, at Albany, N.Y.

SEYMOUR, SAMUEL W.—Age, 26 years. Enlisted, August 9, 1862, at Stillwater, to serve three years; mustered in as private, Co. H, August 14, 1862; captured in action, September 15, and paroled, September 16, 1862, at Harper's Ferry, Va.; mustered out, June 18, 1865, at Richmond, Va. while attached to Light Battery B, First U. S. Artillery.

SHAFT, JOHN H.—Age, 18 years. Enlisted, July 27, 1862, at Saratoga Springs, to serve three years; mustered in as private, Co. G, August 18, 1862; captured in action, September 15, paroled September 16, 1862 at Harper's Ferry, Va.; wounded in action, February 20, 1864, at Olustee, Fla., and May 7, 1864, at Chester Station, Va.; absent since and at muster-out of company.

SHANNON, JOSEPH.—Age, 32 years. Enlisted at Palatine, to serve three years, and mustered in as private, Co A, August 9, 1862; wounded in action, September 12, 1862, at Maryland Heights Md.; transferred to Co. G, Tenth Regiment, Veteran Reserve Corps, September 12, 1863; deserted, September 27, 1864, at Sherburne Barracks.

SHANNON, RICHARD.—Age, 21 years. Enlisted, August 2, 1862, at Canajoharie, to serve three years; mustered in as private, Co. I, August 4, 1862; captured in action, September 15, paroled September 16, 1862 at Harper's Ferry, Va.; wounded in action, February 20, 1864, at Olustee, Fla.; mustered out with company, June 17, 1865, at Raleigh, N.C.

SHAUGHNESSY, MICHAEL.—Age, 25 years. Enlisted at New York City, to serve three years, and mustered in as private, Co. I, March 11, 1865; transferred to Co. H, Forty-seventh Infantry, June 17, 1865.

SHAVER, WEBSTER.—Age, 21 years. Enlisted, August 13, 1862, at Ephratah, to serve three years; mustered in as corporal, Co. E, August 16, 1862; captured in action, September 15, and paroled, September 16, 1862, at Harper's Ferry, Va.; promoted sergeant, February 27, 1863; wounded in action, February 20, 1864, at Olustee, Fla., and May 7, 1864, at Chester Station, Va.; mustered out with company, June 17, 1865 at Raleigh, N.C.

SHAW, JAMES.—Age, 18 years. Enlisted at Northumberland, to serve three years, and mustered in as private, Co. C, August 11, 1862; discharged on writ of habeas corpus, no date.

SHAW, SANFORD W.—Age, 21 years. Enlisted, August 13, 1862, at Mayfield, to serve three years; mustered in as private, Co. E, August 15, 1862; captured in action, September 15, and paroled, September 16, 1862, at Harper's Ferry, Va.; wounded and captured in action, February 20, 1864, at Olustee, Fla.; died, November 10, 1864, in Confederate hospital, at Tallahassee, Fla.

SHAW, WILLIAM H.—Age, 33 years. Enrolled, August 4, 1862, at Fonda, to serve three years; mustered in as captain, Co. E, August 20, 1862; wounded in action, June 3, 1864, at Cold Harbor, Va., and January 15, 1865, at Fort Fisher, N.C.; mustered out with company, June 17, 1865, at Raleigh, N.C.; prior service as captain, Co. F, Seventh Cavalry. Commissioned captain, September 10, 1862, with rank from August 20, 1862, original.

SHAY, LAWRENCE.—Age, 28 years. Enlisted at Brooklyn, to. serve three years, and mustered in as private, Co. F, March 6, 1865; deserted, May 5, 1865, at Raleigh, N.C.

SHEARS, JOHN.—Age, 18 years. Enlisted at Goshen, to serve three years, and mustered in as private, Co. A, February 14, 1865; transferred to Co. A, Forty-seventh Infantry, June 17, 1865.

SHEFFER, LEVI.—Age, 23 years. Enrolled at Saratoga Springs, to serve three years, and mustered in as private, Co. G, July 31, 1862; promoted sergeant, August 18, 1862; first sergeant, no date; mustered in as second lieutenant, November 21, 1863; killed in action, February 20, 1864, at Olustee, Fla.; also borne as Shaffer. Commissioned second lieutenant, May 13, 1863, with rank from March 4, 1863, vice D. H. Graves promoted.

SHEPARD, ALFRED C.—Age, 25 years. Enlisted, July 28, 1862, at Amsterdam, to serve three years; mustered in as private, Co. D, July 30, 1862; captured in action, September 15, and paroled, September 16 1862 at Harper's Ferry, Va.; discharged for disability, August 29, 1863,at Beaufort, S.C., as Shepperd.

SHEPARD, DUANE.—Age, 18 years. Enlisted, August 4, 1862, at Halfmoon, to serve three years, mustered in as private, Co. H, August 14, 1862; captured in action, September 15, paroled September 16, 1862 at Harper's Ferry, Va.; discharged, July 22, 1863, as Shephard.

SHEPPARD, FRANK W.—Age 18 years. Enlisted at Schenectady, to serve three years, and mustered in as private, Co. G, March 3. 1865; transferred to Co. F, Forty-seventh Infantry, June 17, 1865.

SHEPPARD, JOHN.—Age. 28 years. Enlisted at Brooklyn, to serve three years, and mustered in as private, Co. G, September 3, 1863; transferred to the Navy, April 27, 1864.

SHERLOCK, JOHN.—Age, 19 years. Enlisted, August 14, 1862, at Glen, to serve three years; mustered in as private, Co. A, August 18, 1862; captured in action, September 15, and paroled, September 16, 1862, at Harper's Ferry, Va.; again captured in action, August 18, 1864, at Deep Bottom, Va.; paroled, no date; mustered out, August 8, 1865, at New York City, as Shirlock.

SHERMAN, DANIEL C.—Age, 22 years. August 16, 1862, at Charlton, to serve three years; mustered in as corporal, Co. I, August 18, 1862; captured in action, September 15, paroled September 16, 1862 at Harper's Ferry, Va.; died, January 17, 1865, at hospital, Point of Rocks, Va.

SHERMAN, ELIJAH.—Age, 30 years. Enlisted, July 31, 1862, at Milton, to serve three years: mustered in as private, Co. I, August 2, 1862; no further record.

SHERMAN, REUBEN.—Age, 23 years. Enlisted, August 9, 1862, at Moreau, to serve three years; mustered in as private, Co. F, August 19, 1862; captured in action, September 15, and paroled, September 16, 1862, at Harper's Ferry, Va.; died of typhus fever, January 22, 1863, at hospital, Yorktown, Va.

SHIPPER, ZIBA.—Age, 41 years. Enlisted, August 7, 1862, at Day, to serve three years; mustered in as private, Co. F, August 19, 1862; captured in action, September 15, and paroled, September 16, 1862, at Harper's Ferry, Va.; discharged for disability, April 17, 1863.

SHOUTS, HENRY.—Age, 25 years. Enlisted, July 23, 1862, at Halfmoon, to serve three years; mustered in as private, Co. H, August 1, 1862; captured in action, September 15, and paroled, September 16, 1862, at Harper's Ferry, Va.; mustered out with detachment, June 8, 1865, at New Berne, N.C., as Shauntz; also borne as Shants.

SHOUTS, WILLIAM H.—Age, 18 years. Enlisted at Clifton Park, to serve three years, and mustered in as private, Co. H, August 14, 1862; captured in action, September 15, and paroled, September 16, 1862, at Harper's Ferry, Va.; wounded in action, February 20, 1864, at Olustee, Fla., and May 14, 1864, at Drewry's Bluff, Va.; promoted corporal, May 1, 1865; mustered out with company, June 17, 1865, at Raleigh, N.C., as Shants; also borne as Shontz.

SHOWERS, ALEXANDER.—Age, 41 years. Enlisted, August 11, 1862, at Corinth, to serve three years; mustered in as private, Co. F, August 19, 1862; captured in action, September 15, and paroled, September 16, 1862, at Harper's Ferry, Va.; transferred to Veteran Reserve Corps, September 26, 1863.

SHOWERS, JOSEPH H.—Age, 18 years. Enlisted, August 11, 1862, at Corinth, to serve three years; mustered in as private, Co. F, August 19, 1862; captured in action, September 15, and paroled, September 16, 1862, at Harper's Ferry, Va.; died, December 21, 1862, at hospital, Washington, D.C.

SHULER, PETER P.—Age, 23 years. Enlisted, August 14, 1862, at Bleecker, to serve three years; mustered in as private, Co. E, August 15, 1862; captured in action, September 15, and paroled, September 16, 1862, at Harper's Ferry, Va.; died of fever, February 7, 1863, at hospital, Philadelphia, Pa.

SHULTS, FERDINAND.—Age, 21 years. Enlisted at Tarrytown, to serve three years, and mustered in as private, Co. K, March 8, 1865; transferred to Co. K, Forty-seventh Infantry, June 17, 1865.

SHULTS, NICHOLAS.—Age, 21 years. Enlisted at Palatine to serve three years, and mustered in as corporal, Co. A, July 24, 1862; captured in action, September 15, paroled September 16, 1862 at Harper's Ferry, Va.; wounded, July, 1864, at Petersburg, Va.; returned to ranks, no date; discharged for disability, April 28, 1865, at Rochester, N.Y.

SHULTZ, PHILIP M.—Age, 19 years. Enlisted, July 19, 1862, at Minden, to serve three years; mustered in as private, Co. I, August 26, 1862; deserted, August 28, 1862, at Fonda, N.Y.

SHULTZ, RICHARD.—Age, 26 years. Enlisted at Albany, to serve three years, and mustered in as private, Co. F, October 28, 1863; captured, February 9, 1864; paroled, no date; transferred to Co. G, Forty-seventh Infantry, June 17, 1865; also borne as Schultz.

SHULTZ, WILLIAM.—Age, 23 years. Enlisted at Kingston, to serve three years, and mustered in as private, Co. I, February 28, 1865; transferred to Co, I, Forty-seventh Infantry, June 17, 1865.

SHUTE, ALEXANDER B.—Age, 29 years. Enlisted, August 7, 1862, at Florida, to serve three years; mustered in as private, Co. D, August 15, 1862; captured in action, September 15, and paroled, September 16, 1862, at Harper's Ferry, Va.; promoted corporal, no date; mustered out, June 15, 1865, at Albany, N.Y.

SHUTZ, ADOLPHUS.—Age, 21 years. Enlisted, August 15, 1862, at Amsterdam, to serve three years; mustered in as private, Co. G, August 18, 1862; captured in action, September 15, paroled September 16, 1862 at Harper's Ferry, Va.; deserted, October 13, 1862, at Chicago, Ill., as Sholts; also borne as Shultz.

SICKLER, DEWITT.—Age, 19 years. Enlisted, July 18, 1862, at Halfmoon, to serve three years; mustered in as private, Co. H, August 7, 1862; captured in action, September 15, and paroled, September 16, 1862 at Harper's Ferry, Va.; discharged for disability, December 20, 1862, at Chicago, Ill.

SIEGELKEN, FREDERICK.—Age, 31 years. Enlisted at Brooklyn, to serve one year, and mustered in as private, Co. C, February 28, 1865; transferred to Co. D, Forty-seventh Infantry, June 17, 1865; also borne as Seigelbere.

SILK, ANDREW.—Enlisted at Brooklyn, to serve three years, and mustered in as private, Co. I, March 11, 1865; mustered out, August 1, 1865, at McDougall Hospital, New York Harbor.

SILVER, CHARLES W.—Age, 28 years. Enlisted at

Brooklyn, to serve three years, and mustered in as private, Co. C, January 16, 1865; deserted, May 10, 1865, at Raleigh, N.C.; also borne as Silber.

SILVERNAIL, JOHN P.—Age, 41 years. Enlisted, August 12, 1862, at Halfmoon, to serve three years; mustered in as private, Co. H, August 14, 1862; captured in action, September 15, and paroled, September 16, 1862, at Harper's Ferry, Va.; discharged, August 29, 1863.

SIMPSON, JOHN H.—Age, 33 years. Enlisted, August 8, 1862, at Florida, to serve three years; mustered in as private, Co. D, August 15, 1862; captured in action, September 15, and paroled, September 16, 1862, at Harper's Ferry, Va.; wounded and captured in action, February 20, 1864, at Olustee, Fla.; died, April 1, 1864, at Andersonville, Ga.

SIMSON, ERVIN.—Age, 26 years. Enlisted, August 13, 1862, at Hadley, to serve three years; mustered in as private, Co. F, August 19, 1862; captured in action, September 15, and paroled, September 16, 1862, at Harper's Ferry, Va.; wounded in action, February, 20, 1864, at Olustee, Fla.; mustered out with company, June 17, 1865, at Raleigh, N.C., as Irvin Simpson.

SISSON, JACOB A.—Age, 31 years. Enlisted, August 9, 1862, at Moreau, to serve three years; mustered in as private, Co. G, August 18, 1862; captured in action, September 15, and paroled, September 16, 1862, at Harper's Ferry, Va.; promoted corporal, April 4, 1865; mustered out with company, June 17, 1863, at Raleigh, N.C.; also borne as Sesson.

SISTER, ROYAL.—Age, 18 years. Enlisted at Root, to serve three years, and mustered in as private, Co. H, March 2, 1865; transferred to Co. I, Forty-seventh Infantry, June 17, 1865.

SKYM, GEORGE H.—Age 18 years. Enlisted, August 9, 1862, at Moreau, to serve three years; mustered in as private, Co. G, August 18, 1862; captured in action, September 15, paroled, September 16, 1862 at Harper's Ferry, Va.; mustered out with detachment June 24, 1863, at Albany, N.Y., as Skynn.

SLINGERLAND, ELBERT.—Age, 20 years. Enlisted, July 30, 1862, at Amsterdam, to serve three years; mustered in as sergeant, Co. D, August 11, 1862; captured in action, September 15, and paroled, September 16, 1862, at Harper's Ferry, Va.; mustered out with company, June 17, 1865, at Raleigh, N.C.

SLOCUM, AARON C.—Age, 27 years. Enrolled, August 4, 1862, at Fonda, to serve three years; mustered in as second lieutenant, Co. E, August 20, 1862; as first lieutenant, April 7, 1864; as captain, Co. H, February 23, 1865; transferred to Co. E, Forty-seventh Infantry, June 17, 1865. Commissioned second lieutenant, September 10, 1862, with rank from August 20, 1862, original; first lieutenant, May 18, 1864, with rank from April 6, 1864, vice J. L. Haines resigned; captain, May 17, 1865, with rank from February 23, 1865, vice W. Ferguson discharged.

SLOCUM, EDWARD C.—Age, 21 years. Enlisted, August 8, 1862, at Milton, to serve three years; mustered in as private, Co. I, August 9, 1862; captured in action, September 15, and paroled, September 16, 1862, at Harper's Ferry, Va.; wounded in action, February 20, 1864, at Olustee, Fla.; transferred to Veteran Reserve Corps, no date; discharged for disability, March 4, 1865, at Beaufort, S.C., as of Sixty-fourth Company, Second Battalion, Veteran Reserve Corps.

SMEA, MICHAEL.—Age, 20 years. Enlisted at New York City, to serve three years, and mustered in as private, Co. F, August 26, 1863; wounded in action, February 20, 1864, at Olustee, Fla.; again wounded, no date; transferred to Co. G, Forty-seventh Infantry, June 17, 1865.

SMEATON, THOMAS.—Age, 22 years, Enlisted, July 23, 1862, at Root, to serve three years; mustered in as corporal, Co. A, July 24, 1862; captured in action, September 15, and paroled, September 16, 1862, at Harper's Ferry, Va.; returned to ranks, no date; discharged for disability, June 18, 1863, at Hilton Head, S.C., as Thomas B.

SMITH, ABRAM B.—Age, 37 years. Enlisted, August 11, 1862, at Saratoga Spa, to serve three years; mustered in as private, Co. F, August 12, 1862; captured in action, September 15, and paroled, September 16, 1862, at Harper's Ferry, Va.; discharged for disability, February 14, 1863.

SMITH, AHIJAH.—Age, 22 years. Enlisted, July 29, 1862, at Ephratah, to serve three years; mustered in as private, Co. I, August 2, 1862; captured in action, September 15, and paroled, September 16, 1862, at Harper's Ferry, Va.; mustered out with company, June 17, 1865, at Raleigh, N.C.

SMITH, ALONZO.—Age, 18 years. Enlisted, July 30, 1862, at St. Johnsville, to serve three years; mustered in as private, Co. B, August 11, 1862; captured in action, September 15, and paroled, September 16, 1862, at Harper's Ferry, Va.; again captured in action, February 20, 1864, at Olustee, Fla., and reported dead; no further record.

SMITH, ANDREW.—Age, 24 years. Enlisted at Tarrytown, to serve three years, and mustered in as private, Co. D, February 27, 1865; transferred to Co. D, Forty-seventh Infantry, June 17, 1865.

SMITH, ANDREW H.—Age, 19 years. Enlisted, July 22, 1862, at Halfmoon, to serve three years; mustered in as private, Co. H, August 1, 1862; captured in action, September 15, and paroled, September 16, 1862, at Harper's Ferry, Va.; mustered out, May 30, 1865, at Whitehall Hospital, Philadelphia, Pa.

SMITH, BENJOR.—Age, 43 years. Enlisted at Kingston, to serve one year, and mustered in as private, Co. I, February 28, 1865; transferred to Co. I, Forty-seventh Infantry, June 17, 1865; also borne as Benajar Smith.

SMITH, CALEB.—Age, 30 years. Enlisted, August 25, 1862, at Minden, to serve three years; mustered in as private, Co. I, August 26, 1862; deserted, August 27, 1862, at Fonda, N.Y.

SMITH, CARROLL.—Age, 20 years. Enlisted at New York City, to serve three years, and mustered in as private, Co. I, March 7, 1865; transferred to Co. I, Forty-seventh Infantry, June 17, 1865.

SMITH, CHARLES.—Age, 22 years. Enlisted, April 10, 1864, at Schenectady, to serve three years; mustered in as private, Co. K, April 19, 1864; captured, April 14, 1865; paroled, April 30, 1865; mustered out, June 19, 1865, to date, May 14, 1865, at New York City; prior service as private, Co. G, Sixty-second Infantry, as Martin Stock.

SMITH, CHARLES.—Age, 21 years. Enlisted at Brooklyn, to serve one year, and mustered in as private, Co. H, February 23, 1865; deserted, April 1, 1865, at Duplin Roads, N.C.

SMITH, CONRADT.—Age, 41 years. Enlisted at Palatine, to serve three years, and mustered in as private, Co. A, July 30, 1862; captured in action, September 15, and paroled, September 16, 1862, at Harper's Ferry, Va.; wounded in action, January 14, 1865, at Fort Fisher, N.C.; absent at General Hospital since and at muster-out of company.

SMITH, EDWARD.—Age, 21 years. Enlisted at Tarrytown, to serve three years, and mustered in as private, Co. I, October 7, 1863; transferred to the Navy, April 25, 1864.

SMITH, EDWARD.—Age, 20 years. Enlisted at Tarrytown, to serve three years, and mustered in as private, Co. D, October 30, 1863; killed in action, February 20, 1864, at Olustee, Fla.

SMITH, ELI.—Age, 23 years. Enlisted, August 11, 1862, at Caroga, to serve three years; mustered in as corporal, Co. K, August 12, 1862; captured in action, September 15, and paroled, September 16, 1862, at Harper's Ferry, Va.; returned to ranks, no date; discharged, February 6, 1863, at Convalescent Camp, Alexandria, Va.

SMITH, FELIX.—Age, 22 years. Enlisted at Brooklyn, to serve three years, and mustered in as private, Co. C, February 28, 1865; mustered out, July 10, 1863, at New York, N.Y.

SMITH, GEORGE.—Age, 19 years. Enlisted at Mohawk, to serve three years, and mustered in as private, Co. A, July 25, 1862; captured in action September 15, and paroled, September 16, 1862, at Harper's Ferry, Va.; promoted corporal, no date; wounded in action, February 20, 1864, at Olustee, Fla., and August 16, 1864, at Deep Bottom, Va.; transferred to Veteran Reserve Corps, April 1, 1865; mustered out with detachment, June 28, 1865, at Washington, D.C., as of Co. C, Seventh Regiment, Veteran Reserve Corps.

SMITH, GEORGE.—Age, 18 years. Enlisted at Oxford, to serve three years, and mustered in as private, Co. D, March 8, 1865; transferred to Co. H, Forty-seventh Infantry, June 17, 1865.

SMITH, GEORGE H.—Age, 44 years. Enlisted, August 13, 1862, at Ephratah, to serve three years; mustered in as private, Co. E, October 28, 1862; discharged for disability, November 7, 1863, at Beaufort, S.C.

SMITH, GEORGE O.—Age, 18 years. Enrolled, August 5, 1862, at Canajoharie, to serve three years; mustered in as sergeant, Co. I, August 12, 1862; promoted first sergeant, no date; mustered in as second lieutenant, January 27, 1864; discharged for disability, November 4, 1864. Commissioned second lieutenant, April 22, 1864, with rank from January 27, 1864, vice F. D. Barnum promoted.

SMITH, GEORGE S.—Age, 18 years. Enlisted, August 11, 1862, at Canajoharie, to serve three years; mustered in as private, Co. B, August 12, 1862; captured in action, September 15, and paroled, September 16, 1862, at Harper's Ferry, Va.; wounded in action, August 16, 1864, at Deep Bottom, Va.; mustered out, June 29, 1865, at Smithville, N.C.

SMITH, GEORGE W.—Age, 18 years. Enlisted, August 9, 1862, at Moreau, to serve three years; mustered in as private, Co. F, August 14, 1862; captured in action, September 15, and paroled September 16, 1862, at Harper's Ferry, Va.; absent, sick in hospital at Fort Monroe, Va., at muster-out of company.

SMITH, HENRY.—Age, 35 years. Enlisted at New York City, to serve three years, and mustered in as private, Co. D, August 25, 1863; transferred to Co. C, Forty-seventh Infantry, June 17, 1865.

SMITH, HORATIO.—Age, 27 years. Enlisted, July 31, 1862, at Palatine, to serve three years; mustered in as private, Co. I, August 2, 1862; captured in action, September 15, and paroled, September 16, 1862, at Harper's Ferry, Va.; wounded in action, February 20, 1864, at Olustee, Fla.; died, December 11, 1864, at hospital, Fort Monroe, Va.

SMITH, ISAAC E.—Age, 21 years. Enrolled, July 30, 1862, at St. Johnsville, to serve three years; mustered in as sergeant, Co. B, August 11, 1862; as second lieutenant, June 10, 1863; wounded in action, February 20, 1864, at Olustee, Fla.; mustered in as first lieutenant, Co. C. November 28, 1864; as captain, Co. F, June 14, 1865; transferred to Co. E, Forty-seventh Infantry, June 17, 1865. Commissioned second lieutenant, May 13, 1863, with rank from April 16, 1863, vice J. Van De Sande promoted; first lieutenant, November 19, 1864, with rank from November 17, 1864, vice J. Van De Sande deceased; captain, May 17, 1865, with rank from April 29, 1865, vice W. H. McKittrick killed in action.

SMITH, JACOB.—Age, 28 years. Enlisted at Minden, to serve three years, and mustered in as private, Co. H, August 25, 1862; no further record.

SMITH, JAMES.—Age, 44 years. Enlisted, August 9, 1862, at Moreau, to serve three years; mustered in as private, Co. F, August 14, 1862; captured in action, September 15, and paroled, September 16, 1862, at Harper's Ferry, Va.; mustered out, May 15, 1865, at Fort Monroe, Va.

SMITH, JAMES C.—Age, 44 years. Enlisted, August 11, 1862, at Moreau, to serve three years; mustered in as private, Co. G, August 18, 1862; captured in action, September 15, and paroled, September 16, 1862, at Harper's Ferry, Va.; promoted sergeant, no date; returned to ranks, January 18, 1864; wounded and captured in action, February 20, 1864, at Olustee, Fla.; died, August 6, 1864, at Andersonville, Ga.; also borne as James E.

SMITH, JEREMIAH.—Age, 18 years. Enlisted at Schenectady, to serve one year, and mustered in as private, Co. D, September 3, 1864; mustered out with company, June 17, 1865, at Raleigh, N.C.

SMITH, JOHN.—Age, 21 years. Enlisted, August 5, 1862, at Minden, to serve three years; mustered in as private, Co. B, August 12, 1862; captured in action, September 15, and paroled, September 16, 1862, at Harper's Ferry, Va.; transferred to Co. I, October 28, 1862; discharged for disability, no date.

SMITH, JOHN.—Age, 32 years. Enlisted at New York City, to serve three years, and mustered in as private, Co. D, August 28, 1863; transferred to Co. E, Forty-seventh Infantry, June 17, 1865.

SMITH, JOHN.—Age, 18 years. Enlisted at Utica, to serve one year, and mustered in as private, Co. I,

August 22, 1864; mustered out with company, June 17, 1865, at Raleigh, N.C.

SMITH, JOHN.—Age, 23 years. Enlisted at Tarrytown, to serve one year, and mustered in as private, Co. F, March 4, 1865; transferred to Co.—, Forty-seventh Infantry, June 17, 1865.

SMITH, JOHN A.—Age, 18 years. Enlisted at Oppenheim, to serve three years, and mustered in as private, Co. E, August 14, 1862; captured in action, September 15, and paroled, September 16, 1862, at Harper's Ferry, Va.; wounded in action, February 20, 1864, at Olustee, Fla.; absent, wounded at muster-out of company.

SMITH, LEVI.—Age, 23 years. Enlisted at Root, to serve three years, and mustered in as private, Co. A, July 30, 1862; captured in action, September 15, and paroled, September 16, 1862, at Harper's Ferry, Va.; mustered out, June 10, 1865, at Albany, N.Y.

SMITH, LORENZO.—Age, 36 years. Enlisted, August 12, 1862, at Milton, to serve three years; mustered in as private, Co. I, August 19, 1862; captured in action, September 15, and paroled, September 16, 1862, at Harper's Ferry, Va.; discharged for disability, no date.

SMITH, LUCIUS A.—Age, 20 years. Enlisted at Canajoharie, to serve three years, and mustered in as private, Co. B, August 11, 1862; captured in action, September 15, and paroled, September 16, 1862, at Harper's Ferry, Va.; wounded and captured in action, February 20, 1864, at Olustee, Fla.; died of scorbutus, August 8, 1864, at Andersonville, Ga.

SMITH, OLIVER.—Age, 40 years. Enlisted, August 11, 1862, at Saratoga Springs, to serve three years; mustered in as private, Co. G, August 18, 1862; captured in action, September 15, and paroled, September 16, 1862, at Harper's Ferry, Va.; discharged for disability, September 17, 1863, at Washington, D.C.

SMITH, SAMUEL.—Age, 27 years. Enlisted at New York City, to serve three years, and mustered in as private, Co. H, September 2, 1863; transferred to the Navy, April 27, 1864.

SMITH, SIDNEY.—Age, 30 years. Enlisted, August 14, 1862, at Malta, to serve three years; mustered in as private, Co. I, August 18, 1862; captured in action, September 15, and paroled, September 16, 1862, at Harper's Ferry, Va.; mustered out, May 28, 1865, at hospital, Fort Monroe, Va.

SMITH, SOLOMON P.—Age,—years. Enrolled, July 2, 1862, in Saratoga County, to serve three years; mustered in as captain, Co. H, August 26, 1862; wounded in action, August 18, 1864, at Deep Bottom, Va.; discharged for disability, January 14, 1865. Commissioned captain, September 10, 1862, with rank from August 20, 1862, original.

SMITH, THOMAS.—Age, 37 years. Enlisted at Brooklyn, to serve three years, and mustered in as private, Co. G, September 2, 1863; transferred to Co. G, Forty-seventh Infantry, June 17, 1865.

SMITH, WILLIAM.—Age, 40 years. Enrolled at Fonda, to serve three years; mustered in as captain, Co. K, August 26, 1862; wounded in action, September 18, 1862, at Maryland Heights, Md.; dismissed, August 19, 1864, and order of dismissal revoked; again mustered in as captain, Co. K, April 25, 1865; mustered out with company, June 17, 1865, at Raleigh, N.C. Commissioned captain, September 10, 1862, with rank from August 20, 1862, original; recommissioned captain, March 24, 1865, with rank from August 19, 1864, vice himself dismissed.

SMITH, WILLIAM.—Age, 18 years. Enlisted, April 15, 1864, at Rochester, to serve three years; mustered in as private, Co. I, April 20, 1864; transferred to Co. H, Forty-seventh Infantry, June 17, 1865.

SMITH, WILLIAM.—Age, 25 years. Enlisted, August 6, 1862, at Stillwater, to serve three years; mustered in as private, Co. H, August 7, 1862; captured in action, September 15, and paroled, September 16, 1862, at Harper's Ferry, Va.; killed in action, February 20, 1864, at Olustee, Fla.

SMITH, WILLIAM.—Age, 36 years. Enlisted at Eighteenth Congressional District, to serve three years, and mustered in as private, Co. C, April 20, 1864; wounded in action, January 15, 1865, at Fort Fisher, N.C.; transferred to Co. B, Forty-seventh Infantry, June 17, 1865.

SNECK, JAMES.—Age, 18 years. Enlisted, July 30, 1862, at St. Johnsville, to serve three years; mustered in as private, Co. B, August 12, 1862; captured in action, September 15, and paroled, September 16, 1862, at Harper's Ferry, Va.; promoted corporal, January 11, 1864; wounded in action, February 20, 1864, at Olustee, Fla., and August 16, 1864, at Deep Bottom, Va.; absent in hospital since and at muster-out of company.

SNELL, AARON B.—Age, 43 years. Enlisted, July 28, 1862, at Palatine, to serve three years; mustered in as private, Co. I, August 2, 1862; captured in action, September 15, and paroled, September 16, 1862, at Harper's Ferry, Va.; discharged for disability, no date; again enlisted at Utica; to serve one year, and mustered in, August 22, 1864; mustered out with detachment, June 8, 1865, at New Berne, N.C.

SNELL, ABNER.—Age, 30 years. Enlisted, August 9, 1862, at St. Johnsville, to serve three years; mustered in as private, Co. B, August 11, 1862; captured in action, September 15, and paroled, September 16, 1862, at Harper's Ferry, Va.; promoted corporal, May 10, 1863; mustered out with company, June 17, 1865, at Raleigh, N.C.

SNELL, LEANDER.—Age, 24 years. Enlisted at Palatine, to serve three years, and mustered in as private, Co. A, July 25, 1862; captured in action, September 15, and paroled, September 16, 1862, at Harper's Ferry, Va.; mustered out with company, June 17, 1865, at Raleigh, N.C.

SNELL, ORVILLE.—Age, 18 years. Enlisted, August 5, 1862, at St. Johnsville, to serve three years; mustered in as private, Co. B, August 11, 1862; captured in action, September 15, and paroled, September 16, 1862, at Harper's Ferry, Va.; wounded in action, February 20, 1864, at Olustee, Fla.; captured in action, August 16, 1864, at Deep Bottom, Va.; paroled, no date; mustered out, June 9, 1865, at Annapolis, Md.

SNELL, WILLIAM.—Age, 24 years. Enlisted at Schenectady, to serve one year, and mustered in as private, Co. E, September 3, 1864; mustered out with company, June 17, 1865, at Raleigh, N.C.

SNIFFER, MARTIN.—Age, 30 years. Enlisted at New York City, to serve three years, and mustered in as private, Co. D, January 14, 1865; mustered out, July 8, 1865, at Lovell Hospital, Portsmouth Grove, R. I., as Sniffers.

SNOOKS, THOMAS H.—Age, 31 years. Enlisted at New York City, to serve three years and mustered in as private, Co. G, September 2, 1863; wounded in action May 7, 1864, at Chester Station, Va.; discharged for wounds, August 20, 1864.

SNOW, JOSEPH H.—Age, 19 years. Enlisted August 9, 1862, at Edinburgh, to serve three years; mustered in as private, Co. C, August 14, 1862; captured in action, September 15, and paroled, September 16, 1862, at Harper's Ferry, Va.; absent on furlough, at muster-out of company.

SNYDER, ALFRED.—Age, 17 years. Enlisted, April 15, 1864, at Amsterdam, to serve three years; mustered in as private, Co. I, April 20, 1864; killed, July 28, 1864, before Petersburg, Va.; also borne as Alfred C.

SNYDER, ALONZO.—Age, 42 years. Enlisted, August 4, 1862, at Minden, to serve three years; mustered in as private, Co. I, August 26, 1862; deserted August 28, 1862, at Fonda, N.Y.

SNYDER, CHAUNCY.—Age, 45 years. Enlisted July 23, 1862, at Amsterdam, to serve three years; mustered in as musician, Co. D, July 31, 1862; captured in action, September 15, and paroled, September 16, 1862, at Harper's Ferry, Va.; mustered out, June 28, 1865, at Lovell Hospital, Portsmouth Grove, R. I., as Shneider.

SNYDER, JR., CHAUNCY.—Age, 18 years. Enlisted, July 23, 1862, at Amsterdam, to serve three years; mustered in as private, Co. D, July 31, 1862; captured in action, September 15, and paroled, September 16, 1862, at Harper's Ferry, Va.; died of fever, November 3, 1862, at Chicago, Ill.

SNYDER, FRANCIS.—Age, 44 years. Enlisted, July 29, 1862, at Amsterdam, to serve three years; mustered in as musician, Co. D, July 31, 1862; captured in action, September 15, and paroled, September 16, 1862, at Harper's Ferry, Va.; discharged for disability, August 29, 1863, at Beaufort, S.C.

SNYDER, JACOB H.—Age, 23 years. Enlisted, July 28, 1862, at Minden, to serve three years; mustered in as sergeant, Co. B, August 2, 1862; captured in action, September 15, and paroled, September 16, 1862, at Harper's Ferry, Va.; returned to ranks, no date; promoted corporal, May 10, 1863; sergeant, January 1, 1864; mustered out with company, June 17, 1865, at Raleigh, N.C.

SNYDER, JOHN.—Age, 24 years. Enlisted, August 9, 1862, at Glen, to serve three years; mustered in as private, Co. A, August 26, 1862; captured in action, September 15, and paroled, September 16, 1862, at Harper's Ferry, Va.; died of typhoid fever, June 27, 1863, at hospital, Hilton Head, S.C.

SNYDER, NATHAN H.—Age, 22 years. Enlisted, August 11, 1862, at Johnstown, to serve three years; mustered in as private, Co. E, August 13, 1862; captured in action, September 15, and paroled, September 16, 1862, at Harper's Ferry, Va.; promoted corporal, no date; transferred to Co. H, Seventh Regiment, Veteran Reserve Corps, December 9, 1864; mustered out with detachment, June 26, 1865, at Washington, D.C., as of Two Hundred and Forty-third Company, First Battalion, Veteran Reserve Corps.

SOULES, MICHAEL E.—Age, 21 years. Enlisted, August 8, 1862, at Amsterdam, to serve three years; mustered in as private, Co. D, August 16, 1862; captured in action, September 15, and paroled, September 16, 1862, at Harper's Ferry, Va.; discharged for disability, January 21, 1863, at Yorktown, Va., as Soule.

SOULS, ISAAC W.—Age, 28 years. Enlisted, August 12, 1862, at Wilton, to serve three years; mustered in as private, Co. F, August 19, 1862; captured in action, September 15, and paroled, September 16, 1862, at Harper's Ferry, Va.; deserted, November 22, 1862, at Cleveland, Ohio, as Soules.

SOUTHERLAND, EDWARD W.—Age, 18 years. Enlisted August 5, 1862, at St. Johnsville, to serve three years; mustered in as private, Co. B, August 11, 1862; captured in action, September 15, and paroled, September 16, 1862, at Harper's Ferry, Va.; mustered out with company, June 17, 1865, at Raleigh, N.C., as Sutherland.

SOUTHWICK, CLARK.—Age, 18 years. Enlisted at St. Johnsville, to serve three years. and mustered in as private, Co. I, July 31, 1862; captured in action, September 15, and paroled September 16, 1862, at Harper's Ferry, Va.; wounded in action, February 20, 1864, at Olustee, Fla.; died of his wounds March 7, 1864, at Beaufort, S.C.

SPENCER, ANDREW J.—Age, 22 years. Enlisted at Albany to serve three years, and mustered in as private, Co. K, October 29, 1863; wounded in action, February 20, 1864, at Olustee, Fla.; transferred to the Navy, April 27, 1864.

SPIEGEL, CHARLES.—Age, 27 years. Enlisted, August 6, 1862, at Milton, to serve three years; mustered in as private. Co. C, August 8, 1862; captured in action, September 15, and paroled, September 16, 1862, at Harper's Ferry, Va.; wounded in action, February 20, 1864, at Olustee, Fla.; absent, wounded and in hospital, Albany, N.Y., at muster-out of company.

SPRAGUE, RICHARD M.—Age, 35 years. Enlisted, July 29, 1862, at Hadley, to serve three years; mustered in as corporal, Co. G, August 19, 1862; captured in action, September 15, and paroled, September. 16, 1862, at Harper's Ferry, Va. discharged for disability, October 23, 1862 at Chicago, Ill.

SPRINGER, DENNIS.—Age, 36 years. Enlisted, August 6, 1862, at Day, to serve three years; mustered in as private, Co. C, August 14, 1862; captured in action, September 15, and paroled, September 16, 1862, at Harper's Ferry, Va.; killed in action, September 29, 1864, at Chaffin's Farm, Va.; also borne as Dennis B.

SPRUNG, OBEDIAH.—Age, 20 years. Enlisted, August 11, 1862, at Johnstown, to serve three years; mustered in as private, Co. K, August 12, 1862; captured, in action, September 15, and paroled, September 16, 1862, at Harper's Ferry, Va.; wounded in action, May 7, 1864, at Chester Station, Va.; died of his wounds, May 11, 1864, near Petersburg, Va.

STAIRS, THOMAS S.—Age, 25 years. Enlisted, August 4, 1862, at Milton, to serve three years; mustered in as private, Co. I, August 7, 1862; captured in action, September 15, and paroled, September 16, 1862, at Harper's Ferry, Va.; promoted corporal, no date; wounded in action, August 16, 1864, at Deep Bottom, Va.; mustered out with company, June 17, 1865, at Raleigh, N.C.

STANLEY, JEREMIAH.—Age, 43 years. Enlisted, August 25, 1862, at Amsterdam, to serve three years; mustered in as private, Co. K, August 26, 1862; deserted, August 27, 1862, at Fonda, N.Y.

STAPLES, JOHN P.—Age, 29 years. Enlisted, August 6, 1862, at Milton, to serve three years; mustered in as private, Co. I, August 7, 1862; captured in action, September 15, and paroled, September 16, 1862, at Harper's Ferry, Va.; promoted corporal, no date; mustered out with company, June 17, 1865, at Raleigh, N.C.

STARIN, DANIEL.—Age, 24 years. Enlisted, August 6, 1862, at St. Johnsville, to serve three years; mustered in as private, Co. B, August 7, 1862; captured in action, September 15, and paroled, September 16, 1862, at Harper's Ferry, Va.; wounded in action, February 20, 1864, at Olustee, Fla.; mustered out with company, June 17, 1865, at Raleigh, N.C.

STEAD, JOSHUA.—Age, 33 years. Enlisted, August 13, 1862, at Hadley, to serve three years; mustered in as private, Co. F, August 19, 1862; captured in action, September 15, and paroled, September 16, 1862, at Harper's Ferry, Va.; appointed wagoner, no date; wounded and captured in action, February 20, 1864, at Olustee, Fla.; died, June 27, 1864, at Andersonville, Ga.

STEARNS, ADAM.—Age, 26 years. Enlisted, August 6, 1862, at Caroga, to serve three years; mustered in as private, Co. K, August 12, 1862; captured in action, September 15, and paroled, September 16, 1862, at Harper's Ferry, Va.; mustered out with company, June 17, 1865, at Raleigh, N.C.

STEELE, DANIEL T.—Age, 18 years. Enlisted at Mohawk, to serve three years, and mustered in as private, Co. A, August 7, 1862; captured in action, September 15, and paroled, September 16, 1862, at Harper's Ferry, Va.; mustered out with company, June 17, 1865, at Raleigh, N.C.

STEENBERGH, JR., DANIEL.—Age, 24 years. Enlisted, August 15, 1862, at Wilton, to serve three years; mustered in as musician, Co. F, August 19, 1862; captured in action, September 15, and paroled, September 16, 1862, at Harper's Ferry, Va.; discharged for disability, December 30, 1862.

STEENBERGH, MARVIN.—Age 18 years. Enlisted, August 5, 1862, at Halfmoon, to serve three years; mustered in as private, Co. H, August 7, 1862; captured in action, September 15, and paroled, September 16, 1862, at Harper's Ferry, Va.; promoted corporal, May 1, 1865; mustered out with detachment, June 23, 1865, at Albany, N.Y.

STEENBURGH, JEREMIAH.—Age, 34 years. Enlisted, August 12, 1862, at Ephratah, to serve three years; mustered. in as private, Co. E, August 18, 1862; captured in action, September 15, and paroled, September 16, 1862, at Harper's. Ferry, Va.; died, August 26, 1864, at hospital; Fort Monroe, Va.

STEERE, ELISHA A.—Age, 22 years. Enlisted, August 6, 1862, at Saratoga Spa, to serve three years; mustered in as private, Co. F, August 12, 1862; captured in action, September 15, and paroled, September 16, 1862, at Harper's Ferry, Va.; promoted corporal, no date; killed in action, February 20, 1864, at Olustee, Fla.

STEINBAUER, JOHN C.—Age 36 years. Enlisted, August 4, 1862, at Milton, to serve three years; mustered in as private, Co. I, August 7, 1862; captured in action, September 15, and paroled, September 16, 1862, at Harper's Ferry, Va.; wounded and missing in action, February 20, 1864, at Olustee, Fla.; also borne as Sternbaner; no further record.

STEVENS, JOHN.—Age, 29 years. Enlisted at New York City, to serve three years, and mustered in as private, Co. K, March 11, 1865; transferred to Co. K, Forty-seventh Infantry, June 17, 1865; also borne as Stephens.

STEVENS, THOMAS J.—Age, 42 years. Enlisted at Palatine to serve three years, and mustered in as private, Co. I, August 4, 1862; captured in action, September 15, and paroled, September 16, 1862, at Harper's Ferry, Va.; mustered out, June 25, 1865, at Smithville, N.C.; also borne as Stephens.

STEWART, ANDREW.—Age, 33 years. Enlisted, August 11, 1862, at Clifton Park, to serve three years; mustered in as private, Co. H, August 14, 1862; captured in action, September 15, and paroled, September 16, 1862, at Harper's Ferry, Va.; wounded and captured in action, February 20, 1864, at Olustee, Fla.; died, April 5, 1864, at Tallahassee, Fla.

STEWART, NORVAL.—Age, 18 years. Enlisted, August 4, 1862, at Greenfield, to serve three years; mustered in as private, Co. F, August 12, 1862; captured in action, September 15, and paroled, September 16, 1862, at Harper's Ferry, Va.; wounded in action, February 20, 1864, at Olustee, Fla.; killed in action, July 5, 1864, before Petersburg, Va.

STEWART, ROBERT.—Age, 35 years. Enlisted, August 11, 1862, at Johnstown, to serve three years; mustered in as sergeant, Co. E, August 15, 1862; captured in action, September 15, and paroled, September 16, 1862, at Harper's Ferry, Va.; returned to ranks, no date; mustered out with company, June 17, 1865, at Raleigh, N.C.

STEWART, WILLIAM F.—Age, 37 years. Enlisted, August 7, 1862, at Edinburgh, to serve three years; mustered in as private, Co. C, August 14, 1862; captured in action, September 15, and paroled, September 16, 1862, at Harper's Ferry, Va.; died of diarrhea, September 1, 1864, in hospital at David's Island, New York Harbor.

ST. MARIA, JOHN.—Age, 30 years. Enlisted at Eighteenth Congressional District, to serve three years, and mustered in as private, Co. C, February 27, 1865; deserted, April 4, 1865, at Duplin Cross Roads, N.C.

STONE, ALMON E.—Age, 18 years. Enlisted, August 4, 1862, at Halfmoon, to serve three years; mustered in as private, Co. H, August 14, 1862; captured in action, September 15, and paroled, September 16, 1862, at Harper's Ferry, Va.; wounded in action, June or July, 1864, before Petersburg, Va., and January 15, 1865, at Fort Fisher, N.C.; mustered out, June 5, 1865, at Albany, N.Y., as Almond E.

STONE, EZRA F.—Age, 29 years. Enlisted, August 4, 1862, at Waterford, to serve three years; mustered in as private, Co. H, August 18, 1862; captured in action, September 15, and paroled, September 16, 1862, at Harper's Ferry, Va.; wounded in action, February 20, 1864, at Olustee, Fla.; mustered out with company, June 17, 1865, at Raleigh N.C., as Ezra T.

STOWELL, GEORGE W.—Age, 19 years. Enlisted, March 28, 1864, at St. Johnsville, to serve three years; mustered in as private, Co. E, April 12, 1864; transferred to Co. E, Forty-seventh Infantry, June 17, 1865.

STRAIGHT, WILLIAM.—Age, 33 years. Enlisted at Mohawk, to serve three years, and mustered in as private, Co. A, July 25, 1862; captured in action, September 15, and paroled, September 16, 1862, at Harper's Ferry, Va.; absent, sick in hospital, Fort Monroe, Va., since June, 1864, and at muster-out of company; also borne as Strait.

STREIB, CHARLES.—Age, 25 years. Enlisted at Tarrytown, to serve three years, and mustered in as private, Co. H, October 30, 1863; wounded, June or July, 1864, before Petersburg, Va.; and in action August 16, 1864, at Deep Bottom, Va.; transferred to Co. K, Forty-seventh Infantry, June 17, 1865; also borne as Streip.

SUESS, JOHN.—Age, 18 years. Enlisted at Brooklyn, to serve one year, and mustered in as private, Co. K, February 21 1865; transferred to Co. K, Forty-seventh Infantry, June 17, 1865.

SUITS, NOAH.—Age, 26 years. Enlisted, August 15, 1862, at Palatine, to serve three years; mustered in as private, Co. I, August 18, 1862; captured in action, September 15, and paroled, September 16, 1862, at Harper's Ferry, Va.; deserted, October 29, 1862, at Chicago, Ill.

SUITS, WILLIAM H.—Age, 18 years. Enlisted at Northampton, to serve three years, and mustered in as private, Co. E, August 13, 1862; captured in action, September 15, and paroled, September 16, 1862, at Harper's Ferry, Va.; detached to Light Battery B, First U. S. Artillery, June 30, 1863, and mustered out therefrom, June 13, 1865, at Richmond, Va.

SULIVAN, DANIEL.—Age, 22 years. Enlisted at Brooklyn, to serve three years, and mustered in as private, Co. K, February 21, 1865; deserted, May 1, 1865, at Raleigh, N.C.

SULLIVAN, GEORGE.—Age, 22 years. Enlisted, March 28, 1864, at Malta, to serve three years; mustered in as private, Co. C, April 7, 1864; captured in action, August 16, 1864, at Deep Bottom, Va.; paroled, March 16, 1865, at Fayettsville, S.C.; mustered out, June 26, 1865, at Camp Parole, Annapolis, Md.

SULLIVAN, JAMES.—Age, 22 years. Enlisted at Amsterdam, to serve three years, and mustered in as private, Co. I, April 11, 1864; killed in action, July 6, 1864, in front of Petersburg, Va., also borne as Patrick.

SUTLER, WALTER.—Age, 19 years. Enlisted, August 13, 1862, at Hadley, to serve three years; mustered in as private, Co. F, August 19, 1862; captured in action, September 15, and paroled, September 16, 1862, at Harper's Ferry, Va.; transferred to Co. F, Tenth Regiment, Veteran Reserve Corps, September 16, 1863; discharged for disability, October 22, 1864, as Sutliff.

SUTTON, RICHARD E.—Enrolled, August 20, 1862, at Fonda, to serve three years, and mustered in as surgeon, August 27, 1862; discharged for disability, June 17, 1863, at Hilton Head, S.C. Commissioned surgeon, September 10, 1862, with rank from August 20, 1862, original.

SWAN, JAMES A.—Age, 21 years. Enlisted, August 8, 1862, at Caroga, to serve three years; mustered in as corporal, Co. K, August 12, 1862; captured in action, September 15, and paroled, September 16, 1862, at Harper's Ferry, Va.; promoted first sergeant, no date; mustered out with company, June 17, 1865, at Raleigh, N.C.

SWARTWOUT, ORLANDO.—Age, 18 years. Enlisted at Clifton Park, to serve three years, and mustered in as corporal, Co. H, August 14, 1862; captured in action, September 15, and paroled, September 16, 1862, at Harper's Ferry, Va.; wounded in action, February 20, 1864, at Olustee, Fla., and August 16, 1864, at Deep Bottom, Va.; mustered out, June 30, 1865, at hospital, Fort Monroe, Va.

SYLVESTER, REUBEN F.—Age, 23 years. Enlisted at Tarrytown, to serve three years, and mustered in as private, Co. I, September 23, 1863; transferred to Co. I, Forty-seventh Infantry, June 17, 1865.

TAGGART, PHILIP.—Age, 23 years. Enlisted at Brooklyn, to serve one year, and mustered in as private, Co. K, February 21, 1865; transferred to Co. K, Forty-seventh Infantry, June 17, 1865.

TALBOT, ZACHARIAH.—Age, 18 years. Enlisted at Tompkins to serve three years, and mustered in as private, Co. E, March 1, 1865; transferred to Co. E Forty-seventh Infantry, June 17, 1865, as Vilbert.

TAMM, OTTO.—Age, 39 years. Enlisted at Schenectady, to serve three years, and mustered in as private, Co. I, August 1, 1864; transferred to Co. I, Forty-seventh Infantry, June 17, 1865; also borne as Tanner.

TAYLOR, CHARLES.—Age, 19 years. Enlisted, August 7, 1862, at Greenfield, to serve three years; mustered in as private, Co. F, August 14, 1862; captured in action, September 15, and paroled, September 16, 1862, at Harper's Ferry, Va.; wounded and captured in action, February 20, 1864, at Olustee, Fla.; died, August 6, 1864, at Andersonville, Ga.

TAYLOR, JAMES H.—Age, 30 years. Enlisted at Johnstown, to serve three years, and mustered in as corporal, Co. E, August 11, 1862; captured in action, September 15, and paroled, September 16, 1862, at Harper's Ferry, Va.; returned to ranks, no date; wounded in action, February 20, 1864, at Olustee, Fla.; transferred to Veteran Reserve Corps, November 10, 1864.

TAYLOR, JOEL G.—Age, 44 years. Enlisted, August 6, 1862, at Corinth, to serve three years; mustered in as private, Co. F, August 19, 1862; captured in action, September 15, and paroled, September 16, 1862, at Harper's Ferry, Va.; absent, sick, in hospital, New York City, since December, 1864, and at muster-out of company.

TAYLOR, WILLIAM.—Age, 31 years. Enlisted, July 26, 1862, at Clifton Park, to serve three years; mustered in as private, Co. H, August 1, 1862; captured in action, September 15, and paroled, September 16, 1862, at Harper's Ferry, Va.; wounded and captured in action, February 20, 1864, at Olustee, Fla.; died, supposed of his wounds, no date, on the cars between Savannah and Charleston, S.C.

TEATHERS, MICHAEL.—Age, 21 years. Enlisted, August 11, 1862, at Saratoga Springs, to serve three years; mustered in as private, Co. G, August 18, 1862; killed in action, February 20, 1864, at Olustee, Fla.; also borne as Fethers.

TEMPLER, JAMES W. Age, 21 years. Enlisted at Florida, to serve three years, and mustered in as private, Co. D, August 15, 1862; captured in action, September 15, and paroled, September 16, 1862, at Harper's Ferry, Va.; wounded in action, June 12, 1864, at Cold Harbor, Va.; mustered out with detachment, May 11, 1865, at Albany, N.Y.

TERRELL, NATHAN.—Age, 22 years. Enlisted, July 23, 1862, at Mayfield, to serve three years; mustered in as private, Co. A, July 24, 1862; captured in action, September 15, and paroled, September 16, 1862, at Harper's Ferry, Va.; wounded in action, July—, 1864, at Petersburg, Va.; discharged for disability, in 1865, as Tyrrell; also borne as Farrell.

THAYER, CHARLES E.—Age, 18 years. Enlisted, July 28 1862, at Amsterdam, to serve three years; mustered in as private, Co. D, July 30, 1862; captured in action, September 15, and paroled, September 16, 1862, at Harper's Ferry, Va.; mustered out, July 3, 1865, at David's Island, New York Harbor.

THAYER, WILLIAM.—Age, 34 years. Enlisted, August 13, 1862, at Florida, to serve three years; mustered in as private, Co. D, August 15, 1862; captured in action, September 15, and paroled, September 16, 1862, at Harper's Ferry, Va.; wounded and captured in action, February 20, 1864, at Olustee, Fla.; died of diarrhea, September 21, 1864, at Andersonville, Ga.

THOCKRAH, BENJAMIN.—Age, 18 years. Enlisted, August 5, 1862, at Stillwater, to serve three years; mustered in as private, Co. H, August 7, 1862; captured in action, September 15, and paroled, September 16, 1862, at Harper's Ferry, Va.; wounded in action, June 15, 1864, at Petersburg, Va.; discharged for disability, February 28, 1865, at hospital, near Troy, N.Y., as Thockarah.

THOMAS, DANIEL.—Age, place, date of enlistment and muster-in as private, Co. F, not stated; transferred to Co. G, Forty-seventh Infantry, June 17, 1865.

THOMPSON, JAMES D.—Age, 28 years. Enlisted, August 1, 1862, at Milton, to serve three years; mustered in as corporal, Co. C, August 8, 1862; captured in action, September 15, and paroled, September 16, 1862, at Harper's Ferry, Va.; promoted sergeant, no date; first sergeant, May 1, 1865; mustered out with company, June 17, 1865, at Raleigh, N.C.

THORN, GEORGE.—Age, 38 years. Enlisted, August 1, 1862, at Amsterdam, to serve three years; mustered in as private, Co. H, August 5, 1862; surrendered to the Thirty-second Infantry to which he formerly belonged.

THORNE, HENRY C.—Age, 18 years. Enlisted, August 9, 1862, at Edinburgh, to serve three years; mustered in as private, Co. C, August 14, 1862; captured in action, September 15, and paroled, September 16, 1862, at Harper's Ferry, Va.; mustered out with company, June 17, 1865, at Raleigh, N.C.

THORP, ISAAC.—Age, 24 years. Enlisted, August 14, 1862, at Milton, to serve three years; mustered in as private, Co. I, August 15, 1862; captured in action, September 15, and paroled, September 16, 1862, at Harper's Ferry, Va.; wounded in action, January 15, 1865, at Fort Fisher, N.C.; mustered out, June 1, 1865, at hospital, Fort Monroe, Va., as Thorpe.

THORP, RICHARD A.—Age, 30 years. Enlisted at Broadalbin, to serve three years, and mustered in as private, Co. K, August 16, 1862; captured in action, September 15, and paroled, September 16, 1862, at Harper's Ferry, Va.; wounded in action, February 20, 1864, at Olustee, Fla.; mustered out, June 2, 1865, at New York City; also borne as Thorpe.

TIMMINS, MARTIN.—Age, 28 years. Enlisted at Mohawk, to serve three years, and mustered in as private, Co. A, August 5, 1862; captured in action, September 15, and paroled, September 16, 1862, at Harper's Ferry, Va.; wounded and captured in action, August 16, 1864, at Deep Bottom, Va.; paroled, no date; died of his wounds, September 14, 1864, at hospital, Annapolis, Md.

TIPPLE, RODOLPUS H.—Age, 22 years. Enlisted, July 24, 1862, at Glen, to serve three years; mustered in as corporal, Co. A, August 25, 1862; captured in action, September 15, and paroled, September 16, 1862, at Harper's Ferry, Va.; again captured in action, February 20, 1864, at Olustee, Fla., paroled, November 18, 1864, at Millen, Ga.; mustered out, July 15, 1865, at hospital, Annapolis, Md.

TOMPKINS, DENTON C.—Age, 25 years. Enlisted, August 5, 1862, at St. Johnsville, to serve three years; mustered in as private, Co. B, August 11, 1862; captured in action, September 15, and paroled, September 16, 1862, at Harper's Ferry, Va.; wounded and captured in action, February 20, 1864, at Olustee, Fla.; paroled, no date; mustered out with detachment, May 11, 1865, at Albany, N.Y.

TOMPKINS, JAMES C.—Age, 28 years. Enlisted at Johnstown, to serve three years, and mustered in as private, Co. E, August 11, 1862; captured in action, September 15, and paroled, September 16, 1862, at Harper's Ferry, Va.; died of fever, November 4, 1862, at hospital, Chicago, Ill.

TOMPKINS, WILLIAM.—Age,—years. Enrolled at Fonda, to serve three years, and mustered in as second lieutenant, Co. C, August 20, 1862; killed in action, February 20, 1864, at Olustee, Fla. Commissioned second lieutenant, September 10, 1862, with rank from August 20, 1862, original.

TONE, PETER.—Age, 19 years. Enlisted at Brooklyn, to serve three years, and mustered in as private, Co. F, March 6, 1865; transferred to Co. G, Forty-seventh Infantry, June 17, 1865.

TOTTENHOFFER, EDWIN.—Age, 27 years. Enlisted at New York City, to serve three years, and mustered in as private, Co. A, February 27, 1865; transferred to Co. A, Forty-seventh Infantry, June 17, 1865; also borne as Fottenhoffer.

TOURTELLOT, E. BURK.—Age, 23 years. Enlisted, August 11, 1862, at Saratoga Springs, to serve three years; mustered in as private, Co. G, August 21, 1862; captured in action, September 15, and paroled, September 16, 1862, at Harper's Ferry, Va.; discharged for disability, October 22, 1862, at Chicago, Ill.

TRABBLE, PROSPER.—Age, 23 years. Enlisted at Goshen, to serve three years, and mustered in as private, Co. K, November 10, 1863; deserted, March 11, 1864, at Palatka, Fla.

TRAVER, JOHN.—Age, 38 years. Enlisted at Tarrytown, to serve three years, and mustered in as private, Co. K, October 30, 1863; promoted corporal, no date;

wounded in action, July 30, 1864, at Petersburg, Va.; discharged for disability, October 28, 1865, at De Camp Hospital, David's Island, New York Harbor.

TRAVIS, CHARLES F.—Age, 18 years. Enlisted at Schenectady, to serve three years, and mustered in as private, Co. I, March 24, 1864; captured, April 14, 1865, and released, April 30, 1865; mustered out, June 30, 1865, at New York City, as Travace.

TRAVIS, SMITH.—Age, 37 years. Enlisted at Schenectady, to serve one year, and mustered in as private, Co. E, August 13, 1864; died of fever, November 21, 1861, at Tenth Army Corps Base Hospital.

TREPER, STEPHEN S.—Age, 41 years. Enlisted, August 7, 1862, at Broadalbin, to serve three years; mustered in as private, Co. K, August 12, 1862; captured in action, September 15, and paroled, September 16, 1862, at Harper's Ferry, Va.; wounded in action, February 20, 1864, at Olustee, Fla.; mustered out with company, June 17, 1865, at Raleigh, N.C., as Tupper.

TRIESS, PETER.—Age, 35 years. Enlisted at Goshen, to serve one year, and mustered in as private, Co. F, March 6, 1865; transferred to Co. H, Forty-seventh Infantry, June 17, 1865.

TRING, CHARLES.—Age, 21 years. Enlisted, August 11, 1862, at Minden, to serve three years; mustered in as private Co. B, August 12, 1862; captured in action, September 15, and paroled, September 16, 1862, at Harper's Ferry, Va.; died of typhoid fever, August 15, 1863, at Beaufort, S.C.

TRIPP, JAMES A.—Age, 18 years. Enlisted, July 28, 1862, at Florida, to serve three years; mustered in as private, Co. D, August 11, 1862; appointed musician, no date; captured in action, August 16, 1864, at Deep Bottom, Va.; paroled, February 19, 1865; mustered out with company, June 17, 1865, at Raleigh, N.C.

TRUMAN, BENJAMIN.—Age, 18 years. Enlisted, August 5 1862, at Milton, to serve three years; mustered in as private, Co. 1, August 8, 1862; discharged for disability, no date.

TRUMBEL, GEORGE W.—Age, 18 years. Enlisted, August 7, 1862, at Milton, to serve three years; mustered in as musician, Co. C, August 9, 1862; captured in action, September 15, and paroled, September 16, 1862, at Harper's Ferry, Va.; mustered out with company, June 17, 1865, at Raleigh, N.C.

TRUMBLE, CHARLES W.—Age, 23 years. Enlisted, August 14, 1862, at Greenfield, to serve three years; mustered in as private, Co. G, August 18, 1862; appointed musician, no date; absent, detached Brigade Band since October 20, 1864, and at muster-out of company.

TRUMBLE, MARK R.—Age, 18 years. Enlisted, August 13, 1862, at Greenfield, to serve three years; mustered in as private, Co. G, August 18, 1862; captured in action, September 15, and paroled, September 16, 1862, at Harper's Ferry, Va.; died of typhoid fever, August 7, 1863, at hospital, Beaufort, S.C.

TRYON, JOHN S.—Age, 32 years. Enlisted at Brooklyn, to serve three years, and mustered in as private, Co. H, September 2, 1863; discharged for disability, December 1, 1864, at Grant Hospital, New York Harbor.

TUCKER, CHARLES.—Age, 19 years. Enlisted, July 28, 1862, at Minden, to serve three years; mustered in as corporal, Co. B, August 14, 1862; captured in action, September 15, and paroled, September 16, 1862, at Harper's Ferry, Va.; returned to ranks, November 15, 1862; mustered out with company, June 17, 1865, at Raleigh, N.C.

TULLOCK, DANIEL.—Age, 18 years. Enlisted, July 29, 1862, at Florida, to serve three years; mustered in as private, Co. D, August 2, 1862; captured in action, September 15, and paroled, September 16, 1862, at Harper's Ferry, Va.; wounded in action, February 20, 1864, at Olustee, Fla.; mustered out with company, June 17, 1865, at Raleigh, N.C.

TULLOCK, KELLEY S.—Age, 21 years. Enlisted, July 31, 1862, at Florida, to serve three years; mustered in as private, Co. D, August 2, 1862; captured in action, September 15, and paroled, September 16, 1862, at Harper's Ferry, Va.; mustered out with company, June 17, 1865, at Raleigh, N.C., as Tulloch.

TUPER, JOSEPH H.—Age, 22 years. Enlisted at Schenectady, to serve three years, and mustered in as private, Co. H, April 28, 1864; wounded in action, May 14, 1864, at Drewry's Bluff, Va.; transferred to Veteran Reserve Corps, no date.

TURNER, JOHN.—Age, 25 years. Enlisted, August 11, 1862, at Saratoga Springs, to serve three years; mustered in as private, Co. G, August 19, 1862; captured in action, September 15, and paroled, September 16, 1862, at Harper's Ferry, Va.; wounded in action, February 20, 1864, at Olustee, Fla.; absent, sick in hospital, Raleigh, N.C., since May 1865, and at muster-out of company.

TURNER, JOHN.—Age, 18 years. Enlisted, July 23, 1862, at Amsterdam, to serve three years; mustered in as private, Co. D, August 1, 1862; captured in action, September 15, and paroled, September 16, 1862, at Harper's Ferry, Va.; wounded in action, February 20, 1864, at Olustee, Fla.; died of typhoid fever, October 15, 1864, at hospital, Fort Monroe, Va.

TYMESEN, CORNELIUS.—Age, 25 years. Enlisted, August 12, 1862, at Amsterdam, to serve three years; mustered in as private, Co. D, August 13, 1862; captured in action, September 15, and paroled, September 16, 1862, at Harper's Ferry, Va.; absent, sick in hospital, at muster-out of company.

TYMESEN, ELDERT.—Age, 30 years. Enlisted at Amsterdam, to serve three years; mustered in as private, Co. D, August 13, 1862; captured in action, September 15, and paroled, September 16, 1862, at Harper's Ferry, Va.; discharged for disability, January 9, 1863, at Washington, D.C., as Tymeson.

UHLICH, PAUL.—Age, 23 years. Enlisted at Tarrytown, to serve three years, and mustered in as private, Co. E, October 28, 1863; transferred to Co. C, Forty-seventh Infantry, June 17, 1865; also borne as Uplich.

ULMER, CHRISTIAN.—Age, 18 years. Enlisted at Brooklyn to serve one year, and mustered in as private, Co. F, March 6, 1865; transferred to Co. H, Forty-seventh Infantry, June 17, 1865.

VALENTINE, JOHN R.—Age, 21 years. Enlisted, August 11 1862, at Saratoga Spa, to serve three years; mustered in as private, Co. F, August 14, 1862; captured in action, September 15, and paroled, September 16, 1862, at Harper's Ferry, Va.; wounded in action, February 20, 1864, at Olustee, Fla.; mustered out with company, June 17, 1865, at Raleigh, N.C.

VAN ALSTINE, WILLIAM.—Age, 25 years. Enlisted at Glen to serve three years, and mustered in as private, Co. A, August 11, 1862; captured in action, September 15, and paroled, September 16, 1862, at Harper's Ferry, Va.; wounded in action, February 20, 1864, at Olustee, Fla.; mustered out with company, June 17, 1865, at Raleigh, N.C.

VAN ARNAM, JAMES W.—Age, 23 years. Enrolled at Fonda to serve three years, and mustered in as sergeant, Co. A, July 29, 1862; captured in action, August 18, 1864, at Deep Bottom, Va.; paroled, no date; promoted first sergeant, March 6, 1865; mustered in as second lieutenant, April 6, 1865; mustered out with company, June 17, 1865, at Raleigh, N.C. Commissioned second lieutenant, May 17, 1865, with rank from January 21, 1865, vice C. N. Ballou promoted.

VAN AUKEN, JAMES.—Age, 21 years. Enlisted at Johnstown, to serve three years, and mustered in as private, Co. E, August 11, 1862; captured in action, September 15, and paroled, September 16, 1862, at Harper's Ferry, Va.; wounded in action, February 20, 1864, at Olustee, Fla.; mustered out with company, June 17, 1865, at Raleigh, N.C.

VANAUKER, WILLIAM.—Age, 21 years. Enlisted, August 11, 1862, at Johnstown, to serve three years; mustered in as private, Co. E, October 28, 1862; captured in action, September 15, and paroled, September 16, 1862, at Harper's Ferry, Va.; died, January 30, 1863, at hospital, Yorktown, Va.

VANASDALL, WESLEY D.—Age, 23 years. Enlisted at Goshen, to serve three years, and mustered in as private, Co. A, October 18, 1863; captured while on picket, April, 1864, at Pilatka, Fla.; paroled, no date; transferred to Co. A, Forty-seventh Infantry, June 17, 1865; also borne as Vanarsdell.

VAN BROCKLIN, JOHN J.—Age, 18 years. Enlisted at Johnstown, to serve three years, and mustered in as private, Co. A, July 30, 1862; wounded and captured in action, September 15, and paroled, September 16, 1862, at Harper's Ferry, Va.; died of his wounds, October 6, 1862, at Harper's Ferry, Va.; also borne as John, Jr.

VANDERCOOK, GEORGE.—Age, 21 years. Enlisted, August 5, 1862, at Halfmoon, to serve three years; mustered in as corporal, Co. H, August 7, 1862; captured in action, September 15, and paroled, September 16, 1862, at Harper's Ferry, Va.; wounded on picket, August 18, 1864, at Deep Bottom, Va.; discharged for disability, December 1, 1864.

VANDERCOOK, JOHN H.—Age, 18 years. Enlisted, August 13, 1862, at Halfmoon, to serve three years; mustered in as private, Co. H, August 18, 1862; captured in action, September 15, and paroled, September 16, 1862, at Harper's Ferry, Va.; mustered out with company, June 17, 1865, at Raleigh, N.C.

VANDERPOOL, JOSEPH.—Age, 33 years. Enlisted, August 11, 1862, at Caroga, to serve three years; mustered in as private, Co. K, August 12, 1862; captured in action, September 15, and paroled, September 16, 1862, at Harper's Ferry, Va.; wounded and captured in action, February 20, 1864, at Olustee, Fla.; reported died of his wounds, March 16, 1864, at Tallahassee, Fla.

VAN DERVEER, GARRET.—Age,—years. Enrolled at Fonda, to serve three years, and mustered in as captain, Co. A, August 21, 1862; wounded in action, February 20, 1864, at Olustee, Fla.; died of his wounds, February 24, 1864, at Beaufort, S.C. Commissioned captain, September 10, 1862, with rank from August 20, 1862, original.

VAN DE SANDE, JOHN.—Age,—years. Enrolled at Fonda, to serve three years, and mustered in as second lieutenant, Co. B, August 20, 1862; as first lieutenant, April 16, 1863; wounded in action, August 16, 1864, at Deep Bottom, Va.; died of his wounds, September 3, 1864, at Chesapeake Hospital, Fort Monroe, Va.; prior service in Fifth Massachusetts Militia. Commissioned second lieutenant, September 10, 1862, with rank from August 20, 1862 original; first lieutenant, May 13, 1863, with rank from April 16, 1863, vice H. R. Devendorf discharged.

VAN DUSEN, JOHN.—Age, 18 years. Enlisted at Palatine, to serve three years, and mustered in as private, Co. A, August 11, 1862; captured in action, September 15, and paroled, September 16, 1862, at Harper's Ferry, Va.; promoted corporal, March 6, 1865; mustered out with company, June 17, 1865, at Raleigh, N.C.

VAN EPPS, FISHER F.—Age, 20 years. Enlisted, August 8 1862, at Minden, to serve three years; mustered in as private Co. B, August 13, 1862; captured in action, September 15, and paroled, September 16, 1862, at Harper's Ferry, Va.; captured in action, August 16, 1864, at Deep Bottom, Va.; paroled, March, 1865, at Goldsboro, N.C.; mustered out, June 14, 1865, at hospital, Annapolis, Md.

VAN EVERA, ALONZO.—Age, 32 years. Enlisted, July 28, 1862, at Minden, to serve three years; mustered in as wagoner, Co. B, August 2, 1862; captured in action, September 15, and paroled, September 16, 1862, at Harper's Ferry, Va.; promoted corporal, December 30, 1862; mustered out with company, June 17, 1865, at Raleigh, N.C.

VAN EVERA, LUCAS.—Age, 24 years. Enlisted, August 5, 1862, at Canajoharie, to serve three years; mustered in as private, Co. I, August 16, 1862; captured in action, September 15, and paroled, September 16, 1862, at Harper's Ferry, Va.; discharged for disability, no date; also borne as Luckus and Luke.

VAN EVERA, NICHOLAS.—Age, 25 years. Enlisted in Eighteenth Congressional District, to serve three years, and mustered in as private, Co. I, April 25, 1864; died of fever, July, 1864, at hospital, Norfolk, Va.

VAN EVEREN, JOHN.—Age, 23 years. Enlisted, August 18, 1862, at Milton, to serve three years; mustered in as private, Co. G, August 20, 1862; captured in action, September 15, and paroled, September 16, 1862, at Harper's Ferry, Va.; mustered out, June 10, 1865, at Raleigh, N.C., as Van Every.

VAN HOESEN, GEORGE T.—Age, 34 years. Enlisted, August 11, 1862, at Halfmoon, to serve three years; mustered in as private, Co. H, August 14, 1862; captured in action, September 15, and paroled, September 16, 1862, at Harper's Ferry, Va.; wounded in action, February 20, 1864, at Olustee, Fla., and June 30, 1864, at Petersburg, Va.; mustered out with detachment, May 27, 1865, at Foster Hospital, New Berne, N.C.

VAN HORN, JOHN.—Age, 28 years. Enlisted at Schenectady to serve three years, and mustered in as private, Co. H, April 26, 1864; transferred to Co. I, Forty-seventh Infantry, June 17, 1865.

VAN LOON, PETER.—Age, 25 years. Enlisted, August 14, 1862, at Oppenheim, to serve three years; mustered in as private, Co. E, August 15, 1862; captured in action, September 15, and paroled, September 16, 1862, at Harper's Ferry, Va.; wounded in action, January 15, 1865, at Fort Fisher, N.C.; died of his wounds, January 17, 1865, at Regimental Hospital, Fort Fisher, N.C.

VANNUCI, LOUIS.—Age, place, date of enlistment and muster-in as private, Co. G, not stated; transferred to Co. G, Forty-seventh Infantry, June 17, 1865; also borne as Varnuci.

VAN NORDEN, JOHN H.—Age, 30 years. Enlisted, August 12, 1862, at Waterford, to serve three years; mustered in as private Co. H, August 18, 1862; captured in action, September 15, and paroled, September 16, 1862, at Harper's Ferry, Va.; deserted, October 16, 1862, at Chicago, Ill.

VAN OLINDA, WARREN.—Age, 19 years. Enlisted at Halfmoon, to serve three years, and mustered in as musician, Co. H, August 16, 1862; captured in action, September 15, and paroled, September 16, 1862, at Harper's Ferry, Va.; deserted, September 25, 1862, at Annapolis, Md.

VAN RENSSELAER, GEORGE M.—Age, 23 years. Enlisted, August 14, 1862, at Bleecker, to serve three years; mustered in as corporal, Co. E, August 15, 1862; captured in action September 15, and paroled, September 16, 1862, at Harper's Ferry, Va.; promoted first sergeant, November 1, 1862; wounded in action, February 20, 1864, at Olustee, Fla., and August 16, 1864, at Deep Bottom, Va.; absent, sick, at Lovell Hospital, Portsmouth, R.I., since May 12, 1865, and at muster-out of company; also borne as Van Renschler.

VANSKIVOR, ANDREW J.—Age, 26 years. Enlisted at Johnstown, to serve three years, and mustered in as private, Co. K, August 21, 1862; captured in action, September 15, and paroled, September 16, 1862, at Harper's Ferry, Va.; transferred to Co. G, Tenth Regiment, Veteran Reserve Corps, July 15, 1863; promoted corporal, no date; mustered out with detachment, June 28, 1865, at Washington, D.C.

VAN SLYKE, WILLIAM.—Age, 37 years. Enlisted, July 28 1862, at Amsterdam, to serve three years; mustered in as private, Co. G, August 20, 1862; captured in action September 15, and paroled, September 16, 1862, at Harper's Ferry, Va.; mustered out with company, June 17, 1865, at Raleigh, N.C.

VAN STEENBURGH, GEORGE L.—Age, 19 years. Enlisted, August 6, 1862, at Milton, to serve three years; mustered in as private, Co. C, August 8, 1862; captured in action, September 15, and paroled, September 16, 1862, at Harper's Ferry, Va.; wounded in action, February 20, 1864, at Olustee, Fla.; died of his wounds, May 8, 1864, near Hatchers Va.

VAN STEENBURGH, MATHEW.—Age, 34 years. Enlisted, August 12, 1862, at Johnstown, to serve three years; mustered in as corporal, Co. E, August 15, 1862; captured in action, September 15, and paroled, September 16, 1862, at Harper's Ferry, Va.; promoted sergeant, no date; killed in action, February 20, 1864, at Olustee, Fla.; also borne as Van Steensburgh.

VAN TASSELL, GEORGE.—Age, 18 years. Enlisted at Tompkins, to serve three years, and mustered in as private, Co. E,. February 28, 1865; transferred to Co. F, Forty-seventh Infantry, June 17, 1865.

VARNEY, REUBEN.—Age, 28 years. Enlisted, August 6, 1862 at Corinth, to serve three years; mustered in as private, Co. F, August 19, 1862; captured in action, September 15, and paroled, September 16, 1862, at Harper's Ferry, Va.; died, September 18, 1862, while en route from Harper's Ferry, Va., to Annapolis, Md., in hospital at Baltimore, Md.; also borne as Vorney.

VEEDER, JAMES H.—Age, 18 years. Enlisted, August 8, 1862 at St. Johnsville, to serve three years; mustered in as private, Co. B, August 9, 1862; captured in action, September 15, and paroled, September 16, 1862, at Harper's Ferry, Va.; absent, detached to ammunition train at muster-out of company.

VEDDER, J. CLARK.—Age, 19 years. Enlisted, July 25, 1862, at Amsterdam, to serve three years; mustered in as wagoner, Co. D, July 30, 1862; mustered out, June 3, 1865, at Albany, N.Y., as Clark J.; also borne as Clark Vedder, Jr.

VEDDER, JR., JOHN.—Age, 22 years. Enlisted at Schenectady, to serve one year, and mustered in as private, Co. E, August 27, 1864; mustered out with company, June 17, 1865, at Raleigh, N.C.

VIELE, ABRAHAM L.—Age, 28 years. Enlisted, August 11, 1862, at Saratoga Spa, to serve three years; mustered in as corporal, Co. F, August 14, 1862; captured in action, September 15, and paroled, September 16, 1862, at Harper's Ferry, Va.; deserted, October 1, 1862, at Chicago, Ill., as Veiley.

VIELE, STEPHEN S.—Age, 36 years. Enlisted at Schenectady, to serve one year, and mustered in as private, Co. D, September 21, 1864; mustered out with company, June 17, 1865, at Raleigh, N.C.

VOSBURGH, JOHN J.—Age, 21 years. Enlisted at Amsterdam, to serve three years, and mustered in as private, Co. H, August 18, 1862; captured in action, September 15, and paroled, September 16, 1862, at Harper's Ferry, Va.; transferred to Co. D, no date; mustered out with company, June 17, 1865, at Raleigh, N.C.

VOSBURGH, WASHINGTON.—Age, 23 years. Enlisted, August 13, 1862, at Canajoharie to serve three years; mustered in as corporal, Co. B, August 15, 1862; promoted quartermaster sergeant, January 1, 1864; mustered out, June 24, 1865, at Albany, N.Y.

WADSWORTH, JOHN.—Age, 22 years. Enlisted, August 12, 1862, at Wells, to serve three years; mustered in as private, Co. K, August 16, 1862; captured in action, September 15, and paroled, September 16, 1862, at Harper's Ferry, Va.; wounded in action, February 20, 1864, at Olustee, Fla.; mustered out, June 9, 1865, at hospital, Fort Monroe, Va.

WADSWORTH, JOHN H.—Age, 24 years. Enlisted, August 12, 1862, at Wells, to serve three years; mustered in as private, Co. K, August 16, 1862; captured in action, September 15, and paroled, September 16, 1862, at Harper's Ferry, Va.; deserted, June 3, 1863, at Wells, N.Y.

WAGAR, WILBER.—Age, 29 years. Enlisted, August 7, 1862, at Milton, to serve three years; mustered in as private, Co. I, August 12, 1862; captured in action, September 15 and paroled, September 16, 1862, at Harper's Ferry, Va.; wounded and captured in action, February 20, 1864, at Olustee Fla., as Wager; no further record.

WAGER, DANIEL G.—Age, 34 years. Enlisted, August 13, 1862, at Saratoga Springs, to serve three years; mustered in as wagoner, Co. F, August 14, 1862; captured in action September 15, and paroled, September 16, 1862, at Harper's Ferry, Va.; grade changed to private, no date; transferred to Veteran Reserve Corps, July 15, 1863.

WAGER, JAMES A.—Age. 18 years. Enlisted, August 4, 1862, at Milton, to serve three years; mustered in as private, Co. C, August 11, 1862; captured in action, September 15, and paroled, September 16, 1862, at Harper's Ferry, Va.; wounded, no date; died of his wounds, June 6, 1864, at hospital, Hampton, Va.

WAGER, JEREMIAH.—Age, 24 years. Enlisted, August 11, 1862, at Milton, to serve three years; mustered in as private, Co. I, August 15, 1862; captured in action, September 15, and paroled, September 16, 1862, at Harper's Ferry, Va.; wounded and captured in action, February 20, 1864, at Olustee, Fla.; paroled, no date; discharged for disability, no date.

WAIT, CHARLES F.—Age, 21 years. Enlisted, July 30, 1862, at Galway, to serve three years; mustered in as private, Co. I, August 12, 1862; captured in action, September 15, and paroled, September 16, 1862, at Harper's Ferry, Va.; absent on detached service at medical purveyor's office at muster-out of company.

WAIT, GEORGE W.—Age, 18 years. Enlisted, August 8, 1862, at Caroga, to serve three years; mustered in as private, Co. K, August 12, 1862; captured in action, September 15, and paroled, September 16, 1862, at Harper's Ferry, Va.; deserted, September 25, 1862, at Baltimore, Md.

WAITE, WILLIAM.—Age, 26 years. Enlisted, August 1, 1862, at Milton, to serve three years; mustered in as private, Co. I, August 18, 1862; captured in action, September 15, and paroled, September 16, 1862, at Harper's Ferry, Va.; discharged for disability, no date.

WALKER, JOHN W.—Age, 21 years. Enlisted at Eighteenth Congressional District, to serve three years, and mustered in as private, Co. C, April 22, 1864; deserted, May 27, 1864, near Hatchers, Va.

WALKER, WILLIAM.—Age, 18 years. Enlisted at Albany, to serve three years, and mustered in as private, Co. G August 4, 1864; transferred to Co. G, Forty-seventh Infantry, June 17, 1865; also borne as Valker.

WALKER, WILLIAM H.—Age, 23 years. Enlisted at Tarrytown, to serve three years, and mustered in as private, Co. K, October 30, 1863; transferred to Co. A, Forty-seventh Infantry, June 17, 1865.

WALRATH, EZRA E.—Age,—years. Enrolled at Fonda, to serve three years, and mustered in as captain, Co. I, August 20, 1862; as major, November 14, 1863; wounded in action, August 16, 1864, at Deep Bottom, Va.; mustered in as lieutenant-colonel, April 29, 1865; mustered out with regiment, June 17, 1865, at Raleigh, N.C.; prior service as colonel, Twelfth Infantry. Commissioned captain, September 10, 1862, with rank from August 20, 1862, original; major, November 25, 1863, with rank from June 27, 1863, vice P. H. Cowan resigned; lieutenant-colonel, June 17, 1865, with rank from April 29, 1865, vice N. J. Johnson promoted.

WALRATH, JAMES E.—Age, 21 years. Enlisted, August 4, 1862, at St. Johnsville, to serve three years; mustered in as private, Co. I, August 12, 1862; captured in action, September 15, and paroled, September 16, 1862, at Harper's Ferry, Va., and deserted same date, at Frederick, Md.

WALRATH, REUBEN.—Age, 29 years. Enlisted, August 12, 1862, at St. Johnsville, to serve three years; mustered in as private, Co. B, August 13, 1862; captured in action, September 15, and paroled, September 16, 1862, at Harper's Ferry, Va.; wounded in action, October 27, 1864, at Darbytown Road, Va.; reported dead.

WALSH, MICHAEL.—Age, 22 years. Enlisted at Brooklyn, to serve three years, and mustered in as private, Co. H, September 3, 1863; transferred to the Navy, April 27, 1864.

WARD, AARON.—Age, 21 years. Enlisted, August 12, 1862, at Broadalbin, to serve three years; mustered in as private, Co. K, August 16, 1862; captured in action, September 15, paroled September 16, 1862 at Harper's Ferry, Va.; mustered out with company, June 17, 1865, at Raleigh, N.C.

WARD, JOHN N.—Age, 26 years. Enlisted, August 6, 1862, at Oppenheim, to serve three years; mustered in as private, Co. E, August 8, 1862; captured in action, September 15, and paroled, September 16, 1862, at Harper's Ferry, Va.; wounded in action, February 20, 1864, at Olustee, Fla.; mustered out with company, June 17, 1865, at Raleigh, N.C., as John W.

WARD, JOHN W.—Age, 26 years. Enlisted, August 8, 1862, at Oppenheim, to serve three years; mustered in as private Co. H, August 15, 1862; no further record.

WARD, WILLIAM.—Age, 18 years. Enlisted at Poughkeepsie to serve three years, and mustered in as private, Co. D, February 25, 1865; transferred to Co. D, Forty-seventh Infantry, June 17, 1865.

WARMUTH, GEORGE J.—Age, 25 years. Enlisted, August 7, 1862, at Minden, to serve three years; mustered in as private, Co. B, October 28, 1862; captured in action, September 15, and paroled, September 16, 1862, at Harper's Ferry, Va.; mustered out, May 27, 1865, at hospital, Fort Monroe, Va.; also borne as Wormuth.

WARN, ISAAC.—Age, 18 years. Enlisted, July 30, 1862, at Milton, to serve three years; mustered in as private, Co. I, August 8, 1862; captured in action, September 15, and paroled, September 16, 1862, at Harper's Ferry, Va.; died of disease, at Yorktown, Va., no date.

WARNER, JAMES.—Age, 34 years. Enlisted, August 25, 1862, at Amsterdam, to serve three years; mustered in as private, Co. K, August 26, 1862; deserted, August 27, 1862, at Fonda, N.Y.

WARREN, ISAAC.—Age, 18 years. Enlisted, July 30, 1862, at Milton, to serve three years; mustered in as private, Co. I, August 26, 1862; captured in action, September 15, and paroled, September 16, 1862, at Harper's Ferry, Va.; died, January 26, 1863, at hospital, Yorktown, Va.

WASHBURN, ELIAS.—Age, 28 years. Enlisted, August 9, 1862, at Moreau, to serve three years; mustered in as private, Co. F, August 19, 1862; captured in action, September 15, and paroled, September 16, 1862, at Harper's Ferry, Va.; mustered out with company, June 17, 1865, at Raleigh, N.C.

WASHBURN, FRANK.—Age, 21 years. Enlisted, August 6, 1862, at Minden, to serve three years; mustered in as private, Co. B, August 14, 1862; captured in action, September 15, and paroled, September 16, 1862, at Harper's Ferry, Va.; mustered out with company, June 17, 1865, at Raleigh, N.C.

WASHBURN, FREDERICK L.—Age, 20 years. Enlisted, August 7, 1862, at Day, to serve three years; mustered in as private, Co. F, August 19, 1862; captured in action, September 15, and paroled, September 16, 1862, at Harper's Ferry, Va.; deserted, November 29, 1862, on expiration furlough, at Chicago, Ill., since enlisted in Fifth U. S. Cavalry.

WASHBURN, IRA.—Age, 29 years. Enlisted, August 13, 1862, at Hadley, to serve three years; mustered in as private, Co. F, August 19, 1862; captured in action, September 15, and paroled, September 16, 1862, at Harper's Ferry, Va.; died of fever, June 7, 1863, at hospital, Hilton Head, S.C.

WATERMAN, LAFAYETTE.—Age, 21 years. Enlisted at Palatine, to serve three years, and mustered in as private, Co. A, July 28, 1862; captured in action, September 15, and paroled, September 16, 1862, at Harper's Ferry, Va.; wounded in action, February 20, 1864, at Olustee, Fla.; captured in action, August 18, 1864, at Deep Bottom, Va.; died of diarrhea, November 11, 1864, at Salisbury, N.C.

WATSON, JAMES L.—Age, 45 years. Enrolled at Jacksonville, Fla., to serve three years, and mustered in as assistant surgeon, April 4, 1864; discharged, March 22, 1865, for promotion to surgeon, Seventeenth Infantry; prior service as assistant surgeon, One Hundred and Thirty-ninth Infantry. Commissioned assistant surgeon, March 15, 1864, with rank from February 29, 1864, vice H. H. Ingerson resigned.

WATSON, WILLIAM.—Age, 21 years. Enlisted at Bombay, to serve three years, and mustered in as private, Co. F, February 27, 1865; transferred to Co.—, Forty-seventh Infantry, June 17, 1865.

WATT, JOHN R.—Age, 28 years. Enlisted, August 14, 1862 at Halfmoon, to serve three years; mustered in as private, Co. H, August 16, 1862; captured in action, September 15, and paroled, September 16, 1862, at Harper's Ferry, Va.; promoted corporal, January 1, 1863; wounded in action, January 15, 1865, at Fort Fisher, N.C.; promoted sergeant, May 16, 1865; mustered out with company, June 17, 1865, at Raleigh, N.C.

WAYNE, THOMAS.—Age,—years. Enrolled at Amsterdam, to serve three years, and mustered in as first lieutenant, Co. D, August 20, 1862; as captain, October 8, 1864; discharged for disability, February 23, 1865. Commissioned first lieutenant, September 10, 1862, with rank from August 20, 1862 original; captain, November 19, 1864, with rank from October 8, 1864, vice S.D. Lingenfelter resigned.

WEAST, JAMES J.—Age, 22 years. Enlisted, July 26, 1862, at Florida, to serve three years; mustered in as private, Co. B, August 2, 1862; captured in action, September 15, and paroled, September 16, 1862, at Harper's Ferry, Va.; wounded in action, February 20, 1864, at Olustee, Fla.; mustered out with company, June 17, 1865, at Raleigh, N.C.

WEAVER, GEORGE.—Age, 32 years. Enlisted, July 23, 1862, at Amsterdam, to serve three years; mustered in as private, Co. B, July 30, 1862; captured in action, September 15, and paroled, September 16, 1862, at Harper's Ferry, Va.; wounded in action, May 7, 1864, at Chester Station, Va.; mustered out with company, June 17, 1865, at Raleigh, N.C.

WEEKS, GEORGE H.—Age, 27 years. Enrolled, August 11, 1862, at Saratoga Springs, to serve three years; mustered in as sergeant, Co. F, August 19, 1862; promoted first sergeant, no date; mustered in as first lieutenant, June 8, 1865; mustered out with company, June 17, 1865, at Raleigh, N.C. Commissioned first lieutenant, June 27, 1865, with rank from June 8, 1865, vice F. S. Goodrich declined.

WEEPER, CHARLES.—Age, 23 years. Enlisted at Glen, to serve three years, and mustered in as private, Co. A, July 28, 1862; captured in action, September 15, and paroled, September 16, 1862, at Harper's Ferry, Va.; wounded and captured in action, February 20, 1864, at Olustee, Fla.; died, August 26, 1864, at Andersonville, Ga.

WEEPER, WILLIAM.—Age, 21 years. Enlisted at Glen, to serve three years, and mustered in as private, Co. A, July 28, 1862; captured in action, September 15, and paroled, September 16, 1862, at Harper's Ferry, Va.; promoted to non-commissioned officer, no date; returned to ranks, April 1, 1865, for incompetency and continued absence; absent, sick at hospital since July 31, 1864, and at muster-out of company.

WEIGLE, JOHN.—Age, 31 years. Enlisted at Ninth Congressional District, to serve three years, and mustered in as private, Co. H, August 27, 1863; mustered out with detachment, June 8, 1865, at New Berne, N.C., as Weigel.

WEISOON, JOHN.—Age, 17 years. Enlisted at Tompkins, to serve three years, and mustered in as private, Co. E, March 1, 1865; transferred to Co. F, Forty-seventh Infantry, June 17, 1865; also borne as Weissoon.

WELCH, DENNIS.—Age, 18 years. Enlisted, August 11, 1862, at Saratoga Springs, to serve three years; mustered in as private, Co. F, August 14, 1862; captured in action, September 15, and paroled, September 16, 1862, at Harper's Ferry, Va.; promoted corporal, no date; wounded and missing in action, February 20, 1864, at Olustee, Fla.; returned, no date; mustered out, June 2, 1865, at Albany, N.Y.

WELCH, JAMES.—Age, 36 years. Enlisted at New York City, to serve three years, and mustered in as private, Co. E. August 28, 1863; killed in action, February 20, 1864, at Olustee, Fla.

WELCH, ROBERT.—Age, 19 years. Enlisted, August 21, 1862, at Amsterdam, to serve three years; mustered in as private, Co. D, August 25, 1862; captured in action, September 15, and paroled, September 16, 1862, at Harper's Ferry, Va.; wounded in action, February 20, 1864, at Olustee, Fla.; mustered out with company, June 17, 1865, at Raleigh, N.C.

WELCH, WILLIAM.—Age, 21 years. Enlisted, August 15, 1862, at Amsterdam, to serve three years; mustered in as private, Co. B, August 16, 1862; captured in action, September 15, and paroled, September 16, 1862, at Harper's Ferry, Va.; wound in action, February 20, 1864, at Olustee, Fla.; transferred to Veteran Reserve Corps. January 1, 1865.

WELLS, REUBEN T.—Age, 27 years. Enlisted, August 13, 1862, at Mayfield, to serve three years; mustered in as private Co. E, August 15, 1862; captured in action, September 15, and paroled, September 16, 1862, at Harper's Ferry, Va.; mustered out with company, June 17, 1865, at Raleigh, N.C.

WEMPLE, BORNT.—Age, 25 years. Enlisted, August 9, 1862, at Charlton, to serve three years; mustered in as private, Co. G, August 22, 1962; captured in action, September 15, paroled September 16, 1862 at Harper's Ferry, Va.; transferred to Co. I, January 3, 1864; mustered out with company, June 17, 1865, at Raleigh, N.C.

WENDELL, JOHN H.—Age, 21 years. Enlisted at Amsterdam, to serve three years, and mustered in as private, Co. D, August 15, 1862; promoted hospital steward, August 21, 1863; mustered out, July 11, 1865, at New York City.

WESTES, JOSEPH.—Age, 28 years. Enlisted at Tarrytown, to serve three years, and mustered in as private, Co. K, October 30, 1863; discharged, May 1864, for promotion to first lieutenant, First Florida Cavalry; also borne as Wistar.

WESTON, LLOYD.—Age, 41 years. Enlisted, August 4, 1862, at Wilton, to serve three years; mustered in as private, Co. F, August 12, 1862; captured in action, September 15, paroled September 16, 1862 at Harper's Ferry, Va.; wounded and captured in action, February 20, 1864, at Olustee, Fla.; died, October 4, 1864, at Andersonville, Ga.

WHALAN, MICHAEL.—Age, 31 years. Enlisted August 9, 1863, at Tarrytown, to serve three years; mustered in as private, Co. G, October 29, 1963; transferred to Co. F, Forty-seventh Infantry, June 17, 1865.

WHEATON, BENJAMIN.—Age, 32 years. Enlisted, August 8, 1862, at Corinth, to serve three years; mustered in as private, Co. G, August 19, 1862; captured in action, September 15, paroled September 16, 1862 at Harper's Ferry, Va.; wounded in action, June 14, 1864, at Cold Harbor, Va.; mustered out June 10, 1865, at Albany, N.Y., while in hospital at Troy, N.Y.

WHEATON, THOMAS J.—Age, 25 years. Enlisted August 7, 1862, at Edinburg, to serve three years; mustered in as private, Co. G, August 22, 1862; captured in action, September 15, paroled September 16, 1862 at Harper's Ferry, Va.; discharged for disability, October 31, 1862, at Chicago, Ill.

WHERRY, DAVID.—Age, 18 years. Enlisted at Goshen, to serve three years, and mustered in as private, Co. A, October 8, 1863; wounded and captured in action, February 20, 1864, at Olustee, Fla.; paroled, November 26, 1864; promoted corporal, May 1, 1865; mustered out with detachment, June 12, 1865, at Raleigh, N.C.

WHERRY, WILLIAM M.—Age, 18 years. Enlisted at Goshen, to serve three years, and mustered in as private, Co. A, October 8, 1863; promoted corporal, April 1, 1865; sergeant, May 1, 1865; transferred to Co. G, Forty-seventh Infantry, June 17, 1865.

WHITE, WING A.—Age, 32 years. Enlisted at Edinburg, to serve three years, and mustered in as wagoner, Co. E, August 15, 1862; captured in action, September 15, and paroled, September 16, 1862, at Harper's Ferry, Va.; wounded in action, February 20, 1864, at Olustee, Fla.; mustered out with company, June 17, 1865, at Raleigh, N.C.

WHITFORD, THEODORE.—Age, 18 years. Enlisted at Canajoharie, to serve three years, and mustered in as private, Co. I, August 4, 1862; captured in action, September 15, and paroled, September 16, 1862, at Harper's Ferry, Va.; wounded in action, February 20, 1864, at Olustee, Fla., and May 7, 1864, at Chester Station, Va.; mustered out with company, June 17, 1865, at Raleigh, N.C.

WHITNEY, DANIEL J.—Age, 24 years. Enlisted, August 4, 1862, at Minden, to serve three years; mustered in as private, Co. B, August 11, 1862; captured in action, September 15, and paroled, September 16, 1862, at Harper's Ferry, Va.; wounded in action, May 14, 1864, at Drewry's Bluff, Va.; absent on furlough at muster-out of company.

WHOOLERS, HENRY.—Age, 27 years. Enlisted at New York City, to serve three years, and mustered in as private, Co. A, February 27, 1865; transferred to Co. A, Forty-seventh Infantry, June 17, 1865.

WICKINS, JAMES H.—Age, 21 years. Enlisted, August 4, 1862, at Greenfield, to serve three years; mustered in as private, Co. C, August 8, 1862; captured in action, September 15, and paroled, September 16, 1862, at Harper's Ferry, Va.; died of fever, June 17, 1863, at Hospital, Hilton Head, S.C.

WICKS, GILES.—Age, 35 years. Enlisted, August 25, 1862, at Minden, to serve three years; mustered in as private, Co. I, August 26, 1862; captured in action, September 15, paroled September 16, 1862 at Harper's Ferry, Va.; deserted, September 18, 1862, at Frederick, Md.; also borne as Wich.

WIESE, LOUIS.—Age, 21 years. Enlisted at Schenectady, serve three years, and mustered in as private, unassigned, July 22, 1864; mustered out, August 14, 1865, at Albany, N.Y.

WILCOX, MYRON W.—Age, 23 years. Enlisted, August 6, 1862 at Corinth, to serve three years; mustered in as private, Co. F, August 19, 1862; captured in action, September 15, and paroled, September 16, 1862, at Harper's Ferry, Va.; wounded in action, February 20, 1864, at Olustee, Fla.; mustered out with company, June 17, 1865, at Raleigh, N.C.

WILDER, GEORGE C.—Age, 18 years. Enlisted,

August 16, 1862, at Charlton, to serve three years; mustered in as musician, Co. I, August 18, 1862; captured in action, September 15, and paroled, September 16, 1862, at Harper's Ferry, Va.; returned to grade of private, no date; died, September 18, 1862, at hospital, Fort Monroe, Va.

WILDY, GEORGE H.—Age, 22 years. Enlisted, August 7, 1862, at Wilton, to serve three years; mustered in as private, Co. F, August 14, 1862; captured in action, September 15, and paroled, September 16, 1862, at Harper's Ferry, Va.; promoted corporal, no date; wounded in action, June 15, 1864, at Petersburg, Va.; discharged for wounds, April 4, 1865.

WILKS, FRANK.—Age, 23 years. Enlisted at Tarrytown, to serve three years, and mustered in as private, Co. K, October 30, 1863; transferred to the Navy, April 27, 1864.

WILEY, WILLIAM H.—Age, 22 years. Enlisted, July 28, 1862, at Johnstown, to serve three years; mustered in as private, Co. G, August 21, 1862; captured in action, September 15, and paroled, September 16, 1862, at Harper's Ferry, Va.; again wounded and captured in action, February 20, 1864, at Olustee, Fla.; died, September 2, 1864, at Andersonville, Ga., as Whiley.

WILLARD, DANIEL E.—Age, 40 years. Enlisted at Eighteenth Congressional District, to serve three years, and mustered in as private, Co. E, April 7, 1864; wounded in action, July 4, 1864, in front of Petersburg, Va.; mustered out, May 29, 1865, at Albany, N.Y.

WILLIAMS, JAMES H.—Age, 34 years. Enlisted, August 11, 1862, at Caroga, to serve three years; mustered in as private, Co. K, August 12, 1862; captured in action, September 15, and paroled, September 16, 1862, at Harper's Ferry, Va.; wounded in action, February 20, 1864, at Olustee, Fla.; mustered out with company, June 17, 1865, at Raleigh, N.C.

WILLIAMS, JOHN.—Age, 22 years. Enlisted at Tarrytown, to serve three years, and mustered in as private, Co. G, August 25, 1863; transferred to the Navy, April 27, 1864.

WILLIAMS, JOHN.—Age, 38 years. Enlisted at Brooklyn, to serve three years, and mustered in as private, Co. D, March 6, 1865; transferred to Co. D, Forty-seventh Infantry, June 17, 1865.

WILLIAMS, JOHN J.—Age, 21 years. Enlisted, July 25, 1862, at Amsterdam, to serve three years; and mustered in as private, Co. B, July 30, 1862; captured in action, September 15, and paroled, September 16, 1862, at Harper's Ferry, Va.; wounded in action, May 7, 1864, at Chester Station Va.; absent since and at muster-out of company.

WILLIAMS, STEPHEN A.—Age, 20 years. Enlisted, August 30, 1864, at Schenectady, to serve one year; mustered in as private, Co. E, August 31, 1864; wounded in action, no date; mustered out, June 27, 1865, at Albany, N.Y., while in hospital, Troy, N.Y.

WILLIAMS, THOMPSON.—Age, 20 years. Enlisted at Kingston, to serve three years, and mustered in as private, Co. I, March 6, 1865; deserted, April 2, 1865, at Duplin's Cross Road, N.C.

WILLMASER, FRANCIS.—Age, 23 years. Enlisted, August 4, 1862, at Amsterdam, to serve three years; mustered in as wagoner, Co. I, August 5, 1862; captured in action, September 15, and paroled, September 16, 1862, at Harper's Ferry, Va.; wounded in action, August 16, 1864, at Deep Bottom, Va.; mustered out with detachment, May 18, 1865, at White Hall Hospital, Philadelphia, Pa., as Wilmeison.

WILMONT, JOHN W.—Age, 44 years. Enlisted, August 7, 1862, at Amsterdam, to serve three years; mustered in as private, Co. D, August 13, 1862; captured in action, September 15, and paroled, September 16, 1862, at Harper's Ferry, Va.; discharged for disability, August 29, 1863, at Beaufort, S.C.

WILSON, CHARLES.—Age, 25 years. Enlisted at Tarrytown, to serve one year, and mustered in as private, Co. K, March 8, 1865; transferred to Co. A, Forty-seventh Infantry June 17, 1865.

WILSON, JAMES.—Age, 18 years. Enlisted, July 30, 1862 at Halfmoon, to serve three years; mustered in as private Co. H, August 1, 1862; captured in action, September 15, and paroled, September 16, 1862, at Harper's Ferry, Va.; killed in action, February 20, 1864, at Olustee, Fla.

WILSON, JAMES.—Age, 23 years. Enlisted at Brooklyn, to serve three years, and mustered in as private, Co. F, March 6, 1865; transferred to Co. H, Forty-seventh Infantry, June 17, 1865.

WILSON, JAMES H.—Age, 25 years. Enlisted, August 8, 1862 at Greenfield, to serve three years; mustered in as corporal Co. F, August 12, 1862; captured in action, September 15, and paroled, September 16, 1862, at Harper's Ferry, Va.; discharged for disability, May 14, 1863.

WILSON, JOHN.—Age, 24 years. Enlisted at Jamaica, to serve three years, and mustered in as private, Co. H, February 26, 1865; transferred to Co. K, Forty-seventh Infantry, June 17, 1865.

WING, HORACE.—Age, 18 years. Enlisted at Stillwater, serve three years, and mustered in as private, Co. H, August 8, 1862; captured in action, September 15, and paroled, September 16, 1862, at Harper's Ferry, Va.; wounded in action, February 20, 1864, at Olustee Fla.; mustered out with company, June 17, 1865, at Raleigh, N.C.

WINNE, NICHOLAS.—Age, 21 years. Enlisted, August 6, 1862, at St. Johnsville, to serve three years; mustered in as private Co. B, August 7, 1862; captured in action, September 15, and paroled, September 16, 1862, at Harper's Ferry, Va.; mustered out with company, June 17, 1865, at Raleigh, N.C.

WINNEY, BRUCE.—Age, 19 years. Enlisted, August 5, 1862, at Saratoga, to serve three years; mustered in as private, Co. F, August 12, 1862; captured in action, September 15, and paroled, September 16, 1862, at Harper's Ferry, Va.; wounded in action, June 15, 1864, at Petersburg, Va.; mustered out with company, June 17, 1865, at Raleigh, N.C.

WINNEY, JOHN C.—Age, 18 years. Enlisted, August 5, 1862, at Saratoga, to serve three years; mustered in as private, Co. F, August 12, 1862; captured in action, September 15, and paroled, September 16, 1862, at Harper's Ferry, Va.; wounded in action, February 20, 1864, at Olustee, Fla.; mustered out with company, June 17, 1865, at Raleigh, N.C.

WINSMAN, FREDERICK C.—Age, 25 years. Enlisted at Canajoharie, to serve three years, and mustered in as corporal, Co. I, August 20, 1862; captured in action, September 15, and paroled, September 16, 1862, at Harper's Ferry, Va.; died, October 31, 1862, at hospital, Chicago, Ill.

WIRBATZ, HENRY.—Age, 21 years. Enlisted at Brooklyn, to serve—years, and mustered in as private, Co. I, February 2, 1865; transferred to Co. I, Forty-seventh Infantry, June 17, 1865.

WOOD, ALBERT L.—Age, 18 years. Enlisted, August 20, 1862, at Milton, to serve three years; mustered in as private, Co. I, August 21, 1862; captured in action, September 15, and paroled, September 16, 1862, at Harper's Ferry, Va.; mustered out with company, June 17, 1865, at Raleigh, N.C.

WOOD, HENRY.—Age, 21 years. Enlisted at Goshen, to serve three years, and mustered in as private, Co. D, October 8, 1863; wounded in action, February 20, 1864, at Olustee, Fla.; captured in action, May 15, 1864, at Drewry's Bluff, Va.; paroled, no date; transferred to Co. C, Forty-seventh Infantry, June 17, 1865.

WOOD, JESSE F.—Age, 18 years. Enlisted, August 7, 1862, at Corinth, to serve three years; mustered in as private, Co. F, August 19, 1862; captured in action, September 15, and paroled, September 16, 1862, at Harper's Ferry, Va.; again captured in action, August 16, 1864, at Deep Bottom, Va.; exchanged, March 1, 1865; mustered out with company, June 17, 1865, at Raleigh, N.C.

WOOD, JOSEPH.—Age, 37 years. Enlisted, August 14, 1862 at Ephratah, to serve three years; mustered in as private, Co. E, August 15, 1862; captured in action, September 15, and paroled, September 16, 1862, at Harper's Ferry, Va.; died of fever, April 7, 1863, at hospital Hilton Head, S.C.

WOOD, MICHAEL B.—Age, 21 years. Enlisted, August 15, 1862, at Wilton, to serve three years; mustered in as private, Co. F, August 19, 1862; captured in action, September 15, and paroled, September 16, 1862, at Harper's Ferry, Va.; wounded in action, February 20, 1864, at Olustee, Fla.; mustered out with company, June 17, 1865, at Raleigh, N.C.

WOOD, NORMAN.—Age, 42 years. Enlisted, August 20, 1862, at Milton, to serve three years; mustered in as private, Co. I, August 21, 1862; captured in action, September 15, paroled September 16, 1862 at Harper's Ferry, Va.; discharged for disability, no date.

WOODBURY, CHARLES H.—Age, 24 years. Enlisted at Louisville, to serve three years, and mustered in as private, Co. F, February 22, 1865; discharged, May 3, 1865, at Raleigh, N.C.

WOODCOCK, HIRAM.—Age, 20 years. Enlisted, August 7, 1862, at Corinth, to serve three years; mustered in as private, Co. G, August 19, 1862; captured in action, September 15, and paroled, September 16, 1862, at Harper's Ferry, Va.; wounded and captured in action, February 20, 1864, at Olustee, Fla.; died, while prisoner of war, March 3, 1864, at Lake City, Fla.

WOODCOCK, JAMES H.—Age, 18 years. Enlisted, August 7, 1862, at Corinth, to serve three years; mustered in as private, Co. G, August 19, 1862; captured in action, September 15, and paroled, September 16, 1862, at Harper's Ferry, Va.; mustered out, May 25, 1865, at Wilmington, N.C.

WORTMAN, AARON.—Age, 25 years. Enlisted at Schenectady, to serve three years, and mustered in as private, Co. H, April 14, 1864; transferred to Co. K, Forty-seventh Infantry, June 17, 1865.

WRIGHT, HENRY.—Age, 21 years. Enlisted at Johnstown, to serve three years, and mustered in as sergeant, Co. E, August 11, 1862; captured in action, September 15, and paroled, September 16, 1862, at Harper's Ferry, Va.; returned to ranks, no date; transferred to Veteran Reserve Corps, March 15, 1864.

WRIGHT, REUBEN S.—Age, 21 years. Enlisted, August 11, 1862, at Johnstown, to serve three years; mustered in as private, Co. E, August 13, 1862; captured in action, September 15, and paroled, September 16, 1862, at Harper's Ferry, Va.; promoted corporal, no date; died, June 11, 1863, in regimental hospital, at Hilton Head, S.C.

YATES, CHARLES A.—Age, 19 years. Enlisted, August 6, 1862, at Day, to serve three years; mustered in as private, Co. C, August 11, 1862; captured in action, September 15, and paroled, September 16, 1862, at Harper's Ferry, Va.; absent, sick in hospital, Fort Monroe, Va., at muster-out of company.

YATTAN, WILLIAM H.—Age, 28 years. Enlisted, August 11 1862, at Moreau, to serve three years; mustered in as private, Co. G, August 18, 1862; captured in action, September 15, and paroled, September 16, 1862, at Harper's Ferry, Va.; discharged for disability, July 8, 1863, at Hilton Head, S.C.; also borne as Gattow.

YEOMAN, JOHN J.—Age,18 years. Enlisted in Eighteenth Congressional District, to serve three years, and mustered in as private, Co. A, April 4, 1864; deserted, June 20, 1864, near Bermuda Hundred, Va.; also borne as Youman.

YORDEN, JOHN.—Age, 31 years. Enlisted, August 6, 1862, at Mohawk, to serve three years; mustered in as private Co. A, August 26, 1862; captured in action, September 15, and paroled, September 16, 1862, at Harper's Ferry, Va.; deserted November 23, 1862, at Baltimore, Md.; also borne as Yordan.

YOUNG, JAMES.—Age, 44 years. Enlisted at Johnstown, to serve three years, and mustered in as private, Co. K, August 23, 1862; captured in action, September 15, paroled September 16, 1862 at Harper's Ferry, Va.; mustered out with company, June 17, 1865, at Raleigh, N.C.

YOUNG, JAMES M.—Age, 24 years. Enlisted at Fonda, to serve three years, and mustered in as sergeant, Co. I, August 8, 1862; captured in action, September 15, and paroled, September 16, 1862, at Harper's Ferry, Va.; discharged for disability, no date, as Youngs.

YOUNG, WALDO.—Age, 18 years. Enlisted, August 7, 1862, at Milton, to serve three years; mustered in as private, Co. C, August 12, 1862; captured in action, September 15, and paroled, September 16, 1862, at Harper's Ferry, Va.; wounded in action, January 15, 1865, at Fort Fisher, N.C.; mustered out, May 26, 1865, at McDougall Hospital, New York Harbor.

YOUNG, WILLIAM S.—Age, 27 years. Enlisted, August 2, 1862, at Mohawk, to serve three years; mustered in as private, Co. K, August 15, 1862; captured in action, September 15, and paroled, September 16, 1862, at Harper's Ferry, Va.; wounded in action, February 20, 1864, at Olustee, Fla.; captured in action, August 16, 1864, at Deep Bottom, Va.; paroled, no date; absent, sick, at Annapolis, Md., at muster-out of company.

YOUNGER, JOSEPH.—Age, 29 years. Enlisted, August 23, 1862, at Amsterdam, to serve three years; mustered in as private, Co. K, August 25, 1862; no further record.

YOUNGS, GEORGE.—Age, 21 years. Enlisted at Kingston, to serve three years, and mustered in as private, Co. E, October 27, 1863; wounded and captured in action, February 20, 1864, at Olustee, Fla.; paroled, no date; transferred to Co. C, Forty-seventh Infantry, June 17, 1865.

ZIEBOLL, GOTLIEB.—Age, 25 years. Enlisted at New York City, to serve three years, and mustered in as private, Co. G, March 7, 1865; transferred to Co. G, Forty-seventh Infantry, June 17, 1865; also borne as Zeibold.

ZIEGEL, NATHANIEL.—Age, 31 years. Enlisted at Tarrytown, to serve three years, and mustered in as private, Co. B, October 27, 1863; wounded in action, February 20, 1864, at Olustee, Fla.; transferred to Co. A, Forty-seventh Infantry, June 17, 1865; also borne as Ziegle.

Notes

Chapter 1

1. James E. Reid, "The War Against Secessia," p. 1. This is the title Reid used for his series of articles on the 115th New York that appeared weekly in the *Ballston Journal* from March, 1893 through June, 1896.
2. Frederick Phisterer (Ed.), *New York in the War of the Rebellion*, (Albany: J.B. Lyon Company, Third Edition, 1912), Vol. I, pp. 33-34.
3. *The Daily Saratogian*, July 4, July 9, 1862.
4. Colonel Silas W. Burt, Assistant Inspector General, New York State National Guard, *My Memoirs of the Military History of the State of New York During the War for the Union, 1861-65* (Albany: The Argus Company, 1903) pp. 94-98; *The Daily Saratogian*, July 10, 1862.
5. *Ballston Journal*, July 15, July 22, and July 29, 1862.
6. *Ballston Journal*, July 29, 1862; Phisterer, *New York in the War of the Rebellion*, Vol. IV, p. 3346.
7. Reid, "War Against Secessia," p. 1.
8. Burt, *My Memoirs*, p. 54, 97-98; *The Daily Saratogian*, July 10, July 22, August 13, 1862; William H. Shaw, *Fulton County Republican*, April 25, 1889. Captain Shaw wrote several articles on the early days of the 115th that were published in the *Republican* during 1889.
9. Sylvester W. Clemens, letter to James H. Clark in Clark, *Iron Hearted Regiment: Being an Account of the Battles, Marches and Gallant Deeds Performed by the 115th Regiment N. Y. Volunteers* (Albany: J. Munsell, 1865), p. 1, 240; Reid, "War Against Secessia," p. 1; Simeon Sammons, letter c. January 28, 1863, 115th New York Regimental Order and Letter Book, Records of the Adjutant General, Record Group 94, National Archives and Records Administration, Washington, D.C.; Shaw, *Fulton County Republican*, April 25, 1889. Later in the war government bounties increased dramatically.
10. *Illustrated History of Montgomery & Fulton Counties, New York, 1878*, p. 144-145; *Ballston Journal*, August 19, 1862.
11. Shaw, *Fulton County Republican*, May 9, 1889.
12. Reid, "War Against Secessia," p. 1; Shaw, *Fulton County Republican*, June 6, 1889.
13. T. R. Horton, letter of August 30, 1862 in *Fulton County Republican*, September 9, 1862; Clark, *Iron Hearted Regiment*, p. 2.
14. Shaw, *Fulton County Republican*, June 6, 1889.
15. Clark, *Iron Hearted Regiment*, p. 3.
16. Shaw, *Fulton County Republican*, July 4, 1889.
17. Reid, "War Against Secessia," p. 1.
18. Nicholas DeGraff, letter of September 2, 1862, DeGraff Collection, Montgomery County Department of History and Archives, Fonda, New York [hereinafter: MCDHA]. All DeGraff letters cited are from this collection unless otherwise noted. George S. Batcheller, letter of September 4, 1862, George S. Batcheller Collection, Manuscripts & Special Collections, Collection SC11218, New York State Library, Albany, New York [hereinafter: NYSL]; Henry X. Devendorf, letter of September 2, 1862, Manuscripts Department, New-York Historical Society [hereinafter: NYHS]; Reid, "War Against Secessia," p. 1.
19. DeGraff, letter of September 2, 1862; Shaw, *Fulton County Republican*, July 4, 1889.
20. Reid, "War Against Secessia," p. 2.
21. Batcheller, letter of September 4, 1862, NYSL; William J. Jennings, letter in *Ballston Journal*, December 25, 1862.
22. Nicholas DeGraff Memoir, handwritten manuscript in the United States Army Military History Institute [hereinafter: USAMHI], p. 25; Reid, "War Against Secessia," p. 2.
23. Charles Town is also referred to as Charlestown or Charleston in contemporary writings.
24. U.S. War Department, *The War of the Rebellion: A Compilation of the Official Records of the Union and Confederate Armies*, 128 Parts in 70 Volumes (Washington, D.C.: Government Printing Office, 1881-1902), Series I, Vol. XIX, Part I, p. 532 [hereinafter: O.R.; All O.R. references will be Series I except as noted in Chapter 4.]; Reid, "War Against Secessia," p. 2.
25. DeGraff Memoir, p. 25; Batcheller, letter of September 4, 1862, NYSL; DeGraff, letter of September 2, 1862.
26. Batcheller, letter of September 4, 1862, NYSL; Reid, "War Against Secessia," p. 2; Almon E. Stone, letter of September 7, 1862 in *Cohoes Cataract*, September 20, 1862; Devendorf, letter of September 2, 1862, NYHS.
27. Reid, "War Against Secessia," p. 2; *Saratoga County Heritage*, edited by Violet B. Dunn, County Historian (Saratoga County, New York: 1974), p. 346-347. George Sherman Batcheller earned a Harvard law degree at age twenty and won election to the New York State Legislature at age twenty-two. He left the 115th early in 1863 for a career that would include appointments by several presidents to military, cabinet and diplomatic posts.
28. Roger U. Delauter, Jr., *Winchester in the Civil War*

(Lynchburg, Virginia: H.E. Howard, Inc., 1992), p. 40–41, 108.

29. Reid, "War Against Secessia," p. 2; Batcheller, letter of September 4, 1862, NYSL.

30. Batcheller, letter of September 4, 1862, NYSL; Reid, "War Against Secessia," p. 2; Clark, *Iron Hearted Regiment*, p. 5.

31. Reid, "War Against Secessia," p. 2; Sammons, letter of September 9, 1862, Sammons Family Papers, MCDHA; Devendorf, letter of September 2, 1862, NYHS; DeGraff Memoir, p. 25.

32. Shaw, *Fulton County Republican*, July 4, 1889; DeGraff Memoir, p. 29; Batcheller, letter of September 4, 1862, NYSL; Sammons, letter of September 9, 1862, MCDHA; original death certificate of Winslow Burton in author's file.

33. Reid, "War Against Secessia," p. 3; Phisterer, *New York in the War of the Rebellion*, Vol. IV, p. 3305,; William J. Jennings, letter in *Ballston Journal*, December 25, 1862; Shaw, *Fulton County Republican*, July 4, 1889.

Chapter 2

1. Batcheller, letter of September 4, 1862, NYSL. Harpers Ferry is in the part of Virginia that became West Virginia in 1863.

2. DeGraff Diary, September 4, 1862, MCDHA; DeGraff Memoir, p. 29; obituary of John Hubbard, *Mohawk Valley Democrat*, November 3, 1921. A miller before enlisting, Hubbard returned home minus a foot and became a telegraph operator.

3. DeGraff, letter of September 7, 1862; DeGraff Memoir, p. 31. Sibley tents, an 1856 invention of cavalry officer Henry Hopkins Sibley, stood twelve feet tall and eighteen feet in diameter and accommodated twenty men. These seventy-three pound canvas tents served the stationary pre-war army well but were soon discarded by mobile Civil War armies in favor of the shelter half or "pup" tent for field use. (Patricia L. Faust, editor, *Historical Times Illustrated Encyclopedia of the Civil War* (New York: Harper & Row, 1986), p. 687–688.)

4. DeGraff Memoir, p. 31; Reid, "War Against Secessia," p. 3.

5. Reid, "War Against Secessia," p. 3.

6. O.R., Vol. XIX, Part I, p. 533; Phisterer, *New York in the War of the Rebellion*, Vol. III, p. 2188; Shaw, *Fulton County Republican*, July 4, 1889; Michael Aikey, "From Budapest to Bolivar Heights: The Triumphant Rise and Scandalous Fall of Colonel Frederick George D'Utassy," prepublication manuscript, p. 4.

7. Harry W. Pfanz, *Special History Report; Troop Movement Maps, 1862; Harpers Ferry National Historical Park; Maryland–West Virginia* (Denver: National Park Service, 1976), p. 4; Dennis E. Frye, "Drama Between the Rivers: Harpers Ferry in the 1862 Maryland Campaign," in *Antietam: Essays on the 1862 Maryland Campaign*, ed. by Gary W. Gallagher (Kent, Ohio: Kent State University Press, 1989), p. 17–18; Phisterer, *New York in the War of the Rebellion*, Vol. III, p. 2188. Pfanz's report contains a detailed narrative of the September 1862 actions at Harpers Ferry.

8. DeGraff Memoir, p. 33; Clark, *Iron Hearted Regiment*, p. 239–240.

9. Batcheller, letter of September 4, 1862, NYSL; Almon E. Stone, letter of September 7, 1862, *Cohoes Cataract*, September 20, 1862.

10. Clark, *Iron Hearted Regiment*, p. 8–9.

11. DeGraff Diary, September 8, September 11, 1862; DeGraff Memoir, p. 37.

12. James V. Murfin, *The Gleam of Bayonets: The Battle of Antietam and Robert E. Lee's Maryland Campaign, September 1862* (Baton Rouge: Louisiana State University Press, 1965), p. 86; O.R., Vol. XIX, Part II, p. 590. McClellan, a Philadelphian who graduated from West Point in 1846, was placed in command of the Army of the Potomac after the Union defeat at the First Battle of Bull Run. He was a brilliant organizer and much loved by his men but lacked aggressiveness. His dawdling, as well as his Democratic politics, resulted in continuous feuding with President Lincoln. (Faust, *Encyclopedia of the Civil War*, p. 456.)

13. Murfin, *Gleam of Bayonets*, p. 114; O.R., Vol. XIX, Part II, p. 255; Frye, "Drama Between the Rivers," p. 14–17; O.R., Vol. XIX, Part I, p. 787.

14. O.R., Vol. XIX, Part II, p. 603–604.

15. Murfin, *Gleam of Bayonets*, p. 135, 138, 143–144; O.R., Vol. XIX, Part II, p. 603–604; Pfanz, *Troop Movement Maps*, p. 3–6; Frye, "Drama Between the Rivers," p. 19–21. The federal garrison at Martinsburg included two infantry regiments, the 125th New York and the 65th Illinois, the latter of which was added to D'Utassy's brigade at Harpers Ferry.

16. Pfanz, *Troop Movement Maps*, p. 4; Dennis E. Frye, "The Siege of Harpers Ferry," in *Blue & Gray Magazine*, September 1987, p. 13, 18. Dixon Miles had been an ordinary officer through an army career that began with his graduation from West Point in 1824. An inquiry found the charges of drunkenness at First Bull Run to be justified but considered reassignment rather than further proceedings to be in the best interest of the army. (Stewart Sifakis, *Who Was Who in the Civil War* (New York: Facts on File, 1988), p. 447.)

17. General Julius White, "The Surrender of Harpers Ferry," in *Battles & Leaders of the Civil War*, ed. by R. U. Johnson and C. C. Buel, 4 volumes (New York: Century, 1884–1887), Vol. II, p. 612 (hereinafter: *Battles & Leaders*); Frye, "Drama Between the Rivers," p. 17–18; Pfanz, *Troop Movement Maps*, p. 8–9; Murfin, *Gleam of Bayonets*, p. 139–140.

18. Clark, *Iron Hearted Regiment*, p. 19.

19. Frye, "The Siege of Harpers Ferry," p. 19; Pfanz, *Troop Movement Maps*, p. 11–12.

20. Pfanz, *Troop Movement Maps*, p. 12–13; Simeon Sammons, report to Colonel D'Utassy dated September 22, 1862, published in the *Fulton County Republican* of October 14, 1862 with a letter to the editor from Thomas Horton, adjutant of the 115th. A copy is also in the 115th New York Regimental Order and Letter Book. Sammons's report was never published in the Official Records.

21. Frye, "The Siege of Harpers Ferry," p. 19; Pfanz, *Troop Movement Maps*, p. 13–14.

22. DeGraff Memoir, p. 37; Sammons, report to Colonel D'Utassy, September 22, 1862, in *Fulton County Republican*, October 14, 1862; John H. Dye, letter published in *National Tribune*, undated photocopy in Lance Ingmire Collection, Saratoga, New York; William Scorsby, letter published in *National Tribune*, August 21, 1884; Pfanz, *Troop Movement Maps*, p. 22.

23. Pfanz, *Troop Movement Maps*, p. 15–21; Frye, "The Siege of Harpers Ferry," p. 19–20; Phisterer, *New York in the War of the Rebellion*, Vol. IV, p. 3497.

24. O.R., Vol. XIX, Part I, p. 537; Sylvester Clemens, testimony before the Harpers Ferry Military Commission, October 7, 1862, recorded in O.R., Vol. XIX, Part I, p. 576; Clark, *Iron Hearted Regiment*, p. 12–13. Clark claimed to be "suffering from the effects of poison eaten in rebel cake." The Harpers Ferry Military Commission was hastily

convened by the U.S. War Department to determine who was at fault for the surrender of Harpers Ferry.

25. Pfanz, *Troop Movement Maps*, p. 22; O.R., Vol. XIX, Part I, p. 568, 617; Scorsby, *National Tribune*, August 21, 1884; *Mohawk Valley Register*, September 25, 1962.

26. Clark, *Iron Hearted Regiment*, p. 13-14, 250-251; DeGraff Memoir, p. 37-39; Scorsby, *National Tribune*, August 21, 1884; Pfanz, *Troop Movement Maps*, p. 22; O.R., Vol. XIX, Part I, p. 568, 617.

27. Dr. Richard E. Sutton, surgeon of the 115th, testimony before the Harpers Ferry Military Commission, October 9, 1862, O.R., Vol. XIX, Part I, p. 649; William Jennings, letter in *Ballston Journal*, December 25, 1862; O.R., Vol. XIX, Part I, p. 695; Sammons, September 22, 1862 report to D'Utassy, *Fulton County Republican*, October 14, 1862.

28. Dye, *National Tribune*, n.d.; Pfanz, *Troop Movement Maps*, p. 23; Sammons, September 22, 1862 report to D'Utassy, *Fulton County Republican*, October 14, 1862; Clark, *Iron Hearted Regiment*, p. 252; obituary of William Smith, *Johnstown Daily Republican*, February 9, 1891.

29. Simeon Sammons, testimony before the Harpers Ferry Military Commission, October 9, 1862, O.R., Vol. XIX, Part I, pp. 625-627; DeGraff Memoir, p. 39.

30. Sammons testimony, O.R., Vol. XIX, Part I, p. 625-627; Reid, "War Against Secessia," p. 4; Dye, *National Tribune*, n.d.; Scorsby, *National Tribune*, August 21, 1884.

31. Batcheller, letter of September 23, 1862, George S. Batcheller Collection, Manuscripts & Special Collections, Collection SC11218, NYSL; Reid, "War Against Secessia," p. 4.

32. Reid, "War Against Secessia," p. 4; General John G. Walker C.S.A., "Jackson's Capture of Harpers Ferry," *Battles and Leaders*, Vol. II, p. 608; DeGraff Memoir, p. 39.

33. DeGraff Memoir, p. 39; Sammons testimony, O.R., Vol. XIX, Part I, p. 624; Reid, "War Against Secessia," p. 4; Batcheller, letter of September 23, 1862, NYSL.

34. Reid, "War Against Secessia," p. 4; O.R., Vol. XIX, Part I, p. 628; DeGraff Memoir, p. 39.

35. Devendorf, letter of September 24, 1862, Manuscripts Department, NYHS; Clark, *Iron Hearted Regiment*, p. 15.

Chapter 3

1. Reid, "War Against Secessia," p. 4-5; Batcheller, letter of September 23, 1862, NYSL; O.R., Vol. XIX, Part 1, p. 953, 980.

2. Reid, "War Against Secessia," p. 5; DeGraff Memoir, p. 41; Batcheller, letter of September 23, 1862, NYSL.

3. William J. Jennings, letter in *Ballston Journal*, December 25, 1862.

4. Reid, "War Against Secessia," p. 5; Batcheller, letter of September 23, 1862, NYSL; William Jennings, letter in *Ballston Journal*, December 25, 1862.

5. Reid, "War Against Secessia," p. 5; DeGraff Memoir, p. 41; Scorsby, *National Tribune*, August 21, 1884; O.R., Vol. XIX, Part I, p. 980.

6. Reid, "War Against Secessia," p. 5; O.R., Vol. XIX, Part I, p. 45.

7. Pfanz, *Troop Movement Maps*, p. 33-34; O.R., Vol. XIX, Part I, p. 720.

8. O.R., Vol. XIX, Part I, p. 45, 721; Pfanz, *Troop Movement Maps*, p. 34.

9. Batcheller, letter of September 23, 1862, NYSL; Reid, "War Against Secessia," p. 5.

10. Batcheller, letter of September 23, 1862, NYSL; Dye, *National Tribune*, n.d.

11. Frye, "Drama Between the Rivers," p. 28; O.R., Vol. XIX, Part I, p. 580, 596-599, 665; Pfanz, *Troop Movement Maps*, p. 42.

12. O.R., Vol. XIX, Part I, p. 599; Aikey, "From Budapest to Bolivar Heights," p. 4, 17ff.

13. William Jennings, letter in *Ballston Journal*, December 25, 1862; Batcheller, letter of September 23, 1862, NYSL.

14. Reid, "War Against Secessia," p. 6; Batcheller, letter of September 23, 1862, NYSL; Clark, *Iron Hearted Regiment*, p. 15.

15. DeGraff Diary, September 14, 1862; O.R., Vol. XIX, Part I, p. 980; Sammons report to Colonel D'Utassy, September 22, 1862, in *Fulton County Republican*, October 14, 1862; Batcheller, letter of September 23, 1862, NYSL; Reid, "War Against Secessia," p. 6; Dye, *National Tribune*, n.d.

16. DeGraff Memoir, p. 43; William Jennings, letter in *Ballston Journal*, December 25, 1862.

17. Captain Greenlee Davidson, C.S.A., *Diary and Letters 1851-1863*, ed. by Charles W. Turner (Verona, Virginia: McClure Press, 1975), p. 52; DeGraff Memoir, p. 43; Batcheller, letter of September 23, 1862, NYSL.

18. Almon E. Stone, letter of September 22, 1862, in *Cohoes Cataract*, October 4, 1862; DeGraff Memoir, p. 43-45; Frye, "Drama Between the Rivers," p. 32; O.R., Vol. XIX, Part I, p. 980.

19. Clark, *Iron Hearted Regiment*, p. 20; Reid, "War Against Secessia," p. 5, 6.

20. DeGraff Memoir, p. 45; Reid, "War Against Secessia," p. 6; Clark, *Iron Hearted Regiment*, p. 20.

21. General Julius White, "The Surrender of Harpers Ferry," in *Battles & Leaders*, Vol. II, p. 613-614; O. R., p. 598-599.

22. Thomas R. Horton, letter of September 21, 1862, in *Fulton County Republican*, September 30, 1862; Clark, *Iron Hearted Regiment*, p. 20; Sammons, report to Colonel D'Utassy, September 22, 1862, in *Fulton County Republican*, October 14, 1862; Batcheller, letter of September 23, 1862, NYSL. The casualty figure is from Sammons's report to D'Utassy. It includes the losses sustained at Maryland Heights, but excludes the subsequent mortal wounding of Private Vanbrocklin.

23. Horton, letter of September 21, 1862, in *Fulton County Republican*, September 30, 1862; Reid, "War Against Secessia," p. 7.

24. Captain William T. Poague, C.S.A, *Gunner with Stonewall*, ed. by M. F. Cockrell (Wilmington, N.C.: Broadfoot Publishing Company, reprint 1987), p. 44; Dye, *National Tribune*, n.d.; Sammons, report to Colonel D'Utassy, September 22, 1862, in *Fulton County Republican*, October 14, 1862; Batcheller, letter of September 23, 1862, NYSL.

25. Dye, letter in *National Tribune*, n.d.; Sammons, report to Colonel D'Utassy, September 22, 1862, in *Fulton County Republican*, October 14, 1862; William Smith, letter of October 6, 1862; Margaret Vanbrocklin, letter of October 1862; J. G. Van Burkalow, letter of October 31, 1862. Photocopies of the Smith, Vanbrocklin, and Van Burkalow letters are in the collection of James Morrison, Gloversville, New York; the original letters are in the collection of William G. Loveday, Jr., Gloversville, New York.

26. Frye, "Drama Between the Rivers," p. 33; O.R., Vol. XIX, Part I, p. 539; DeGraff Memoir, p. 51; Dye, *National Tribune*, n.d.

27. Reid, "War Against Secessia," p. 7; DeGraff Memoir, p. 45.

28. Devendorf, letter of September 24, 1862, NYHS.

29. Reid, "War Against Secessia," p. 7; Batcheller, letter of September 23, 1862, NYSL.

30. Reid, "War Against Secessia," p. 7; Batcheller, letter of September 23, 1862, NYSL; Thomas Horton, letter of September 22, 1862, in *Fulton County Republican*, October 14, 1862.

31. DeGraff Memoir, p. 47; Clark, *Iron Hearted Regiment*, p. 24; O.R., Vol. XIX, Part I, p. 553; Sammons testimony, O.R., Vol. XIX, Part I, p. 629; DeGraff, letter in *National Tribune*, n.d.; Clark, *Iron Hearted Regiment*, p. 24; *Mohawk Valley Register*, September 25, 1862. Twenty-two years later one veteran wrote that the flags had been saved by Mrs. Bertrand "secreting them on her person," but the weight of evidence appears to belie this romantic memory. (Scorsby, *National Tribune*, August 21, 1884).

32. Dye, *National Tribune*, n.d.; Clark, *Iron Hearted Regiment*, p. 21; DeGraff Memoir, p. 45.

33. Reid, "War Against Secessia," p. 7; Frye, "The Siege of Harpers Ferry," p. 53. Paroles and exchanges of captives were common practice in the first two years of the war.

34. Frye, "The Siege of Harpers Ferry," p. 53; DeGraff Memoir, p. 45.

Chapter 4

1. Reid, "War Against Secessia," p. 8; Chaplain Sylvester Clemens, letter of October 6, 1862, in *Cohoes Cataract*, October 18, 1862; George Batcheller, letter of September 23, 1862, NYSL; DeGraff Memoir, p. 51.

2. Reid, "War Against Secessia," p. 8; Clark, *Iron Hearted Regiment*, p. 27; Scorsby, *National Tribune*, August 21, 1884.

3. DeGraff, letter of September 17, 1862.

4. Batcheller, letter of September 23, 1862, NYSL; John Reardon Memoir, September 18 and 19, 1862; Clark, *Iron Hearted Regiment*, p. 27-31. John Reardon's diary-format memoir, his self-edited transcription of his wartime diaries, are referenced by date. The Reardon memoir appeared in weekly installments in the *St. Johnsville News* from February 5 to July 15, 1908.

5. DeGraff Memoir, p. 53-61.

6. Sylvester Clemens, letter of October 6, 1862 in *Cohoes Cataract*, October 18, 1862; Reid, "War Against Secessia," p. 9.

7. Clark, *Iron Hearted Regiment*, p. 31-32. Clark puts the number of parolees already present when the 115th arrived at 16,000. Reid (p. 9) estimated the number as 20,000, and DeGraff (Diary, September 21, 1862) put it at 80,000. The term "Camp Parole" is used by Lieutenant Colonel Batcheller in his letter of September 23, and by Lieutenant Henry X. Devendorf in his letter of September 24. There are also numerous references to "Camp Parole" in the *Official Records*.

8. Clark, *Iron Hearted Regiment*, p. 31; DeGraff Memoir, p. 61-63; Reid, "War Against Secessia," p. 10.

9. Batcheller, letter of September 23, 1862, NYSL; DeGraff Memoir, p. 61.

10. Frye, "The Siege of Harpers Ferry," p. 53; James H. Clark, letter of September 22, 1862 in *Cohoes Cataract*, October 18, 1862; DeGraff Memoir, p. 61.

11. Devendorf, letter of September 24, 1862, NYHS; Reardon Memoir, September 22, 1862; Reid, "War Against Secessia," p. 10; O.R., Series II, Vol. IV, p. 550; DeGraff Diary, September 25, 1862.

12. Clark, *Iron Hearted Regiment*, p. 33; Reardon Memoir, September 25, 1862; DeGraff Memoir, p. 63; Devendorf, letter of September 30, 1862, Manuscripts Department, NYHS; Sylvester Clemens, letter of October 6, 1862, in *Cohoes Cataract*, October 18, 1862. Riots in which both federal troops and civilians were killed erupted in Baltimore in April 1861 when Union regiments first marched through the city en route to fight the Confederacy. The violence was suppressed by military force and Baltimore remained under military occupation throughout the war. (Faust, *Encyclopedia of the Civil War*, p. 37.)

13. DeGraff Memoir, p. 65; Clark, *Iron Hearted Regiment*, p. 35; Sylvester Clemens, letter of October 6, 1862 in *Cohoes Cataract*, October 18, 1862; Devendorf, letter of September 30, 1862, NYHS; Reid, "War Against Secessia," p. 10.

14. Clark, *Iron Hearted Regiment*, p. 34-36; Reid, "War Against Secessia," p. 10; DeGraff Memoir, p. 69; Reardon Memoir, September 28, 1862.

15. Reid, "War Against Secessia," p. 10; DeGraff Memoir, p. 69; Devendorf, letter of September 30, 1862, NYHS; Reardon Memoir, September 28, 1862.

16. Reid, "War Against Secessia," p. 11; Reardon Memoir, September 29, 1862; Clark, *Iron Hearted Regiment*, p. 36-37; Devendorf, letter of September 30, 1862, NYHS.

17. *Ballston Journal*, October 7, 1862.

18. I.N. Haynie, *A History of Camp Douglas: A Prisoner of War Camp at Chicago, Illinois, 1861-1865* (from a Report by the Adjutant General of the State of Illinois, Volume 1, Containing Reports for the Years 1861–66, reprint, Little Rock, Arkansas: Eagle Press, 1991), p. 4–5, 10; DeGraff Memoir, p. 71; Frye, "The Siege of Harpers Ferry," p. 53. Stephen A. Douglas is best known for his defeat of Abraham Lincoln in the 1858 race for the U.S. Senate following a series of debates whose main subject was slavery. He subsequently failed in an effort to gain the 1860 Democratic nomination for president and died on June 3, 1861.

19. Reid, "War Against Secessia," p. 11; Reardon Memoir, September 29–30, 1862; Clark, *Iron Hearted Regiment*, p. 38; DeGraff, letter of September 29, 1862. One account from another regiment claims the former Confederate prisoners left Camp Douglas "empty of everything but filth, rats and other vermin not to be named to ears polite." Arabella M. Wilson, *Disaster, Struggle, Triumph: The Adventures of 1000 Boys in Blue from August, 1862 to June, 1865*, the regimental history of the 126th New York (Albany: The Argus Company, 1870), p. 107.

20. DeGraff, letters of September 29 and October 13, 1862; Reardon Memoir, October 7, 1862.

21. Reid, "War Against Secessia," p. 11–12; Clark, *Iron Hearted Regiment*, p. 39; Dr. Richard E. Sutton, letter to Colonel Sammons, November 3, 1862, Adjutant General's Correspondence and Petitions, Series B0462, New York State Archives [Hereinafter: NYSA].

22. Devendorf, letter of October 5, 1862, Manuscripts Department, NYHS; DeGraff Memoir, p. 71, 91; Reardon Memoir, October 4 and October 29, 1862; DeGraff, letter of October 13, 1862.

23. Reardon Memoir, October 7, 10, 23–25, 1862; DeGraff, letter of October 25, 1862; DeGraff Memoir, p. 95–97.

24. DeGraff, letter of October 13, 1862; Devendorf, letter of October 5, 1862, NYHS.

25. DeGraff Memoir, p. 71, 85.

26. Reid, "War Against Secessia," p. 11.

27. DeGraff Memoir, p. 81; Reardon Memoir, October 8, 1862; DeGraff, letters of October 13 and 31, 1862.

28. O.R., Volume XIX, Part I, p. 576, 625, 649.

29. Regimental Order and Letter Book, National Archives.

30. *Ballston Journal*, October 2, 1862; DeGraff Memoir,

p. 75; Reid, "War Against Secessia," p. 12; Reardon Memoir, October 16–17, 1862; DeGraff, letter of October 9, 1862; John Kneeskern, letter of October 12, 1862, collection of Richard Bellinger, St. Johnsville, New York; Reid, "War Against Secessia," p. 12.

31. O.R., Series II, Volume IV, p. 596; Reid, "War Against Secessia," p. 12; Clark, *Iron Hearted Regiment*, p. 39; DeGraff Memoir, p. 81–83; John Kneeskern, letter of October 12, 1862, collection of Richard Bellinger.

32. Sammons, letter of January 27, 1863 to Secretary of War E.M. Stanton, Regimental Order and Letter Book, National Archives; Sammons, letter of November 4, 1862 to Thomas Hillhouse, Adjutant General of New York, Adjutant General's Correspondence and Petitions, Series B0462, NYSA; Reardon Memoir, October 18–22, 1862; Clark, *Iron Hearted Regiment*, p. 39–40; Reid, "War Against Secessia," p. 12.

33. Reid, "War Against Secessia," p. 12; DeGraff Memoir, p. 81, 85, 91; DeGraff, letter of October 31, 1862; DeGraff Diary, October 14, 1862, Clark, *Iron Hearted Regiment*, p. 38.

34. Sammons to Morgan, November 3, 1862, Sammons to Hillhouse, November 4, 1862, Sutton to Sammons, November 3, 1862, all NYSA; Clark, *Iron Hearted Regiment*, p. 38.

35. DeGraff Memoir, p. 93.

36. DeGraff, letter of November 19, 1862.

37. Clark, *Iron Hearted Regiment*, p. 41; DeGraff Memoir, p. 99.

38. Reid, "War Against Secessia," p. 12; records of a Court of Inquiry conducted at Camp Douglas November 22–26, 1862, National Archives, Record Group 94, File T-681; Reardon Memoir, November 20, 1862.

39. Reid, "War Against Secessia," p. 12; DeGraff Diary, November 20, 1862; Reardon Memoir, November 20, 1862; Clark, *Iron Hearted Regiment*, p. 40, 51–52.

Chapter 5

1. DeGraff Diary, November 23, 1862; Reardon Memoir, November 23, 1862; Clark, *Iron Hearted Regiment*, p. 42. The U.S. Sanitary Commission developed Soldier's Relief facilities, usually located near major railway depots, to offer food and temporary shelter for Union soldiers. The Commission was a civilian organization supported by volunteers and fund raising that provided such shelters and many other services including nursing, ambulances, medicine and clothing. (Faust, *Encyclopedia of the Civil War*, p. 656.)

2. Joshua White Ripley, letter of December 4, 1862, Manuscripts & Special Collections, Call Number 14818, NYSL; DeGraff Memoir, p. 103; Clark, *Iron Hearted Regiment*, p. 43.

3. Reid, "War Against Secessia," p. 12; Clark, *Iron Hearted Regiment*, p. 42; Reardon Memoir, November 24–25, 1862.

4. Ripley, letter of December 4, 1862, NYSL; DeGraff Memoir, p. 109.

5. DeGraff, letter of December 1, 1862; Clark, *Iron Hearted Regiment*, p. 43; DeGraff Memoir, p. 107; Reardon Memoir, November 28, 1862.

6. Reardon Memoir, December 1–2, 1862; DeGraff Memoir, p. 111; William McKay, letter of February 1, 1863, in *Ballston Journal*, February 17, 1863. The highly accurate British-made Enfield rifles saw wide use by both sides in the Civil War. The .577 caliber weapon fired a smooth sided minie' bullet. (Faust, *Encyclopedia of the Civil War*, p. 244.).

7. DeGraff Diary, November 27–December 11, 1862; Reardon Memoir, November 27–December 11, 1862, Reid p. 12.

8. Reid, "War Against Secessia," p. 12; Clark, *Iron Hearted Regiment*, p. 44–45; DeGraff, letter of December 18, 1862; Colonel Simeon Sammons, letter of December 21, 1862, MCDHA.

9. Martin McMartin, letter in *Fulton County Republican*, December 27, 1863; DeGraff Memoir, p. 123–125.

10. Sammons, letter of December 27, 1862, MCDHA; DeGraff, letter of December 30, 1862; Dr. Richard Sutton, letter of January 15, 1863, collection of Richard Bellinger.

11. Sammons, letter of December 27, 1862, MCDHA; DeGraff Memoir, p. 123–125.

12. Sammons, letter of December 27, 1862, MCDHA; DeGraff Memoir, p. 127; Reid, "War Against Secessia," p. 13.

13. DeGraff Memoir, p. 128; Clark, *Iron Hearted Regiment*, p. 46–47; Reardon Memoir, December 31, 1862.

14. Dr. Richard Sutton, letter of January 9, 1863, collection of Richard Bellinger; "Septimus," letter of January 16, 1863, in *Fulton County Republican*, January 27, 1863.

15. Clark, *Iron Hearted Regiment*, p. 47.

16. Reid, "War Against Secessia," p. 14; DeGraff, letter of January 18, 1863; Clark, *Iron Hearted Regiment*, p. 50; DeGraff Memoir, p. 132.

17. DeGraff, letter of January 6, 1863; Reid, "War Against Secessia," p. 13.

18. "True Soldier of the 115th," letter of January 8, 1863, in *The Daily Saratogian*, January 22, 1863; McKay, letter of February 1, 1863, in *Ballston Journal*, February 17, 1863; O.R., Volume XVIII, p. 124.

19. Reid, "War Against Secessia," p. 14; DeGraff Memoir, p. 135; *Fulton County Republican*, January 27, 1863.

20. Reid, "War Against Secessia," p. 14; DeGraff Memoir, p. 136–137.

21. DeGraff Memoir, p. 137–138; Reid, "War Against Secessia," p. 14.

22. DeGraff Memoir, p. 141; McKay, letter of February 1, 1863, in *Ballston Journal*, February 17, 1863; E.D. Townsend, Assistant Adjutant General, U.S. War Department, letter to General John A. Dix, commander at Fortress Monroe, January 7, 1863, Record Group 94, Muster Rolls, Returns, Regimental Papers, National Archives.

23. Reid, "War Against Secessia," p. 14.

24. DeGraff Memoir, p. 141.

25. Reid, "War Against Secessia," p. 15.

26. Reid, "War Against Secessia," p. 14–15; Clark, *Iron Hearted Regiment*, p. 54; DeGraff Memoir, p. 148; Simeon Sammons, letter to Dr. A.C. Hamlin, August 11, 1863, Regimental Order and Letter Book, National Archives, p. 51; Jacob B. Brown, letter of February 6, 1863, collection of Lance Ingmire, Saratoga, New York.

27. Clark, *Iron Hearted Regiment*, p. 55; Reid, "War Against Secessia," p. 15; Simeon Sammons, letter to Dr. A.C. Hamlin, August 11, 1863, Regimental Order and Letter Book, National Archives, p. 51.

28. The record of the Court of Inquiry is located at the National Archives in Record Group 94, Letters Received 1862, File T-681. This record is the source of the material in this section unless specifically noted otherwise.

29. McKay, letter of February 1, 1863, in *Ballston Journal*, February 17, 1863; Daniel Doxtater, letter of February 24, 1863, in *Herkimer County Journal*, March 12, 1863; DeGraff, letters of November 19, 1862 and February 9, 1863; Sammons to Governor Morgan, November 3, 1862,

NYSA; Sammons to Adjutant General Hillhouse, November 4, 1862, NYSA.

30. Daniel Tyler served fifteen years in the army after his graduation from West Point in 1819, moving into private industry after only having obtained the rank of first lieutenant. At the outbreak of the Civil War he returned to the army as a brigadier general of Connecticut volunteers but mustered out again after a poor performance at the First Battle of Bull Run. He returned again in March 1862 and served in the western theater before being moved through a number of administrative posts, including a brief stint as commander at Camp Douglas. (Ezra J. Warner, *Generals in Blue: Lives of the Union Commanders* (Baton Rouge: Louisiana State University Press, 1964), p. 514.)

31. DeGraff, letter of February 9, 1863; DeGraff Memoir, p. 150.

32. Sammons, letter to Secretary of War Edwin Stanton, n.d., Regimental Order and Letter Book, National Archives, p. 22–24.

33. David Kittle, letter to Secretary of War Edwin Stanton, n.d., Regimental Order and Letter Book, National Archives, p. 24.

34. Frank Barnum, letter to Secretary of War Edwin Stanton, n.d., Regimental Order and Letter Book, National Archives, p. 25; Washington Vosburgh, letter of February 10, 1863, Wash Vosburgh Letters, Bentley Historical Library, University of Michigan.

35. Sammons, letter to Major General David Hunter, commander of the Tenth Corps at Hilton Head, February 26, 1863, Record Group 94: Muster Rolls, Returns, Regimental Papers, National Archives; *Herkimer County Journal*, March 12 and March 19, 1863; Clark, *Iron Hearted Regiment*, p. 56; *The Daily Saratogian*, March 19, 1863; DeGraff, letter of March 17, 1863.

36. Reid, "War Against Secessia," p. 29.

37. William F. Fox, *Regimental Losses in the American Civil War, 1861–1865* (Albany: Albany Publishing Company, 1889), p. 226. Fox compiled a listing of the three hundred Union Civil War regiments that suffered the most casualties during the war, a listing that became known as the Fighting 300.

Chapter 6

1. Robert Carse, *Hilton Head Island in the Civil War: Department of the South* (Columbia, South Carolina: The State Printing Company, 1961), p. 1–2, 10ff.

2. Clark, *Iron Hearted Regiment*, p. 59.

3. *The Free South*, January 17, 1863; Clark, *Iron Hearted Regiment*, p. 60. Soldiers could subscribe to *The Free South* for three months for fifty cents. *The New South* cost five cents per copy, "invariably cash" according to its masthead. Sutlers were civilian businessmen officially appointed to sell goods to the troops. Their merchandise included anything a soldier might need, from food and toiletries to tobacco and contraband whiskey.

4. Reardon Memoir, February 10, 1863; Sammons, letter of May 17, 1863, MCDHA; DeGraff Memoir, p. 147.

5. DeGraff, letter of February 9, 1863; Sammons, letter to Dr. Augustus C. Hamlin, Medical Inspector of the Department of the South, August 11, 1863, Regimental Order and Letter Book, National Archives, p. 51; DeGraff Memoir, p. 148; Reardon Memoir, February 23—February 28, 1863; Garret Van Derveer, letter of March 16, 1863, Lewis Leigh Collection, USAMHI.

6. Reid, "War Against Secessia," p. 17.

7. DeGraff Memoir, p. 147; William H. Bennett, grandson of Nicholas DeGraff, letter to author of February 15, 1995.

8. Sammons, letter of May 15, 1863, MCDHA.

9. Clark, *Iron Hearted Regiment*, p. 56–58; DeGraff Memoir, p. 154.

10. Jacob Brown, letter of February 6, 1863, collection of Lance Ingmire; Clark, *Iron Hearted Regiment*, p. 58–59; Reardon Memoir, March 19, 1863.

11. Reid, "War Against Secessia," p. 17.

12. Seely Conover, letter of May 26, 1863, reprinted in the *Amsterdam Evening Recorder*, May 29, 1913; DeGraff, letter of April 7, 1863; Reid, "War Against Secessia," p. 16.

13. Carse, *Hilton Head Island in the Civil War*, p. 24–25; DeGraff Memoir, p. 170.

14. Sammons, letter of April, 11, 1863, MCDHA.

15. Seely Conover, letter of May 26, 1863, reprinted in the *Amsterdam Evening Recorder*, May 29, 1913. Conover later served as a school teacher, school superintendent, and Mayor of Amsterdam.

16. Reardon Memoir, March 1, 1863.

17. DeGraff Memoir, p. 140, 170; Dudley T. Cornish, *The Sable Arm: Negro Troops in the Union Army, 1861–1865* (New York: W.W. Norton & Co., 1966), p. 79ff.

18. Reuben Wells, letter of June 4, 1863, William Gladstone Collection, USAMHI; Clark, *Iron Hearted Regiment*, p. 64.

19. Stephen R. Wise, *Gate of Hell: Campaign for Charleston Harbor, 1863* (Columbia, South Carolina: University of South Carolina Press, 1994), p. 29.

20. Wise, *Gate of Hell*, p. 30–32; Garrett Van Derveer, letter of April 13, 1863, Lewis Leigh Collection, USAMHI.

21. DeGraff, letters of February 9, March 24, April 7, June 6, 1863; DeGraff Memoir, p. 144, 150, 164, 170.

22. O.R., Vol. XIV, p. 463; Wise, *Gate of Hell*, p. 52–53. The 54th Massachusetts, its role in the Darien raid, and Shaw's reaction were dramatized in the 1989 film *Glory*.

23. William E. Flint, letter of June 4, 1863, Lewis Leigh Collection, USAMHI.

24. *The New South*, June 6, 1863; O.R., Volume XIV, p. 309; "True Soldier of the 115th," letter of June 8, 1863, in *The Daily Saratogian*, June 25, 1863; Reardon Memoir, June 3, 1863. Reardon recorded the date incorrectly.

25. "True Soldier of the 115th," letter of June 8, 1863, in *The Daily Saratogian*, June 25, 1863.

26. "True Soldier of the 115th," letter of June 8, 1863, in *The Daily Saratogian*, June 25, 1863; Simeon Sammons, letter to Dr. Augustus C. Hamlin, Medical Inspector of the Department of the South, August 11, 1863, Regimental Order and Letter Book, National Archives, p. 51.

27. Reid, "War Against Secessia," p. 17–18; Clark, *Iron Hearted Regiment*, p. 68; DeGraff Memoir, p. 170; Reardon Memoir, June 30, 1863; *The Free South*, June 27, July 4, 11, 18, 25, August 1, 1863. The lists of soldier deaths in these six weekly issues included 14 men of the 115th, but these lists were incomplete.

28. Wise, *Gate of Hell*, p. 185–186; Simeon Sammons, letter to Dr. Augustus C. Hamlin, Medical Inspector of the Department of the South, August 11, 1863, Regimental Order and Letter Book, National Archives, p. 51.

29. Kelley S. Tulloch, letter of November 7, 1863, collection of Lance Ingmire.

30. Reid, "War Against Secessia," p. 18; Wise, *Gate of Hell*, p. 34; O.R., Volume XXVIII, Part I, p. 9, 13; Warner, *Generals in Blue*, p. 176.

31. Wise, *Gate of Hell*, p. 15.

32. O.R., Volume XXVIII, Part I, p. 12–27; Fred S. Goodrich, letter of October 14, 1863, Fred S. Goodrich

Collection, Bentley Historical Library, University of Michigan; Wise, *Gate of Hell*, p. 114, 211; Phisterer, *New York in the War of the Rebellion*, Vol. III, p. 2357; DeGraff Memoir, p. 178.

33. Cornish, *The Sable Arm*, p. 155–156.

34. Wise, *Gate of Hell*, p. 113; Reid, "War Against Secessia," p. 18; DeGraff Memoir, p. 179; *The Free South*, July 25, 1863.

35. *The Free South*, August 8, 1863.

36. DeGraff Memoir, p. 159.

37. Reid, "War Against Secessia," p. 18.

38. Garret Van Derveer Diary, collection of the Fultonville Lodge No. 531, Free and Accepted Masons, Fultonville, New York, November 9, 1863; Dr. Carrington Macfarlane, *Reminiscences of an Army Surgeon* (Oswego, New York: Lake City Print Shop, 1912), p. 39; DeGraff Memoir, p. 190–191; Faust, *Encyclopedia of the Civil War* p. 225–226. The draft law touched off opposition and protest including violent riots, most notably in New York City and Troy, New York. It resulted in adding 46,000 conscripts and 118,000 substitutes to the Union army, just 6% of the total force.

39. Reid, "War Against Secessia," p. 18; DeGraff Memoir, p. 188.

40. DeGraff Memoir, p. 185.

41. Proceedings of the General Court Martial against Colonel Simeon Sammons, National Archives, Record Group No. 153, NN-271 Box 1535; Sammons, letter of October 8, 1863, MCDHA.

42. Colonel C.H. Van Wyck, letter to Captain Walton W. French, September 14, 1863, Adjutant General's Correspondence and Petitions Series B0462, NYSA. Van Wyck was commander of the 56th New York and president of the Sammons court martial. This letter forwarded the quoted statement from Saxton's adjutant, Captain Stewart M. Taylor.

43. Sammons, letter of October 8, 1863, MCDHA; DeGraff, letter of September 5, 1863; DeGraff Memoir, p. 175, 185.

44. Proceedings of the General Court Martial against Colonel Simeon Sammons, National Archives; Millham's tribute is transcribed in *Illustrated History of Montgomery and Fulton Counties, New York, 1878*, p. 146; Reid, "War Against Secessia," p. 18; *The Free South*, December 5, 1863.

45. Sammons, letters of October 8, December 4, December 6, 1863, MCDHA; DeGraff Memoir, p. 193.

46. DeGraff Memoir, p. 189; Sammons, letter of December 6, 1863, MCDHA.

47. Carrington Macfarlane, *Army Surgeon*, p. 4, 31, 36–37.

48. Reid, "War Against Secessia," p. 19; DeGraff Memoir, p. 198; John Kneeskern, letter of January 10, 1864, collection of Richard Bellinger. William B. Barton was a New Jersey native, son of a Presbyterian minister, and graduate of Princeton (Barton obituary, *New York Tribune*, June 14, 1891).

Chapter 7

1. Sammons, letter of January 24, 1864, MCDHA.

2. Richard McMurry, "The President's Tenth and the Battle of Olustee," *Civil War Times Illustrated*, January 1978, p. 14.

3. McMurry, "The President's Tenth," p. 14–15; William H. Nulty, *Confederate Florida: The Road to Olustee* (Tuscaloosa, Alabama: The University of Alabama Press, 1990), p. 69–72; Mark F. Boyd, "The Federal Campaign of 1864 in East Florida," *Florida Historical Quarterly*, Volume 29, July 1950, p. 4; David Herbert Donald, *Lincoln* (New York: Simon & Schuster, 1995), p. 478–484.

4. O.R., Volume XXXV, Part I, p. 278, 292.

5. O.R., Vol. XXXV, Part I, p. 279; Nulty, *Confederate Florida*, p. 58, 66.

6. O.R., Vol. XXXV, Part I, p. 280; Macfarlane, *Army Surgeon*, p. 43. Macfarlane penned this lyrical description long after he had done his bloody work with the expedition's casualties. Truman Seymour was the son of a Vermont preacher who attended West Point then served in the Mexican and Seminole Wars. He commanded Union troops at Fort Sumter, the Peninsula, and Second Bull Run before leading the bloody July 18, 1863 assault on Fort Wagner. (Warner, *Generals in Blue*, p. 432–433.)

7. Clark, *Iron Hearted Regiment*, p. 69–70; Reardon Memoir, February 7, 1864.

8. Boyd, "Federal Campaign," p. 6–7; O.R., Vol. XXXV, Part I, p. 280; Derveer Diary, February 5, 1864; Reardon Memoir, February 5, 1864; Macfarlane, *Army Surgeon*, p. 43; Nulty, *Confederate Florida*, p. 81; Clark, *Iron Hearted Regiment*, p. 71; DeGraff Memoir, p. 200.

9. Reardon Memoir, February 7, 1864; DeGraff, letter of February 13, 1864.

10. DeGraff Memoir, p. 200; O.R., Vol. XXXV, Part I, p. 295–296, 330; McMurry, "The President's Tenth," p. 16; Boyd, "Federal Campaign," p. 7.

11. Macfarlane, *Army Surgeon*, p. 44; Clark, *Iron Hearted Regiment*, p. 72; DeGraff, letter of February 13, 1864; Reardon Memoir, February 9, 1864.

12. Van Derveer Diary, February 9, 1964; McMurry, "The President's Tenth," p. 16–17; O.R. p. 296.

13. O.R., Vol. XXXV, Part I, p. 296.

14. DeGraff Memoir, p. 200; Reid, "War Against Secessia," p. 19; Macfarlane, *Army Surgeon*, p. 44.

15. Van Derveer Diary, February 11–12, 1864; DeGraff Memoir, p. 202; O.R., Vol. XXXV, Part I, p. 282, 296.

16. O.R., Vol. XXXV, Part I, p. 283, 291.

17. O.R., Vol. XXXV, Part I, p. 277, 282–283, 291; *New York Times*, February 23, 1864.

18. Nulty, *Confederate Florida*, p. 109, 111.

19. Reid, "War Against Secessia," p. 19.

20. DeGraff, p. 202; Macfarlane, *Army Surgeon*, p. 45.

21. Nulty, *Confederate Florida*, p. 111; DeGraff Memoir, p. 202; Reid, "War Against Secessia," p. 24.

22. DeGraff, p. 202; Clark, *Iron Hearted Regiment*, p. 79–80; *Illustrated History of Montgomery & Fulton Counties, New York, 1878*, p. 76.

23. Reid, "War Against Secessia," p. 19.

24. O.R., Vol. XXXV, Part I, p. 281, 296; McMurry, "The President's Tenth," p. 16; Reardon Memoir, February 9–27, 1864.

25. O.R., Vol. XXXV, Part I, p. 277, 282, 284, 285–286; Boyd, "Federal Campaign," p. 13; Truman Seymour, letter to Brigadier General John T. Sprague, New York State Adjutant General, March 26, 1864, Record Group 94, Entry 159, General's Papers (Second Series), National Archives.

26. O.R., Vol. XXXV, Part I, p. 299; Boyd, "Federal Campaign," p. 15–17; Reid, "War Against Secessia," p. 19; Clark, *Iron Hearted Regiment*, p. 80.

27. O.R., Vol. XXXV, Part I, p. 288, 299, 303; Boyd, "Federal Campaign," p. 17; Reid, "War Against Secessia," p., 21; DeGraff Memoir, p. 204. The 1st North Carolina was composed of former slaves recruited around New Bern, North Carolina.

28. Boyd, "Federal Campaign," p. 17; Nulty, *Confederate Florida*, p. 126; Clark, *Iron Hearted Regiment*, p. 80–81.

29. Nulty, *Confederate Florida*, p. 119–121; Boyd, "Federal Campaign," p. 9, 11, 14; O.R., Vol. XXXV, Part I, p. 331.

30. Nulty, *Confederate Florida*, p. 125–131; Boyd, "Federal Campaign," p. 17–19; O.R., Vol. XXXV, Part I, p. 287–288, 303, 307, 349, 352; Reid, "War Against Secessia," p. 20.

31. Nulty, *Confederate Florida*, p. 134–145; Reid, "War Against Secessia," p. 20.

32. O.R., Vol. XXXV, Part I, p. 302; DeGraff Memoir, p. 204; Clark, *Iron Hearted Regiment*, p. 83; Reid, "War Against Secessia," p. 20.

33. *New York Times*, March 1, 1864; Boyd, "Federal Campaign," p. 24; Reid, "War Against Secessia," p. 20; Clark, *Iron Hearted Regiment*, p. 84.

34. O.R., Vol. XXXV, Part I, p. 302; DeGraff, letter of February 23, 1863; Clark, *Iron Hearted Regiment*, p. 83; DeGraff Memoir, p. 204; Boyd, "Federal Campaign," p. 25.

35. Reid, "War Against Secessia," p. 20; Clark, *Iron Hearted Regiment*, p. 85; *New York Tribune*, March 1, 1864; DeGraff, letter of February 23, 1864; Benjamin K. Northrup, letter of February 23, 1864, in *Cohoes Cataract*, March 5, 1864.

36. Reid, "War Against Secessia," p. 20; Clark, *Iron Hearted Regiment*, p. 84; O.R., Vol. XXXV, Part I, p. 337.

37. DeGraff Memoir, p. 204; DeGraff, letters of February 23 and March 7, 1864. Levi Lingenfelter was a cousin of Captain Sidney Lingenfelter.

38. Northrup, letter of February 23, 1864, in *Cohoes Cataract*, March 5, 1864.

39. Reid, "War Against Secessia," p. 22, 24.

40. James H. Clark, "At Their Country's Call," published in the program of the 35th Reunion of the 115th New York Volunteer Infantry Association, August 26, 1916, Glens Falls, New York, collection of Hector J. Allen, Town Historian Oppenheim, New York, p. 20.

41. Clark, "At Their Country's Call," p. 20–21.

42. Clark, *Iron Hearted Regiment*, p. 88.

43. Macfarlane, *Army Surgeon*, p. 46; O.R., Vol. XXXV, Part I, p. 299.

44. Reid, "War Against Secessia," p. 21.

45. Sergeant Cyrus N. Ballou, letter of February 23, 1864, undated newspaper clipping in author's file; *Montgomery County Republican*, March 8, 1864; Van Derveer Diary, March 18, 1863 and below February 13, 1864; O.R., Vol. XXXV, Part I, p. 289; Simeon Sammons, letter to N.Y.S. Adjutant General John T. Sprague, February 25, 1864, Adjutant General's Correspondence and Petitions, Series B0462, NYSA; Batcheller, letter of March 16, 1864, in *Montgomery County Republican*, March 22, 1864.

46. Obituary of Captain William Smith, *Johnstown Daily Republican*, February 9, 1891; *New York Tribune*, March 1, 1864.

47. DeGraff, letter of February 23, 1864; Clark, *Iron Hearted Regiment*, p. 233–234; Truman Seymour to N.Y.S. Adjutant General John T. Sprague, February 27, 1864, Record Group 94, Entry 159, General's Papers (Second Series), National Archives; *Illustrated History of Montgomery & Fulton Counties, New York, 1878*, p. 146; affidavits of Simeon Sammons and Dr. Thompson Burton, Sammons Family Papers, MCDHA; O.R., Vol. XXXV, Part I, p. 289.

48. Joseph Hawley, 7th Connecticut, "Comments on General Jones's Paper," in *Battles & Leaders*, Vol. IV, p. 80; General Samuel Jones, C.S.A., "The Battle of Olustee, or Ocean Pond, Florida," in *Battles & Leaders*, Vol. IV, p. 78; Nulty, *Confederate Florida*, p. 162–163; James M. Nichols, 48th New York, *Perry's Saints, or the Fighting Parson's Regiment in the War of the Rebellion* (Boston: Lathrop, 1886), p. 194; O.R., Vol. XXXV, Part I, p. 344, 349–350; Boyd,

"Federal Campaign," p. 24; Northrup, letter of February 23, 1864, in *Cohoes Cataract*, March 5, 1864; Lorenzo Lyon, 48th New York, letter of February 23, 1864, Lorenzo Lyon Letters, NYHS.

49. Reid, "War Against Secessia," p. 20–21; Boyd, "Federal Campaign," p. 24.

50. DeGraff Memoir, p. 206.

51. Reid, "War Against Secessia," p. 20; Clark, *Iron Hearted Regiment*, p. 85; Boyd, "Federal Campaign," p. 25; Nulty, *Confederate Florida*, p. 158.

52. O.R., Vol. XXXV, Part I, p. 302; DeGraff Memoir, p. 206; Clark, *Iron Hearted Regiment*, p. 86; Northrup, letter of February 23, 1864, in *Cohoes Cataract*, March 5, 1864; William H. Shaw, letter of February 24, 1864, in *Johnstown Independent*, March 25, 1864.

53. O.R., Vol. XXXV, Part I, p. 302, 308–309; Nulty, *Confederate Florida*, p. 170–173; *New York Times*, March 1, 1864; Reid, "War Against Secessia," p. 21, 23; Macfarlane, *Army Surgeon*, p. 46; DeGraff, letter of February 23, 1864. Several Confederate reports characterized the Union withdrawal as a precipitous flight, assertions clearly disproved by the weight of evidence (see Hawley, "Comments on General Jones's Paper," *Battles & Leaders*, Vol. IV, p. 80).

54. Macfarlane, *Army Surgeon*, p. 46–47.

55. O.R., Vol. XXXV, Part I, p. 300; DeGraff Memoir, p. 206; Macfarlane, *Army Surgeon*, p. 46.

56. Clark, *Iron Hearted Regiment*, p. 88–89.

57. William Gardner, letter published in *National Tribune*, October 23, 1884.

58. Reid, "War Against Secessia," p. 25–27; Andersonville Cemetery Records. Baker's February 1865 return to the regiment is described in Chapter 14.

59. Reardon Memoir, February 20–21, 1864; Clark, *Iron Hearted Regiment*, p. 90. Twenty-three-year-old Lieutenant Isaac E. Smith, a farmer from Minden in Montgomery County, survived his shoulder wound and rose to captain near the war's end. (Clark, *Iron Hearted Regiment*, p. 250).

60. O.R., Vol. XXXV, Part I, p. 328; Boyd, "Federal Campaign," p. 28–29; DeGraff Memoir, p. 208; *New York Times*, March 1, 1864.

61. Oliver W. Norton, letter of February 29, 1864, *Army Letters, 1861-1865* (Dayton, Ohio: Morningside House, 1990), p. 199; DeGraff Memoir, p. 208.

62. Truman Seymour, letter of March 26, 1864, National Archives.

63. Warner, "Generals in Blue," p. 433.

64. Phisterer, *New York in the War of the Rebellion*, Vol. IV, p. 3347; Reid, "War Against Secessia," p. 21.

65. DeGraff, letter of February 23, 1864; Norton, *Army Letters*, p. 198, 200. After the war Norton authored a well-known study of the Battle of Gettysburg, *The Attack and Defense of Little Round Top* (New York: Neale Publishing Company, 1913).

66. Grady McWhiney and Perry D. Jamieson, *Attack and Die: Civil War Military Tactics and the Southern Heritage* (University, Alabama: University of Alabama Press, 1982), p. 11; Nulty, *Confederate Florida*, p. 203.

67. John J. Hennessy, *Return to Bull Run: The Campaign and Battle of Second Manassas* (New York: Simon & Schuster, 1993), p. 175–186.

68. Alan D. Gaff, *Brave Men's Tears: The Iron Brigade at Brawner Farm* (Dayton, Ohio: Morningside House, 1985), p. 157; O.R., Vol. XXXV, Part I, p. 298; Truman Seymour, letter of February 27, 1864, National Archives.

69. O.R., Vol. XXXV, Part I, p. 289; Truman Seymour, letter of February 27, 1864, National Archives.

70. *New York Times*, March 1, 1864; *New York Herald* report, reprinted in the *Mohawk Valley Democrat*, March 5, 1864.

71. Shaw, letter of February 24, 1864, *Johnstown Independent*, March 25, 1864; Reid, "War Against Secessia," p. 28; Clark, *Iron Hearted Regiment*, p. 84.

Chapter 8

1. Reid, "War Against Secessia," p. 27; DeGraff, letters of February 29 and March 7, 1864 Reardon Memoir, March 4, 1864.
2. O.R., Vol. XXXV, Part II, p. 15; Nulty, "Confederate Florida," p. 188, 200.
3. Reardon Memoir, March 9-10, 1864; DeGraff Memoir, p. 210; Reid, "War Against Secessia," p. 27.
4. Pension affidavits, Sammons Family Papers, MCDHA; Clark, *Iron Hearted Regiment*, p. 236.
5. Phisterer, *New York in the War of the Rebellion*, Vol. III, p. 1873; John J. Hennessy, *The First Battle of Manassas: An End to Innocence* (Lynchburg, Virginia: H.E. Howard, Inc., 1989), p. 20-22, 26; Franklin Hough Papers, Box 36 Folder 3, NYSL.
6. Phisterer, *New York in the War of the Rebellion*, Vol. III, p. 1886, and Vol. IV, p. 3358; Ezra L. Walrath, letter to "My Old Friend Boz," January 30, 1864, Adjutant General's Correspondence and Petitions, Series B0462, NYSA; Sammons, letter to Adjutant General Sprague, February 25, 1864, NYSA; Sprague to Sammons, March 25, 1864, Sammons Family Papers, MCDHA.
7. DeGraff, letter of March 20, 1864.
8. Reid, "War Against Secessia," p. 28; DeGraff, letter of March 20, 1864; O.R., Vol. XXXV, Part I, p. 376-377, 382.
9. Benjamin Thackrah, "Capture of a Bushwacker Outpost" in, W.F. Beyer and O.F. Keydel, editors, *Deeds of Valor: How America's Civil War Heroes Won the Congressional Medal of Honor* (Stamford, Connecticut: Longmeadow Press, 1992 reprint), p. 310-312; Benjamin Thackrah Medal of Honor File, National Archives; O.R., Vol. XXXV, Part I, p. 382-383. *Deeds of Valor* was originally published in 1903.
10. Benjamin Thackrah Medal of Honor File, National Archives.
11. Reardon Memoir, April 6-8, 1864, April 13, 1864.
12. Ulysses S. Grant, *Personal Memoirs* (New York: Charles L. Webster & Company, 1885), Vol. II, p. 129, 556; William S. McFeely, *Grant: A Biography* (New York: W.W. Norton & Company, 1981), p. 157.
13. William Glenn Robertson, *Back Door to Richmond: The Bermuda Hundred Campaign, April-June, 1864* (Baton Rouge: Louisiana State University Press, 1987), p. 14; McFeely, *Grant: A Biography*, p. 157; Grant, *Personal Memoirs*, Volume II, p. 129-132, 143; David Herbert Donald, *Lincoln* (New York: Simon & Schuster, 1995), p. 499.
14. DeGraff, letter of April 18, 1864; Reid, "War Against Secessia," p. 29; Reardon Memoir, April 18-20, 1864.
15. Clark, *Iron Hearted Regiment*, p. 103; Dallas F. Paul, letter of April 26, 1864, collection of Lance Ingmire; Macfarlane, *Army Surgeon*, p. 52.
16. John A. Porter, *76th Regiment Pennsylvania Volunteer Infantry, Keystone Zouaves: The Personal Recollections 1861-1865 of Sergeant John A. Porter*, ed. James A. Chrisman (Wilmington, North Carolina: Broadfoot Publishing Company, 1988), p. 48; Herbert M. Schiller, *The Bermuda Hundred Campaign: Operation on the South Side of the James River, Virginia, May, 1864* (Dayton: Morningside, 1988), p. 39-40, 336. John W. Turner was born near Saratoga but grew up in Chicago. He graduated from West Point in 1855 and served in numerous posts before the Civil War. (Warner, "Generals in Blue," p. 512).
17. Warner, "Generals in Blue," p. 60-61.
18. Schiller, *Bermuda Hundred Campaign*, p. 25-27; Grant, *Personal Memoirs*, p. 132, 563; Benjamin F. Butler, *Butler's Book* (Boston: A.M. Thayer & Co., 1892), p. 628-631.
19. Reardon Memoir, May 4-6, 1864; Clark, *Iron Hearted Regiment*, p. 103; Schiller, *Bermuda Hundred Campaign*, p. 41; Reid, "War Against Secessia," p. 29; Robertson, *Back Door to Richmond*, p. 57; DeGraff Memoir, p. 220.
20. Reardon Memoir, May 6, 1864; Reid, "War Against Secessia," p. 30; Clark, *Iron Hearted Regiment*, p. 104.
21. Herbert M. Schiller, "Beast in a Bottle: The Bermuda Hundred Campaign, May, 1864," *Blue & Gray Magazine*, October 1989, p. 15.
22. Robertson, *Back Door to Richmond*, p. 79-82; Schiller, *Bermuda Hundred Campaign*, p. 81, 85; O.R., Vol. XXXVI, Part II, p. 519.
23. DeGraff Memoir, p, 220; Reardon Memoir, May 7, 1864; Schiller, *Bermuda Hundred Campaign*, p. 82; Robertson, *Back Door to Richmond*, p. 85-86.
24. Robertson, *Back Door to Richmond*, p. 86; O.R., Vol. XXXVI, Part II, p. 87, 101; Nichols, *Perry's Saints*, p. 206; John A. Porter, *76th Regiment*, p. 50.
25. Reid, "War Against Secessia," p. 30; DeGraff Memoir, p. 220; Reardon Memoir, May 7, 1864; Clark, *Iron Hearted Regiment*, p. 105.
26. Reid, "War Against Secessia," p. 30, 33.
27. Macfarlane, *Army Surgeon*, p. 54.
28. Reid, "War Against Secessia," p. 30-31; Reardon Memoir, May 7, 1864; DeGraff, letter of May 8, 1864.
29. DeGraff Diary, May 7, 1864; Reid, "War Against Secessia," p. 31; O.R., Vol. XXXVI, Part II, p. 251-2; Clark, *Iron Hearted Regiment*, p. 106.
30. Reardon Memoir, May 7, 1864; DeGraff, letter of May 8, 1864; Reid, "War Against Secessia," p. 31; Clark, *Iron Hearted Regiment*, p. 107; DeGraff Memoir, p. 220. While these sources all mention taking cover behind a row of bushes in the field opposite the railroad, the men variously described the terrain as a "ditch," a "line of brushwood," a "small stream," a "brook," or a "slight ridge." Its nature may have varied at different points on the 115th's line.
31. Reid, "War Against Secessia," p. 31; O.R., Vol. XXXVI, Part II, p. 251.
32. Reardon Memoir, May 7, 1864.
33. Reid, "War Against Secessia," p. 34; Clark, *Iron Hearted Regiment*, p. 256; DeGraff Memoir, p. 222.
34. DeGraff, letter of May 8, 1864; Reardon Memoir, May 7, 1864; O.R., Vol. XXXVI, Part II, p. 133, 521-522; Robertson, *Back Door to Richmond*, p. 89.
35. O.R., Vol. XXXVI, Part II, p. 74-75, 124-125, 133; Reid, "War Against Secessia," p. 32-33; DeGraff Memoir, p. 220.
36. Reid, "War Against Secessia," p. 31; Reardon Memoir, May 7, 1864; DeGraff, letter of May 8, 1864; Peter Keck, letter quoted in Reid, "War Against Secessia," p. 33; Clark, *Iron Hearted Regiment*, p. 108.
37. Reid, "War Against Secessia," p. 33; Clark, *Iron Hearted Regiment*, p. 108.
38. Reardon Memoir, May 7, 1864.
39. DeGraff Memoir, p. 220; Reid, "War Against Secessia," p. 35; DeGraff Diary, May 7, 1864.
40. Reid, "War Against Secessia," p. 33, 35; DeGraff Memoir, p. 222; Phisterer, *New York in the War of the Rebellion*, Vol. IV, p. 3347; Reardon Memoir, May 7, 1864; Schiller, *Bermuda Hundred Campaign*, p. 98.

41. Robertson, *Back Door to Richmond*, p. 89; Schiller, *Bermuda Hundred Campaign*, p. 97.
42. DeGraff Diary, May 9–10, 1864; Clark, *Iron Hearted Regiment*, p. 110; Reardon Memoir, May 10, 1864; DeGraff, letter of May 17, 1864.
43. Robertson, *Back Door to Richmond*, p. 139–142; Schiller, *Bermuda Hundred Campaign*, p. 163–164.
44. Robertson, *Back Door to Richmond*, p. 142–3, O.R., Vol. XXXVI, Part II, p. 11–12, 691; Butler, *Butler's Book*, p. 652; Reardon Memoir, May 8, 1864.
45. O.R., Vol. XXXVI, Part II, p. 36, 151; Robertson, *Back Door to Richmond*, p. 143–145.
46. Reardon Memoir, May 12, 1864.
47. Robertson, *Back Door to Richmond*, p. 147; Reardon Memoir, May 13, 1864; DeGraff, letter of May 17, 1864.
48. DeGraff, letter of May 17, 1864.
49. DeGraff Memoir, p. 224; Reardon Memoir, May 14, 1864.
50. Schiller, *Bermuda Hundred Campaign*, p. 203; Robertson, *Back Door to Richmond*, p. 170; William H. Borden, letter of May 25, 1864, collection of Lance Ingmire.
51. Reid, "War Against Secessia," p. 36.
52. Schiller, *Bermuda Hundred Campaign*, p. 203.
53. O.R., Vol. XXXVI, Part II, p. 103; Nichols, *Perry's Saints*, p. 215–219; DeGraff, letter of May 17, 1864; Reid, "War Against Secessia," p. 37–38; DeGraff Memoir, p. 226.
54. Robertson, *Back Door to Richmond*, p. 209–213; Clark, *Iron Hearted Regiment*, p. 119; Reid, "War Against Secessia," p. 38.
55. DeGraff, letter of May 17, 1864; Phisterer, *New York in the War of the Rebellion*, Vol. IV, p. 3347; Clark, *Iron Hearted Regiment*, p. 119; Schiller, *Bermuda Hundred Campaign*, p. 285–286; Reardon Memoir, May 16, 1864.
56. Schiller, *Bermuda Hundred Campaign*, p. 295; Grant, *Personal Memoirs*, Vol. II, p. 568.
57. Borden, letter of May 25, 1864, collection of Lance Ingmire; Reid, "War Against Secessia," p. 38; Reardon Memoir, May 16, 1864. Modern historians have rendered much the same judgment of Butler's campaign as the men of the 115th New York.

Chapter 9

1. Reid, "War Against Secessia," p. 38; David H. King, *History of the Ninety-Third Regiment New York Volunteer Infantry* (Milwaukee: Association of the 93rd New York State Volunteers, 1895), p. 597–598; N.Y.S. Adjutant General John T. Sprague, letter to Colonel Sammons of March 25, 1864, Sammons Family Papers, MCDHA.
2. Reid, "War Against Secessia," p. 38; DeGraff Memoir, p. 230.
3. Robertson, *Back Door to Richmond*, p. 221; Clark, *Iron Hearted Regiment*, p. 121; Reardon Memoir, May 20, 1864; Reid, "War Against Secessia," p. 39; DeGraff Memoir, p. 230.
4. Reid, "War Against Secessia," p. 39; Clark, *Iron Hearted Regiment*, p. 121; Robertson, *Back Door to Richmond*, p. 221–222; Reardon Memoir, May 20, 1864; DeGraff Memoir, p. 230.
5. DeGraff Memoir, p. 230.
6. DeGraff Memoir, p. 230; Colonel William Barton, letter of May 24, 1864, Nathan J. Johnson, letter of May 28, 1864, Solomon P. Smith, letter of July 19, 1864, Ezra Walrath, letter of July 9, 1864, and General John Turner, letter of July 27, 1864, all in N.J. Johnson Service Record, National Archives; Sammons, letter of July 18, 1864, MCDHA.
7. DeGraff Diary, May 17–26, 1864; Reid, "War Against Secessia," p. 39; Schiller, *Bermuda Hundred Campaign*, p. 320.
8. Noah Andre Trudeau, *Bloody Roads South: The Wilderness to Cold Harbor, May–June 1864* (Boston: Little, Brown and Company, 1989), p. 341; R. Wayne Maney, *Marching to Cold Harbor: Victory and Failure, 1864* (Shippensburg, Pennsylvania: White Mane Publishing, 1995), p. 49, 63.
9. Reid, "War Against Secessia," p. 39; Schiller, *Bermuda Hundred Campaign*, p. 321–322; Ernest B. Furgurson, *Not War But Murder: Cold Harbor 1864* (New York: Alfred A. Knopf, 2000), p. 58.
10. DeGraff Diary, May 26–31, 1864; Reardon Memoir, May 26–31, 1864; DeGraff Memoir, p. 234–235; Clark, *Iron Hearted Regiment*, p. 124; Reid, "War Against Secessia," p. 40.
11. Grant, *Personal Memoirs*, Vol. II, p. 259, 264; Trudeau, *Bloody Roads South*, p. 261–263.
12. Trudeau, *Bloody Roads South*, p. 266–267; General William F. Smith, "The Eighteenth Corps at Cold Harbor," in *Battles & Leaders*, Vol. IV, p. 230; DeGraff Diary, May 31, 1864; Louis J. Baltz III, *The Battle of Cold Harbor: May 27–June 13, 1864*, (Lynchburg, Virginia: H.E. Howard, Inc., 1994), p. 81; O.R., Vol. XXXVI, Part I, p. 999.
13. Archibald McGlachlin, letter in *National Tribune*, December 25, 1886; DeGraff Diary, May 31–June 1, 1864; Reardon Memoir, June 1, 1864; General William F. Smith, "The Eighteenth Corps at Cold Harbor," p. 222–223.
14. O.R., Vol. XXXVI, Part I, p. 999.
15. McGlachlin, *National Tribune*, December 25, 1886; Smith, "The Eighteenth Corps at Cold Harbor," p. 230; Furgurson, *Not War But Murder*, p. 94–95; Clark, *Iron Hearted Regiment*, p. 125.
16. John Reardon, letter of June 2, 1864, typescript at Richmond National Battlefield; Reid, "War Against Secessia," p. 40; O.R., Vol. XXXVI, Part I, p. 1000; Robert E.L. Krick, Michael Andrus, and David Ruth, "Grant and Lee, 1864: From the North Anna to the Crossing of the James," in *Blue & Gray Magazine*, April, 1994, p. 44–46. The original of Sergeant Reardon's June 2 letter is in the possession of his grandson, Karl Reardon of Buffalo, New York.
17. Reid, "War Against Secessia," p. 41; O.R., Vol. XXXVI, Part I, p. 1019–1020; Clark, *Iron Hearted Regiment*, p. 125–126; DeGraff Memoir, p. 236; *New York Times*, June 7, 1864.
18. Clark, *Iron Hearted Regiment*, p. 125; Reid, "War Against Secessia," p. 41; McGlachlin, *National Tribune*, December 25, 1886; Reardon, letter of June 2, 1864, typescript at Richmond National Battlefield. The men's estimates of the width of the field across which they charged vary greatly. General Smith and Colonel Barton recorded the width as 1200 and 1250 yards, respectively (O.R., Vol. XXXVI, Part I, p. 996, 1018), but the estimates from the 115th are lower.
19. Reardon, letter of June 2, 1864, typescript at Richmond National Battlefield; Clark, *Iron Hearted Regiment*, p. 126; *New York Times*, June 7, 1864; O.R., Vol. XXXVI, Part I, p. 1020.
20. Clark, *Iron Hearted Regiment*, p. 125; Reardon, letter of June 2, 1864; *New York Times*, June 7, 1864.
21. McGlachlin, *National Tribune*, December 25, 1886.
22. Reid, "War Against Secessia," p. 41; Reardon, letter of June 2, 1864; DeGraff Memoir, p. 236.
23. *New York Times*, June 7, 1864; Reid, "War Against Secessia," p. 41; DeGraff Memoir, p. 236. Colonel Barton reported that his brigade took 400 prisoners (O.R., Vol. XXXVI, Part I, p. 1018).

24. Clark, *Iron Hearted Regiment*, p. 126; O.R., Vol. XXXVI, Part I, p. 1019; Abraham Palmer, *Forty-Eighth Regiment, N.Y.S. Volunteers*, p. 150-151; DeGraff Memoir, p. 236; Reid, "War Against Secessia," p. 40.

25. Macfarlane, *Army Surgeon*, p. 55; Reid, "War Against Secessia," p. 40-41; DeGraff Memoir, p. 236; O.R., Vol. XXXVI, Part I, p. 179, 1018. Colonel Barton reported 224 casualties in his brigade for the entire Cold Harbor campaign of June 1-12, 1864, including 18 in the 115th New York. Separate figures are not available for June 1.

26. Fred Mosher, letter to James Reid, quoted in Reid, "War Against Secessia," p. 41; Reid, "War Against Secessia," p. 41; Clark, *Iron Hearted Regiment*, p. 125.

27. Krick, Andrus, and Ruth, "Grant and Lee, 1864," p. 46, 50; Smith, "The Eighteenth Corps at Cold Harbor," p. 224-225; Furguson, *Not War But Murder*, p. 110, 133, 150; DeGraff Diary, June 2, 1864; Reardon Memoir, June 2, 1864.

28. Smith, "The Eighteenth Corps at Cold Harbor," p. 225.

29. Faust, *Encyclopedia of the Civil War*, p. 150; Reardon Memoir, June 3, 1864; DeGraff Memoir, p. 238; Grant, *Personal Memoirs*, Vol. II, p. 271, 276.

30. Reid, "War Against Secessia," p. 41; DeGraff, letter of June 11, 1864; Reardon Memoir, June 7, 9, 10; DeGraff Memoir, p. 238-240; Clark, *Iron Hearted Regiment*, p. 128-129, 132.

31. Reardon Memoir, June 3, 1864.

32. Reid, "War Against Secessia," p. 41-42.

33. DeGraff, letter of June 11, 1864; DeGraff Memoir, p. 238; Reid, "War Against Secessia," p. 41.

34. Trudeau, *Bloody Roads South*, p. 307-308; Reardon Memoir, June 6, 1864; DeGraff, letter of June 11, 1864.

35. DeGraff Memoir, p. 240; Clark, *Iron Hearted Regiment*, p. 129; Reardon Memoir, June 6, 1864; DeGraff, letter of June 11, 1864.

36. Trudeau, *Bloody Roads South*, p. 309-310; Maney, *Marching to Cold Harbor*, p. 196; Reardon Memoir, June 8, 1864.

37. Clark, *Iron Hearted Regiment*, p. 133.

38. Clark, *Iron Hearted Regiment*, p. 130; Reardon Memoir, June 7, 1864.

39. Reardon Memoir, June 3, 10, 1864.

40. DeGraff, letter of June 11, 1864; DeGraff Memoir, p. 240.

41. O.R., Vol. XXXVI, Part I, p. 22; Noah A. Trudeau, *The Last Citadel: Petersburg, Virginia, June 1864–April 1865*, (Boston: Little, Brown and Company, 1991), p. 16.

42. Trudeau, *Bloody Roads South*, p. 313; Grant, *Personal Memoirs*, Vol. II, p. 284-288; Reid, "War Against Secessia," p. 43.

43. Clark, *Iron Hearted Regiment*, p. 134; Reardon Memoir, June 12, 1864; Furguson, *Not War But Murder*, p. 249-251.

44. DeGraff Memoir, p. 242; Reardon Memoir, June 13, 14, 1864; Reid, "War Against Secessia," p. 44; DeGraff Diary, June 14, 1864; Clark, *Iron Hearted Regiment*, p. 134.

45. Clark, *Iron Hearted Regiment*, p. 134-135; Reardon Memoir, June 15, 1864; Reid, "War Against Secessia," p. 44.

46. DeGraff Memoir, p. 244; Reardon Memoir, June 17, 1864; Phisterer, *New York in the War of the Rebellion*, Vol. IV, p. 3346.

47. Trudeau, *Bloody Roads South*, p. 341; O.R., Vol. XXXVI, Part I, p. 179, 180, 188, 1018; DeGraff, letter of June 19, 1864; Reid, "War Against Secessia," p. 41.

Chapter 10

1. Thomas J. Howe, *Wasted Valor: The Petersburg Campaign, June 15-18, 1864* (Lynchburg, Virginia: H.E. Howard, Inc., Second Edition, 1988), p. 24, 27, 51-52; Trudeau, *The Last Citadel*, p. 38, 43, 46-50; O.R., Vol. XL, Part II, p. 131-132. The 115th was coming into contact with Beauregard for the second time; he had held overall command of the Confederate defenses of South Carolina, Georgia, and Florida when the 115th supported the campaign against Charleston and fought at Olustee. The ubiquitous Louisiana Creole, West Pointer, and Mexican War veteran had also served the South at Fort Sumter, First Bull Run, and Shiloh. (Faust, *Encyclopedia of the Civil War*, p. 51-52.)

2. Reid, "War Against Secessia," p. 47; Reardon Memoir, June 17, 1864; DeGraff Memoir, p. 244; Clark, *Iron Hearted Regiment*, p. 136.

3. DeGraff Memoir, p. 244-246; DeGraff, letter of June 19, 1864; Reardon Memoir, June 17, 1864.

4. Reid, "War Against Secessia," p. 47.

5. Reardon Memoir, June 18, 1864; DeGraff Memoir, p. 246-248; Reid, "War Against Secessia," p. 52.

6. DeGraff Memoir, p. 248; Reardon Memoir, June 22, 1864.

7. Palmer, *48th New York*, p. 156; DeGraff Memoir, p. 250; Trudeau, *The Last Citadel*, p. 70-71.

8. Reid, "War Against Secessia," p. 52; DeGraff Diary, June 24, 1864; Clark, *Iron Hearted Regiment*, p. 137.

9. O.R., Vol. XL, Part II, p. 368-369; John Kneeskern, letter of July 15, 1864, collection of Richard Bellinger.

10. Reid, "War Against Secessia," p. 53, 55.

11. Reid, "War Against Secessia," p. 53; Kneeskern, letter of July 15, 1864, collection of Richard Bellinger; Clark, *Iron Hearted Regiment*, p, 187.

12. Reid, "War Against Secessia," p. 53; Noah Andre Trudeau, *Bloody Roads South: The Wilderness to Cold Harbor, May-June 1864* (Boston: Little, Brown and Company, 1989), p. 54; DeGraff Memoir, p. 250; Reardon Memoir, June 24, 1864.

13. Reid, "War Against Secessia," p. 53-54; O.R., Vol. XL, Part II, p. 400.

14. Reid. p, 54; DeGraff Memoir, p. 252; O.R., Vol. XL, Part II, p. 426.

15. O.R., Vol. XL, Part II, p. 428; Reardon Memoir, June 25, 1864; DeGraff Memoir, p. 252.

16. O.R., Vol. XL, Part II, p. 538-539; DeGraff Memoir, p. 256; O.R., Vol. XL, Part I, p. 703; Reid, "War Against Secessia," p. 56.

17. O.R., Vol. XL, Part II, p. 538; Barton obituary, *New York Tribune*, June 14, 1891.

18. DeGraff Memoir, p. 260; Reid, "War Against Secessia," p. 55-56.

19. Reid, "War Against Secessia," p. 57.

20. DeGraff Memoir, p. 260; Reid, "War Against Secessia," p. 56.

21. DeGraff, letter of July 27, 1864.

22. DeGraff Memoir, p. 252-254.

23. Reid, "War Against Secessia," p. 53.

24. Reardon Memoir, June 24, 1864; Reid, "War Against Secessia," p. 55.

25. Kneeskern, letter of July 15, 1864, collection of Richard Bellinger; Reid, "War Against Secessia," p. 58.

26. Macfarlane, *Army Surgeon*, p. 56.

27. Reardon Memoir, July 24, 1864; Reid, "War Against Secessia," p 58.

28. Reid, "War Against Secessia," p. 57; Phisterer, *New York in the War of the Rebellion*, Vol. IV, p. 3347; DeGraff, letter of July 11, 1864; DeGraff Memoir, p. 258.

29. DeGraff Memoir, p. 260; DeGraff, letter of July 27, 1864.
30. DeGraff Memoir, p. 185, 256, 266.
31. DeGraff Memoir, p. 262-264; Reid, "War Against Secessia," p. 58, 59.
32. Reid, "War Against Secessia," p. 59.
33. Reid, "War Against Secessia," p. 58-59; McGlachlin, *National Tribune*, December 25, 1886.
34. DeGraff Memoir, p. 258.
35. Reardon Memoir, June 27, 1864.
36. Clark, *Iron Hearted Regiment*, p. 213-216.
37. DeGraff Memoir, p. 258; Clark, *Iron Hearted Regiment*, p. 141.
38. Clark, *Iron Hearted Regiment*, p. 142-143; DeGraff Memoir, p. 260.
39. Reid, "War Against Secessia," p. 57.
40. Reid, "War Against Secessia," p. 56-57.
41. Clark, *Iron Hearted Regiment*, p. 251-252; William Smith Service Record, National Archives; DeGraff Memoir, p. 264; Macfarlane, *Army Surgeon*, p. 56-57.
42. Sammons, letter of July 18, 1864, MCDHA.
43. Reid, "War Against Secessia," p. 59.
44. O.R., Vol. XL, Part III, p. 544. Twenty-seven-year-old Louis Bell was a lawyer from Farmington, New Hampshire and the son of New Hampshire Governor Samuel Bell. (Roger D. Hunt, *Colonels in Blue: Union Army Colonels of the Civil War; The New England States* (Atglen, Pennsylvania: Schiffer Military History, 2001), p. 159).
45. DeGraff, letter of August 3, 1964; Reid, "War Against Secessia," p. 59, 67.
46. DeGraff, letter of July 19, 1864; Trudeau, *The Last Citadel*, p. 100; O.R., Vol. XL, Part II, p. 396-397; Michael A. Cavanaugh and William Marvel, *The Battle of the Crater, The Horrid Pit: The Petersburg Campaign, June 25-August 6, 1864,* (Lynchburg, Virginia: H.E. Howard, Inc., Second Edition, 1989), p. 4ff.
47. O.R., Vol. XL, Part I, p. 556-557.
48. O.R., Vol. XL, Part III, p. 476; Cavanaugh and Marvel, *The Horrid Pit*, p. 14ff.; Trudeau, *The Last Citadel*, p. 106.
49. Reid, "War Against Secessia," p. 59; DeGraff Memoir, p. 274; Macfarlane, *Army Surgeon*, p. 59.
50. DeGraff Memoir, p. 274; Reid, "War Against Secessia," p. 59; Macfarlane, *Army Surgeon*, p.59.
51. DeGraff Memoir, p. 274; Cavanaugh & Marvel, *The Horrid Pit*, p. 37-39; Reid, "War Against Secessia," p. 61.
52. Reid, "War Against Secessia," p. 62; letter of August 2, 1864 by a soldier of the 115th whose name is withheld by request of descendants who own his collection of letters [hereinafter: Unnamed]; Clark, *Iron Hearted Regiment*, p. 146; O.R., Vol. XL, Part I, p. 558, 788.
53. Reid, "War Against Secessia," p. 62; DeGraff Memoir, p. 274; Clark, *Iron Hearted Regiment*, p. 146; O.R., Vol. XL, Part I, p. 280; Cavanaugh & Marvel, *The Horrid Pit*, p. 41.
54. Clark, *Iron Hearted Regiment*, p. 147; DeGraff, letter of August 3, 1964; Reid, "War Against Secessia," p. 63; Macfarlane, *Army Surgeon*, p. 60.
55. Cavanaugh & Marvel, *The Horrid Pit*, p. 42.
56. Cavanaugh & Marvel, *The Horrid Pit*, p. 20ff.; Trudeau, *The Last Citadel*, p. 107-111.
57. Cavanaugh & Marvel, *The Horrid Pit*, p. 58.
58. Reid, "War Against Secessia," p. 63; DeGraff, letter of August 3, 1864; Clark, *Iron Hearted Regiment*, p. 148; Cavanaugh & Marvel, *The Horrid Pit*, p. 17, 58.
59. O.R., Vol. XL, Part I, p. 699; Cavanaugh & Marvel, *The Horrid Pit*, p. 53.
60. O.R., Vol. XL, Part I, p. 699; Clark, *Iron Hearted Regiment*, p. 149, 223-224; Reid, "War Against Secessia," p. 63; "N," letter published in *Montgomery County Republican*, August 16, 1864; DeGraff, letter of August 3, 1864.
61. DeGraff, letter of August 3, 1864; Reid, "War Against Secessia," p. 63.
62. Reid, "War Against Secessia," p. 63-64; Clark, *Iron Hearted Regiment*, p. 150.
63. DeGraff, letter of August 3, 1864; Cavanaugh & Marvel, *The Horrid Pit*, p. 53, 88-89.
64. DeGraff, letter of August 3, 1864; "N," letter published in *Montgomery County Republican*, August 16, 1864.
65. DeGraff, letter of August 3, 1864; O.R., Vol. XL, Part I, p. 704; Reid, "War Against Secessia," p. 64.
66. Clark, *Iron Hearted Regiment*, p. 151, 224; Reid, "War Against Secessia," p. 64; DeGraff Memoir, p. 276; "N," letter published in *Montgomery County Republican*, August 16, 1864.
67. DeGraff Memoir, p. 276; affidavit of Ezra Walrath, Sammons pension file, Sammons Family Papers, MCDHA; "N," letter published in *Montgomery County Republican*, August 16, 1864.
68. DeGraff Memoir, p. 276; Phisterer, *New York in the War of the Rebellion*, Vol. IV, p. 3347; O.R., Vol. XL, Part I, p. 249.
69. DeGraff Memoir, p. 276-277; Reid, "War Against Secessia," p. 65.
70. DeGraff Memoir, p. 276; O.R., Vol. XL, Part I, p. 700, 704; Reid, "War Against Secessia," p. 65.
71. Reid, "War Against Secessia," p. 64; O.R., Vol. XL, Part I, p. 699, 704.
72. Reid. p. 65; DeGraff, letter of August 3, 1864; "Unnamed," letter of August 2, 1864.

Chapter 11

1. Clark, *Iron Hearted Regiment*, p. 156-157, DeGraff Memoir, p. 280; DeGraff, letter of August 3, 1864; Reid, "War Against Secessia," p. 66. None of the three men who died from sunstroke were in the 115th; they were from other units in the same division.
2. Reid, "War Against Secessia," p. 66; Reardon Memoir, August 8, 1864; Clark, *Iron Hearted Regiment*, p. 157-158.
3. Reid, "War Against Secessia," p. 66; Clark, *Iron Hearted Regiment*, p. 158; DeGraff Memoir, p. 290; Reardon Memoir, August 8, 1864.
4. Trudeau, *The Last Citadel*, p. 146; Grant, *Personal Memoirs*, Vol. II. p 321; O.R., Vol. XLII, Part II, p. 136.
5. Trudeau, *The Last Citadel*, p. 67, 145-152; John Horn, *The Destruction of the Weldon Railroad: Deep Bottom, Globe Tavern and Reams Station, August 14-25, 1864* (Lynchburg, Virginia: H. E. Howard, Inc., 1991), p. 9-16; Reid, "War Against Secessia," p. 68. Hancock was a West Pointer and career officer who served prominently throughout the Civil War. William and David Birney were sons of an antislavery Alabamian who moved his family to Cincinnati in 1838. Both were lawyers and volunteer officers. Terry was a Connecticut militia officer who stayed in the regular army after the Civil War. He was George A. Custer's commanding officer during the 1876 Little Big Horn campaign. (Warner, *Generals in Blue*, p. 54-55, 202-204, 497-498).
6. Reid, "War Against Secessia," p. 68; DeGraff Memoir, p. 290; O.R., Vol. XLII, Part II, p. 188; Macfarlane, *Army Surgeon*, p. 61; Reardon Memoir, August 14, 1864.
7. Trudeau, *The Last Citadel*, p. 153; Horn, *Destruction*

of the Weldon Railroad, p. 20; O.R., Vol. XLII, Part I, p. 218; Reid, "War Against Secessia," p. 68.

8. Reid, "War Against Secessia," p. 68; Macfarlane, *Army Surgeon*, p. 61; DeGraff Memoir, p. 290; Horn, *Destruction of the Weldon Railroad*, p. 24.

9. Horn, *Destruction of the Weldon Railroad*, p. 26, 31–41; Trudeau, *The Last Citadel*, p. 155–157; O.R., Vol. XLII, Part I, p. 688, 728, 755. One Second Corps brigade operated with the three brigades of Terry's Division on August 16.

10. The 169th New York, also part of Bell's Brigade, was on detached duty at Dutch Gap at this time.

11. DeGraff, letter of August 18, 1864; Reid, "War Against Secessia," p. 69; O.R., Vol. XLII, Part I, p. 765.

12. DeGraff, letter of August 18, 1864; Reid, "War Against Secessia," p. 69; Horn, *Destruction of the Weldon Railroad*, p. 41. Major Walrath had commanded the 115th since Colonel Sammons's wounding at the Crater. Lieutenant Colonel Johnson, though released from arrest on July 28, had not yet rejoined the regiment.

13. Horn, *Destruction of the Weldon Railroad*, p. 41; DeGraff Memoir, p. 292–294; Reid, "War Against Secessia," p. 69.

14. Clark, *Iron Hearted Regiment*, p. 159; Reardon Memoir, August 16, 1864; DeGraff, letter of August 18, 1864; Reid, "War Against Secessia," p. 69; O.R., Vol. XLII, Part I, p. 120; Phisterer, *New York in the War of the Rebellion*, Vol. IV, p. 3347.

15. DeGraff, letter of August 18, 1864; Reardon Memoir, August 16, 1864; Reid, "War Against Secessia," p. 69–70; Charles L. Clark, affidavit dated July 27, 1887, in Peter J. Keck Pension File, National Archives; James H. Clark, "At Their Country's Call," p. 22.

16. Reardon Memoir, August 16, 1864; DeGraff, letter of August 18, 1864; Reid, "War Against Secessia," p. 69–70. Captain McKittrick's words are from a letter of his that is quoted at Reid, "War Against Secessia," p. 70. Reid does not give the date of McKittrick's letter, but it had to date from between August 16, 1864, when the described action took place, and September 29, 1864, when McKittrick was killed in action.

17. William McKittrick, letter in Reid, "War Against Secessia," p. 70; DeGraff, letter of August 18, 1864; Horn, *Destruction of the Weldon Railroad*, p. 43–45.

18. McKittrick, letter in Reid, "War Against Secessia," p. 70.

19. Phisterer, *New York in the War of the Rebellion*, Vol. IV, p. 3347; Clark, *Iron Hearted Regiment*, p. 159, 236–237, 246–248, 266; DeGraff Memoir, p. 296.

20. Clark, *Iron Hearted Regiment*, p. 261–262.

21. DeGraff Memoir, p. 292; Reardon Memoir, August 16, 1864; Seely Conover, letter of December 28, 1864, collection of Lance Ingmire.

22. DeGraff Memoir, p. 292, 295.

23. Macfarlane, *Army Surgeon*, p. 61–62.

24. Reid, "War Against Secessia," p. 70; DeGraff Diary, August 16, 1864; DeGraff, letter of August 18, 1864.

25. DeGraff, letter of August 18, 1864.

26. Horn, *Destruction of the Weldon Railroad*, p. 48; Proceedings of General Court Martial in the Case of Lieutenant Colonel Nathan J. Johnson, September 4, 1864, in N.J. Johnson Service Record, National Archives (hereinafter: Proceedings of Johnson's Court Martial), p. 6; DeGraff Diary, July 28, 1864.

27. DeGraff Memoir, p. 296; Reid, "War Against Secessia," p. 70; Horn, *Destruction of the Weldon Railroad*, p. 49; N.J. Johnson, letter of September 30, 1864, in N.J. Johnson Service Record, National Archives.

28. Horn, *Destruction of the Weldon Railroad*, p. 49; Trudeau, *The Last Citadel*, p. 160–161; O.R., Vol. XLII, Part I, p. 220, 678.

29. DeGraff, letter of August 24, 1864; Reid, "War Against Secessia," p. 70; Proceedings of Johnson's Court Martial, testimony of William Shaw (p. 3), written statement of Nathan Johnson (Appendix A, p. 1A), testimony of Captain Thomas B. Eaton, 169th New York (p. 18), testimony of Captain Egbert B. Savage, Company G, 115th New York (p. 24). Shaw was senior captain of the 115th and therefore in command of the regiment at this time because Lieutenant Colonel Johnson headed the brigade and Major Walrath remained absent due to his August 16 wounding.

30. Proceedings of Johnson's Court Martial, testimony of Captain George B. Dyer, 9th Maine (p. 8) and Lieutenant Hugh S. Sanford, 115th New York (p. 20); Private John Reed's account of his scout with Lieutenant Colonel Johnson appears in Corporal James Reid's "War Against Secessia." James Reid and John Reed first became acquainted during the 115th's original muster at Camp Mohawk when James responded to John's name at roll call (Reid, "War Against Secessia," p. 70–71).

31. DeGraff, letter of August 24, 1864; Proceedings of Johnson's Court Martial, testimony of Captain Julius Weiss (p. 12).

32. Proceedings of Johnson's Court Martial, testimony of Weiss (p. 12–13), Brastow (p. 7) and Dyer (p. 9), and statement of Johnson (Appendix A, p. 2); DeGraff, letter of August 24, 1864; Reid, "War Against Secessia," p. 71; DeGraff Memoir, p. 296–298.

33. Proceedings of Johnson's Court Martial, especially testimony of Shaw (p. 3, 5–6), Dyer (p. 9–10), Weiss (p. 13), Captain Fred Mosher, 115th New York (p. 6), and Captain Robert Gray, 9th Maine (p. 6); Reid, "War Against Secessia," p. 71; DeGraff Memoir, p. 296.

34. Reid, "War Against Secessia," p. 71. Within a few days the regiment's strength climbed back up to 132, according to Private Joseph Abeel of Company C (letter of August 23, 1864 to "Friend Morgan," collection of Lance Ingmire).

35. DeGraff, letter of August 18, 1864; Horn, *Destruction of the Weldon Railroad*, p. 51.

Chapter 12

1. DeGraff Memoir, p. 301; DeGraff, letter of September 9, 1864; Reid, "War Against Secessia," p. 73.

2. McKittrick, letter of August 29, 1864, quoted in Reid, "War Against Secessia," p. 74; Reid, "War Against Secessia," p. 74.

3. DeGraff, letter of September 22, 1864.

4. DeGraff Memoir, p. 305.

5. Reardon Memoir, September 3, 1864; DeGraff Memoir, p. 302–303.

6. Reardon Memoir, September 9, 19, 1864; Reid, "War Against Secessia," p. 75; DeGraff Memoir, p. 306. Sherman entered Atlanta on September 2, 1864, after a hard fought campaign that began in Chattanooga during the first week in May in coordination with the Army of the Potomac's initial movement south toward Richmond and the Army of the James's movement up the James River to Bermuda Hundred. Sheridan whipped the rebels at Winchester on September 19 in the opening victory of his successful campaign to destroy the Shenandoah Valley's utility to the Confederacy.

7. Reid, "War Against Secessia," p. 80.

8. DeGraff, letter of September 22, 1864; DeGraff Memoir, p. 307–308; McKittrick, letter of September 28, 1864, quoted in Reid, "War Against Secessia," p. 75.
9. DeGraff Memoir, p. 308; William Jennings, letter of October 22, 1864 in *Ballston Journal*, November 8, 1864.
10. Grant, *Personal Memoirs*, Vol. II, p. 333.
11. Richard J. Sommers, *Richmond Redeemed: The Siege at Petersburg* (New York: Doubleday & Co., 1981), p. 5; Grant, "General Grant on the Siege of Petersburg," in *Battles & Leaders*, Vol. IV, p. 577.
12. Sommers, *Richmond Redeemed*, p. 21; Reid, "War Against Secessia," p. 77; William C. Davis and the Editors of Time-Life Books, *Death in the Trenches: Grant at Petersburg* (Alexandria, Virginia: Time-Life Books, 1986), p. 139–140; Reardon Memoir, September 29, 1864. Robert S. Foster was an Indianan who volunteered for the army at age 27 at the outbreak of the Civil War and rose to colonel in the 13th Indiana, then to Brigadier General leading a division in the Tenth Corps. He later served on the military commission which tried the Lincoln assassination conspirators. (Warner, *Generals in Blue*, p. 158–159.)
13. O.R., Vol. XLII, Part I, p. 760; DeGraff Memoir, p. 308; Reardon Memoir, September 29, 1864; *New York Herald*, October 2, 1864.
14. *New York Herald*, October 2, 1864; O.R., Vol. XLII, Part I, p. 760.
15. O.R., Vol. XLII, Part I, p. 760, 769.
16. DeGraff, letter of October 9, 1864 to "Aunt Mollie," published in *Mohawk Valley Democrat*, June 11, 1989; Clark, *Iron Hearted Regiment*, p. 161. Several of DeGraff's wartime letters were published in the *Mohawk Valley Democrat* in 1989 to celebrate Memorial Day.
17. O.R., Vol. XLII, Part I, p. 760–761; DeGraff, letter of October 4, 1864.
18. O.R., Vol. XLII, Part I, p. 769; Sommers, *Richmond Redeemed*, p. 83–85.
19. DeGraff Memoir, p. 308; DeGraff, letter of October 4, 1864; Sommers, *Richmond Redeemed*, p. 85–86; O.R., Vol. XLII, Part I, p. 761.
20. O.R., Vol. XLII, Part I, p. 761; DeGraff, letter of October 4, 1864; DeGraff Memoir, p. 308–309.
21. *New York Herald*, October 2, 1864; O.R., Vol. XLII, Part I, p. 761, 769; Sommers, *Richmond Redeemed*, p. 87.
22. DeGraff Memoir, p. 309; Phisterer, *New York in the War of the Rebellion*, Vol. IV, p. 3347; DeGraff, letter of October 4, 1864.
23. Reid, "War Against Secessia," p. 78–79; Clark, *Iron Hearted Regiment*, p. 257; Jennings, letter of October 22, 1864 in *Ballston Journal*, November 8, 1864. Walrath's tribute to McKittrick is transcribed in Reid, "War Against Secessia," p. 78.
24. Reid, "War Against Secessia," p. 79–80; Scorsby, *National Tribune*, August 21, 1884.
25. Reid, "War Against Secessia," p. 80.
26. Clark, *Iron Hearted Regiment*, p. 266–267; DeGraff Memoir, p. 309. Sergeant Kline received a promotion to second lieutenant during a four month convalescence in a hospital at Fortress Monroe, remained in the army on detached service, and re-joined his comrades in the 115th just in time to journey home with them at the war's end.
27. N.J. Johnson, letter of September 30, 1864 and Dr. C. Macfarlane, affidavit of September 30, 1864, both in N.J. Johnson Service Record, National Archives.
28. Clark, *Iron Hearted Regiment*, p. 226–227.
29. O.R., Vol. XLII, Part I, p. 761; Davis et al, *Death in the Trenches*, p. 147–148.
30. Trudeau, *The Last Citadel*, p. 213; Davis et al, *Death in the Trenches*, p. 149–150; DeGraff Memoir, p. 309.

31. U.S. Grant, "General Grant on the Siege of Petersburg," in *Battles & Leaders*, Vol. IV, p. 577.
32. Reardon Memoir, October 6, 15, 1864; Reid, "War Against Secessia," p. 82; DeGraff, letters of October 14 and 24, 1864.
33. Reardon Memoir, October 11, 1864; Reid, "War Against Secessia," p. 82; DeGraff Memoir, p. 312.
34. DeGraff, letter of October 14, 1864; Reid, "War Against Secessia," p. 82.
35. O.R., Vol. XLII, Part III, p. 331.
36. O.R., Vol. XLII, Part III, p. 332, 366–368; Reid, "War Against Secessia," p. 83.
37. DeGraff, letter of October 31, 1864; Reid, "War Against Secessia," p. 82–83; O.R., Vol. XLII, Part I, p. 762–763, 769; O.R., Vol. XLII, Part III, p. 367.
38. Reid, "War Against Secessia," p. 83; DeGraff, letter of October 31, 1864.
39. Clark, *Iron Hearted Regiment*, p. 161–161; Reid, "War Against Secessia," p. 83; Macfarlane, *Army Surgeon*, p. 62.
40. Reid, "War Against Secessia," p. 83.
41. O.R., Vol. XLII, Part I, p. 769–770; Reid, "War Against Secessia," p. 83–84; DeGraff, letter of October 1, 1864; *New York Herald*, October 31, 1864.
42. Reid, "War Against Secessia," p. 83–84; DeGraff, letter of October 31, 1864.
43. O.R., Vol. XLII, Part I, p. 770; DeGraff, letter of October 31, 1864; Reid, "War Against Secessia," p. 84; Phisterer, *New York in the War of the Rebellion*, Vol. IV, p. 3347; Clark, *Iron Hearted Regiment*, p. 161.
44. Trudeau, *The Last Citadel*, p. 229–250.
45. DeGraff Memoir, p. 315-6; Trudeau, *The Last Citadel*, p. 248; Reid, "War Against Secessia," p. 84.
46. Reid, "War Against Secessia," p. 82; Reardon Memoir, October 12, 1864; Jennings, letter of October 22, 1864 in *Ballston Journal*, November 8, 1864; DeGraff Memoir, p. 316.
47. DeGraff Memoir, p. 311; Trudeau, *The Last Citadel*, p. 252–253; Reid, "War Against Secessia," p. 82.
48. Reardon Memoir, November 2, 1864; Reid, "War Against Secessia," p. 84; DeGraff, letter of November 8, 1864.
49. DeGraff, letters of November 16 and 27 and December 6, 1864; Reid, "War Against Secessia," p. 86; O.R., Vol. XLII, Part III, p. 691.
50. DeGraff, letter of November 27, 1864; Reardon Memoir, November 27, 1864; O.R., Vol. XLII, Part III, p. 734, 816.
51. Reardon Memoir, November 27–28, 1864; Reid, "War Against Secessia," p. 86; DeGraff Memoir, p. 321.
52. Reid, "War Against Secessia," p. 86; O.R., Vol. XLII, Part III, p. 761.
53. Reardon Memoir, December 7–8, 1864.

Chapter 13

1. Rod Gragg, *Confederate Goliath: The Battle of Fort Fisher*, (New York: Harper Collins, 1991), p. 3, 12.
2. Gragg, *Confederate Goliath*, p. 34–35; Chris Fonvielle, "The Last Rays of Departing Hope: the Fall of Wilmington, Including the Campaigns Against Fort Fisher," *Blue & Gray Magazine*, December 1994, p. 15–16.
3. Gragg, *Confederate Goliath*, p. 35–37; Dr. Jay Luvaas, "The Fall of Fort Fisher," *Civil War Times Illustrated*, August 1964, p. 6; Fonvielle, "Last Rays of Departing Hope," p. 19.
4. Captain Thomas O. Selfridge, Jr., U.S. Navy, "The

Navy at Fort Fisher," in *Battles & Leaders*, Vol. IV, p. 662; Reid, "War Against Secessia," p. 87; O.R., Vol. XLII, Part I, p. 967, 972–973, 981.

5. Macfarlane, *Army Surgeon*, p. 66; Clark, *Iron Hearted Regiment*, p. 162; Reardon Memoir, December 8–14, 1864; Reid, "War Against Secessia," p. 87, 91–93.

6. Reardon Memoir, December 15, 1864; Gragg, *Confederate Goliath*, p. 46; Macfarlane, *Army Surgeon*, p. 67.

7. Reid, "War Against Secessia," p. 87; Reardon Memoir, December 16, 1864.

8. Macfarlane, *Army Surgeon*, p. 67.

9. O.R., Vol. XLII, Part I, p. 967; Gragg, *Confederate Goliath*, p., 49; Reardon Memoir, December 21–24, 1864.

10. Fonvielle, "Last Rays of Departing Hope," p. 19–21; Gragg, *Confederate Goliath*, p. 41, 49–53; Selfridge, "The Navy at Fort Fisher," p. 655.

11. Gragg, *Confederate Goliath*, p. 63–64; O.R., Vol. XLII, Part I, p. 994; Fonvielle, "Last Rays of Departing Hope," p. 21, 48; Colonel William Lamb, C.S.A., commander of Fort Fisher, "The Defense of Fort Fisher," in *Battles & Leaders*, Vol. IV, p. 646.

12. Lamb, "The Defense of Fort Fisher," p. 643; Fonvielle, "Last Rays of Departing Hope," p. 14; Gragg, *Confederate Goliath*, p. 18–19; O.R., Vol. XLVI, Part I, p. 407; Nathan J. Johnson, letter of January 30, 1865 to Colonel John S. Crocker, Crocker Papers, Manuscripts & Special Collections, Collection SC18227, NYSL.

13. Reid, "War Against Secessia," p. 89; Macfarlane, *Army Surgeon*, p. 68.

14. Gragg, *Confederate Goliath*, p. 73.

15. Macfarlane, *Army Surgeon*, p. 68; Reid, "War Against Secessia," p. 89; O.R., Vol. XLII, Part I, p. 1004; Fonvielle, "Last Rays of Departing Hope," p. 48.

16. Gragg, *Confederate Goliath*, p. 79–80; Reid, "War Against Secessia," p. 89; Macfarlane, *Army Surgeon*, 68.

17. Reid, "War Against Secessia," p. 89; Reardon Memoir, December 25, 1864; Macfarlane, *Army Surgeon*, p. 68.

18. Gragg, *Confederate Goliath*, p. 82–83; O.R., Vol. XLII, Part I, p. 982; Reardon Memoir, December 25, 1864.

19. Reardon Memoir, December 25, 1864; Gragg, *Confederate Goliath*, p. 83; Fonvielle, "Last Rays of Departing Hope," p. 49.

20. O.R., Vol. XLII, Part I, p. 982–983; Gragg, *Confederate Goliath*, p. 83; Reid, "War Against Secessia," p. 90; Fonvielle, "Last Rays of Departing Hope," p. 49.

21. O.R., Vol. XLII, Part I, p. 983; Gragg, *Confederate Goliath*, p. 87–88; Beyer and Keydel, *Deeds of Valor*, p. 469–471; Reardon Memoir, December 25, 1864.

22. Reid, "War Against Secessia," p. 91; Reardon Memoir, December 25, 1864; Macfarlane, *Army Surgeon*, p. 69.

23. Reid, "War Against Secessia," p. 91; Fonvielle, "Last Rays of Departing Hope," p. 49; Gragg, *Confederate Goliath*, p. 95–96.

24. Luvaas, "The Fall of Fort Fisher," p. 7–8; Fonvielle, "Last Rays of Departing Hope," p. 49; Gragg, *Confederate Goliath*, p. 103–104; O.R., Vol. XLII, Part I, p. 971–972.

25. Reid, "War Against Secessia," p. 92; Reardon Memoir, December 30, 1864–January 3, 1865.

26. Gragg, *Confederate Goliath*, p. 105–109; Chris E. Fonvielle, Jr., *The Wilmington Campaign; Last Rays of Departing Hope*, (Mechanicsburg, Pennsylvania: Stackpole Books, 1997, 2001) p. 192–193.

27. Reardon Memoir, January 3–15, 1865; Reid, "War Against Secessia," p. 93; Clark, *Iron Hearted Regiment*, p. 163.

28. Fonvielle, "Last Rays of Departing Hope," p. 52.

29. Reardon Memoir, January 13, 1865; Fonvielle, "Last Rays of Departing Hope," p. 52; O.R., Vol. XLVI, Part I, p. 396–397.

30. O.R., Vol. XLVI, Part I, p. 394–397; Fonvielle, "Last Rays of Departing Hope," p. 53.

31. Selfridge, "The Navy at Fort Fisher," p. 658; Fonvielle, "Last Rays of Departing Hope," p. 53.

32. Nathan J. Johnson, letter of January 30, NYSL.

33. O.R., Vol. XLVI, Part I, p. 397–398; Gragg, *Confederate Goliath*, p. 171–172.

34. Selfridge, "The Navy at Fort Fisher," p. 659; Gragg, *Confederate Goliath*, p. 134.

35. O.R., Vol. XLVI, Part I, p. 398; Gragg, *Confederate Goliath*, p. 141; Fonvielle, "Last Rays of Departing Hope," p. 54; Selfridge, "The Navy at Fort Fisher," p. 659.

36. Nathan J. Johnson, letter of January 30, 1865, NYSL; Colonel William Lamb, C.S.A., "The Defense of Fort Fisher," in *Battles & Leaders*, Vol. IV, p. 649–650; Fonvielle, "Last Rays of Departing Hope," p. 54–55.

37. Lamb, "The Defense of Fort Fisher," p. 650; O.R., Vol. XLVI, Part I, p. 398, 418–419; Fonvielle, "Last Rays of Departing Hope," p. 55–56; Gragg, *Confederate Goliath*, p. 175–182.

38. Gragg, *Confederate Goliath*, p. 185–186.

39. Major Ezra L. Walrath, report in O.R., Vol. XLVI, Part I, p. 422.

40. Gragg, *Confederate Goliath*, p. 191–199.

41. Nathan J. Johnson, report in O.R., Vol. XLVI, Part I, p. 421; Fred Mosher, letter transcribed in Reid, "War Against Secessia," p. 96.

42. Nathan J. Johnson, report in O.R., Vol. XLVI, Part I, p. 421; Ezra L. Walrath, report in O.R., Vol. XLVI, Part I, p. 422; Peter J. Keck Pension Record, National Archives.

43. Ezra L. Walrath, report in O.R., Vol. XLVI, Part I, p. 422; Nathan J. Johnson, report in O.R., Vol. XLVI, Part I, p. 421; Johnson, letter of January 30, 1865, NYSL; Mosher, letter in Reid, "War Against Secessia," p. 96.

44. Gragg, *Confederate Goliath*, p. 203–216; Fonvielle, "Last Rays of Departing Hope," p. 56; Reardon Memoir, January 15, 1865.

45. DeGraff Memoir, p. 323; Johnson, letter of January 30, 1865, NYSL; Reid, "War Against Secessia," p. 96.

46. Fonvielle, "Last Rays of Departing Hope," p. 56; Mosher, letter in Reid, "War Against Secessia," p. 96; Johnson, letter of January 30, 1865, NYSL.

47. *Harper's Weekly*, February 4, 1865, p. 2.

48. Macfarlane, *Army Surgeon*, p. 69; Johnson, letter of January 30, 1865, NYSL; Reardon Memoir, January 15, 1865.

49. Reid, "War Against Secessia," p. 94, 96; Reardon Memoir, January 15, 1865; DeGraff Memoir, p. 330; O.R., Vol. XLVI, Part I, p. 405; Gragg, *Confederate Goliath*, p. 235. The 115th had 274 men present for duty at Fort Fisher (DeGraff Memoir, p. 326).

50. Phisterer, *New York in the War of the Rebellion*, Vol. IV, p. 3347; Reardon Memoir, January 15, 1865.

51. *The Saratogian*, January 26, 1865; Fonvielle, "Last Rays of Departing Hope," p. 56; Clark, *Iron Hearted Regiment*, p. 164.

52. Reid, "War Against Secessia," p. 98.

53. Reardon Memoir, January 16, 1865.

54. Fred Mosher, letter in Reid, "War Against Secessia," p. 98; Johnson, letter of January 30, 1865, NYSL; Macfarlane, *Army Surgeon*, p. 70.

55. Reid, "War Against Secessia," p. 98.

56. *The Saratogian*, January 26, 1865; Reardon Memoir, January 16, 1865; Reid, "War Against Secessia," p. 98; *St. Johnsville Enterprise & News*, January 17, 1934. Getman and his descendants kept the surviving shoe for many decades after the war. Today it is on display, together with Getman's Civil War drumsticks, at the Reaney Library in St. Johnsville, New York.

57. Reardon Memoir, January 16, 1865; Reid, "War Against Secessia," p. 99; Macfarlane, *Army Surgeon*, p. 70.
58. *The Saratogian*, January 26, 1865; Reardon Memoir, January 16, 1865; Reid, "War Against Secessia," p. 99.
59. Reid, "War Against Secessia," p. 99; Reardon Memoir, January 16, 1865; *The Saratogian*, January 26, 1865; Macfarlane, *Army Surgeon*, p. 70; Phisterer, *New York in the War of the Rebellion*, Vol. IV, p. 3347; O.R., Vol. XLVI, Part I, p. 405. The number of casualties the 115th suffered from the explosion is derived as the difference between the casualty figures listed in Phisterer, which records the total of losses in both the battle and the blast, and the O.R., which tallies only the battle casualties of January 15.
60. O.R., Vol. XLVI, Part I, p. 425–431.
61. Reid, "War Against Secessia," p. 99; Clark, *Iron Hearted Regiment*, p. 231; Walrath, letter of February 8, 1865, *Mohawk Valley Democrat*, February 28, 1865. Walrath's letter to Widow Van Derveer, and the piece of flag it forwarded to her, are today in the possession of Donald Oakley of Amsterdam, New York.
62. Johnson, letter of January 30, 1865, NYSL.
63. Reardon Memoir, January 17–19, 1865; Reid, "War Against Secessia," p. 99.
64. DeGraff, letter of February 8, 1865.
65. Reid, "War Against Secessia," p. 100; Fonvielle, "Last Rays of Departing Hope," p. 57.

Chapter 14

1. O.R., Vol. XLVII, Part I, p. 18, 909–910; Grant, *Personal Memoirs*, Vol. 2, p. 400–413; Fonvielle, "Last Rays of Departing Hope," p. 57–58; Mark L. Bradley, "Last Stand in the Carolinas," *Blue & Gray Magazine*, December 1995, p. 10; Warner, *Generals in Blue*, p. 425.
2. DeGraff Memoir, p. 322–326, 347; DeGraff, letters of December 6, 14, 21, and 30, 1864, January 15, and February 8, 1865.
3. O.R., Vol. XLVII, Part I, p. 910; Fonvielle, "Last Rays of Departing Hope," p. 57.
4. Fonvielle, "Last Rays of Departing Hope," p. 58; Phisterer, *New York in the War of the Rebellion*, Vol. IV, p. 3346; DeGraff Memoir, p. 330; Reid, "War Against Secessia," p. 100.
5. O.R., Vol. XLVII, Part I, p. 910; O.R., Vol. XLVII, Part II, p. 427; Fonvielle, *The Wilmington Campaign*, pp. 349–352; DeGraff Memoir, p. 330.
6. O.R., Vol. XLVII, Part I, p. 910; Fonvielle, "Last Rays of Departing Hope," p. 58; Reardon Memoir, February 14, 1865; Reid, "War Against Secessia," p. 100; DeGraff Memoir, p. 330.
7. O.R., Vol. XLVII, Part I, p. 910; Reardon Memoir, February 17–18, 1865; DeGraff Memoir, p. 331; Reid, "War Against Secessia," p. 101.
8. O.R., Vol. XLVII, Part I, p. 910; Reid, "War Against Secessia," p. 101; Fonvielle, "Last Rays of Departing Hope," p. 59; DeGraff Memoir, p. 331.
9. Reardon Memoir, February 20, 1865; Reid, "War Against Secessia," p. 101; DeGraff Memoir, p. 331.
10. Reid, "War Against Secessia," p. 101.
11. Reid, "War Against Secessia," p. 102; DeGraff, letter of February 28, 1865; Reardon Memoir, February 22, 1865; Macfarlane, *Army Surgeon*, p. 71.
12. DeGraff, letter of February 28, 1865; O.R., Vol. XLVII, Part I, p. 924; Reardon Memoir, February 22, 1865.
13. O.R., Vol. XLVII, Part II, p. 1179; Reid, "War Against Secessia," p. 102; DeGraff Memoir, p. 332.
14. Reid, "War Against Secessia," p. 102; DeGraff, letter of February 28, 1865.
15. Macfarlane, *Army Surgeon*, p. 72; DeGraff Memoir, p. 332; DeGraff, letter of February 28, 1865.
16. DeGraff Memoir, p. 332; O.R., Vol. XLVII, Part I, p. 164–165.
17. Reardon Memoir, February 26, 1865.
18. Reid, "War Against Secessia," p. 25–27, 102.
19. Reardon Memoir, March 1, 1865; DeGraff Memoir, p. 336.
20. Macfarlane, *Army Surgeon*, p. 74.
21. O.R., Vol. XLVII, Part I, p. 924; Reid, "War Against Secessia," p. 102; Reardon Memoir, March 2–March 14, 1865.
22. O.R., Vol. XLVII, Part I, p. 924; Bradley, "Last Stand in the Carolinas," p. 10–12.
23. Reardon Memoir, March 21, 1865; DeGraff Memoir, p. 337–338; Bradley, "Last Stand in the Carolinas," p. 67.
24. Reardon Memoir, March 22–23, 1865; DeGraff Memoir, p. 338–339; Reid, "War Against Secessia," p. 103.
25. Reid, "War Against Secessia," p. 103.
26. DeGraff, letter of March 28, 1865; Reardon Memoir, March 24, 1865.
27. Reardon Memoir, March 26, 1865.
28. DeGraff Memoir, p. 339.
29. General Henry W. Slocum, "Final Operations of Sherman's Army," in *Battles & Leaders*, Vol. IV, p. 754–755; O.R., Vol. XLVII, Part I, p. 28–30.
30. Reardon Memoir, April 8, 1865; Reid, "War Against Secessia," p. 104; Slocum, "Final Operations of Sherman's Army," p. 755.
31. Reid, "War Against Secessia," p. 104–105; Reardon Memoir, April 12, 1865.
32. Reardon Memoir, April 15, 1865; DeGraff, letter of April 15, 1865.
33. DeGraff, letters of April 24 and May 1, 1865; Reid, "War Against Secessia," p. 105.
34. Slocum, "Final Operations of Sherman's Army," p. 756; DeGraff Memoir, p. 343.
35. Slocum, "Final Operations of Sherman's Army," p. 757–758.
36. Macfarlane, *Army Surgeon*, p. 79; Reid, "War Against Secessia," p. 107; Phisterer, *New York in the War of the Rebellion*, Vol. IV, p. 3346–3347.
37. Clark, *Iron Hearted Regiment*, p. 304. The total enrollment figures cited do not include 203 recruits who arrived in the 115th's camp just two weeks before the war ended (DeGraff Memoir, p. 340; Reid, "War Against Secessia," p. 104).
38. Clark, *Iron Hearted Regiment*, p. 169, 304; DeGraff Memoir, p. 345.
39. Reid, "War Against Secessia," p. 108.
40. Macfarlane, *Army Surgeon*, p. 80; Reid, "War Against Secessia," p. 99; Clark, *Iron Hearted Regiment*, p. 231; Program for the Forty-Fifth Reunion, 115th and 153rd Regiments N.Y. Vol. Infantry, August 26, 1925, collection of James Morrison, Gloversville, New York, p. 31–32. The flags were turned in to state authorities. Today the late-war replacement New York State flag is in the collection of the New York State Military Museum. Their collection inventory also lists a second 115th flag but it is either missing or it is out of sight in the back of the cabinet, covered by other flags that are in such a state of deterioration that the curator is unwilling to handle them.
41. DeGraff Memoir, p. 346, 350; Reid, "War Against Secessia," p. 108; *Mohawk Valley Democrat*, July 4, 1865; Clark, *Iron Hearted Regiment*, p. 310.

42. Reid, "War Against Secessia," p. 108; Macfarlane, *Army Surgeon*, p. 81.
43. Macfarlane, *Army Surgeon*, p. 80; DeGraff Memoir, p. 350; Clark, *Iron Hearted Regiment*, p. 169.

Chapter 15

1. James E. Reid, "Annual Reunion of the 115th N.Y. Regiment," *Ballston Journal*, September 2, 1893. The annual meetings ran through at least 1925.
2. Program of the 35th reunion of the 115th New York, August 25, 1916, collection of Hector J. Allen, Town Historian, Oppenheim, New York; James E. Reid Pension File, National Archives.
3. Reardon Memoir, May 9, 1865.
4. Karl Reardon, grandson of John Reardon, telephone conversation with author, January 1995; *St. Johnsville News*, June 10, 1908. Mr. Reardon, of Buffalo, New York, has his grandfather's original diaries, as well as 122 of his wartime letters. He is seeking to have them published and would not make them available for this work.
5. *Mohawk Valley Democrat*, October 10, 1865.
6. Civil War Letters folder in the Sammons Family Papers, MCDHA. The enlisted men's farewell letter to Sammons is dated May 5, 1865, and the officers' meeting was held May 7, 1865, four months after the January 6 date of Sammons' printed farewell. By May the war had ended and the 115th was stationed in Raleigh, North Carolina, after the campaign between Fort Fisher and Raleigh. It is possible that the colonel's formal farewell message did not reach the regiment until that time or that he did not get it printed until that time.
7. *Illustrated History of Montgomery & Fulton Counties, New York, 1878*, p. 145–146; *The Amsterdam Democrat*, August 31, 1899.
8. DeGraff Memoir, p. 347, 350.
9. William H. Bennett, grandson of Nicholas DeGraff, letters to author of February 2, 1995 and April 13, 1997.
10. Program of the 45th reunion of the 115th New York, August 26, 1925, collection of James Morrison, Gloversville, New York.

Appendix B

1. Annual Report of the Adjutant General of the State of New York for the Year 1903: Registers of New York Regiments in the War of the Rebellion, Serial No. 35. (Albany, New York: Oliver A. Quayle, 1904).

Bibliography

Voices of the 115th

This section of the bibliography lists the writings of the sixty-seven veterans of the 115th New York whose first-hand accounts were used in preparation of this history of their regiment. Multiple works by the same author are listed in chronological order when their date is known. Undated items follow dated items and are listed in alphabetical order by title.

Abeel, Joseph C. Letter to "Friend Morgan" of August 23, 1864. Collection of Lance Ingmire, Saratoga, New York.

Adams, Henry. Testimony at court martial of Colonel Sammons on September 8, 1863. Record Group No. 153, File NN-271 Box 1535, National Archives, p. 48.

Baker, William H. Testimony at court martial of Colonel Sammons on September 5 and 8, 1863. Record Group No. 153, File NN-271 Box 1535, National Archives, p. 35, 52.

Ballou, Cyrus N. Letter of February 23, 1864. Undated newspaper clipping.

Barnum, Francis D. Letter to Secretary of War Edwin Stanton regarding Chicago barracks fire, n.d. 115th N.Y. Regimental Order and Letter Book, National Archives, p. 25.

Batcheller, George Sherman. Letters to his sister of September 4 and 23, 1862. George S. Batcheller Collection, Manuscripts & Special Collections, Collection SC11218, New York State Library.

———. Letter to T.R. Horton of March 16, 1864, lamenting the death of Captain Van Derveer. *Montgomery County Republican*, March 22, 1864.

———. Letter of April 13, 1889. Benjamin Thackrah Medal of Honor file, National Archives.

Borden, William H., Jr. Letter of May 25, 1864, to "Friend Fannie" regarding Bermuda Hundred. Collection of Lance Ingmire, Saratoga, New York.

Brown, Jacob B. Letter to his brother of February 6, 1863. Collection of Lance Ingmire, Saratoga, New York.

Clark, Charles L. Affidavit dated July 27, 1887, concerning August 16, 1864, action at Deep Bottom. Peter J. Keck Pension File, National Archives.

———. Letter regarding Peter Keck. Quoted in Reid, *The War Against Secessia*, p. 33.

Clark, James H. Letter to the editor of September 22, 1862, regarding Harpers Ferry. *Cohoes Cataract*, October 18, 1862.

———. *The Iron Hearted Regiment: Being an Account of the Battles, Marches and Gallant Deeds Performed by the 115th Regiment N. Y. Volunteers*. Albany: J. Munsell, 1865.

———. "At Their Country's Call." Program of the 35th Reunion of the 115th New York Volunteer Infantry Association, August 26, 1916, Glens Falls, New York. Collection of Hector J. Allen, Town Historian, Oppenheim, New York.

Clemens, Sylvester W. Letter to the editor of October 6, 1862, regarding the 115th's journey from Harpers Ferry to Chicago. *Cohoes Cataract*, October 18, 1862.

———. Testimony before the Harpers Ferry Military Commission, October 7, 1862, recorded in O.R., Vol. XIX, Part I, p. 576.

———. Testimony at court martial of Colonel Sammons on September 8, 1863. Record Group No. 153, File NN-271 Box 1535, National Archives, p. 44.

———. Letter ca. June 1865 to James H. Clark. Clark, *Iron Hearted Regiment*, p. 240.

———. Miscellaneous official correspondence. Sylvester Clemans (sic) Papers, File 17732, New York State Archives.

Conover, Seely. Letter of May 26, 1863. *Amsterdam Evening Recorder*, May 29, 1913.

———. Letters of July 24, November 19 and December 28, 1864. Collection of Lance Ingmire, Saratoga, New York.

Cowen, Patrick H. Letter of February 2, 1863, to Secretary of War Edwin Stanton claiming personal innocence in the Camp Douglas arson. Adjutant General's Correspondence and Petitions, File 6635, New York State Archives.

DeGraff, Nicholas. Diaries. (Three pocket diaries covering the periods September 1, 1862, through January 22, 1863; May 4 through December 12, 1864; and January 1 through June 26, 1865.) DeGraff Collection, Montgomery County Department of History and Archives.

_____. Letter to the editor supporting increase in veteran pensions. *National Tribune*, March 19, 1919.

_____. Letters. DeGraff Collection, Montgomery County Department of History and Archives, Fonda, New York. This collection contains 129 letters DeGraff wrote to siblings and parents between August 1862 and June 1865. He collected the letters and numbered them after returning home and used them in compiling his memoir.

_____. Letters. *Mohawk Valley Democrat*, June 11, 1989.

_____. Letter to the editor regarding Harpers Ferry. *National Tribune*. Undated photocopy in collection of Lance Ingmire, Saratoga, New York.

_____. Memoir (handwritten manuscript in a paginated ledger book). United States Army Military History Institute, Carlisle, Pennsylvania. DeGraff's lengthy memoir in diary format was compiled using his wartime diaries and correspondence.

Devendorf, Henry X. Letters to his wife of September 2, 24, 30, October 5, 1862. Manuscripts Department, New-York Historical Society, New York, New York.

Disbrow, William. Testimony at court martial of Colonel Sammons on September 8, 1863. Record Group No. 153, File NN-271 Box 1535, National Archives, p. 51.

Doxstater, Daniel B. Letter to the editor of February 24, 1863, regarding the Camp Douglas arson charges. *Herkimer County Journal*, March 12, 1863.

Drake, Ezra W. Letter to sister of October 4, 1862. Collection of Lance Ingmire, Saratoga, New York.

Dye, John H. Letter to the editor regarding Harpers Ferry. *National Tribune*, undated photocopy in collection of Lance Ingmire, Saratoga, New York.

Farrar, George H. Letter to "Dear Cousin" of November 13, 1862. Collection of Lance Ingmire, Saratoga, New York.

Flint, William E. Letter of June 4, 1863 to "Respected Friends." Lewis Leigh Collection, Book 10-72, U.S. Army Military History Institute, Carlisle, Pennsylvania.

Gardner, William. Letter to the editor claiming that his father, James Gardner, also of the 115th, may have been the oldest man to serve. *National Tribune*, October 23, 1884.

Garner, Elijah H. Testimony at court martial of Colonel Sammons, September 8, 1863. Record Group No. 153, File NN-271 Box 1535, National Archives, p. 50.

Goodrich, Fred S. Letter of October 4, 1863, to "Dear Uncle" regarding the July 18, 1863, battle at Fort Wagner, South Carolina. Fred S. Goodrich Collection, Bentley Historical Library, University of Michigan.

Haines, Jacob L. Testimony at court martial of Colonel Sammons on September 8, 1863. Record Group No. 153, File NN-271 Box 1535, National Archives, p. 42.

Harlow, Job J. Letter of March 1863 to "Mr. Webster" regarding conditions at Hilton Head. *Mohawk Valley Register*, March 19, 1863.

Horton, Thomas R. Letters to the editor of August 30 and September 2, 1862. *Fulton County Republican*, September 9, 1862.

_____. Letter to editor of September 21, 1862. *Fulton County Republican*, September 30, 1862.

_____. Letter to editor of October 8, 1862. *Fulton County Republican*, October 14, 1862. Horton's October 8 letter appended a copy of Colonel Simeon Sammons's September 22, 1862, report to brigade commander Colonel Frederick D'Utassy concerning events at Harpers Ferry.

Jennings, William J. Letter to "My Old Friend" regarding Harpers Ferry, undated. *Ballston Journal*, December 25, 1862.

_____. Letter to the editor of October 22, 1864, regarding Fort Gilmer. *Ballston Journal*, November 8, 1864.

Johnson, Nathan J. Letter to General John Turner of May 28, 1864, requesting release from arrest. N.J. Johnson Service Record, National Archives.

_____. Written statement in records of his court martial August 30–September 3, 1864. N.J. Johnson Service Record, National Archives, Appendix A, p. 1A.

_____. Letter to Captain and Assistant Brigade Adjutant B. Dyer, of September 30, 1864, requesting leave. N.J. Johnson Service Record, National Archives.

_____. Testimony before the board of inquiry investigating the magazine explosion at Fort Fisher, January 21, 1865. O.R., Vol. XLVI, Part 1, p. 427.

_____. Letter of January 30, 1865, to Colonel John S. Crocker regarding Fort Fisher. Crocker Papers, Manuscripts & Special Collections, Collection SC18227, New York State Library.

_____. Official Report on Fort Fisher. O.R., Vol. XLVI, Part 1, p. 421.

Keck, Peter J. Letter regarding Port Walthall Junction. Quoted in Reid, *The War Against Secessia*, p. 33.

_____. Memoir. (Brief handwritten manuscript.) Collection of Lance Ingmire, Saratoga, New York.

Kittle, David M. Letter to Secretary of War Edwin Stanton regarding Chicago barracks fire, n.d. 115th N.Y. Regimental Order and Letter Book, National Archives, p. 24.

Kneeskern, John P. Letters (ten) to Gordon Hough, dated between October 1862 and September 1864. Collection of Richard Bellinger, St. Johnsville, New York.

Lingenfelter, Sidney D. Testimony at court martial of Colonel Sammons on September 4 and 5, 1863. Record Group No. 153, File NN-271 Box 1535, National Archives, p. 22.

Macfarlane, Dr. Carrington. Affidavit of September 30, 1864, regarding Lieutenant Colonel Johnson's wounding at Fort Gilmer, N.J. Johnson Service Record, National Archives.

_____. *Reminiscences of an Army Surgeon*. Oswego, New York: Lake City Print Shop, 1912.

McGlachlin, Archibald. Letter to the editor regarding Cold Harbor. *National Tribune*, December 25, 1886.

McKay, William W., Letter of February 1, 1863, to the *Amsterdam Recorder* regarding the Camp Douglas arson charges. *Ballston Journal*, February 17, 1863.

McKittrick, William H. Undated letter and letters of August 29 and September 28, 1864. Quoted in Reid, *The War Against Secessia*, p. 70, 74, 75.

_____. Testimony at court martial of Lieutenant Colonel Johnson on September 1, 1864. N.J. Johnson Service Record, National Archives, p. 20.

McMartin, Martin. Testimony at court martial of

Colonel Sammons on September 4, 1863. Record Group No. 153, File NN-271 Box 1535, National Archives, p. 25.

———. Letter in *Fulton County Republican*, December 27, 1863.

Millham, George. Speech delivered November 28, 1863, at a ceremony in tribute to Colonel Sammons. *Illustrated History of Montgomery and Fulton Counties, New York, 1878*, p. 146.

Mosher, Frederick S. Testimony at court martial of Lieutenant Colonel Johnson on August 30, 1864. N.J. Johnson Service Record, National Archives, p. 6.

———. Testimony before the board of inquiry investigating the magazine explosion at Fort Fisher, January 22, 1865. O.R., Vol. XLVI, Part 1, p. 430.

———. Undated letters excerpted in Reid, *The War Against Secessia*, p. 41, 96, 98.

"N." Letter to the editor regarding the battle of the Crater. *Montgomery County Republican*, August 16, 1864.

Northrup, Benjamin K. Letter to his brother of February 23, 1864, regarding Olustee. *Cohoes Cataract*, March 5, 1864.

Paul, Dallas. Letters to his brother of April 26 and November 27, 1864. Collection of Lance Ingmire, Saratoga, New York.

Reardon, John. Letter to his sister of June 2, 1864, regarding Cold Harbor. Typescript at Richmond National Battlefield. The original of Sergeant Reardon's June 2 letter is in the possession of his grandson, Karl Reardon of Buffalo, New York, together with over one hundred other wartime letters and his original diaries.

———. Memoir. Published in weekly installments in the *St. Johnsville News* between February 5 and July 15, 1908. The memoir is in diary format. It was prepared by Reardon while on his deathbed using his wartime pocket diaries. Reardon died just before finishing the memoir and his daughter, Susie Frances Reardon, completed the work. A scrapbook collection of the Reardon memoir is in the DeGraff Collection at the Montgomery County Department of History and Archives in Fonda, and a typescript is in the Reaney Library in St. Johnsville.

Reid, James, E. *The War Against Secessia*. Regimental history published as a series of weekly articles in the *Ballston Journal* from March 4, 1893, through June 6, 1896. Reid used his own diaries and recollections, correspondence with many other 115th veterans, and postwar publications to compose this voluminous work. A scrapbook containing all of the articles comprising *The War Against Secessia* is in the Saratoga Springs Public Library. The scrapbook was donated in 1961 by the grandson of a 115th veteran. The page numbering used in the text notes refers to the numbering entered by this author (Mark Silo) on his photocopy of the scrapbook; another photocopy using this pagination has been donated to the U.S. Army Military History Institute in Carlisle, Pennsylvania.

Rich, Frank E. Testimony at court martial of Colonel Sammons on September 5, 1863. Record Group No. 153, File NN-271 Box 1535, National Archives, p. 41.

Ripley, Joshua White. Letter of December 4, 1862, to "Dear Brother & Sister" regarding the camps in Virginia. Manuscripts & Special Collections, Call Number 14818, New York State Library.

Sammons, Simeon. Letter of August 15, 1862, to New York State Adjutant General Thomas Hillhouse regarding departure of 115th from Fonda. Adjutant General's Correspondence and Petitions, File 5915, New York State Archives.

———. Report to Colonel Frederick D'Utassy dated September 22, 1862, concerning events at Harpers Ferry. *Fulton County Republican*, October 14, 1862. Published with a letter to the editor from Thomas Horton, adjutant of the 115th. A copy is also in the 115th New York Regimental Order and Letter Book, National Archives. Sammons's report was never published in the *Official Records*.

———. Testimony before the Harpers Ferry Military Commission, October 9, 1862, O.R., Vol. XIX, Part I, pp. 625–627.

———. Letter of November 3, 1862, to Governor Morgan of New York State regarding conditions at Camp Douglas. Adjutant General's Correspondence and Petitions, Series B0462, New York State Archives.

———. Letter of November 4, 1862, to New York State Adjutant General Thomas Hillhouse regarding conditions at Camp Douglas. Adjutant General's Correspondence and Petitions, Series B0462, New York State Archives.

———. Letter of February 26, 1863, to Major General David Hunter, commander of the Tenth Corps at Hilton Head, regarding the 115th's exoneration from the arson charges. National Archives.

———. Written statement in records of his court martial at Hilton Head, September 1863. Record Group No. 153, File NN-271 Box 1535, National Archives, Appendix C, p.59.

———. Speech delivered November 28, 1863, at a ceremony at Hilton Head during which the men of the 115th presented gifts to Colonel Sammons. *Free South*, December 5, 1863.

———. Letter of February 15, 1864, to New York State Adjutant General Sprague regarding Olustee. Adjutant General's Correspondence and Petitions, Series B0462, New York State Archives.

———. Farewell statement to the regiment, January 6, 1865. Sammons Family Papers, Montgomery County Department of History and Archives.

———. Letters. Sammons Family Papers, Montgomery County Department of History and Archives, Fonda, New York. This collection contains 56 letters Sammons wrote to his wife and daughters.

———. Letters and miscellaneous official documents. Copies in the 115th New York Regimental Order and Letter Book, National Archives.

Sanford, Hugh S. Testimony at court martial of Colonel Sammons on September 3, 1863. Record Group No. 153, File NN-271 Box 1535, National Archives, p. 17.

———. Testimony at court martial of Lieutenant Colonel Johnson on September 1, 1864, N.J. Johnson Service Record, National Archives, p. 19.

Savage, Egbert B. Testimony at court martial of Lieutenant Colonel Johnson on September 1, 1864. N.J. Johnson Service Record, National Archives, p. 23.

Scorsby, William H. Letter to the editor regarding Harpers Ferry. *National Tribune*, August 21, 1884.

"Septimus." Letter to the editor of January 16, 1863, regarding the early movements of the 115th. *Fulton County Republican*, January 27, 1863.

Shaw, William H. Testimony at court martial of Colonel Sammons on September 5, 1863. Record Group No. 153, File NN-271 Box 1535, National Archives, p. 36.

____. Letter of February 24, 1864, regarding Olustee. *Johnstown Independent*, March 25, 1864.

____. Testimony at court martial of Lieutenant Colonel Johnson on August 30, 1864. N.J. Johnson Service Record, National Archives, p. 3.

____. Articles in *Fulton County Republican*, April 25, May 9, June 6, July 4, 1889. Captain Shaw's humorous articles concerned the early days of the 115th.

Smith, Solomon P. Letter of July 19, 1864. N.J. Johnson Service Record, National Archives.

____. Letter of March 28, 1889. Benjamin Thackrah Medal of Honor file, National Archives.

Smith, William. Letter of October 6, 1862, to G.F. Mills advising of the death of private John Van Brocklin due to wounds from an artillery shell at Harpers Ferry, September 15, 1862. Photocopy in collection of James Morrison, Gloversville, New York; original in collection of William G. Loveday, Jr., Gloversville, New York.

____. Testimony at court martial of Colonel Sammons on September 8, 1863. Record Group No. 153, File NN-271 Box 1535, National Archives, p. 53; affidavit dated January 28, 1875 regarding Colonel Sammons's wounding at The Crater, pension folder, Sammons Family Papers, Montgomery County Department of History and Archives.

Stewart, Robert. Testimony at court martial of Colonel Sammons on September 3, 1863. Record Group No. 153, File NN-271 Box 1535, National Archives, p. 13.

Stone, Almon E. Letter to the editor of September 7, 1862, regarding Harpers Ferry. *Cohoes Cataract*, September 20, 1862.

____. Letter of September 22, 1862, to editor *of Waterford Sentinel* regarding Harpers Ferry. *Cohoes Cataract*, October 4, 1862.

Sutton, Dr. Richard E. Testimony before the Harpers Ferry Military Commission, October 9, 1862. O.R., Vol. XIX, Part I, p. 649.

____. Letter of November 3, 1862, to Colonel Sammons regarding the health of the 115th at Camp Douglas. Adjutant General's Correspondence and Petitions, Series B0462, New York State Archives.

____. Letters to Gordon Hough of St. Johnsville of January 9 and 15 and February 3, 1863. Collection of Richard Bellinger, St. Johnsville, New York.

Templer, James W. Testimony at court martial of Colonel Sammons on September 5, 1863. Record Group No. 153, File NN-271 Box 1535, National Archives, p. 31.

Thackrah, Benjamin. "Capture of a Bushwacker Outpost." In W.F. Beyer and O.F. Keydel (eds.), *Deeds of Valor: How America's Civil War Heroes Won the Congressional Medal of Honor*. Stamford, Connecticut: Longmeadow, 1992.

____. Correspondence and statements. Benjamin Thackrah Medal of Honor File, National Archives.

"True Soldier of the 115th." Letter to the editor of January 8, 1863, regarding raid on West Point, Virginia. *Daily Saratogian*, January 22, 1863.

____. Letter of June 8, 1863, to "Friends Potter & Judson" regarding the raid on Bluffton, South Carolina. *Daily Saratogian*, June 24, 1863.

Tulloch, Kelley S. Letter of November 7, 1863. Collection of Lance Ingmire, Saratoga, New York.

Van Derveer, Garret. Letters of March 16 and April 13, 1863, to "Bro." Lewis Leigh Collection, U.S. Army Military History Institute, Carlisle, Pennsylvania.

____. Letter of October 31, 1863, to "My Bro Will." Folded into 1863 diary. Collection of the Fultonville Lodge No. 531, Free and Accepted Masons, Fultonville, New York.

____. Diaries for the years 1863 and 1864 through Van Derveer's mortal wounding on February 20, 1864. Collection of Fultonville Lodge No. 531, Free and Accepted Masons, Fultonville, New York. This collection is in the possession of Donald Oakley, Amsterdam, New York.

Vosburgh, Washington. Letters. Wash Vosburgh Letters, Bentley Historical Library, University of Michigan. The collection contains 43 letters to Vosburgh's fiancée, Ella. They are primarily personal in content.

Walrath, Ezra L. Testimony at court martial of Colonel Sammons on September 8, 1863. Record Group No. 153, File NN-271 Box 1535, National Archives, p. 55.

____. Letter to "My Old Friend Boz" seeking influence with promotion, January 30, 1864. Adjutant General's Correspondence and Petitions, Series B0462, New York State Archives.

____. Letter of July 9, 1864, to Assistant Adjutant General C. Hale regarding Lieutenant Colonel Johnson's release from arrest. N.J. Johnson Service Record, National Archives.

____. Eulogy tribute to Captain William McKittrick. Transcribed in Reid, *The War Against Secessia*, p. 78.

____. Official Report on Fort Fisher. O.R., Vol. XLVI, Part 1, p. 422.

____. Testimony before the board of inquiry investigating the magazine explosion at Fort Fisher, January 21, 1865. O.R., Vol. XLVI, Part 1, p. 428.

____. Letter of February 8, 1865, to "My Dear Captain" regarding the 115th's flags. *Mohawk Valley Democrat*, February 28, 1865.

____. Letter ca. February 1865 to the widow of Captain Garrett Van Derveer. Collection of Donald Oakley, Amsterdam, New York. In the collection with the letter is the piece of the 115th's flag the letter forwarded to her.

Weeks, George H. Testimony at court martial of Colonel Sammons on September 8, 1863. Record Group No. 153, File NN-271 Box 1535, National Archives, p. 45.

Wells, Reuben T. Letters of June 4 and 5, 1863, to "Most Dear and Afectionate Wife." William Gladstone Collection, U.S. Army Military History Institute.

____. Letters of August 3, 1863, and March 3, 1864,

to his wife. Collection of Lance Ingmire, Saratoga, New York.

Other Manuscript Sources

Adjutant General's Correspondence and Petitions, 1821–1896. Series B0462, New York State Archives, Albany, New York.

Aikey, Michael. "From Budapest to Bolivar Heights: The Triumphant Rise and Scandalous Fall of Colonel Frederick George D'Utassy." Unpublished manuscript.

Bennett, William H. Letters to author, 1993–1998. Bennett was the grandson of Lieutenant Nicholas DeGraff of the 115th New York.

Hough, Franklin. Papers. Box 20 Folder 7, and Box 36 Folder 3, New York State Archives, Albany, New York.

Lyon, Lorenzo. Letters. New-York Historical Society, New York, New York. Lyon was a sergeant in the 48th New York Infantry.

Records of a Court of Inquiry conducted at Camp Douglas November 22–26, 1862. Record Group 94, Letters Received 1862, File T-681, National Archives. Proceedings of the tribunal investigating the 115th's fault in the fire that consumed the regiment's barracks as it departed Chicago.

Regimental Order and Letter Book, New York 115th Infantry. Records of the Adjutant General, Record Group 94, National Archives, Washington, D.C.

Seymour, Truman. Olustee letters to New York State Adjutant General John T. Sprague. Record Group 94, Entry 159, General's Papers (Second Series), National Archives.

Documents and Pamphlets

Annual Report of the Adjutant General of the State of New York for the Year 1903. Registers of New York Regiments in the War of the Rebellion, Serial No. 35. Albany, New York: Oliver A. Quayle.

Haynie, I.N. *A History of Camp Douglas: A Prisoner of War Camp at Chicago, Illinois, 1861-1865*. Little Rock, Arkansas: Eagle, 1991.

Pfanz, Harry W. *Special History Report: Troop Movement Maps, 1862; Harpers Ferry National Historical Park, Maryland–West Virginia*. Denver: National Park Service, United States Department of the Interior, 1976.

Program of the 35th reunion of the 115th New York, August 25, 1916. Collection of Hector J. Allen, Town Historian, Oppenheim, New York.

Program for the 45th reunion of the 115th and 153rd Regiments N.Y. Vol. Infantry, August 26, 1925. Collection of James Morrison, Gloversville, New York, pp. 31–32.

U.S. War Department. *The War of the Rebellion: A Compilation of the Official Records of the Union and Confederate Armies*. 128 Parts in 70 Volumes. Washington, D.C.: Government Printing Office, 1881–1902.

Newspapers

Amsterdam Democrat. Amsterdam, New York.
Amsterdam Evening Recorder. Amsterdam, New York.
Ballston Journal. Ballston Spa, New York.
Cohoes Cataract. Cohoes, New York.
Daily Saratogian. Saratoga Springs, New York.
Free South. Union occupied Hilton Head, South Carolina.
Fulton County Republican. Johnstown, New York.
Harpers Weekly. New York, New York.
Herkimer County Journal. Little Falls, New York.
Johnstown Daily Republican. Johnstown, New York.
Johnstown Independent. Johnstown, New York.
Mohawk Valley Democrat. Fonda, New York.
Mohawk Valley Register. Fort Plain, New York.
Montgomery County Republican. Fultonville, New York.
National Tribune. New York, New York.
New South. Union occupied Hilton Head, South Carolina.
New York Herald. New York, New York.
New York Times. New York, New York.
New York Tribune. New York, New York.
Palmetto Herald. Union occupied Hilton Head, South Carolina.
St. Johnsville Enterprise & News. St. Johnsville, New York.
St. Johnsville News. St. Johnsville, New York.

Magazines

Blue & Gray Magazine. September 1987; October 1989; April 1994; December 1994; December 1995.
Civil War Times Illustrated. August 1964; January 1978.
Florida Historical Quarterly. Vol. 29, July 1950.

Books

Illustrated History of Montgomery & Fulton Counties, New York. F.W. DeBeers, 1878.

Baltz, Louis J., III. *The Battle of Cold Harbor: May 27–June 13, 1864*. Lynchburg, Virginia: H.E. Howard, 1994.

Beyer, W.F., and Keydel, O.F., eds. *Deeds of Valor: How America's Civil War Heroes Won the Congressional Medal of Honor*. Stamford, Connecticut: Longmeadow, 1992. Reprint of 1903 edition.

Burt, Silas W. *My Memoirs of the Military History of the State of New York During the War for the Union, 1861–65*. Albany: Argus, 1903. Bound in one volume with another book: Hugh Hastings, *New York and the War with Spain: History of the Empire State Regiments*.

Butler, Benjamin F. *Butler's Book*. Boston: A.M. Thayer, 1892.

Carse, Robert. *Hilton Head Island in the Civil War: Department of the South*. Columbia, South Carolina: The State Printing Company, 1961.

Cavanaugh, Michael A., and Marvel, William. *The Battle of the Crater, "The Horrid Pit": The Petersburg

Campaign, June 25–August 6, 1864. Lynchburg, Virginia: H.E. Howard, 1989.

Clark, James H. *The Iron Hearted Regiment: Being an Account of the Battles, Marches and Gallant Deeds Performed by the 115th Regiment N. Y. Volunteers.* Albany: J. Munsell, 1865. Regimental history of the 115th New York by one of its officers.

Cornish, Dudley T. *The Sable Arm: Negro Troops in the Union Army, 1861–1865.* New York: W.W. Norton, 1966.

Davidson, Greenlee. *Diary and Letters 1851–1863.* Ed. by Charles W. Turner. Verona, Virginia: McClure, 1975.

Davis, William C., and the editors of Time-Life Books. *Death in the Trenches: Grant at Petersburg.* Alexandria, Virginia: Time-Life, 1986.

Delauter, Roger U., Jr. *Winchester in the Civil War.* Lynchburg, Virginia: H.E. Howard, 1992.

Donald, David Herbert. *Lincoln.* New York: Simon & Schuster, 1995.

Dunn, Violet B., ed. *Saratoga County Heritage.* Ballston Spa, New York: Saratoga County, 1974.

Faust, Patricia L., ed. *Historical Times Illustrated Encyclopedia of the Civil War.* New York: Harper & Row, 1986.

Fonvielle, Chris E., Jr. *The Wilmington Campaign: Last Rays of Departing Hope.* Mechanicsburg, Pennsylvania: Stackpole, 1997, 2001.

Fox, William F. *Regimental Losses in the American Civil War, 1861–1865: A Treatise on the Extent and Nature of the Mortuary Losses in the Union Regiments.* Albany: Albany Publishing Company, 1889.

Frye, Dennis E. "Drama Between the Rivers: Harpers Ferry in the 1862 Maryland Campaign." In Gallagher, Gary W., ed., *Antietam: Essays on the 1862 Maryland Campaign.* Kent, Ohio: Kent State University Press, 1989.

Furgurson, Ernest B. *Not War But Murder: Cold Harbor 1864.* New York: Alfred A. Knopf, 2000.

Gaff, Alan D. *Brave Men's Tears: The Iron Brigade at Brawner Farm.* Dayton, Ohio: Morningside House, 1985.

Gragg, Rod. *Confederate Goliath: The Battle of Fort Fisher.* New York: HarperCollins, 1991.

Grant, Ulysses S. *Personal Memoirs.* New York: Charles L. Webster, 1885.

Hennessy, John J. *The First Battle of Manassas: An End to Innocence.* Lynchburg, Virginia: H.E. Howard, 1989.

_____. *Return to Bull Run: The Campaign and Battle of Second Manassas.* New York: Simon & Schuster, 1993.

Horn, John. *The Destruction of the Weldon Railroad: Deep Bottom, Globe Tavern and Reams Station, August 14–25, 1864.* Lynchburg, Virginia: H.E. Howard, 1991.

Howe, Thomas J. *Wasted Valor: The Petersburg Campaign, June 15–18, 1864.* Lynchburg, Virginia: H.E. Howard, 1998.

Hunt, Roger D. *Colonels in Blue: Union Army Colonels of the Civil War, The New England States.* Atglen, Pennsylvania: Schiffer Military History, 2001.

Johnson, R.U., and Buel, C.C., eds. *Battles & Leaders of the Civil War.* New York: Century, 1887–88.

King, David H. *History of the Ninety-Third Regiment New York Volunteer Infantry.* Milwaukee: Association of the 93rd New York State Volunteers, 1895.

Macfarlane, Carrington. *Reminiscences of an Army Surgeon.* Oswego, New York: Lake City Print Shop, 1912.

Maney, R. Wayne. *Marching to Cold Harbor: Victory and Failure, 1864.* Shippensburg, Pennsylvania: White Mane, 1995.

McFeely, William S. *Grant: A Biography.* New York: W.W. Norton, 1981.

McWhiney, Grady, and Jamieson, Perry D. *Attack and Die: Civil War Military Tactics and the Southern Heritage.* University, Alabama: University of Alabama Press, 1982.

Murfin, James V. *The Gleam of Bayonets: The Battle of Antietam and Robert E. Lee's Maryland Campaign, September 1862.* Baton Rouge: Louisiana State University Press, 1965.

Nichols, James M. *Perry's Saints, or the Fighting Parson's Regiment [48th New York] in the War of the Rebellion.* Boston: D. Lathrop, 1888.

Norton, Oliver W. *Army Letters, 1861–1865.* Dayton, Ohio: Morningside House, 1990.

Nulty, William H. *Confederate Florida: The Road to Olustee.* Tuscaloosa: University of Alabama Press, 1990.

Phisterer, Frederick, ed. *New York in the War of the Rebellion.* Albany: J.B. Lyon, 1912.

Poague, William T. *Gunner with Stonewall.* Ed. M.F. Cockrell. Wilmington, NC: Broadfoot, 1987.

Porter, John A. *76th Regiment Pennsylvania Volunteer Infantry, Keystone Zouaves: The Personal Recollections 1861–1865 of Sergeant John A. Porter.* Ed. James A. Chrisman. Wilmington, NC: Broadfoot, 1988.

Robertson, William Glenn. *Back Door to Richmond: The Bermuda Hundred Campaign, April-June, 1864.* Baton Rouge: Louisiana State University Press, 1987.

Schiller, Herbert M. *The Bermuda Hundred Campaign: Operations on the South Side of the James River, Virginia, May, 1864.* Dayton: Morningside House, 1988.

Sifakis, Stewart. *Who Was Who in the Civil War.* New York: Facts on File, 1988.

Sommers, Richard J. *Richmond Redeemed: The Siege at Petersburg.* New York: Doubleday, 1981.

Trudeau, Noah Andre *Bloody Roads South: The Wilderness to Cold Harbor, May-June 1864.* Boston: Little, Brown, 1989.

_____. *The Last Citadel: Petersburg, Virginia, June 1864–April 1865.* Boston: Little, Brown, 1991.

Warner, Ezra J. *Generals in Blue: Lives of the Union Commanders.* Baton Rouge: Louisiana State University Press, 1964.

Wilson, Arabella M. *Disaster, Struggle, Triumph: The Adventures of 1000 Boys in Blue from August, 1862 to June, 1865.* Regimental history of the 126th New York. Albany: Argus, 1870.

Wise, Stephen R. *Gate of Hell: Campaign for Charleston Harbor, 1863.* Columbia: University of South Carolina Press, 1994.

Index

Numbers in **_bold italics_** indicate pages with photographs.

Abeel, Joseph 84, 95, 185
Aiken's Landing, Virginia 151
Alback, Philip 129
Albany, New York 8, 9, 190, 192, 196
Alexandria, Virginia 45
Amboy, New Jersey 9
ambulance corps 181–182
American Revolution 7
Ames, Gen. Adelbert 106, 109, 160, 168, 179, 180, 183, 184
Amsterdam, New York 8, 24, 41, 57, 70, 93, 155, 196, 199
Andersonville, Georgia 82, 84, 129
Annapolis, Maryland 34, 35, 36, 145, 156, 193, 199
Antietam, Battle of 34
Antietam Creek 27, 32, 34
Appomattox Court House, Virginia 188
Appomattox River 96, 98, 107, 119, 121, 122, 138, 151
Arlington Heights, Virginia 43
Army of Northern Virginia 12, 19, 96, 111, 114, 120, 161
Army of the James 64, 95–96, 103–107, 111, 114, 120, 157, 159, 160, 163
Army of the Potomac 27, 32, 34, 51, 86, 94, 96, 104, 110, 111, 112, 115, 117, 118, 119, 149, 157, 160, 181, 186
Atlanta, Georgia 129, 150, 161, 186

Bailey's Creek 139
Baker, Charles Nathaniel 84, 185
Baldwin, Florida 71, 73, 85
Ballston Journal 37, 40, 41, 155, 159, 192
Ballston Spa, New York 6
Baltimore & Ohio Railroad 10, 15, 36, 43
Baltimore, Maryland 10, 15, 36
Barber's Plantation, Florida 71, 72, 73, 74, 75, 83, 85
Barksdale, Gen. William 22, 24
Barnum, Lt. Frank 50–51, 82
Barton, Col. William 59, 67, **_67_**, 76, 82, 89, 91, 98, 110, 121, 124, 130, 285n.48 (ch. 6)
Barton's Brigade 67, 69, 70, 74, 76–78, 80, 81–82, 86, 87–88, 94, 95, 98, 100, 101, 103, 104, 106, 110, 113–115, 119, 121–124
Batcheller, Lt. Col. George Sherman 11–13, **_11_**, 29, 31, 32, 33, 35, 36, 39, 65, 81, 90, 93, 279n.27 (ch. 1)

Battery Anderson 167, 168
Battery Gatlin 167, 168
Battles and Leaders of the Civil War 192
Beaufort, North Carolina 163–164
Beaufort, South Carolina 59–61, 62, 64, 66, 67
Beauregard, Gen. P.G.T. 120, 289n.11 (ch. 10)
Beefsteak Raid 150
Belgian rifles 10
Bell, Col. Louis 131, 134, 137, 141, 158, 173–174, 180, 290n.44 (ch. 10)
Bell's Brigade 131, 133, 136–137, 141, 152, 157–158, 160, 168, 170, 173
Bennett, Laura DeGraff 199
Bennett, Norman 199
Bennett, William 199–200
Bentonville, North Carolina 186
Bermuda Hundred 96, 98, 102, 103, 104, 106–107, 108, 110, 111, 114, 118, 119, 120, 121, 122, 138, 139, 146, 148, 149, 151, 160, 181, 182
Bermuda Hundred Landing, Virginia 96, 160, 170
Bertrand, Lewis 30, 116, 155
Bertrand, Lucy 30
Birney, Gen. David 139, 151, 290n.5 (ch. 11)
Birney, Gen. William 139, 141, 143, 145, 147, 152, 290n.15 (ch. 11)
Bisbee, J.H. 49
black soldiers 56, 58, 69, 72, 74, 75, 82, 133–137, 147, 151, 160
Blackburn's Ford, Virginia 90
Blackwood, George **_196_**
blockade 52, 161, 180
Bluffton, South Carolina 59
boarding party (Fort Fisher) 173
Bolivar Heights 13, 15–18, 21–24, 26–31
bombproofs 125, 165, 166, 173, 175
Bona, Sgt. Louis 49
Borden, William H. 105
Boston, Massachusetts 192
bounties 6, 7, 62
Bovee, Jeremiah 40
Brastow, Capt. Billings 147
Brawner Farm 88
Brice, Charles 98
Broad River 66
Brown, Amos 177
Brown, Jacob 123
Brown, John 13

Brown, Sgt. Orrin 101
Buddle, Edward C. **_189_**
Bull Run, First Battle of 18, 21, 88, 90
Bull Run, Second Battle of 5, 12, 19, 21, 87
bumming *see* foraging
burial detail 126
Burnside, Gen. Ambrose 133
Burton, Winslow 13, 62
Butler, Gen. Benjamin F. 94, 95–96, 98, 104, 106–107, 111, 119, 120–121, 122, 157, 159, 163, 164, 167, 168, 169

Callahan Station, Florida 72
Camp Chase 43–44, 47
Camp Douglas 36, 37, 38–42, 43, 50, 128
Camp Finegan 70–71
Camp Fonda *see* Camp Mohawk
Camp Mohawk 8, **_9_**, 44, 189, 192, 199
Camp Parole 35–36
Camp Vermont 45, 47
Canajoharie, New York 56
Cape Fear River 161–163, 165–166, 168, 170, 173, 182–183, 184
Cape Hatteras, North Carolina 190
Carolinas Campaign 170, 186–188
Cayadutta Cornet Band 9–10
Cedar Mountain 87
Chaffin's Farm *see* Darbytown Road
Chambersburg, Pennsylvania 139
Charles Town, Virginia (later West Virginia) 11–13
Charleston, South Carolina 52, 56, 57, 60–62, 69, 186
Chase, U.S. Secretary of the Treasury Salmon P. 68
Chattanooga, Tennessee 129, 186
Chesapeake & Ohio Canal 10, 15
Chesapeake Bay 36, 45, 95, 96, 111, 139, 163, 190
Chesterfield Heights, Battle of *see* Port Walthall Junction
Chesterfield Heights, Virginia 106
Chicago 36, 37, 38, 42, 43, 48, 50, 54, 145
Chickamauga 87, 186
Christie, Sgt. Harvey C. **_60_**
Christie, Philip 55
Cincinnati, Ohio 28
City of Norwich 36
City Point, Virginia 111, 119, 129, 139, 190

303

Index

Clark, Lt. Charles L. 143
Clark, James H. 9, 23, 52, 55, 56, 83, 85, 117, 193
Clemens, Samuel **105**
Clemens, Rev. Sylvester W. 18, 23, 36, 37, 91, 127, 139, 145
Clifton Park, New York 9, 144, 193
Coan, Col. William 130, 131
Cockran, Mark 116–117
Cohoes Cataract 18
Cohoes, New York 143
Cold Harbor 111–116, **115**, 118, 119, 120, 127, 146, 155, 170
Colored Troops *see* black soldiers
Colquitt, Gen. Alfred H. 75
Columbia, South Carolina 186
Comstock, Lt. Col. Cyrus 182
Conover, Sgt. Frank 144–145
Conover, Corp. Seely 55, 56, 145, **145**
conscription 62, 156, 285n.38 (ch. 6)
contrabands 55, 56
Coosaw River 66
Copperheads *see* Peace Democrats
Corinth, New York 95
Cornell, Samuel 156
Cornell, Corp. Sidney T. 78–79, 156
Countryman, Corp. Jadua 178
covered ways 124–125, 127, 133
Coy, Jeremiah 177
Crampton's Gap 27
Crater, Battle of the 133–137, **134**, 138, 139, 146, 193
Crimean War 28
Cropsey, Edward 117
Curreen, George 39, **40**
Curtis, Gen. N. Martin 168, 173

D-Day (Normandy) 170
Daily Saratogian 5, 51, 59
Darbytown Road 157–159, 176
Darien, Georgia 58–59
Davis, Pres. Jefferson 19, 95
Deep Bottom, Second Battle of 141–144, 145, 146, 148, 152, 185
Deep Bottom, Virginia 139, 149, 151, 152, 169
DeGraff, Capt. Alonzo 118
DeGraff, John 196
DeGraff, Nicholas 10, 11, 19, **19**, 22, 35, 36, 38, 39, 41, 42, 57–58, **58**, 62, 64, 65, 72, 78, 85, 90–91, 100, 102, 104, 110, 114, 117, 118, 121, 125, 126, 127, 128, 136, 145, 146, 148, 149–150, 151, 153, 155, 156, 159, 175, 181–182, 184, 187, 196–197, 199, **200**
Delacteur, Martin 179
Delaware 69
Delphos, Ohio 37
DeMolay 111, 170
Department of North Carolina 181
Department of the South 48, 52, 56, 57, 60, 64, 68, 69, 95
desertion 40–41, 150, 156, 161
Devendorf, Lt. Henry X. 25, 32, 37, 39
Devens, Gen. Charles 113, 116
disease 41, 54, 59–60, 82, 185, 189
Dixie 117
Dodds, Sylvanus 39
Douglas, Sen. Stephen A. 38, 39, 282n.18 (ch. 4)
draft law *see* conscription
Drake, Col. Jeremiah 113, 114
Drewry's Bluff 105, 106, 110
Duckett, John 79
Dunk, James 158
Dunning, Albert 114, 127–128

D'Utassy, Col. Frederick 17–18, 21, 25, 28, 29, 30, 31
Dye, John 22, 29, 31

Early, Gen. Jubal 139
Eighteenth Corps 95, 104, 110, 111, 112–114, 115, 116, 118, 119, 121, 122, 151, 156, 157, 158, 160
8th Connecticut 100, 103
8th New York Cavalry 11, 13
8th U.S. Colored Troops 74, 76–77, 85
81st New York 67
83rd Pennsylvania 86
election of 1864 68, 149, 157, 159, 161
Enfield muskets 10, 43, 283n.5 (ch. 5)
English, James 13, **14**
Ephratah, New York 177
Erie Canal 6
euchre 62
execution, military 74, 150

Fayetteville, North Carolina 186
Fellows, Sgt. Charles 134, 136, 155, 179
Ferguson, Lt. Willett 23, 33
Fernandina, Florida 71
Fifth Corps 115, 159
5th Georgia Cavalry 93
54th Massachusetts 59, 61, 69, 75, 82, 284n.22 (ch. 6)
55th Massachusetts 74, 89
Fighting Three Hundred *see* Fox's Fighting Three Hundred
Finegan, Gen. Joseph 75
fire, Camp Douglas barracks 42, 48–51, 54, 66, 146
1st Maine Heavy Artillery 123
1st Maryland 22
1st Massachusetts Independent Cavalry 69
1st North Carolina 74, 82, 285n.27 (ch. 7)
flags 8, 32–33, 34, 101, 134, 136, 143, 155, 168, 173, 174, 179–180, 189, 190, 294n.40 (ch. 14)
Flint, William 59
Florida, Atlantic & Gulf Railroad 71
Florida Railroad Company 68, 71
Fonda, New York 5, 6, 7, 8, 9, 12, 19, 179, 189, 194
Fonda, Sgt. Raymond 101–102
foraging 186–187
Ford, Col. Thomas 23
Fort Anderson 182, 183
Fort Donelson 38
Fort Fisher 161–183, **165**, **166**, 186, 189, 193
Fort Garibaldi 12
Fort Gates 91, **92**, 93–94, 141
Fort Gilmer 152–156, **153**, 157, 170
Fort Gregg 61
Fort Harrison 151–152, 156
Fort Plain, New York 23, 144
Fort Pulaski 59
Fort Sumter 56
Fort Wagner 61, 82, 85, 87, 88, 95
Fort Wayne, Indiana 37
40th Massachusetts 72, 110
Fortress Monroe 45, 47, 96, 111, 119, 127, 144, 160, 163, 169, 193
43rd Alabama 122
47th New York 67, 76, 82, 98, 111, 114, 174
48th New York 59, 61, 67, 76, 82, 88, 98, 100, 103, 114, 123, 130, 131, 174
48th Pennsylvania 131
Foster, Gen. Robert 152, 292n.12 (ch. 12)

Fourmile Creek 139
14th New York Heavy Artillery 118
4th New Hampshire 131, 141, 168, 176, 182
Fox, Robert 33, 82
Fox's Fighting Three Hundred 51, 284n.37 (ch. 5)
Francisco, Lt. Francis 84, 144
Franklin, Gen. William 27
Frederick, Maryland 20, 27, 34
Free South 54, 59, 60, 61, 66
French, Capt. Walton W. 65
friendly fire 158
Fulton County, New York 6, 7, 56
Fulton County Republican 46, 47
Fultonville, New York 91, 192
furlough 35, 64, 128, 182, 188
Fussell's Mill, Battle of *see* Deep Bottom, Second Battle of
Fussell's Mill, Virginia 139, 140, 146

Gainesville, Florida 71, 72
Gainesville, Virginia 88
Galway, New York 155, 185
Gardner, James 83–84
Gardner, James, Jr. 84
Garibaldi Guards *see* 39th New York
Getman, James 177, **178**
Gettysburg 62, 87, 138
Gillmore, Gen. Quincy 60–62, 69, 71–72, 74, 85, 86, 95, 139
Gloucester Point, Virginia 95
Glover, William 127
Goldsboro, North Carolina 181, 184, 186, 187
Goodrich, Fred 61
Goodrich, Henry 116
Goodrich, Menzo 116
Gorr, Heinrite 156–157
Grand Army of the Republic 197
Grand Reviews 188
Grant, Corp. Daniel 82, 83
Grant, Gen. Ulysses S. 94, 96, 104, 107, 110–111, 112, 115–116, 117, 118, 120, 121, 132, 133, 137, 139, 148, 151, 156, 157, 159, 163, 169, 170, 180, 181, 187, 188
Granville, New York 108

Halfmoon, New York 61, 79
Halleck, Gen. Henry W. 20
Halltown, Virginia (later West Virginia) 11
Hamilton County, New York 6, 144
Hampton Roads, Virginia 52, 100
Hancock, Gen. Winfield Scott 139, 140, 290n.5 (ch. 11)
Hanna, James A. 78–79
Hanner, Corp. Albon 174
Hansow, John 126
Hare's Hill 122, 123, 125, 128, 131, 149
Harlow, Smith 136
Harpers Ferry Investigation Commission 39, 41
Harpers Ferry, Virginia (later West Virginia) 10, 11, 13, 15–28, **16**, 30–32, 34–39, 41–42, 51, 77, 88, 146, 179
Harper's Weekly 175
Harrisburg, Pennsylvania 15
Harrison, Col. George P., Jr. 75
Hatch, Gen. John 93
Hatcher's Run 159
Hay, John 68–69
Haze 163, 167, 169, 170
Heaton, Sgt. Henry 178
Henry, Col. Guy 70–71
Hill, Gen. Ambrose P. 30, 32

Index

Hillhouse, N.Y.S. Adjutant Gen. Thomas 41
Hilton Head, South Carolina 47, 48, 50, 51, 52–60, 65, 67, 72, 74, 80, 81, 84, 89, 90, 91, 94, 199
Himes, Corp. James 143
Hogan, John 129
Home, Sweet Home 184
Horton, Lt. Thomas 8, 30, 31
Hubbard, John A. 15
Hudson River 6, 9, 36, 190
Hudson Valley 9
Hunter's Creek 45
U.S.S. *Huron* 164
Hutchinson, John 62

Illinois State Fairground 38, 51
Iron Brigade 88
Iron Hearted Regiment 193
Island Number Ten 38

Jackson, Gen. Thomas J. (Stonewall) 12, 18–21, 24–27, 29–30, 32, 37, 87
Jacksonville, Florida 69–72, 73, 74, 84, 85, 89
James River 19, 52, 96, 104, 105, 107, 111, 118, 119, 120, 121, 132, 139, 146, 148, 151, 156, 157, 160, 169, 190
Jenkins, Charles 79
Jennings, William 26, 155, 158
Johnson, Lt. Col. Nathan J. 108–110, **109**, 131, 137, 146–148, 155, 170, 174, 179, 180
Johnston, Gen. Joseph E. 19, 186–188
Johnstown, New York 31
Joint Committee on the Conduct of the War, U.S. Congress 169
Jones Neck 139

Keck, Sgt. Peter 101, **102**, 143, 174, 179
Keenholt, Christopher 100
Kershaw, Gen. Joseph 22, 24
Key West, Florida 52
Keyes, Gen. Erasmus 46–47
Kinnicut, George 174
Kittle, Capt. David 50
Kline, Sgt. Charles 155
Kneeskern, Capt. John 41, 194

Lake, William **87**
Lake Michigan 38
Lamb, Col. William 167, 170, 173, 174
Laurel Hill Church 152
Lee, Gen. Robert E. 12, 19, 20, 24, 27, 32, 34, 96, 104, 110–112, 114, 118–121, 132, 139, 141, 148, 151, 156, 161, 181, 187, 188
Lee, Whitney **103**
lice 126, 170
Lima, Ohio 37
Lincoln, Pres. Abraham 5, 6, 20, 56, 68–69, 94, 122, 149, 159, 161, 163, 187, 188
Lingenfelter, Sgt. Levi 78
Lingenfelter, Capt. Sidney 65, 127
Link, Philip 79
Long Bridge 43
Loudoun Heights 15, 17, 20, 21, 24, 26, 29
Louisiana 163–164
Luffman, George 99, 100

Macfarlane, Dr. Carrington **66**, 67, 72, 78, 79, 83, 99, 126, 130, 132, 140, 145, 158, 163, 168, 178, 179, 185, 190
Madison County, New York 90

magazine explosion (Fort Fisher) 176–179
Majer, Dr. Adolph 79
March to the Sea (Sherman) 161, 170
Martinsburg, Virginia (later West Virginia) 20
Maryland Heights 10, 15, 17, 20–29, 31, 81, 130
Matanzas 47
Mayfield Corners, New York 56
McClellan, Gen. George B. 5, 19, 20, 27, 29, 31, 34, 46, 149, 159, 280n.12 (ch. 2)
McGlachlin, Archibald 112, 113, 114
McKay, William 57
McKittrick, Capt. William 47, 123, 127–128, 149, 151, 154–155, **154**
McKnight, John 40
McLaws, Gen. Lafayette 20, 21, 24, 26, 27
McMartin, Lt. Martin 194
Meade, Gen. George G. 117
Medal of Honor 93–94, 168
Mexican War 123, 154
Meyer, Corp. Fred 177, **179**
Miles, Col. Dixon S. 17, 20, 21, 22, 23, 27, 28, 30, 31, 280n.16 (ch. 2)
Millham, George 39, 66
mine *see* Petersburg mine
Mobile Bay 163
Mohawk River 6
Mohawk Valley 8, 91, 193
Montaney, James 9
Montgomery, Col. James 74, 82
Montgomery County, New York 6, 23, 144, 194, 200
moon-blindness 129–130
Moreau, New York 7
Morgan, Gov. Edward 5, 6, 8, 41, 50
Morris, Stephen 23
Morris Island 61
Mosher, Capt. Fred 114, **115**, 158, 174, 175, 177, 179
Mound Battery (Fort Fisher) 165
Mount Vernon 45
Mulliken, Corp. Charles 79
Musgrove, Corp. Abbot 143
Myrtle Sound 182

Nashville, Tennessee 181
Naval Battery (Maryland Heights) 21, 23, 24, 28
Nelliston, New York 177
New Bern, North Carolina 181
New Castle, Virginia 112, 118
New Market Heights, Virginia 139, 151
New Market Road 152, 154, 156
New Orleans, Louisiana 95
New South 54, 59
New York Central Railroad 192
New York City 9, 13, 124, 190
New York Herald 88, 152, 154, 158
New York Times 72, 83, 88, 113, 114
New York Tribune 78, 177
Newton Center, Massachusetts 192
93rd New York 108
97th Pennsylvania 109, 131, 174
Ninth Corps 118, 122, 131–136, 159
9th Maine 131, 141, 147, 158, 182
9th U.S. Colored Troops 144, 147
9th Vermont 17, 38, 42, 48–50
North Anna 111
North Carolina Junior Reserves 164
North Point 190
Northampton, New York 174
Northeast Bastion (Fort Fisher) 165, 173, 164, 176

Northeast Station, North Carolina 184–185
Northern Light 94–95
Northrup, Benjamin 78
Norton, Lt. Oliver W. 86
Nutt, Bill 35, 126

Ocean Pond 75
Official Records 192
Olney, Lt. Stephen 175
Olustee 74, 75–83, **77**, 85, 86, 87, 89, 90, 91, 108, 127, 129, 146, 156, 175, 176, 180, 185, 193
Olustee Station, Florida 75, 82
100th New York 98, 103
111th New York 13–14, 17
125th New York 41
126th New York 22
142nd New York 168
153rd New York 44
169th New York 131, 168, 176, 180, 182
Opequon Bridge 11, 13
Osborn, Col. Francis 141
Oswego, New York 67
oysters 36, 46, 56, 199

Palatka, Florida 89, 91, 93, 94, 141
Palmer, Corp. Henry 49
Palmetto Herald 54
Pamunkey River 47, 111, 119, 170
Park Barracks 9
parole 33, 41, 184
Paul, Dallas 95
Peace Democrats 149, 159
Pennypacker, Col. Galusha 173–174
Petersburg mine 131–132, 136
Petersburg, Virginia 96, 106, 107, 118, 120–122, 126, 127, 129, 130, 131–133, 138, 139, 148, 149–152, 157, 159–161, 181, 189, 190
Philadelphia 9, 10, 15
Philadelphia Inquirer 117
Philadelphia Soldier's Retreat 9
picket duty 125, 127
Pickett, Gen. George 138
pioneers 173
Pittsburgh, Pennsylvania 37
Plaisted, Col. Harris 98, 100
Pleasants, Col. Henry 131–132
Point of Rocks, Virginia 119, 122, 138, 151
pontoon bridge 139–140, **140**, 148, 151, 170, 184, 185
Pope, Gen. John 12, 19, 20, 37
Port Hudson 87
Port Royal Island, South Carolina 57, 59, 62, 65, 66
Port Royal Sound 52, 56, 59, 61
Port Walthall Junction 98–103, 143
Port Walthall, Virginia 98
Porter, Admiral David Dixon 163, 170, 173
Potomac River 10, 12, 15, 17, 19, 20, 21, 22, 23, 27, 28, 43, 45
powder ship (Fort Fisher) 163–164, 167
prisoner exchange 42, 44
prisoners-of-war returns 184–185, 190
Proctor's Creek 104

Raleigh, North Carolina 187–188
Rapidan River 111
Reardon, Edmund 118, 193
Reardon, John 39, 55, 73–74, 84, 89, 100, 101, 103, 104, 113–114, 118, 122, 128, 145, 150, 163, 177–178, 185–187, 192–193

Reardon, Susie Frances 193
Reed, John 147
Reid, James E. 6, 29, 35, 36, 38, 46, 62, 78, 84, 102, 105–107, 114, 121, 129–130, 137, 140, 145, 148, 156, 158, 168, 169, 177, 185, 192
Rhodes, Edwin 125
Rice, Michael 37
Richardson, Col. Israel 90
Richmond & Petersburg Railroad 98, 103, 120
Richmond-Petersburg Turnpike 104, 109
Richmond, Virginia 5, 19, 33, 46, 47, 94, 95, 96, 103, 104, 105, 107, 111, 118, 120, 122, 132, 139, 148, 151–152, 156, 157, 159, 161, 169, 181
rifle pits 125, 158
Ripley, Joshua W. 30 43
Rock City Falls, New York 7

St. Augustine, Florida 68
St. John's River 69, 89, 91
St. Johnsville, New York 37, 41, 193
St. Johnsville News 193
St. Mary's River 71
St. Philips Island 52
Salvor 119
Sammons, Col. Simeon 7–8, **8**, 10, 16, 22, 23, 24, 29, 30, 32, 35, 37, 38, 41, 42, 46, 47–51, 55–56, 57, 59, 64–66, 68, 72, 76, 81, 90, 82–83, 110, 130–131, 136–137, 193–196, **195**
Sanderson, Florida 71, 75
Sandy Hook, Maryland 10, 22, 23
Sanford, Lt. Hugh 174
Saratoga County, New York 6, 9, 40, 41, 78, 84, 99, 144, 155, 185, 193
Saratoga Springs, New York 6, 7, 60, 175, 179
Savannah, Georgia 52, 161, 170, 181, 186
Saxton, Gen. Rufus 56, 65
Schenectady, New York 8, 60, 174
Schofield, Gen. John McAllister 181, 183, 187
Schoolhouse Ridge 29
Seabrook, South Carolina 54
Second Corps 51, 118, 132, 139–140, 148
2nd Illinois Light Artillery 27
2nd New York Heavy Artillery 118
2nd Wisconsin 88
Selfridge, Capt. Thomas 164
Seven Pines 19
7th Connecticut 74, 75–77, 83
7th New Hampshire 74, 76–77
76th Pennsylvania 95, 98, 111, 114, 174
77th New York 100
Seymour, Gen. Truman 69, 71–72, 73, 74–76, 80, 81, 82, 85–86, 88, 93, 146, 285n.6 (ch. 7)
Sharpsburg, Maryland 32
sharpshooters 150
Shaw, Col. Robert Gould Shaw 59
Shaw, Capt. William 8, **17**, 147, 194
Shenandoah River 29
Shenandoah Valley 10, 12, 15, 20, 94, 139, 148, 150, 151, 161
Sheridan, Gen. Philip 111–112, 139, 150, 151, 161
Sherman, Daniel 40
Sherman, Gen. William T. 94, 129, 150, 161, 170, 181, 186–188
Sherrill, Col. Eliakim 23
Shiloh 17, 38

Sibley tents 16, 45, 280n.3 (ch. 2)
Sing Sing Prison 28
Sixth Corps 112–113, 115, 120–121
60th Ohio 17
65th Illinois 28
66th New York 57
Slingerland, Sgt. Elbert **58**
Smith, Capt. Isaac E. 85, **85**, 286n.59 (ch. 7)
Smith, Capt. Solomon 79, 91, 93, 110, 141, 144
Smith, Capt. William 24, 31, 81, 130, 194
Smith, Gen. William F. 110, 112, 116, 123–124
Smithville, North Carolina 183
Snell, Orville 185
Snyder, Alfred 128
Snyder, Chauncey, Jr. 41, 128
Snyder, Chauncey, Sr. 41, 128
Snyder, Francis 128
Solomon's Gap 21–22
South Mountain 20, 27, 32
Southside Railroad 157, 159
Spiegel, Charles 72, 155
Spotsylvania 87, 100, 111
Sprague, N.Y.S. Adjutant Gen. John T. 86, 88
Stannard, Col. George 48–50
Stanton, U.S. Secretary of War Edwin 36, 163
Stickney, Lyman D. 68–69
Stillwater, New York 79
Stone, Almon 18, **18**, 136
Stones River 87
Stonewall Brigade 87
Strawberry Plains *see* Deep Bottom, Second Battle of
substitutes 62, 95, 156
Sugar Loaf Battery 168, 182, 183
Summit Point, Virginia 11, 13
Susquehanna River 37
Sutton, Dr. Richard 31, 38, 41, 67
Suwannee River 71, 74, 75, 86
Syracuse, New York 90

Tenth Corps 95, 104, 108, 119, 121, 122, 133, 139–141, 148, 149, 151–152, 156, 157, 158, 160, 170
Terry, Gen. Alfred 139, 141, 170, 175, 181, 186–187, 290n.5 (ch. 11)
Terry's Provisional Corps 182, 183, 186
Thackrah, Benjamin 91–93, 136; awarded Medal of Honor 93–94
3rd Rhode Island Artillery 89
3rd Virginia 138
13th Indiana 109, 128, 131, 141, 157–158, 168, 173, 174, 179, 182
32nd Georgia 78
32nd Ohio 17, 22
39th New York 17, 22, 28, 38, 41, 42, 49, 50
Thomas Way 190
Thorne, Harry 135–136, **135**, 140
Tompkins, Lt. William 80
Toronto, Ontario 199
Tribes Hill, New York 57, 199
Troy, New York 18, 156
Tulloch, Kelley 60
Turner, Gen. John W. 95, 104, 110, 122, 128, 130, 134, 137, 287n.16 (ch. 8)
12th New York 90
Twenty-third Corps 181, 183

Twenty-fourth Corps 160
24th Massachusetts 141
24th New York 67
Twenty-fifth Corps 160
29th Maine 45
203rd Pennsylvania 174
205th Pennsylvania 160
Tyler, Col. Daniel 48–50, 284n.30 (ch. 5)

U.S. Naval Academy 35
U.S. Navy 57, 61, 95, 161–173, 182, 183, 184
U.S. Sanitary Commission 129, 283n.11 (ch. 5)
U.S. War Department 39, 50, 51, 56, 69, 72, 93–94, 163, 192

Vanbrocklin, John 31
Van Derveer, Capt. Garret 54, 57, 80, **80**, 90, 91, 108, 180
Van De Sande, Lt. John 144, **144**
Van Epps, Fisher 185
Van Evera, Corp. Alonzo 56
Van Steenberg, George 100, 102
Veterans Association, 115th New York Volunteer Infantry 192, 197
Vicksburg 62
vidette duty 125
Virginia Peninsula Campaign 5, 19

Wager, James 99
Walker, Gen. John G. 20, 24
Walling, Lt. William 168
Walrath, Maj. Ezra 62, 81, 90, **90**, 99, 101, 108, 121, 131, 141–143, 144, 155, 175, 177, 179, 180, 194
War of 1812 7, 83, 102
Ware Bottom Church 109
Washington, George 45, 46
Washington County 108
Washington, D.C. 10, 15, 20, 39, 41, 42, 43, 50, 54, 68, 93, 94, 117, 139, 161, 163, 188
Washington D.C. Soldier's Relief 43
Waterford Sentinel 190
Watt, Corp. John Robert **189**
Wayland, Rev. Dr. John 7
Wayne, Lt. Thomas 42, 57, 100
Weitzel, Gen. Godfrey 163, 167
Weldon Railroad 148
Wells, Reuben 56
West Point, Virginia 47
White House Landing, Virginia 111, 112, 118–119
White's Ford 19
Whiting, Col. William C. 106
Wilderness 87, 111, 117
Williamsport, Maryland 20
Wilmington, North Carolina 160–164, 168, 169–170, 181, 182–187
Winchester Railroad 10
Winchester, Virginia 11–13, 150
winter quarters 43, **44**, 45, 47, 159, 160, 169
World War II 200
Wright, Gen. Horatio 120

Yankee Doodle 117
York River 19, 47, 46, 95, 96, 111, 119
Yorktown, Virginia 45, 46, 47, 95, 199
Young, Waldo 177

www.ingramcontent.com/pod-product-compliance
Lightning Source LLC
Chambersburg PA
CBHW081025240426
43661CB00074B/2822